# COMING
# TO OUR
# SENSES

W9-BRA-275

# BANTAM NEW AGE BOOKS

This important imprint includes books in a variety of fields and disciplines and deals with the search for meaning, growth and change.

Ask your bookseller for the books you have missed.

THE AGES OF GAIA by James Lovelock
ANGELS FEAR: TOWARDS AN EPISTEMOLOGY OF THE SACRED
   by Gregory Bateson and Mary Catherine Bateson
BEYOND EINSTEIN: THE COSMIC QUEST FOR THE THEORY OF THE
   UNIVERSE by Dr. Michio Kaku and Jennifer Trainer
BEYOND SUPERNATURE by Lyall Watson
THE CEREBRAL SYMPHONY: SEASHORE REFLECTIONS ON THE
   STRUCTURE OF CONSCIOUSNESS by William H. Calvin
COMING TO OUR SENSES: BODY AND SPIRIT IN THE HIDDEN
   HISTORY OF THE WEST by Morris Berman
THE COSMIC CODE by Heinz R. Pagels
COSMIC COINCIDENCES: DARK MATTER, MANKIND, AND
   ANTHROPIC COSMOLOGY by John Gribbin and Martin Rees
THE DANCING WU LI MASTERS by Gary Zukav
DOLPHIN DREAMTIME: THE ART AND SCIENCE OF
   INTERSPECIES COMMUNICATION by Jim Nollman
THE DREAMS OF REASON: THE RISE OF THE SCIENCES OF
   COMPLEXITY by Heinz R. Pagels
ECOTOPIA by Ernest Callenbach
ENTROPY, Revised Edition by Jeremy Rifkin with Ted Howard
THE HOLE IN THE SKY by John Gribbin
IN SEARCH OF SCHRODINGER'S CAT by John Gribbin
IN SEARCH OF THE BIG BANG: QUANTUM PHYSICS AND
   COSMOLOGY by John Gribbin
IN SEARCH OF THE DOUBLE HELIX: QUANTUM PHYSICS AND
   LIFE by John Gribbin
INFINITY AND THE MIND by Rudy Rucker
THE LIVES OF A CELL by Lewis Thomas
THE MEDUSA AND THE SNAIL by Lewis Thomas
METAMAGICAL THEMAS: QUESTING FOR THE ESSENCE OF MIND
   AND PATTERN by Douglas R. Hofstadter

MIND AND NATURE by Gregory Bateson
THE MIND'S I by Douglas R. Hofstadter and Daniel C. Dennett
THE OMEGA POINT: THE SEARCH FOR THE MISSING MASS AND
   THE ULTIMATE FATE OF THE UNIVERSE by John Gribbin
ORDER OUT OF CHAOS by Ilya Prigogine and Isabelle Stengers
OUT OF WEAKNESS: HEALING THE WOUNDS THAT DRIVE US TO
   WAR by Andrew Bard Schmookler
PERFECT SYMMETRY by Heinz R. Pagels
QUANTUM HEALING by Deepak Chopra, M.D.
RECOVERING THE SOUL: A SCIENTIFIC AND SPIRITUAL SEARCH
   by Larry Dossey, M.D.
THE REENCHANTMENT OF THE WORLD by Morris Berman
SCIENCE, ORDER AND CREATIVITY by David Bohm and
   F. David Peat
SHAMBHALA: THE SACRED PATH OF THE WARRIOR by
   Chogyam Trungpa
SPACE-TIME AND BEYOND (THE NEW EDITION) by Bob Toben and
   Fred Alan Wolf
SPIRITUAL ECOLOGY by Jim Nollman
STAYING SUPPLE by John Jerome
SYNCHRONICITY: THE BRIDGE BETWEEN MATTER AND MIND
   by F. David Peat
THE TAO OF PHYSICS, Revised Edition by Fritjof Capra
THE TURNING POINT by Fritjof Capra
UNCOMMON WISDOM: CONVERSATIONS WITH REMARKABLE
   PEOPLE by Fritjof Capra
"WHAT DO YOU *CARE* WHAT OTHER PEOPLE THINK?"
   by Richard P. Feynman
ZEN AND THE ART OF MOTORCYCLE MAINTENANCE by
   Robert M. Pirsig

# COMING TO OUR SENSES

BODY AND SPIRIT IN THE
HIDDEN HISTORY OF THE WEST

## MORRIS BERMAN

BANTAM BOOKS
NEW YORK · TORONTO · LONDON · SYDNEY · AUCKLAND

*This edition contains the complete text
of the original hardcover edition.*
NOT ONE WORD HAS BEEN OMITTED.

COMING TO OUR SENSES: BODY AND SPIRIT IN THE HIDDEN HISTORY OF THE WEST

*A Bantam Book / published by arrangement with
Simon and Schuster*

*PRINTING HISTORY*
*Simon and Schuster edition published 1989*
*Bantam edition / August 1990*

*Grateful acknowledgment is extended to the following for permission to reprint copyrighted material:*

Macmillan Publishing Company for lines from fragments of Anaximenes and Heraclitus in *The Presocratics* by Philip Wheelwright, copyright © 1966 by Macmillan Publishing Company.

Robert Bly for permission to reprint "I am not I" by Juan Ramón Jiménez, translated by Robert Bly, in *Light and Shadows: Selected Poems of Juan Ramón Jiménez*, ed. Dennis Maloney and published by the White Pine Press, copyright © 1987 by Robert Bly; for lines from Poem Number 5 of *The Kabir Book*, version by Robert Bly, published by Beacon Press, copyright © 1971 by Robert Bly; and for Poem XVII by Antonio Machado, translated by Robert Bly, in *Times Alone: Selected Poems of Antonio Machado*, published by Wesleyan University Press, copyright © 1983 by Robert Bly.

Judith H. Ciardi for one line from *An Alphabestiary* (J. B. Lippincott Co.), copyright © 1965 by John Ciardi. Reprinted by permission of the estate of John Ciardi.

White Pine Press for permission to reprint "What an immense rip" by Juan Ramón Jiménez, translated by D. Maloney and C. Zlotchew from *Light and Shadows: Selected Poems of Juan Ramón Jiménez*, copyright © 1987 White Pine Press.

Yale University Press for lines from "Song. To Celia" by Ben Jonson, in *Ben Jonson: The Complete Poems*, ed. George Parfitt, copyright © 1982 Yale University Press.

Viking Penguin Inc. for lines from "A Doe at Evening" by D. H. Lawrence, in *The Complete Poems of D. H. Lawrence*, collected and edited by Vivian de Sola Pinto and F. Warren Roberts. Copyright © 1964, 1971 by Angelo Ravagli and C. M. Weekley, Executors of the Estate of Frieda Lawrence Ravagli. All rights reserved. Reprinted by permission of Viking Penguin Inc.

Simon and Schuster, for lines from Christopher Marlowe, *The Tragedy of Doctor Faustus*, ed. Louis B. Wright and Virginia A. LaMar (New York: Washington Square Press, 1959).

Doubleday for one line from "In a Dark Time," copyright © 1960 by Beatrice Roethke as administratrix of the estate of Theodore Roethke. From *The Collected Poems of Theodore Roethke* by Theodore Roethke. Reprinted by permission of Doubleday, a division of Bantam Doubleday Dell Publishing Group, Inc.

North Point Press for an excerpt from *Break the Mirror*, copyright © 1987 by Nanao Sakaki. Published by North Point Press and reprinted by permission.

Robert Phillips, Literary Executor for the Estate of Delmore Schwartz, for one line from "The Heavy Bear Who Goes With Me" by Delmore Schwartz, in *Summer Knowledge*, published by Doubleday in 1959.

*All rights reserved.*
*Copyright © 1989 by Morris Berman.*
*Cover art copyright © 1990 by Leo and Diane Dillon.*
*No part of this book may be reproduced or transmitted
in any form or by any means, electronic or mechanical,
including photocopying, recording, or by any information
storage and retrieval system, without permission in
writing from the publisher.*
*For information address: Simon and Schuster,
1230 Avenue of the Americas, New York, New York 10020.*

**Library of Congress Cataloging-in-Publication Data**

Berman, Morris, 1944–
   Coming to our senses : body and spirit in the hidden history of
the West / Morris Berman.—Bantam ed.
   p.   cm.
   Reprint. Originally published: New York : Simon and Schuster, c1989.
Includes bibliographical references.
   ISBN 0-553-34863-9
   1. Mind and body—History. 2. Gnosticism—History. 3. Dualism—
History. 4. Civilization, Occidental. I. Title.
[BF161.B475  1990]
128'.2'09—dc20
                        89-49180
                          CIP

*Published simultaneously in the United States and Canada*

*Bantam Books are published by Bantam Books, a division of Bantam Doubleday Dell Publishing Group, Inc. Its trademark, consisting of the words "Bantam Books" and the portrayal of a rooster, is Registered in U.S. Patent and Trademark Office and in other countries. Marca Registrada. Bantam Books, 666 Fifth Avenue, New York, New York 10103.*

PRINTED IN THE UNITED STATES OF AMERICA

FFG    0  9  8  7  6  5  4  3  2  1

FOR MY PARENTS,
HARRY AND LIBBIE BERMAN

# ACKNOWLEDGMENTS

A great number of people have contributed to making this book possible, and it is a pleasure for me to acknowledge my debt to them at this time. My decade-long dialogue with the American video artist Paul Ryan has greatly enriched these pages, as have my discussions with Jack London, a student of the mind/body relationship for more than fifty years now. Michael Fellman of Simon Fraser University read several chapters of the manuscript in its early stages and offered some very helpful criticisms and suggestions. Sandra Campbell did the same for the entire text of the final draft, as did Agehananda Bharati of Syracuse University, thereby saving me the embarrassment of a number of egregious errors. Robert Asahina, my editor at Simon and Schuster, helped me to reorganize the book in ways that improved it immensely. I was fortunate to have the help of Jocelyne Laflamme in wading through the extensive literature on the Cathars, and the assistance of Angelika Arend, Gisela Dumka, and Karen Robertson with source materials in German. Kevin O'Keeffe and Beth Bosshard were also generous with their time in the capacity of research assistants, and I wish to thank Joe Jones, librarian at the University of British Columbia, for similar help. At the University of Victoria, where I taught from 1982 to 1988, I received a great deal of bibliographical and reference help from colleagues Tom Saunders and Angus McLaren in History, and Mike Doyle and Mel Faber in English. (In all of these cases, errors of fact or interpretation are, as usual, strictly my own.) Susan Dehnel and Sandra Campbell assisted me in typing the manuscript; John Oliphant helped in preparing the illustrations; and Carol White compiled the index. My agent, John Brockman, has been a staunch ally, and Don Babcock, a wise man and good friend, provided a great deal of emotional support and helped me through the process of getting acquainted with my own body. To all these friends, and more, I can only say Thank You for your interest, encouragement, and generous assistance over the years.

*M.B.*
*Seattle, 1988*

# CONTENTS

Acknowledgments    9
List of Illustrations    13

PART ONE: THE SOURCES OF FRAGMENTATION                    17
1. The Basic Fault    19
2. The Wild and the Tame: Humans and Animals
   from Lascaux to Walt Disney    63

PART TWO: SPIRITUAL POLITICS                              105
3. The Body of History    107
4. The Gnostic Response    136
5. Jews and Christians    156
6. Cathars and Troubadours    178
7. Science and Magic    221
8. The Twisted Cross    253

PART THREE: BREAKING THE MIRROR                           295
9. The Gesture of Balance    297
10. The Two Faces of Creativity    319

Epilogue: Coming to Our Senses    341

Notes    345
Index    413

# LIST OF ILLUSTRATIONS

1. Large bull and running horses, Lascaux    67

2. Deer, Altamira    67

3. Scene from Walt Disney's *Cinderella* (1950)    68

4. *The First Stage of Cruelty*, by William Hogarth (1751)    74

5. *The Temptation of St. Anthony* (detail), by Hieronymus Bosch (ca. 1500)    75

6. Testing detergents for eye irritation (on rabbit)    84

7. Testing effect of electric shock and anxiety on growth of ulcers (on monkeys)    85

8. Monkey undergoing morphine withdrawal    86

9. Slaughter of buffalo in the nineteenth century    87

10. Engraving of London Zoo by Scharf, ca. 1836    88

11. Rodeo event: taming the "outlaw" bronc    93

12. Advertisement for Nocona boots, showing destruction of a rattlesnake    Not shown in this edition.

13. The pleasure of curiosity: children and spiders    101

14. Enlarged hands in Cathar iconography; carving on a sarcophagus in Domazan, France    201

15. Robert Fludd's "divine monochord," symbolizing the ladder of ascent from earth to heaven (1617)    242

16. Fludd's illustration of the three "octaves," showing the path of descent and reascent of the soul (1619)    244

17. Fludd's illustration of a diatonic scale mapped onto the path of ascent to the heavens (1621)    245

18. The evolution of verticality    250

19. Albert Speer's lighting effects at the Nazi Party rally at Nuremberg    287

20. *Persimmons*, attributed to Mu Ch'i (thirteenth century)    336

THE PROBLEM OF THE REALITY OF THE BODY
IS SHOWN TO BE THE CENTRAL PROBLEM, AND
UPON ITS SOLUTION EVERYTHING ELSE DEPENDS.

—Gabriel Marcel,
*Metaphysical Journal*


THE BRAVE NEW WORLD TO BE EXPLORED BY THE
TWENTY-FIRST CENTURY IS THE IMMENSE LABYRINTH
OF THE SOMA, OF THE LIVING, BODILY EXPERIENCE
OF HUMAN INDIVIDUALS. AND WE OF THE LATTER
THIRD OF THE TWENTIETH CENTURY HAVE BEEN
APPOINTED DISCOVERERS AND EARLY CARTOGRAPHERS
OF THIS SOMATIC CONTINENT.

—Thomas Hanna,
*Bodies in Revolt*

# PART ONE:
# THE SOURCES OF FRAGMENTATION

---

I AM NOT I.
        I AM THIS ONE
WALKING BESIDE ME WHOM I DO NOT SEE,
WHOM AT TIMES I MANAGE TO VISIT,
AND WHOM AT OTHER TIMES I FORGET;
WHO REMAINS CALM AND SILENT WHILE I TALK,
AND FORGIVES, GENTLY, WHEN I HATE,
WHO WALKS WHERE I AM NOT,
WHO WILL REMAIN STANDING WHEN I DIE.

                    —From Juan Ramón Jiménez,
                      *Light and Shadows*,
                      translated by Robert Bly

# 1

# The Basic Fault

> *What happens when I look in my [mirror]*
> *is that I, who am nothing here, place*
> *myself there where I am a man, and project*
> *him back upon this centre. Now this is*
> *only a specially lucid case of self-observation*
> *in general; my glass does for me what my*
> *friends do, only with fewer complications. . . .*
> *What occurs everywhere obscurely occurs*
> *plainly here. . . . Between us, the glass and*
> *I achieve a man. . . .*
>
> —D. E. Harding,
>    *The Hierarchy of Heaven and Earth*

> *The hole of my life flashed before my eyes.*
> —John Lennon

SOME OF THE EARLIEST CHILDHOOD MEMORIES I HAVE involve family gatherings, when members of the extended family would assemble for some sort of holiday or celebration, or when a few family members would come over to our home simply for the purpose of getting together. As a child, I often enjoyed these gatherings; there was usually a lot of warmth and reassurance in them. Looking back, however, one thing that strikes me about much of this socializing was a marked absence of silence. As is frequently true of such get-togethers, the talking was almost constant. I am sure there were some exceptions to this, but they do not stand out in my mind. As a family we rarely, if ever, sat around just "being" with each other; that never seemed to happen. The unstated rule seemed to be that empty space was uncomfortable, and that it was necessary to fill it up. Silence—not of the hostile variety, but rather of the kind that simply expresses beingness—was apparently, and I believe unconsciously, seen as threatening. It was as though something potentially dangerous would emerge if the talking were to stop for anything longer than half a minute or so.

I suppose this situation is typical of almost all gatherings, not just family ones. The dinner party is the most obvious example. It is as though silence could disclose some sort of terribly frightening Void. And what is being avoided are questions of who we are and what we are actually doing with each other. These questions live in our bodies, and silence forces them to the surface. If such questions ever get openly asked, the family often falls apart, and the dinner party usually breaks up in a strained and embarrassed way.

It is these types of situations that lay bare the nature of a culture most profoundly, for they go down to the root of our existence. They echo the lessons learned in our bodies from childhood, in a daily and repetitive way, and they are microcosms of our entire civilization. My family experience, in one form or another, was probably not very different from your own; and this despite the fact that there are many cultures on this planet for which silence is a comfortable fact of life rather than a difficulty. The difference may finally be one of embodiment, for if you are in-corporated, if you are in your body most of the time, the Void is not so threatening. If you are out of your body, on the other hand, you need a substitute for the feeling of being grounded. Much of what passes for "culture" and "personality" in our society tends to fall into this substitute category, and is in fact the result of running from silence, and from genuine somatic experience.

The problem of hollowness, then, of a-Voidance, is really one of secondary satisfactions, the attempt to find substitutes for a primary satisfaction of wholeness that somehow got lost, leaving a large gap in its place. The British novelist John Fowles calls this emptiness the "nemo," which he describes as an anti-ego, a state of being nobody. "Nobody wants to be a nobody," writes Fowles. "All our acts are partly devised to fill or to mark the emptiness we feel at the core."[1]

When we look around at our society today, it is hard to escape the truth of this judgment. It is especially through the experiences of alcohol, drugs, and sex that most of us are able to re-create a state of undivided consciousness, of the primary satisfaction of unity with our environment. Food, romantic love, religious ecstasy, and even video screens (televisions or home computers) also serve to produce the same effect. In a sense, these things are not as secondary as they might seem, since their effect is so dramatic in their ability to make the nemo go away (for a while). The conflict, the a-Voidance, gets melted down in short order and, for reasons that I believe are rooted in our bodies, we seek that experience desperately.

Many of us, of course, back away from going the drug or alcohol route, or at least from doing so completely, and as a result our lives are filled with activities designed to cover up the emptiness Fowles refers to. We raise children, pursue careers, go to football games, or write books (not that these things cannot be done in a nonneurotic way). We especially knock ourselves out trying to get other people to love us, so that somehow we will be able to love ourselves. But in the end, it is "looking for love in all the wrong places," as one popular song puts it. Sándor Ferenczi, the Hungarian psychoanalyst, wrote that our real aim in life is to be loved, and that any other observable activity is really a detour, an indirect path toward that goal.[2] All of this follows from the emptiness at the core.

I do not mean to suggest, however, that the search for primary satisfaction is merely a private one, or even a collective private one. The scope of all this is much larger than personal anguish or individual dilemmas. Our social and political life is a charade as well, asking us to take substitute activity seriously. This is particularly true in the case of the world's dominant ideologies, which are obvious candidates as "nemo-stuffers." In the capitalist nations, the search for love often takes the form of the drive for success, which we think will get others to love us (it usually has the opposite effect). This ideology of achievement and productivity extends to virtually every activity, even the writing of poetry. Ambition is, for us, unquestionably "good." The poet who is "not producing" is invariably inferior, in our eyes, to the one who has a "prodigious literary output." The problem with this ideology, as well as with socialism or any other, is that it finally does not work. If the real goal is to recover a lost primary experience, then worldly or financial or artistic/literary success is all beside the point. Achieving in order to feel whole makes about as much sense as hanging a cross up on your living room wall in order to precipitate an ecstatic experience (as people such as Saint Francis have told us down through the centuries). Our ideologies are as hollow as our organized religions. The millionaire dies a bitter and lonely man; the famous athlete finds that nobody cares about his great track record of decades past. Success, as the Swiss therapist Alice Miller demonstrates so powerfully in *Prisoners of Childhood*, is one of the hollowest ideologies around.[3]

Ideologies arise when people feel they have no real somatic anchoring. The person who is truly grounded in him- or herself as a biological organism may espouse a cause, but they do not need it in order to feel that their existence is validated. God and country, feminism and sexism, Judaism and anti-Semitism, the religious fundamentalism of Bible Belt Baptists and the self-conscious intellectualism of *The New York Review of Books*—any ism you care to name, really—are all attempts to create meaning for human beings who, if they had not suffered some sort of primary loss early on, would not need it. For the (extremely rare) healthy person, life is its own meaning; they do not need an ism to stuff the gap, to feel OK. In our society, however, isms and ideologies are as widespread, and as addictive, as any drug one can think of.

On some level, we all know this; it is the common somatic heritage we all share. But modern Western culture in particular is a conspiracy not to talk about the world of primary satisfaction, or even about the body at all. Since that is excluded from discussion, we are required to take the world of secondary satisfaction seriously. Blowing the whistle on the game, refusing to take it seriously, declaring that the emperor has no clothes—such behavior has fairly serious penalties in the cerebral societies of Western industrial culture. (Try doing it at work, if you don't believe me.) Devotion to secondary satisfaction is intense precisely *because* it ultimately provides no satisfaction, and pointing this out generates a terrific amount of rage. If you won't shut up, and insist on discussing this issue in public, you are finally going to wind up in serious trouble, of which loss of employment is probably the mildest form. "Success," career, reputation, money, and the accumulation of material goods are the most obvious forms of secondary satisfaction, although there are many more that are equally hollow and equally "sacred": spectator sports, patriotism and war, organized religion, and even a good deal of artistic or creative activity. As already noted, none of this ultimately works because it fails to penetrate down to the primary somatic layer. But because that layer has long since been given up on, our secret attitude is: what else is there? And our defeat shows in our bodies: we either "prop ourselves up," so to speak, or slump in a posture of collapse; and this has a profound effect on the nature of the culture we create. It is thus a civilizational problem, not just a personal or individual one, although these are two sides of the same coin. As the Austrian psychiatrist Wilhelm Reich pointed out, characterology and culture go hand in hand. What appears in the infant body is created by the surrounding culture and in turn creates (reproduces) that culture.

There is, then, a larger cultural and historical dimension to all of this, one that I shall be discussing at great length (in fact, it is the subject of this book). To date, however, the problem of the nemo and its existence as a somatic fact of human life has not, at least in theoretical terms, been the territory of the historian (a major omission, in my view), but principally of the psychologist. In particular, the analysis of human ontology and ontogeny in terms of a gap, or fundamental psychic break, is the principal contribution of a number of French scholars, such as Jacques Lacan, Maurice Merleau-Ponty, and Henri Wallon (dealt with later on in this chapter), as well as of the so-called British "object-relations school," which includes analysts such as Michael Balint and Donald Winnicott (Ronald Laing's teacher and therapist). This "nemological" approach was also picked up by the Hungarian anthropologist Géza Róheim, whose book *The Origin and Function of Culture* was a path-breaking attempt to interpret human culture in these terms.[4] It is my bias as well; and I am convinced that neither a somatic interpretation of the past nor the construction of a healthy somatic future (which would be the point of this exercise) is possible without a thorough understanding of the infant origins of this phenomenon of the nemo and the way that the resulting dynamic unconsciously permeates our entire adult life. In all cultures, at all times, human identity is heavily conditioned by what happens to the infant body; this is where it all begins. I ask you, then, to sit back and let yourself go on a journey, a journey back in time, both personal and cultural, to the heart of human existence itself. And if, in the course of this journey, memories of your own childhood and infancy come up for you, that is all to the good. If that happens, put this book down, close your eyes, and try to recall as much of those early events as you can. For Reich was right: our cultural history is encoded in our bodies, and as you begin to sort one out, you will sort the other out as well. Let yourself move back and forth, then, between your own bodily history and an examination of larger cultural processes and assumptions. It is in this back-and-forth movement, I am convinced, that real understanding takes place.

One of the most important contributions to this whole discussion was the book published by Michael Balint, *The Basic Fault*, the title of which, he believed, captured the essence of the human condition. There is a double entendre here: by "fault," Balint did not just mean a mistake; his analogy was that of a geological fault, a gap or crevice in the earth that produces earthquakes under conditions of sufficient stress. The fault is also a default; in terms of the human condition, there is some way in which, during the early childhood of most (if not all) of us, the person who was closest to us (usually our mother) failed to move in harmony with our needs. She was frequently absent when we needed her, or intrusive when we needed to be left alone. In either case, a mismatch occurred, what the Austrian psychoanalyst Otto Rank called a case of faulty mirroring, which tends to be the rule rather than the exception. The "fit" between ourselves and our first human environment was off, and from that point on, relations between ourselves and the world, Self and Other, were disturbed. This surfaced in our psyche as the feeling that something was not quite right, was somehow missing. A crevice, an abyss of sorts (John Fowles' nemo) had irrevocably opened up in our soul, and we would spend the rest of our lives, usually in an unconscious and driven way, attempting to fill it up.[5]

The enormous power of this feeling of hollowness, as I indicated earlier, derives from the fact that the basic fault has a biological foundation. It is laid down in the tissues of the body at a primary level, and as a result can never quite be eradicated. To get down to the "ground level," we have to retrace the steps of human ontogeny and see what happens to the human infant in the course of its early development. The actual appearance of the nemo—the vague perception that something is missing, that one is split, or empty—would appear to date from the third year of life. Can you recall your first conscious moment? Can you recall how old you were when it occurred? (This is a valuable exercise; you might wish to stop and do this for a few minutes, before continuing. Try to recall that moment in as much detail as possible.) I have found, in working with people over the years, that the dating varies anywhere from four months to four years, but that the first memory we have usually dates back to some point between two and three years of age. And I have also found that although the content varies—what one perceived in that moment can literally be anything—the form is always the same. Thus my own first conscious moment was the perception of folding glass doors, with latticework in them, in my parents' house when I was almost exactly thirty months old. For one student in my class, it was a portrait of John Lennon, and for another, it consisted of wearing a new dress and whirling around on the grass in the afternoon sun. Exactly where one comes to consciousness is totally arbitrary; the thing that remains constant is the awareness that "I" am "here" and that "that" (whatever one is looking at, or is outside of one) is "there." To use a bit of technical jargon, the ego crystallizes out of an amorphous and undifferentiated matrix. Up to this point, all of us feel ourselves more or less continuous with the external environment. Coming to consciousness means a rupture in that continuity, the emergence of a divide between Self and Other. With the thought "I am I," a new level of existence opens up for us. There is a tear in the fabric, so to speak, and Self vs. Other remains the issue that we shall have to negotiate for the rest of our lives.

Preconscious unity with the environment, a state of "symbiosis" that has been called by many names—"cosmic anonymity" (Erich Neumann), "infant-world unity" (Kurt Goldstein)—has been taken by psychoanalytic theory as a given of early human life.[6] The question is, however, how early? Research on newborn babies during the past twenty years has pushed the "symbiotic" phase further and further back; it now appears that infants can imitate parental gestures within the first few days of life, and can, if they heard their father's voice while *in utero*, recognize that voice within the first hour or two of life.[7] There is of course the question of whether behavior of this sort amounts to true self-awareness (an issue I shall deal with later on); but in any case, it suggests that if we wish to argue for the existence of a somatic memory or primary wholeness or unity, we may have to chase our subject back into the womb, and possibly to the first few weeks of fetal life. Much of what we today call mysticism may be nothing more than a type of body memory that contemporary science regards as impossible; yet certain types of practices seem to dislodge these very early memories. LSD research, Reichian bodywork, and rebirthing techniques (a kind of yogic breathing method) are the major sources of "direct" information here. ("[I]f we consider flesh neurologically," writes Charles Brooks, ". . . it surely represents the most 'spiritual' aspect of the cosmos!")[8] The German physician Kurt Goldstein suggested, in 1957, that embryonic life itself undergoes psychic experiences, that it registers conditions of order and disorder (shock, anxiety)[9]—a suggestion that thirty years ago had the flavor of an old wives' tale (attend concerts while pregnant and your child will grow up to be a concert pianist, etc.). Today, it is not so easily dismissed; we have a good bit of data on the subject of prenatal memory. A few words on this subject are thus in order.

From a somatic point of view, truly undifferentiated existence may be very brief. As the fetus begins to be formed out of zygote and blastula, it "confronts" its first Other—the placenta. Yet because of the harmonious role of the placenta vis-à-vis the fetus, especially during the first trimester, it is only dimly perceived as an Other, if at all. The fetus is nourished and fed by the placenta and provided with oxygen, and its blood is cleansed of wastes and carbon dioxide. It lives in its environment like a fish in water, or an adult human in air. "Foetus, amniotic fluid, and placenta are . . . a complicated interpenetrating mix-up of foetus and environment-mother," wrote Michael Balint.[10] Balint, following other psychologists such as Otto Rank (*The Trauma of Birth*), Phyllis Greenacre (*Trauma, Growth and Personality*), and Nándor Fodor (*The Search for the Beloved: A Clinical Investigation of the Trauma of Birth and Prenatal Conditioning*), believed that intrauterine life was one of pure bliss, and that birth was traumatic, the archetypal separation, the loss of Eden. Undoubtedly, birth is traumatic, but recent fetal research tends to suggest that the womb is not without its disturbances. Evidence collected by the Toronto psychiatrist Thomas Verny (*The Secret Life of the Unborn Child*) suggests that the pattern of symbiosis-to-differentiation is real, but that Neumann, Goldstein, and others (including Freud) were wrong about the dating.[11] Any stress experienced by the pregnant mother is communicated to the fetus, and this (argues Verny) contributes the first stirrings of Other-awareness. (One wonders why Other-awareness can't occur through sensations of pleasure.) By the eighth week, the fetus will kick vigorously if it finds itself inconvenienced, and its heartbeat picks up if the mother has an anxious moment. But, says Verny, one should not necessarily regard all stress as negative; in some form, he claims, stress makes the awareness of Otherness possible in the first place. Experiments with stress have established the emergence of Self/Other awareness in the fetus somewhere between the fourth and sixth month. Maternal anxiety, writes Verny, can be beneficial. Communicated to the fetus, it "disturbs his sense of oneness with his surroundings and makes him aware of his own separateness and distinctness." All of this jolts fetal serenity and leaves a somatic memory trace; cosmic anonymity is interrupted by a moment of focused awareness. Again, this is not "bad"; the real isue is whether this primitive ego-crystallization occurs in a context that is loving or hostile. There is, says Verny, such a thing as intrauterine bonding; good postpartum bonding (a rarity these days) can merely be a continuation of an organismic memory experience of good intrauterine bonding. Nevertheless, there is a duality of experience here; the drama of good Self and Other-I'm-not-too-sure-about, of merger vs. separation, probably begins at a very early point.

As for the birth trauma, it would seem that regardless of prenatal differentiation experience, and of the possibly liberating aspects of the birth process, it nevertheless remains the most fundamental discontinuity of our lives. The water bag breaks; a new world begins. Verny calls it "the first prolonged emotional and physical shock the child undergoes," and adds that the child never forgets it. "Even in the best of circumstances," he continues, "birth reverberates through the child's body like a seismic shock of earthquake proportions."[12] The "best of circumstances" are those of truly natural childbirth, practiced in tribal and traditional cultures, and recently revived by doctors such as Frederick Leboyer and Michel Odent.[13] The goal of these "soft" birthing practices, which may include having the delivery in warm water, in a dimly lit room, with no use of anesthetics or forceps, and with no slapping of the baby to get it to draw its first breath, is to preserve the continuity of the intrauterine bond, to minimize the physical experience of separation as much as possible. From the point of view of human connectedness, the twentieth-century hospital practice of industrial societies is the most barbaric; the fact of separation is seared into the infant body in a way that it will never forget. The American therapist Arthur Janov has argued that the traumas surrounding birth today are so great that lifetime careers of overeating, smoking, alcoholism, and every other form of neurotic splitting and dependence are laid down at this time, because the feeling of unity that the womb offers is ruptured in so brutal a way.[14] As Michael Balint put it, "[i]n my experience the yearning for this feeling of 'harmony' is the most important cause of alcoholism or, for that matter, any form of addiction."[15] If the basic fault was slowly initiated during the fetus-placenta interaction (which is, of course, debatable), it is definitely established under modern conditions of birth. Janov's observations echo those of Ferenczi when he writes that the neurotic product of such a birth can never be loved enough: "All of the rest of life is but a poor substitute; a symbolic ploy to the unconscious to try to 'pretend' that the fulfillment has really occurred."[16]

We cannot be sure, of course, of what is really going on in fetal life on a psychic level; but if some slight Self/Other differentiation has begun, birth is certainly the climax of that. Once that occurs, the newborn baby ideally stabilizes in its adjustment to its surroundings, and the cycle of increasing differentiation and climax begins again.

The next major climax or "punctuation" is the definitive emergence of ego-consciousness during the third year of life. In this sense, ego-crystallization is the intellectual recognition of an earlier somatic event. The awareness that one is a separate entity, a Self in a world of Others, is merely the later recognition of an awareness that has been present in the body for a long time already. It is the point at which the child begins to work out consciously what was imprinted on its tiny body at an earlier time: that it is a separate Self. From age two or so, this conscious awareness is accompanied by a growing understanding that this fact has certain emotional consequences.

The education into the world of Self vs. Other is a process that is completely dependent on the bodies of other people. If it does occur in the womb, it depends on the mother, via her "representative," the placenta. But from the time of birth, in any case, one is involved with the bodies of others in terms of gesture, gaze, and touch. The core experience of this differentiation process is the phenomenon of mirroring, i.e., the growth of self-recognition through the medium of other people. Mirroring includes the phenomenon of observing oneself in a reflecting surface, such as water or silvered glass, but this is only a special case of a larger process. It is this larger process that lies at the heart of identity formation.

A major pioneer in the clinical investigation of the mirroring phenomenon was the British psychoanalyst and pediatrician Donald Winnicott. Even more than Balint, Winnicott placed a heavy emphasis on the "fit" between the child and the mother. What he called the "good enough mother" was, in his view, central to a healthy mirroring experience; and the mirroring experience was for him the prototype of the entire human experience. Hence his famous remark, "There is no such thing as an infant," by which he meant that the primary unit is infant-and-mother, or infant-plus-environment. For Winnicott, object relations began at birth, and it was this interaction, he believed, that had to be studied in the clinical situation.[17]

What exactly is observed in the clinical situation? The baby sees the mother's face, and what her face portrays is related to what she sees in *its* face. Thus for the baby, the mother's face acts as a mirror; she gives back to the baby its own self. "[I]n individual development," wrote Winnicott, "the precursor of the mirror is the mother's face."[18] The mother's mirroring of her baby is a crucial factor in the development of the sense of self; the Self that results bears the imprint of the mirroring experience.[19] The effect of a "not-good-enough mother" can be seen in a recent experiment with very young infants, in which

mothers were instructed to look into their babies' faces without reg-
istering any emotion. The babies' expressions and gestures became
hectic and disorganized; the infants rapidly went into a situation of
distress.[20] One can well imagine what the resulting Self would be like
if this experiment were daily fare. Both the American sociologist
C. H. Cooley (Human Nature and the Social Order) and the philosopher/
psychologist George Mead (Mind, Self and Society) argued that this sort
of mirroring is the crucible of self-formation. Cooley introduced the
concept of the "looking-glass self," which refers to an individual seeing
himself or herself in the ways in which others see him or her. Mead
similarly argued that self-concept is the result of the person's concern
about how others are reacting to them.[21] As R. D. Laing once put it,
there is no Self without Other. The phenomenon of mirroring and
that of human identity seem to be closely tied together.

To what extent is the presence of an actual, *physical* mirror a factor
in all of this? For Jacques Lacan, the "French school," and a number
of other psychologists and writers, the fact of a reflected presence—
the "specular image," as it is called—constitutes a critical factor in the
formation of human identity and self-consciousness. The question of
how the child sorts out the significance of his or her physical reflection,
and the importance of that process for psychic development, is, to
these researchers, absolutely crucial, and investigation of the issue
actually goes back to Charles Darwin, who studied his own child with
a view to this question in 1877. Rightly or wrongly, the mirror was
taken, from that date, as an archetype, a pure case of what went on
in a more diffuse and general way in a social setting. Hence one
American psychologist writes that "even before the experience with
an actual mirror, a long experience of emotional 'mirroring' has taken
place";[22] and Paul Guillaume, an early (1920s) French student of the
subject, argued that the presence of a mirror can accelerate self-
recognition, but that because of social interaction, children eventually
come into self-recognition with or without it.[23] I shall have to say more
about the history of the mirror as an artifact of Western civilization
later on, because its archetypal significance is probably open to question if it cannot be shown to be ubiquitous. For now, however, I wish
to review the mirror studies of infant development that have been
done since Darwin's first investigation of the subject.

Darwin's observation was actually fairly elementary. He found that
when his son reached nine months of age and was called by name
when in the presence of a mirror, he turned to the mirror and said
"ah." Darwin speculated that this was an indication of self-recognition

on the part of the child. A few years later, the psychologist William Preyer concluded that his own child attained self-recognition at fourteen months of age when it recognized its mother in the mirror—presumably since this would imply a Self/Other distinction. Such early studies were pure guesswork, but nevertheless vitally important, for Darwin and Preyer were not only searching for signs of self-recognition, but were also trying to puzzle out what the criteria for such an event would consist of.[24]

The first systematic study of infant self-recognition was done in the 1920s by Paul Guillaume in the form of a series of observations on his infant daughter, Louise.[25] The first few weeks of life found Louise grimacing in the mirror, or just staring at her reflection. The next stage involved recognizing things in the mirror that were situated next to her (prompted by tactile or auditory sensation). At five months and seventeen days, according to Guillaume, she began turning around to try to see the real person whose image she glimpsed in the mirror. At eleven months and eighteen days, Louise came upon her image in the mirror while wearing a straw hat (which she had had on since morning) and put her hand to her head to touch it. Guillaume took this as an obvious moment of self-recognition, but it was one that did not stabilize: six weeks later Louise was not able to perform on herself, in front of the mirror, acts that she performed on others (pinching the nose, for example). It was only at two years of age that Louise, dressed in a new coat, went to the mirror to check herself out. At two years and eight months, Louise was shown a photo of a group of children, in which she was included; she knew who all of them were except herself. Guillaume told her it was her; the next day, exactly the same thing happened. "We can see, then," wrote Guillaume, "how very tenuous is the precise notion of one's own visual form, in spite of what the child learns from looking into a mirror."

Finally, the first *scientific* study of this sort, i.e., one done with other people's children, and not "anecdotally" with one's own, was conducted by yet another French psychologist, Henri Wallon, over a period of several years beginning in the 1930s.[26] During the first six months of life, he found, the infant's relationship to the specular image is one of "sociability"—it regards its reflection as a playmate of sorts, and as late as thirty-five weeks of age it registers surprise when it reaches out to this "playmate" and its hand touches glass. Clear signs of self-recognition—as with Louise and the straw hat—emerge at around one year of age, but (as in the case of Louise) this momentary insight does not stabilize. By and large, Wallon's findings were not very dif-

ferent from those of Guillaume. In particular, he confirmed the tenuous and nonlinear quality of the whole process. From twelve to fifteen
months of age, he found, children will practice certain movements in
front of the mirror (experiment with the image, in effect), exploring
and checking out what this other self represents. This sort of play and
experimentation, he discovered, can go on up to thirty-one months
of age. There is something about our body image, and the Self/Other
distinction, that is never finished. Accounts are never closed here—
a fact that has serious consequences for adult life.

As the reader might expect, research of this sort has expanded
dramatically since the days of Guillaume and Wallon, and has (pre-
dictably) taken a heavily scientific direction, especially in the United
States. Child behavior laboratories attached to major universities now
conduct large-scale, long-term experiments, employing a massive
technological apparatus: video monitoring, split-screen photography,
and, of course, computer analysis.[27] In the four major studies conducted in the United States in the 1970s, the criteria for self-recognition
included any or all of the following: (a) with a mark (e.g., of rouge)
applied to the infant's nose, the infant looked in the mirror and touched
the rouge mark; (b) the infant said its name in response to the mother
pointing to its reflection and saying, "Who's that?"; (c) the infant
displayed embarrassed or self-admiring behavior in front of the mirror,
including being silly or coy. Although the occasional nine-month-old
met the criteria for self-recognition, the overwhelming majority of
infants began to display these signs only after eighteen months of age,
thus moving the Guillaume-Wallon threshold ahead by about six
months. But other than that, it is not clear that these modern scientific
studies have altered the conceptual mapping of the two French psychologists in any significant way. Beyond the issue of more precise
dating, the conclusions are fairly similar: movement and "practice" in
front of the mirror (what are now called "contingency clues") accelerate the process of self-recognition; it takes a long time for such
recognition to stabilize; it all seems to occur in a nonlinear way, i.e.,
in stages (although there is some debate about this);[28] and the process
never really ends. The sequence thus remains as Wallon pegged it:
"sociability" (treating the specular image as a playmate); moments of
self-recognition, followed (later) by experimentation with the image;
stabilization of the insight that the image *is* a reflection; and (by thirty
months of age) only occasional interest in the image, or in playing
with it.

Modern researchers have also spent a great deal of time investigating the process by which the infant mirrors its environment (including its mother) and have, as a result, been able to push the phase of "cosmic anonymity" further and further back. As Daniel Stern, a leading student of the subject, puts it, "[n]ew infant capabilities are being revealed at an astounding rate."[29] A newborn can imitate the mother within the first six days; if she sticks her tongue out, so will the baby—an action that requires sophisticated visual-tactile correlation. At two to three weeks of age, infants can visually recognize an external object (e.g., a cube) which they had only experienced through touch (i.e., in the mouth, while blindfolded). At three months, they can differentiate between categories of color. At four months, shown two films and a sound track, they will look at the film appropriate to the sound track. Clearly, the newborn is not the amorphous blob of Id postulated by classical psychoanalysis. This recent research reveals a *curious* infant, an *exploring* one. The infant does not "awaken" to object relations, but rather is born ready for a perceptual-motor-affective dialogue with its mother, or whoever acts as the central caretaker in its life. "Infants," concludes Daniel Stern,

> appear to be predesigned by nature, in the form of perceptual and cognitive preorganization, such that salient natural categories such as self and other are not left to be slowly and painstakingly learned "from scratch"; rather, they are prestructured emergent entities that result from the interaction between a prestructured perceptual and cognitive organism and natural events in a predictable external world.

What these studies do *not* address was what Wallon, in his more philosophical passages, tried to come to grips with, namely, what is the psychological and ontological significance of all this? In all of the above studies, no agreed-upon relationship was ever worked out among self-recognition, imitation behavior, and interior awareness (existential identity). That a six-day-old infant can stick its tongue out when its mother does does not prove the existence of Self/Other differentiation. It may be part of the biopsychic process of such differentiation—en route to it, so to speak—but more than that we cannot say. Even Daniel Stern qualifies his discussion of early infant abilities by saying that the research in question deals only with sensorimotor schemata, not with "representations capable of symbolic transformations." In other words, infants cannot, on this evidence, be said to have prestructured categories of Self and Other, which "are categories and experiences of enormous complexity, requiring redefinition at each point in development."[30]

The same thing can be said of many of the mirror studies discussed here. The problem with drawing substantial inferences for self-aware-ness from evidence of self-recognition is that a number of animal species, including chickens and goldfish, display a great interest in mirrors. William Preyer concluded, from his observation that his four-teen-month-old child could recognize its mother in the mirror, that this was evidence for self-recognition; but a macaque can do this as well.[31] It is also clear that chimpanzees display self-recognition be-havior. Thus the key criterion in the four studies cited above—rec-ognition of a rouge or dye mark on the face—was met by chimpanzees in a study done in 1970. The chimps were marked while anesthetized; later on, shown a mirror, they used it to guide themselves to the dye mark and then inspected their fingers.[32] It seems difficult to maintain that any of these animals have a growing sense of "I"-awareness or existential inwardness that increasingly guides their lives, and thus it becomes problematic to determine what all of these self-recognition studies amount to, beyond playing the role of a halfway house or developmental stage.[33] Infants also acquire language in the second year of life; this does not make them poets, but they cannot become poets without it.[34] Hence the authors of the most extensive of the four studies cited, Michael Lewis and Jeanne Brooks-Gunn, admit that the presence of self-recognition is at most a "window on the emerging concept of self."[35]

These scientific studies are useful in showing that there is an alter-nating slow and fast buildup of increasing self-recognition, and of Self/Other differentiation; but the shift to true self-awareness is completely discontinuous—a "catastrophe point," as these events are sometimes called. "I am I" is a different level of existence, and it raises questions about ontology and the basic fault that "objective" clinical analysis simply cannot deal with. But what should be clear from all this research is that the body contains, by age three, a dialectic of continuity/dis-continuity that is very deeply felt. As a result, crossing the catastrophe point into existential awareness (and it is not, in childhood, crossed "once and for all") is closely tied up with body image, with the mind's perception of the body. Mirroring has a purely physical (tactile) aspect, which I shall discuss later on; but even in the case of the infant con-fronting its specular image, we recognize that it is a *body* image we are talking about. Body image and interiority, or self-awareness, are two sides of the same coin—we cannot hope to understand one without the other. "The ego is first and foremost a body ego," as Freud once put it.[36] The onset of self-recognition, and finally self-awareness, is a bodily phenomenon and revolves around the body image, even if neither of these generates a lot of measurable clues for the behavioral scientist. When one talks about the basic fault, or the nemo, one is talking about a somatic process.

So if birth is the moment that the physical body is released into the world, a body that has been in preparation for nine months, the "I am I" experience is the moment that the body image is born, an image that was "conceived" in the process of self-recognition. The physical body is conceived as a zygote and then carried to term and delivered. The psychic body—the body image—is similarly "conceived" during self-recognition and "delivered" at the moment of self-awareness a year or so later on. The pregnancy of the mother with the child's physical body is in a sense replicated by the "pregnancy" of the child with its body image. In this latter case, the mother acts as a midwife; this is what the general process of mirroring is all about. The physical mirror merely generates a faster "delivery."

We are, I realize, in murky territory here, so let me summarize the argument thus far. Basically, three points emerge, facts that are closely related to each other. The first is that like self-recognition, self-awareness is a discontinuous process. The second point is that it is not amenable to scientific verification. The third point is that this development is somatic; it is only partly a matter of conceptual or intellectual understanding. Before I go on to discuss the implications of all this for human identity, it might be helpful to say just a few more words about these three points.

Recall the exercise I suggested earlier, of trying to remember your first conscious moment. Now add the following exercise: try to remember your *second* conscious moment. Over the years, as a teacher or lecturer, I have given these exercises to people only to discover that recall of their first conscious moment is fairly easy, and recall of their second moment typically nonexistent. Can you recall your second conscious moment? Probably not; and the reason for this is that just as in the case of Louise Guillaume and her straw hat, or her examining herself in a group photograph, existential self-awareness—despite an initial "I am I" experience—is something that grows over time. It is nonlinear, it weaves in and out. The first experience is only the beginning in a series of memories that become increasingly frequent.

The reason that the Self is not amenable to scientific verification is that it does not exist as a discrete entity, but is in fact a process; it can never be a clinical object, never be localized in space or time. Thus, whereas self-recognition is trackable via contingency (i.e., movement) clues, rouge marks, and so on, the Self (soul, in the Middle Ages) lies outside the bounds of scientific observation. To begin with, although the experience of "I am I" typically occurs in the third year of life, many people report the experience happening anywhere from four months to thirteen years (!), so the whole thing lacks stable definition.[37] It is also definable in terms of what is not—what I shall refer to later on as the problem of binary opposition. "I am I" can never flash through your consciousness without the simultaneous sense of "I am not *that*" (i.e., Other). In all the cases I know of—including my own experience with the glass doors—the subject recalled being aware that they were "here" and that the object or situation perceived was "over there." This phenomenon of contrast invariably emerges in studies done on the subject of existential self-awareness, and we are forced to conclude that the real experiential category is not Self, but Self/Not-Self; these two only occur in a bipolar constellation. Whatever the Self is, it is part of a force field; there is no separate entity called the Self. But it exists, lack of hard evidence notwithstanding.[38]

Of course, the sense of "I" finally does stabilize, usually around eight years of age, though it is still not scientifically verifiable.[39] But interviews with eight-year-olds reveal a clear possession of a sense of inner self. This is the point at which "conscious deception becomes a possibility for the child, because the child is able to manipulate the relation between external and internal reality."[40] It knows it can have a facade, in other words. The shift that began at about six months of age, from participating consciousness (the experience of Self as being immersed in the world) or what Kurt Goldstein called "concreteness" or "immediacy," to what he called "abstractness" (discrimination), is finally complete.[41] By age eight, the magical or animistic world is finished for children; participating consciousness becomes the exception rather than the rule.

As for our third point, the tie-in of all this to visual experience is the fact that self-awareness is awareness of one's own body as a separate entity, or as a specular image. The concept of the "I," even as a first, momentary flash, is a fully embodied event—as embodied, let us say, as an orgasm. The Self is a body self; it has no other root than a visceral one. Yet although it remains tied to the body until death, it gets elaborated in such a way as to take a viewpoint on the body, have a conception of it. It is here that our problems begin. The body image lies at the heart of all human self-awareness; neither the basic fault nor the human history that flows out of it can be understood without understanding what the body image is or how it operates in our early (and subsequent) lives.

What does it mean, then, to look in the mirror and understand, for the first time, but in a clear and unequivocal sense, that what you are seeing is nothing other than what other people see when they look at you? For the "French school" of philosophy and child psychology—Henri Wallon, Maurice Merleau-Ponty, Jacques Lacan—this moment, which marks the birth of your identity as a being in the world, also marks the birth of your alienation from the world. The full understanding of a distinction between Self and Other sets up a tension in the psyche, requiring you to make a decision in favor of one or the other in terms of this identity. Alienation, or what Wallon called "confiscation," involves a shift that can be described in various ways: from Self to Other; from the kinesthetic to the visual; from the authentic (inward) to the social (exterior); or, to use the language of Laing and Winnicott, from the true self to the false one. All of this is not without long preparation; it has been building in all of the stages of self-recognition discussed above. But it is in the leap from self-recognition to self-awareness that the psyche is torn in two. The shock is not that an Other exists, but that you realize that *you are an Other for other Others*. What now opens up, and deepens until age eight, and is something you are condemned to deal with for the rest of your life, is that an interpretation can be put upon you that is antagonistic to what you feel about yourself. It is not merely that the Self is something that remains unfinished; it is, more significantly, that its validity, its very existence, can be thrown into question.

Confiscation, then, is another way of talking about the basic fault. What happens inside—the emergence of the nemo—is the very same thing that happens outside, namely the Self/Other dichotomy. *These two events are the same process*, not just two "aspects" of a single process. The inside "tear" is the outside tear; that is what it means to say, "there is no Self without Other." As infants, we move from "syncretic sociability" (Wallon), the confusion between ourselves and the Other, to the emergence of a "lived distance" that now divides us.[42]

The loss involved in the shift from kinesthetic to visual awareness, which lies at the heart of confiscation, is no small thing. It amounts to a revolution in consciousness, the crucial feature of which is the decision to distrust the evidence of our senses. Seen in this way, Hans Christian Andersen's tale "The Emperor's New Clothes" takes on archetypal significance, and this is inevitable if identity is a function of social mirroring. In order to win membership in the human race, we are asked to pay a "small" price: everything. We are asked to give up our basic, and most trustworthy, way of knowing the world in favor of a phony charade of polite agreement. This is a colossal mutilation, and it accounts for much of the rage and pain that all of us carry and that erupts periodically in orgies of war and barbarism. It also, as we shall see in Part II, accounts for much of the religious history of the West and the whole cycle of orthodoxy and heretical rebellion that is the major key to the way reality itself is coded and organized in this civilization.[43] For regardless of what visual con game goes down, the kinesthetic level always remains. "Through smell, taste, touch," writes Lawrence Durrell, "we apprehend each other, ignite each other's minds; information conveyed by the body's odours after orgasm, breath, tongue-taste—through these one 'knows' in quite primeval fashion."[44] We know each other physically—by the way we move, the way we smell, by the sound of the voice, etc.—before we come to know any of this information (or attempt to fog it over) intellectually. This is why as a young child you could sense an atmosphere, or have an intuitive grasp of a social situation, much better than you now can as an adult, and why adults in social situations have to keep talking constantly, so that (visceral) reality will not break through. As Merleau-Ponty puts it, there exists for all of us, initially, a state of precommunication in which our intentions play across the body of another, and vice versa.[45] But the truth of the matter is that this never goes away; our intentions *always* play across each other's bodies, whether we choose to recognize this or not.

Because the kinesthetic precedes the visual, because of the deep archaic origins of merger, as opposed to separation, the "lived distance" that divides us occasionally tends to break down, though these situations are regarded as potentially taboo or hazardous by "visual" society. Both psychic boundaries, as Freud noted in the opening pages of *Civilization and Its Discontents*, and somatic ones (i.e., the body image), as Paul Schilder pointed out in his classic work, *The Image and Appearance of the Human Body*, are highly labile, influenced by a great number of factors and always extending beyond the physical boundaries of the skin or any psychic entity we may choose to call ego or Self.[46] This is why, for example, clothing—what Erasmus of Rotterdam called "the body of the body"[47]—is a controversial issue in nearly every society, and why departure from the norm (e.g., hippies, beatniks, punks) generates such a storm. Any public shift to the kinesthetic threatens to blow the whistle on the agreed-upon visual game, which a somatically alienated culture both longs for and fears. (Ever wonder why corporate executives make money and mime performers do not?) Situations of intense relatedness—romantic love, psychosis, mystical experience—involve a "regression" to syncretic sociability, wherein it is impossible to distinguish where Self ends and Other begins (a "confusion at the core of a situation that is common to us both," comments Merleau-Ponty[48]). We long for this, but it is the ultimate horror as well, the collapse back into the abyss. "Lived distance," so carefully preserved, collapses, or explodes to include the entire world. Ecstatic experience is one of total kinesthesia; everything is alive, quivering, embodied, and it is noteworthy that mystics down through the ages have insisted that the experience is essentially cognitive, a mode of knowing.[49] (What is it that they know? That Self and Other are identical.) Schizophrenia is a situation that can be called totally visual: the person feels transparent as glass, a being completely confiscated, completely determined by the look of the Other.

Most of our experiences, of course, lie somewhere between these two extremes; in daily life, the line between Self and Other, or kinesthetic and visual, is constantly being negotiated. We are always, in some sense, being "confiscated," and this is a dance that is played around the basic fault.[50] But this whole set of behaviors depends on the final recognition of what the specular image represents. "At the same time that the image of oneself makes possible the knowledge of oneself," writes Merleau-Ponty,

it makes possible a sort of alienation. I am no longer what I felt myself, immediately, to be; I am that image of myself that is offered by the mirror. To use Dr. Lacan's terms, I am "captured, caught up" by my spatial image.

Thus a split opens up between a real, lived me and an imaginary one. "In this sense," Merleau-Ponty writes,

I am torn from myself, and the image in the mirror prepares me for another still more serious alienation, which will be the alienation by others. For others have only an exterior image of me, which is analogous to the one seen in the mirror. Consequently others will tear me away from my immediate inwardness much more surely than will the mirror.

Inevitably, he goes on,

there is a conflict between the *me* as I feel myself and the *me* as I see myself or as others see me. . . . The acquisition of a specular image . . . bears not only on our *relations of understanding* but also our *relations of being*, with the world and with others.[51]

So alienation involves the imposition of a constructed me—one visible at a distance—on the immediately lived me. This is the essence of the confiscation, and it anticipates the later confiscation of me by others. "The visual makes possible a kind of schism between the immediate *me* and the *me* that can be seen in the mirror."[52] All deep relations with others, as a result, inevitably generate psychological insecurity.

A powerful description of confiscation occurs in Pär Lagerkvist's novel, *The Dwarf*, which captures perfectly the fear that is involved here. The dwarf lives in the house of the Prince; the great artist, Bernardo (Leonardo da Vinci), has been commissioned to paint a portrait of the Princess, which she does not want to have painted. "I understand her only too well!" the dwarf says to himself.

> One may contemplate oneself in a mirror, but on leaving it one does not wish the reflection to remain there so that somebody else can take possession of it. . . .
>
> No one possesses himself! Detestable thought! No one possesses himself! Thus everything belongs to the others! Don't we own even our faces? Do they belong to anybody who chooses to look at them? And one's body? Can others own one's body? I find the notion most repellent.
>
> I, and I alone, will be the sole possessor of that which is mine. Nobody else may seize it, none outrage it. It belongs to me and nobody else. And after my death I want to continue to own myself. Nobody is going to poke about in my entrails. I do not wish them to be seen by strangers. . . . It is as though I were no longer sole owner of myself. . . .[53]

It is interesting that Native Americans have a fear of being photographed, a fear that the possessor of their picture has in some way confiscated their soul. As one psychologist has written, "whenever we deal with the mirror phenomenon, we are dealing with something enigmatic, uncanny. . . ."[54] Sartre said that for the adult, the image is a "quasi-presence." Even for the adult, the specular image "is mysteriously inhabited by me; it is something of myself."[55] This is why stepping on a photograph is something we feel uneasy about, unless we do it as a deliberate act of aggression. Intellectual understanding is useless here; the "uncanny" nature of the specular image cannot be removed by a course in optics; the "quasi-presence" of the snapshot cannot be eliminated by being told it is merely photographic paper. The whole world of objects and object relations is not a neutral one; it is soaking in questions of ontological survival.

True recognition of the specular image is acquired very slowly. It is not the sort of knowledge on the order of $2 + 2 = 4$ or Paris is the capital of France. Self/Other cognition is never settled; it haunts us all our lives; it cannot be solved by imposing a binary yes/no framework (although we often attempt to do this). Rather, it involves great uncertainty. The specular image acquires a marginal existence only very slowly, and this is why it still exerts a hold over us when we are adults. To the end of our days we continue to check ourselves out in front of the mirror or search ourselves out in a group photograph, to "see what we look like." Similarly, this quality of "presence" implicates our relations with others. The things that really matter in life all have this quality; they can never really be "known."[56]

This finally indefinite quality of our visual image has not deterred behavioral scientists from examining this phenomenon, but as already noted, measurable data prove to be elusive. Scientists such as Seymour Fisher and Franklin Shontz have made major contributions to this field, though their crucial discovery seems to be how extremely plastic the body image really is.[57] The ABD, or adjustable body distorting mirror—a full-length mirror that enables manipulation of the body image by pressure (bowing)—has been a useful tool of research, but experiments with it have yielded peculiar results. Subjects typically forget what they actually look like, and come up with a wide range of reflections that are all different and yet, to the subjects, all valid representations of their bodies! The ABD has proven to be more of a Rorschach test than anything else.[58]

Our inconclusiveness about what we look like, and therefore about who we are, is also the result (in part) of the uniqueness of the specular image. Wallon noted that the child sitting in front of a mirror with its father has before it two visual images that it can compare, but in the case of its own body it has only one. It cannot look at its own body as a whole *except* in a mirror.[59] Both Guillaume and Wallon noted that this particular visual image is an exceptional phenomenon. Grasping it, said Wallon, requires displacing your own image in order to stand outside of yourself, which is a complex task as long as the image is still felt kinesthetically.[60] Knowing oneself and confiscation—which confuses the knowing—seem to be completely inseparable. If the Uncertainty Principle has finally stood classical physics on its head, a similar sort of effect operates in psychology to an even greater degree.

Jacques Lacan has gone over much of the same territory Merleau-Ponty has, being much more aggressive than other psychologists about what he regards as the catastrophe of the gap, or Self/Other split.[61] The consequence of this split, he says, is that the ontological structure of human life is paranoid (the Self can always be invaded by the Other). The kinesthetic-to-visual shift means the irrevocable fragmentation of the body: "paranoiac alienation . . . dates from the deflection of the specular I onto the social I." An ego is constructed to paper over this gap, making it (the gap), in repressed form, the dynamic force of our lives. In other words, we attempt to heal the basic fault by identifying with a visual image of ourselves. What most psychologists regard as a sign of health, viz., a strong ego structure, Lacan thus regards as the symptom of a disturbed psyche. The authority of the ego over our psychic life is itself the symptom of our problem and the basis of our unreal relations with ourselves, he says, and it is the mirror stage (stade du miroir), as he calls it, that generates the ego as an entity modeled on the body image. For Lacan, the ego is rooted in what he calls the realm of the Imaginary, the world of images, doubles, mirrors, and specular identification. It emerges as an either/or relationship, a construct founded on the opposition and identity between Self and Other, and as such is paranoid. For our fundamental relationship with the world is one of connection; the stade du miroir, the whole process of specular identification, tricks us into believing that the Other is something to be feared. Hence Einstein's reply to a reporter who had asked him if there was a single crucial question that the human race had to answer: "Yes," said Einstein, "it is this: Is the universe friendly?" For Lacan, the realm of the Imaginary marks the attempt of the Self to master trauma through the "mirage of self-sufficiency." "The mirror or visual me," writes Michael Eigen, "the actor for an audience, comes to be used as a defence against authentic body feelings, especially one's vulnerability and insufficiency."[62]

There is, however, in all this discussion of images and perception, one aspect of mirroring that must not be overlooked, and that is the factor of touch, which includes libidinal attachment. Of all of our French psychologists, Jacques Lacan has had the most to say about this, for he has pointed out that all of what we learn about the Self/ Other dynamic in infancy occurs in an affective, tactile, and emotive context—it is not merely a question of gazing into eyes or silvered glass.[63] Hence Lacan's word for the gap, the Self/Other separation, is *sevrage*, a word that means "weaning" as well as "severance." When we talk about object relations, we are not talking about just any objects, but—among other things—hands, faces, and breasts. The nemo emerges in a context that is erotic, fleshy, libidinally charged. From a Freudian viewpoint—and Lacan and Winnicott can certainly be put in this camp— this is *the* crucial issue in the matter of separation and attachment. It was for this reason that Winnicott argued that the real drama was not Self vs. Other but Self vs. Mother—a theme recently reworked, from a feminist perspective, by another Freudian writer, Dorothy Dinnerstein (*The Mermaid and the Minotaur*).[64] It is in this highly emotive context that the infant has to work out the ontological puzzle of self-identification, and this is why—Piaget and modern science notwithstanding—cognition and emotion are closely bound up with one another, for adults as well as for children. Object loss triggers not just terror of the Void, but a heavy component of rage, pain, and sadness, which reflect the energy of sexual attachment. So there is more to this whole thing than meets the eye.

For the most part, the object-relations theorists did not have much to say about human sexuality. Balint held that object relations are completely independent of erotogenic zones,[65] and even Winnicott, when faced, in his pediatric practice, with the fact that the play that goes on in transitional space is sometimes sexual in nature, preferred to ignore it.[66] Object relations sees the basic issue of the human condition as being one of meaning and cognition, and object loss (loss of Other) as being fundamentally the loss of a comprehensible world. As such, object relations seems to be primary in the hierarchy of human needs, and in fact there is much to suggest that this is true. John Holt, the American educator, has argued that children come into the world with a desire to make sense of it—what we might call the "cosmological urge." He claims that this urge is biological, stronger than the need for food. Infants who are feeding, for example, will stop and look up with great curiosity if something interesting (i.e., meaningful) happens in their environment.[67] Since feeding is, in psychoanalytic theory, a libidinal activity, we can see already that it is capable of being usurped by a deeper hunger, namely the search for a comprehensible world.[68] Consider also the couple that stays together, year after year, without engaging in sexual activity or even in the occasional touch or caress, simply because something bad is preferable to nothing at all. "Nothing at all," as the object-relations school would argue, is the worst thing we think we can face.

I am, however, not completely convinced by all this, because in actual practice, sexuality and ontology tend to run together from a very early point, in particular if one takes sexuality in its broadest sense to mean a sensual and erotic relationship with the world. From birth, some degree of physical contact with others is so strong an aspect of our ontological development that prolonged absence of it later in life makes us feel that life is meaningless without it (to me, a reasonable conclusion). By the time the infant is into the mirror stage and the process of self-recognition, it is immersed in a libidinal network. I believe it is for this reason that the two energies, ontological and erotic, often seem to be so similar. Both have a fierceness to them, as well as a quality of "drawing one in." The person with a new guru, new therapist, or new philosophy of life is visibly animated and excited, and this often has a sexual feel to it. The crossover between sexuality and religious ecstasy is a well-known phenomenon, whatever religious context it occurs in. No matter how "spiritual" the cosmological urge may seem, it is, I want to emphasize, thoroughly grounded in the tissues of the body; meaning is part of the bodily self.

So a "pure" object-relations position is difficult to maintain. Infants literally die if they are not held; just being looked at lovingly isn't enough.[69] Paul Schilder's empirical studies revealed that the construction of the body image is libidinal as well as social, and that those parts of the body that are erotogenic are perceived by subjects to be closer to them in terms of physical distance than nonerotogenic parts.[70] Michel Odent reports ecstatic states and orgasmic gratification of women at the moment of birth (at least in the case of completely natural childbirth);[71] and Frederick Leboyer's description of how the newborn should be caressed upon delivery is frankly erotic:

> Our hands travel over the infant's back, one after the other, following each other like waves. One hand still in contact as the other begins. Each maintaining its steady rhythm until its entire journey is concluded. Without rediscovering this visceral slowness that lovers rediscover instinctively, it is impossible to communicate with the child.
>
> But, people will say, you're making love to the child!
> Yes, almost.

To make love is to return to paradise, it is to plunge again into the world before birth, before the great separation. It is to find again the primordial slowness, the blind and all-powerful rhythm of the internal world, of the great ocean.[72]

The importance of touch as a form of (positive) mirroring, and therefore as a source of self-creation and ontological security, was explored very fully in one of the most significant essays to appear in the English language in recent years, *The Continuum Concept* by Jean Liedloff.[73] Liedloff began to understand the role of being held in human identity-formation as a result of living with the Yequana Indians of Brazil for about two years' time. Yequana babies are held—"in arms," as she puts it—twenty-four hours a day for at least the first two years of their lives. The result is that they grow up not experiencing any gap, or sense of having an empty space within themselves. They do not, she says, spend their entire lives trying to prove that they exist, or trying to make up for a missing sense of Self. Confiscation is a rupture in the continuum of life, which is a biological continuum. The Yequana, apparently, get only very mild doses of this, or perhaps none at all. So where we moderns spend most of our lives trying, indirectly and unconsciously, to repair a ruptured continuum, the Yequana never have to think about it—they can just live and enjoy life. For us, the Self comes to be defined as wanting, the Other as withholding. From birth to "I"-consciousness and confiscation, we learn that life is lonely and full of pain and that the universe is most definitely *not* friendly. We have an abyss, says Liedloff, where a rich sense of Self might have existed. Our basic orientation to life is future-oriented: "I'd be all right *if . . . ,*" "I'll be happy *when . . . ,*" etc. This desire for tactile mirroring, for physical reassurance, says Liedloff, is not about sex—at least not in the narrow sense of the term. In fact, the modern Western preoccupation with sex is really a symptom of continuum rupture. Sex is only a nodal point on an erotic, object-relations continuum. The search for a universe that is loving (not just friendly) is the real issue here. This is what Liedloff supplies that Wallon and others tend to omit: a friendly universe gazes approvingly on the infant, whereas a loving universe *holds* it. The search for the lost Other is first and foremost an ontological, or cosmological, project, but in practice it turns into an erotic one as well. By itself, then, object-relations theory is incomplete.[74]

We need, finally, to be able to relate all of this to questions regarding the nature of culture and society at large. Before we can do that, however, a few words concerning the mirror as a physical object would not be out of place. For up to this point, our discussion has been primarily psychological in nature, and psychology often tends to assume that human beings are fundamentally, in all places and at all times, the same. History, on the other hand, does not necessarily bear this out. To put the issue directly: silvered glass is not that old, historically speaking. It is, in fact, a relatively recent invention. If so, much of this psychological material, including discussions of confiscation and alienation, is really (as Ivan Illich puts it) epoch-specific and therefore suspect. It may only represent a modern pathology, not "the human condition." Of course, it would seem to be the case, as I have already indicated, that the physical mirror is only an archetype, or condensed instance, of the larger phenomenon of human mirroring, and the researches of Darwin, Preyer, Guillaume, Wallon et al. tend to bear this out. The physical mirror—specifically, silvered glass—can thus be seen to "reflect" the accelerated condition of modern times. But how do we know this? Before we can turn to the consequences of the phenomenon of mirroring for culture at large, it will be necessary to examine the history of the mirror as a physical object. Just how archetypal is it? is a question that can only be answered by means of historical investigation.

To anticipate for a moment, the history of the physical mirror would seem (as far as I can determine) to run parallel to the development of consciousness itself; it itself mirrors the larger cultural milieu of which it is a part. For the evolution of reflecting surfaces is not really about technology, but about psyche and soma. Its real significance is that it is an icon of the kinesthetic/visual balance at any moment in time. The mirror *grows* as an archetype, in other words, although the process is (as with consciousness) not a linear one. Periods of strong self-awareness are curiously accompanied by sharp increases in the use, distribution, or manufacture of mirrors, with the heaviest emphasis occurring in the modern period. Thus the mirror emerges, strangely enough, both as an archetype *and* as an indicator of pathology. The torn condition of modern man, in other words, is an extreme case of a situation that is, at the very least, dormant in the human condition, though there are societies that tend not to trigger the phenomenon of confiscation, if at all. Let me elaborate on this in greater detail.[75]

The use of reflecting surfaces is probably as old as the human race itself. Going back even beyond those civilizations that used polished metal disks, we find the practice of spitting on a dark, flat stone and rubbing it to give it a shiny, reflecting surface, or simply the use of pools of water. Some Indian tribes used the glistening body of a fish that had recently been pulled out of the water. Paralleling this usage are stories and myths about mirrors, present in numerous cultures around the world. The Narcissus myth of ancient Greece undoubtedly has a number of antecedents, though its very pointed message—the gods finally got annoyed with this beautiful youth who fell in love with his reflection, and so turned him into a flower—suggests that ancient cultures found this sort of behavior (when it existed) aberrant.

In the case of both the mirrors and the stories about them, however, precise dating is not possible. Plaques of mica, pierced with a hole so that they could be hung in some way, have been found in predynastic Egyptian tombs (i.e., possibly as far back as 4000 B.C.), and they reflect quite well. The earliest identifiable mirror, unearthed in the 1920s about 250 miles south of Cairo, dates from before 4500 B.C., and is made of selenite (a variety of gypsum). A copper one was also found, dating from 2920–2770 B.C. It is probably of Asian origin, and is now in the Sydney Museum. The use of bronze mirrors began ca. 2100 B.C. In general, Egyptian mirrors had a handle, and were typically used for grooming, but were also included in tombs, where they were placed close to the body. Representations of mirrors also occur in tombs, with the famous Egyptian "magical eye" painted on the disk.

There are certain Aegean artifacts (Cycladic culture) that may be mirrors, dating from about 2500 B.C., and there are two mirrors that were found at Mycenae that date to about 1500 B.C. As in the case of the Egyptians, there is evidence that the Greeks used mirrors for grooming, and mirrors were also placed in Bronze Age tombs in Crete and Mycenae. It is, however, from the sixth century B.C., when one sees the growing appearance of ego-consciousness in Greece, that Greek mirror production really took off. The Romans continued this, being the first people in Europe to produce glass mirrors, which art they learned from the Egyptians. Mirrors became so popular in Rome that they were even owned by servants; and Seneca (first century A.D.) reported his disgust at one Hostius Quadra, who had himself constantly surrounded by mirrors.

Mirror production in Europe went into abeyance after about A.D. 100; and after Saint Augustine's development of the mirror as a metaphor for the soul, the mind, Holy Scripture, etc. (this about the early fifth century), little more was heard about mirrors until the twelfth century. This dormancy coincided roughly with a loss of interiority, or self-consciousness, during the early Middle Ages. I discuss this in detail in Part II of this book; but briefly, human self-awareness, for reasons not entirely clear, seemed to disappear during this time and then mysteriously reappeared in the eleventh century. Behavior during the period A.D. 500–1050 had a kind of "mechanical" or robotic quality to it, as a result, and the interest in reflection, in both the physical and the metaphysical sense, was correspondingly low. Thus there was a reference to mirrors by Isadore, Bishop of Seville, in the seventh century; and in 625, Pope Boniface IV sent a mirror to the queen of Edwin of Northumbria; but that is about all. Reference to mirror manufacture reappeared only in the twelfth century, in Alexander of Neckam's *De Naturis Rerum*, in which he talked about glass sheets being backed with lead. The intense self-awareness of the troubadour period (also discussed in Part II), which gave rise to a great interest in finding a romantic partner, or soul mate, to "reflect" one's innermost thoughts and feelings, was matched by a great popularity of mirrors, which were often decorated with scenes of love and gallantry. The knight sometimes carried a sword with a mirror mounted on the hilt as he rode to the defense of his lady, and medieval love lyric is filled with mirror imagery.

Increasing skill in manufacture accompanied all of these developments. The Germans discovered a cylinder process that enabled them to make glass in flat sheets, and they also began to manufacture small convex mirrors out of glass. The art of backing glass with metal, known to some ancient cultures, was rediscovered in the twelfth century. Dutch mirror manufacture also blossomed at this time; in the late thirteenth century, an elaborate Venetian glass guild system moved over to the Isle of Murano, and the use of metallic leaf pressed onto glass appeared for the first time.

From what we can guess, early cultures regarded the specular image in the same way that modern infants do until about two years of age: it was an Other, the manifestation of a deeper reality. It was seen, in other words, as the soul—hence the frequent centrality of the mirror in religious ceremonies and burial rites. One Egyptian term for the mirror was *ankh*, life, and it was used in an anointing ritual that helped preserve the body for future life. It was also seen as capable of receiving the *ka* (double, Other); the Etruscans similarly regarded it as a vehicle for the soul. All of this suggests, however, that confiscation was regarded as a possibility. Mirrors formed an important part of magical and mystical practices in antiquity and the Middle Ages, and one of the dangers associated with such practices, such as autohypnosis induced by prolonged self-contemplation, was that the Self could get lost. Premodern peoples, very likely, had less of a nemo, or basic fault, to worry about, though as one student of the subject has written, "[w]orldwide myths warn of the hazard of having one's soul stolen by a mirror." One psychoanalyst has recorded a number of cases in which her psychotic patients stared into mirrors in an attempt to *recover* their lost souls.

The sixteenth century was the turning point for all of this, although there had been a period of incubation prior to this lasting about four hundred years. From about 1500 on, the manufacture and distribution of silvered glass increased exponentially. Mirrors began to appear everywhere, along with the "rise of the individual" that so clearly characterized the Renaissance. We find a sharp simultaneous increase in self-consciousness and in the quantity and technical quality of mirror production. The rise of modern mirror manufacture coincided with the rise of the nation-state, large standing armies (even in peacetime), the notion of perspective in art, the emergence of the self-portrait as an independent genre, and the early phase of the Scientific Revolution, which spelled the end of the magical worldview. At the same time that this was going on, Murano was beginning to supply small, cheap glass mirrors to the general public, and widespread usage of mirrors occurred in England after 1550. The process of "mirror foiling" (use of tin amalgam) was developed early in the century, and became dominant in the Venetian industry. In *The History of Manners*, the German historian Norbert Elias describes how the sixteenth century in particular witnessed the rise of self-conscious etiquette books that discussed table manners from the viewpoint of how one was being observed by others. (We take this for granted today, but it was a novelty in the 1500s.) Some of these made explicit use of the mirror analogy: *A Mirror for Magistrates*, for example, or *The Mirour of Good Manners*. Around 1550, books were manufactured with small mirrors inside of them; hand and pocket mirrors were worn in dress.

All of this is about the discovery of the Self; it has to be related to the larger issue of mirroring by the eyes of other persons. Elias' example of how our manners and body language slowly came to be controlled in this way is a good one. It is likely that, just as most of the cultures of antiquity were not terribly concerned with mirrors, or regarded preoccupation with self-appearance as aberrant, they were also not terribly concerned with how they appeared in the view of the Other. The Other was much less of an Other; the Self, not a very developed thing. As Elias says, even in the Middle Ages spontaneity was much greater; Self and Other were far more mixed up than today.

People tended to be "immersed" in each other more—not so confiscated. The increasing interest in and production of mirrors as we approach modern times suggests the emergence of an increasing psychic distance between human beings, and *within* human beings. Self/Other unity begins to break down in the modern period, and mirror manufacture parallels this psychic development. Nation-states, armies, self-portraits, perspective, the collapse of magic—all of these represent an increasing preoccupation with boundaries, with sharp Self/Other distinctions, and the interest in the mirror is really an icon of the whole process. The seventeenth century witnessed the introduction of plate glass, and this stimulated the use of large stationary mirrors as part of the household furniture. The upper classes began to indulge in mirror decoration as a fetish, culminating in the Hall of Mirrors at Versailles. By 1599 Catherine de' Medici of France had a mirror room constructed with 119 Venetian mirrors. Mirror rooms and galleries were popular from the seventeenth century on, and by the mid-nineteenth century such rooms were taken up by the middle classes. This type of affectation is surely the product of the torn or mutilated condition referred to above, being as it is so totally Other-directed and Self-preoccupied at one and the same time. We are at the gates of the existential era now; who "I" am is a matter of paramount importance. But we can see that the "French school"—writers such as Lacan and Wallon—overdid its indictment of the human condition, making the modern, acute form of confiscation a kind of norm. All societies probably confiscate to some degree, but not all mutilate, as Lacan has argued. Differences of degree, after all, finally do become differences of kind.

To sum up, then, the story of the physical mirror is really a profile of the evolution of psychic process. Understanding that evolution gives us a certain type of handle, a kind of "cultural psychology," as it were. The outlines, for sure, are gross, but the pattern is nevertheless clear enough. The mirror is indeed an archetype, but the modern period shows the archetype in its most extreme form. When we talk about the development and diffusion of mirrors, then, we are not merely discussing some aspect of the history of technology or of economic history, but the evolution of certain mental structures, specifically of human self-consciousness. This is a first step toward formulating a relationship between individual ontogeny—our private somatic drama—and the larger culture and society of which it is a part.

A second step in this direction—specifically, in relating the basic fault to the origins of culture—can be found in the work of Donald

Winnicott, to whom we have already referred. Winnicott's approach was, like the history of the mirror, still too gross in nature (at least for historical purposes), and yet his contribution to our understanding of issues such as these was literally enormous. For Winnicott, culture was finally a product of how individuals dealt with the gap, or nemo, and he attempted to demonstrate this in a remarkable (and by now classic) essay of 1951, "Transitional Objects and Transitional Phenomena."[76] In specific terms, the paper was, in effect, a study of the teddy bear; more generally, of how children come to select an object by means of which they negotiate the basic fault. Even more than the mirror, for Winnicott, the Transitional Object (T.O.) was the material manifestation of the whole confiscation process; its career in the child's life was the way in which the gradualness of the identification of the specular image actually expressed itself. The teddy bear (or any such object the child might choose) was the intermediary between me and not-me; it served to keep inner and outer reality separated and yet related. Winnicott defined Transitional Objects as "objects that are not part of the infant's body yet are not fully recognized as belonging to external reality." The T.O. is an agent of continuity, a defense against anxiety. As such, it has a definite addictive quality for the child; he or she is obsessive, for example, about taking it to bed at night, or along on a trip; and its loss can precipitate severe anxiety or even hysteria.[77]

Interestingly enough, Winnicott regarded such attachment as healthy and necessary. The T.O., he said, made all relations with an Other possible; it provided a secure or neutral area of experience. The real sign that the T.O. was a healthy phenomenon, for Winnicott, was that if things went well, the T.O. got "decathected" over time and the libidinal energy consequently diffused over "the whole cultural field." In other words, the infant loses interest in his or her teddy bear and goes on to things that are more complex, such as writing books. In what could have been a flash of inspiration Winnicott brought together a whole series of phenomena that arose when the T.O. was finally decathected. "At this point," he wrote,

> my subject widens out into that of play, and of artistic creativity and appreciation; and of religious feeling, and of dreaming, and also of fetishism, lying and stealing, the origin and loss of affectionate feeling, drug addiction, the talisman of obsessional rituals, etc.

*transitional object*

In infancy, the teddy bear is the T.O. Later on, the child and adult graduates to more sophisticated toys: drugs, alcohol, art, religion, and creative scientific work. The T.O. is potentially a very powerful concept, for it would seem to be the bridge between what we have been talking about up to now—kinesthetic, somatic "microhistory"—and the level of the visible, i.e., the stuff that makes it into the newspapers and the history books. Winnicott had essentially arrived at a position similar to that of Géza Róheim, that human beings create culture to keep the wolves from the door. What he failed to ask, however, was this: what kind of culture? If the same impulse lies behind heroin addiction, lying and stealing, organized religion, and the paintings of van Gogh, then I suggest that there is something seriously wrong with a culture that includes all of these things. Winnicott wrote that by learning to play in transitional space, the infant "slides out of playing into cultural experience of every kind." In this way, he said, "the whole torch of culture and civilization is handed on."[78] As one commentator, Arthur Efron, notes, what Winnicott failed to see was that "this slide may not be altogether a good thing." The " 'whole torch,' " adds Efron, "is exactly the problem."[79] As in the case of the mirror, we have to be careful about turning the T.O. into an archetype. Winnicott assumed that the teddy bear (in some form) was a constant of all cultures everywhere, and this is not necessarily the case. Nevertheless, Winnicott finally takes us to the door of the issue I am trying to raise here: history—or at least *history of a certain type*—arises in the space that opens up between the kinesthetic body and the specular image, and is in fact the product of a desire Lacan describes as the desire for the (imaginary) Other, the desire to close down the gap once and for all. This dynamic is revealed most markedly in situations such as addiction or romantic love, situations that possess a structure that is one of total mirroring. We are, in these cases, in the curious position of running around "trying to find a hole to fill up a hole."[80] ("There is no end to desire," as an old yogic saying puts it.) A choice is implied here, each path having very different implications for culture at large. Option One: abandon the Self, so that Other ceases to be a problem; Option Two: attempt to destroy the Other, allowing Self to reign supreme; and Option Three: work your way back to a Self/Other relationship that is not founded on opposition or confiscation. In the first case, history disappears; in the second case, it continues to be what it has been for about ten thousand years now; and in the third case, it takes on a very different form from what we have known in the West. These choices are always available on the individual level; what is possible on a cultural level is something I shall come back to a number of times in the course of this book.

We are, nevertheless, finally in a position to say something more specific regarding the relationship between individual psychology and the characteristics of the culture in which the individual is embedded. For the body image, which is a function of both affective and visual mirroring, and which is highly unstable, arises out of confiscation and our early experience of life, and can be used, along with the idea of the gap and the T.O., to understand history and culture in a new way. All of this is very tentative, but we should be able to generate a few preliminary sketches.

Actually we do not have very far to look for data or examples, at least not in the case of modern society. I have a tendency to do my writing in cafés. As it turns out, I am sitting in one of my favorite haunts right now, and the waiter, a young man of about eighteen years, brings me my coffee. As he turns and goes back to the counter or kitchen, I notice a label on his jeans: "Calvin Klein." I know these jeans are expensive; they may cost anywhere from forty to eighty dollars. The young man may have had to work a full day, possibly two days, to own them. If he would forgo the Calvin Klein label, which consists of a small piece of fabric stitched to the back pocket, he could get a pair of jeans for as little as a third of what he paid for them. But he is not willing to do so; the Klein label is crucial. Furthermore, if I were to ask him *why* he spent so much money on having the Klein label, he would very likely get defensive or angry, and perhaps tell me that it was none of my goddamn business. I think it is very unlikely that he would sit down at my table and tell me that from early childhood, for reasons he couldn't understand, he felt that something was somehow missing, that his life was somehow "wrong" or empty, and that wearing Calvin Klein jeans makes no *logical* sense but is clearly a Winnicottian Transitional Object, enabling him to feel less anxious about his life. Also, that it hasn't worked; he felt OK for two days after he bought the jeans, but then found that the sense of unease and emptiness returned.

Anyway, my waiter departs. At the next table, a man of about sixty is telling the fellow sitting with him how, when he was a boy growing up in Scotland, people were respectful to the flag. At the conclusion of a movie, they stood at attention while "God Save the Queen" was played; some even sang along. Today, the Union Jack is seen as a kind of joke. People leave movie theaters at the end of the film, he says—walk out right in the middle of the national anthem! He shakes his head and sighs. Continuing my fantasized scenario with the waiter, I lean over to this man's table and ask him why he needs the British monarchy to create meaning in his life; what difference a hackneyed song or piece of cloth could possibly make to the issues really confronting him. The likely outcome is that he calls me a communist and gives me a black eye. Less likely, he tells me that Samuel Johnson was right when he called patriotism the last refuge of the scoundrel; and admits that by identifying with this larger cause, the Fatherland, he feels much less like the loser he knows, at heart, he really is.

Finally, the waiter and the patriot notice that I have been busy writing in this café for several weeks now, and come over and ask me what I'm writing about. I briefly summarize what I am trying to communicate in this book. They ask me how writing a book which suggests I understand the human condition better than they do, or having the social label "author," is any different, when you really get down to it, from flashing a Calvin Klein label or a Union Jack. Isn't it an attempt to mitigate the very anxiety I am talking about, to create meaning on a psychological level as a substitute for a somatic at-oneness with the world that I don't feel in my body? At this point I get very defensive, call them anti-intellectuals, and leave in an insulted, self-righteous huff, my manuscript (read: T.O.) tucked safely under my arm.

What is involved in these scenarios is much more than the "mundane details" of our daily lives; the truth is that this is where history is ultimately made. For these "details" are finally translatable into socioeconomic and historical events. Far more than the use of sex in advertising, capitalism relies heavily on the anxiety centered around the nemo to generate sales and cash flow in the market.[81] By being able to identify with Calvin Klein, a prestigious (what does "prestige" really mean? That which is "successfully" Other-defined) fashion designer, you simultaneously promote your Self and submerge it, paradoxically, in the Other, in this case the *haut monde* of Calvin Klein. The game works for a while, and when it wears off, don't you worry: the folks on Wall Street and Madison Avenue will have something *else* for you to buy. There is no way that capitalism could function without the psychological fuel of this dynamic, and a number of historians and political scientists have pointed this out. Yet the fact that this is a *somatic* event never gets discussed. Somehow, in studies of the modern economy from *Das Kapital* to the *New Left Review*, the body gets curiously omitted.

Much the same can be said of the patriot. He is easily persuaded that war is necessary and just, when the whole enterprise is in fact a way of obliterating nemonic pain by submerging yourself in a larger Cause that—for the duration of the war at least—erases the Self/Other split (all is now Other). You may have some problems when peace is finally restored; but between wars, at least, you can sit in cafés and bemoan the decline of patriotism. And never fear, after enough time the nemonic itch will bring about the next cycle of destruction, and you can identify with the heroic Fatherland once again.

As for our pathetic author, he probably makes the least difference of all, at least on the larger historical level. His activity is not translatable into the economy or the political arena, though I suppose it can be seen as an aspect of "intellectual culture" or some such thing. In any case, "knowing" why other people behave as they do is, one suspects, merely a means of generating feelings of superiority. It changes nothing, is largely self-serving, and is in the final analysis only subject matter for cocktail parties (if that), soon to be discarded for the next "new" analysis of the human condition. And so it goes. As Lacan says, so much of what we are doing is a disguised attempt to embrace the body of the specular image; to end the basic fault once and for all. But it doesn't go away, and our games merely take new forms. Nor, apparently, is anything else possible. For as long as our interpretation of ourselves is visually based, i.e., made from the viewpoint of the Other (as first occurred in the mirror stage), we can never really get back to the body, and so continue to go in circles.

A similar endless, and useless, game that is rooted in the basic fault and that gets played out in a historical and cultural way is the supposed human tendency (it is actually only about ten thousand years old, as I shall argue in Chapter 2) to see the world in terms of black and white. Things are divided into Good vs. Evil, Us vs. Them, Male vs. Female, Old vs. Young, Conscious vs. Unconscious, Sacred vs. Secular, and so on. The strategy here is simple, as the psychotherapist Melanie Klein described it many years ago: if I can split the world into good and bad, and keep good "inside" and bad "outside," I resolve the problem of Self vs. Other by protecting myself from invasion (which is what, dialectically, I secretly yearn for).[82] It is a position of grim determination: let Self remain Self and Other remain Other; at least we know where we stand. The whole thing works in a rather convoluted way. Since the world is actually gray, rather than black and white, events are constantly intruding on the framework. Yet instead of modifying it, or undermining it, these events only serve to fuel the splitting mechanism even further. Energy must be mobilized to expel the intruder and get the lines of demarcation straight once again. The reason that this whole system ultimately fails is that engagement with the Other, which is systematically denied, is what is somatically desired. Victory on one level turns into defeat on another, more fundamental level.

This type of splitting is easily observable in contemporary politics. Since the early fifties, America has been run by leaders who, to varying degrees, have been obsessed with "containing" (Harry S. Truman's word, I believe) the "godless communists" who allegedly seek to destroy our way of life. Consider John F. Kennedy's constant harping on the theme of "missile gap" (there was none, as it turns out) during his election campaign—a phrase that immediately appealed to the Self/Other fears of the American public, because it was really an echo of the nemonic gap. With Richard Nixon and Ronald Reagan, this Manichaean worldview reached its pathological apogee. But "pathology" is a curious name for this, in that Reagan was reelected to office in 1984 by a landslide margin. So Reagan was quite simply a mirror of the American somatic dilemma: the American people went to the polls and elected themselves to office. This is how, at least in gross outline, unresolved somatic dilemmas work themselves out on the larger historical stage.

Turning to the "good guys," we often find changes in content but not in form. Ecological fundamentalists, if so they can be called, similarly divide the world into two camps, in this case the evil technologists and those out to save Mother Earth. Now this schema may in fact have some validity, just as the dichotomy of communist/capitalist may; but the problem is the way in which this set of ideas is held. In the Nixon-Reagan case, psychic integrity itself is maintained by the splitting mechanism, and *this* is the real problem, not "the enemy." In the same way, many eco-radicals are in the position of making their psychic lives possible by means of an ideology. It is this somatic tension that is the real issue, culturally speaking, far and above any evil technocrats that (as far as I can see) certainly do abound. In historical terms, it is the somatic drama that will determine much more than the loss or victory of either side in the debate, or of the particular set of ideas in question.

Of course, this type of "nemological analysis" is a bit coarse; somatic history will have to do better than merely laying everything at the door of the basic fault. And one way of refining the analysis is to investigate the implications of body image and body boundaries. For the two are not the same; as Paul Schilder argued, the body image always extends beyond the physical limits of the skin.[83] This generates the possibility of an interactive influence, a kind of moving somatic (and morphogenetic, as Rupert Sheldrake would say)[84] field. The psychologist Seymour Fisher, a pioneer in research in body perception, argues that the immediate experience of one's body has a powerful impact on every social situation, and that the image changes depending on whom we meet, what moods we are in, or what circumstances we encounter.[85] Schilder's empirical studies of the human body led him to conclude not merely that the body image was highly plastic, but that it was completely inseparable from social interaction. How did that incomparable actor and mime, Jean-Louis Barrault, once put it?

> The whole of life consists in either pulling toward oneself,
> or else pushing away from oneself,
> and Oneself is the navel.[86]

Another version of this was recently voiced by the French Canadian writer, Jean-Claude Dussault (following Schilder), who wrote that a "relation between two personalities is first and foremost a relation between two bodies."[87] But this leads us to ask: what about two cultures, or two subcultures, or two periods (eras) within the same culture? Much has been written, for example, in the history of science or art, about shifting worldviews; but suppose two different worldviews reflected two different mind/body (body image) experiences? How did Montezuma experience the body language (including the dress) of Cortés? What if the very fabric of modern Mexican history were woven on the somatic level? Is there any possibility that it is *not*? Perhaps such questions are not as ridiculous as they at first seem. Sociologist John O'Neill writes:

> We seek out other bodies in society as mirrors of ourselves . . . because our own bodies are the permeable ground of all social behavior; our bodies are the very flesh of society. . . . What we see in the mirror is what others see. Here is the *incarnate bond between self and society*.[88]

A similar analysis might apply to movements of political unification: Garibaldi and the Risorgimento, the forces behind Bismarck, or the nineteenth-century American preoccupation with "manifest destiny." Is it not likely that all of this is based on the somatic identification with the nation as the body politic, and that the underlying "goal" of such activity is bodily integrity and a secure body boundary? This is reflected in the familiar custom of calling the central part of a nation the "heartland," and I suspect that more than just metaphors are involved here. In the same way, moves toward decentralization or balkanization might involve a local urge toward having a unified body, one that seems manageable, and not on the verge of fragmentation. Geopolitics, in the end, may be a branch of somatic history.

Schilder's work makes it possible to examine things such as the layering or texture of a culture, principally because of his emphasis on the plasticity and communal nature of the body image. The body image, he argued, is not given once and for all, but is subject to a series of creations and decreations; we are constantly building it up, but we also tear it down to some extent.[89] There is, in each culture, a dominant image (what Reich called the "modal personality"), but there are different layers of body images underneath this, and even a single interaction with an object suffices to modify it.[90] "Object" here can mean a lot of things. It can be another body image, but also clothing or even an emotion.[91] How do you react to someone who is heavily tattooed, for example? Could you imagine yourself getting tattooed in such a way? Why not?

Similarly, what do you think would happen to you if you systematically copied the body language of a schizophrenic? A ditchdigger? A famous artist? To what extent do we unconsciously begin to do this when we encounter someone (anyone)? Is this why we feel uncomfortable about tattoos, or class lines? In his book *Class*, Paul Fussell writes that the central reason why you can't escape your socioeconomic class is that the key to it is training in body language that goes on from infancy. The upper classes typically have restricted movements, arms kept close to the torso, while the lower classes are less controlled and more expansive. Hence, if you set out to mimic an Oxford accent, wear the right clothes, and even imitate body language, you'll eventually be found out, because training in class affiliation is total, early, and somatic, and sooner or later you'll slip and give yourself away.[92] Here again is an example of the link between the somatic microlevel and the historical or sociological macrolevel. And we can easily imagine expanding such an analysis: think of the difference between the mode of physical movement (and, we can guess, body image) of the residents of Yorkshire and those of Calabria, for example, or of that of Germany as opposed to that of Jamaica.

Body image extends beyond the borders of the body, as I mentioned earlier, and it can also include objects once connected with the body, such as voice, breath, blood, hair, and semen.[93] A friend of mine who teaches voice to actors once said to me, "The voice *is* the body." (We all know this intuitively.) Control of the breath has played a key factor in Japanese military history. In a famous scene in Akira Kurosawa's film *The Seven Samurai*, two swordsmen square off and watch each other's breathing for a long time, until one falters. At that moment, the other samurai cuts him down in a single stroke. Similarly, the drinking of blood has historically and anthropologically been a very significant ritual, and not merely for symbolic reasons. Drinking blood undoubtedly alters your feelings and perceptions of your body. In the same way, drinking semen has historically been a central rite in a number of gnostic sects, and it very likely goes on today among certain occult groups. All of this extension of the body image is, once again, part of the lability and communality of that image. Schilder wrote:

> There exists a deep community between one's own body-image and the body-image of others. In the construction of the body-image there is a continual testing to discover what could be incorporated into the body. . . . The body is a social phenomenon.[94]

To influence someone in any serious way, it seems to me, is to have an impact on that person somatically. This may actually be what the word "influence" means.

All of this remains, to date, largely hidden, but as Thomas Hanna says (see the second epigraph to this volume), a whole continent awaits our exploration. Consider this bit of hidden somatic history: years ago I had a friend, an older man, a German Jew who left Germany after Hitler's accession to power and for a few years (1933–38) wound up living in Italy. A biologist, he became a member of the newly formed cinematographic research institute in Rome, where he was an early pioneer in time-lapse photography. A short, stocky man used to show up once a week for a private viewing of popular American films, and my friend would see him dimly through a small window in the door of the auditorium, sitting all alone, sort of huddled up, looking at whatever film they showed him that week, or whatever he had requested. "Who is that man?" he finally asked the director of the institute. "Benito Mussolini," was the reply. "He's afraid of crowds, so he comes here to see movies by himself."

Mussolini afraid of crowds! The man who spent his adult political career addressing huge rallies was terrified of possible body contact.

And his favorite movies? Laurel and Hardy films, the humor of which—they were pioneers of American film slapstick, after all—depended on physical touch: pushing, shoving, tripping, pies in the face, etc. What a difference all this must make for modern Italian history. But I have never read a book on the rise of Italian fascism that mentions any of this, or even tries to work out the physical nature of the Italian people in its relation to political events. And no wonder; the body is (literally) beneath our consideration.

In a work written by Seymour Fisher in 1973 (Body Consciousness), the author extends his empirical and theoretical understanding of body image and body behavior to a number of important cultural phenomena.[95] Fisher found a larger predominance of weak body boundaries in his studies of numerous experimental American subjects, and speculates that this fact might account for the creation of a car culture in the United States—having a steel structure around one is a backup for those weak boundaries. Similarly, he wonders whether the isolationist posture of certain cultures (e.g., the Japanese before World War II) might be related to fear of boundary invasion, and whether certain monastic orders have some of their origin in a similar fear and distrust. (If so, the medieval monastic practice of self-flagellation would represent not merely an attempt to degrade the body, but more importantly, a way of feeling the body that had been desensitized via religious repression.) In cases such as these, it may be possible that the situation of the basic fault creates a kind of porosity in the body image, with a corresponding need to deal with it in neurotic ways that get institutionalized as cultural patterns. How a nation (or culture) treats the bodies of its children, says Fisher, may have its echoes in the behavior of the entire national (cultural) body.

It may also be meaningful to look at race relations and culture contacts in somatic terms. This is why my example of tattooing is not as strange as it seems. Fisher suggests that racial prejudice gets part of its energy from the fear of any human body that is significantly different in appearance from our own. There is, he says, some scientific evidence to indicate that we experience anxiety in the presence of different bodies or body distortions, and that the energy one has toward this different body is a function of the negative self-feeling generated in one's own body, which one then unconsciously seeks to "unload" on that other body. The supposedly eternal war between the sexes, it seems to me, may also reflect some of this dynamic. I believe this is also why, in the fairy tales of almost every culture in the world, the liberator or liberating agent of the person stuck in a difficult (symbolic) situation is either an animal—the frog that must be kissed to get the prince—or a witch, a disfigured hag, who must be loved or married to release a spell or curse. In the famous nineteenth-century case of the Elephant Man, the freaks discussed by Leslie Fiedler in his book on the subject (Freaks: Myths and Images of the Secret Self), or the people so starkly photographed by Diane Arbus, we are offered redemption from our confiscation, our alienation, by having the Other shoved in our face in its most extreme form. Here is the *distorting* mirror, the lure of which we can't resist; and in the case of Diane Arbus, in fact, she eventually was led to get sexually involved with many of her subjects, in an attempt to break out of the Self in which she felt trapped.[96] The fear of a different body, says Fisher, expresses itself in attitudes toward entire races, dwarves, people who are crippled, the aged, as well as toward menstruating women. A special class of monster images, he continues, haunts each culture— just consider how we treat some of these groups—and all of this because we have such a difficult time with our own bodies.

What about mass spectacles and identical uniforms that appear in times of crisis—the swastika and brown shirt, or the Rajneesh necklace and accompanying red and orange outfit? The goal of all this, says Fisher, may be to assuage doubts about the stability of the body. Mass rallies in mass uniforms demonstrate to the participants that their bodies are all alike: it is all right now, you are secure. It is no accident that the horror of miscegenation—body pollution—was central to Nazi cosmology (see Part II), and that it remains a keystone of all racist thought.

Much more could be said about the micro/macro connection and the issue of somatic history; all of the above is by way of suggestion as to how such research might proceed. However, what I would like to do now, before making any further suggestions of this sort, is turn the present essay on its head. Splitting, binary thinking, and Self vs. Other translate, in our culture, into a whole spectrum of intellectual thought systems that are sharply dualistic in nature. I am very suspicious of this. It reminds me of the old adage about there being two types of people, those who believe there are two types of people and those who don't. Consider the rigid dualism of The Communist Manifesto, for example ("Free man and slave, patrician and plebeian, lord and serf . . . in a word, oppressor and oppressed . . ."), or how, in the work of Freud and Jung, reality gets divided up into categories of conscious and unconscious. In anthropology, Claude Lévi-Strauss has made binary opposition the theme of culture itself—The Raw and the

*Cooked*, the primitive and the civilized. In Rousseau similarly, and to some extent in Wilhelm Reich, we have natural man hidden under his armored counterpart ("born free, everywhere in chains"); and the whole object-relations school, on which this chapter is based, is itself a binary mode of regarding the human condition, from Melanie Klein's good and bad breast to Winnicott's and Laing's true and false self. This binary thinking may be right, but what does "right" mean, except that all of these thinkers are giving voice to a common somatic experience?

As in the case of the mirror, we have to be cautious about turning epoch-specific situations into transcultural archetypes. As already noted, other cultures, and earlier eras, do (did) not experience the basic fault in the same way modern Western society does, and some may not (have) experience(d) it at all. I have already suggested that the Transitional Object, the use of which Winnicott believed was inherent in human nature and essential to healthy development, is apparently absent in certain cultures, such as the Yequana, as well as among Australian aborigines, who "cathect" the earth, i.e., nature itself, and have no need for substitutes.[97] In point of fact, the toy *qua* toy—an object manufactured specifically for a child to entertain itself with—is only two hundred years old.[98] Thus the American psychiatrist Simon Grolnick argues that T.O.'s are very likely the product of modern times, and attributes the phenomenon to the fact that it is only over the last few centuries, in the West, that children have been made to sleep alone.[99]

All of this suggests a need for caution with regard to archetypes. Alice Miller has argued (as have others) that Freud's theories of oedipal rivalry and sexual repression were "correct," but that he was studying a sick society and taking it as the norm; hence the theories were only correct for that type of society. Surely the same can be said of Winnicott. His subjects were not the happy children of a healthy society, but the depressed and anxious youngsters of modern Britain. One can project the Oedipus complex back to the Stone Age and the Primal Horde, as Freud did, and one can call the cave paintings of Lascaux Transitional Objects, and perhaps in some way they were; but I sense a tremendous ahistoricity in such an approach. In fact, I suspect that the epochal changes that take place across historical "fault lines," such as Michel Foucault and a few other historians have explored (see Chapter 3), are precisely about shifts in the subjective experience of the body—i.e., about differences in the mind/body relationship. As we now know, practices over long enough periods—i.e., certain disciplines of yoga, meditation, and breath control—can radically deepen a person's sense of mind/body relationship and ontological security in the world. If something so fundamental proves to be experimentally plastic, then surely we must conclude that the size and nature of the basic fault is not a historical constant. The behaviors that Jean Liedloff identifies with Western culture—escalating addictive patterns, "if-onlyism" and delayed gratification, self-hatred and self-sabotage—are, perhaps, exclusively modern phenomena. A sophisticated somatic history would not lump everything into the basic fault, but rather chart the changing relationship of mind and body over time. The gap is not of constant dimensions; its career over time, the different ways of treating it, and its translation into a (changing) body image may be the real hidden history of civilization.

In Part II of the present volume I shall try to uncover some of this hidden history (in particular, religious history) by means of somatic analysis, and so chart the changing mind/body relationship in the West over the last two millennia. This is a tall order, I realize, and I doubt I can be more than marginally successful with it. The present section of this book, however, deals with the sources of our fragmentation, and more needs to be said about that before this sort of grand-scale somatic reconstruction can be attempted. If mirrors, T.O.'s, Self/Other oppositions, and basic faults are all artifacts in some sense, it remains for us to try to figure out whence such things arose. How old are these things? Were human beings really, really different at some earlier point? Was there (as some have alleged) a prehistoric Golden Age, during which time the human race was not beset by war, madness, and internal conflict? It is to these issues that I now wish to turn.

# 2

# The Wild and the Tame: Humans and Animals from Lascaux to Walt Disney

*Every swarming thing that swarms*
*upon the earth is an abomination. . . .*

—Leviticus 11:41

*If all the beasts were gone, we would die*
*from a great loneliness of spirit, for whatever*
*happens to the beast, happens to us. All things*
*are connected. Whatever befalls the earth,*
*befalls the children of the earth.*

—Chief Sealth

OUR BRIEF HISTORY OF THE MIRROR, provided in the previous chapter, suggested that the basic fault is not so basic as we might first imagine. As a psychic entity, the gap is something like an accordion, historically speaking; Self/Other boundaries can be hard, soft, or even—as the American psychologist Julian Jaynes argues with some success—non-existent.[1] As an expression of the psyche, the evolution of the mirror and its vicissitudes in terms of quality and popularity can serve as a rough guide to the history of the Self/Other relationship. Yet as we have seen, the omnipresent availability of reflecting surfaces leaves us ignorant as to exactly when or why Self/Other opposition first arose. I am not suggesting that participating consciousness, or complete Self/Other merger, was the consciousness of all of human prehistory. Jaynes argues this, and so have I; but it may only apply to the period of Great Mother worship that existed for part of the time during the great agricultural civilizations. Self/Other *distinction*, it seems to me, can exist without turning into Self/Other *opposition*, in other words; a differentiated universe can still be friendly. But we are still left with the problem of causes and origins, and our study of the mirror can only take us so far.

The same thing is true, I think, for Transitional Objects; these are also lost in the mists of time. But one thing that can be more helpful here, and that I believe goes right to the root of the problem, is the historical relationship between human beings and animals. This is a more reliable "mirror" than the mirror per se, not only because more data are available, but also because the nonhuman living world is the most obvious Other around, and has been so since human beings first separated out of the animal kingdom. (God, what a slip! I actually wrote that! Human beings *never* separated out of the animal kingdom!) Human/animal relations would seem to be isomorphic to mind/body relations, or Self/Other relations. To be close to the animal kingdom is to not see the body—that thing in the mirror—as an Other, and so not to suffer the basic fault; whereas for many centuries now, and I suspect many millennia, "we" (i.e., our minds) have regarded our bodies as somehow untame, unruly—animalistic. They give birth, they die, they generate stomach aches or menstrual cramps, they contract diseases, they tingle with excitement, they get tired, and all without "our" voluntary control. Like animals, they don't "listen to reason." And so in animal species we see reflections of our own physicality. How we relate to animals over time can, I believe, even more than the mirror, serve as a way into our hidden somatic history.

That animal species might be a key to a secret or subterranean history of the human race is not a new idea, although the equation is not widely known. But a number of scholars have stated (or assumed) it in various forms. The British anthropologist Roy Willis wrote of the "concealed significance in the man-animal relation," which he likened to a code or "secret cipher" of human society.[2] Francis Klingender, in *Animals in Art and Thought to the End of the Middle Ages*, has argued that animals were symbolic of the secret urges of society.[3] Elizabeth Lawrence, an American veterinarian who studied rodeos extensively, has demonstrated that the treatment of animals in rodeo/rancher culture is an excellent "roadmap" of the American psyche, replaying, at each rodeo event, the "winning of the West" theme so central to American history (or at least American mythology).[4] Anthropologists Paul Shepard and Edmund Leach have explored this type of relationship in radical and innovative ways, as does the British historian Keith Thomas in his book *Man and the Natural World*.[5] Finally, anthropologist Mary Douglas has pointedly argued that traditional academic scholarship could not possibly penetrate a culture by an analysis of its rituals, because there could easily be a set of hidden rituals, revealed in the relationship with certain animals, that contradicted what appeared to be going on on the surface.[6] She adds that only some kind of subjective intuition could really reveal the nature of a culture; and it is this sort of somatic understanding that I hope to bring to bear on the objective historical data that we do have available on the human/animal relationship. To expand on what I stated above, I shall take it as a legitimate analytical key that how we relate to animals is emotionally and cognitively isomorphic to how we relate to our own bodies, and that knowledge of this takes us directly into the Self/Other relationship, which in turn "unpacks" the culture in question, or the historical period being studied. Of course, there is no way I can *prove* the validity of this methodology, and so I hope the reader will forgive me if I occasionally sound as if I know what I am talking about. All I can say is that it "smells" valid and (I believe) leads to some interesting results. Let me, in any event, try to do this, and see what turns up.

Animal mythologies go back to the earliest Paleolithic societies. Belief in human descent from animals, as well as tales of human/animal transformations, are probably as old as the race, and part of the age-old view of animals as sacred beings. John Berger, in an essay entitled "Why Look at Animals?," suggests that the mirroring function of the animal is a crucial one because the look of an animal is so unlike the look of another human being. The eyes of an animal considering a man, he says—and he is explicitly excluding a pet or zoo animal here—are wary, and man "becomes aware of himself returning the look." The animal's silence, and its distance, hold a secret for man, and in Paleolithic times this resulted in the animal's being seen as a possessor of power.[7] D. H. Lawrence was inspired to write the following lines upon seeing a wild doe, which capture what Berger is talking about:

> . . . I looked at her
> And felt her watching;
> I became a strange being . . .[8]

This strangeness we ourselves feel is the result of the power of a nonhuman mirror, and it probably accounts for the fact that the first art, which can be seen in the caves of Altamira and Lascaux, is about animal subjects rather than human ones (Plates 1 and 2). Otherness is a miracle; for hunter-gatherers, this was a source of celebration and awe, not fear. The fundamental distinction made by humans from Neolithic (agricultural) times onward—about 8000 or 9000 B.C.—was the division between the Wild and the Tame, a distinction not made by human beings for the million or million and a half years preceding the advent of the domestication of animals.

All of this falls into the category of what Paul Shepard calls "totemic culture." Totemic cultures, he says, assume the separateness of animals, a separateness that shakes us loose from ourselves and enables us to see ourselves from the outside. In this way, animals become constituents of the Self.[9] If human identity, as I have argued in Chapter 1, is so heavily shaped by the phenomenon of mirroring, it becomes obvious how different a culture that has a nonhuman mirror available is going to be from one that does not. It is not for nothing that the American poet, John Ciardi, called zoology "the science most like a looking glass."[10]

There is, of course, a second category, viz., that of domestic culture. Since all domestic cultures are descended from totemic ones, it is no surprise that our language still contains animal metaphors ("wolfing" one's breakfast down, chasing one's tail, and so on) or serves up Walt Disney as a major source of entertainment for children. But this is to go too fast, for this is the final watering down of totemism in modern industrial life. Between cave art and Walt Disney, whose animals display heavy human imprinting (non-Otherness; see Plate 3) lies a total revolution, if not inversion, of human consciousness, which occurred in a long and complex set of stages. Exposure to animals was one of the first experiences an infant in preagricultural societies had, and there was something direct and unmediated about it. This experience broke the homogeneity of human mirroring from a very early age, and this was the case for most of the history of the human race. There is something tedious and narcissistic about a strictly human world, and hunter-gatherer societies managed to avoid this. It is thus no surprise that the first symbols were animal ones; that the use of animal

1. Large bull and running horses, Lascaux. From Paolo Graziosi, *Paleolithic Art*, courtesy of R. C. S. Sansoni Editore.

2. Deer, Altamira. From Paolo Graziosi, *Paleolithic Art*, courtesy of R. C. S. Sansoni Editore.

3. Scene from *Cinderella*, ©1949 The Walt Disney Company. From Frank Thomas and Ollie Johnston, *Disney Animation: The Illusion of Life*.

imagery for charting the experience of the world is universal.[11] Animals and cave art were, in some sense, the first Transitional Objects; which may be a way of saying that for most of human history, the T.O. didn't really exist. As Shepard puts it, the "cave ceremonies were a continuation of good mothering practices. . . ."[12]

In fact, animal life was everywhere, even in the skies. The constellations were identified as animal forms from earliest times; and as late as the seventeenth century, when twenty-two new constellations were added (i.e., identified as such) to the forty-eight existing Ptolemaic ones, nineteen of them were given animal names.[13]

Animal movement, the animal body, was the model of human expression in hunter-gatherer society. It is very likely that Hugh Brody's description of the hunt among contemporary Indians of British Columbia depicts a very old pattern, psyche, and way of life:

> Above all they are still and receptive, prepared for whatever insight or realization may come to them, and ready for whatever stimulus to action might arise. This state of attentive waiting is perhaps as close as people can come to the falcon's suspended

flight, when the bird, seemingly motionless, is ready to plummet in decisive action.[14]

Agricultural and industrial man formulates a plan and then goes about carrying it out.[15] Paleolithic men and women took their cues from body feelings and the movements of animals. This was a life governed by shifting moods rather than the demands of the ego. The ego, very likely, was a tool; it didn't run the show. Nor was there any interest in obliterating it, as developed later on, in what would come to be known as Great Mother culture.

The hunting and eating of animals did not contradict the fact that they were regarded as sacred beings. In fact, just the reverse was true. Paleolithic hunter-gatherers would in all likelihood have little sympathy for modern vegetarian and animal rights groups, for the hunt was seen as sacred activity, an act of communion and reciprocity with the animal kingdom. They understood that death was a part of life; animals occasionally killed men, and men occasionally killed animals. There was no need to take it personally.[16] The tracking and killing of a wild animal requires great identification. To catch it, you must learn its habits in your body; you must *become* it, in a sense; and all tribal cultures have or had rites of wearing animal skins or animal masks.

Similarly, eating an animal was a sign of profound respect. By eating the animal, you absorbed its power, its characteristics. (The same is true of cannibalism.) Eating is the most fundamental form of Self/Other relationship, the incorporation of the body of another into your own body.[17] And the cutting up of the animal body, as Paul Shepard says, taught the children of Paleolithic societies about the insides of things, and therefore about their own insides. One's innards were not a source of uneasiness, but of pleasure. All of this adds up to a *reverence* for life.[18] The animal was hunted, eaten, worshipped, and, above all, used for transformation. The Plains Indians of the nineteenth century sought animal encounter, or vision encounter, with a wide range of creatures, to obtain a guardian spirit and, thereby, personal power.[19] The animal could also enter the seeker's body, it was believed, and become part of his spirit strength. The famous Sioux medicine man, Black Elk, claimed that many of his healing powers came from the bear.[20]

We get some idea, then, of how deeply hunter-gatherer cultures were immersed in animal life as an agent of sorting out Self/Other relationships and the meaning of human life. Properly speaking, human life for them had no special significance apart from the animal world.

As Paul Shepard writes, men "have always suspected that certain animals are masters and keepers of important secrets: metamorphosis, birth, puberty, healing, courtship, fertility, and protection."[21] When we think about how disturbed all of these processes or rituals are in contemporary society, we get some idea of what the loss of animals as sacred Others has meant for human life.

Animal cults and symbolism continued into the Neolithic period, still strongly coloring human processes of cognitive and psychological development.[22] Animal divinities abounded in Egypt and Mesopotamia, and animal images figured in the earliest scripts.[23] Greek deities were believed to be able to assume animal form and cohabit with humans;[24] the story of Leda and the swan was part of a whole genre. Astrology, which probably arose during the period of the archaic civilizations, incorporated animal signs as a matter of course, and the folklore of these cultures is filled with sacred beasts and animals in human form. Mesopotamian monuments are covered with animal representations, which come off looking much more real and lifelike than the depiction of human beings; that was true of Egyptian art as well. Animals were also central to divination—e.g., the reading of entrails and viscera—the practice of which continued throughout the period of the Roman Empire and probably even later.[25]

Despite all this evidence for continuity, the Neolithic revolution was an enormous break with the past, since it altered a way of life that had lasted for more than a million years. The fact of agriculture meant the end of nomadic life, the rise of more or less permanent settlements, the planting of grain, and the domestication of animals. This last development was, psychologically speaking, probably the most profound. Domestication means, by definition, that the Wild is made Tame; that the Other becomes more like yourself. Or rather, a distinction is made between the Other that is now regarded as "me" and the Other that is identified as "not-me." The first part of this equation generates a certain kind of safety, but it makes boredom inevitable. Once animals got subsumed under human categories, they could not, by definition, be as sacred or mysterious as they once had been. Domestication altered the polarity between Self and Other; it created a kind of flattening effect in one direction, and an effect of heightened opposition in another. The "friendly"part of the animal kingdom started almost to disappear from view, whereas the "unfriendly" part now stood out in stark relief. This binary tendency, of flattening and heightening, proved, in an agricultural context, to be both alluring and irreversible. But it meant that the mirroring phenomenon was starting to become primarily a human one, and with this, human development took a very different turn.

Why domestication arose at all has never really been clarified, but what is clear is that it entrenched a binary form of reasoning that was probably not present, or only mildly present, in Paleolithic times. If the animal was a sacred Other, it is also likely that the boundaries between natural and supernatural were fairly blurry for hunter-gatherers.[26] I shall return to this in Part II, but very briefly, hunter-gatherer society was not "religious" in the way agricultural society was. If there was no sharp divide between Wild and Tame, or Self and Other, there was also no such divide between sacred and profane, or heaven and earth. Again, it was not (I do not think) a question of everything getting melted down into the "One," or the "All," as in Great Mother societies—which bespoke a need to *transcend* a gap—but rather that fault lines and distinctions were lived with without very much difficulty, and were not, in any case, constructed or perceived in a binary fashion. Paleolithic society was characterized by *polymorphic* thought, which moved in a slow, kaleidoscopic way, as the quote from Hugh Brody (above) would suggest.

Domestication changed all this. The fundamental categories that presented themselves now were two—Wild and Tame—and eventually all forms of thought, down to the present day, came to be based on this model (the raw and the cooked, in Lévi-Strauss' terminology). It is a coarse model, and one lacking in subtlety, especially in the West. (Asian civilizations modified it somewhat by positing a Taoistic or dialectical relationship between polar opposites. This is why, in the West, thinkers such as Jung or Marx or William Blake have almost prophetic status.) Thousands of plants that are very different from each other, for example, all get lumped into one category, "edible," or its opposite, "inedible." In a similar fashion, most animals now become enemies, partly because they were a menace to crops.[27] The sheep (domesticated about 9000 B.C.) and the dog (about 7500 B.C., but perhaps earlier) are "good"; the wolf and the leopard are "bad."[28] The major psychic fallout for human beings is that Self and Other now constitute an antagonism rather than a polarity. Self is tame, "good"; Other is wild, "bad." It is very likely that Paleolithic society did not know war; that the concept of an enemy, an unfriendly Other, is a Neolithic invention.[29]

The process of domestication thus had important psychological consequences. Much of the animal kingdom seemingly disappeared; the greater part of it was turned into an Other that had to be resisted,

tamed, or (inevitably) conquered, overcome. As Paul Shepard has
written, the duality of Wild and Tame constituted a "jarring alteration
in world view." Domestication was a profound redirection of human
reason, from the subtle to the coarse, i.e., from polymorphous and
kaleidoscopic thinking to that which is binary, mechanical, ideological.[30] Animals were regarded with awe in hunter-gatherer societies
because the Wild/Tame distinction did not exist, or constituted a fairly
soft boundary. Once this distinction arose, or got hardened, awe got
transformed into fear. This is what it means to have an enemy. In this
sense, industrial civilization is continuous with agricultural civilization, but with one important exception: archaic societies made their
fears explicit, whereas we repress them. This is why, strictly speaking,
archaic societies did not know what we call "the unconscious." Fear
was as phenomenologically real as a spider; the latter did not "represent" the former in the sense that we now mean by this term. Thus,
if the shift from hunter-gatherer society was a mistake in the sense of
creating an enemy and a system of binary logic, agricultural civilization
had—at least in comparison with industrial society—one saving grace,
that the attendant tension and anxiety were publicly discharged, not
forced down into nightmares and psychosomatic illness.

The iconography and folktales of archaic civilizations become very
significant keys to hidden history if they are read within this framework. A whole range of demons arose in Mesopotamia, monsters
formed out of combinations of animals or of animals and humans.
The divine pantheon in Mesopotamia included a man-fish, a man-
scorpion, and a man-bull. The female demon Lamashtu, who attacked
infants, had the head of a lioness and the claws of a bird of prey. In
southern Turkey, at Çatal Hüyük, the site of the largest Neolithic
settlement known (flourished ca. 6500 B.C.; site excavated in the 1960s),
the Great Mother, as goddess of death, appears represented by vultures, which sometimes had human legs.[31]

Strictly speaking, these civilizations were not matriarchies, but (as
we have noted) were dominated by Great Mother worship, with its
attendant emphasis on fertility cults and the obliteration of Self/Other
distinctions. These distinctions, now sharpened into antagonisms, became emotionally difficult to endure, so the goal became "cosmic consciousness," return to the Primal Unity (hence the emergence of cults
and religion in general). The Great Mother in many cultures was regarded as the mistress of animals, and this had both a destructive and
a creative side to it. As bearer of life, the fertility goddess was often
associated with bulls and rams; as bearer of death, the Great Mother

was associated with vultures and boars. Under the aegis of the Great Mother, animals could often represent demonic powers, and getting transformed into an animal was seen for the first time as a curse, a form of damnation. In the *Odyssey*, Odysseus' men are transformed into pigs by Circe; and the whole concept of negative enchantment by means of witchcraft, in which human consciousness is trapped in an animal body, was part of the oral culture of the archaic civilizations and can be traced through the Middle Ages. Apuleius' *Golden Ass* (second century A.D.), as well as Kafka's *Metamorphosis,* revolves around this theme. In *The Golden Ass*, in fact, the hero is finally redeemed by the goddess Isis, and becomes a priest in her cult.[32]

The themes of negative enchantment, metamorphosis, and monsters (including human and animal combinations) formed an important aspect of the magical tradition, as well as the larger consciousness, of medieval Europe. There was a tremendous fear of, and fascination with, this whole murky world; and treatment of animals, which was often brutal, reflected this. It was because of the occult power attributed to animals, especially cats (the witch's "familiar"), that they were often tortured or burned alive; and this lasted, among the lower classes in particular, through the eighteenth century (Plate 4).[33] Yet it is doubtful whether this dynamic of terror and retaliation can be ascribed to the lower classes alone. After dreaming that the animals in his private menagerie were planning to eat him, Henry III of France personally killed them all, on January 20, 1583.[34] This was a significant event, it seems to me, and perhaps a kind of symbolic turning point. As rationalism began to permeate western Europe, the unconscious was born as a concept, and thus (given its self-creating nature) as a fact; and animals, representative of human fears of Otherness, were banished to it. Prior to this, on the eve of the Scientific Revolution, the making of human fears explicit by means of freakish animal imagery reached its peak in the chaotic and disturbed iconography of painters such as Hieronymus Bosch (Plate 5).[35] But after this, making fear explicit in this way is abandoned. It survives in fairy tales, in which human freaks, people with gross deformities, often appear, as we have said, as agents of liberation (the hag-witch who, if treated with respect, gives the wandering hero the secret he needs to slay the dragon, for example). It also survives in dreams. But all of this is "for children"; adults need not bother about it, supposedly. Thus fear of the animal Other acquires a whole new dimension during the modern period; it becomes vague, unspecified, repressed, and all the more terrifying as a result.

4. *The First Stage of Cruelty*, by William Hogarth (1751). Reproduced by Courtesy of the Trustees of the British Museum.

5. *The Temptation of St. Anthony* (detail), by Hieronymus Bosch (ca. 1500). Courtesy of the Museu Nacional de Arte Antiga, Lisbon.

So if the Neolithic revolution, through the process of domestication, succeeded in turning the human/animal, Self/Other relationship around, making the Other into an object of fear, at least it retained its capacity for awe by making those fears explicit. The language of psycho-analysis—repression, projection, etc.—may not really apply to Great Mother civilizations, in which distinctions between inner and outer were often absent, and to which the language of the occult and sha-manistic traditions is more appropriate than Freudian or even Jungian terminology. But the last remnants of participating consciousness, or complete merger with the environment, got routed with the rise of Renaissance humanism and the Scientific Revolution. It became "ir-rational" to have irrational fears. Hybrid monsters and fabulous beasts seemed to vanish under the glaring light of the new science. In reality, they only scurried away, found a place to hide in the recesses of the mind. The language of psychoanalysis and depth psychology, which may *partially* apply to the period from Homer to Hieronymus Bosch, now starts to make much more sense. Fear expressed is very different from fear repressed.[36]

Before we deal with the modern period, however, it will be useful for us to obtain a clearer notion of the nature of all this fear. It was surely not only a function of the economic danger that wild animals pose to crops in agricultural civilizations. That was part of it, but I doubt it was the most important part. The problem lies in the nature of binary logic itself. Once Wild and Tame were established as cate-gories of life, so that Self and Other necessarily became antagonistically related, the "problem" of what to do with intermediate forms surfaced as a problem. To take our earlier example, if hunter-gatherer society had only one category of vegetation, viz., "plants," each member of which possessed unique and interesting properties, agricultural civil-ization now had two: edible and inedible. (This distinction *was* known in hunter-gatherer societies, but it did not receive sharp emphasis.) All well and good; but what do you do with the plants that are poi-sonous unless prepared in a special way, which then renders them magical, i.e., capable of transmitting power? How do you classify that which is intermediate, or transformable; that which literally lies on the fault line of the basic fault (where before none existed)? To put this another way, whereas hunter-gatherer societies "cathected" (a true anachronism here) the entire environment, or more accurately, did not *have* Transitional Objects, Neolithic civilization opened up the whole world of the T.O. by generating an opposition between the Self and the World. Children born during the last few millennia inevitably inherit the tendency to interpret the Other as fearful or hostile; this is part of the (relatively recent) history of the race, as is the Transitional Object. A bridge, a form of safety, is now required to negotiate the space between Self and Other, and it had better be a reliable one. It must (to be a true T.O.) have the characteristics of both me and not-me, and in the context of domestication, tame animals are an obvious choice. The horse, even if not human, represents safety, whereas the tiger is danger; all of this is clear. (It is not an accident that modern T.O.'s take the form of teddy bears or other animal representatives.) But what about snakes, or scaly anteaters? There is a way in which their position is intermediate, unclear, and thus threatens to usurp transitional space. These are like "semi-edible" plants, and it is unclear what to do with them. The answer is that they are relegated to the category of taboo, the untouchable, but with a curious flip: they are also, simultaneously, sources of power, bearers of sacred relationship. As crazy as this seems, it is perfectly understandable, for the moment you force the world into a system of binary logic, a logic that does violence both to reality and the human mind, you make paradox and dialectical relationship absolutely inevitable, as a kind of safety valve. If horses are going to be safe, and tigers dangerous, you will eventually get a William Blake who will tell you that "The tigers of wrath are wiser than the horses of instruction," or that "The wrath of the lion is the wisdom of God."[37] Something deeply buried then echoes within you; you know that this is true.

This is even more true for forms that, unlike the lion or the tiger, are clearly, if disturbingly, "intermediate." It is why snakes are revered in so many cultures, and why our own attitude to the serpent in the Garden of Eden story is not so clear-cut. It is why the Egyptians regarded the beetle as a sacred animal. It is why I once awoke from a dream, in which I put a scorpion into my briefcase, with a tremendous sense of power and liberation. (In waking life, when I discovered a scorpion in my hotel room in Venice one evening, I simply stepped on it, and that was that. There was no question of sticking it in my briefcase. But thinking back on it now, I kind of wish I had done so.) It is why the Egyptians hunted that great intermediate creature, the crocodile, that somehow moves on both land and sea. Regarded as a force hostile to human life, the crocodile was hunted because such activity was a demonstration of courage. And *because* it was fearful, it was sacred; i.e., the successful crocodile hunter absorbed the animal's power, and became somewhat marginal himself.[38] (Witch doctors also have this status.) The "combination animals" (animal/animal and human/

animal) of Egypt and Mesopotamia also displayed this dialectical relationship, the paradoxical equation of that which is not-me and yet disturbingly resonant with something within me. Freud termed this the experience of the "uncanny" or "creepy"—*unheimlich* in German, that which is not familiar (literally, not of the home).[39] But it *is* familiar, nonetheless; griffins, minotaurs, and mermaids are not so easily dismissed as Other precisely because of their intermediate quality. And it is precisely these uncanny animals that carry a load of sacred power. Hence, lion *tamer*, but snake *charmer*. Our language reflects our unconscious attitudes.[40]

The notion of intermediate forms and the sacred/taboo equation takes us to the core of the Self/Other relationship and ultimately to the heart of the whole issue being discussed here. Both Edmund Leach and Paul Shepard have commented on this phenomenon and agree that the key to it is the way in which marginality (ambiguity and anomaly) functions as a violation of binary cognition or binary classification. In fact, this syndrome, if so it may be called, extends to a great deal of organic life, including substances such as blood, semen, saliva, a whole variety of foods, and even "dirt"—that which symbolically stands for disorder.[41] And to be disordered, from the Neolithic revolution onward, has been to fall outside the categories of Self and Other. Leach argues[42] that we only arrive at conceptual clarity (read: binary classification) by repressing things that are ambiguous, i.e., by making them taboo; and he explicitly ties this to the world of object relations, the Self vs. World crystallization that finally occurs in the third year of life. Around this separation, this gap, he says, every culture constructs its own code, or "grid," of discontinuities. It may be arbitrary, it may vary widely from culture to culture, but any culture can be counted on to defend its own particular grid, because it believes—and on one level, it is correct—that if the grid is compromised in any way, psychic integrity will be lost and the entire culture will go down the drain. As played out in the animal world, the grid gets mapped in such a way as to create an isomorphism between the set

Self/Sister (or Brother)/Cousin/Neighbor/Stranger

and the set

Self/Pet/Livestock/Game/Wild Animal

Even within this spectrum, interstices exist; and because they consist of suppressed things, it is precisely these that are a source of anxiety and interest, simultaneously dangerous/filthy and powerful/sacred. Fluids that come out of the human body, such as blood and semen, are taboo because they echo the fundamental problem of the infant: where does me end and not-me begin? Intermediate substances leave the boundaries of the body unclear,[43] and this can evoke a primal fear. This is why such substances, and even such animals, are associated with witches' brews. Typical recipes call for newts' eyes, for example, or cocks' eggs. In Basel in 1474, a cock was sentenced to be burnt alive for the "heinous and unnatural crime" of laying an egg. A similar such prosecution occurred in 1730. Historian of science Joseph Needham argued that only a culture capable of putting a cock on trial for supposedly laying an egg, and thereby violating natural law, could be capable of generating modern science, a system committed to the existence of (binary) laws of nature in the first place.[44] Thomas Kuhn was right to argue that scientific revolutions were born out of anomalies that finally couldn't be ignored, but he failed to grasp why such anomalies were disturbing.[45] Witches are deviant beings precisely because they deal in intermediate substances and transitional zones, threatening to usurp them. They can assume animal form, and they possess spirit familiars, all of which renders seemingly ordinary dogs and cats dangerous. And they themselves are marginalized (i.e., put in the interstices) by society, and in times of stress get burnt en masse. Mary Douglas writes:

> Witches are social equivalents of beetles and spiders who live in the cracks of the walls and wainscoting. They attract the fears and dislikes which other ambiguities and contradictions attract in other thought structures, and the kind of powers attributed to them symbolise their ambiguous, inarticulate status.

In effect, the scientific anomalies Kuhn was talking about are the intellectual equivalents of beetles and witches. We thus get some sense of the cultural origins of our fragmentation, and understand why anything that emphasizes it or (simultaneously) threatens to repair it is, for us, a source of fascination and anxiety. (Just consider how much "culture" and "history" revolves around Self, Other, and the relationship between them.)[46]

The same process of marginalization also befalls those who live "too long" in another culture, or to psychologists who spend too much time in transitional space. No society can tolerate much heresy, and certainly not the greatest heresy of all, namely the assertion that its

cultural grid is lacking in any particular, transcendent validity; that
the only reality is the creative flame of transitional space, and that
even that "reality" may be relatively recent (twelve thousand years or
so). In the Soviet Union, such heretics wind up in psychiatric hospitals.
In western Europe and North America they are awarded the dubious
status of harmless kooks who sit in cafés filling page after page with
scribblings that virtually no one is ever going to read. The masses
must be fed the illusion of Us vs. Them at all costs; it is what makes
films such as Rambo or White Nights (appropriately termed "warnog-
raphy" by the Russian poet Yevgeny Yevtushenko) a multimillion-
dollar business. A traitor or a heretic is one who transgresses categories. It is no accident that such a person is called a "snake in the
grass," that heretics in the Middle Ages were referred to as "vermin,"
or that those animals that push the boundaries of our reality (our body
boundaries) are termed "creepy" and make us "edgy." As Leach puts
it, the "hostile taboo is applied most strongly to creatures that are
most anomalous in respect of the major categories, e.g., snakes—land
animals with no legs which lay eggs."[47]

Insects, spiders, and reptiles all fall into the category of the ambiguous or the anomalous, and that is why the Bible tells the Jews not
to eat them. Such animals, says Paul Shepard,

> offend the necessity of clear distinction. These animals live in
> cracks that are the zones of separation, or under things, the sur-
> faces between places. The flying insects swarm around our heads,
> near the body orifices, which are themselves marginal areas. Par-
> asites on human and animal bodies seem like indeterminate forms,
> neither internal nor external, neither part of us nor free. Insects
> crawl, which is betwixt walking and swimming. . . . [T]hey sug-
> gest a seething, secret world of transformations, menacing in
> fecundity and frightening in their metamorphoses.[48]

The fear that the world will somehow "dissolve" in insects, get over-
run by things that crawl, is a popular one in the horror genre, and it
may even have some basis in ecological or evolutionary fact. Once
again, our language betrays our anxieties: "going bugs," "bughouse,"
"bugs in the system," "iron the bugs out," and so on.

So if the world gets sliced up into Self and Other, and the breach
can only be negotiated by Transitional Objects, there exists a real
danger that intermediate animals and substances could usurp transitional space, without control over which we fear a fall into chaos.[49]

The idea of transitional space, after all, is that the human being starts life off with a neutral area of experience that won't be challenged; a kind of safety zone that has intermediate status (is both "me" and "not-me"). Jungian analyst James Hillman argues that we fear insects and snakes because they have autonomous psyches;[50] they are *most* in a position to usurp transitional space, and thus they evoke the greatest horror. But this is only a problem for a consciousness that splits the world into Wild and Tame. For Paleolithic society, such animals were, no less than lions and tigers, imbued with divinity, partly because there were no categories to be violated. For Neolithic civilization, this divinity got mixed up with anxiety, which unleashed the whole dialectical game of taboo and sacred. For us moderns, anxiety plays the heaviest role, though such animals often remain dialectical in our dreams.

Mary Douglas has gone over much of the same territory in her classic study, *Purity and Danger*, noting how "dirt" is a symbolic category that includes anything that is out of place, that violates systemic ordering.[51] Thus, when a monstrous birth occurs, the dichotomy between human and animal is threatened, and hence every culture has some mechanism for dealing with this. *Kadosh*, in Hebrew—"holy"—also means "separated," that which keeps categories distinct. Thus Leviticus enjoins against eating things that "swarm," because such activity is an indeterminate form of movement, cutting across basic lines of classification (it occurs in air, in water, and on land). And the Jews themselves are told, at various points in the Hebrew liturgy, not to associate or assimilate (especially not to cohabit) with the *goyim*—other nations—since it will pollute their racial purity; an injunction hardly limited to Jews as a social and racial practice.[52]

Concern with dietary laws, and with sexual or bodily contact—consider the widespread injunctions regarding menstruating women, for example—is no accident, and it is a concern of virtually all cultures, not just the Jews. As we have seen, animal and bodily fears are isomorphic. "The body," writes Douglas, "is a model which can stand for any bounded system. Its boundaries can represent any boundaries which are threatened or precarious." The orifices of the body symbolize its especially vulnerable points. Insects can crawl or fly in, mucus or saliva can leak out. Spiders and semen become sacred precisely because of their intermediate status. They appear as the symbols of creative formlessness, of loss of control; they have the power to overturn the established order. Here we begin to move out into history at large. All orthodoxies need heresies, all political regimes need dissenters, not only to jail or burn them, but also to co-opt them. For as marginal figures, they hold the secret of creative transformations. If anomalies can be plowed back into the system—"composted," as Mary Douglas puts it—the system becomes stronger; if you eat your enemy, you absorb his power. If, on the other hand, you insist on purity, you become like a body without orifices, which means you die very quickly.

It should be clear, then, that how any culture relates to animals says much about how the people in that culture feel about their bodies. This in turn reveals the essential structure of the Self/Other relationship, and does much to explain the particular history of that culture, the "body politic." Western industrial society is as much a candidate for this kind of somatic analysis as are the Jews of Leviticus or the denizens of medieval Europe, with their fears of witches and monsters. It is to the modern period, then, that I finally wish to turn. And it is in technological societies that we find the greatest terror of the organic, in fact, the deepest hatred and fear of life that this planet has ever known. As in the case of the history of the mirror, we have to be careful of archetypal analysis. Belief in the categories of "purity and danger," or Self and Other, or Tame and Wild, is certainly a characteristic of all cultures; but the degree of preoccupation with this, the sharpness of the boundaries, is so severe in the modern period as to catapult it into a different category of existence. It deserves, as a result, a separate section all its own.

Perhaps the central feature of the shift from a medieval to a modern world, or from a sacred to a secular one, was the rise of what has been called the mechanical philosophy, the idea that everything in the world, from atoms to galaxies, is composed of material particles and operates on the model of a machine. This change of outlook is, philosophically speaking, the most obvious characteristic of seventeenth-century thought. There is no reason why animals should have been exempted from this worldview, and in fact, they were especially vulnerable to it. According to that great mechanistic thinker, René Descartes, animals were nothing more than automata; they did not suffer pain any more than did a clock. From this time on, experimentation of live animals became widespread in western Europe. If animals were nothing more than clocks, their suffering could be dismissed as mere noise, and they were routinely nailed to boards for vivisection or for illustrating anatomical facts such as the circulation of the blood.[53] The nineteenth century saw the rise of animal protection societies, partly in reaction to this. Apparently, the first antivivisection society in Europe was founded by the wife and daughter of the famous experimental biologist Claude Bernard, following their discovery that the good doctor had vivisected the family dog. Bernard regarded any discussion of animal suffering as totally unscientific, and therefore as being beneath any serious consideration; and despite the rise of animal protection societies, that attitude continues to be the dominant (or "official") mode of thought in the West.[54] Peter Singer, who has documented the torture of animals carried out in the name of scientific progress, states that it is in the twentieth century that we probably inflict more pain on animals than at any other time in history—and this includes the period of the Roman Empire, when animals were routinely slaughtered in gladiatorial combats for popular entertainment. As Singer points out, millions upon millions of animals are routinely tortured every year in the United States and Europe within the framework of experiments that are motivated by nothing more than goalless curiosity—i.e., in experiments that haven't the remotest prospect of any medical or scientific benefits. Many more experiments are carried out for commercial purposes, such as the testing of cosmetics or food coloring agents. And both types of experiments are frequently barbaric, involving prolonged electric shocks, techniques for making animals crazy or depressed, starvation, poisoning, heating to death, and so on.[55] (See Plates 6, 7, and 8.)

My aim here is not to get the reader to join an animal rights group, although I suppose one could do worse. My point is that animals are now regarded as laboratory tools, experimental "equipment," no more significant on an invoice or order sheet than test tubes or graduated cylinders. They are literally "stuff," and this is the nadir of the Self/ Other relationship; it is the flattening effect taken to its logical conclusion. Whereas the animal Other was once sacred, it is now literally garbage, waste material, and this seems to spill over into the human realm. Assembly-line genocide and the treatment of the human body as a medical specimen are two obvious expressions of this. If Other is nothing more than scratch paper, so to speak, Self is finally going to be regarded in a similar way.

The Scientific Revolution destroyed animals theoretically, as it were; the Industrial Revolution that followed on its heels removed them from the environment almost completely. It is difficult to realize how recent all of this is; that going back only a few generations, animals— and I don't mean pets—were still very much a part of the social surroundings, even in large urban centers. Hogs routinely roamed the

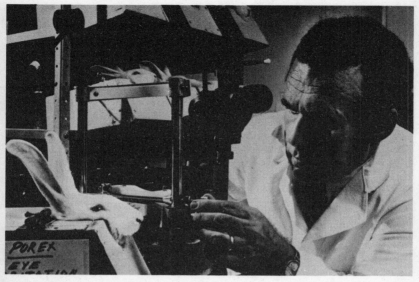

6. Testing detergents for eye irritation (on rabbit). Courtesy of the Bettmann Archive.

streets of New York, about ten thousand of them, as late as 1842. Cattle were a street "hazard," and horses were everywhere, largely for the purposes of transportation.[56] But the removal of animals from the environment began in Europe in the early modern period, when farmers started moving animals out of their houses and into separate quarters, newly built for the purpose. Yet domestic relations between humans and animals persisted; after all, it had been going on for ten or twelve millennia. "In the [English] towns of the early modern period," writes Keith Thomas, "animals were everywhere, and the efforts of municipal authorities to prevent the inhabitants from keeping pigs or milking cows in the street proved largely ineffective." The famous health commissioner and reformer Edwin Chadwick found in the course of his investigation of 1842 that birds were commonly reared in town bedrooms, and that horses were often kept indoors as well.[57]

The fact that relationships with domestic animals, even in terms of their individual personalities, had been going on for such a long time, and then collapsed in the space of a few generations, made the change nothing less than a psychic bombshell. This might have been fine if it had meant a return to the sacred otherness of hunter-gatherer society, but of course it was just the reverse. Animals became, literally

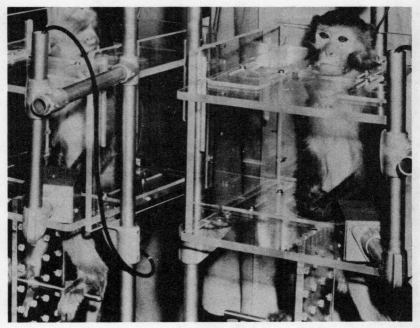

7. Testing effect of electric shock and anxiety on the growth of ulcers (on monkeys). Courtesy of Wide World Photos.

and conceptually, nonexistent. The nineteenth century saw the slaughter of nearly sixty million (!) buffalo in the United States, with Buffalo Bill being regarded not as a madman or a butcher, but as a hero.[58] (See Plate 9.) Draft animals, increasingly regarded as inferior machines, were removed from the street and the factory and replaced with real machines. Organic life doesn't fit well into urbanized, technological societies, and the result was that it got removed from them, creating what John Berger calls a "new solitude." Nonhuman Otherness is not merely degraded now, but absent; and so, in a sense, are we.[59]

Patterns of human food consumption also changed accordingly, for everything eventually got subsumed under the model of industrial mass production. In a brilliant film by Frederick Wiseman, entitled *Meat* (he also made the film *Primate*, about the treatment of laboratory animals at the Yerkes Primate Laboratory in Atlanta, Georgia), it becomes clear that "meat"—mechanically processed flesh—is a twentieth-century invention. The assembly-line slaughtering procedures of agribusiness and factory farm, like large-scale scientific ex-

8. Monkey undergoing morphine withdrawal. Courtesy of Universal Features.

periments, reduce animals to "stuff," inert matter. At the consumer end of this process, described by Peter Singer in horrifying detail,[60] we purchase this "stuff" in plastic packages wrapped in cellophane; and in an emotional sense, container and contents are roughly equivalent. There is no reason to associate this package with animal life. Self and Other are completely flattened now; this is really the end of the line. The ingestion of an animal in hunter-gatherer society was done to absorb its power; it followed the principle "you are what you eat." According to that logic, the urbanized human being is turning into mass-produced schlock. Even at mealtimes, he or she has no opportunity to interact with real animal (or even organic) existence.

In modern times, two institutions have arisen to compensate for the absence of animal life, for the truth is that we cannot lose nonhuman

9. Slaughter of buffalo in the nineteenth century. Courtesy of the Glen-bow Archives, Calgary.

Otherness without literally going berserk. One institution is the zoo; the other is the pet. I wish to discuss these briefly before going on to consider the terrible fear of animals that now exists in our society, a fear that is pervasive in the same proportion that animals are now physically absent from the scene.

Strictly speaking, the keeping of aviaries, menageries, or other animal collections is not new. Some of this activity goes back to the time of the archaic civilizations.[61] Archaeological remnants of zoos date back to 4500 B.C. (significantly, the date of the earliest identifiable mirror). There were royal collections of sacred animals—lion, baboon, and ibis—in Egypt, which were protected in parks and temples; and we know that a zoo established during the Old Kingdom (ca. 2800–2250 B.C.) included the ibex, the antelope, and the gazelle. Ramses II (fl. 1250 B.C.) collected giraffes. The Greeks began to keep wild animals captive by the seventh century B.C., and by the fourth century all of the city-states had animal collections, including aviaries. Alexander the Great established a large zoo in Alexandria, which subsequently grew to enormous size under the rulership of Ptolemy II. The Romans also had zoos, since they had to house animals for the gladiatorial shows; and they kept animals in private collections as well.

With the fall of Rome, the age of large-scale animal collections was

10. Engraving of London Zoo by Scharf (ca. 1836). From Solly Zuckerman, *Great Zoos of the World*, publ. Weidenfeld & Nicolson.

over. Medieval menageries, such as that of Henry I at Oxford in the twelfth century, were small affairs. They tended to be a mark of splendor; the goal was to acquire exotic specimens, and monarchs would send these to each other as gifts. With the Commercial Revolution of the sixteenth century—an age very much interested in novelty and discovery—large menageries and royal collections flourished once again.

In a technical sense, however, none of these collections were really zoos. That is, they were the private collections of the rich or of royalty. They were not established for public attendance; and given the pervasive presence of animals in the average person's daily life, the idea of a zoo as a public institution, even to house wild and exotic animals, never seemed to arise. Even the foundation of the Paris Zoo, which took place when the menagerie at Versailles (founded 1665) was moved to the Jardin des Plantes in 1793, was undertaken for the purpose of scientific study, not popular exhibition. The first institution for this purpose, the Schönbrunn Zoo in Vienna, was established in 1765, and the zoos of London (Plate 10) and Berlin followed within a century (1828 and 1844, respectively). The early nineteenth century saw the first demand for the zoo as a public institution, and no less then twenty-six zoos were established between 1828 and 1865.[62]

The timing of all of this is rather obvious.[63] The period of 1800–1850 saw the Industrial Revolution and the urbanization process swing into high gear. The removal of animals from the environment, and from the sphere of human activity, which had begun at a slow pace in the seventeenth century, was now entering its final phase. The sudden interest in zoos on the part of the general population can be read as an unconscious drama, and is very similar to the outcry over the destruction of whales in the late twentieth century. This latter phenomenon, I believe, reflects the (real) fear that scientific rationalism is overtaking human life, and that the destruction of the whale—the "deep brains of the sea"—represents the end of any unconscious forces in the natural world, and thus the end of life as we know it. In the same way, the demand for zoos in the early nineteenth century reflected a fear that the new industrial regime was wiping wildness from the face of Europe, and that without it human beings would no longer be human beings. I believe that that sentiment was right, and that this fearful, unstated prediction is coming true; but zoos seem, at best, to be a sop to the whole process. They hardly managed to stem the tide, and in an eerie sense they represent our defeat. There is no wildness present in zoos; as John Berger says, we observe the animals rather than the reverse. The nonhuman mirroring function I mentioned earlier in this chapter is now completely gone. The zoo environment is an illusory one; the animals are indifferent. You cannot, says Berger, encounter the look of an animal in a zoo, for the animals look sideways, their gaze flickers. They know they have been marginalized by human society, and in a way that renders them innocuous, rather than sacred or taboo.

"For adults," writes Keith Thomas,

> nature parks and conservation areas serve a function not unlike that which toy animals have for children; they are fantasies which enshrine the values by which society as a whole cannot afford to live.[64]

Thomas, of course, has captured something important here, but there are at least two things wrong with his argument. The first is that zoos really do not enshrine the values of wildness, which I assume he is arguing. Once in captivity, wild animals get imprinted by human keepers in such a way that makes it impossible for them to return to the wild, where they would die. The fallacy of the zoo is that a species can be removed from an ecosystem and still remain the same species.

It is an atomistic outlook, an extension of the mechanical philosophy itself. "Zoos," write David Phillips and Sandra Kaiser, "are giving a false impression that species can be saved even if the wild is destroyed." But the truth is that a "caged animal is a shadow of its natural self. . . ."[65]

The second problem with Thomas' argument is that he assumes that society cannot afford the values of wildness and wilderness, whereas the truth is that society cannot afford to live *without* these values. I am reminded of a remark made by Lewis Thompson in his book, *The Deepest Ground*: "All fantasy is a failure of sensuality."[66] The same period that saw the popular rise of the public zoo saw the manufacture of the first stuffed animals, with Walt Disney only a few decades away. We are back to the Transitional Object here, except that the reduction of the sacred animal to a human security blanket fails, in the end: we wind up, in reality, much less secure. Zoos and game parks warp wilderness, warp the Self/Other polarity.[67] The zoo is in fact part of a much larger process engendered by industrial society, which puts art in galleries, poetry between covers of books, Indians on reservations, the mad and retarded in asylums, and even tends to segregate children from adults. It simply wants Other out of the way. It is a mistake to assume that we can afford to live without all this, or that it is all right for these things to be ornamental. As Mary Midgley notes, Saint Paul's injunction to put aside "childish" things has been fulfilled with a vengeance; we have wound up putting aside the things that matter most in life.[68] The zoo and the stuffed animal are symbolic of this entire process.

And so, of course, is the pet. It is no use arguing that human beings have always had pets, and therefore that this is nothing new. The pharaoh of Egypt may have kept a tame monkey in his rooms, but as in the case of zoos, the real issue is a statistical one, and that puts us squarely into the nineteenth and twentieth centuries. Most writers on the subject acknowledge that on the scale at which it now exists, pet-keeping is a relatively recent phenomenon, and in fact a rather eccentric one. In England, pets now number about half the human population of the country, and over sixty percent of American households keep such animals.[69] Historically, this is unprecedented; there is simply nothing we can compare this to.

Yet what it is all about is not hard to imagine. Pets now have a major rehabilitative role for some psychiatric patients.[70] They are essentially bonding objects, and "pet-facilitated therapy" has become a major aspect of the whole mental hygiene field, which makes no bones

about how pets are essential to reduce the alienation of urban, technological life, compensate for the collapse of the extended family and
the rise of a confused, middle-class life, and so on.[71] It is obvious to
many therapists, however, that we are essentially talking about living
teddy bears, and that the "cure" for alienation here may be more
pathological than the disease. Thus studies reveal that pet owners
tend to be a great deal more brittle and neurotic than nonowners; that
pets are detrimental to effective social relations; and that loss of a pet
can result in lasting mental disturbances, so much so that a separate
profession of "pet bereavement counselors" has arisen to help people
cope with this sort of loss.[72] By 1970, the United States had something
like four hundred pet cemeteries.[73] In her book *Petishism*, Kathleen
Szasz concluded that people are apparently not capable of loving each
other and have anthropomorphized pets to replace their relationships
with human beings.[74]

In his essay "The Pet as Minimal Animal," Paul Shepard effectively
sees this inability of humans to love each other, and this ferocious
bonding behavior, as part of the historical process of the removal of
animals from human cognitive and emotional development. Alienation is not just the simple outcome of the rise of technoindustrial
society. It reflects the breakdown of a complex series of steps, an
identity-forging process that requires the presence of nonhuman mirrors at crucial stages of human development. We have lost this, but
we retain, at least subliminally, an awareness that psychic damage
occurs without it. This is why, suggests Shepard, millions of people
have pets: they are "fumbling with the paraphernalia of totemic
thought." "Keeping pets is a hopeless attempt to resurrect crucial
episodes of early growth that are lost forever. If the modern child
needs a puppy in order to encounter birth and death," he concludes,

> then that child is in serious jeopardy already and the welcome
> benefits of the puppy, however real, should perhaps be seen as
> the kind of catch-up measures that characterize most of modern
> medicine. . . .[75]

The pet, adds John Berger, provides a nonhuman mirror, but as in
the case of the zoo animal, the reflection is distorted. We get a hu-
manized form of ourselves, not a true Other, and in consequence, we
don't know who we are.[76]

In terms of our relationship with animals, there exists only one
modern institution bent on preserving a notion of who we are by

means of dramatic emphasis on the Wild/Tame dichotomy, and that is the rodeo. On the surface, it has nothing to do with zoos or pet-keeping, which institutions ranchers often regard with amusement or contempt. Yet as in the case of zoos and pets, it too is a recent (nineteenth-century) institution, and emerges out of a similar social matrix, i.e., the elimination of any sort of wildness from our lives. It is, in short, another sop, another nonsolution to the same deep, underlying problem. The rite of the rodeo also mirrors our relationship with our bodies and encapsulates, in a somatic way, some crucial themes of American history. (The bullfight would be the European, or at least French and Spanish, equivalent, but that is a whole other story.) I therefore wish to spend just a brief moment discussing this phenomenon before turning to the larger issue of direct evidence for the fear of organic life.

According to Elizabeth Lawrence (*Rodeo*, 1982), rodeo/rancher culture is not a small or aberrant phenomenon in the United States.[77] The rodeo entertainment industry is big business. Millions attend every year, and it plays out a major drama embedded in the American psyche (and perhaps the European psyche as well, given the expansionist and control-of-nature character of modern European history). In emphasizing the sharp distinction between Wild and Tame, the rodeo, as we have already noted, symbolically reenacts the "winning of the West," and even, it seems to me, the process of domestication that signaled the end of hunter-gatherer society. The important element here, represented by the bucking bronco, is that of unpredictability. The bronc has "outlaw" (true Other) status; it is to be domesticated, brought under human control (Plate 11). Events of this sort are quite violent, and bodily injury is a common occurrence. This injury, however, is a badge of pride; rodeo stars will typically refuse medical treatment, and may even seek to emphasize their injuries, for example by setting off a lost finger by wearing a ring on the stump. What is going on here, contends Lawrence, is that the mastery of injury and pain—i.e., the mastery of the physical body—displays a mastery of Self, and is the key to the mastery of the environment (Other). The Other is hated, has "outlaw" status, and it is the obsession of rodeo/rancher culture to break its spirit, bring it under human domination. Yet there is something heroic about this "outlaw" that won't be tamed, this "rebel" bronc. He can heroically be identified with as well.

The primary emotion with respect to the organic world is thus fear, but as in the case of pets and zoos, the emotion is repressed and shows up in a different form. In this case, it surfaces as machismo, a "hard-

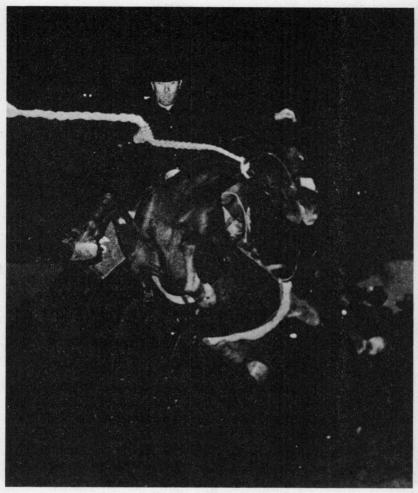

11. Rodeo event: taming the "outlaw" bronc. From Elizabeth Atwood Lawrence, *Rodeo*.

nosed" and swaggering attitude toward a recalcitrant body, which is itself seen as a kind of outlaw or wild animal needing to be tamed. Yet the dialectical identification with the wild is crucial, because it is unconsciously understood that a totally tame world is a dead one—the world of pets, zoos, and "city folk." Lawrence found that the most feared representative of the wilderness was the rattlesnake; that ranchers had a deep fear and hatred of the rattler as the embodiment of the alien, the Other (Plate 12)*. Yet perhaps the most popular constituent of rancher clothing and accoutrements is rattlesnake skin. Belts, boots, wallets, and key holders, to name but a few items, are made from the rattler and sold by the ton. There is a desire to identify with wildness, in other words, and to do so in a bodily way (clothing). Rodeo/rancher culture thus manages to have it both ways.

In a like manner, ranchers embody the anti-ecological thrust of the whole of modern, and especially recent, history. They loathe coyotes, eagles, and bears, and favor extermination of all animals regarded as predators. The coyote is hated because it can outwit human beings, the eagle because of its power of flight, the bear for its elusiveness. In this regard it is interesting to compare the attitudes of the Plains Indians, who admired the coyote for its cleverness—it was often the hero ("trickster") of their tales—and who saw the bear and eagle as having mysterious powers, ones to be absorbed rather than "controlled" or mastered.

Lastly, the rite of the rodeo includes an enormous emphasis—usually carried out in a raunchy, humorous way—on such things as feces, urine, blood, saliva, milk, and hair. Lawrence provides numerous examples of this sort of humor from her own experience, and seeks to explain it by means of Leach's analysis of intermediate substances. In a world of sharp dichotomies between Wild and Tame, or man and animal, items that blur that boundary or occupy intermediate space surface as a source of anxiety, as taboo. The rodeo, she says, is dedicated to showing that we are masters of the animals, separate from them. The emphasis on intermediate substances serves as a counter-motif, defusing the situation by showing that, in fact, we *are* linked to animal life. She may be right, and she certainly is in good anthropological company, echoing as she does Gregory Bateson's themes of "schismogenesis" (certain systems move ineluctably toward climax or breakdown) and "end linkage" (the climax may be avoided by the introduction of categorical inversions);[78] but I personally find this a bit too elaborate, especially since mastery of animals is a way of joining with them (making Other into Self). My own guess is that the public joking about and emphasis on intermediate substances is akin to the hybrid monsters and fabulous beasts of the Middle Ages: repressed anxiety about the Wild, the Other, is discharged by making it explicit,

*This illustration, an advertisement for Nocona boots, shows a man stepping on a rattlesnake and holding a large knife in his hand. Illustration appears in original hardcover edition of this book only (Simon & Schuster, 1989); permission for further use was withdrawn by the Nocona Boot Co.

bringing it out into the open. Rattlesnake belts may serve the same function. Yet it is all projected fear, fear that is unacknowledged. One never admits to fear in this culture; it is "feminine" weakness, a badge of shame. The "uptightness" of rancher culture over the Wild and the Other may get a bit defused, but it is never really faced; and I think the social, historical, and ecological consequences of this are clear. When you get down to it, the rodeo is a microcosm of much of what goes on in society today, in the same way that zoos and pets are. Animal treatment, body treatment, the Self/Other definition, and finally the social and ideological pattern of the modern period are all part of the tail end of the same long (somatic) history.

All of this, as I have said, constitutes indirect evidence for what is going on in the modern period. Evidence for the increasing fear of organic life that is a bit more direct emerges in Keith Thomas' important study, *Man and the Natural World*, and it is to Thomas' credit that he sees this fear as linked to feelings about the body.[79] Speaking of England in the period from 1500 on, he notes that "most people were taught to regard their bodily impulses as 'animal' ones, needing to be subdued." In fact, given Thomas' discussion, a good case could be made that the American rodeo represents the modern history of British—and probably European—sensibilities on the Wild/Tame distinction in a more compressed form. "Wherever we look in early modern England," writes Thomas, "we find anxiety, latent or explicit, about any form of behaviour which threatened to transgress the fragile boundaries between man and the animal creation." Again, the issue is one of repression, for previously this anxiety was made explicit in the form of frog-prince stories and bestiaries of hybrid creatures, and it had even been traditional for certain English families to claim ancestry from wild animals. "The early modern period," says Thomas, "swarmed with missing links, half-man, half-animal." The modern period sought to suppress all this, and to keep the Wild/Tame categories free of blurry intermediates. The rising emphasis on cleanliness, which became a Victorian fetish, is explicable in the sense that lack of it was regarded as bestial. It also became "bestial" to be hairy. Traditional tales about the metamorphosis of humans into animals were condemned, and the possibility that this line might be crossed became a source of horror. One argument raised against vaccination in the nineteenth century was that inoculation with fluid from cows would "animalize" human beings. From the seventeenth century on, there was increasing comment on bestiality as the worst of crimes, and it became a capital offense for most of the period of 1534–1861. Incest, by way of comparison, was not a secular crime until the twentieth century.

There was, however, one notable exception to the taboo on tales of human/animal metamorphosis, and it became something of a major preoccupation from the late fifteenth century on, climaxing in an internal Self/Other tale that epitomized all the fears and anxieties of the new sanitized society, namely *Dr. Jekyll and Mr. Hyde*, the story of which came to its author in a dream. At the very same time that the machinery for persecuting witches began to fall into place, the literate classes of western Europe became obsessed with werewolves. The European peasantry had always believed in the existence of such creatures, but now leading intellectuals found themselves pondering the nature of this bizarre "phenomenon," roughly over the period 1485–1700. Werewolves were, for example, a subject of discussion of the Royal Society of London in 1663, and the late sixteenth century saw a number of werewolf trials, especially in France. One tradition had it that the werewolf was laid low by silver, something that resurfaced in the twentieth-century story of Superman, who was vulnerable to a mineral known as "kryptonite." (Why did the Lone Ranger use silver bullets, I wonder?) As far as fiction goes, between the first century A.D., which saw the printing of a Latin novel, *Satyricon*, that dealt with the werewolf theme, and the nineteenth century, there was almost nothing—one novel, in fact, *Monsieur Oufle*, by the Abbé Bordelon, in 1710. But with the emergence of the new industrial, animal-free society in earnest, the werewolf genre saw a rapid development. *The Phantom Ship*, by Marryat, was an early example (1839); George Reynold's serial, *Wagner the Wehrwolf*, published in 1846–47, had phenomenal success. By 1894, K. F. Smith was able to publish a bibliographical survey of the werewolf in fiction. In general, this literature played on the deepest fears of the age, that one could, like the good Dr. Jekyll, suddenly be taken over by an animal form, reduced to a hairy, instinctual beast—a Mr. Hyde, the ultimate outlaw, or transgressor of rational categories. The figure of Hyde, in fact, stalks Victorian society; his repulsiveness is the source of his fascination. It was Robert Louis Stevenson's wife, as it turns out, who pointed out to her husband that Jekyll/Hyde was Everyman, which precipitated a full-scale domestic uproar. When the dust settled, Stevenson admitted to his wife that she was right, and subsequently rewrote the story, in which form it was finally published in 1886.

All of this fear of the animalistic had immediate social and historical echoes, for anything that could be put in the animal category was singled out for special, nonhuman (inhumane) treatment. The Other easily included "primitive" peoples, such as Indians and blacks, as well as the Irish, the poor, infants and women (childbearing and nursing were regarded as being animal-like). Beggars and madmen were obvious targets, says Keith Thomas: "the image of animality haunted the madhouse." Just as animals were removed to separate quarters, so were such categories of people, and the techniques of animal domestication often served as models for treatment of them.

At the same time, at the level of the intellectual and scientific middle and upper classes, the repression of animal Otherness was creating an obvious backlash. The new scientific naturalism encouraged a more detached way of looking at animal life, but it was easier said than done. In the seventeenth century, Cambridge Platonist Henry More commented on how loathsome spiders and caterpillars were, and naturalist John Ray wrote of snakes: "I have such a natural abhorrency of that sort of animal that I was not very inquisitive after them." Robert Boyle said that he could not look at a spider "without feeling a notable commotion in my blood. . . ."[80] Reptiles, insects, and amphibians (let us recall their role as category violators) were especially hated, although the reasons for this loathing were seldom understood or articulated. Oliver Goldsmith's comment (*An History of the Earth and Animated Nature*, 1774) that many people, himself included, "have an invincible aversion to caterpillars and worms of every species" was fairly typical of the period. Thomas reiterates what I have already suggested, that much popular thinking revolved around the distinction between Wild and Tame, and that encroachment of the former on the latter was viewed with alarm. Pets, zoos, rodeos, the rise of the vegetarian movement, and the fear of the body all have to be seen against this background.

Fear of vaccination because of its supposed potential to "animalize" humans, or remarks by More and Ray on the fear of worms and snakes, are surely the tip of the iceberg. Fear of organic life and the existence of the Tame/Wild distinction is so central and pervasive a feature of modern technological societies that it is, paradoxically, almost invisible. Like the basic fault, and the mind/body split, it is virtually everywhere, so it seems to be nowhere. And like these, it runs much of our lives, and determines much of our relationships and our social and cultural history. Modern technological society rests on the repression of these fears, and may even be an expression of them. But this means that it rests on a shaky foundation, and it is getting visibly shakier every year. As in the case of the mirror, we see dramatic changes in the human/animal relationship, both institutional and psychological, from the sixteenth century on. Ours is the first civilization in the history of the human race not to possess a nonhuman model of Otherness. Children in this culture do not typically get raised with animals around them (pets excepted). This is a radical departure in the history of child rearing, and it implies a very serious alteration in our relationship to an internal or external Other—an interference with the natural processes of the human psyche that is having profound consequences.[81] It is part of the same process that has turned the basic fault, or the phenomenon of confiscation, into a full-blown disease. For we have botched the problem of Otherness, and have thus created the "problem" of Self. It isn't an overstatement, to my mind, to say that if we don't somehow reverse this botch—and pets and zoos are not going to cut it—we are headed for suicide.

If I were a historian who had survived a nuclear holocaust, I think I might explain the event according to the schema given in Table 1 ("Why the Modern World Came to an End"). It doesn't require much by way of explanation, given what we have already said; but I wish to point out that nuclear holocaust is really a scientific vision of utopia, in which the world is finally expunged of the messy, organic, and unpredictable by being wiped out—"purified." Suicide, whether on the political, environmental, or personal level, is the ultimate (and most effective) solution to the problem of Otherness, a "problem" that should never have become one in the first place. The terror over creepy-crawlies is merely an icon. It is isomorphic to the anxiety over the body, and finally attains a visible, historical dimension in the yearning for *Vernichtung* (extermination), *Gleichschaltung* (leveling, homogenization), to use the terminology of National Socialism. We shall not merely "solve" the problem of intermediate substances, body fluids, and ambiguous animals, in this view; we shall solve it *all*, destroy any vestige of wild, disorganized Other *entirely*, so that Self now reigns supreme in a pure, dead, and totally predictable world. This, I believe, is the real meaning of our disturbed relationship with organic life at this time, and it shows where the sources of fragmentation are finally taking us. Hatred and destruction of life is the inevitable outcome.

What would *love* of life look like? If the times were different, the answer to this question would form the bulk of this chapter, and what came before would amount to no more than a few paragraphs. Unfortunately, the reverse is true here; but it is, nevertheless, a start. For it is important to make the attempt, to envision a world that would

Table 1

WHY THE MODERN WORLD CAME TO AN END

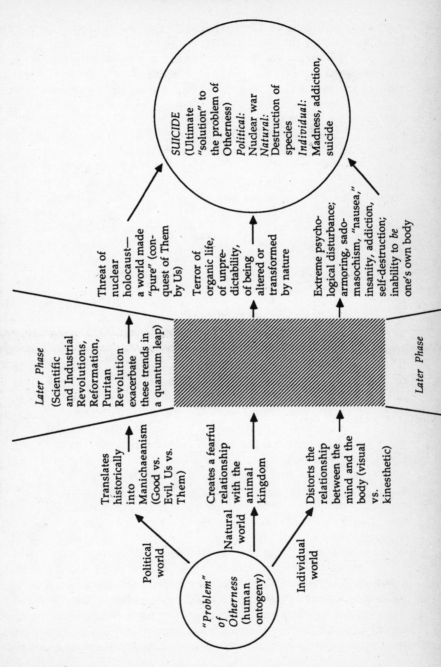

*"Problem" of Otherness* (human ontogeny)

Political world → Translates historically into Manichaeanism (Good vs. Evil, Us vs. Them)

Natural world → Creates a fearful relationship with the animal kingdom

Individual world → Distorts the relationship between the mind and the body (visual vs. kinesthetic)

*Later Phase* (Scientific and Industrial Revolutions, Reformation, Puritan Revolution exacerbate these trends in a quantum leap)

→ Threat of nuclear holocaust—a world made "pure" (conquest of Them by Us)

→ Terror of organic life, of unpredictability, of being altered or transformed by nature

→ Extreme psychological disturbance; armoring, sado-masochism, "nausea," insanity, addiction, self-destruction; inability to *be* one's own body

*Later Phase*

*SUICIDE* (Ultimate "solution" to the problem of Otherness)
*Political:* Nuclear war
*Natural:* Destruction of species
*Individual:* Madness, addiction, suicide

embody love of life, and to keep it before us as an ideal. This is part of what I see as the somatic reconstruction of our culture, which I regard as the major task before us in the late twentieth century.

I witnessed a good example of love of life a few years ago, one that startled me into a clear awareness of the whole phenomenon. I was dating a woman who had a lovely two-year-old daughter. The little girl, Danielle, often carried a small stuffed cat with her, "Fluffy," a classic T.O. Whenever Susan and I would eat in a restaurant, and Danielle wanted to go off and explore other tables, she would take Fluffy with her, for security. One day, the three of us were out for a walk and unexpectedly came across a cat—a real one. (A pet, true enough, but you take what you can get.) Danielle's interest in Fluffy vanished in less than two seconds. With a cry of glee, her eyes lit up and she stretched her hand out toward the real thing, wanting to engage it, touch it, encounter it. (The cat ran off.) It was a very stark incident, and I thought about it for many weeks after.

Love of life is the uninhibited expression of interest, or curiosity—the "cosmological urge" I referred to in Chapter 1. It is known as *jīvitindriya* (roughly, "life force") in certain schools of Buddhism, or what Dorothy Dinnerstein, in *The Mermaid and the Minotaur*, calls "enterprise" (more on this in Part III). It can perhaps be seen most nakedly with young children in a sudden, unexpected encounter with animals (Plate 13). This is a response to the world that is not driven by fear or even need, if such a thing can be imagined. It is *not* the response of the infant to Transitional Objects, which is rooted in insecurity (the desire to fill the gap), but a response rooted in trust, which tends to be spontaneous and immediate, not hurried or driven. It is significant to recognize how central the animal is to this process, the nonhuman Other that we reach out to out of wonder and curiosity; and it was with some interest that I learned that, in a curious parallel with cave art, young children (ages three through seven) dream not about humans or family members, but about animals and animal life. These dream animals are *not* familiar ones, i.e., pets, but farm animals, such as horses, cows, and pigs, or wild species that may still be in the environment, e.g., frogs, birds, and deer. At this age too, children like to tell animal stories, and in the telling the child and the animal will often get exchanged. Animals decline in dream life after age seven, coinciding with the point at which self-representation starts to occur.[82]

It is possible, I suppose, to argue that this animal interest is conditioned, that it comes out of a lot of exposure to Walt Disney cartoons and animal-illustrated wallpaper in nurseries; but it seems to me that

13. The pleasure of curiosity: children and spiders. Copyright by Karen Patkau 1985 from *Don't Eat Spiders* by Robert Heidbreder (Oxford University Press).

this only begs the question. We know animals are important to children, so we make their images available as best we can. But how do we know this? Mary Midgley argues that even children who have not had any animal acquaintanceship or early nonhuman imprinting actively seek it. "Animals," she says, "like song and dance, are an innate taste." Children find them irresistible not because they regard them as simplified human beings, but because they find them "radically foreign, and it is just that foreignness which attracts a child." Pets may be pathological, but the desire for contact with animals is not. In their spontaneous response to animals, says Midgley, children display an "eager reaching-out to surrounding life," and this persists in a few adults throughout their lives: a desire to play, explore, make objects for pleasure—which is the basis of at least some forms of creativity.[83] This is a situation in which the Other is a source of awe or excitement, not of fear; and it makes a deep sense of confidence in the body possible—an ontological confidence, one that is not going to develop into a need to "purify" the world by destroying it.

It is this kind of trust that makes a person comfortable with the body image and with changes in it. Paul Shepard writes that transformation stories that enable children to "become" different forms or animals also enable them to experiment with the not-me, and therefore with the plasticity of the Self. The body image, and therefore the mind, avoid the static quality of a fixed personality.[84] The person comes to see change as central to his or her being—something very difficult if you are raised with human or physical mirrors alone. The essence of Self is then not this or that particular persona or identity, but has the principle of transformation directly within it. Different Others become interesting rather than threatening. Ideology is avoided as boring. And fear, hatred, and the urge toward the destruction of organic life never enter the mind.

I believe it is this sort of consciousness, rare as it is, that can properly be called Love of Life.

# PART TWO:
# SPIRITUAL
# POLITICS

_____

[COUNTER-HISTORY IS] THE BELIEF THAT THE
TRUE HISTORY LIES IN A SUBTERRANEAN TRADI-
TION THAT MUST BE BROUGHT TO LIGHT. . . .
[THE COUNTER-HISTORIAN] AFFIRMS THE
EXISTENCE OF A "MAINSTREAM" OR "ESTABLISH-
MENT" HISTORY BUT BELIEVES THAT THE VITAL
FORCE LIES IN A SECRET TRADITION.

—David Biale,
*Gershom Scholem:*
*Kabbalah and Counter-History*

# 3

# The Body of History

*The secret life of belly and bone . . .*

—Delmore Schwartz,
"The Heavy Bear Who Goes With Me"

WHAT IF IT TURNED OUT THAT most of what was in the history books, or even in the daily newspapers, had nothing to do with life as it was actually lived? This seems a most curious suggestion; after all, what could all that stuff that fills much of the world's libraries be about, if not "the human story"? And yet I do not believe this suggestion is as strange as it sounds. Let us explore this possibility, just for a moment.

I was born and raised in upstate New York. During my high school years, we were required, as part of the history sequence of our education, to spend time learning about local and regional history. Our textbook had a chapter about the Colonial period, another about the defeat of the Iroquois, still another about the building of the Erie Canal, as well as ones on the rise of the steel and textile industries. For all I remember, there may even have been chapters on working-class movements, strikes, the formation of labor unions, possibly something on the life of Emma Goldman (though I doubt it).

That I *don't* remember is largely the point here. It was all crushingly boring; it seemed to have little relevance to anything that really mattered, to me or any of the other students forced to study this material. Yet it never occurred to me that there was anything wrong with this, because *all* of high school—or, I should say, the part devoted to formal education—was boring. Chemistry and Latin were no different from history, even though history was supposedly about "real life." Yet none of us were deceived about what actually constituted real life. Real life was your awkwardness in front of the opposite sex, your relations with your peers, your struggle to cope with what went on in your family. And for many of us, fear played a large part in all of these dramas. Yet none of this was in the history books; why (white) people bothered killing Indians or building canals remained a total mystery, and not a very interesting one at that. History, no less then chemistry or Latin, was a set of abstractions, a bunch of formulas to be learned and later repeated. Which is what we did.

It will of course be argued that all of high school is a disaster, generally for everyone, and that my use of textbooks written for teenagers is an unfair example. But is it really? Pick up almost any history monograph today, including ones written by sophisticated or "sympathetic" historians, and you will generally confront the problem of reading about things that somehow fail to resonate with what is most familiar to you. And what is that? In a word, your emotions, or more broadly, your "spiritual" and psychic life. These things are what your real life is about; they reflect the things that matter the most to you, for they are experienced in the body. The human drama is first and foremost a somatic one. How is it, then, that things such as emotions, or more generally the life of the body, gets left out of academic history? How is it that historians remain oblivious to the anemia of their enterprise in its present form? How is it that that which is *most* important in human life gets omitted from virtually all accounts of the past?

To say this is a curious blind spot is a bit of an understatement. Practically speaking, I should have titled this chapter not "The Body of History," which subject I have already discussed (in part) in Chapters 1 and 2, but "The Amputation of History," for it is more precisely about the "limbs" that got hacked off, to the point that what now passes for written history is really a history of the head—of the ego. Things such as the basic fault, Self/Other opposition, somatic experience and the like somehow do not exist for historians today (for the most part), and the lay public has no choice but to buy into this distorted version of the past. The point of this chapter, then, is to address the problem of historical explanation or methodology and its relevance to lived experience, and to make the case, theoretically, for the crucial importance of somatic analysis. That being done, we can get down to specific cases in Chapters 4–8. My goal in these latter chapters will be to show, from a somatic point of view, how we arrived at our present situation; how hidden somatic forces have in fact shaped our history. But before we can deal with that, it will be necessary to examine the problem of contemporary historical methodology in some detail.

I have to admit, of course, that much has changed in the world of historical explanation since I had to learn about the Erie Canal thirty years ago. Since 1965 in particular, there has been a conscious attempt in academic circles to effect a marriage of the abstract and the concrete by means of interdisciplinary work in history and social anthropology. Social anthropology operates on an intimate level; it studies face-to-face and day-to-day interactions of individuals in particular communities.[1] But until recently it made no attempt to fit this material into a coherent whole or extrapolate it backward into the past; and historians never saw this material as having any value for their own discipline. In the last twenty years, however, there have been important efforts in these directions. British and French historians in particular have attempted to use the "stuff of daily life" to create long-range studies (three or four centuries) of things such as family relations, religious movements, and the practice and persecution of witchcraft. In addition, the study of *mentalité*, as it is called, has done much to probe the nonrational foundations of human history (more on this below). Yet in all this work, and even in the work of the social anthropologists, there remains a failure of resonance. Anthropologists, for example, will talk in terms of rights and obligations within kinship groups, but words such as "love" and "hate" never surface in their analyses.[2] The life of the body, the life of our emotions, remains mysterious, unpredictable. Thus, although I find many of the developments in historiography since 1965 intellectually fascinating, I am convinced that the major historiographical revolution is yet to come. Western academic understanding, including philosophy and anthropology as well as history, tacitly assumes that the body has nothing to tell us, has no knowledge or "information"; that for all practical purposes, it isn't even there. And yet the life of the body is our real life, the only life we have.

Contrasts with "nonliterate" civilizations can be very instructive on this point. I put the word in quotes because our own civilization equates literacy with literature, i.e., with the printed text; it does not *consciously* understand that there is such a thing as body literacy (on an unconscious level it understands this very well). Some time ago, I saw the premiere of a dance concert called *Rainforest*, performed by a Vancouver group called the Karen Jamieson Dance Company. The choreography was so raw that I often felt as if I had stuck my finger into an electric light socket. The vignettes in this work are taken from the life of the Northwest Indians, principally the Haida, and they weave a cosmology that is entirely body-based. Gesture and grimace, blood and sexuality, darkness and light tumble out in a shifting kaleidoscope, stunning the audience relentlessly with what they already know: this is your real life, no matter what else you pretend. The director, Karen Jamieson, performs two of the vignettes by herself: one of a tour guide pointing to satellite maps of the earth and saying, "You are here," the other of a "correctly" dressed anthropologist with a microphone narrating a museum survey of Indian artifacts. In this latter vignette, the anthropologist loses her grounding as the cord from the mike gets coiled around her ankles; and the implication of the tour guide's "You are here," in contrast to the Haida, who are *truly* present on the earth, is obvious. "You are nowhere" with this mode of rootless, disembodied analysis; to leave your body and believe you can still know anything at all is quite literally a form of madness. The boredom of our schools testifies to the fact that none of us are fooled by this charade.

Regardless of what a person visibly presents to the world, they have a secret life, one that is grounded in their emotions, their bodily relationship to the world and to themselves. History has failed to tell us about these things because as a discipline it moves along the lines of external description. The academic study of human life, despite the various efforts in the field of psychohistory (work that is very often highly formulistic), proceeds on the assumption that only the visible is real. The reason this work is so limited is that from a certain vantage point it all amounts to the same book, written over and over again, but in different guises. Academic discourses generally lack the power to shock, to move the reader; which is to say, they lack the power to teach. They fail to address the felt, visceral level of our being, and so possess an air of unreality.

History gets written with the mind holding the pen. What would it look like, what would it read like, if it got written with the *body* holding the pen? I suspect it would be a very different story, one that would revolve around the hidden, somatic roots of our more visible behavior. Such a history would open us to our own emotional life; it would lead us into a world of visceral identification, tangible resonance. It would read like a good novel, but it would not be invented. This "subjective" experience is "what actually happened"; writing about the past in this way would be "objective" in the truest sense of the word. At present, however, no historian, myself included, has really explored this possibility to any great extent, though a few have made promising beginnings—writers such as Carlo Ginzburg and Norbert Elias, among others (discussed below). And in almost all of these cases, the historian recognized that he had come up against a methodological wall; that the possibility of a new, emergent type of history required the simultaneous emergence of new criteria for assessing what happened in the past. Opening the door on a new world requires a completely new set of procedures for negotiating the threshold; it has always been this way. Hence, we find a growing number of historians arguing that the epistemological or "scientific" dimensions of the discipline itself are too confining, and that the notion of "objectivity" as it has evolved over the last few centuries actually works against true understanding. But (as always) the obstacles to pushing into this new territory are formidable. Before we can get an idea of what a somatic or visceral history would consist of, it might be useful to understand what some of these obstacles are.

The major obstacle to understanding the past in the way I am suggesting is, curiously enough, the problem of living in the modern period itself, i.e., during the time in which history became a professional discipline, modeled along the lines of the natural sciences. Previous to this time, history was by and large a mode of storytelling. This is not to say that it was "merely" (note how loaded our terms are!) fiction, though its concern with "the facts" was certainly far less greater than our own. It would be more accurate to say that it had a very different sense of what "the facts" were. In this mode, "the facts" were first and foremost what happened on a psychic and emotional level; indeed, if this got left out, it was fair to say that *nothing happened*—there was no story to tell. The essential truth was an interior one; to omit this was to give the reader, or listener, no significant information whatsoever. In the transition to modernity, this emphasis on interior knowing was severely attenuated.

When I say "modern period," I am talking about the stretch of time from the Scientific Revolution—say, the mid-sixteenth century—to the present. A whole series of disciplines has grown and flourished over the last four hundred years. Alchemy gave way to chemistry, astrology to astronomy, mythology to psychoanalysis, and, as noted, storytelling to professional academic history. Most of us would agree that this shift represents an increase in our mode of understanding the natural and social world, specifically, a gain in what we call "objectivity." And the essential feature of this mode of understanding is that of psychic distance, the existence of a rigid barrier between observer and observed. If you get emotional about a subject you are analyzing, if you do experience identification or resonance, you disqualify yourself as a professional observer or analyst. "Emotional" in the modern period has the same force as "unreliable"; it means you are biased, that your judgment cannot be counted on. I suspect most of us would agree with this; I am only trying to suggest that our agreement is part of a culturally conditioned process. Prior to 1600, *lack* of identification was regarded as strange. Perception and cognition emerged primarily from the body, which is why, to borrow a term from the anthropologists, everything possessed *mana*, was alive. In this sense, it is difficult to imagine how profoundly different, almost totally disparate, oral and written cultures are. The former had a somatic base so solid that their reality was totally different from our own.[3]

An interesting discussion of somatic/oral culture is provided by Eric Havelock in his book *Preface to Plato*, in which he describes the mode of education in pre-Homeric Greece. Havelock writes that *mimesis*, or active emotional identification with a speaker or chorus, was the way in which the knowledge of the culture was passed on. This knowledge, in the form of poetry, was recited before a large audience that memorized the verses in a state of autohypnosis. *Mimesis*, the root of our words "mime" and "mimicry," was the submission to the spell of the performer, and was a process with physiological effects that were at once relaxing and erotic. Learning went on at the level of the body. Knowledge was, in consequence, directly experiential; there was no (or little) separate intellectual analysis that commented on the world or regarded it from a distance.[4]

A similar mode of understanding prevailed during much of the Middle Ages. This form of participating consciousness, to which I have already referred, was very likely not so pure as that of pre-Homeric Greece, but it existed nonetheless. A whole host of crafts and disciplines had an absorbing, repetitive, trancelike aspect to them, and were highly mesmerizing and sensuous in nature. This was especially true of the occult sciences, such as alchemy and witchcraft; and Thomas Goldstein, the medieval historian, makes the same point about cathedral building.[5] In all of these cases, the route to true understanding was to be found in that absorption, in the loss of psychic distance. Participation, or identification, is highly sensuous in nature, and it is a mode of knowing that cannot be intellectually refuted because of its immediate, visceral quality.

It can, however, be intellectually *rejected*, or intellectually repressed, which was what much of the Scientific Revolution was about. Yet if the truth be told, it is not that the emotional life got repressed, but that one particular emotion triumphed above all the rest. "Emotionless" activity, e.g., scientific or academic detachment, is driven by a very definite emotion, viz., the craving for psychological and existential security.[6] The increasing preoccupation, in Europe, with psychic distance can be seen in most areas of human activity from the Renaissance on; this is closely related to the rise of the mechanical philosophy briefly referred to in Chapter 2. In art we have the discovery of perspective, a device that assumes a neutral spectator looking at the painting from the outside, at a distance. The shift from alchemy to chemistry, and what that symbolized, meant that emotional identification was also abandoned in favor of psychic distance. Similarly, a good astrologer must know how to feel a situation out emotionally; a good astronomer, on the other hand, takes care not to let his emotions influence his observations (and is generally unaware that detachment is an emotion).

This shift took a long time, and it represented an increasing "masculinization" of culture and consciousness. Some of this was a good thing; to be constantly immersed in Great Mother consciousness is hardly the best state the psyche can be in, and as already noted, hunter-gatherer societies probably had a much more balanced consciousness. But this "masculinization" was heavily reactive in nature, and ultimately it went completely overboard. Physics was affected first; then chemistry, biology, and finally the study of human life. By the middle of the eighteenth century the work of Isaac Newton had become the model for the social sciences, and in the nineteenth century Comtean positivism affected history and sociology alike. Psychology in its turn was a branch of biology, itself conceived of as a subdivision of physics.

The heavy professionalization of history began in the nineteenth century. Leopold von Ranke, the noted German historian, set the tone for historical research by asserting that the job of the historian was nothing more or less than to give a straight account of the facts; to report "what actually occurred." Despite a few deviations from this theme, it is a goal most historians still share, and it has at its core the notion of psychic distance, of a past "out there" that is somehow, miraculously, independent of our interpretations of it. Interpretation of the facts is of course necessary, but this is not really seen as changing the "hard bedrock of reality." Emotional identification with the facts, however, is totally out of the question; it smacks of participating consciousness, and is to be avoided at all costs. The triumph of the Scientific Revolution in the realm of historical understanding meant that things must never be examined except from the outside. And this, *mutatis mutandis*, is where we still are today. The body and its feelings have no apparent relationship to the historical process; the "inside" simply doesn't count. History is, quite literally, a superficial discipline.[7]

The result of all this is that a lot of historical analysis today is simultaneously orthodox in methodology and unbelievable in content. I could easily turn this chapter into a review article of such works, but let me instead cite one or two examples from my own experience.

Some years ago I had a colleague who was studying eighteenth-century German Pietism, and was collecting data on how many people went to church in some small village in Hesse or Baden (the exact location slips my mind) over a period of several decades. Attendance, according to the parish register, was very high, and my colleague used this to argue for a high degree of religious sentiment in that region. I voiced my doubt as to whether the two things were necessarily related. That is, statistics are fine, but what did they tell us about what those German villagers were *feeling* about God or the life of the spirit? They may have been in church for other reasons besides God; and thus the real objectivity here, if any sort of *Geistesgeschichte* were being attempted, had to be intensely subjective—i.e., focus on the inner life. Well, as this sort of information is methodologically invisible to traditional historical analysis, my colleague regarded my question as meaningless. I, in turn, regarded the methodology itself as meaningless, or, at the very least, seriously misapplied; and there is no way I know of resolving this conflict of viewpoint.

A similar incident occurred with another colleague who was doing a computer analysis of medieval saints. The project, which had no trouble attracting grant support, struck me as being fundamentally wacky. His method was to compile all kinds of data on these religious figures—social class, country of origin, age at which they had their major ecstatic experience ( if at all)—and run the information through a computer. It was as though he somehow hoped to compute the cubic volume of the soul, to distill the essence of mystical experience and yet manage to escape the direct loss of consciousness that makes the experience meaningful at all (because ineffable). The project seemed stereotypical, a classic product of what one of my friends calls "the Age of Quantitative Mysticism." When I suggested to my colleague that he might possibly learn more about sainthood from thirty seconds of religious ecstasy than three hundred hours of FORTRAN time, he effectively told me that I must be crazy. Yet where does sanity lie in all this? That is indeed the crux of the matter. Who knows more about medieval sainthood—the historian who compiles data on age and nationality, or the one who goes to a monastery and sits in a cell for several months in complete silence? What does it mean, "to know," anyway? Again, there is a conflict of viewpoint here that is completely unresolvable.

The whole problem of inside vs. outside, and its consequences for knowing, was raised some time ago by Lewis Mumford in a critique of academic studies of ancient civilizations. Mumford attacked the notion, promoted in particular by the discipline of archaeology, that man was first and foremost a tool user—*homo faber*. This is no surprise, Mumford said, given the fact that the artifacts of the discipline are by and large material items that do not perish easily, e.g., stone hammers and flint arrowheads. But, he went on, suppose some ancient culture had a fantastic mode of conflict resolution, or a brilliant technique of dream analysis? What if it were the case—and Mumford believed this—that Paleolithic human expression came through the body, in activities such as mime, dance, song, and ritual, as well as symbolically, via gesture or cave painting? By the very nature of these activities, no artifacts would be left, and in fact, when the first cave paintings were discovered in Spain in 1879, anthropologists denounced them as a hoax. This emphasis on "hard data," from the viewpoint of common sense, makes no sense at all. As Mumford put it, "this apparently solid evidence is full of holes. . . ." "Material artifacts may stubbornly defy time," he wrote, "but what they tell about man's history is a good deal less than the truth. . . ." Contemporary Australian bushmen, for example, have a very rudimentary technology but very complex religious ceremonies, kinship organization, and language. Future archaeologists caught up in the *homo faber* model will inevitably dismiss them as a nonculture, as we have done with preagricultural and even some ancient agricultural societies. Yet it is precisely these somatic and symbolic activities that very likely constituted the major part of the life of Paleolithic humans. These are the things that were most representative of their value system, the things in which they invested most of their energy. But as Mumford noted, these essential, "interior" activities are invisible to traditional academic analysis.[8]

A similar situation can be found in the field of evolutionary biology. Certain hard-shelled animals—crustaceans such as the horseshoe crab, for example—have an extremely tough exoskeleton, and it is this shell that gets deposited in mud and rock to form the visible record of the creatures' evolution. Allowing for what Darwin called "imperfections in the geological record," these fossils enable the biologist to draw a fairly neat evolutionary picture. The problem is that the exoskeleton is essentially the defense system of these animals; eyes, digestive apparatus, and nervous system are contained within the soft, gushy interior, the part that rapidly decomposes upon death. This gushy interior is *not* preserved in the fossil record. Paleontological reconstructions based on the exoskeleton are very similar to archaeological reconstructions based on arrowheads and implements of war. It becomes very easy in both cases to conclude that the essential activity of the horseshoe crab or human being is attack and defense. But this is *not* the exclusive or essential activity of either organism; the larger part of their lives goes on inside the gushy interior. Darwin anticipated Mumford, in a way, when he wrote: "No organism wholly soft can be preserved."[9] Organisms or cultures that are partially soft can very easily fool the biologist, the archaeologist, and the historian. Which approach, then, should we trust—a "hard-nosed" methodology that is blind to what is essential, or a commonsense evaluation that points to what is being left out?

"On the surface, an intelligible lie," says one of Milan Kundera's characters in *The Unbearable Lightness of Being*; "underneath, the unintelligible truth." Certainly, if these are our only choices, we might as well forget the whole thing right now. If we want the historical truth, we are going to have to set aside our obsession with "objectivity" and its attendant methodologies and come up with a completely different approach, one that can reliably take us into the center of the gushy interior. And what we find there are those topics tied up with the body, the emotions, and inner psychic perception: religious experience, love and sexuality, humor, anger, insults, play and fantasy, sound (not the history of music, which is a very different thing), boredom, depression, fun, crying, sneezing, gesture, the treatment of body hair, anxiety, addiction, suicide, creativity (not simply the history of art), oedipal tensions, incest, and so on. The Chilean biologist, Francisco Varela, once remarked that the hard sciences deal with the soft questions and the soft sciences deal with the hard ones. What I am calling for is a new type of historical "science" that can deal with the hard—that is to say, truly significant—issues of human life. For such a methodology, studying religious feeling through parish records, or ecstatic experience through computer correlations, would be completely softheaded.

An interesting discussion of what I am talking about is provided by the British psychiatrist R. D. Laing in his classic work, *The Divided*

*Self.*[10] Pointing out that in the English language the word "merely" never precedes the word "objective," Laing goes on to give the example of Alfred Kinsey, the pioneering sexologist who spent his life gathering information on American sexual behavior. Through surveys, questionnaires, and interviews, Kinsey painstakingly compiled data on (among other things) the frequency of intercourse among married couples. But let us stretch this a bit; let us assume that he wanted to be even *more* objective, *absolutely* certain of his data. Imagine, then, Alfred Kinsey tiptoeing across suburban lawns every evening, peering into windows and recording the incidence of sexual activity, until finally he could produce the "hard" statistics he was looking for, e.g., "the American middle-class couple engages in intercourse an average of 3.4 times per week."

The scene then shifts to Laing's consulting room, where a patient is explaining to the doctor that for years he hasn't "really" been having sex with his wife. Yes, penis has gone into vagina an average of 3.4 (or whatever) times per week, but during this act the patient has been disconnected from the activity and has mentally been floating on the ceiling watching the activity go on. He has, in fact, been observing his wife having sex with his *imago*, or detached bodily image, and observing her thinking that she is engaged in intercourse with him. But he (at this point Laing begins to put the word "he" in quotation marks) knows better.

Now who is "he"? Has this man *really* been making love to his wife all these years? If the answer is yes, then what's the problem? Why is he consulting a psychiatrist? For surely his activity satisfies all the tests for reality that objective, nonparticipating scientific analysis requires. And this is precisely the problem: Kinsey was dealing with *merely objective evidence*; his data tell us nothing about American sexuality. And the reason for this is that sexuality is part of the gushy interior; the crux of it is where the mind is in relation to the body, as anyone who has ever made love knows. Wiring people up à la Masters and Johnson could only happen in an age caught in the grip of quantitative mysticism.

It now becomes clear why I was bored in high school—and why you probably were as well (at least in class). Historical "objectivity" is not merely boring; it is also, quite simply, wrong, and on some level the body knows this. This is why we found it difficult even to sit still in school. That restlessness is the body's way of flashing us an essential message: "This is bullshit," the body is saying; "don't listen to this." Pick up a recent copy of virtually any academic history journal (add sociology, psychology, etc., etc.) and the chances are good that your body will have the same reaction it once did in high school.

I once heard the American poet Robert Bly read one of his poems and admit that he didn't know what the concluding line meant. But, he added, he knew that the line belonged there, because as he wrote it, he felt a twinge in his gut. Of course, history is not poetry, and I very much doubt that "gut-twingeing" can serve as an adequate methodology for historians. But to be honest, I don't think it's a bad start. History is _made_ somatically; to be accurate, then, it should be _written_ somatically. If a twinge doesn't add up to a methodology, it can at least be an indicator of inner accuracy; which is, I think, the point Bly was trying to make.

I know of two modes of reportage about the past that produce the kind of twinge Bly was talking about. One is mythology, specifically, fairy tales; the other is historical fiction, at least some of it. I am not suggesting that history be converted into fairy tales or fiction; that is too easy a way out, or so it seems to me. But I want to dwell on these for a moment because as indicators, they do point in the direction of a deeper understanding of the human condition.

The problems I have been wrestling with up to this point can be made very palpable by attending the meetings of a learned society, where people stand up and read papers, and then attending a session of storytelling, especially when the latter deals with myths or fairy tales. Historians typically say to each other at the conclusion of a professional conference (usually _sotto voce_) that they learned more chatting over coffee than they did from the formal sessions, and they laugh. There is nothing surprising about this; the laughter is understandable. For we are bodies as well as minds, and the formal sessions tend to deal with topics, and deal with them in such a way, that leaves the body out. By contrast, at storytelling conferences (and these are getting increasingly popular of late) the body and its concomitant emotions are immediately engaged, along with the mind. So deep does this material cut that an audience can typically be found howling with laughter or in a state of panic. It is not that the mind is left out here; it's just that it is not examining things strictly from the outside. Storytellers make an assumption that historians rarely do, namely that human beings are _not_ rational, that they cannot be understood in terms of "objective" analysis, and that their deepest and most significant experiences are lived on a level that is largely invisible, a shadowy region where the mind and the body move in and out of each other in an infinite number of elusive combinations, and that can only be evoked through allusion, feeling tone, rhetoric, and "resonance." And these storytelling conferences also assume what academic history must by definition deny, that this shadow world is what human life is really about, and is the crucible in which history, in the final analysis, is really made.

As for fiction: how shall we study, let us say, the Russian revolution of 1905, or the German occupation of Rome? There have been numerous analyses of both these events. In the case of the former, for example, we learn about wage-price spirals in the closing years of the nineteenth century, the social backgrounds of revolutionary groups, military skirmishes, ideological debates, and the effectiveness of the czar's army in squelching the revolt. Footnotes refer us to newspapers, subversive tracts, economic indices, police reports, letters and correspondence of relevant individuals. All of this is well and good; it is certainly "real," in that it refers to events that "actually occurred," as Ranke said. Yet I never had any sense of the 1905 revolution until I read Andrei Bely's novel *Petersburg*, which zeros in on the generational conflict between a father, who is highly placed in the czarist bureaucracy, and his son, who inadvertently gets caught up in the revolutionary movement. As events move toward their climax, Bely presents us with a surreal dream sequence, in which the son experiences his mind separated from his body, floating through the cosmos. As the narrative proceeded from that point, I began to feel the twinge Bly spoke of. In fact, I was mesmerized; my own critical faculties were suspended as my body started to go through a mild anxiety reaction and somehow entered into the events of 1905. It is easy to say that this is simply a testimony to Bely's literary talents, and that the whole thing is an excellent imaginative reconstruction; but anyone who knows about anxiety reactions—and all of our bodies know it, and know it well—recognizes that if this did not actually take place as Bely describes it, then *something* like it must have, because this surreal "onlooker" experience is always triggered when your moorings come undone, or when you come face to face with impending psychic death. Revolution is not a rational event; it cannot be grasped or even "explained" in terms of ideological debates or wage-price spirals. In fact, many years ago I heard the British historian Eric Hobsbawm—a student of revolution if there ever was one—give a lecture at the London School of Economics in which he candidly admitted that he had no idea why revolutions occurred, and that as far as he could make out, they were large-scale "happenings." Bely has, quite simply, captured an essential component of what goes on during such a happening.[11]

A second example is afforded by Elsa Morante's novel *La Storia* (History), which is about the German occupation of Rome, and which revolves around the rounding up of the city's Jews on October 16, 1943. The central character, a schoolteacher named Ida Mancuso, happens to stumble upon the Tiburtino railway station more or less by accident during the event. The scene is one of cattle cars and chaos, and at the level of immediate perception, Ida has no idea of what is going on. For months, a demented woman has been wandering around the Jewish ghetto (where Ida occasionally does her shopping) hysterically proclaiming that the Jews would be shipped off and destroyed. Ida's infant son Useppe, whom she holds in her arms as she stands on the platform, suddenly turns to her and stares into her eyes with a look of questioning horror. Months later, Ida returns to the now-abandoned station, wanders into one of the nearby apartments, its windows broken, the corners of the rooms filled with cobwebs, and sits down. Suddenly, involuntarily, the words escape from her body, as it were: "They're all dead," she says aloud, allowing herself finally to acknowledge verbally what she knew viscerally on October 16. It is a *tour de force*, this moment; I felt my whole body quivering, on the edge of tears and immense grief. Again, it is no use claiming that this is merely a question of literary power. It *is*; but whether Ida actually existed or not is much beside the point. Morante cites a number of historical studies of the fate of the Italian Jews in her bibliography, but she has captured something which they, I suspect, have not: evil has something to do with somatic disturbance, and the recognition of evil has something to do with somatic awareness. It is not for nothing that she called her book *History*. This *is* La Storia—the real story.[12]

Again, I am not suggesting that academic history departments be absorbed into those of creative writing, or that the American Historical Association devote its annual meeting to fairy tales. It might be an improvement of sorts, but I don't think that the cure for scientism is complete subjectivity. That would merely be the perpetuation of the mind/body dichotomy in a different form. But I do think these examples may help us on our way. By dealing directly with the non-rational, with the body, they give us a glimpse of what a *truly* objective historical reconstruction might necessarily include.

There is a small group of academic historians that has struggled with the role of the nonrational in human history, an offshoot of the so-called French *Annales* school (whose writings date from the 1920s), though it includes two of the *Annales* founders, Lucien Febvre and Marc Bloch.[13] More recent exponents, such as Emmanuel LeRoy Ladurie or the Italian historian Carlo Ginzburg, have followed in the tradition of Febvre and Bloch, focusing their attention on subjects such as heresy, sorcery, peasant and popular culture, and in general the mindscape of the late Middle Ages. Febvre's pioneering study was of the problem of religious belief (actually, unbelief) in the sixteenth century; Bloch first set out to explore the cultural and symbolic significance of the medieval belief that the king's touch could heal scrofula.[14] In focusing on what Febvre called the "collective mental baggage" of a civilization, these historians moved far beyond what had passed, up to that point, for the mental life of a culture. They were not interested in intellectual history as such, but in *fundamental* outlooks; ones that reached, like a geological formation, far below the visible level. This was not, then, the history of ideas, but the history of psychic life in general; what they chose to call *mentalité*. I should add that this was not the same thing as psychohistory, i.e., psychoanalysis applied to history. Febvre, Bloch, and others did not reduce the nonrational to the strictly sexual, and did not approach their subjects with an a priori theoretical structure (Freudian or otherwise). Furthermore, they focused on entire cultures and civilizations rather than on single, significant individuals (which psychohistory tends to do).[15]

The implications of this were at least twofold. One, such investigations tended to break down the distinction between "high" and "low" culture, even to suggest that what went on in the minds of ordinary people in any age was more significant, historically, than what went on in the minds of leading intellectuals or literary figures. Second, their work began to reveal (or suggest) the presence of serious mental discontinuities between successive periods of history. In mapping the psychic contours of the sixteenth century, for example, Febvre and Bloch were able to demonstrate the existence of a kind of mental watershed between the medieval and modern worlds. "Sacred" and "secular" are not just convenient intellectual categories; they are lived experiences, and neither can be understood from the outside. To live in a world in which a person's touch was believed to be able to (could?) cure a specific disease is a very different psychic experience than to live in a world in which such things are regarded as impossible (and, perhaps as a result, do not occur).

All of this enlarged the possibilities for historical understanding quite dramatically, and in recent years vast territories of invisible history—"unintelligible truth"—have started to emerge into view. Most notable in this regard are Michel Foucault, who dealt with madness, sexuality, and the experience of punishment, and Philippe Ariès, who focused on childhood and death.[16] In *Les Mots et les choses* (Words and Things, translated into English as *The Order of Things*), Foucault took as his subject matter the nature of cognition itself, showing how, as a code or "mode of discourse" through which the world was perceived, premodern cognition was based on symbol and analogy, so that the world reflected itself in terms of feeling tone and resonance. It was Don Quixote's world, in which windmills could reasonably be giants, and in which walnuts, which resembled the brain in appearance, were in some sense small cerebrums and eaten as "brain food." For Foucault, writes the American historian Patrick Hutton, these modes of discourse "are the verbal expression of the mental structures (the 'words and things') through which man organizes his activities and classifies his perceptions of the world."[17] And again, the discourse of modernity is radically different from that of the sacred, medieval world; we are talking about two discontinuous orders of reality. Work of this sort finally opened the possibility of moving across this watershed, of recapturing past experience in the sense that it was actually lived, rather than through the filter of the post-sixteenth-century mode of discourse.

And yet this did not happen. Foucault denied the possibility of crossing the watershed precisely *because* the forms of discourse were radically incommensurate; which meant, of course, that he was unable or unwilling to suspend his own consciousness. And this is the problem with virtually all studies in the field of *mentalité*: they stop short of the attempt to recreate a previous consciousness, and opt instead for describing it from the vantage point of our own conceptual categories. In the last analysis *mentalité* remains abstract, preserving the psychic distance so central to modern cognition. Mind and body, fact and value, still wind up on opposite sides of the fence. The history of mentalities reflects the great divide set up by the Scientific Revolution, and it in fact understands this. To remedy the situation, however, it goes on a journey that is ultimately baroque and convoluted. In this sense, the field of *mentalité* does have some similarities to Freudian psychoanalysis and a good bit of psychohistory. That is to say, it attempts to recover the body by making a journey within the mind. In *Laws of Form*, Cambridge mathematician G. Spencer-Brown— whose intellectual ancestry includes Lewis Carroll—pegs this exactly. The mind, he says, semi-deliberately cuts itself off from what it knows and then goes on an elaborate circular voyage to find it.[18] As Freud said, we know and we don't know, and we play this game of hide-and-seek all our lives (as Freud himself did). This peekaboo structure—itself a variant on the theme of psychic distance—has finally emerged as the real structure of modern cognition, and so long as the subjective experience of the body and the emotional life is excluded from historical understanding, we shall continue to go around in circles. Not that this is necessarily bad; at least it seems to me that not all circles are vicious. But we do have to ask what lies outside the circle; what it would be like to step outside of it and into something else.

We come, then, to a boundary, and one that has a curious irony, or paradox, attached to it. In order to cross over to the premodern period, we have to abandon modern consciousness, at least temporarily; and this means to abandon a certain type of egoic personality structure, allowing the mind to sink into the body, as it were. But that merger *is* premodern consciousness, or at least a good part of it. To explicate past consciousness we must *become* it; and if we are terrified of doing that, we are condemned to move in an endless circle, our discourse finally beginning to resemble that of deaf mutes discussing harmony, as Somerset Maugham once put it. It has been the fate of the history of mentalities, as historiography's cutting edge, to take us right up to the limits of traditional historical analysis and throw it into question. It is clear that psychic distance must now be abandoned as the criterion of truth, and that other criteria must be put in its place. This is the inevitable direction to go in; there are no other alternatives. But it is most unclear how to do this. The question of *Quo vadis?* is inextricably linked with the one of How shall we get there?

In the remaining pages of this chapter I shall make some suggestions that will undoubtedly strike professional historians (among others) as very much beyond the pale. But I wish to repeat what I stated earlier, that already a number of historians have commented on the nature of the crossroads at which we have finally arrived, and the enormity of the problem involved in this transition. To take just one example, this whole methodological conundrum surfaced recently in the footnotes of a book on sixteenth-century heresy, *The Cheese and the Worms* by Carlo Ginzburg. Ginzburg begins the book with an epigraph taken from the French author Louis-Ferdinand Céline: "Everything that is interesting happens in the shadows; we know nothing of the real life of the human race." Searching in the shadows is both the major theme and the methodological undercurrent of the story that Ginzburg skillfully unfolds for us, that of Domenico Scandella, a peasant who was burned at the stake in 1599. Concerning Scandella, or Menocchio, as he was called, we learn two important facts: that his heretical cosmology emerged (or so Ginzburg argues) from an oral peasant tradition; and that he shot off his mouth on the subject for thirty years in the Friuli (the northernmost part of the Venetian provinces) without getting turned in, and when he *was* finally turned in, it was by a priest. Menocchio was thus very likely the tip of the iceberg, the bulk consisting of an ancient animistic tradition existing beneath the surface of a Church-dominated society, and which the Church had apparently failed to eradicate. The life of the shadows, then, becomes the real life of the Friuli—the psychic, social, and intellectual life all rolled into one. This is history from the inside, then; yet how are we to know that Ginzburg's guesswork is correct? After all, Menocchio could conceivably be an aberration, as some critics have argued.[19] Here, in a footnote, Ginzburg counters with something that might be seen as a cop-out, but that opens up the very possibility I am discussing. Arguing for the existence of a reciprocal relationship that obtains between written and oral culture, or between the visible and the hidden, Ginzburg says that it

> imposes on the historian standards of proof different from the usual. This is due to the fact that dominant culture and subordinate culture are matched in an unequal struggle, where the dice are loaded. Given the fact that the documentation reflects the relationship of power between the classes of a given society, the possibility that the culture of the subordinate classes should leave a trace, even a distorted one, in a period in which illiteracy was so common, was indeed slim. At this point, to accept the usual standards of proof entails exaggerating the importance of the dominant culture. . . . [T]o assure that every scrap of written evidence . . . is of greater validity in the reconstruction of Menocchio's ideas than a "purely" oral tradition . . . means deciding the issue in advance in favor of one (the more privileged) of the contenders on the field. In this way we inevitably finish by "demonstrating" the traditional thesis that ideas by definition originate *always and only* in educated circles . . . in the heads of monks and university professors, certainly not of millers or of peasants. . . . [I]t would be advisable to develop new criteria of proof specifically suited to a line of research based on so thoroughly a heterogeneous, in fact unbalanced, documentation. That a new field of investigation alters not only the methods but the very criteria of proofs in a given discipline is shown, for example, in the history of physics: the acceptance of atomic theory has ne-

cessitated a change in the standards of evidence that had developed within the sphere of classical physics.[20]

The interesting thing, as many physicists have noted, is that quantum mechanics, in contrast to classical physics, recognizes no independent observer. The scientist is part of his or her own experiment; his or her very presence changes the course of the events. If modern historiography continues to evolve, and if it follows its own historical trend of imitating the methodology of contemporary physics, it could conceivably develop a participant or interactive mode. It could understand that on the "subatomic" level, so to speak, there are no independent observers, and that experiential identification is dialectically the route to objective understanding.[21]

To take a single example: some time ago I received a letter from a colleague informing me that he had just completed a history of anger. I was very excited by the possibility of such a text; a history of anger would have been inconceivable even fifteen years ago. But my basic reaction was this: there are two possible books that could be written on this subject. One is the one in which my colleague would simply obtain, from written documents, information on how anger functioned in the past and how its expression evolved over time. In the other book, my colleague would do all of this, but one thing more as well: he would spend a long time exploring his own anger, experiencing it, watching when and how it surfaced or got repressed, and observing what the consequences of this expression or lack of same are. It seems to me that the second book would be a very different one from the first; and although I cannot prove it, because the events are "subatomic," I submit that this work would be a lot closer to the historical truth than the first one.[22] There are dangers here, of course, the most obvious being the one of projecting one's own anger onto historical situations that would not have involved anger, or a particular mode of expressing anger, as part of their pattern. This remains a genuine pitfall, and will need a lot of methodological discussion. My own belief here about the validity of this approach is based on a dialectical premise as to how the body operates. Unlived or repressed emotions have different consequences from ones that get expressed. Having direct, personal experience of anger enables one to write a very different sort of history than not having such experience. The difference is an *interior* experience—one of empathy, and therefore of insight. But as noted, there is no way I can prove I am correct about this. At this point in the evolution of modern historiography, my suggestion of experiential identification remains only that, a suggestion, but nevertheless one that I think we ought to play around with. As the historian Theodore Zeldin puts it, the "quality of a historian's personal experience is ultimately decisive in determining the quality of his writings." But it is more than that; and Zeldin adds that he looks forward to the day when "the historian who can discover the links between his own life and what has happened in past centuries, who can express in a new way how the past is alive, or who can give it a new colouring through the sieve of his own idiosyncracies, will no longer be idiosyncratic."[23] I suspect that day will not be here for a while yet, but I am convinced it is coming nonetheless.

Undoubtedly, the issue of experiential identification will have to be worked out in specific ways and in particular historical contexts. A history of anger in its entirety, for example, would be too cosmic to deal with between the covers of a single book. But before we go on to consider such possible contexts, an obvious question presents itself: why do this at all? Why concern ourselves with interior "microevents" of this sort? What difference does the history of anger, laughter, or play, or topics such as these, make for the "real" events of history, the major historical dramas?

The popular comic strip by Lynn Johnston, "For Better or For Worse," put this question rather starkly on one occasion. Mother is sitting in front of the radio listening to the news report; young daughter, home from school, is babbling to her about what happened in school that day ("And then Johnny took a frog out of his pocket, and . . ."). Finally, mother turns to daughter and says, "Elizabeth, be quiet! Can't you see I'm trying to listen to the news?" Elizabeth goes to her room, thinking to herself: "I thought that's what I was *telling* you!"

What is "the news"? What are "real events"? How is it that the story of the plane hijacked in Costa Rica (or wherever) is "news," but the one about Johnny and the frog is not? I am not making some sort of moral point here about how we should pay attention to our kids. My point is cognitive and analytical: what happens on an immediate, local, and experiential level is primary, and it finally determines macroevents such as wars and hijackings. We have been deluded as to what the "real dramas of history" are.

An analogy with the history of modern psychiatry might be helpful here. Until very recently, psychoanalysts assumed that neurotic behavior was the result of early traumatic events, and much therapeutic practice was preoccupied with helping the patient work through these traumas. After several decades of this approach, a number of therapists began to experiment with another possibility (although the trauma model, to be sure, can hardly be dismissed): the real neurotic scars are less the result of onetime traumatic shocks than they are of the daily habits of family life. Personality is generally a posture of defense, and one learns what one must defend oneself against in the context of what is regular rather than aberrant. What forms the core of the adult personality is thus, in this later theory, that which was, in the formative years, not traumatic but daily, repetitive, even boring. Like grain dropping upon grain, as one character in a Beckett play says, the whole structure is slowly built up, out of almost invisible micro-events. And it is these that must be investigated if the larger structure is to be understood. What *sustains* laughter, play, anxiety, or anger? These are the icons of personality, and it is on this level that the riddle of personality has to be unraveled.

Historical studies, it seems to me, have to begin entertaining the notion that an analogous procedure is going on, and therefore that an analogous shift of focus will have to take place. Historians typically study economic depressions, political revolutions, the impact of greater or lesser thinkers; they look at patterns of population, the distribution of wealth, the statistics of immigration, the occurrence of major or minor wars. Most of this falls into the "trauma" category and, as in the case of the psychoanalytic situation, it can hardly be called unreal. But the less visible may be, as I have suggested, more real, or at least more significant. Claude Charron, a former Quebec politician, wrote of his disenchantment with politics because of its tendency to create a "deforming prism," by which one comes to believe that history consists of mass movements, broad categories of people, and large-scale events. According to this view, wrote Charron, people

> are workers, they are the elderly, they are people on welfare, they are natives, they are people from the Gaspé, they are union members, they are people on the margins of society. No politics can be done without the abbreviation of differences, no government would know how to act without these indispensable categorizations; these categorizations make the newspapers live, and no one officially denies them.
>
> . . . These clusters, we say, make history: we mention the Bastille, we point to insurrections.

But, he says, this mode of analysis is a duplicity, for these clusters are only heightened episodes that explode out of the real events of life, events that are hidden and subterranean, and that remain imperceptible when we insist on viewing history from a great height. The truth, he concludes, is that

> history is not made by parties, unions, groupings, demonstrations. It is discreetly woven in the souls and hearts, the successes, failures, pains and joys of which are a thousand times nearer to the daily life of each person.[24]

The argument here, to put it in its most extreme form, is that the life of the body, and the emotions, and the subjective experience of how mind and body interact, constitute the real events of our lives, and condition, if not cause, everything that happens "historically." The challenge for history (i.e., for historical analysis), as far as I am concerned, is to start seeing the larger dramas in these somatic and "subatomic" terms, and to come up with a methodology that convincingly relates the visible to the invisible.[25]

In Chapters 1 and 2 I tried to generate examples of what a somatic history might look like; what kinds of topics it would select, and how it might go about dealing with them. I shall, as already indicated, work one such topic out in Chapters 4–8 in specific detail. Let me, however, close the discussion here with three examples (two of which were mentioned very briefly in Chapter 1) of what a somatic analysis might look like. The first example is taken from a lecture I attended in 1983 by Brian Sutton-Smith, Professor of Education at the University of Pennsylvania. His talk was entitled "The Role of Toys in the Modern World."[26] He pointed out that in the previous ten years (i.e., roughly 1972–82) in the United States, toys had become a six-billion-dollar industry; that seventy percent of them were purchased for children by parents at Christmas, suggesting that they served a form of bonding function for the family at a stressful time; but that their essential function was to induce separation or isolation, for most toys are designed to be played with by the child in a solitary situation ("Go play by yourself," we typically say to a youngster). Sutton-Smith also pointed out that a toy in this sense, something designed and manufactured by adults to enable or encourage children to be by themselves, is a very recent invention. Down to 1750, the historical pattern was *group* play, *group* toys. This phenomenon thus constitutes a real historical break, a break with tribal culture and custom. From 1750 on, the tendency has been to induce solitariness in children, which really amounts to teaching them to tolerate loneliness by means of diverting themselves with objects. If we want, then, to understand how modern Western culture managed to inculcate values of individuality and achievement ("success"), how it essentially managed to make people "happy" with isolation instead of relatedness, a history of toys might be an important place to look. Sutton-Smith also noted that toys have been fatal to street games, which have disappeared except among the lower classes. The result, he said, is a fatality for the body, for the physical self. The body gets left behind by an entire generation mesmerized by video games; and the consequences for a culture getting disposed or softened (conditioned) to certain larger, more "visual" (nonkinesthetic) possibilities are enormous. So the history of toys is really a history of the body; and my guess is that it can tell us quite a lot about the causes of what we customarily call "real" history, i.e., the stuff that makes it into the six o'clock news and the textbooks.

Yet to understand the psychic dimension revealed by toys, something more is needed here. Sutton-Smith, or whoever chooses to approach the modern isolated psyche and the cult of individualism in terms of toys, would need to endow the research with a special kind of quality by trying to relive in their own mind their own childhood experience with toys. This need not necessarily be part of the final published work on the history of toys (though it might); the point is to enter into your own experiment, to break down the methodological principle of psychic distance. What will emerge as a result, I cannot say; but to sit for several weeks playing with the wooden toys of our youth, as well as with the plastic toys of today's youth—to feel the difference physically, in one's hands—is (I suspect) to open the door to a very different sort of historical understanding. To some extent, a history of the body reflected in the evolution of toys has to be a history of *your* body (i.e., the author's body) as you experienced them in your own life. How exciting it would be to read a history textbook or monograph that resonated with this kind of energy!

A second possible example of embodied history occurred to me after I ran across a quotation from a German child-rearing manual published in 1787, reproduced in Alice Miller's book, *For Your Own Good*. The author, J. Oest, pointed out the need for sex education among children, but added that such information would typically inflame the childhood imagination. Children, he said, should be given a knowledge of what the genitals of the opposite sex look like; but how to do this safely? Pictures are far too provocative, he maintained. Herr Oest's solution was as follows:

All these worries disappear if one makes use of a lifeless human body for this purpose. The sight of a corpse evokes solemnity and reflection, and this is the most appropriate mood for a child under such circumstances. By a natural association of ideas, his memory of the scene will also produce a solemn frame of mind in the future. . . . [E]very teacher can . . . impart the necessary instruction in [this] manner. . . . There is often opportunity to see a corpse.[27]

Now suppose this manner of sex education actually took hold after 1787 and lasted through the nineteenth century and into the twentieth. (I have no idea whether this was the case or not.) Suppose, through an investigation of other child-rearing manuals, or by means of interviews with German and Austrian octogenarians, or school records of field trips to morgues, we could establish that historically, this mode of instruction was widespread. I would suggest to you that such an investigation would tell us infinitely more about the Third Reich and the Holocaust than any number of psychobiographies of Hitler, no matter how valuable. That Hitler was psychotic, that women had to defecate on him in order for him to be able to make love, is all very titillating, but it tells us nothing about why such an individual managed to pluck a responsive chord in an entire population. But Hitler's appeal would be a lot more understandable if it turned out that a number of generations prior to 1933 had a sexual education in childhood that taught them to associate sex with death.[28] This is history of the body of a more profound and convincing sort. One might also wonder, if Oest's book had a wide following in Austria, whether Freud's theory of the death instinct, and of civilization being a war of Eros and Thanatos, did not have its roots in the clinical results of such upbringing among adults. The death instinct always struck me as the weakest stone in the Freudian edifice, but it is not so strange an invention if the entire culture in which Freud lived had been trained to associate sex with death on an unconscious level. In this way too, such a study would enable us to make better sense of the intellectual history of that period.

Once again, there is a further subjective step to be taken here. How does the investigator feel about his or her own sexuality? Granted, they may not have learned about the facts of life in a morgue (although interestingly enough, generations of American medical students had their first exposure to the subject in autopsy rooms); but how precisely does their own psyche differ from the German one? What do their dreams tell them about this? What are their specific fears regarding sexual behavior and expression? How about making a trip to the morgue today? What sorts of reactions do they have to the genitals of a corpse? Again, there is a lot that has to be worked out here methodologically; one reason that I am groping in the dark is that we do not *have* methodologies of feeling, only ones of analyzing. But a start has to be made.

My final example is that remarkable book by Norbert Elias (briefly referred to in Chapter 1), *The History of Manners*, which falls into the category of *mentalité* and which was first published (in German) in 1939. What Elias was able to do was to chart the emergence of a phenomenon he called the "advancing threshold of shame" in the transition from medieval to modern Europe. He took as his subject the daily, repetitive habits of table manners, including such things as nose blowing, farting, the use of utensils, burping, and so on. From the point of view of almost any school of historiography, it is a most bizarre book. Yet the exploration of the daily details of etiquette enabled him to show that the major form of control that emerged in modern society was a form of social distancing—not unrelated to modern scientific or historical methodology, as it turns out—whereby you modify your behavior based on how you see yourself being seen through the eyes of those around you. This "mirroring" phenomenon, whereby people became increasingly self-conscious, began to have its echoes in the etiquette books of the time, such as *De Civilitate Morum Puerilium* (On Civility in Boys, 1530), by Erasmus of Rotterdam. Thus Erasmus wrote: "Some people put their hands in the dishes the moment they have sat down. Wolves do that. . . ."[29] Other quotations, especially after 1600, reveal a preoccupation with how one will appear to an external observer—a preoccupation that requires taking a position on yourself as a "specimen," an object of contemplation. Very slowly, said Elias, the European upper and middle classes came to be detached observers of their own behavior, in contrast to the more spontaneous and "blurry" behavior of the Middle Ages.

So far so good; and as a history of the body, and of mind/body relationships, the book has a lot to commend it. But to his credit, Elias did not stop there; he extrapolated from this minute, daily behavior to a major cultural shift, namely the Scientific Revolution itself:

The development of the idea that the earth circles around the sun in a purely mechanical way in accordance with natural laws— that is, in a way not in the least determined by any purpose relating to mankind, and therefore no longer possessing any great emotional significance for men—presupposed and demanded at the same time a development in human beings themselves toward increased emotional control, a greater restraint of their spontaneous feeling that everything they experience and everything that concerns them takes its stamp from them. . . .

Herein lies one of the keys to the question of why the problem of scientific knowledge took on the form of classical European epistemology familiar today. The detachment of the thinking subject from his objects in the act of cognitive thought, and the affective restraint that is demanded, did not appear to those thinking about it at this stage as an act of distancing but as a distance actually present, as an eternal condition of spatial separation between a mental apparatus apparently locked "inside" man, an "understanding" or "reason," and the objects "outside" and divided from it by an invisible wall.[30]

The implications of such a suggestion are enormous. The rise of modern science has been studied from the vantage point of the history of ideas, or in terms of concomitant social and economic factors; and there is no doubt that both of these approaches have been fruitful. But it has never been studied as a *bodily* phenomenon, and surely Elias—whose suggestion was never picked up—was on to something very important. What he grasped was the "subatomic" stratum, the possibility that the educated classes of western Europe learned the phenomenon of detachment and observation *in their bodies* for two centuries preceding Newton; and that a Newton (or a Copernicus, or a Galileo) could not have arisen or been comprehensible in a culture that had not had such a visceral apprenticeship. In a like manner, the success of the heliocentric theory, or of atomism, required of people a radical distrust of sensory evidence (it still does), a kind of detachment that was simply not part of the medieval European psyche, probably for reasons discussed by Elias. In this regard, it is interesting to note that to this day the modern scientific paradigm has made the least headway among those cultures whose table manners, from our point of view, are the sloppiest.

What else might Elias have done? I think back to a course I once took in sixteenth-century Italian court dance. As background, we began the first class with medieval dance. The movements were light, and the dances were all done in group formation, similar in style to the

Virginia reel; there was no partner dancing. We then switched to the dances of the late Renaissance, and the difference in physical sensation was immediate and dramatic; one felt it most clearly in the pelvis. The sensation was: "This is *my* space I am standing on, *my* property." The sense of deliberateness, aggressiveness, and privatization (individuality) was unmistakable, and I would never have experienced it merely from reading about the history of dance. Have I been deceived? Possibly; but possibly also, I understand something about the physicality of modernity that I would otherwise have missed.

In the same way, Elias pointed out that medieval people struck postures (we can see this in paintings) that seem very strange to us, e.g., standing on one leg for long periods of time. (There are tribes in various parts of Africa that still do this.) Why not suggest to readers that they go and do this before reading any further? Why not, as a historian, do this himself? Or to take another example, he charted the evolution of the spoon, from the large round pewter soup spoon used almost exclusively in the Middle Ages to the tapered teaspoon more shaped to the mouth today (this evolution can be seen at the Victoria and Albert Museum in London). Why is this significant? Because as part of the history of manners, the large spoon was sloppier, much less efficient; it reflected the spontaneity of eating during the Middle Ages, whereas the tapered spoon reflects the self-conscious eating and etiquette of the modern period. To understand that spontaneity, to really feel it in your body, you would have to eat with a large spoon for several weeks, feeling how it stretched your mouth, at first uncomfortably, until finally the sensation of throwing the mouth wide open—the grimace of the medieval gargoyle—seemed perfectly natural. Perhaps Elias could have instructed his publisher to attach such a spoon to every copy of the book, with instructions to readers that they should eat all of their meals with it for the next few weeks (having first, presumably, done so himself).

It is easy to dismiss all of this as sheer idiocy, but I am not so sure. Recent research in neuropsychology has tended to confirm the notion that personality changes in individuals precipitate serious alterations in their physical bodies. It seems likely to me that the reverse is also true—that bodily changes or conditioning would create serious alterations in personality; and moreover, that on such a basis, the "personality" and therefore the history of an entire culture could undergo profound shifts in orientation as well. Toys, sex education, and eating habits are all good examples of slow, cumulative body training that can finally make a profound difference in the definition of reality itself. What Elias had to say about scientific detachment, for example, could equally apply to the emergence of perspective in art, to which I have already alluded, where the observer stands outside the painting and perceives objects or lines all converging upon himself or herself as the neutral spectator; as well as to modern historical analysis, where the historian arranges a linear chronology of events, events of a particular kind, namely those experienced in a detached fashion, and where subjective experience of them is seen to violate the canons of the discipline itself. If Elias' book seems bizarre to most historians, and my extrapolation of it idiotic, perhaps we ought to reflect, once again, upon where our standards of the "reasonable" and "sensible" come from. For they are rooted in a commitment to psychic distancing and somatic nonengagement, and that commitment is learned by us physically, as young children. What took Europe several hundred years to assimilate in terms of table manners has now been compressed into the first five or six years of life for those of us born in the twentieth century. The historian who finds these suggestions ridiculous may only be acting out, on an "adult" and "mature" intellectual level, the effects of that early visceral apprenticeship. There may be more than one way to look at all this.

The issue of visceral apprenticeship, then, is something that must start to apply to ourselves in the investigation of historical or cultural phenomena; only then will the criteria of historical proof start to change. *Mentalité* is fine, an immense advance over what came before and over what still remains the historical mainstream. But as Carlo Ginzburg notes, we are finally up against the methodological edge of the old paradigm, and in my view we need to take a leap to what we might call *corporéalité*, a visceral approach to history that puts the mind and body back together again. Once again, I have to say that this is not necessarily a reversion to storytelling or to archaic modes of understanding; the goal should be a post-Cartesian paradigm, not a pre-Cartesian one. But this new methodology would involve our bodies as well as our minds; it would create bodily and emotional echoes in the person who reads historical studies reconstructed on its basis. It would elaborate on a suggestion made many years ago by Wilhelm Reich, that the way we hold our bodies—what he called the "character structure"—"is the congealed sociological process of a given epoch";[31] and that as a result, our bodies might be the key to the historical dramas we seek to understand. Above all, *corporéalité* would link the visible with the invisible, put the macrocosm back together with the microcosm. We are in murky territory here, in the same way that the physicists are; no physicist I know of has managed to construct a methodology that directly involves the experimenter in their own experiment. But that day may not be far off. Our history has been disembodied long enough; the time has come to flesh it out.

# 4

# The Gnostic Response

*If you want the truth, I will tell you the truth:*
*Friend, listen: the God whom I love is inside.*

> —Kabir, fifteenth century, version
> by Robert Bly

*Tout commence en mystique et tout finit en politique.*
*(Everything begins in mysticism and ends in politics.)*

> —Charles Péguy

IN PART I OF THIS BOOK I attempted to demonstrate that the body is the hidden ground of history, and that an examination of certain phenomena, such as the use and availability of mirrors, the human/animal relationship, and manifestations of body image, to name but a few, is useful in unpacking the nature of the mind/body relationship over time and indeed of Western culture itself. The next few chapters continue to develop this theme, that history is finally an activity of the flesh, but I seek now to apply the techniques of somatic analysis to one particular problem in the history of Western civilization: the presence of a heretical or countercultural tradition that is rooted in bodily experience and that rejects the cerebral, or formulistic, way of life of the dominant culture (orthodoxy). This tradition, despite relentless persecution, has refused to go away; and despite (or perhaps because of) its somatic and subterranean quality, it has managed to influence and, in an important sense, shape the dominant culture over the last two thousand years.

The topic of heresy may seem, at first, a rather specialized one, and one chosen only as a case study, with a view to demonstrating the effectiveness of somatic analysis. And indeed, that is an important aspect of this section of the book. Heresy has generally been treated as an ideological debate, a conflict over the divinity of man, the corporeality of Christ, and a host of related issues. Understood from a somatic point of view, these disagreements over matters of theological dogma recede into the background; the fact that heresy was a bodily activity puts the whole thing in a very different light. But beyond that is the fact that heresy is no "specialized topic" in the history of the Christian West; indeed, that is precisely what the orthodoxy would have us believe, a kind of "nuisance theory" of history. The truth—and I believe it can *only* be seen from a somatic point of view—is that the subject of heresy is finally about the cognitive and perceptual history of the West—about its entire *Weltanschauung*, its way of coding reality. An analysis of the subject thus provides a skeleton key to the whole Western reality-system, to a whole set of beliefs and mental structures. To examine this "mirror" of Western culture is, in effect, to comprehend the last two millennia as a whole, and in a new and synthetic way. A rather difficult project, as I've already admitted, but somatic history is (or ought to be) the attempt to grasp such large configurations without sacrificing critical analysis or historical detail. Only the reader can judge whether I have been successful, and if so, to what extent.

The topic is also important in that, more than anything discussed in Part I, the chronic or even cyclical recurrence of heresy implies the possibility of a different future, i.e., of a major cultural shift occurring once again in the future as it has occurred at several points in the past. This possibility is shown to be especially viable by the demonstration that a lot of what we take to be archetypal, part of "human nature," is in reality epoch-specific. A new era, a new future, is thus not all that farfetched. To that end, my goal in this section is to establish a *typology* of heresy—to show that the interaction between politics and spirituality falls into four very distinct patterns—and then to use this as a guide to possible future developments. This is a tricky business, and as far as the future goes, I have left it to be dealt with, as best as I can manage it, in a separate section (Part III); but clearly it is a crucial question to ask. Real cultural shifts are of this order, discontinuous breaks with the past, as Michel Foucault argued. If it seems unlikely that such an event might take place over the next hundred years or so, it is nevertheless the case that Western history has undergone a discrete number of serious ruptures, or realignments, and also the case that these were rarely anticipated by those living at the time. Although, as I shall explain in Part III, I have problems with the whole "paradigm-shift" concept that has become so fashionable in recent years, it is nevertheless likely that we are in the midst of some sort of morphogenetic (literally, the birth of a new form) transformation, and the real issue is *what* sort, and whether, from an understanding of past models, we can successfully throw our weight behind certain tendencies and pull away from others that seem less desirable. I honestly don't know; but the hope that this may be possible has motivated much of this work. In what follows I wish to discuss the nature of heresy in general—what Eric Voegelin has called the "gnostic response"—and then turn to the subject of the political contexts that have shaped that response in radically different directions. Only then will we be in a position to make some guesses about "paradigm-shifts" and the heretical agenda of the twenty-first century.[1]

Although it is not often stated directly or even understood, the attempt to restore body cognition to the center of human consciousness is a central feature of most heretical movements in the history of the Christian West. Much of the argument of heresy vs. orthodoxy revolves around belief in God vs. the actual *experience* of God, something that can only be brought about by somatic practices, ascetic or otherwise. Gnosis is not about belief, but about tangible proof of the existence of "larger forces," which Western mystics over the centuries have claimed to have obtained by means of certain somatic techniques of breathing, chanting, meditation, and so on. That all of this gets translated into doctrinal debates only reflects the fact that heretics rarely got to speak for themselves; we glean most of our knowledge about them through their orthodox opponents or persecutors, men who, untouched by the spirit (i.e., the body), were literally unable to grasp what these "apostles of the Antichrist" were on about.[2]

The tendency to see ancient or medieval religious debates in modern ideological terms easily lends itself to seeing our ancestors as mental defectives, people who would persecute each other or go to war over what often seem to be issues of spelling or word usage. Thus at the Council of Nicaea in 325, the doctrine of the Trinity was effectively canonized by declaring that Christ was of the same substance as the Father—"consubstantial." The Greek word for this is *homoousios*; the alternative position—what came to be known as the Arian heresy— was that Christ was *homoiousios*, of *similar* substance. The dispute was bitter, and it lasted another 125 years and beyond. And all, seemingly, over the Greek letter iota. In his classic work, *The Decline and Fall of the Roman Empire*, Edward Gibbon castigated the early Christians for generating an endless debate that was "not worth one iota." Viewed in purely doctrinal terms, nothing could be more senseless.[3]

From a somatic perspective, however, the debate may not be quite so absurd. What if it were the case that there were certain esoteric techniques, possibly of Asiatic origin, dating from at least the second century B.C., that continued to permeate the Greco-Roman Empire and that enabled the practitioner to have a direct experience of God? And what did Christ really mean when he said, "I am the Way"? If Christ was *homoousios*, then he was not a man but a god—*was* God, in effect (consubstantial)—and thus any sort of ecstatic or visionary experience had by those of us here on earth was a delusion. His divinity was a one-time event, and all us mortals could ever hope to do was believe in him ("I am the Way"). Insert the iota, and a very different state of affairs ensues. Then Christ was a man who had a transformative experience. Other men and women can have this experience too, if they follow his example ("I am the Way"). From a spiritual point of view, the two paths are radically different, and they have different political implications as well. In the first case, a priesthood is necessary to guide the faithful onto the paths of righteousness. In the second, a shaman might be useful, but a hierarchy of priests, bishops, and deacons would be a positive hindrance. Somatically and politically speaking, this was an iota worth fighting for. Since direct (bodily) experience of God (or "God") seems to be the crucial issue here, a few words about this subject at the outset would not be out of place.

When I say that much heretical, or gnostic, or mystical experience (they are not necessarily identical, as I shall discuss below) in the West is somatically based, I mean by that that Western spiritual experience is characterized by the "great rush," the flash of white light or moment of illumination that takes over the body completely and that can, if the experience is strong enough, change the course of a person's life. If modern analyses of heresy fail—seeing the debates as purely doctrinal or ideological, for example—it is because they ignore the underground somatic current that lies at the heart of all gnostic systems. As already noted, *gnōsis*, in Greek, refers to a kind of direct internal or visceral (spiritual) knowledge rather than to rational-analytic knowing. Even one hour of yogic breathing exercises can suffice to give one at least a hint that something much deeper is involved.

I once had such a hint as a result of going through a process called rebirthing, which involves a type of breathing apparently derived from an ancient practice known as kriya yoga. It occurred after many sessions of this: my body suddenly dissolved into light. Of course, my rebirther didn't see this, and in that sense I remained fully corporeal. But *I* saw it; I *was* it, and that is the issue here. It is one variety of gnostic "illumination," so to speak, and is variously reported in mystical and gnostic literature.[4] And it is an amazing experience; one retains, from that point on, the memory of the possibility that one is ultimately a "body of light." The same sort of turnaround occurs with classical "oceanic" experiences, such as have been reported by Jakob Boehme, William Blake, Teresa of Avila, and many other less famous (or notorious) individuals. Experiences like this are so immediately real, in a somatic and cognitive sense, that one begins to understand why the Christian West spent so much of its history arguing over iotas or burning dissidents at the stake—an unwitting parody, or inversion, of turning the body into "light."

What follows is thus going to seem kind of strange, especially from the vantage point of traditional studies of heresy and gnosticism, for I am going to take the mystical or magical spokesmen and spokeswomen at their word. They *did* ascend to heaven, or turn into light, or whatever; all of this is not reducible to "brain chemistry," which is a very low-level understanding of altered states of consciousness. Such an approach, I believe, can potentially open up Western religious and political history in a dramatic way. It is not my intention, however, to filter the somatic or spiritual events involved here strictly through my own experience, which is limited at best. We have to turn to a more general understanding of gnostic mind/body practices, such as are recorded in heretical, occult, or yogic literature. There are many texts that could be consulted at this point; I have chosen to use the schema outlined by the American psychologist Robert Masters in his essay "The Way of the Five Bodies" because of its relative clarity and accessibility.[5] It should be noted that the idea of five levels of consciousness is (despite what any system claims) almost arbitrary. Yoga traditionally speaks of seven, as does ancient Indian medicine (the seven chakras), the ancient cult of Mithras (seven gates), or that of Isis (the initiate removes seven garments or animal disguises). The process could be a harrowing one, and was called *palingenesia*, or rebirth.[6] But exactly how many levels or bodies we have is not the point. The central issue is that there is a somatic and experiential bridge strung, like a rope ladder, across Winnicottian transitional space. That is to say, much of heresy is about the direct experience of "God" rather than about the Transitional Object and its numerous manifestations in terms of substitute gratification. Its greatest enemy, as a result, is organized religion and the concept of God that such religions peddle to the masses; for in the name of God, which can be a direct experience, the Church (*any* church) gives you a formula, a T.O. to play with (cross on the wall, mezuzah on the door, etc., etc.). It is thus the traditional God that is most despised by gnostic cults over the centuries, and this is why a central tenet of Catharism, Manichaeanism, and all the major Christian heresies is that the ruler of this world is in reality the Prince of Darkness who usurped the throne, and that the real god is a *deus absconditus*—a god who has gone into hiding. The world, as Christopher Hill once put it in his study of seventeenth-century English sects, is perceived to have been inverted, turned upside down.[7] Heretical practice is first and foremost a body practice; its emphasis is always on essence as opposed to form.

The essence/form distinction is, of course, a manifestation of the deeper kinesthetic/visual split discussed in Chapter 1. All of the following pairs are variations of the distinction between spirituality and religion, God-realization and dogma:

| ESSENCE | FORM |
| --- | --- |
| Love/sex | Marriage |
| Learning | School |
| Health | Hospital |
| Creativity | Academy, genre |
| Motivation | Career |
| Social relations | Government |
| Friendship | Club, organization |
| Playfulness | Entertainment |

In the heretical worldview, the items on the right arise when the items on the left fail. As Lao-tzu says somewhere in the *Tao Te Ching*, "Law" and "Justice" become important when love and trust have collapsed.[8]

In order to begin to understand that we possess more than one body, we have to give up the notion of body as being a strictly physical thing.[9] This is not easy; it takes a little practice. The first step lies in recognizing that we can deliberately move our consciousness around, into various parts of our body or even into the objects around us. Consider the following exercises, and perhaps try them out before continuing your reading:

(1) With your eyes closed, sit in a comfortable chair, and relax your muscles as much as you can. Now put your attention into your right thumb. Do not *observe* the thumb; rather, project your consciousness *into* it. *Be* your thumb. After a while, allow your consciousness to move to the top of your head. Feel the sensations in your scalp. Then slowly move your consciousness downward, allowing it to inhabit the surface of the skin on your face. Now let it descend along the surface of your entire body, part by part. Finally, as best you can, try to feel your internal organs: nasal passages (you can do this by following your breath inward), heart, ribs, liver.

(2) Staying in the same position, again with your eyes closed, remove your consciousness entirely from your body. Let it float outside of yourself, as it were, or above yourself, and observe your body from a distance. (In this case, you do observe; your consciousness remains *outside* of your body.)

(3) Still with your eyes closed, project your consciousness into an object in the room. (It might be easier to begin by imagining that the object is similar to an item of clothing, and that you are wearing it.) As in the case of (1), this is identification rather than observation. Really feel that you are the flower, desk, doorknob, or whatever.

(4) Finally, do the same thing you did in (3) with a complete stranger or casual acquaintance. As they speak to you, empty yourself of all self-attention and place your consciousness within theirs, so that you can identify completely with what they are saying. Notice how they are relating to you as a result.

Practiced often enough, exercises such as these create a consciousness that you can snap into almost at will. This consciousness will finally have the feel of a separate body; it will seem to acquire a solidity no less tangible than your physical body. And no matter how disparate the various "underground" traditions are, they all depend on exercises such as these for creating a ladder of ascending states, or bodies, which one can learn to inhabit voluntarily.[10]

What, then, are these various bodies? The first, very obviously, is the body of Western science and medicine. Much to the discredit of these disciplines, the physical body is all they recognize; a state of affairs that once led a Chinese doctor to conclude that Western medicine was essentially about corpses. The physical body has a brain but no mind, and is therefore not the body of our actual experience. The body actually experienced is the second body—what I have called the body image, the physical body as it is experienced by the mind. It is one's personality, or "aura"; the force field that surrounds the physical body. You can feel the aura as you get physically close to another person; contact is made even though the two of you aren't "actually" touching. The Egyptians called this the *ka*, or etheric double. It is this that separates out at the moment of death, which is why all cultures, including our own, have a network of established rituals for dealing with the demise of the physical body.

These two bodies are essentially the only two that Western philosophy has chosen to recognize. Lacan, Wallon, Merleau-Ponty, and others have assumed that the gap or nemo boils down to the separation between the second body—which they have called the mind—and the physical body. While it is true that mind/body distortion originates from the mirror stage and the process of confiscation, it is also the case that the gap contains more than this simple hiatus. In the theory of the five bodies, our alienation is really an illusion. The gap is filled with the five bodies, strung across transitional space, but one has to develop them in order for the mind (second body) to recognize this. The situation is thus fairly complex; no one could become whole merely by grasping the specular image. The real work of the *ka* is to contact, and develop, the third or unconscious body, which can be observed in trance and drug states, as well as in dreams (it is sometimes called the astral body). It is this body that Jung called the (Higher) Self, and in this he was far ahead of Freud, who could only see the unconscious as a reservoir of dangerous and repressed forces. These certainly are in the unconscious, but if we work with them properly, these forces can be turned into allies. (The snake one dreams about, for example, can become a spirit ally.) Contact between the etheric double and the unconscious body can be developed through certain kinds of exercises that "freeze" the *ka* or get it out of the way: meditation and hypnosis, for example. In such situations, the *ka* is really an incipient kind of Higher Self; it works in the direction of the unconscious body.

The unconscious body, says Masters, also contains one's individual fate; one's dream, in the sense of the destiny that is "dreaming" one's conscious life. Ignoring this body means dreaming the mass dream, such as is projected onto the mind from the television screen. In the gnostic tradition, failure to awaken this body means that one lives someone else's life, not one's own; something that can be seen, for example, at a football game or any form of mass entertainment (more than one hundred million people in the United States watched the Super Bowl on TV last year) or in organized religion. Hence, according to the gnostic tradition, most people are zombies, robots; or in the jargon of that tradition, "sleepers." Those who are "awake" have contacted their own individual destiny by means of the unconscious body. The higher role of the *ka*, as an incipient Higher Self, is to become a detached observer of the unconscious world; to recognize the existence of a larger Mind. In the language of medieval theology, it is to find the soul; and taking the trouble to fill the gap by "growing" a soul is, in all mystical traditions, the activity that most decisively sets off the "wakers" from the "sleepers."

The myth or destiny of each person is shaped by the fourth level, that of the magical body. It is this body that is capable of generating paranormal effects. In the magical tradition, there are no such things as inanimate objects. Mind exists in matter and can be contacted by other (human) minds, so that supposedly impossible events become possible. Those who master this level can make objects move by concentrating on them, walk barefoot on glowing coals without being harmed, or bend metal merely by the force of their minds—phenomena that have been widely reported and that are by now common knowledge.[11] Such people can apparently dematerialize objects and rematerialize them (this is less well known). All of this is the sensationalist side of magical practice. Adepts in this category can turn water into wine, multiply loaves and fishes, heal by touch, and, as a result, attract very large crowds.

The fifth level is that of the spiritual body. It is at this point that the gnostic practitioner accumulates enough personal power that he (it is usually a he, which is a significant point) can influence thousands of individuals, even millions, and therefore alter the course of history. This is what Hegel, whose philosophical sources were heavily magical and Vedic in nature, meant by the phrase "world-historical individual." Hitler and Gandhi are obvious examples of this, and their cases suggest that psychic power by itself is neutral: it can be used for great good or great evil. These cases also reveal how the great teacher works: he speaks directly to the unconscious body, and thereby awakens in his listeners the possibility of living out a more (apparently) authentic dream. His charisma is irresistible because his experience with the five bodies enables him to pluck this chord in the masses. It is the spiritual body that controls the so-called kundalini energy of the body, the "coiled serpent" at the base of the spine, which it can uncoil and raise to the top. One has only to see the stoned adoration of the crowds in Leni Riefenstahl's movies of the 1930s to realize that this was what was going on in Nazi Germany (see Chapter 8). In that particular case, the dream or destiny attached to this process and reawakened by Hitler was the dream of Aryan glory, so evocative an issue for people whose spirit had been severely humiliated in recent decades. In Gandhi's case, it was the dream of a true homeland, free of cultural violation by an occupying power. These two were not "great men" in the sense of somehow being able to do these things by themselves. Rather, there was enough coherence and unity of somatic experience among Germans or among Indians that their respective "gaps" had a fairly similar configuration. A religious figure (who is often, also, a political one) becomes great by intuitively knowing this configuration, expressing it or echoing it publicly, and convincing his audience that he can close (or fill) the gap for them. He thus embodies salvation, the promise of an end to their collective nightmare of alienation.

Finally, the five bodies are not independent of each other. They interact back and forth along a chain, and there are numerous examples of this. Thus Masters points out that the body parts of any given person do not wear out uniformly. The four "subtle bodies" have an enormous influence on the physical one. Unconsciously, we choose our mode of death and probably the time of it as well. It is not an accident, for example, that one person has lower back pain while another "prefers" ulcers. These are only the particular physical manifestations of the ensemble of bodily relations.

For our purposes, however, the most important body is the fifth, or spiritual body—Hegel's *Zeitgeist*, the somatic and psychic configuration of a society at any given time. In the case of gnostic illumination, or what I am going to refer to in this volume as the experience of ascent, the five bodies momentarily collapse into one. In fact, the fifth body "invades" the first two. This is why the experience is both physically ecstatic (body boundaries dissolve, and one is merged with the universe) and cognitive (it is a mode of knowing). This "recognition of the Absolute" affects all five levels of existence; one is never the same after that. It becomes impossible to remain a strict rationalist; unconscious "programming" gets seriously rearranged. How did Ronald Laing once put it? "I have seen the Bird of Paradise, she has spread herself before me, and I shall never be the same again."[12]

These, then, are the five bodies that potentially inhabit the gap that all of us possess. This is also why heresy is not about ideology. Gnostic experience means engaging in some form of spiritual/bodily practice that will take one, step by step, up the ladder to illumination, the direct experience of "God." It is because of the five bodies that what we call "influence" is even possible, and why influence spreads in ways that can never be measured scientifically. Hegel was at least partly right in arguing for a *Zeitgeist*, a concept that has been resurrected in semi-scientific garb by Rupert Sheldrake with his notion of "morphogenetic fields."[13]

What both Hegel and Sheldrake omit, of course, is the somatic basis of it all. Their vision is much too spiritual, and in this sense Marx and other historians were right to reject Hegel's notion that consciousness creates the world. The problem is, however, that every age or epoch does seem to possess a kind of controlling spirit, or dominant metaphor. Seen in terms of psychic effects grounded in body image, Lacan's mirror stage, and the psychophysical dramas of early infancy, the Hegel/Sheldrake notion is less easily rejected, because the "spirit of an age" does emerge out of our bodily configuration, even if it doesn't remain there. What is really happening in events such as the spread of heresy (or even the telling of jokes and stories) is a somatic rippling effect: bodies influencing other bodies. I realize it sounds strange, but I suspect we are going to have to start accepting a peculiar idea (peculiar, at least, for our culture), that consciousness, or psychic energy, can "float," and that ultimately an entire culture can undergo profound changes from the transmission of this energy. Culture and history themselves may, in the last analysis, prove to be the products of viscerally embodied morphogenetic fields. Once the chain of five bodies that stretches across the gap starts vibrating, it acquires the ability to cause other people's "chains" to vibrate sympathetically as well. The effect is quite powerful because it goes so deep. It holds out to all of us the possibility of becoming a fully "realized" person, of closing down the gap. This is, I believe, what the word "influence" really means, and it has had quite a dramatic career in the history of religion and even the history of ideas, though historians generally don't use this word in the sense being used here. It also underlies the basic orthodox/heterodox distinction. The goal of the Church (any church) is to obtain a monopoly on this vibratory experience, to channel it into its own symbol system, when the truth is that the somatic response is not the exclusive property of any given religious leader or particular set of symbols. But if a church can convince the populace that its monopoly is legitimate, that *extra ecclesiam nulla salus* (there is no salvation outside the church), it can acquire enormous temporal power.

Politically speaking, the major problem, of course, is the gnostic distinction between "sleepers" and "wakers." Fritz Perls, the father of gestalt therapy, once said that certain people are "poisoned"; they are so damaged that self-awareness has become impossible for them. Freud went so far as to say that most people were "worthless"; they would never get free of their conditioned behavior. In the gnostic tradition, "sleeping" means being unconscious, being run by this conditioned behavior. The unconscious body has effectively gone to sleep, and has been taken over by forces such as childhood traumas or childhood conditioning. The tradition assumes, at least theoretically, that all beings *can* become conscious, can "wake up." But given the way of the world, this is a vision that is often difficult to maintain. In his later years, for example, Plato gave up on his dream of a republic ruled by philosopher-kings who guided a populace toward some form of enlightened behavior. This is, of course, an authoritarian vision, albeit a benevolent one; but his final version of this was unabashedly totalitarian—a state in which the rulers had effectively "given up" on the populace, and in which the citizens were viewed as nothing more than robots whose every move had to be monitored for their own good.[14] The same gloomy outlook informs a number of leading dystopian novels, such as *Brave New World* and *1984*, and is also the substance of the famous "Grand Inquisitor" section of Dostoevsky's *Brothers Karamazov*. In that debate, the Grand Inquisitor tells Christ (who has returned to earth incognito) that he (Christ) expected too much from people. Very few, he says to Christ, can seriously do the work of self-realization, and the Church, i.e., the orthodoxy, knew this ("the everlasting craving of humanity," he tells Christ, is "to find someone to worship"). So it eased their burden: it enabled them to identify with the experience of the vibrating chain in a symbolic way, without actually having to go through the process itself. If a cross on the wall cheats them of genuine spiritual experience, it lets them lead a "happy," programmed life. This is the best they can do, and anything else would make them miserable. So why don't you (he effectively says to Christ) buzz off?

Orthodoxy, in other words, opts for map instead of territory, for the travelogue instead of the trip. If this is the eventual source of its political power—its ability to acquire a large membership by making it easy for potential converts to enter the fold (when was the last time anyone got high from being baptized?)—it is also its Achilles' heel. For heretics can always shout "fraud," and they will usually be right.

And if they can produce a leader who can vibrate the somatic chain, not just allude to it, then it is only a matter of time before a schism is in the making. As a result, Western religious experience is essentially schismogenic in nature. There is no end to this game, and it is still with us today in the form of charismatic movements, "born-again" Christians, cults and sects of various sorts, and even political splinter groups. A cult, after all, is merely a religion that hasn't won popular acceptance. If or when it does gain this, it will inevitably begin to play down the importance of actual somatic experience. This in turn opens the door to the next cycle of authentic realization and heretical rebellion. The problem is that this may be a *revolving* door, and this puts the phenomenon of ecstasy and vision-quest in a whole different light. Whether other alternatives are possible is something I shall deal with in the final part of this book.

Within the matrix of Neolithic society, and the categories of Self/ Other, or Tame/Wild, discussed in Chapter 2, the schismogenic cycle is quite inevitable. Western consciousness is deeply influenced by dualism, or Manichaeanism (one of the oldest Christian heresies); its unconscious body is that of a dream, a dream of the war between Light and Dark, and this war has become its destiny. Robert Masters notes that the unconscious body—the destiny—*can* be altered, but it is a fearfully difficult task. In the meantime, everything in the West is cast in terms of binary structures. The possibility that form and essence, orthodoxy and heterodoxy, are bipolar, are actually necessary for each other's existence, is one that continues to elude us (even though, as in Taoism, this would still be binary). Hence, we continue to replay what Erich Neumann called the twin brothers' war in our religious life and in everything else (see Chapter 10). As a result, the response to this patriarchal framework is inevitably female revolt, the voice of the Great Mother Representative. If male consciousness wants to make separations, the Great Mother Representative wants to make connections, to the point of total merger (ecstatic experience). The "underground stream" of the West—witchcraft, alchemy, and most forms of gnosticism and heresy—is essentially a feminine stream.[15] Its goal is to undo the process of alienation; to get back to kinesthetic origins, or the True Self, which got confiscated by society, in this case represented by the Church. In that process of confiscation, so the argument goes, order and chaos got reversed. The public order is thus purely visual, *le monde d'apparence*, and is cemented together by fear. To get in touch with deeper, somatic realities, and to translate them into the political realm, requires the destruction of this phony order.

Historically, heretical movements thus often act as agents of cultural meltdown, but the problem is that these "feminine" values usually get colonized for "male" purposes. Victorious heresies tend to harden, to supplant previous symbol systems with ones of their own. These latter frequently wind up being more rigid and formulistic than the orthodoxies they replaced. For better or worse, the "politics of aura" has not worked out. But the whole dynamic is not easily dispensed with, because the debate between form and essence goes on within each individual psyche. We are all of us popes and heretics, and oscillate between the two poles. The heretic is typically our "shadow" self, the internal Other we fear. It is this split phenomenon, operating dialectically, that accounts for the passion of heresy, the fierceness of those who have persecuted it, and the backlash effect of hardening or colonization.

All of this would seem to make the war of heresy vs. orthodoxy, or Self vs. Other, completely inevitable, an innate psychic structure; but as we saw in Chapter 2, this is not the case. For those societies that antedated the great agricultural civilizations, the dichotomous game of Tame vs. Wild was feeble or nonexistent, and T.O.'s and transitional space did not manifest themselves. It is no accident that Paleolithic societies, as opposed to Neolithic ones, were not preoccupied with religious questions (e.g., "Where is heaven and how do I get there?"). For the gap between heaven and earth is obviously a projection of an internal gap, of transitional space, and as we have seen, this is a comparatively recent phenomenon. According to one student of the subject, S. N. Eisenstadt, hunter-gatherer societies did not possess or recognize a tension between a mundane, "lower" world and a "higher," transcendental one.[16] Instead, the two worlds were built on the same principles, so there was no need to cross over from one to the next. Salvation, in short, was not an issue. As is the case in certain schools of Buddhism, the point is what is actually in front of you, not what lies "beyond." Eisenstadt believes that such two-world tendencies did exist among Paleolithic peoples, but that it was only with the rise of the great civilizations—Israel, Greece, Iran, China—that a clear distinction was made between the transcendent and the mundane. This in turn made possible the institutionalization of the split, as well as the rise of various sects as agents of change. For once the split opened up, the question of how to bridge the two worlds became paramount, and this directly implicated the individual personality and gave rise to some form of rebirth eschatology. Whereas in hunter-gatherer societies death was simply a part of life, in the great agricultural civilizations how to get to the "higher" world—i.e., conquer death—became a central concern. It implied the search for utopia, the need to reconstruct the personality, and a corresponding emergence of sectarian tendencies. Priesthoods followed very rapidly, as well as a distinction between an inner and outer social order. The psychic, the religious, and the political all tended to emerge simultaneously.

From this point on, the politics of heresy became unavoidable. Any resolution of the tension between the two worlds, Eisenstadt notes, was inevitably incomplete and contradictory. There was always room for alternative interpretations, always a place for spokesmen of those interpretations. Hence we get Jewish prophets (and priests), Greek philosophers and Sophists, Hindu Brahmins, and so on. These men were not shamans, integrated into their societies in an immediate and concrete way. No; they spoke for a transcendent god and an autonomous vision. The inflation of issues was impressive. What had once been tribal differences were now, says Eisenstadt, "missionary crusades for the transformation of civilizations." Salvation, bridging the two worlds, reconstructing the human personality—things that had never occurred to hunter-gatherer societies—suddenly became crucial to the future of (Neolithic) civilization.

All of this, Eisenstadt continues, existed in the East as well, but it received its most extreme formulation under Judaism and Christianity. In these latter religions, great emphasis is placed on the clarity of doctrinal boundaries and their ritual application. In Buddhism, by way of comparison, these things are not as important. As a result, it is possible to talk about Buddhism in terms of sectarian tendencies and different schools, but not in terms of heresy as such. In the West, on the other hand, doctrinal struggles (and, I would add, somatic practice) got translated into attempts at psychological, cultural, and political reconstruction. As a result, as the German sociologist Max Weber was one of the first to argue, heresy has been a major force in the history of Western civilization. I believe this is so firstly because our biological legacy, and the events of our infancy, generate a definite energy field; and secondly because this energy field has historically been deployed in various ways. In particular, a typology of heretical formation can be mapped out, such that we come to see that one of four models is always running our psychological life, even down to the present day. Cultural upheavals in the West have the heresy/orthodoxy conflict at their very core.

Before elaborating on these four models of heresy, it might be help-ful to say a few words about the terminology I shall be using in this discussion, since from the viewpoint of what would probably be a more discriminating historical analysis, many of these cultural mani-festations cannot be shoved into the same category. I have used the label "gnosticism" in an umbrella-like fashion, and strictly speaking, this is inaccurate. Gnosticism, Catharism, magic, Fascism, alchemy and witchcraft, heresies of all sorts—these are not equivalent and may not really add up to an alternative tradition. For example, they cannot all be responses to Christianity, since many of them antedated the birth of Christ. Not all heresies are gnostic; not all gnostics actually become heretics. "Heresy" is, like "insanity," a social label. Magic is not necessarily gnostic in nature, since it is not particularly dualistic, and it never includes the notion of an outside savior or redeemer, which gnosticism (especially in its early forms) sometimes does. The High Middle Ages saw a very wide range of heresies, and these cannot all be reduced to gnosticism; and in the case of the early modern period, it is likely that things such as cabala and alchemy were part of an older tradition, not simply a response to the Church. I have, then, hardly been precise in my definition of terms up to this point, and this may cause obvious problems in the attempt to analyze such a phenomenon as heresy or to map a typology of its forms.

How to escape from this terminological confusion, then? The answer is that despite what a more discriminating analysis might want, there may *be* no escape, and this is due to the somatic nature of the phe-nomena involved. Umberto Eco writes: "There is a mysterious wisdom by which phenomena among themselves disparate can be called by analogous names. . . ."[17] The things I have (correctly and incorrectly) labeled "gnosticism" are somatic phenomena—lived experience. In practice, they often run together. They resist the neat categorization that a student of ideology, let us say, might "reasonably" insist upon. In his review article on magic in early Christianity, for example, his-torian David Aune points out that despite the various distinctions that have been made between magic and religion, they cannot be distin-guished in actual practice. *Social* definitions and distinctions exist, but all classifications made in terms of *Wesen* (essence, Being) fail—as the great historian of religion, A. D. Nock, once argued years ago.[18] In a similar fashion, an international colloquium that was held in Sicily in 1966 to settle the question of what Gnosticism (i.e., the gnosticism of the Mediterranean basin in late antiquity) actually was, failed. After six days of wrangling, leading scholars in the field were not able to isolate a few elements that could be said to constitute the essentials of Gnosticism. As one scholar, Th. P. van Baaren, pointed out, Gnosticism is a purely historical phenomenon, whereas gnosis is phenomenological. One can find gnosis existing without gnosticism, for the former is a lived practice, not a network of beliefs. Thus gnosticism is not shamanism; and if it is always dualistic, it is also the case that there are numerous types of dualism. It is somewhat amusing, for example, to see these scholars "titrating" the Gnosticism vs. Judaism of the Dead Sea Scrolls, trying to get an idea of exactly how Jewish or Gnostic the sect at Qumran (presumed to be the Essenes) actually was. Hans Jonas, one of the experts on the subject, further argues that gnosticism contains mood elements—e.g., elements of revolt or rebellion—that are not part of the conceptual doctrine per se, but that are nevertheless crucial to it.[19]

There is, then, no winning this game from a strictly academic angle; my indiscriminate umbrella may actually be a more reliable way to go about it. Furthermore, the real goal here is not to generate a definitive treatment of the subject, which I take to be an impossible task, but rather to offer a suggestion, or venture upon an exploration, and see if it provides a certain amount of insight or enables us to reflect more deeply on the culture in which we live. As far as I can see, there is, historically and psychologically speaking, something that can be called a "gnostic response" to life, and it is grounded in a somatic configuration peculiar to human beings. Tantra, Catharism, and Western witchcraft are certainly worlds apart—I doubt that their respective practitioners would bother spending more than two minutes in each other's company—but all such systems and traditions do have one crucial thing in common: some form of somatic practice, some direct experience with the theory of the five (or more, or less) bodies, lies at the heart of their cosmology. And at various points in history, for the dominant culture, which has always sought the triumph of the visual over the kinesthetic, this overlap is "good enough"; it all represents the same specter of "chaos and communism," the same threat to the established order. Witches and Manichaeans alike got put to death (albeit in different centuries); and despite the great differences among alchemy, astrology, the cabala, and trance experience, all of the Italian thinkers discussed in Chapter 7 found themselves accused of heresy and suffered for their beliefs. The Church was never too fussy about the doctrinal differences that existed among its enemies.

The purpose of the typology that follows is to take the somatic energy as a given and assess what happens to it in different social and historical situations. The result is, as the reader will see, still a lumping together of the phenomena, but along historically differentiated lines that are undoubtedly unconventional. More importantly, I think that it shows that deeper forces rule our lives than we tend to recognize, and that if we can, via this typology or some other, better one, understand how those forces operate, we might be able to get some idea of what kinds of obstacles we are up against today.

I shall be dealing with each of these historical types in separate chapters, but to summarize the argument in advance, what we have are four basic categories of heretical formation: (a) world religion (Christianity); (b) defeat/co-optation (the Catharist heresy of southern France, and the ideology of romantic love); (c) a new science (the occult revival of the Renaissance that led to the rise of the experimental method); and (d) Fascism (Nazi involvement in the occult tradition and alternative worldviews). All four of these were an assault on orthodox Christianity to varying degrees; except, of course, the first, which emerged as part of a very long tradition of somatic and doctrinal conflict within Judaism. It should be obvious that this hardly exhausts the actual number of heresies that have existed in the West during the past two thousand years; my argument, rather, is that these four each display a characteristic political pattern, and that most, possibly all, of the heresies we have seen in the history of the West fall into one of these four basic categories. To put it another way, although the "gnostic response" is always present as an underground phenomenon, it clusters or intensifies at certain nodal points and becomes "overground" in a distinct set of historical patterns.[20]

The first model, or archetype, is Gnosticism proper (capital G), a set of beliefs that were widespread in the Mediterranean basin during (and after) the time of Christ and that have been clearly identified in the texts discovered in a cave near the village of Nag Hammadi in Egypt in 1945. These texts reveal that early Christianity was a much more supple and complex affair than was previously assumed. The Christ of these long-hidden gospels argues that the spiritual world is the only reality and that the material world, including its political institutions, is illusory. In his view, the world is transformable only through an inner transformation of the individual soul. Furthermore, entry into the Christian cult was probably gained by means of a secret initiation that had powerful psychological effects, and that was derived from the ancient mystery religions. A number of scholars have thus argued that Christianity was a Gnostic/magical (possibly Essene) cult within Judaism, i.e., that it was a Jewish heresy accelerated under the pressure of hellenizing influences. I call this, then, the "Greek" model, and it is that of some type of mystery cult, possibly proto-Gnostic in nature, managing to become a world religion. How it managed to do so is an important aspect of the "colonization" process referred to earlier.

The second major nodal point is characterized by the emergence of a group known as the Cathars (or Albigensians) in the south of France, perhaps as early as the eleventh century. Catharism was a heresy that seems to have been rooted in an earlier Manichaean doctrine, and that, in the form of some sort of overlap with the troubadours of Languedoc (it is still a moot point), generated the concept of romantic love—the "coded" form of the heretical doctrine. By the thirteenth century, however, the Cathars were defeated, partly through a series of massacres (the most notorious being the ones at Béziers in 1209 and Montségur in 1244), partly by means of the Inquisition (established for this purpose), and finally through a process of co-optation. The emphasis on the courtly love of an unattainable lady was undercut by the Church by means of the Cult of the Virgin Mary. Gnostic experience thus got contained by the Church, channeled back into the dominant institution. This then might be called the "French" model, essentially characterized by a process of repression, co-optation, and reabsorption.

The third resurgence of gnosticism occurred during the Renaissance, and was especially oriented to the occult sciences. I call this case the "Italian" model, due to the profound immersion of a significant number of late-Renaissance figures in magical practice, such as Marsilio Ficino, Girolamo Cardano, Pico della Mirandola, Giordano Bruno, and Tommaso Campanella, to name the most famous of these. In this case the outcome was not a world religion, or romantic love/co-optation, but modern science. Of course, the origins of modern science, which have been debated *ad infinitum*, cannot be attributed to any single factor, but many historians now recognize the importance of magic in the whole process, in that magical thinking enabled the thinkers of the Renaissance to break with the passivity of medieval Scholasticism in favor of a program that encouraged the active manipulation of nature. This in turn opened the door to the experimental method.[21]

The fourth model is perhaps a detour, although an important one to note. Nazism was, in a very profound sense, a Christian heresy (cf. the swastika as the "twisted cross") rooted in a return to pagan tradition and an occult worldview (if not actual occult practice). Thus

Otto Rahn was dispatched by the Nazi elite to Montségur to recover the Holy Grail, and various leaders of the Third Reich, including both Hitler and Himmler (head of the SS), were fascinated by magic in various forms, as well as by Teutonic, non-Judeo-Christian mythology. This form of heresy may have been the inner reality that lay at the heart of the Nazi worldview, and it is significant that both Jung and Heidegger were probing classical Gnostic themes and flirting with Nazi ideology (which was really a cosmology) at the same time.

The mechanism of all this, it seems to me, is fairly clear. Because of their direct contact with actual somatic experience, gnostic beliefs and practices serve to melt down accepted cultural and religious assumptions, and give rise to a "new" set of assumptions that manage to replace the dominant ones, with varying degrees of success. But successful or not, all of these heresies in turn manage to harden into orthodoxies. The Gnosticism of the early Church soon congealed into a set of rituals (baptism, communion, the Mass) designed to extract a commitment from potential converts who had not had the transforming experience themselves. By the time of Isaac Newton's death (1727), and certainly by the late eighteenth century, science had become a fairly rigid worldview, as many writers have pointed out. Romantic love is still with us, and for millions in the West it operates as an addiction that literally dominates their lives.[22] And in the German case, the ban on repressed emotions that Hitler was able to lift unleashed an energy that was then cleverly channeled into a regime of authoritarian control and terror. There is, then, a psychic alternation of dissolution and hardening that has gotten translated, at least up to this point in time, into the historical and political realm in four distinct patterns. Let us begin, then, with the first of these, and come to terms with the heresy of ancient Palestine, a heresy that had its roots in the mystery cults of Greek civilization.

# 5

# Jews and Christians

*The Vision of Christ that thou dost see*
*Is my Visions Greatest Enemy . . .*
*Thine is the Friend of All Mankind,*
*Mine speaks in parables to the Blind . . .*

—William Blake,
"The Everlasting Gospel"

EXACTLY WHEN EGO-CONSCIOUSNESS FIRST AROSE will probably never be known. What is clear is that it has been present to different degrees in different epochs, and in different civilizations. I have suggested that Paleolithic society may have had a "balanced" consciousness, a blend or kaleidoscope of discrimination (psychic distance) and participation (immersion in the Other). In the agricultural civilizations dominated by Great Mother worship, as Julian Jaynes has shown, discrimination tended to be relatively absent; participating consciousness tended to be the rule. As Great Mother civilization began to disintegrate, greater emphasis was placed on the existence of a separable Self, or I-consciousness, that could be moved around at will. All magical, occult, or gnostic practice requires such a Self, and usually a major goal of the practice is to bury it, to reimbed this Self into the Absolute, the larger reality. In this sense, all magical practice operates in the shadow of the Great Mother.

In the last millennium before Christ, mystery cults, which preserved the secret practices of Great Mother civilization, arose in Greece, and were organized around the opposition between mind and body, or

Self and Other, that by now—certainly by 600 B.C.—was a fact of conscious existence. Julian Jaynes writes:

> It is now the conscious subjective mind-space and its self that is opposed to the material body. Cults spring up about this new wonder-provoking division between *psyche* and *soma*. It both excites and seems to explain the new conscious experience, thus reinforcing its very existence. The conscious *psyche* is imprisoned in the body as in a tomb. It becomes an object of wide-eyed controversy. Where is it? And the locations in the body or outside it vary. What is it made of? Water (Thales), blood, air (Anaximenes), breath (Xenophanes), fire (Heraclitus), and so on, as the science of it all begins in a morass of pseudoquestions.
>
> So dualism, that central difficulty in this problem of consciousness, begins its huge haunted career through history, to be firmly set in the firmament of thought by Plato, moving through Gnosticism into the great religions, up through the arrogant assurances of Descartes to become one of the great spurious quandaries of modern psychology.[1]

So Western philosophy *is*, as Alfred North Whitehead once remarked, a series of footnotes to Plato, or at least to the gnostic insight that got coded into the *Dialogues,* and Jaynes has captured the essence of the development exactly. This gnostic or occult insight was, however, inverted by Plato, such that gnosis became, in his scheme of things, not a moment of ecstatic insight, but rather one of heightened rational and intellectual awareness.[2] Plato's great enemy was participating consciousness, and the *Dialogues* only make sense if read against the particular context of Classical Greece. The championing of ego-awareness has to be seen, as the Greek scholar Eric Dodds has argued, against a background of almost "institutionalized" ecstatic experience—a whole network of cults and shamanic practices bent on annihilating the Self that Plato was so desperate to preserve.[3] The mysteries of Eleusis, Orpheus, and Dionysus punctuate the Classical period; those of Mithra, Isis, Attis, and Cybele/Magna Mater, the Hellenistic one.[4] Most of these cults probably had prehistoric roots,[5] and were characterized (among other features) by initiations that precipitated a strong rebirth experience, or (as noted in the previous chapter) what the Greeks called *palingenesia* (or palingenesis).[6] It is no wonder that belief in metempsychosis (reincarnation) always accompanied this, and we should not be surprised to find the doctrine in Plato. The

famous Parable of the Cave (*Republic*, Book VII) is, on one level, a
story of palingenesis.

According to Dodds the soul, prior to Plato, was regarded as the
*spirit* of the body, not as its prisoner. With Plato, this began to change;
a type of puritanism characteristic of certain gnostic doctrines—what
Frances Yates calls "pessimistic gnosticism"—now entered the picture. This was the oppositional structure I talked about in Chapter 2,
which obviously had a long time to incubate. The soul and the body
were pitted against one another in mortal combat, and this sharply
negative dualism later on became, in the hands of the Catholic Church,
an important part of the Western psyche and cultural heritage.[7] It also
served to emphasize the need for salvation, for finding a bridge between heaven and earth, which I referred to in Chapter 4. If the human
being had a detachable soul or Self that could, via certain psychophysical exercises, be withdrawn from the body at will, it began to
seem likely that this occult entity would outlast the physical body after
death. Thus the line from Plato most frequently quoted by the Church
(especially in the Middle Ages) occurs in the dialogue *Theaetetus*: "we
should make all speed to take flight from this world to the other, and
that means becoming like the divine so far as we can . . . ."[8] The
destiny of the soul, in other words, is to ascend, to leave the body
and merge into the Godhead—a fundamental precept, and practice,
of all pessimistic gnostic systems.

Finally, Plato canonized not only the mind/body dichotomy, but
also the "sleepers/wakers" one, which was a necessary corollary to
the former. It was an elite group of "wakers"—men who had knowledge of the occult Self and its survival of bodily death—that could
teach the sleeping masses to see certain things, and thus take them
out of the "cave" of darkness that they inhabited. One could, in this
way, die to the mundane world, the world of "shadows" and material
phenomena, and be reborn into higher consciousness. ("I am the Way,
the truth, and the life.") This was the "examined life" for Plato, the
only one worth living.

Ideas such as these soaked through the cultures of the Mediterranean basin in the centuries before and after the birth of Christ. Places
such as Jerusalem and Alexandria were, culturally speaking, soupy
mélanges of Gnostic beliefs and practices, well into the period of the
Roman Empire. The texture was a rich one of merchants and traders,
rabbis and centurions, speakers of Aramaic, Latin, and Greek, of jug-
glers and prostitutes and effete aristocrats. It was in this context that
Hellenism and Judaism came face to face, creating a dialogue about

psyche and soma, epistemology and ethics, ecstatic experience and the exigencies of daily life.[9] In such a context, it would have been quite surprising if Christianity had *not* arisen, and it was the major argument of the so-called History of Religions school, in particular, the German philologist Richard Reitzenstein, that Christianity was only one of a number of magical or possibly Gnostic (it is still a matter of debate) sects; that it owed much to the "underground" religions of the Roman Empire.[10] The essential position of the History of Religions school was summarized by Marcel Simon as follows:

> Early Christianity, which . . . was but a Jewish messianic sect, was transmuted, once St. Paul established it on Graeco-Roman ground, into a salvation religion, the exact counterpart of the pagan Mystery religions. The Christian "mystery," as Paul presents it, is focused on the saving efficacy of Christ's death and resurrection. Mystical assimilation, achieved through Baptism and the Eucharist, makes the faithful a participant in Christ's destiny and opens to him the gates of eternal life. The Christian's relation to his savior is closely akin to that which unites the pagan initiate to the gods of the oriental mysteries, who like Christ, and with the only exception of Mithra, suffer, die and rise again and who, by uniting the initiate to this experience of death and life, become to him savior gods.[11]

Recent scholarship has tended to back away from the idea of any direct connection between Christianity and the mystery religions of antiquity.[12] The central claim of the History of Religions school was that of a connection between early Christianity and the pre-Christian notion of a Gnostic redeemer who came to earth to show humans the way back to heaven. But Gnosticism proper—whatever that might be—was apparently post-Christian; and the idea of a redeemer does not appear in pre-Christian material. This may, however, be irrelevent, a case of historical or doctrinal nitpicking, for there may be no escaping the existence of a redeemer syndrome in general terms, i.e., in the terms of what Claude Lévi-Strauss would call "mythic structures." The Greco-Roman world did share a common underground mythic structure, if not a specific myth, viz., that of an intermediate figure bridging the two worlds of heaven and earth, and mediating between them, by means of ascent.[13] (The structural similarity between all of this and the gap/T.O. phenomenon discussed in Chapter 1 is, I think, rather obvious, and I shall return to it at the conclusion of this chapter.)

The classic work on the heavenly journey was published by Wilhelm Bousset at the turn of the century, and it still remains a definitive essay.[14] Bousset pointed out that the ecstatic trance journey was, for its practitioners, only an anticipation of the journey of the soul after death. It is this, says the historian Alan Segal, that constitutes the almost universal structure of the ascent myth. The "structural similarity between the ecstatic journey and the final journey of humans after death," writes Segal, "is so widespread as to be crucially important."[15] Anthropologically speaking, the ascent resolves the tension between heaven and earth, or finitude and immortality, by giving the adept a kind of "sneak preview" of life everlasting, paradise to come. Segal is able to show how pervasive this initiatory pattern was in the ancient world, including the Jewish community. Apocryphal and apocalyptic texts, such as Enoch or the Ascension of Isaiah, are based on an underlying ascent structure. "[M]artyrdom, ascension and resurrection," says Segal, "are the themes that serve as the cradle of christology."[16]

The subject of the ascent and visionary experience is discussed at some length in the work of this century's greatest authority on Jewish mysticism, the late Gershom Scholem.[17] Scholem notes that the roots of the cabala—Jewish number mysticism—go back to ancient Palestine, and points out that it is still unclear to what extent the growth of Gnostic tendencies within Judaism preceded their development in early Christianity. The Jewish tradition itself concerned the mysteries of God's throne; and this, says Scholem, set the pattern for Jewish mysticism in its early forms. The goal of ecstatic trance was the perception of the throne on its chariot, as described in the first chapter of Ezekiel; and this came to be known as *merkabah,* or chariot, mysticism.[18] In the early centuries of the Christian era, *merkabah* literature became very explicit regarding the ascetic preparation necessary to ascend to the upper world (which consisted of seven firmaments) and see God, sitting on His throne. The aspirant placed his head between his knees (which would facilitate self-hypnosis) and recited hymns of a repetitive, ecstatic character—hymns that, as it turns out, bear a linguistic affinity to the liturgy of the Qumran sect (see below). The literature also describes the experiences that various aspirants reported going through during their ascent—typically, sensations of being on fire.[19]

It is in these later years that more specifically Gnostic themes were elaborated. An identity of substance between the savior and the soul of the believer was postulated, for example. In the text known as the

Ascension of Isaiah, part of which is pre-Christian and part post-Christian (i.e., post-Christ), the "Beloved of the Father" descends through the seven heavens and assumes the form of the residents of the earth, so as not to be recognized. He then reascends to heaven, after witnessing the events of Jesus' life. In general, the divine in man gets identified with the divine in God; theodicy begins to turn into individual psychology and the adept is seen as immortalized by means of the ecstatic ascent. The historian Morton Smith, in fact, has argued that heavenly ascent, or soul travel, was the secret doctrine of Christianity from the very beginning.[20]

It would be impossible at this point to provide anything more than the barest bibliography of studies of the mystery cults and occult or Gnostic techniques of late antiquity; they have been examined in exhausting detail.[21] But since Christianity did emerge as a Jewish heresy, it will be necessary to obtain some idea of the nature of Jewish magic and how it developed under the impact of Greek philosophy and religion.[22]

Our story begins in 586 B.C., the year of the destruction of the Temple in Palestine by the Babylonian king Nebuchadnezzar. This inaugurated the Diaspora—"scattering of the seed," in Greek—which refers to a location (that which is outside of Palestine) as well as an event. In the ensuing centuries, some Jews did return to Palestine, but most remained outside it. The Temple was eventually rebuilt, and eventually destroyed again, by the Roman Emperor (as of A.D. 79) Titus, in A.D. 70. (Coins struck during this time bear Jewish motifs, such as candelabra, along with the legend, *Judea capta*.)

The intervening centuries represented a period of increasing hellenization. Palestine was under Greek rule, or at least Greek influence, from the time of Alexander the Great (d. 323 B.C.), who was responsible, via his military conquests, for the intense hellenization of the Mediterranean basin. Alexander himself was friendly to the Jews, but in terms of cultural integrity, the Jews were very wary of the hellenization process. Nevertheless, the brilliance, as well as the omnipresence, of Greek culture and philosophy proved to be overwhelming. The book of Ecclesiastes, for example, written in the third century B.C., demonstrates the heavy influence of Greek Stoicism. By the beginning of the second century, a Greek-oriented upper class had emerged among Palestinian Jews, a class that was very interested in assimilation. Fluency in Greek (as opposed to just Aramaic) was the key to moving up the social scale, although this always carried a hint of betrayal to it. Thus the Hasidim—a sect dating from about 300 B.C.—

reacted with increasing conservatism, campaigning for a pious, devoted, and legalistic observance of Jewish life as outlined in the Torah. This ritualistic or legalistic observance was known as *halacha*, and it was popularly based. The Hasidim, as it turns out, were the sect from which the Pharisees would later emerge.

In 175 B.C., Greek succession brought the Seleucid governor Antiochus IV (Seleucia was a Greek colony in Syria) to power. With the help of Jewish factionalism—the existence of an upper crust that wanted Jerusalem turned into a Greek polis—Antiochus effectively began a war against Judaism as a religion, outlawing all religious observances. The next twelve years were among the bloodiest in Jewish history. The Hasidim threw in their lot with a leader named Mattathias and his sons, notably Judah Maccabee—the Hasmonean family. These years were characterized by a full-scale guerrilla war, heavy torture of Jewish rebels, and finally, the defeat of Antiochus and the establishment of a Jewish state in 164/163 B.C. Chanukah, the "Festival of Lights," is the celebration of the Hasmonean victory.

Once in power, however, the Hasmoneans discovered that the honeymoon was over. Politically speaking, they saw that they had to operate in a Greek context. Although Greek influence was much less than it had been previously, it was impossible to escape it. All political and economic negotiations across the border, for example, had to be carried out in Greek; Aramaic was hardly an international language. By about 150 B.C. the Hasidim splintered, as two groups in particular were disgusted with the lack of a strong anti-Greek policy in Jerusalem. One believed in separatism. These were the Essenes, an ascetic sect located at Qumran, on the Dead Sea, whose records are those of the Dead Sea Scrolls, and who were led by the so-called Teacher of Righteousness.[23] The other, also anti-Greek, was the Pharisees, ancestors of the rabbis of the second century A.D., who believed one had to work "with the establishment," i.e., within the given political situation. And during this time, a version of Judaism emerged that was, at least ostensibly, not concerned with *halacha* but with prophecy, especially in its millennarian and apocalyptic form. Very clearly, religion and politics were—the Essenes notwithstanding—becoming inseparable.

(As a postscript, we should note that the period from 175 B.C. to A.D. 135 was one of chronic rebellion and suppression. Even after the destruction of the second Temple, Jewish revolts continued, down to the Bar Kochba rebellion of A.D. 135, which was brutally put down by Rome. After this, the Diaspora began in earnest.)

What does all this have to do with the origins of Christianity? As many scholars have recognized, the tension of hellenization vs. *halacha* set the stage for the emergence of Christianity; it is the proto-Gnostic aspect of Hellenism and Judaism together that made Christianity possible. Thus Christianity has long been regarded as a syncretistic phenomenon within the context of Greco-Roman paganism, but it is necessary to remember that it emerged as a heresy within a particular religious context, viz., that of what might be called "normative" Judaism. Yet what *was* "normative" Judaism? The heavy hellenization of Judaism in the two centuries preceding Christ make it very difficult to sort out the predominant cultural-religious context, if indeed there was one. Thus nearly a century before the discovery of the Dead Sea Scrolls or the Nag Hammadi manuscripts, the French historian Ernest Renan argued that Christianity was basically Essenism taken out into the larger world. He asserted that John the Baptist (often thought to have been an Essene) was involved in yogic practice. Renan speculated on possible Buddhist influence, and saw the Essenes and their Teacher of Righteousness as being modeled on an Eastern format of guru and cult following.[24] Similarly, Charles Guignebert, also antedating the discovery of esoteric and Gnostic documents, argued that Judaism had become penetrated by Oriental cults, producing a Jewish syncretism and Gnosticism that finally "sprang" Christianity. Early on, Guignebert posed the question of what to take as the Jewish mainstream. This mainstream, he said, feared mysticism; yet "the traditional faith proved receptive to actively polytheistic ideas."[25] Following L. Blau's work of 1898, *Das altjüdische Zauberwesen*, which remains the standard treatment of ancient Jewish magic, Guignebert argued that the Jews were reknowned throughout the Greco-Roman world for their skill in the magic arts which, he said, they probably learned from the Chaldeans. Essenism was a variant on this theme, one of many. Thus numerous sects arose at this time, Christianity among them. But it was the one, for whatever reason, that "made it." Hence, Renan's central point: "Christianity is an Essenism which has largely succeeded."[26]

Essenism seems to have been part of a widespread anti-Pharisaic heresy, then—the "larval" stage of Christianity.[27] Yet for all of this, we have yet to understand (a) the inner core of the heresy, and its relationship—somatic or otherwise—to early Christianity; and (b) the political mechanism of how the heresy got "sprung" from its matrix. Both of these questions require a clear definition of "normative" Judaism, and it is just this that seems to elude us. If it is simply Pharisaism—ritualistic and legalistic Judaism—then Jesus is largely a miracle; which is certainly what the Church, even today, would have us believe, but which makes no sense historically (miracles don't just happen, they have contexts). If it is a heavily gnosticized Judaism, Jesus is thoroughly explicable—one Jewish magician among many—but then there seems to be no reason for Christianity's sectarian success, short of good public relations. The answer seems to lie somewhere in between, but nobody, as far as I can see, has been able to pin it down in a definitive way.

One of the most important efforts in this direction came from a Protestant scholar who taught at Yale, Erwin Goodenough, whose thirteen-volume *Jewish Symbols in the Greco-Roman Period* (1953–68) constitutes a major contribution to the whole debate. In part, Goodenough was reacting against the view of his teacher, G. F. Moore, who saw normative Judaism as Pharisaic/rabbinic. To Moore, *halacha* was what the Jewish nation *always* stood for: law, reason, and ethics. Piety, as embodied in works such as the Mishna and the Talmud, circumscribed the right sort of life for a human being, which was guided by ritual and observance.[28] This way of life Goodenough characterized as the "horizontal path." Its primary characteristic is that it is continuous rather than apocalyptic; so continuous that it can even include the prophetic tradition. The horizontal path deals with linear time and slow, incremental progress. Redemption occurs at the *end* of time, when the Messiah will finally appear. In the meantime, life is about ethics, charity, ritual observance, and social organization. As Goodenough pointed out, all religions offer the experience of the horizontal path; and indeed, it is impossible to imagine any sort of society without it.

The problem, Goodenough went on to argue, is that all religions also offer another, very different sort of experience—what he termed the "vertical path"—and in the case of Judaism, he said, the predominance of this has been overlooked. The vertical path is discontinuous, visionary, or ecstatic. It involves, to refer back to our earlier discussion, a process of psychic ascent. Through certain disciplines, the individual soul can ascend to heaven, find God, encounter death, learn the course of history, etc., and return to tell (and presumably liberate) the world. It was this aspect of Judaism, said Goodenough, that most interested early Christians, and the truth is, he added, that *it was the vertical path that was normative*. In effect, Goodenough inverted G. F. Moore's thesis almost completely. The norm is *not* rational, he claimed, and those who finally codified it—Plato in the Greek case, Philo Judaeus (an

Alexandrian philosopher, first century A.D.) in the Jewish—were merely the tip of the iceberg, building on a vast underground tradition of soul travel, astral projection, and other standard occult techniques. In order for Christianity to become so completely hellenized and gnosticized so shortly after Christ's death, he argued, Judaism must have been fairly well along in *its* hellenization by the time Christ came along. Because of a later rabbinical whitewash, a suppression of Apocryphal texts occurred in Judaism, in the same way that the Gnostic gospels uncovered at Nag Hammadi got suppressed by the Church fathers. We have inherited a version of Judaism, claimed Goodenough, that is as "safe" as it is inaccurate. In the context of early Christianity, he said, the mystical Judaism of someone like Philo Judaeus was the norm, and the Pharisaic horizontal path the exception. Goodenough thus contrasted a small number of "uptight," literate rabbis with an oral magical tradition, so large that it could scarcely be called "underground." It had become underground only because the rabbinate had managed, via control of the written word, to literally paper it over with the *halachic* tradition. But it was *not* the norm, Goodenough claimed, and Jesus can thus indeed be seen as one more Jewish holy man.[29]

It seems an incredible thesis, but we have to remember that our own image of Judaism *has* been formed by a certain victorious orthodox tradition, and that books such as Jubilees, Maccabees, and Enoch were excluded from the Bible. (Daniel, which deals with dream interpretation, is the only book in this genre that got included, although Ezekiel is also in an alternative tradition.) We may have a clear impression of Judaism as being essentially Talmudic/rabbinical, but this proves nothing about Judaism at the time of Christ. Furthermore, there is no doubt as to *how* the whitewash took place. The Jewish scholar William Green, for example, in his study of Honi the Rainmaker, a first-century-B.C. magician, shows how textual descriptions of the latter succeeded in turning him into a kind of rabbi, dispensing pious wisdom instead of actually going into trance.[30] Goodenough's argument, that it is literally impossible that the mass of the Jewish population in late antiquity was rabbinic in its orientation, seems to carry some weight.

But: were all these Jews engaged in magic? Was Philo really the tip of the iceberg of some Jewish cargo cult, as it were? The problem is that Goodenough was unable to demonstrate that Philo was at all typical; and outside of Philo's own references, there exists no evidence for widespread mystic Jewish cultism. To make things worse, Gershom Scholem was able to show that the mystical tradition was not alien to rabbinic Judaism. Apparently, a number of leading rabbis experimented with soul travel, trance, and what was in effect the theory of the five bodies discussed in Chapter 4.[31] For example, one of the most famous ascent stories is recorded in the Talmud, the so-called *pardes* (garden, or paradise) story of four rabbis who undertook the practice and saw God as a result. Ben Zoma, the Talmud tells us, went crazy; Simeon ben Azzai died; Elisha ben Avuyah (or Abuyah) left Judaism and apparently became a Gnostic;[32] and Rabbi Akiva (or Akiba) "ascended in peace and descended in peace." Akiva, in short, became representative of mysticism contained within the boundaries of rabbinic Judaism; and in fact, Scholem points out that the tale is *halachic* in nature: the authors of this story are hardly heterodox.[33] In any event, if *merkabah* mysticism was fully integrable into the rabbinic tradition, it becomes difficult to maintain the dichotomy of a small group of uptight, *halachic* rabbis as opposed to a vast, "liberated," magical Jewish populace. We come back to a problem that plagues all of hidden or invisible history, viz., what, in normative terms, was the visual/ kinesthetic balance? In each culture, or era, there will be a typical ecology of personality that integrates the Self/Other, mind/body, or "pope/heretic" relationship in a particular way. This is the somatic secret of any society and any era, and if one wants, for example, to know the origins of Christianity, it is to this ecology that one must refer. But how can we know it? The truth is that Goodenough's horizontal and vertical paths exist, but only as Ideal Types. If one path is about ecstasy and the other about law, then in Christ we apparently have a figure whose message was that ecstasy was to be the new law. But where did he come from, and how did he manage to collapse these categories? Goodenough's rigid distinctions don't permit much of a working answer.

Certain qualifications have to be made, therefore, and these suggest not two totally unrelated paths, but a kaleidoscope of possibilities. Expressions of Judaism between 200 B.C. and A.D. 100 were in fact very diverse. As one scholar, Michael Stone, has written, "the creativity of Judaism in the period before and after Christ may well be its outstanding feature."[34] Or to quote Morton Smith, Goodenough wanted "a sharp division between rabbinic and anti-rabbinic Judaism, whereas actually there seems to have been a confused gradation."[35] As Ideal Types, the two paths are mutually exclusive. In actual practice, legalism and mysticism often managed to occupy the same sect and even, at times, the same psyche. Such was, apparently, the case among the Essenes. In general, the tension between the two paths lies at the center of Jewish philosophy and Jewish cultural expression, and despite the ultimate victory of the rabbinical tradition, the creative spark of Judaism is traceable to an unwillingness to resolve the tension at all—which Gershom Scholem saw the Christian millennarian movement trying to do.[36] In the context of that time, however, as the Jewish scholar Jacob Neusner has written, the mystic groups and the rabbinic ones were in effect "modulations" of Jewish Hellenism.[37] Can we, then, advance on Goodenough's typology, and get a clearer notion of what these intermediate modulations looked like, and how they interacted?

One of the most sensitive attempts to sort these issues out is provided by the German historian Martin Hengel in his very dense and closely argued book, *Judaism and Hellenism*.[38] In some ways, it is a rerun of the Goodenough argument, but made much more specific and much less rigidly dichotomous. The Jews, he says, had long been in possession of a prophetic tradition, which told them that they would be redeemed through history. To this, from the time of Greek rule (ca. 360 B.C.), was added an apocalyptic tradition. The prophetic tradition was based on a "Torah ontology," in which the Old Testament was seen as a kind of world map, or divine plan, and in which the march of time and events was taken to be linear and continuous. The apocalyptic tradition, on the other hand—a variant of Goodenough's vertical path—saw history as divided into a series of discontinuous stages (usually four), with all but the last stage having taken place. It was an Orphic idea, and possibly an Oriental gnostic one as well; and from 360 B.C. onward it became increasingly popular. The apocalyptic view of history included the notion of popular revolt and rebellion, led by a deliverer, and it was strongly present in the culture from the time of the Hasmonean revolt to the last days of the Bar Kochba rebellion; not, as we have seen, as a specific myth, but as a generalized mythic structure (that of heavenly ascent). This view of history, via direct experience with the five bodies, included the notion of being able to undertake soul travel, learn the Mystery of the Kingdom, and return to earth. In the Book of Enoch, for example—fragments of which are found in the Dead Sea Scrolls—we find the first mention in Judaism of a journey of the soul after death, and its subsequent incarnation, an idea that was as Greek as it was Jewish.[39] Side by side, Gnostic notions and apocalyptic ones added up to an obvious image: the deliverer would necessarily be a magus who would be able to sweep gradualism and Torah ontology aside. He would be able to travel between heaven and earth—even after physical death—and through his magic power (a combination of all of the five bodies, really) liberate the Jews from the yoke of foreign domination. Imperialism has at its root the interpretation of Self by Other, the imposition of a visual interpretation on an original kinesthetic one. A colonized people intuitively knows this, and this is why magic is frequently resorted to as a weapon: it is a tool for doing away with the visual interpretation and reinstating the kinesthetic one. Especially in the context of late antiquity, liberation very naturally implied spiritual politics. If one wants to speak of a body politic here, one has to deal with all five bodies. This is the hidden (somatic) dimension, it seems to me, of the beginnings of Christianity.

One of Hengel's major points, however, is the compatibility of the horizontal and vertical paths. This can be seen, for example, in the Sermon on the Mount, in which Christ says that he came to complete or fulfill the law, not to destroy it (Matthew 5:17). In the works of Philo, as well as in the beliefs of the Essenes, we find the notion of the Torah as the divine plan (world map) *and* the notion of four discontinuous stages of history as part of God's secret plan for the salvation of Israel. The Pharisees themselves took over the notion—and, it seems obvious, the practice—of soul travel and debated it up to the time of Christ. Jewish magic was, as one commentator has pointed out, "scarcely distinguishable from its pagan counterpart."[40] The Essenes, for example, argued that history was in its final crisis, and that salvation would come through both Gnostic practices (though they would not, obviously, have used that phrase) and the pursuit of *halacha*. Hence, devotion to the law was part of the apocalyptic vision; and this is why Christ's statement about fulfilling the law, as well as being "the Way," was not strange to certain contemporary ears.

In any event, the involvement of Jews, rabbis included, in magical/ somatic practice was rife at this time, and has been documented by a number of scholars in addition to Scholem. According to Jack Lightstone, for example, the Jews spawned a great number of shamanistic "holy men," and some of them practiced techniques that aspired to achieving a total union with Jahweh. Extant magical papyri reveal Judaic rites aimed at self-divination, i.e., getting God's spirit to enter one's body (in the terms of the previous chapter, collapsing body number five into body number one)—an idea that occurs in the writings of Paul as well. In the Diaspora especially, Jewish magicians were no fringe element, but often set up shop in the synagogue itself. The Pharisees were active as exorcists; as late as the fourth century A.D. Christians went to synagogues to obtain the services of Jewish holy men for these purposes.[41] Five-body practice (in effect) was a popular pursuit, for it was commonly believed that spirits of the dead could travel to the upper worlds, and that a downward flow of sacred power was also possible. Communal incantation, as well as the cultic meal as a medium of communion with the dead—possibly the origin of the Eucharist—were commonly taken up. In general, the "cult of Jahweh" in the Hellenistic period was focused on the career of the dead and the traffic of the soul between heaven and earth.[42] The esoteric/rabbinic *merkabah* tradition, in fact, can be translated very easily into five-body theory: the soul (body number three) leaves the body (body number one) by means of practices that "freeze" the mind (body number two) and ascends to heaven (body number five), after which it descends and reenters the body (number one).

All of this ties into apocalypse very neatly: the ascent of the soul to heaven is, in a sense, the end of the historical process, the rupture with the past, and (psychologically) the beginning of a "new age," a rebirth. Thus Hengel notes that apocalyptic literature had a living source: it was derived from actual visions and ecstatic experiences, and these got interpreted in terms of time, history, the future of the Jews, etc. None of this is surprising: because of our biology, ecstatic experience is ecstatic experience; what system of symbols it gets translated into is a matter of context. In this particular context, it did have the aspect of a cargo cult attached to it, i.e., deliverance from oppression. So interest in chanting and fasting was intense up to the time of Christ and after; vision and ecstasy were the touchstones of the true wise man, the proof of his divine gifts. Apocalyptic literature such as Daniel, Enoch, and Jubilees was in this tradition, and the Essenes were the climax of it. They in particular created a "systematic" apocalypse, one that combined law, wisdom, salvation, and community.

Where, then, is the heresy in Christ? Surely he was just one more Palestinian holy man, no? The answer is yes, but not entirely. No matter how sectarian, diverse, and magical Judaism managed to get, it had one unifying point, viz., the Torah. No movement could remain *in* Judaism if it criticized the Torah fundamentally; to do so meant heresy and exclusion. Hence, a kind of bifocal image existed, and it is this, I believe, that lies at the heart of Goodenough's two paths and his confusion about them. Despite the immense syncretism that permeated all sectors of the Jewish community, the Jews knew, then as now, that survival in a non-Jewish context depended upon presenting a closed, united, and therefore legalistic front to the outside world. It was absolutely necessary to do this. The problem was that it generated heretics where it might have absorbed them, for the political need for a united front based on the Torah sharply circumscribed theological debate. Christ's real message was not necessarily heretical—at least not initially. It was merely that the Torah had lost its original psychic power and needed a bit of revitalizing. For all their magical practice, the Pharisees still tended to see the Torah as the exclusive medium of revelation. This was a frozen position, and it was inevitable that it would precipitate a number of breakaway movements based on cultivating a direct (somatic) experience of God. Primitive Christianity, says Hengel, finally burst the framework of prophetic (i.e., gradualist) Torah ontology.[43] Christ may not have really been outside of the law, although he certainly, because of a large popular following, had the elements of a potential troublemaker, at least as far as Rome and the Jewish establishment were concerned. Paul, of course, quickly passed the point of worrying about whether *halacha* was violated or not.

What can we conclude from all this? In a curious way, both Erwin Goodenough and his teacher, G. F. Moore, were correct: normative Judaism, in an oppressive political context, was both vertical *and* horizontal. It was magical on the inside, legalistic on the outside. Within the spectrum of these two poles, all kinds of strange combinations and relationships ("modulations") were possible. The strong conversion reaction, for example, such as happened to Saul on the road to Damascus, is a classic flip from one pole to the opposite. *Halachic* Saul hated his Gnostic "shadow" until it rose up and overpowered him—actually blinded him for three days. But most Jews were not so black and white in their behavior. As Scholem has argued, the two poles existed in a dialectical relationship. Mysticism was not a separate current in Jewish history, but often flourished at the heart of legal, rabbinic Judaism. In fact, it was because of this that the *halachic* tradition retained any vitality at all. What happened with Christ, apparently, was that during this time, for reasons internal (Scholem) or external (Hengel) to Judaism itself, dabbling with the vertical path got so widespread that the overall ecology of Judaism tipped over into something else. The result was an official reaction against the new tendency, but by then it was too late. Through morphogenetic ripples produced by somatic experience, and in a political context hungry for a deliverer, a kind of spiritual "takeoff" occurred—as has been said of the Industrial Revolution of eighteen hundred years later—into self-sustained growth. There is an uneasy tension between the prophetic tradition and the apocalyptic one. The latter can certainly serve to revitalize the former; but if enough people actually go through altered states based on experimentation with the five bodies, a morphogenetic field can develop and become irreversible. This undoubtedly required a certain political context to sustain itself, and this is what the Roman persecution of the Jews provided. Somatic experience along ecstatic lines convinced enough people, rabbis included, that Torah ontology and prophetic gradualism were shadow rather than substance. The door to heaven could be forced, as it were, and the fourth stage of history finally entered upon, by means of a psychopolitical rupture with the past. FREEDOM NOW!, it turns out, is a very old slogan.

How did Christianity come to make a bid for becoming a world religion? How did it finally succeed in doing so? It turns out that all previous experimentation with the occult or separable Self or with the five bodies was done in the context of cultures that were bioregional, highly local in perception and worldview. The Egyptians, for example, regarded Egypt as the mirror of heaven, and believed that if a person died outside of its geographical boundaries, his or her soul would wander for eternity, with no hope of ever being incarnated. But the cultic development of the five bodies, especially of the third body, which could travel, spelled the birth of what would eventually become cosmopolitanism. The Gnostic notion of a great, transpersonal Self into which all individual consciousness eventually merged rendered local variations meaningless. Despite the fierce nationalism of the Pharisees, says Hengel, Judaism developed tendencies toward becoming a world religion, especially in the context of a populace living in a state of imminent eschatological expectation. This cosmopolitan apocalyptic shattered the narrow obsession with the Torah; and with the rise of primitive Christianity, Christology replaced Torah ontology—just as narrow, when you really get down to it, except that the cosmopolitan element was now a major feature. Christ was now the revelation of God in history, on a global scale. Thus Hengel concludes that "primitive Christianity is to be seen as an eschatological and revolutionary movement in which the 'salvation-historical' task of the people of God" was fulfilled by a universalism. This was immensely ecumenical, especially in the hands of someone like Paul, who began to baptize non-Jews and sacrifice matters of content in order to get everyone under the umbrella of the new religion. When, early in the fourth century, the Roman emperor Constantine himself converted to Christianity, it was the political culmination of an earlier somatic tendency. In terms of organization, administration, and Church hierarchy, Christianity began to look, even by the second century, more like the Roman Empire than anything else. Its experimental phase lasted a few decades, at best.[44]

To review our somatic-political schema, then, the first factor in this whole process was the severe oppression of the Jews from 175 B.C. to A.D. 135; a history, as Hengel says, of blood and tears. This in turn had the background of foreign occupation that sharpened the Self/Other split, and generated an apocalyptic deliverer syndrome, polarizing the Jews around the question of the law. Each Jew felt this internally, and the problem was deepened by the availability of direct experience of God via five-body practice. The second factor, then, was the heresy itself, apostasy from the law in favor of Gnostic experience that emphasized the here and now. This, coupled with a doctrine that closed down the Self/Other split, propelled it into a phase of "takeoff" into self-sustained spiritual activity. Phenomena such as glossolalia (speaking in tongues) kept occurring in various Christian communities; the energy was there to attract followers, an attraction that was deepened by the persecution by Rome, which sharpened the Self/Other split and thereby deepened the spiritual experience. Finally, the Church, especially under the leadership of Paul, was organizationally very clever. *Pari passu*, as the spiritual flame waned, the organizational side of things was stepped up, so that the Church was able to gain followers on a purely social and ritualistic basis. Eventually it concluded pacts with Constantine and later Clovis. By then, it stabilized even more rigidly than Judaism had long ago: it became a purely horizontal path. The later models of heresy we shall discuss were, at least in part, attempts to rupture the framework once again. In this sense Catharism, Hermeticism, and Fascism (see Chapters 6–8) can all be seen as violent dialogues with Christianity.

Could the early Christian model be repeated in our own time? The somatic, or energetic part of the equation seems to be a very familiar one. It is five-body practice, and the Self/Other dynamic, that makes visionary or ascent experience possible, and all this is certainly going on today, especially among those sects and cults that have rejected (or claim to have rejected) the dominant culture. Occasionally, very large followings can be generated, and to take just one recent example, it was at the height of his influence (just before the total collapse of the movement) that Bhagwan Rajneesh declared that his aim was to convert the entire world.[45] I am not suggesting that the Rajneeshee and the earliest Christians were somehow identical; for it seems to me that Christ did have a specific ethical message about how to treat other human beings (the horizontal path) that is lacking in virtually all the

New Age cults that have appeared on the scene today (despite their claims to the contrary). But the somatic/magical pattern (the vertical path) is surely identical, rooted as it is in a body that has not changed very much in two thousand years. The somatic part of the equation thus remains constant, and I shall need to say a few words about this, and about the whole phenomenon of psychic interiority, before we can explore our next model of heresy. But what creates these different models of heresy is the political context of the energy, the way it gets channeled. Despite Rajneesh's fond hopes of replacing Christianity, it is clear to me that he never had much of a chance, because the Greek model, that of a heresy turning into a world religion, is unique— probably a one-shot deal. It requires a very particular arrangement of social and political factors, including colonial oppression and sustained and intense persecution, that is just not present within the borders of the Western industrial nations; at least not normally. Cargo cults only become dominant under such conditions, and those conditions would seem to be absent in Europe and North America. Yet who knows? If the West is to survive at all, it will in all likelihood have to pass through a severe crisis, a civilizational breakdown, including plague (already beginning), famine, and massive economic depression, in its transition to a new culture. Anything could happen during such a situation, including the emergence of Roman-style governments, if the period of breakdown is of sufficient intensity and duration. So if the Greek model is not likely, it is nevertheless not to be dismissed out of hand.

Before we can move on to the French model, the eruption of heresy in the eleventh century, three topics have to be briefly addressed: the psychological and anthropological interpretation of all this; the relation of such an interpretation to earliest Christianity, as reported in the Gnostic gospels; and the solidification of the Church into pure form, certainly by the time of Augustine (d. A.D. 430), such that the phenomenon of interiority that is so strongly present in the case of Gnostic or five-body practice finally got shut down. All of these things overlap to some extent, and so exposition of them can be a bit difficult. But some clarification must be attempted here, so that the dramatic nature of Catharism, and medieval heresy in general, as the sudden re-emergence of interiority into a world that could only regard it as a species of insanity, can really be appreciated.

The matter of the interpretive framework has, in fact, already been dealt with in Chapter 2, in which I discussed the Tame/Wild distinction and the historical origins of dichotomous consciousness. I say *historical* origins because Lévi-Strauss was certainly wrong in seeing this mode of consciousness as inherent in the human psyche, but he correctly pointed out that humans have conceived of intermediate categories or substances—e.g., honey and tobacco—that seemingly bridge the gap between the Wild and the Tame, or what he referred to as the raw and the cooked.[46] But all of this arose only with the domestication of animals, and this is why ritual and religion are so central to the great agricultural civilizations. Religion comes into being when the basic fault that arises in the human psyche gets projected onto the external world, so as to create a corresponding gap, or fault line, between heaven and earth, sacred and profane. This projected gap is the source of all rebirth eschatology, the search for salvation or immortality. Becoming a priest, or a pope, means that you achieve the socially sanctioned role of a T.O.—you are given the right to act as an intermediary between these two worlds. But this requires a further opposition between two intermediaries—the heretic is the "failed pope," the potential usurper of transitional space. Like a snake, he is transformative, and within "rational" cultures the intermediate figure can be venerated as sacred or become the focus of that society's fear and rage, e.g., in the form of crucifixion. The Greek ascent structure is, as Alan Segal points out, the basic binary pattern described by Lévi-Strauss, except, as far as I am concerned, there is nothing inherent about it. Western mystical experience is not universal, and it is not the only way of coding reality, as we shall see in Part III. But it is the source of our own particular binary pattern, and in that sense Western mysticism and rationalism actually have a lot in common.[47]

If ascent experience, or Self/Other merger, is rooted in biological tendencies that are combined with cultural conditioning, it is nevertheless the case that its archetypal possibilities can be quite powerful, and quite beautiful. This emerges very clearly in the famous Gnostic gospels discovered at Nag Hammadi, a discovery that has thrown into doubt any claims regarding the original existence of a "real" or orthodox Christianity. The manuscripts, in fact, reveal a Christianity as diverse and complex as the Judaism of late antiquity. If there was a rabbinical whitewash of Jewish mystical tendencies after A.D. 70, there was certainly a corresponding one on the part of the Church fathers, such as Hippolytus and Irenaeus, to bury all traces of early Christian Gnosticism. This also had its climax in the fourth century, when the Council of Nicaea effectively declared that the career of body number three (the soul) would be decided by Church doctrine rather than private (occult) experimentation. From that point on, fooling around with altered states could get you into serious trouble. The Church was by then interested in political and numerical progress; the Gnostics and soul travelers who had once made it possible were, even by the late first century, something of an embarrassment—a pattern that gets repeated in every heretical cycle.

Consider, in any event, the following statement of Christ in the Gospel of Thomas:

> *When you make the two one, and*
> *when you make the inside like the outside*
> *and the outside like the inside, and the above*
> *like the below, and when*
> *you make the male and the female one and the same,*
> *so that the male not be male nor*
> *the female female; when you fashion*
> *eyes in place of an eye, and a hand*
> *in place of a hand, and a foot in place*
> *of a foot, and likeness in place of likeness;*
> *then will you enter [the Kingdom].*[48]

What else could he be talking about here but the mirror stage, the split into Self and Other which we struggle to resolve and which haunts us our entire lives? The inside like the outside, a likeness (image) in place of a likeness . . . here is the insistence that one will not be interpreted from the outside, that one will not allow one's experience to be mystified. That Christ never read Lacan or Wallon should not deter us. Intuitively, he is appealing to a psychodynamic that is inaccessible to academic historical analysis, a psychodynamic that goes back to our earliest visceral experience, the evolution of body image and body awareness. The emergence of a political figure who promises, in one way or another, to validate the kinesthetic dimension is going to be, in certain contexts, a momentous event.

What else is in the Gnostic gospels?[49] In the Gospel of Philip, Jesus is portrayed as a sexual being, and in fact the God of these gospels is both masculine and feminine. In the Testimony of Truth, we get the Garden of Eden story from the viewpoint of the serpent—that marginal, taboo, intermediate animal that sheds its skin periodically and that appears in our dreams (and in this gospel) as a symbol of divine wisdom. In the Gospel of Thomas, Jesus often sounds like a Jungian analyst, and effectively tells his audience that to know oneself at the deepest level is to know God. God is not *ganz anderes* (to use the phrase of Rudolf Otto), wholly Other, but inside of you—right now!

This Jesus speaks not of sin and repentance, but of illusion and en-lightenment (know that you are not the specular image). Walter Bauer, in *Orthodoxy and Heresy in Earliest Christianity* (1934), argued that these early heresies were not really heresies at all, but simply various forms of the new religion—other (valid) manifestations of early Christian life as it began to separate out from its Jewish context. In effect, "her-esy" *preceded* orthodoxy. What we now call Christianity is merely a few sources selected as orthodox (literally "straight opinion" in Greek) from dozens of others. But the choice was not arbitrary. By violating the kinesthetic in favor of the visual, Christianity was able to accom-modate literally everybody who wanted in. What remained of its living content is well known.

This brings us, finally, to the issue of interiority, for the experience of Self is surely a prerequisite to the direct experiencing of "God." It is clear, for example, that the issue of interiority was central to the debate within Judaism at the time of Christ. The word "Pharisee" is used today to refer to someone who thinks the life of the spirit is merely a question of ritualistic observance; and Christ's famous re-mark, that the kingdom of heaven is within, reflects his commitment to what we have called the vertical path. The problem is that the period of visionary experience cannot last forever, and it is at that point that a cult has to decide whether it will go under, or metamorphose into something else, or try to become a church. But this last choice means losing the interior experience that made the cult different from the surrounding religious context in the first place. In the first century, conversions to Christianity came via vision and trance; the experience of "influence," as already discussed, was at its height, with somatic energy passing through a congregation like electricity.[50] By the second half of the second century, the Church saw this as an embarrassment. It chose to argue that the ecstasies of Christ and Paul were quite enough, and that no further testaments to the spirit were needed. The "Holy Ghost was now a potential hazard," writes the American his-torian Frederick Turner. But the Gnostic gospels reveal that the various Christian cults that continued to spring up regarded what would later be called the orthodox position, which argued that the Church office itself conferred holiness on its occupants, as ridiculous. These Gospels call such holders of ecclesiastical office "waterless canals,"[51] and an early Church father, Tertullian, who spent years attacking these her-esies, finally defected to one of them (the Montanists), warning the Church that its tendency to substitute dogma and ecclesiastical hier-archy for actual inward experience was a dead end. In his *De Anima*

(On the Soul), written at the end of his life, Tertullian praised ecstatic vision as the key to the true spiritual life.[52]

The process of constructing an orthodoxy began toward the end of the second century, and solidified within a century or so, compiling a history of heresy based on deviations from its own (i.e., the orthodox) position. In the fourth century, the imperial state became the enforcement agency of Christian orthodoxy.[53] The decisions of Nicaea (325) and Chalcedon (451) continued this trend of expanding organization and shrinking spirituality; they represent a massive attack on the human soul. As already noted, the *homoousian* creed meant that Christ was to be venerated as an object of faith, not imitated as a true exemplar. By the fifth century, there were roughly one hundred active statutes against heresy; experience with the "God within" was effectively closed off. The early Middle Ages form a coherent, if completely closed, cultural unity; truly "dark," or, as the historian Peter Brown has written, "singularly monochromatic."[54]

It is really Saint Augustine who sounds the death knell for the voice of interiority. His career was the mirror image of Tertullian's. A Manichaean for no less than nine years, Augustine finally went over to the orthodox side, and ultimately—this is so typical of converts—outdid the Church in zeal, advocating the use of torture by the state in the rooting out of heresy. By the end of his life Manichaeanism, the last manifestation of Gnosticism in the ancient world, was spent, and would not reappear in the West until the neo-Manichaean movements of the eleventh and twelfth centuries. As Paul Johnson has written, in the intervening centuries the "Church was cocooned within the authoritarian tradition of Augustine."[55]

And society was cocooned as well. In the stiff iconography of Carolingian art we see a frozen body, and a frozen God. Having had several centuries of intense and turbulent interiority, the psyche, Jewish as well as Christian, was exhausted. As noted in Chapter 1, a loss of interest in mirrors occurred at the same time, and did not get revived until the simultaneous rediscovery of the Self in the eleventh and twelfth centuries. And this rediscovery was the next episode in the history of countercultural, or somatic, awareness.

# 6

# Cathars and Troubadours

> [W]e have learned to take such phenomena as the
> Crusades, the Inquisition, and kindred forms of
> religious persecution as more or less normal stages
> in the growth of our civilization, however attended
> by violence they have been. Generally we have not
> thought these might be symptoms of a deep spiritual
> pathology that has prevented us from experiencing
> more authentic forms of renewal.
>
> —Frederick Turner,
>   *Beyond Geography*

> . . . this may be his weal
> That ecstasy his soul shall softly steal.
>
> —Aimeric de Belenoi, thirteenth century

THE RELATIVE DISAPPEARANCE OF HERESY down to the eleventh century is a curious fact. I say "relative" because given the obvious continuity of the human body over these five or six centuries, it would seem almost certain that many people engaged in spiritual exercises that generated an ascent through the five bodies and opened the door to ecstasy, vision, soul travel, and the like. How could such a powerful somatic tradition simply die out? According to such a view, heresy would have been rife, but so completely underground that it never came under public scrutiny; which meant that the culture would have been severely schizoid—something like modern Britain or, if you prefer, Japan. People, on this view, would have been busy putting a good face on things, while leading lives of quiet desperation. Then, in the eleventh century, they just couldn't take it any more; the demand for direct experience of God exploded, went public again, giving birth to the second major cycle of heretical activity in the West.

It is certainly a plausible thesis; the alternative would be to imagine an entire culture without interiority, without conscience, thoughts, feelings, or even intentionality. As we have seen, Julian Jaynes has argued this for the period down to about 900 B.C. or so, after which we get the *Odyssey* and the rise of a whole language of interior experience and intellectual soul-searching.[1] It seems almost impossible, however, to accept such a state of mind for, let us say, the tenth century A.D. Yet in very recent years, a number of medieval historians have begun to argue exactly this. Since this has obvious implications for the nature of the Self, and for Self/Other relationships in general, as well as for the question of what heresy ultimately is, it will be useful to elaborate on this argument a bit before turning to the culture of Languedoc and the rise of Catharism, interiority, and romantic love.

One of the most important articles in the "noninteriority" genre appeared in 1978, and was written by the American historian Charles Radding.[2] Radding takes the approach of the French historians of *mentalité* (discussed in Chapter 3) that certain cognitive shifts can occur in a civilization that are so profound that there seems to be almost no mental continuity between one epoch and the next. This is not a question of one age having a different set of ideas from the next, or even a different set of beliefs or values. It is rather a total revolution in perception, a whole shift in the way reality presents itself to the eyeballs and the brain. The shift from magic to science, from a living world to a dead one, such as occurred during the Scientific Revolution, is such a shift because there is, for example, nothing an alchemist and a chemist can meaningfully say to each other. It is not merely a question of conflicting theories that is at issue here; rather, what is actually seen, felt, and experienced in the world is radically different. And the result, as writers such as Owen Barfield and Julian Jaynes have argued, is that the world *is* radically different; the notion of a sharp boundary between inner and outer as a fact of all human life is a delusion.[3] According to Radding, what happened after Augustine, and lasted down to about 1050, was the disappearance of interiority—not the *repression* of interiority, but the actual disappearance of it. The interiority of something like Augustine's *Confessions*, says Radding, was simply not present in the early Middle Ages. Monastic practice, for example, was essentially the performance of ritual, pure and simple. Much the same was true of legal practice during this time (say, 500–1050); there was virtually no discussion of the issue of intentionality in a criminal act. It was only the *act* that counted, the overt physical behavior.

This curious feature of the early Middle Ages is thrown into relief when one begins to compare it to the period that followed. In the case of penance done for sins, for example, there was no interest in probing the mind of the sinner—obtaining interior repentance (what was later called *contritio*)—until the twelfth century. All that was important was behavioral reparation (*satisfactio*), and you could even have a third party perform it for you, if you wished. The issue was only that the penance got done. The Church had absolutely no interest in knowing that you had "searched your soul" and come to see the error of your ways. It simply did not think in those terms.

The same tendency can be seen in the case of doctrinal debates that arose within the Church. There are no references to direct spiritual experience such as Tertullian (when he finally became a Montanist) was making, nor is there even any intellectual argumentation in the later sense of the term. Doctrine was regarded as if it were exterior to one's mind; faith and dogma were experienced as being identical. In the case of a doctrinal dispute, one was not called upon to formulate an intellectual reaction, but rather to bombard one's opponent with quotations from the Church fathers and the Bible.

Now none of this really proves the absence of interiority; it could have just gone into hiding. As the cliché goes, absence of evidence is not evidence of absence. But the almost total lack of any documents from this period that show signs of interiority or intentionality is a bit creepy. It is paralleled by the fact that there are only two references to mirrors in the extant literature over a period of several hundred years (discussed in Chapter 1). There is no evidence, says Radding, that this purely literal or "materialist" mentality was straining with internal contradictions. What Radding uses as evidence here is not really evidence, but as an analogy it is eerily suggestive, and that is the parallel between the evolution of medieval culture and the ontogeny of modern childhood.

In *The Moral Judgment of the Child* (1932), Jean Piaget reported that his own work with young children (specifically, boys) revealed an attitude of what he called "moral realism."[4] Asked questions about the rightness and wrongness of certain actions, his subjects focused on the actual material conditions involved, not on issues such as whether the person in the hypothetical story knew he was doing wrong, intended to do wrong, etc. Thus Piaget told his subjects first a story in which a boy climbed into a cupboard to get some jam and knocked over a cup, which fell and broke, and then another story in which a child, who was called to dinner, opened the door to the dining room, accidentally knocking over a tray and breaking fifteen cups. Children aged six to seven, Piaget found, focused on the amount of damage (breaking fifteen cups was worse than breaking one); whereas children over ten were interested in the intention present or absent in these acts. "Moral realism" lacks this interior dimension; it is about material conditions in the most literal sense of the word.

Following up on this work, the American psychologist Lawrence Kohlberg, along with other researchers, was able to establish the existence of six stages of moral reasoning that ranged from Piaget's "moral realism" to a growing awareness of the role of the intentions of others to an emphasis on abstract principles of human rights and justice. These researchers also found that these stages were developmental, not cultural: individuals in every culture they studied went through the same stages, though the timing of the stages was occasionally different. Thus twenty percent of sixteen-year-old American boys, they discovered, continued to use the nonintentional reasoning of early childhood, whereas fifty percent of the sixteen-year-old boys studied from a contemporary peasant culture used it. It could be the case, in other words, that certain types of societies accelerate certain types of *mentalité*, and that an entire society can undergo "arrested" development, even though the programming is innate. The birth of both language use and ego-identity follows this pattern of what some biologists call "gene-culture coevolution."[5]

Was the period from 500 to 1050, then, one long case of "arrested" development? Certainly, the contrast with the period that followed this is a striking one. I have already mentioned the totally disparate notions of penance involved in the shift from the *satisfactio* to the *contritio*, but there is much more that we can point to and that historians such as Marie-Dominique Chenu and Colin Morris have elaborated upon.[6] From 1050 onward, monasticism showed obvious signs of interiority, and the law started to emphasize the relationship between intentionality and ethics; and these were two of the most crucial institutions of medieval society. In the eleventh century as well, for the first time in several centuries, heretics arose who denied the efficacy of ritual. They argued that a baptism, to be efficacious, required inward belief; and in general, by 1050 monastic communities were beginning to awaken to the idea of intense personal commitment. In the area of doctrinal debates, the eleventh century saw the development of logic (Peter Abelard, for example), as opposed to argument from authority. The period emphasized emotion—in particular romantic love—and the idea arose that to be real, love had to be voluntary and reciprocal. By 1200, homicide with malice aforethought was singled out for special punishment. "It's the thought that counts," we say today; a mind-set that has its roots in the High Middle Ages.

Radding's work (leaving Piaget and Kohlberg aside) has received some support, and documentation, from the historian John Benton, who points out that the Socratic dictum (it actually belongs to Solon) "know thyself" had a nonlinear career from the time of Socrates down to the twelfth century.[7] A "graph" of self-awareness, he says, would show a decline from Augustine and then a sharp rise in the twelfth century, with not much in between. Even then, the nature of the twelfth-century awakening, or reawakening,[8] is problematic. It is unclear whether the twelfth century produced anything quite as soul-searching as Augustine's *Confessions*. Figures who attempted this (e.g., the Benedictine abbot Guibert of Nogent in 1115) tended to be more naive than self-aware; and even if we include writers like Peter Abelard, says Benton, "a great leap in subjectivity separates medieval Europe from the eighteenth century." Medieval accounts of dreams, for example, are not tied to self-examination, because dreams were regarded as imposed experiences, external to the dreamer. The search for Self was really the search for God; it was not an inward search in a twentieth-century existential sense.[9]

That being said, Benton is nevertheless quite clear "that the practice of self-examination was deeper and more widespread in twelfth-century Europe than at any time since the fifth century." There was a growing *institutional* interest in introspection and in the examination of one's conscience, either in private meditation or, increasingly, by means of a spiritual adviser. Guilt became a dominant theme, and by the early thirteenth century the role of the priest as confessor was pretty well established. Inwardness flowered in a whole variety of forms. Intention, which had been a legal concern in the late Roman Empire and which had declined thereafter, was rediscovered or reinvented in the twelfth century.[10] A growing canonistic agreement had it that consent rather than coitus made a marriage. Individual portraiture, which had been popular in antiquity, was largely absent from Carolingian art or Romanesque sculpture, and then made a reappearance in the art of the twelfth century. Where Saint Benedict, in the sixth century, held that monks should obey the commands of their abbot virtually as a reflex action—a framework that dominated the religious structure of monastic Europe for the next six centuries—Saint Francis wrote that service should be rendered willingly and mutually. And for what might be inferred from a word, the Latin term *persona* meant "mask," in the literal, physical sense (something an actor used); there was no medieval word for "personality." Radding would concur that what all of this adds up to is a single historical movement. "The novelty of the twelfth century in the history of medieval mentalities," he writes, "lies in the sudden predominance of cognitive structures that were different from those of the early Middle Ages."[11]

What was the cause of all this? Benton gives a list of possible factors for the reemergence of interiority—social, economic, political—but as in the various attempts to explain the rise of heresy in the twelfth century (which is part of the same movement), none are conclusive.[12] Radding suggests that the shift in *mentalité* may have been due to the rise of larger social groups that broke down kinship structures, and thus set up situations in which one had to know what the other person was thinking in order to deal with them.[13] Culture contact may indeed be a factor; Jaynes suggests something similar for the awakening of interiority in the archaic period. But the cause may not be all that important. What remains fascinating is the suggestion that the shift in *mentalité* that occurred between the tenth and the twelfth centuries parallels the moral-stage-shift from, say, age five to ten in the modern child. For if this parallel is more than an analogy—and it is a big "if"— then we are, once again, not describing a culture that represses things such as love, friendship, intentionality, logical argumentation, and other signs of interiority, but rather one that simply doesn't *have* these things; that simply has no experience of inwardness. We accept this in very young children; why not in an entire civilization?

If Radding is right, it is possible for an entire culture to be "visual," nonkinesthetic in the sense discussed in Chapter 1. We can even go so far as to remove the Whiggish (i.e., modernist) bias present in his or Kohlberg's notion of the six stages—which does, despite his own disclaimer, have the assumption of emotional progress (increasing sophistication) in it—and simply say that there are a number of types of *mentalité* available to human beings, and that the one of pure "visualness" or Otherness does not *necessarily* involve the sort of confiscation or alienation Wallon described. "Arrested" development is a loaded term; it is possible to be so totally confiscated that you never know it, and in this sense nothing is lost. This would also mean that the charge made by heretics against the orthodoxy, of being empty vessels, or "waterless canals," disappears not because the heretics go underground, but because interiority itself disappears. Orthodox, ritualistic behavior is thus not always phony; interiority may require, for its awakening, the using of the body in a certain way, or the practicing of certain exercises. If all five bodies are not engaged, the last three—perhaps even the last four—go dormant. It is only from the point of view of interiority that such behavior is "robotic." From *its* point of view, or from the viewpoint of the early Middle Ages, there may be nothing amiss. But it is impossible to know exactly what is going on. Some people, for example, never fall in love because of the fear of losing control. Others just simply never fall in love; it's not part of their makeup, and they really don't feel they are missing anything. Viewed from the outside, however, there is no way to tell the difference.[14]

Let me try to put this another way. Some years ago, the Polish-American author, Jerzy Kosinski, wrote a novel called *Being There*, in which the central character, Chance, was raised from birth with almost no contact with the outside world except via a television set. (This was subsequently made into a film with Peter Sellers in the leading role.) His total experience of life, in other words, was visual; he had literally no kinesthetic or inward experience whatsoever. At age twenty-five or thirty, as a fully grown adult, he is forced to change his situation due to a set of external circumstances, and he is suddenly thrust out into the outside world. One would think that this culture contact would be a disaster; instead, Chance becomes an immense success. No one in American society can imagine that this is a person totally lacking interiority; but as everything he says and does is purely literal, or one-dimensional, those around him project their own interiority onto him. He is quickly credited with being a brilliant economist, a polyglot, even a sensitive lover; finally, he is nominated as the Republican candidate for vice-president. It is all a satire, of course, a future look at a sort of robotic society that Kosinski feels the United States might be drifting toward. It is funny precisely because the reader, or filmgoer, *possesses* interiority, and thus finds the strange interactions that result when people have to deal with someone like Chance— virtually a denizen of another species—often hilarious. But if the reader or filmgoer did not possess interiority—was, in effect, like Chance— there would be no joke, because all of this would come under the heading of normal behavior. (In fact, it would be all of the *other* people in the book or film who would be strange.) This (autistic or even schizophrenic) behavior would simply be what being human *was*. The trick is to imagine, historically, an entire culture without a Self, and behaving like this for centuries. If such things do exist, problems only arise at the interface between two cultural formations. The period from about 450 to 1050 might well be called "Radding space." At one end of this space (or just before it), you get an Augustine advocating the use of torture to extinguish the remaining possessors of interiority. At the other end of it (or just after), you have a neo-Manichaean revival arguing that the sacraments are empty rituals. Between these two poles: silence.[15]

In any event, the relevance of all this to the history of heresy should be obvious. If Radding is right, then heretics, in the eyes of the faithful, are not so much threatening as insane (a charge that was occasionally made). They are to be pitied rather than persecuted. But if Radding is wrong, and interiority never really died, then heretics would evoke rage, because they would remind the orthodoxy of its betrayal of its own interiority. Thus Radding would seem to be wrong—rage was the typical reaction—except for one thing: the reaction of rage grew very slowly in the eleventh century, gained momentum in the twelfth, and was in full force by the thirteenth. This would tend to suggest that heretics were the avant-garde of interiority, and that the Middle Ages was gradually coming out of its literal or materialist "slumber." The awakening to interiority was, once again, based on body practice, and moved out in social ripples, like a morphogenetic field. We moderns persecute our own psychological avant-gardes (Wilhelm Reich is perhaps the best example); the same probably obtained in the Middle Ages.

And yet the real question is why persecution exists at all. The awakening to interiority means, in effect, the awakening of the Self/Other dynamic, or kinesthetic/visual polarity, previously discussed. It means confiscation as Wallon defined it is once again possible; it means that society becomes complex—a whole range of allegiances emerges depending on the degree of inwardness each person "chooses" to emphasize. This breaks down the "monochromatic unity" of the early Middle Ages, and it is no surprise that a bodily metaphor used by Saint Augustine to describe heresy, viz., disease—especially leprosy—was revived in the twelfth century. Catharism, for example, was described as a disease infecting the limbs of Christ; heresy was to the soul what leprosy was to the body.[16] There are many reasons why leprosy would be chosen as a metaphor here, notably, I suppose, its ability to spread via contagion. In *The Name of the Rose*, Umberto Eco argues for a different possibility, viz., that the leper, with his decaying flesh and bleeding eyes, is the essence of the Other, or the marginal creature who is *unheimlich*, like us but not like us. "The lepers," he writes, "are a sign of exclusion in general." "All heresies," he continues, "are the banner of a reality, an exclusion. Scratch the heresy and you will find the leper." The problem is that we are defined by what we exclude; the Self/Other game is a dialectical one. Hence everyone is simultaneously heretical and orthodox, no one is totally certain of where he or she stands, and anyone can serve as an unpleasant reminder, a mirror, or shadow.[17] To confront the heretic, or the leper, is generally to confront your excluded kinesthetic Self, that nags at you to be "real," as reality is now defined. It echoes the whole *stade du miroir* of Lacan; it simultaneously beckons you to admit to the interior world you've rejected *and* to stamp it out in its projected form. At least, this is how the West has chosen to respond, and this is why major segments of Western history can be seen to be politically "coded" along the lines of interiority, or somatic understanding, or—what I believe it is—an underground feminine current.

The female nature of this interior awakening is a crucial issue, and one that has to be addressed if we hope to understand medieval heresy. Twelfth-century monks began to conceive of Christ as having breasts and nursing his followers. The God of Rules that dominated the early Middle Ages was replaced by a God(ess) of Love in the thirteenth century—initially a heretical personage or archetype (Sophia, or gnostic wisdom), later one adopted (or, more accurately, co-opted) by the Church (Mary). We shall return to the question of female consciousness later on. But in general, the intensity of inward experience represented by heretical developments from the eleventh century gave birth (or rebirth, more likely) to two psychological developments that are still with us today: the concept of romantic love and the notion of the crime of conscience—"thought crime." In what follows, I am going to develop the former theme in more detail than the latter; but it turns out that the famous Cathar-troubadour link argued for by Denis de Rougemont in *Love in the Western World* is probably part of a wider development that had interiority at its root; that crimes of conscience and the Inquisition were part of this same development; and that a certain model of heresy, based on a combination of co-optation and repression, emerges from this study that is distinctly different from our first, or Greek, model (the rise of a world religion) and is one that we are still living with, when you really get down to it. It is also the case, as already noted, that the appearance of interiority in the period after 1050 revived a logic of opposition, of Self vs. Other, that had apparently disappeared (because Self had disappeared) between 500 and 1050. It was, furthermore, revived with a vengeance, and this represents the third bit of psychocultural fallout of what I call the French model, namely that in destroying the culture of Languedoc, the Church—and hence the West—absorbed much of the dualistic and gnostic cosmology so central to Cathar and Manichaean thought. It became what it hated; and in secular form, this oppositional logic has proven to be the real cross on which Western culture, and the individuals in it, get crucified. And this, finally, raises the question of whether, in order to escape this logic, we have to return to a monochromatic society—a world of Chances—or whether something else may yet be possible for us today. Let us begin, however, with the Catharist heresy and the institutional response to it. This will enable us to clarify, as we did in the case of our first model, the exact nature of the interaction of political context and spiritual/somatic energy.

Dualist heresy began to reemerge—or at least be noticed—in the early part of the eleventh century. In "the visions of the mystics," argued Paul Alphandéry many years ago,

> in the symbolism of medieval literature, in the peculiar hierarchies constructed by such heretics as Eon de l'Etoile and Tanchelin . . . ancient dualistic concepts were preserved, often deep in the communal unconscious, which . . . burst out into the open air as heresies in the eleventh century.[18]

On an intellectual level, at least, dualism had a lot to commend it, because, as was the case with the Marcionites and other dualist heresies of antiquity, it had an answer to the problem of evil in the world—a problem with which the orthodox Church was notoriously unsuccessful.[19] Whereas the latter had difficulties in explaining how or why a benevolent deity could permit the existence of evil, dualistic doctrines had more of a problem explaining the presence of good (!). These doctrines, were, in short, very pessimistic. In absolute form, dualism saw the cosmos as a war between good and evil, with neither having the upper hand. Sometimes one won, sometimes the other; but if either could be credited with greater potency, it would be evil, specifically the creator God of the Old Testament. For the evidence of the evil of His creation was everywhere. Yet in each material body, according to Gnostic tradition, the divine spark had somehow gotten embedded, in the process of incarnation, and the goal of any person in this life was to shun the material in favor of a purely spiritual existence. As with medieval alchemy, it was a process of successive refinement; but in this case, from one life to the next. When the soul finally got completely purified, it didn't need to be reincarnated any longer, and so, upon the death of the body, it went up to heaven and got reabsorbed into the Absolute. For Christian dualists, Christ was the perfect example of this. He was a body in spirit only, yet he was not divine. Rather, he was a teacher, and his teaching was a salvation, consisting of the liberation of the soul from matter. This was not an article of faith, but something every human being could do for him- or herself.[20]

Certain practices followed directly from this. If matter is to be shunned, then the sacraments, including baptism, are empty rituals. The only true baptism is the baptism of the Spirit. Flesh foods are to be avoided;[21] sexual intercourse only procreates the material world, and is therefore not to be engaged in. Animals must never be killed, a fortiori human beings, because these all contain souls. Only the strictly ascetic life can be counted on to lead one to heaven. Hence the name "Cathar," from the Greek word *katharos*—pure.[22]

Of course, this was a pretty exacting regimen, and thus almost all dualist sects allowed for certain classes of believers. Usually there were two: an elite, which was actively adhering to the precepts of the cult— these were called the Perfect (*Parfaits*, or, more colloquially, *bons hommes*—good men) in the case of the Cathars—and then simply the believers (*croyants*, or in Latin, *credentes*), who paid homage to the elite but who could carry on more or less ordinary lives. In this way, a dualist sect could attract a large following, since only a small percentage of any group could be counted on to lead a life of total abstinence. Leniency in these matters was thus a boon to membership, but it must be said that asceticism was as well. In the context of a corrupt and decadent orthodoxy, especially on the local level, the presence of a group of *Parfaits* leading exemplary lives that seemed to be truly Christian in the original, apostolic sense had a great impact.

The return to the apostolic ideal was the guiding theme of the eleventh and twelfth centuries. It is likely that a number of heresies, perhaps even that of the early Cathars, were originally Christian reform movements with a bit of dualist cosmology thrown in. Thus the historian Jeffrey Burton Russell writes that "the orthodox reform movement and the heterodox search for purity [were] cut from the same bolt of cloth," and that "only the width of a hair separated a Valdes from a Francis of Assisi. . . . "[23] The early pattern was one of a cult following organized around a dominant personality who was preaching the apostolic ideal and accusing the Church of spiritual bankruptcy and corruption.[24] These wandering preachers tended to live what they preached, and their major focus of attack was that at some point the Church had taken a wrong turn, and that a need for a return to the true church of Christ was long overdue.

Despite orthodox attempts to outflank this development, the apostolic movement continued to gain momentum. With the rise of Catharism, the heretical pattern shifted from that of cult following to full-blown organization. The first Cathar church made its appearance in northern Italy in the eleventh century; when Bernard of Clairvaux visited the region around Albi (from which the name "Albigensians" is derived) in the south of France a century later, he found the sect everywhere, heavily integrated into the political, religious and cultural life of Languedoc.[25] The heresy had become corporate in nature, i.e., it did not depend on any individual charismatic figure for its continuation, was organized around a coherent "anti-tradition," and had links with similar groups in other countries. By 1200, and probably as early as 1150, Occitania—the south of France—was largely a Cathar state.

Why Occitania? What was it about Languedoc in particular that lent itself to "Eastern" ideas? The answer to this has never been clear. But the Midi was, in the eleventh and twelfth centuries, Europe's cultural avant-garde; it was the first region to break out of the "monochromatic unity" of the Dark Ages, to awaken to interiority. The German historian Friedrich Heer spoke of "the feminine culture of the South,"[26] and there is no doubt that it possessed a very receptive and supple character. The Midi had become a cultural mélange not unlike the culture of Palestine at the time of Christ. It was experimental, open to new possibilities, very much oriented to the mystical and mythological. By southern standards, the north was a totally different, and largely alien, country: rural, crude, and agricultural, as opposed to the urban and cosmopolitan character of the south. The *langue d'oc* was understood in Barcelona, but not in Paris.[27] The south was culturally syncretic, a potpourri of Moorish poetry and medicine, Jewish number mysticism (the cabalistic revival), troubadours and traveling minstrels whose lyrical ballads spoke of love and satire. Schools of medicine, philosophy, and astronomy were active in cities such as

Narbonne, Avignon, Montpellier, and Béziers long before the foundation of universities, and Aristotle was first taught in the West, via
Arabic translation, in Toulouse.[28] The Cathars were part of this kaleidoscope of culture contact and (if Charles Radding is right) concomitant awakening to interiority. Moving from town to town in their
black robes, pale and thin from continual fasting, the Perfect, notes
historian M. D. Lambert, appeared to the believers to be a race of
restored angels.[29] They told myths, sang poems of love and joy, re-
counted visionary experiences, and healed the sick.[30] In such a context,
their intense and organized heresy clearly fell on fertile ground.

In this context also, Catharism was not seen as such a sharp rival
to the Church. Occitania was a *tolerant* place; Catholics and heretics
lived side by side in relative harmony. Every family typically had some
member who had joined the Cathar fold, and when the Church, and
the north, decided to make war on the south, this proved to be the
crucial difficulty.[31] The enormous resistance of the south was at least
partly due to the whole network of friendly and familial relationships
that was tied into Catharism on a grass-roots level. It was not easy
for the local nobility to make war on heresy, on behalf of the king and
pope, when half of their family and friends were involved in it.

The Midi, was, finally, a very physical culture—the most "Latin"
of all of Europe. It felt life with its entire body (still true today); and
that meant it was open to contrary influences, not so stuck in fixed
forms. To this day, the south is a land of contrasts, of hot and cold,
humid and dry. It was, perhaps, the ideal place for heretical somatic
experience, and a deepening awareness of interiority, to flower. It
may have even been the site of ancient pagan religions that never
completely died out, despite the thin veneer of Christianity that had
been laid over them in the intervening centuries.[32] It was also, says
Walter Wakefield, a major crossroads geographically, an area with
easy contact with other regions, and this permitted ideas—and the
people carrying them—to circulate freely throughout the culture.[33] If
the British historian Steven Runciman is right about the chronic refueling of Western heresy by means of Eastern influences (something
also argued by Hans Jonas in *The Gnostic Religion*),[34] we can see that
it would be in the south that these influences would be most likely to
be felt, as well as in northern Italy. "Catharism was now [in the late
twelfth century] much less Christian and less Western in temper,"
wrote Friedrich Heer; "Oriental and non-Christian elements replaced
poverty and the apostolic way of life as its dominating features."[35]

The outlines of Cathar history are fairly well known, and the story can be summarized briefly.[36] Disturbed by the strong Cathar presence in the south of France, the Church had sent two preaching missions to the region between 1145 (which included Bernard of Clairvaux) and 1180, but these had proved to be obvious failures, and hardly served to alter the heretical pattern. There had also been *some* show of force: Pope Lucius III and the Emperor Frederick Barbarossa had condemned the Cathars in 1184, and the papal bull, *Ad abolendam*, had even established a procedure for inquisition. But it was not until the papacy of Innocent III (1198–1216) that a real war on the south began in earnest. The murder of the papal legate, Peter (or Pierre) de Castelnau, in January of 1208, served as the focal point, triggering the idea of a crusade; and this idea was eagerly picked up by the nobles of the north, who saw in it an opportunity for territorial gain at the expense of their southern counterparts. As so often happens in such cases, the religious issue became blurred with political and economic ones.[37]

The story of the actual military campaign, under the leadership of Simon de Montfort, is a famous (or notorious) one, and has been told many times. Along with the Inquisition that followed (officially instituted at Toulouse in 1233), it is one of the darkest periods of European history and a blot upon the history of the Church, from which it never really recovered, despite its "victory." The losses of the south during the first fifteen years of the crusades have been estimated to have been one million dead, and in many ways the worst was yet to come.[38] Whole towns, starting with Béziers in 1209 (a suspected Cathar stronghold), were put to the sword; holocausts of the Perfect followed in the wake of these massacres. No political or territorial motives can explain the rage and fury of the crusaders, who butchered babies with glee. Having awoken to interiority, and the consequent pain of a spiritual vacuum that ached to be filled, the military agents of the king and the pope went on a killing orgy, their targets being precisely those people who were *not* spiritually bankrupt (or simply "blank") and who were in touch with a living, somatic mythology. When Arnold Amalric (or Arnaud Aimery), Bishop of Cîteaux, was asked by the crusaders what they should do with the (Catholic) citizens of Béziers, he was reported to have replied: "Kill them all, God will recognize his own." The new papal legate was quite happy to report to the Pope that twenty thousand people were put to death—the entire population of the town.[39]

"Christian civilization," writes Frederick Turner,

embarked on [a] concerted effort at regeneration through sacri-
ficial violence, offering the mutilated bodies of its enemies as gifts
pleasing to a god whose son had once appeared as the Prince of
Peace.[40]

And it was this enemy, this Cathar heresy with its core of the Perfect
capable of profound somatic experience, vision and trance and ecstasy
(see below), that had demonstrated what authentic renewal was about,
that served as a terrifying kind of mirror, and that provided a focus
of attack for what the crusaders feared and hated most: their bodies,
the natural world, the wild and the primitive, the interior Other who
now threatened them at every turn. The war lasted twenty years, and
was resumed in the 1240s, years that saw many of the southern nobility—the real Cathar protectors—go up in flames, and that witnessed
the fall of Montségur in 1244, which concluded with a mass burning
of two hundred Perfect. The thirteenth century increasingly got caught
up in a cyclone of hysteria, as the definition of heresy kept slipping
and sliding, as torture was officially added to the interrogation process
in 1252, and as townspeople denounced each other to the Inquisition;
and all of this, says Turner, fueled by a violently uncorked spiritual
drive, the frenzied desire "to purge civilization of the vast hidden
army of Christ's enemies." Yet in many ways, the issue of heresy
almost fell from sight. The war very quickly stopped being one against
heresy per se, and turned into one of the north versus the south. The
Albigensian crusade was finally a clash of two cultures, really two
mentalités.[41] At issue during these years, writes Turner, "was the shape
and content of the psychic geography of the West."[42]

It was, in any event, all over by 1350. The Midi lay in ruins; the
remaining Cathars fled to Italy; the exquisite Provençal tongue was
eventually rendered archaic and obsolete; the "feminine" culture of
the south had been seemingly snuffed out forever, to be replaced by
national unification under the banner of the French language and the
Capetian kings. It was worse than Sherman's march to the sea in
American history, and left scars that have never healed, for (as in the
case of the American south) this part of the country has never been
emotionally integrated with the rest of the nation, regardless of what
is printed on the map.[43]

The destruction of the Cathars is surely one of the great lost op-
portunities in the history of the West. Arnold Toynbee once remarked
that the introduction of Buddhism—and perhaps we should say of
Eastern thought in general—to the West would be seen by future

historians as one of the turning points in our civilization. In a way, Steven Runciman and Hans Jonas echo this when they say that the story of Western heresy is that of a perpetual refueling from Eastern influences. The synthesis of East and West is perhaps in some metaphysical sense one of the major goals toward which the history of the world has been ineluctably moving. Such a synthesis may in fact lie at the heart of every healthy creative endeavor, a theme I shall elaborate upon in Chapter 10. But it has been an enormously painful process, one that has been resisted as bitterly as it is needed, because (I suspect) East and West are mirrors for each other. This mirroring phenomenon, I have argued, is central to the human dilemma since the rise of agricultural civilization, and it is the pivot on which the entire heresy/orthodoxy dynamic swings. In a Manichaean framework—and the Church is as riddled with Manichaeanism as any dualistic sect—this dynamic is one of rage. Zbigniew Herbert writes of the destruction of the Cathars:

> A flourishing civilization moving towards an important synthesis of oriental and occidental elements was destroyed at the very heart of Christian Europe. The obliteration from the religious map of the world of the Albigensian faith—which might have played as significant a role in the shaping of the human race's spirituality as Buddhism or Islam—is connected with the founding of a centuries-long institution called the Inquisition.

"There is no doubt that in their heresy," he adds, ". . . the voice of the Orient can be heard."[44]

For all the violence of the Crusades, it was really the Inquisition, with its grinding persistence, that destroyed the cultural integrity of the south. The arrival of the Inquisition, both in terms of its organizational model and in terms of its *modus operandi*, was the real death knell of the Languedocian way of life. By 1227 the Church had instituted a primitive police system, in which people were appointed to report on their neighbors. The procedure was exacting and meticulous—a good example of "banality of evil," as Hannah Arendt put it in another context. The sign of repentance was to name other suspects. Long lists were accumulated, lists that included anybody who had even spoken to a heretic. These lists were then checked against other lists. Penalties were graded, which also helped with the process of denunciation, for you could get off lightly with fast cooperation. As of 1233 inquisitors had autonomous power (i.e., they were responsible only to the pope); prisons were constructed to house for life those who simulated conversion to the Church; and the testimony of criminals was approved in cases of heresy. Almost anyone, in fact, could be a "reliable" witness, and witnesses were typically examined behind closed doors. The goal was to weave a network of secrecy, suspicion, and terror, and in this the Inquisition was very successful.[45]

Even in the face of all this, popular uprisings occurred. The Inquisition had to be suspended during 1238–41. The latter part of the thirteenth century also saw sporadic uprisings against the institution, in Italy and Germany as well as the south of France, for it was seen as foreign, vicious, and intrusive. But with the added pressure of torture legalized by Pope Innocent IV in 1252, the kinship and network structure of the south simply couldn't hold. The Perfect typically went to their deaths in silence; believers could not be counted on to share this ascetic courage, and in fact they were often, legitimately, confused. The open society of the twelfth century was becoming increasingly closed. Denunciation of heretics was made a duty, and the identity of the person doing the denouncing did not have to be revealed. The Inquisition proceeded in a relentless and bureaucratic fashion—"built up slowly, piece by piece, to the point where it became a merciless machine." Even the dead were not exempt. It often turned out that someone was posthumously tried and convicted of heresy, in which case the body was exhumed and burnt.[46]

What were the Cathars actually *doing*, to deserve all this? At the level of the believers, probably not very much. The Church was primarily concerned with the spread of the "infection," and so was most concerned with contacts and influence. By the thirteenth century, in fact, Catharism was getting fairly tame; as in the case of the early Church, ritual and hierarchy were starting to receive a lot more emphasis than personal illumination.[47] The ritual of the Consolamentum (see below) seemed very similar to extreme unction, and the Cathar service included the Lord's Prayer and the communal meal.[48] Beliefs also seemed to overlap, for Catholicism is, psychologically speaking, a very dualistic or Manichaean religion; it possesses, as does Catharism, strong antisexual attitudes; and it too sees body and soul as somehow antagonistically related, despite its doctrinal emphasis on incarnation. Given these similarities, it was easy for ordinary Catholics to stray onto heretical ground without even knowing it, and suddenly get caught up in a complicated ecclesiastical machinery that pressured them to admit to certain practices or ideas that they were not clear were wrong, and to supply a list of names of those who had behaved or believed similarly.

The situation with the Perfect, however, was altogether different. They were the living core of the religion, and their training was always directed toward personal illumination, especially in the twelfth century. Indeed, without this it is very unlikely that the Cathars would have had the magnetic power to attract a following. The problem for the historian, however, can (once again) be put very simply: on a somatic level, what were they actually doing?

This brings us face to face with a crucial methodological problem, viz., that the medieval heretics, of which the Cathars were the most organized and historically significant, were so closemouthed about their esoteric practice that we do not have a lot of evidence that it even existed. Very little surfaced under investigation or torture by the Inquisition; written Cathar documents give oblique hints, but nothing actually explicit; and even when someone like Rainer Sacconi (or Raynier Sacchoni), who had been a Cathar for seventeen years (and a Perfect to boot), finally defected (he eventually became Grand Inquisitor of Lombardy), he had no great revelations to make about a set of secret bodily practices beyond that of the Consolamentum. "We look in vain," writes Zbigniew Herbert, "for traces of magic, initiation rites or gnosis in Cathar ritual."[49]

We thus come to the central methodological problem of what I have called hidden history, that the techniques of analysis developed by historiography in the last two centuries are designed to verify (or falsify) only a certain type of assumption; and if we insist that there nevertheless is an invisible or somatic layer beneath the drama we are investigating, there seems to be no way in which this can be consensually validated. Heretical and sectarian phenomena are particularly maddening in this regard, because they open up to an instinctual "feel" that seems to strike home and yet slips through the net of any and every traditional mode of analysis. One historian, George Shriver, thus asserts: "Grappling with various facets of the Cathar story, one is well aware that much of life escaped the documents, [and] that there must be a place for intuitive perception at times." It was in this spirit that Déodat Roché, the greatest spokesman for Catharism in modern times, constructed a history of the Cathar phenomenon based on the esoteric system of Rudolf Steiner, thereby proposing a comparative method that would enable the historian to uncover a deeper history.[50] Yet his major conclusion—that there is a clear unbroken chain of identical esoteric practice from the Manichaeans, and ultimately from the Essenes, right through to the Cathars, remains, as far as I am concerned, an unwarranted assumption. "Hidden history" is plagued by the problem that it is easy to *invent* a past while claiming, in the name of intuitive perception, to uncover one. The question of continuity of influence between the Cathars and the earlier heresies thus has to be briefly examined.

In terms of similarity of doctrine, the argument for direct links between the heresy of the High Middle Ages and the Gnosticism of antiquity seems to be fairly solid. The same themes occur over and over again, and Runciman, for example, has used them to trace Catharism, via the Bogomils of the Balkan countries, back to third-century Manichaean and earlier Gnostic sources.[51] In the second century, notes Runciman, Iranaeus called the cultic initiates "Adepts of the Great Mother," and this identification of interiority with the Earth Goddess persisted through the fourth century. Adepts also saw their practice as closely intertwined with magic. Their form of baptism, for example, was magical practice; and the initiate became, via some form of direct identification with God, a type of magician. Cultic organization, from Marcion to Mani to the Bogomils and Cathars, divided the church into the Elect and the Believers (or "Hearers"), with the Elect following the regimens of fasting, vegetarianism, and sexual abstinence. The key doctrine, in all cases, was that of light being imprisoned in matter, and of salvation consisting in its release. In the tenth century, all of the same doctrines emerged in the heretical sect known as the Bogomils (literally, "Beloved of God"), who claimed that the sacraments were empty rituals and that the cross should be despised rather than venerated.[52] Many historians of heresy believe that it was the Bogomils who, traveling to the West, established the Cathar heresy there. Others hold that there was a native dualistic tradition in the West, though, like Runciman, they generally conclude that this tradition was continually reinforced from the East.[53]

The link with the Bogomils is undoubtedly correct; there is a good deal of concrete evidence that Cathar ideas originated with them, and most historians of the subject regard Catharism as clearly traceable to this Eastern, tenth-century source. But going much beyond the tenth century is a dubious venture; no genuine causal (i.e., not just thematic) links to Manichaeans, Gnostics, Essenes, and so on have ever been verified. It is also the case, as Russell points out, that the thesis of a continuous countercultural history based on themes or ideas leaves the question of receptivity—why did Catharism take hold so dramatically?—unanswered.[54] This is where history of ideas and somatic history have to part company, for in somatic terms, heresy represents a deeper truth than any set of ideas could ever convey or contain, as Al-Hallaj tried to say to his executioner.[55]

More convincing than the usual chain-of-influence approach is the methodology adopted by Rudolf Otto in his famous study, *Mysticism East and West*, that similar ideas need not arise from a common source or be causally related. Otto argued, rather, that patterns of religious thought were not culturally peculiar, but that they "occurr[ed] in unrelated areas and circumstances with parallel or similarly structured dynamics and logic."[56] The most likely explanation for this is that these patterns have an underlying somatic basis to them, for then a kind of independent and spontaneous recovery of information is possible. For example, in antiquity, as we saw in Chapter 5, concepts such as the presence of an occult, separable Self and a region of heaven to which this Self can travel were flesh and blood in nature. Through certain kinds of somatic practice, the doctrines got embodied; people actually experienced the regions described in five-body theory. Ideas do not spread or endure without this type of energetic content (and context); and the fact that it is always there to be tapped would explain both the similarity of the doctrines over time and their spontaneous, periodic recurrence. From a somatic point of view, in other words, the question of mental or material causality and continuous influence is a nonissue. We do, however, have to attempt to explicate exactly what sort of esoteric, somatic practice the Cathars engaged in, in order to verify that an "independent and spontaneous recovery of information" was in fact going on.

As far as I can see, evidence for a hidden, somatic substrate principally falls into two categories: (a) the existence of certain rituals practiced by the Cathars, which we know for certain were practiced, that (given the nature of human physiology) would have to have generated mild to severe altered states of consciousness; and (b) the centrality, within the Cathar sect, of an ancient document known as the Ascension of Isaiah (see Chapter 5) which deals with soul travel (i.e., astral or third-body travel) as it had been practiced in ancient Palestine. I deal with each of these in turn.

The Perfect of the sect apparently practiced meditation in order to bring about a state of trance, and there is some contemporary testimony regarding this.[57] To the Perfect alone, also, was granted the right to recite the Pater Noster, which they did numerous times each day in long, repetitive chains (called the double, or *dobla*) that in effect amounted to a hypnotic mantra. Fasting, a tried-and-true method of generating visionary or altered states, was a major activity of the Perfect, and it was interspersed with a vegetarian diet. Three days a week, the Perfect ate only bread and water; they also engaged in three forty-day-long fasts of this kind each year. All this was bound to have mental, or spiritual, effects.[58]

In general, the period of emergence into interiority, which began in the eleventh century, was characterized by certain types of yogic practice. A fourteenth-century document on the Messalian sect of the Byzantine Empire, for example, reveals that its monks reported that by means of a certain breathing technique and mechanically repeated prayer, they were led to a sensory vision of God.[59] Pierre Mauri, who turned in Pierre Bélibaste (a Perfect) to the Inquisition at Pamiers in the early fourteenth century, described how he observed the latter, one night when they lodged together, getting up several times during the night to go through a series of ritual genuflections and gestures, which sound rather yogic to the modern reader.[60] Another testimony at Pamiers described a series of body movements performed during prayer that seems similar to the so-called "sun worship" cycle of hatha yoga, performed in this case to the point of fatigue, and accompanied by the utterance of the words *Adoremus Patrem.*[61] All this is, perhaps, not much to go on, but it does demonstrate that body practice of some sort was part of the esoteric training of the Cathars. In general, the Cathars, like the Gnostics of the first century A.D., regarded the orthodoxy as "waterless canals," who talked of God without experiencing Him. As in the case of a number of other Cathar sources or testimonies, Pierre Bélibaste argued that Catholic baptism by water had no value because it was performed mechanically (usually on preconscious infants) and not received voluntarily and spontaneously. Popes in the days after Peter, he told Pierre Mauri, lacked any real spiritual power because they did not follow the practice of the sort carried out by the Cathars. Only the Cathars, he said, were actually passing the Spirit from person to person (i.e., from Perfect to Perfect) in the same way that Christ passed it on to the Apostles, and he "proved" this to Mauri by recounting for him the story of the Ascension of Isaiah. This story, in fact, probably says more about esoteric Cathar practice than anything else.[62]

The passing on of the Spirit occurred during the central Cathar rite of initiation, the Consolamentum, and it involved the laying on of hands, a practice that certainly goes back to antiquity. This the Perfect regarded as the only valid baptism; and there are enough hints to the effect that the ritual was modeled on the practice of ancient soul travel or heavenly ascent, and in particular on the Ascension of Isaiah. I referred to this text briefly in Chapter 5. It is a composite Jewish-Christian work, technically part of the Apocrypha, dating in its present form from the third century A.D., although most of it probably originated in the second century B.C. Chapters 6–11, entitled "The Vision of Isaiah," are a later (Christian) interpolation, probably dating from the early part of the second century A.D., and undoubtedly inserted to support the claim that the prophets of the Old Testament foretold the coming of Christ. In this story, Isaiah's soul is taken on a journey through the seven heavens (read: the seven—or five—bodies), where it sees the future, including the story of Jesus and the crucifixion. The vision includes an ecstatic experience, a taste of paradise to come in the afterlife. ("Paradise," when you get down to it, is a state in which one is in a never-ending oceanic experience and somehow remains conscious at the same time, in this occult tradition.) The angel that guides Isaiah through this tells him that he (i.e., his soul, or third body) has left his (first) body, but will return to it after he witnesses the events of Christ's life.[63]

In terms of the actual somatic practice that precipitated the visionary experience, it would be interesting to know whether Cathar practice depended at all on the cabala, which existed contemporaneously in Spain, Provence, and Languedoc. These techniques of ascent, for example, are discussed at length in the mystical *Maaseh Merkabah* (The Working of the Chariot), which Gershom Scholem reproduces (in the original Hebrew) in his book *Jewish Gnosticism, Merkabah Mysticism and Talmudic Tradition,* and to which we have already referred. The text repeats formulas that were recited to generate a successful ascent, and has long discussions of the proper way of recitation. These prayers typically involved long strings of nonsense words chanted in highly repetitive patterns, which would put the speaker into a hypnotic state.[64] Cabalist texts began to emerge in Provence around 1150, although (says Scholem) there were earlier stages in this development that were connected with *merkabah* mysticism. In fact, the first centers of cabala in the Christian world were in the Cathar strongholds of Languedoc, although the relations between Jews and Cathars are certainly obscure. It is also interesting that in the thirteenth century Abraham Abulafia (ca. 1240–92) in Spain led a movement toward ecstatic/prophetic cabala and described the ascent techniques quite explicitly. These included the use of music and breathing exercises, the repetition of divine names, and meditations on colors. Subjects reported seeing flashes of light, the appearance of an ether or aura, and also the appearance of an inner spirit guide.[65] This is somatic evidence at its best, it seems to me, and although we have very little direct evidence that such practices were going on among the Cathars, it would be remarkable if this were not the case; there is simply too much circumstantial evidence to the contrary. Let me be more explicit about this.

It was a common belief during the twelfth and thirteenth centuries that the Cathars were in possession of a central, occult secret, or revelation, that was imparted to the initiate during the Consolamentum with the laying on of hands. The first written statement of this is probably that of Ekbert (or Eckbert) of Schönau, archbishop of Cologne between 1159 and 1167, who published a series of thirteen sermons against the Cathars in 1163. Ekbert, in fact, coined the term *Cathari*, and believed that they were Manichaeans. He reported—though he was not a direct witness—that the room became illuminated at the moment of initiation; a "white light" experience that is in fact quite common, even today.[66] Although the Consolamentum was the critical moment for this, there is some testimony that it could strike at any time. Thus in 1321, one witness before the Inquisition at Pamiers reported that a certain Perfect he knew had been troubled by religious doubts, which were cleared up by a vision. In this vision, according to what he had told the witness, he mounted the shoulders of an angel and went through the seven heavens to the Father (presumably not Jehovah), where he saw the brilliance of the uppermost layer. The Father told him he must descend to earth and preach the (Cathar) faith.[67]

It would seem to be the case, however, that most visionary experience occurred at the moment of initiation, following a rigorous period of fasting and spiritual preparation; and that the "Vision" section of the Ascension story was the crucial guidebook, as it were. Roché argued that the goal of the Perfect was to reproduce the journey of Isaiah, and this seems to be fairly likely. In the Ethiopian version of the text (see note 63), it is reported that at the moment of the laying on of hands, Isaiah was given the gift of prophecy; and the text frankly discusses being in and out of the body.[68] Contemporaries such as Rainer Sacconi and Moneta of Cremona (author of *Adversus Catharos et Valdenses*, 1244) explained that in the Cathar schema, the physical hand was symbolic of an invisible hand, which carried the Holy Ghost, and thus that this invisible baptism conferred a spiritual regeneration.[69] The idea here was that the visionary experience that was granted the initiate at the moment of the laying on of hands was a "sneak preview"

14. Enlarged hands in Cathar iconography; carving on a sarcophagus in Domazan, France. From René Nelli et al., *Les Cathares*.

of what happened at the time of death, when the soul of the Perfect ascended to heaven and reunited with the Absolute. The initiation was thus a present realization of a future celestial life, anticipating the later process of the soul leaving the body. In certain Inquisition documents there are recitals that were inspired by the Ascension, and in these the name of Isaiah is replaced by the words *bonus homo*, i.e., Perfect. Cathar iconography contains the occasional image of a person with extremely enlarged hands (see Plate 14), suggesting the impor-

tance of this experience.[70] Thus at Orléans in 1022, a group appeared
that was, in all likelihood, Cathar, and that was reported on in a
document donated by a knight named Aréfaste to the abbey of Saint-
Père de Chartres six years later, describing promises that were made
to him by this sect. He was told that the laying on of hands would
take him through the gate of salvation; that he would be nourished
by the divine spirit, and thus filled from the inside; that he would
have angelic visions and be able to travel to wherever he wished.[71]

This possible facility of leaving the body may account for a particular
testimony that occurs over and over again in various contemporary
accounts of the Cathars, viz., their apparent ability to go to the stake
and not suffer pain. Observers occasionally reported that they went
to their deaths cheerfully. One Cathar text even states: "There is no
happier death than the death by fire."[72] The suggestion here is that
they could simply leave their bodies at will, and so get burnt alive
and not feel the pain. Thus when the group at Orléans were (in 1022)
burnt at the stake, they actually claimed, just before this, that they
would survive the fire intact.[73] The same claim was repeated three
centuries later to the Inquisition at Pamiers, that the Cathars believed
that when the Perfect were burnt the fire did not hurt their flesh.[74]
Similarly, during the height of the Albigensian crusade, four hundred
Perfect were burnt en masse at Lavaur, and they stepped into the
flames singing.[75]

What to make of all this? It could be the case, as one historian has
claimed, that the whole set of ascension stories was written up indirectly, by scholars, in an academic manner;[76] but it is just not likely
that this is so. Such an argument strains credibility much, much more
than the argument for actual ascent experience. The sect survived for
nearly three hundred years, and on an underground basis probably
longer. It seems impossible that it could have done so on the basis of
rumor and ideology alone. The possession of a "central secret," i.e.,
direct visionary experience that was trained for on a somatic basis,
seems extremely probable, and the circumstantial evidence, at least,
would seem to be overwhelming. I think it is safe to say that we have
penetrated down to the hidden, or invisible, layer of history here, and
found, at the core of it—the human body.

What were the Cathars really guilty of, when you get down to it?
I believe that the real "crime" of the Cathars, and the real drama of
the period 1050–1350, was the discovery of interiority. Early medieval
society worked insofar as it was circumscribed by Piaget's "moral
realism," lack of intentionality, and the absence of any Self/Other

dynamic. Its icons, as I have said, were the stiff figures of Carolingian paintings and the uniform voices of Gregorian chant. It was a beautiful society, in many ways, and probably, in the absence of culture contact, infinitely stable. It is for this reason that I believe that all discussions of the origins of medieval heresy have to be subsumed under a general awakening to piety and inwardness, of which heresy and romantic love were the most intense forms of expression. But it can be seen in a whole variety of forms: the beginning of the Crusades in the late eleventh century, the rush to new monastic orders, the call for apostolic purity, the enthusiasm for church building, the cult of relics and of saints, and the flowering of religious art and architecture. Polyphonic music is also part of this general trend, breaking up, as it does, the "monochromatic unity" of Gregorian chant.[77] Medieval mysticism gained increasing momentum as men such as Tauler and Eckhart (thirteenth and fourteenth centuries), as well as female mystics such as Teresa of Avila (sixteenth century) experimented with the five-body theory and tried to deal with the Self/Other dynamic by arguing that God exists within, that the soul can be annihilated by means of total concentration on God. "To adore God from love alone," wrote Louis Massignon in his biography of Al-Hallaj,

> is the crime of the Manichaeans. . . . These adore God with a *physical* love, through the magnetic attraction of iron to iron, and their particles of light are impelled like a magnet back toward the focus of light whence they came.[78]

Such discoveries are not easily assimilated by a civilization that has been living without interiority for more than five hundred years, and the reaction, as we have seen, was correspondingly harsh. As a result, the legacy of the period 1050–1350 has not been a healthy one.

In the first place, the Albigensian crusades resulted in a model of political unification, the nation-state, that has heralded the nationalisms of the modern (post-sixteenth-century) period. With the annexation of the southern territory by the king of France, that country became the most powerful state in Europe for the next five centuries. The Midi became a backwater; Provençal became "quaint," finally forgotten. This is a key feature of the modern age: the homogenization of culture, the defeat of subcultures with their alternative languages, ways of life, and modes of consciousness. Life became less diverse, and therefore less rich and more precarious.

Secondly, the emergence of inwardness was dealt with in police terms, as I have already noted. The "crime of conscience" was born, as belief rather than act became the central issue. This required a major institution, viz., the Inquisition, to examine the ins and outs of particular beliefs. "From the outset," writes Fredric Cheyette,

> the inquisitors . . . were exclusively devoted to this task. They kept continuous records of the depositions they heard and in time developed "handbooks for heretic-hunters" summarizing the knowledge gained over years of activity. With these data and an organization that reached all over Europe, they had resources roughly comparable with those of a modern police organization; they could track suspects wherever they went and could threaten even the descendants of accused persons (who risked losing their inherited property). Any suspect could be put under oath to testify to his or her beliefs, participation in forbidden rites, and knowledge of other suspects.[79]

It is not that all of this was "roughly comparable" with a police state. Rather, *the Inquisition is the origin of the modern police state*, its most terrifying legacy. And as the United States saw during the McCarthy era, even a so-called open or democratic society is hardly above using these tactics if it gets caught up in a fever of heretical or ideological hysteria. The network of mental control that circumscribes the Western industrial nations, and that rears its head in times of political instability, is the single most destructive result of the Inquisitional response to the awakening of interiority. Administrative violence remains, to this day, the ultimate guarantor of mind control in the West, of conformity and uniformity of opinion. As Joseph Strayer says, pressure, penalties, torture, and encouragement of betrayal were techniques picked up by the European states during this time, and they survive intact down to the present.[80]

The spirit that was crushed, where did it go? For the fourteenth century was not a repeat of the fifth. The Self/Other dynamic did not shut back down to several centuries of monochromatic unity; far from it, in fact. All of the heretical sects went underground, only to resurface centuries later, when it was relatively safe, and then in the very same places where they had been stamped out.[81] The heretical idea never died: the idea of a counterculture based on the body and the use of the spirit; the belief that the dominant culture is a con game and a betrayal; the direct experience of ecstasy, vision, and personal illumination; the attempt to build a true community of Christ. And dialectically enough, the destruction of the Cathars by the Church, by the West, led to the absorption or reinforcement of some of the key Cathar ideas, most especially the notion that the world is a battleground of good and evil. Dualism and Manichaean thinking, of course, are very old, certainly pre-Christian, and hardly needed the Cathars for their continuance. But the all-or-nothing, God-vs.-the-Devil war that the Crusades and the Inquisition represented put dualistic thinking into the Western mainstream in a dramatic and irrevocable way. It might be reasonably stated that the oppositional structure of Western consciousness, which we discussed in Chapter 2 as the dichotomy between Tame and Wild, became "official" in the thirteenth and fourteenth centuries. The psyche became disconnected from the body, and all feelings of aliveness were thereafter based on the adrenaline "rush" that comes from engaging in some form of conflict. By now it is so habitual that we cannot imagine any other way of thinking or living. (Perhaps it is no accident that coffee became a popular beverage in Europe from the sixteenth century on.)

Finally, the most pervasive result of the French model, as I call it, was the birth of romantic love in the West and its subsequent co-optation by the Church (the Cult of the Virgin Mary) and by secular culture at large. As Denis de Rougemont has pointed out, for most people in the West today, falling in love is literally the one ecstatic or mystical experience left open, and it serves as a haven from the culture of repression and control that grew up at the same time. It is the one tiny portion of their lives in which they can be truly kinesthetic rather than visual; in which they can (theoretically, at least) live true selves as opposed to false ones. This is no small legacy, in my opinion; despite its heavy co-optation and exploitation, it remains, for millions, the only real counterculture they can enjoy, the only expression of inwardness left in the modern world. It is, according to de Rougemont, the increasingly desperate attempt of *eros* "to take the place of mystical transcendence by means of emotional intensity."[82] It will be necessary, then, for us to conclude this section on medieval heresy and the French model by examining de Rougemont's thesis on the heretical origins of romantic love, and so see how politics and the life of the body interacted to shape the modern consciousness in so indelible a fashion.

It was the claim of de Rougemont, in *Love in the Western World*, that the real legacy of the Catharist heresy was the firm entrenchment of romantic love in the psyche of the West. At first glance, the thesis seems incredible: the ideal of the Perfect included, after all, sexual abstinence. But de Rougemont's thesis takes on greater weight when one comes face to face with the fact that at the heart of both Catharism and romantic love is the concept, and the feeling, of longing, or yearning; something that was experienced in somatic terms and that can be summarized in the paradoxical expression "erotic asceticism." This discipline of unfulfilled desire, of course, informed the love lyrics of the troubadours, those poets and minstrels of the south; and it was de Rougemont's claim that it was here that the link between love and Catharism became concrete: many troubadours, he argued, were really Cathars in disguise, and the lyrics were actually coded forms of esoteric doctrine.

De Rougemont wrote his original essay in 1938, without any notes, in an intense burst of creative activity, over a period of four months. Yet the love/heresy thesis actually has a long ancestry, to which de Rougemont occasionally referred.[83] Thus, in 1832, Gabriele Rossetti (the father of the painter) published a work in which he argued that courtly or romantic love was actually the vehicle of religious dissent; that the troubadours were members of a secret, anti-Catholic fraternity; that (this came in a later work) writers such as Dante, Petrarch, and Boccaccio were part of a "love sect" that exploited the language of erotic love for the propagation of Catharist beliefs, and that in fact the troubadours were ministers of the Albigensian heresy.[84]

Some years later, the French writer Eugène Aroux claimed that the troubadours were part of a vast proto-Protestant conspiracy, and that their poetry was actually a description of the trials and achievements of the Perfect.[85] Finally, with the work of Otto Rahn in 1933, the thesis was stated in its strictest form: all troubadours were Cathars (and vice versa), and the love lyrics were nothing more than disguised heretical messages.[86] De Rougemont did not formulate the argument in so absolute a way, but central to it was the notion that religious experience as practiced by the Cathars and the feelings involved in romantic love were essentially the same.

It might be useful, at this point, to clarify what is meant by courtly or romantic love, before elaborating on de Rougemont's argument. The term itself, *amour courtois*, was not used in the Middle Ages, but was coined by Gaston Paris in 1883 to refer to the love between Lancelot and Guinevere.[87] He saw it as a kind of idolatry, an illicit attachment that nevertheless had religious overtones. Grounded in sexual passion, it nevertheless was a kind of mental, or even moral, discipline. Thus F. X. Newman writes: "It is the special mark of *amour courtois* that it entails the simultaneous acceptance of contradictory notions . . . courtly love is a doctrine of paradoxes. . . ."[88] It is, then, to be distinguished from caring or affection; and following the typology set out by Anders Nygren (*Agape and Eros*), de Rougemont points out that he is talking about *eros* rather than *agape*; about being in love, rather than simply loving. In recent times, this distinction has perhaps been most clearly elaborated by Dorothy Tennov in her book *Love and Limerence*. Love, she says, is simply caring for someone, having a close attachment to them and being concerned for their welfare. It is essentially unselfish. Limerence, on the other hand, is altogether different. The term is derived from the Anglo-French word *limer*, which refers to a dog that is kept on a leash (cf. *lien* in French). Once again we have the theme of being hooked, dependent, drawn in. There is nothing relaxed (or unselfish) about this state of mind; the condition is one of preoccupation, or total obsession, with the beloved. Being in love means that there is nothing else you wish to do except be with the object of your desire. It involves jealousy, drama, fear of loss, suffering in his/her absence. Above all, it thrives on obstacles, and this gives it a paradoxical aspect. Hence, "parting is such sweet sorrow." It is an agony that generates exquisite pleasure. It is shot through with the dynamics of anxiety, desperation, and relief, because it is somatically rooted in the nemo, the gap, and in the possibility of completing (or losing) the isolated Self "once and for all." Love is *affection* for the beloved; limerence is *adoration* of him or her. In fact, romantic love is effectively a religious experience, in which the deity worshipped is the beloved. Hence, to lose one's love is to lose one's life; is to lose the entire world.[89]

The relationship of all this to heresy starts to become clear when we realize that heresy in the Christian West was typically dependent on Oriental influences; and translated into Occidental terms this usually meant some form of Neoplatonism. For that reason, it becomes crucial to consider how Plato regarded love, and this emerges most clearly in his famous dialogue, the *Symposium*, in particular in a speech that Plato puts into the mouth of the Athenian playwright Aristophanes. Aristophanes recounts a parable, or allegory, of the earliest days on earth, when the world was populated by a collection of male, female, and androgynous wholes, or "blobs," of some sort. They were proud blobs, and for this sin of hubris Zeus bisected them all and mixed up all the resulting parts. Each unit was now half an original person, condemned to search the earth for its missing half. Love, says Aristophanes, is "the desire and pursuit of the whole," the attempt to regain a former state of bliss by finding and uniting with the lost Other. In fact, he adds, echoing the mystery religions on which so much of Plato's work was based, the ultimate object of love is the vision of absolute beauty that the soul had before it was incarnated in a body. The relationship of the lover to the "love object," in effect, is that of the believer to God, or of the soul seeking to free itself of its material prison and to return to the Absolute from which it came.[90]

Love, in the sense of limerence, is clearly no pleasure, or at least no unalloyed pleasure. Too much is at stake, which is why it has such a keen edge of desperation. It is clearly an erotic asceticism, as we have said, because so much discipline is called for, so much pain is part of the game. The connection to Cathar doctrine, especially the notion of fleeing matter to attain the Spirit, should be obvious; and if one substitutes Erich Neumann's phrase "cosmic anonymity" for the word "Spirit" or "Absolute," it becomes clear that we are talking the language of object-relations theory: Transitional Objects, specular images, kinesthetic awareness, and so on. This is why romantic love is at root not a sexual experience but a sacred (biopsychic) one; why love is really the key to Plato's entire metaphysics; and why, if Western philosophy is indeed a series of footnotes to Plato, so much of the history of Western consciousness boils down to an attempt to find love/God through indirect means. Love denied, and the somatic experience of that denial, is—as de Rougemont recognized—the hidden, and gnostic/heretical, thread of Western history.[91]

We can guess, then, what happened to de Rougemont (which he hints at), and what enabled him to produce a book that has been the source of such widespread outrage and condemnation, only to remain, after half a century, the single most important volume on the subject of love in the West. Unlike virtually all his critics, or the many writers who have studied love from a kind of intellectual (or "reasonable") viewpoint (Erich Fromm, for example), de Rougemont had known these states of "mind" from the inside (that is to say, somatically). There is every indication both that he had had a mystical experience *and* that he had been, at one point, deeply in love, and saw that in his body the two (altered) states were not very different. He had the courage to live his life at the messy core, not at the clean, theoretical periphery, and this enabled him to generate an essay that has proven to be maddeningly irrefutable, despite the fact that he was not able to generate a strictly causal argument. Indeed, many of his critics begin their rebuttals by empirical refutation of the thesis, only to wind up in an unwitting position of fundamental, if unacknowledged, agreement. For whether Cathars and troubadours formed some sort of "holy alliance" in the High Middle Ages is ultimately neither here nor there. What is clear, as a leading authority on the Cathars, René Nelli, has pointed out, is that love lyric and Cathar practice are sister phenomena, daughters of a common milieu.[92] Troubadour poetry and Catharism were effectively part of the same mode of discourse; they were both carried by a common (vernacular) language.[93] The entire region of Languedoc was soaking in the same set of ideas for something like two hundred years, and it is inevitable that troubadours and Cathars were *au courant* with each other's mode of expression. Thus, says Nelli, courtly love was one of Catharism's social forms, an accommodation of the heresy to the feudal-aristocratic exigencies of a particular locale.[94] But beyond that regional configuration is one that is translocal, transpersonal, and finally somatic: to hunger like that is to hunger for God. A spokesman for a related tradition (see below, on the Arabic thesis), Jalal ed-Din Rumi, a Sufi mystic of the thirteenth century, put it this way:

> There is both amber and lodestone.
> Whether thou art iron or straw,
> thou wilt come to the hook.[95]

Let us now turn to de Rougemont's formulation of the love/heresy relationship, as first developed by Rossetti, Aroux, and Rahn.[96]

According to de Rougemont, feudal society was cemented by a code of allegiance between a knight and his lord. The lord gave his protection; the knight put himself at the service of his lord, especially in terms of loyalty to the latter and willingness to go into battle on his behalf, should the occasion arise. This obtained in Europe roughly down to the twelfth century, and was celebrated in poems and ballads known as *chansons de geste*, which were primarily celebrations of military exploits and victories. All of this largely reflected the "monochromatic" and masculine quality of the period down to about 1050 or 1100.

The second half of the twelfth century saw the emergence of an alternative code of chivalry that conflicted with the older one, and that is perhaps most clearly evident in the prototypical love story, *Tristan and Iseult* (or *Isolde*). In this alternative, or "courtly," code, the knight became, in his own mind, the vassal of some chosen lady, and the sole basis of his loyalty to her was love. This lady was, however, distant and unavailable, in fact usually married to the knight's lord;

hence the typical structure of this triangle was an "adulterous" relationship that was never consummated. Thwarted passion was thus
built right into the structure of courtly love. "Drink to me, only, with
thine eyes," wrote Ben Jonson in his song to Celia (sixteenth century),
"And I will pledge with mine." But although this love took place at
a distance (or *because* it did), it was seen as superior to marriage, and
ultimately incompatible with it, because it was freely given, spontaneous, whereas marriage was an arrangement, imposed from without.
As a Catholic sacrament, marriage was very much like the Church,
i.e., preoccupied with form and ritual rather than content and internal
feeling. Romantic love, on the other hand, was like heresy: both were
concerned with essence, both emerged out of a true inner feeling that
then manifested itself externally. As the power of this spontaneous
feeling grew more widespread in the twelfth century, the *chanson de
geste* was replaced by the *chanson d'amour*, and the lyrics of the troubadours reflected the new sensibility. Chrétien de Troyes (twelfth
century) wrote of this new feeling: ". . . I am so pleased to want thus
that I suffer agreeably, and have so much joy in my pain that I am
sick with delight." This paradox of "love-pain," or "sweet cautery,"
as one of the troubadours put it, was central to the whole psychological
structure of courtly love.[97]

What lovers love, in this new configuration, is the psychological
structure itself, which is to say they love the state of being in love.
Hence, "love is blind"; Tristan and Iseult do not really know each
other, or even want to know each other. "Their need for one another,"
says de Rougemont, "is in order to be aflame." So obstacles become
crucial here, because without them there would be no tale (*roman*,
romance); and this is as true of *Romeo and Juliet* as it is of *West Side
Story*. As Dorothy Tennov says, limerence that is quickly satisfied
quickly dies. Certainly, as far as European literature goes, happy love
has no history.

The whole phenomenon of an altered state of consciousness that
constitutes the bliss of being in love is not, of course, unique to twelfth-
century Europe, or to the troubadours of Occitania. It becomes part
of the Western cultural mainstream after that, but falling in love has
occurred, very probably, in all cultures and at all times, as extant
fragments of ancient Egyptian love poetry, or the Song of Songs,
would suggest. However, like the presence of ego structure, it varies
from culture to culture; and in antiquity, or in China or India, limerence
was regarded as aberrant, a form of madness, not unlike the aberration
of Narcissus.[98] Its roots, says de Rougemont, lie in ancient dualistic

mythologies, such as Manichaeanism (third century A.D.), and, before that, Iranian and Orphic mystery religions. All of these dualistic cosmologies saw matter, and this world, as evil; and they developed body practices and disciplines that trained the mind to leave the body and ascend to the heavens. This yogic search for the Absolute, says de Rougemont, lies at the heart of the Western problem of romantic love. In a word, the sources of our own limerent behavior are Eastern and Gnostic. Yet as soon as we say this, we are confronted with a paradox: in the East, limerence is relatively unknown. Love is seen simply as pleasure; there is no great interest in passion as such. How is it that our own erotic asceticism has Eastern sources, yet as a state of mind is largely foreign to Eastern cultures?

The situation is complicated further by the fact that the Western mystical tradition is epithalamian, i.e., it aims at a *marriage* between the soul and God, whereas the Eastern variety is unitive—its goal is a *fusion* of the soul with God. Gerard Manley Hopkins, for example, is a Catholic poet clearly within the epithalamian tradition, whereas the Sufis are a good example of the unitive type of mysticism. Heresy in the West largely consists of being too "Eastern," i.e., of describing your experience as that of *becoming* God. It was this sort of thing that got Meister Eckhart into trouble, and that always made it difficult for the Church to classify one mystic as a saint and another one as a troublemaker. But the point here, insofar as love is concerned, is that epithalamian mysticism is equivalent to *agape*, and unitive mysticism, which involves total merger, to *eros*. Hence once again we are faced with a curious paradox that as things worked out in actual practice, it was the West that got caught up in a "terrestrial form of the cult of Eros," and the East that cleanly divided love into physical pleasure, on one hand, and *caritas*, or compassion, on the other.

There are a number of reasons for this strange reversal, and among them, said de Rougemont, is the fact that Christianity, from very early days, sought to extirpate dualistic and pagan beliefs, which included the worship of the Great Mother, Sophia (wisdom), or Woman as a prophetic being. The result of this was not the elimination of these beliefs, but the driving of them underground. In this process—a process that Joseph Campbell has called "the collapse of the mythological layer"—the archetypal level of the ancient worship got dislocated, and a kind of category error occurred: the ordinary woman, as love object, came to be experienced as Sophia; or, in Jung's terminology, as the anima. In this way romantic love, as a profane form of archaic religious experience, began to spread through Western culture. Friedrich Heer captured something important here when he wrote, "We cannot hope to understand the atmosphere surrounding the courtly romances unless we accept as fact this close union of the primeval and magical with hard-headed practical politics."[99] The East, somehow, worked its archetypes differently. By and large, nothing got classified as heresy and hence there was no repression of religious beliefs. As a result, woman remained woman and the Great Mother, as well as the anima, remained archetypes. A woman didn't have to be put on a pedestal in order to be loved, and hence the style was one of *caritas* rather than idealization. In a similar vein, the East, and for that matter the female world, has not been preoccupied with heroes, Grail legends, and in general, vision-quests; something we shall have to return to at the conclusion of this book.[100]

De Rougemont's second argument for the dialectical switching between East and West is that in unitive mysticism, the soul can reach God; hence the soul's career is a happy one and a vocabulary of passion and longing is unnecessary. In the epithalamian version, however, such a vocabulary is necessary because the soul can never reach its divine goal. Love becomes something that takes one out of the world, something that leads to ultimate understanding (*conoscenza*, in Provençal), in troubadour poems or (later) in the language of mystics such as Saint John of the Cross or Saint Teresa of Avila. The talk is necessarily that of an agony over separation and of a fusion that is cruelly denied. Once again, the crushing of heresy by the Church drove all this underground, where it invaded the European mind in "shadow" form and got picked up in language and literature. Modern love songs, as well as emotional attitudes, are thus the secular expression of the debris of the ancient mystery religions.

Where do the Cathars fit into this? Of all the repression of heretics during the Middle Ages, the Church attack on the Albigensian heresy was the worst. Of course, by now we can recognize how courtly love echoes the life and beliefs of the Perfect: the yearning for God, the desire to escape matter (a concrete, flesh-and-blood woman) in favor of spirit (an archetype), the emphasis on inner feeling (*eros*) rather than ritual observance (marriage, *caritas*), the practice of sexual abstinence, and so on. And we can also recognize the coincidence of time and place: both Catharism and courtly love made their most dramatic appearance in the Midi in the twelfth century. True, said de Rougemont, the troubadour poems never explicitly referred to Catharist beliefs, but this was because it was dangerous to do so. However, he claimed, the woman being addressed in these poems was the anima, which appeared to men in the course of their spiritual/heretical practice as a female entity, or feminine principle. It was only a category confusion that subsequently transferred an archetype onto real persons. How do we know this? Of course we don't, and although some troubadours were undoubtedly Cathars, or Cathar sympathizers, it is not necessarily the case that many or most were.[101] But de Rougemont was not constructing an absolute relationship, as did Otto Rahn; his argument, at least in later editions of the book (see note 104), was that courtly poetry was inspired by Cathar mysticism as an indirect influence: gnostic dualism permeated the air of Occitania, and both the Cathars and troubadours breathed the same atmosphere. For this reason, the famous "Arabic thesis" on the origins of courtly love—that it came to Occitania via the Moors, and represented an Islamic mystical tradition—is not really a refutation of the argument for the influence of Catharism. De Rougemont was certainly not opposed to the Arabic thesis, and it is very likely the case, as one writer notes, that courtly love was a "phenomenon produced by the interaction of Latin and Moorish elements with the social conditions of Provence. . . . "[102] The point is that the cosmopolitanism of the south left it open to mystical influences; that Sufis and Cathars alike talked in terms of a yearning for the Godhead; that the heretical Islamic tradition involved the same mind/body duality that the heretical Christian tradition did, and if it was an influence on Provençal poetry, this was only because the Midi was already susceptible to such an influence. Thus René Nelli argues that it is not really a matter of philosophical system, insofar as the troubadours were concerned; it is not likely that they even *had* one. They effectively borrowed parts of those metaphysical systems, such as Catharism or Islamic mysticism, that agreed with their imaginations.[103] It was a case of somatic resonance, part of what de Rougemont called a "twelfth-century psychic revolution" that involved a widespread awakening to the feminine principle. "It shared in the epiphany of the *Anima* which . . . marked the reappearance in Western man of a symbolical East."[104] The central importance of this reappearance of a symbolical East, and, it would seem, a symbolic feminine, was perhaps best summarized by Friedrich Heer, in a passage worth quoting at length:

> [M]edieval civilization, particularly during its "open" period, is to be understood as a coexistence of highly improbable opposites. . . . This paradoxical civilization found in the figures, symbols and "adventures" of the *roman courtois* the artistic and formal

expression ideally suited to it. As in a tapestry, the motifs inter-
twine in complex arabesques of meaning, drawn from many different worlds. Historians, theologians and philologists . . . have
all tried their hands at drawing out a single thread, be it of Christian, Persian, Gnostic, Cathar, druidical or Islamic origin. These
invidious attempts are understandable, and can in a sense be
justified. But they are an injustice perpetrated against the living
reality of a work of art and the compelling power of its "symbolic"
figures. It is, in fact, the veil of form and symbol that gives the
*roman courtois* its power . . . [T]he theme of the great romantic
epics . . . is initiation, dedication, metamorphosis and absorption
into a higher and fuller life, at once more human and more divine.

All Chrétien's work, indeed all Arthurian romances of the first
rank, were attempts at expounding the processes of man's interior
development. . . . The remedies prescribed for the man who has
strayed a thousand times into the jungle of his immature passions
are women, "nature," *mysterium.* In the *romans,* therefore, a woman
is always at hand to transform and ennoble a man. Through his
relationship with the woman the man gains access to his own
soul, to the deeper layers of his "heart." . . . [105]

The notion of a psychic revolution in the West, based on Eastern
influences and a revaluation of the archetypal feminine, gets us to the
heart of what I have been pursuing in this chapter on heresy as a
secret, somatic "skeleton key," as it were, to the history of Western
consciousness at large. It amounts to a breakthrough to interiority, an
overturning of a previous "masculine" *mentalité* at certain nodal points
in our political history; and it is the immediate political context that
shaped, in each case, what happened to the immense psychic energy
that got released. In the case of our Greek model, it had (in my view)
an unfortunate ending: amidst the rich diversity of Greek philosophy
and shamanism, Jewish ethics and magic, and Oriental Gnostic practices that made the culture of the Mediterranean basin so exciting and
heterogeneous, one system managed to triumph. Christianity was
victorious over its competitors, including the Roman Empire, only to
become a Roman Empire of the mind for the next several hundred
years. When the next challenge to it arose, it could only respond as
a political monolith, repressing the opposition and/or co-opting it by
means of the Cult of the Virgin Mary (more on this below). The French
model has as a major characteristic the creation of unintended side
effects that are still with us today: the rise of the nation-state; the final
canonization of dualistic thinking, which is ultimately simplistic; the

legitimizing of investigation into "thought crime," and the administrative persecution of it (to varying degrees); the unexpected channeling of the gnostic impulse of moving toward union with God into
the love of another human being as a secular/ecstatic experience. Both
romantic love and mind control get institutionalized as a result of the
Church's repression and co-optation of the Cathars. This process of
a rebellious heresy actually playing into the hands of the powers that
be is what I take to be the central feature of the French model, and it
is certainly one capable of being repeated today.[106]

We must be clear, then, as to what the whole "love thing" was
about. Despite the outrage of de Rougemont's critics, it can now be
seen that his broader thesis, that of the second edition (1956) of his
work, was actually quite bland. Thus he argued in his 1972 postscript
to the book "that troubadours and Cathars cannot be understood
*separately*, outside of the broad religious—or psychosocial—phenomenon which includes them and carries them from the twelfth to the
fourteenth century."[107] That phenomenon was the awakening of interiority, which includes the sermons of Bernard of Clairvaux on the
Song of Songs, the redefinition of friendship and of piety (spiritual
commitment), and the "discovery of the individual," as historian Colin
Morris once put it, which had romantic love as its most intense, and
obvious, expression. Paul Alphandéry was certainly right when he
said that the whole development constituted a breakup of church-
feudal authoritarianism, that mysticism "penetrated the masses," and
that this lay mysticism constituted a major step in the development
of the human personality in the West. What happened to this flowering of interiority in the hands of the Church is another story; but
we still live in the psychic fallout of this remarkable somatic rediscovery.[108]

A word, then, must be added regarding the Church co-optation of
Catharism and romantic love by means of the Cult of the Virgin, before
we move on to the next major breakthrough of heretical activity in
the sixteenth century. De Rougemont described it as follows:

In order to counter this powerful and almost universal rise of
Love of the cult of Idealized Woman, the Church and clergy were
bound to set up a belief and worship which met the same profound desire, as this sprang up out of the communal spirit of the
time. While the Church had to fall in with that desire, the Church
had also to "convert" it and lead it into the strong stream of
orthodoxy. . . . Hence the repeated attempts from the beginning

of the twelfth century onwards to institute a worship of the Virgin. It is from that time that Mary has generally received the title of *Regina coeli*. . . . [109]

The co-optation of romantic love by the Church, i.e., the diverting of this gnostic experience into a specific Catholic archetype, was a far greater victory for the Church than its physical destruction of heresy, though the two processes went hand in hand. Archetypes, as Jung pointed out, guide our individual destinies. We (usually unwittingly) live out our major dramas in their terms, which is to say, in terms of the third body. More than that, if these archetypes acquire the dimensions of a political movement (essentially de Rougemont's argument about romantic love), they start to operate on the level of the fifth body; i.e., they become public and dominant, not just privately transpersonal. Enormous power then hangs in the balance, and it was this that the Church intuitively understood. The process of co-optation was thus one of interior colonization; it was not merely about the Lady of the Cathar heresy or the love object of the Provençal poet vs. the Virgin Mary, but about *the process of interiority itself*; about its guiding symbols and images, ones that direct the energy of the human personality. The flip side of Inquisitional thought crime was the symbolic control and manipulation of this unconscious energy. As Hitler was to demonstrate much later on (see Chapter 8), there is no greater political power than this.

Two things become crucial to understanding the dynamics of this battle, and why it was Mary specifically who was used by the Church for its ends. One is that in a male-dominated society—i.e., one in which institutional control was almost uniformly (except in the south of France, significantly enough) in the hands of men, the third body, or soul, or interior voice, presented itself as a woman—not surprising from a Jungian perspective, at least. The second reason is one that might seem bizarre at first, except when we realize that the symbolism of all of Christendom revolved around the Eucharist, the eating of Christ's body: the relationship of the soul to God was frequently one of ingestion, or swallowing. I shall deal with each of these in turn, before returning to the Marian co-optation of romantic love.

The concept of the soul (*anima*) as female did not require a Catharist or troubadour heresy for its formulation. Indeed, in the Cathar religion, the soul was sexless, or even masculine before its reabsorption into the Absolute. The discovery of an interior feminine from the eleventh century on was quickly made part of the Christian mainstream. In this category, for the twelfth century at least, it was Bernard of Clairvaux who led the way, especially in his famous series of sermons on the Song of Songs, no less than eighty-six of them, "that together form one of Christian mysticism's most astonishing masterpieces."[110] The Song of Songs, which probably dates from the fifth century B.C., focuses very clearly on the subjective experience of desire. In Bernard's hands, it is a mystical system in which one is transfigured by love. The love here, despite Bernard's claim to be speaking about *agape*, is clearly erotic, with sexuality as the guiding metaphor for ecstatic union. But it is the Virgin who symbolizes this union, who is seen as having attained this (spiritual) perfection. Bernard makes her personal; she becomes "the private sweetheart of monks and sinners." His commentaries draw heavily on the fusion terminology of both Plato's *Symposium* and the Song of Songs, as "metaphors of merging, dissolving, fusing, [and] absorbing swim in his stream of consciousness." Hard masculine boundaries are lost; the man's armor melts away as he surrenders to the internal, and often maternal, feminine.[111] Already by the eleventh century, Saint Anselm used the phrase "Christ, my mother," and Bernard's own experience of God was a mixture of the maternal and the erotic. "Bernard's sermons," writes one commentator, ". . . are forcible reminders that medieval male Christians, in so far as they spoke of themselves as a soul before God, spoke of themselves as *female*."[112] Historian Caroline Walker Bynum agrees: twelfth-century religious writing, she says, "shows an outburst of mystical theology after hundreds of years of silence about it and a great increase in devotion to female figures." Nuptial themes were similarly popular among male mystical writers in the twelfth century. God was now becoming loving and accessible; and to men, this meant that both She and the soul were female. From the twelfth century on, erotic and sexual imagery was used to describe the union of the soul with Christ.[113]

The connection to eating or swallowing, our second point, should be pretty obvious. A maternal god is a nurturing one; she has breasts as well as flesh, and feeds her children from both. Medieval texts use the image of the soul eating God; a few English writers even describe the soul as possessing a mouth, gums, and teeth. Julian of Norwich, in the fourteenth century, speaks of the soul *swallowing* God. The assumption in these writings, as in certain mystery cults of antiquity, is that the tasting of God leads to spiritual knowledge of Him (or Her).[114] This point was not lost on one of Catholicism's greatest defenders, John Henry Cardinal Newman, many centuries later, when he explained that a major reason for his conversion to the Roman Church was its emphasis on orality. He could, he said, only believe in a god whom he could eat, directly absorb into his body.[115] What comes home here is the sheer physicality of religion, i.e., religion that is experienced as a bodily phenomenon. True spiritual experience is about transformation, and perhaps nothing is so immediately transformative as the physical incorporation of some external substance into one's body. As Caroline Walker Bynum puts it, eating is "the most basic and literal way of encountering God."[116]

By the twelfth, and especially the thirteenth, century, Mary, and Christ as mother, became very popular images in terms of metaphors for love, *eros*, fusion, nursing, and eating. A cult of the Virgin's milk had surfaced; men and women were also seen as drinking from the breast of Jesus. Bernard urged the monks at Clairvaux to suck the breasts of the crucified Christ. Christ's blood was also seen as nourishment, and his crucified body was equated with food. Eating his flesh was thus the redemption of humanity. In feeding the world with his blood and flesh, he was regarded as mother.[117]

The process of co-optation was not that difficult for the Church. Whereas the Cathar and troubadour Lady was often vague, unspecified, and "decentralized," the Church had a ready-made love object that was familiar and specific, and that had been growing in popularity since the tenth century. Its ability to capture the somatic/archetypal imagination was very strong, even in the Midi, especially once the back of Catharism had been broken. From the twelfth century, hymns to the Virgin, addressing her as queen or agent of mercy, began to circulate, including the hauntingly beautiful *Salve Regina*, which speaks of exile and inwardness.[118] Crusaders may have sung it on the battlefield, and we see how all of this—Crusades, Marian hymns, and the awakening of interiority—was all of a piece. It is about a new spiritual energy, the discovery of being exiled from God, and the search for something to plug the resultant (somatic) gap. Bernard ached for the Virgin; in the twelfth century, the Cistercian order established hundreds of abbeys devoted to her, and numerous cathedrals were built in her honor. Convents multiplied in Occitania, as did the Virgin cult, and after the Albigensian crusades Mariolatry became mixed in with secular love lyric. The erotic asceticism of Languedoc was invaded by this worship of Mary, who became, according to the medieval historian Marina Warner, nothing more than "an establishment prop." The whole thing, she says, was "one of the Church's most successful intellectual operations," viz., the "transference of yearning and desire to the figure of the Virgin. . . . " The next generation of troubadours began to shift their focus to Mary; she became Notre Dame, and a lot of potentially heretical energy was transmuted, or siphoned off. "The heresy of the troubadours," writes Marina Warner, " . . . had been trampled underfoot, and [Mary's] name invoked in the battle."[119]

Let us, then, summarize the French model of heresy before moving on to the next one. The real development of the eleventh to the thirteenth centuries is the recovery of interiority, of which heresy and romantic love, both rooted in a powerful somatic experience, constitute the most dramatic public expression. The reaction of the dominant culture—a culture profoundly cut off from body experience—was a combination of repression and co-optation, and the fallout includes the emergence of thought crime and the corresponding need for bureaucratic persecution of it; the secularization of romantic love; the collapse of cultural pluralism, and the accompanying rise of centralization and the nation-state as fact and concept; and the "official" absorption of dualist cosmology (the world is a battleground of Good vs. Evil) into the mainstream of Western Christendom and, really, Western thought. All of this fallout, with the possible exception of the destruction of cultural pluralism, was unintended; it was the unplanned by-product of the Church's assault on the Catharist heresy.

There are certain similarities between the Greek and French models in terms of preconditions. In both cases, we have (a) a situation of cultural pluralism overlaid by a dominant establishment; and (b) a situation of repression triggered by a perceived threat to that establishment. The big difference, however, is that the French model rests on the emergence of an entire culture into interiority, a shift in *mentalité* that was a profoundly dislocating development. And this plays a key role in our evaluation of whether the French model could be repeated today. Emerging into interiority is not possible for us; we are *already* a self-conscious people. Yet the great lesson here is the one of co-optation, and it seems to me that this *is* repeatable. Points (a) and (b) exist for us in the form of a technological, industrial culture that has largely taken over the globe and has, in terms of a dominant reality system associated with Western science, colonized our consciousness. The emergence of an alternative reality system is perceived as a threat at those points where power or authority is involved: holistic vs. allopathic medical practice in hospitals, "soft" energy options vs. nuclear power, the revival of the occult sciences, or the emergence of a "new paradigm" literature vs. mechanistic/materialistic science (and social science) as taught in educational institutions. And it is possible, in those situations, not that the new "heretics" will be burnt at the stake, but that the dominant establishment has its own version of Marian symbolism and can use those symbols to suck up the energy of the opposition and actually strengthen its own domination and control as a result. Unlike the Greek model, this scenario is a strong possibility, and one that we shall return to in Chapter 9. Before we can discuss it, however, we need to look at the rise of modern science itself, which was, at least in part, the product of an initially diffuse heretical movement.

# 7

# Science and Magic

*I hold the search for essences to be equally
impossible and futilely exhausting in the case
of elementary substances which are to hand, as
for celestial substances which are very distant
. . . I do not understand the true essence of
earth or fire any better than I understand that
of the moon or the sun: such knowledge awaits
us when we have come to the state of heavenly
bliss, and only then.*

—Galileo Galilei,
*Letters on Sunspots*

*Every one who has lived since the sixteenth
century has felt deep distrust of every one
who lived before it . . .*

—Henry Adams,
*Mont-Saint-Michel and Chartres*

THE HERETICAL CYCLE IS, at least in very broad terms, invariable. There
is a form that has outlived its ability to provide any genuine spiritual
experience; a group arises that points this out, and demonstrates its
own ability to deliver the goods (the essence); it finally succeeds,
becoming the new orthodoxy; and in the space of a century or less,
it itself has forgotten about essence and is preoccupied with form. As
a result, it evokes a new heretical challenge . . . etc. Pharisaic Judaism,

bogged down in ritual observance, spawned magical and ascent practice in its midst; this led to a breakaway movement organized around the memory (or legend) of Jesus Christ; and by the time the Roman emperor converted to the new religion—actually, long before this—it had ossified into the most rigid and monolithic structure the world has ever known. Enter the Cathars several centuries later, and the cycle begins again; although the Cathars were wiped out before the cycle could run its natural course.

What I shall call, in this chapter, the "Italian model" is about the rise of modern science, and it follows the general outline of the heretical cycle pretty closely. In this case, the form or cultural crust that had to be broken was Church Aristotelianism and academic Scholasticism, which, by the sixteenth century certainly, had completely lost touch with the natural world that it purported to describe. One story has it that anatomical demonstrations at medical schools in the late Middle Ages had the operator cutting open a human body with one hand and holding a copy of Galen's anatomy (second century A.D.) in the other, proclaiming, "This is a liver!" as he plucked out a kidney and held it up before the credulous students. By 1620, when Francis Bacon published *Novum Organum* (New Instrument), calling for interaction with nature instead of mere discussion of nature, the new consciousness was slowly but steadily gaining ground.

But why should this be linked with heresy? True, Galileo's trial was a heresy trial, but this is not the sort of heresy we are dealing with in this book. Where do ascent, magical practice, gnosticism, and the like fit into the rise of modern science? Although it is still a matter of some debate, many historians have been forced to conclude that such esoteric doctrines and practices were crucial to the emergence of the scientific worldview.[1] There is much magic in Bacon's work, for example, and in the sixteenth century, distinctions between magic and science were (from a modern viewpoint) scrambled, very difficult to sort out.[2] For what the two traditions had in common proved to be more significant historically than what they later had apart; and what they had in common was an outlook that encouraged an active posture toward the natural world. Science and magic are hardly identical, to be sure, but both have a strong manipulative component, and it is in this sense that magic came to serve as the midwife of modern science. The occult/craft tradition that led to the experimental method of modern science constantly appealed to the "powers of nature" as well as to the power of man as an operator upon nature. Aristotelianism and

Scholasticism were seen as moribund, providing only academic descriptions of the natural world. Magic, and later science, proposed instead to tap its energies; and as in the case of the Cathars and romantic love, we are now living with the fallout (literally, in the case of science) of this psychic and intellectual reorientation.

To what extent ascent practice, in particular, was relevant to these events is unclear. Certainly, magic was relevant; and I have called this model "Italian" because there was a tendency, from the late fifteenth century, for Italian thinkers in particular to become disenchanted with medieval Scholasticism and begin to experiment with the magical worldview and its manipulative aspects. Once again, the body is the point at issue, because magical practice is highly concrete and sensual, engaging the senses of taste, smell, sound, and touch, and not merely vision, which is more "purely" scientific (telescope, microscope, etc.) in holding things at a distance for detached observation. Alchemy, for example, was typically tied to practices of breathing and chanting.[3] The revival of the occult that began during the Renaissance opened up the possibility of a dynamic and multifaceted reality, one that, as in the case of Catharism, was somatically based. Yet the context in which it emerged rendered such a vision completely unstable: the "crack between worlds" was all that the magical worldview finally amounted to, as western Europe went from one system of rationality— the Church Aristotelianism of Thomas Aquinas—to another, viz., the mechanical worldview of modern science. In a sense, this too was a case of co-optation, as in the case of the French model, but with a curious twist: there was no "co-opter," unless the co-opter can be identified as capitalism and the rising bourgeoisie. What I really mean, of course, is that there was no "conspiracy" going on. It was rather that the political and economic fortunes of Europe were moving toward stability, and in such a context magic was far too fragile to endure qua magic. The tendency to reify it proved to be too strong, with the result that science and technology effectively became the magic of the modern era.[4] The Italian model is thus one of the loosening of one system of rationality by an involvement in magical and somatic awareness, only to result in a congealing of that awareness into a new system of rationality; specifically, a new science. As in the case of the Greek and French models, my primary interest, which I shall deal with later, is whether this is a unique case or whether it has elements that are repeatable in our own time.

As already noted, the first stage in this process was a disenchantment with the older forms of thought, especially in terms of their practical inability to *do* anything. Once again, the social context of this cannot be ignored, for this was the age of exploration and travel, the rise of mercantile capital and of early industrial expansion, especially in the areas of mining and shipbuilding. This commercial revolution was widespread throughout western Europe, with the Italian states becoming centers of banking, trade, financial enterprise, and military consolidation. In all of these countries, magic had strong associations with "the arts," i.e., with crafts and technology; and in this new, proto-capitalist context, its active and manipulative aspects made it extremely attractive. In Christopher Marlowe's version of the Faust story, for example, he has Doctor Faustus sitting in his study, circa 1590, reading the works of Aristotle and becoming increasingly bored. "Is to dispute well logic's chiefest end?" he finally says out loud; "Affords this art no greater miracle?/Then read no more. . . . "[5] It is at this point that Faustus invites supernatural forces in, but this path had been, by 1590, well trodden for more than a century, especially in Italy. In the fifteenth century, the Florentine Academy, under Marsilio Ficino—who had already (in 1463) translated the old occult lore, the *Hermetica,* or Hermetic corpus, from Greek into Latin—dabbled heavily in astrology, Jewish number mysticism, and related arts. Inevitably, this opened up the world of fantasy, dream, and intense sensual experience, and gave these men a lever by which to pry themselves loose from the sterile concepts of medieval Scholasticism.

The thesis that magic was the midwife of modern science is perhaps most closely identified with the British historian Frances Yates (see note 1). According to her, it was the function of the will that was most affected by this activity. She writes that "the real function of the Renaissance Magus in relation to the modern period . . . is that he changed the will. It was now dignified and important for man to operate [on nature]. . . . " Yates continues:

> It was this basic psychological reorientation towards a direction of the will which was neither Greek nor mediaeval in spirit, which made all the difference.
>
> What were the emotional sources of the new attitude? They lie . . . in the religious excitement caused by the rediscovery of the *Hermetica,* and their attendant Magia; in the overwhelming emotions aroused by the Cabala and its magico-religious techniques. It is magic as an aid to gnosis which begins to turn the will in the new direction.[6]

This new orientation was hardly the exclusive property of Italy; yet again and again, it was the Italian magicians/scientists who seemed to form the cultural avant-garde: Giordano Bruno, Marsilio Ficino, Bernardino Telesio, Girolamo Cardano, Francesco Giorgi, Pico della Mirandola, Tommaso Campanella, Giambattista della Porta, et al. And the role of heresy in all of this is well established: during their lifetimes, most of these men were in trouble with the Church authorities to varying degrees, ranging from censure to imprisonment, torture, and—in the case of Bruno—death.

Where do ascent and soul travel fit into all of this? As in the case of the Cathars, much of the evidence is circumstantial, and not that easy to uncover; but there are a few case studies that strongly suggest that five-body practice was going on. The case of Giordano Bruno is as good a place to start as any. Born in the city of Nola, near Naples, in 1548, Bruno became a Dominican and soon after that a teacher of a branch of magic known as the memory art.[7] His travels were always marked by controversy, and the period 1583–85 found him in England, attached to the retinue of the French ambassador. During this period he wrote his major works, in dialogue form (as Galileo was to do not too many years later), including *La Cena de le ceneri* (The Supper of Ashes, or Ash Wednesday Supper), which was his defense and exposition of the heliocentric, or Copernican, theory of the universe. In 1592 he returned to Italy, strangely convinced that he could convert the pope to the ancient Hermetic philosophy, which he regarded as the "true" Christianity. He was soon arrested by the Inquisition and imprisoned for eight years, during which time his apparently heretical views were examined on a number of occasions. On February 17, 1600, scoffing at his executioners and refusing to look at the crucifix held up before him, Bruno was led out to the Campo dei Fiori in Rome and burnt at the stake.[8]

We might get confused if we regard Bruno's Copernicanism as strictly, or even largely, scientific in nature. After all, why would a book on heliocentricity be called *Ash Wednesday Supper*? *Cena*, in fact, refers to the Eucharist, or the Lord's Supper (in Italian, da Vinci's masterpiece is called *Il Cenacolo*). The light in the center of the universe is hardly an optical one for Bruno (though it could be); it is more specifically the divine light present in every human being, and accessible by means of magical practice; which was (he believed) what the Mass, and the Eucharist—i.e., the miracle of transubstantiation—originally were. The Copernican sun was for Bruno an ancient Egyptian light, one that would dispel the present darkness of the world. Heliocentricity—the

physical fact of a sun-centered universe (or, at least, solar system)—
was thus for Bruno the astronomical confirmation of an ancient magic,
and his ill-fated trip to Italy was an attempt to get the pope to "see
the light," the Egyptian/Hermetic core of the original Christian religion, from which, he asserted, the Roman Church had strayed. Hence
also his refusal to look at the cross when taken out to die: the Church
was using this symbol to deny the real (magical) content of its own
religion—as the Cathars, among other heretics, had argued repeatedly.[9]

The blur between science and magic becomes clear when we read
*Ash Wednesday Supper* and examine Bruno's discussion of certain optical
thought experiments with opaque and luminous bodies. From a modern scientific viewpoint he is occasionally correct (but more often not),
but his goal was not science as we understand the term; *nobody's* goal
was this in 1583, with the exception of a very few thinkers. In addition
to regarding Copernicus as a reviver of the Hermetic tradition, Bruno
believed in the gnostic doctrine of soul travel, and was in all likelihood
a practitioner of it; his language, at once magical, poetic, and ecstatic,
is very revealing on this score.[10] In *Ash Wednesday Supper*, Bruno claimed
to be a prophet of the new Hermetic movement because he had had
the ascent experience; and he saw the Copernican theory, which did
away with the crystalline spheres of the heavens of medieval Aristotelian (or Ptolemaic) astronomy, as facilitating this process. Thus
Bruno writes that he had "pierced the air, penetrated the sky, toured
the realm of stars, [and] traversed the boundaries of the world. . . ."[11]
Bruno, writes Frances Yates, "has made the gnostic ascent, has had
the Hermetic experience, and so has become divine, with the Powers
within him." And we should not be surprised—shades of de Rougemont—that Bruno uses the language of romantic love to describe the
gnostic trance, in which the soul leaves the body and ascends to God.
Love, in fact, was central to Bruno's entire cosmology.[12]

For Bruno as well as other contemporary thinkers, soul travel and
ascent experience lay at the heart of the heretical and magical challenge
to Church Aristotelianism, at the center of this new mode of investigating nature. Thus Lawrence Lerner and Edward Gosselin
write:

> the Hermeticists believed man had descended voluntarily from
> the non-material world of the Divine Mind to earth and continued
> to partake of the divine nature that had been his before the de-
> scent. There was indeed a channel for continual communication

between man in his divine aspect and God. This channel could be deepened and widened by acquiring a kind of recondite knowledge we would call occult. . . . As a result of the curious juxtaposition of belief in magic and in reason as paths to knowledge of God, many serious scholars, including Dee, Gilbert, Ficino and Paracelsus, took part simultaneously (and with no sense of incongruity) in magical and scientific investigations.

This mystical connection, they continue,

provided a means for manipulating the universe. If God could use the connection in a "downward" fashion to perform supernatural deeds as well as natural ones, man could do the same by working "upward" through the performance of magic. From this standpoint the boundary between magic and scientific investigation, which in modern times is clear, becomes indistinct. The Neoplatonists saw no inconsistency between the two activities; indeed, they were regarded as being complementary and mutually reinforcing.[13]

In a word, the control of nature, which lies at the heart of the modern scientific paradigm, has its historical roots in the Renaissance-Hermetic version of soul travel, or ascent.[14] The basis of the magic/science overlap, of the manipulation of the natural world (macrocosm) for the benefit of human beings (the microcosm) was that there was a real and experiential channel between this world and the next one. This later got converted into an ideology (Newtonian Puritanism, as well as the natural theology tradition—"through nature up to nature's God"), and the esoteric/somatic kernel fell by the wayside. Yet all of (pure) science is the search for God, and remains so to this day (though this is rarely admitted); and Bruno's optical thought experiments can clearly be understood in this way.[15] When he discussed the illumination of opaque bodies, for example, he was talking about the "lighting up" of the host by the divine light of Christ; he was saying to his readers—as he foolishly attempted to say to the pope and the Inquisition—that gnostic illumination is the crux of Christianity and must be restored to its rightful place. Similarly, heliocentricity is important because it implies that the universe has more than one center, and by extension, so does the mind of the human being. In Hermetic practice and philosophy, the mind becomes what it contemplates; hence, by this mystical means, the "man-microcosm becomes universe-microcosm and as a result is brought closer to the Creator."[16] In other words, heliocentricity is, among other things, a way of confirming the Gnostic/Hermetic theory of two worlds united through soul travel, i.e., through the ancient doctrine of ascent, which, as we have seen, is the centerpiece, or hidden somatic doctrine, of all previous heretical thought. Modern science, again, is the shell of this insight, with, however, the notion of a descent of celestial influence strongly present as well. In brief, it is the ideology of Hermetic soul travel with the esoteric or somatic core left out.

The notion of soul travel and science being linked through the philosophy and practice of magic is an intriguing one, and the link can be found in other thinkers of the Italian Renaissance in addition to Giordano Bruno. Pico della Mirandola (1463–94), for example, gave evidence of this link in his manifesto of Renaissance magic, the famous *Oration on the Dignity of Man*.[17] The magus, he said, marries earth to heaven. Natural magic is the practical part of natural science, and through the use of the cabala, which establishes links between heaven and earth, natural magic is strengthened. In particular, he said, one can go straight to God, without using intermediary causes; and Pico described the trance state in which this direct communication occurs, and in which, in a state of ecstasy, the soul leaves the body and ascends to heaven. Pico, says Yates, was very preoccupied by this experience; he was probably speaking out of direct acquaintance with it, not out of theoretical abstractions. Pico, in fact, learned the techniques from Spanish Jews, who—at least in the thirteenth century (see the previous chapter)—had been very explicit about these techniques and their effects and had even described them in printed texts.[18] "Through the intensive cult of angels," writes Frances Yates, "cabala reaches up into religious spheres. . . . " In general, she adds, the cabalistic system is a ladder to God, which one climbs by means of meditative techniques. By means of magic, she continues,

> man has learned how to use the chain linking earth to heaven, and by Cabala, he has learned to manipulate the higher chain linking the celestial world, through the angels, to the divine Nature.[19]

It was the somatic awareness of the phenomenon of ascent, the very possibility of soul travel, that for Pico constituted the true "dignity of man." Pico thus spoke of man as an operator, a controller of heaven and earth. Frances Yates concludes that

the Dignity of Man as Magus, as operator . . . and the magical
power of marrying earth to heaven rests on the gnostic heresy
that man was once, and can become again through his intellect,
the reflection of the divine *mens*, a divine being. The final revaluation of the magician in the Renaissance is that he becomes a
divine man.[20]

This was, it seems to me, the first, and necessary, stage of the
Scientific Revolution, and we should not be surprised that Pico was
soon accused of heresy. He had to appear before a commission appointed by Pope Innocent VIII, finally flee to France, and, inevitably,
spend time in prison. But clearly the cat was out of the bag: the dignity
of man lay not in Aristotelian contemplation, but in somatic techniques
that catapulted man to the status of a god, using cabala and "natural
magic" to control his destiny and, ultimately, the destiny of the world
(body number five). This reversion to ancient Gnosticism, this "going
backward to go forward," constituted the key in the lock of modern
science.

Pico and Bruno, along with others such as Marsilio Ficino, Francesco
Giorgi, and the English alchemist Robert Fludd, were (to use Arthur
Koestler's terminology) prewatershed figures.[21] Their goal was explicitly magical. Figures who can be labeled "watershed," in that their
goal (conscious or unconscious), or at least their effect, was to reduce
magic to science, include John Dee, Ralph Cudworth, Henry More,
Tommaso Campanella, Giambattista della Porta, Girolamo Cardano,
Johannes Kepler, and the early Isaac Newton. Figures who are postwatershed include Galileo, Marin Mersenne (though not completely),
and the later Newton. While it is not possible to discuss any of these
men in detail (I have already done so elsewhere in the case of Newton),[22] a brief survey of their work is necessary in order to trace the
evolution and eventual fate of the ascent/descent doctrine and the
whole question of soul travel as it got transmuted from direct experience (magic) to mathematical and mechanical analogy (modern science).

A good deal, of course, could be said (and has been said) about
each of these figures, and thus I have to be fairly selective in my
approach. Ficinian magic, for example, has been treated in detail by
D. P. Walker and Frances Yates, and there is no doubt of Ficino's
interest in magical practice, especially in incantations and hymns, to
draw down the "celestial influence."[23] The theory is the classic Neo-
platonic/Gnostic one, that the soul or astral body or etheric vehicle

begins in a pure state, or one of fire, and becomes heavy and impure as it descends down through the various stars and spheres to become incarnated in an earthly body. Our job on this earth is to repurify that body, get it back up to heaven, and this can be done by a series of practices: fasting, incantation, the use of incense, prayers and images, and so on.[24] Ficino was particularly interested in the role of music in this process, and this was especially emphasized in the work of Francesco Giorgi, whose *De Harmonia Mundi* of 1525 outlines a system of numerical harmony by which one can rise through the stars to the angels. Heavily cabalistic in nature, the book constantly refers to "the One," the Source, to which it is man's spiritual destiny to return.[25] The book is remarkable for its mixture (again from our viewpoint) of science and magic. Thus Giorgi discussed the nature of ascent and ecstatic trance, and at the same time gave what might be the most explicit statement to date regarding the manipulation of nature. The art of numerology, he told his readers, will give the practitioner *vis operandi et dominandi*—the power of operating and dominating. The link between the occult/craft tradition and technology as a philosophical outlook is epitomized by this "slogan" of the early modern era. As in the case of Pico, this power of operating upon nature and dominating it, which was at first occult and later mechanistic, was regarded as the key to the dignity of man.[26]

Another important figure in this tradition was Tommaso Campanella, whose career embodied changing attitudes to magic and what we would today call paranormal phenomena.[27] Campanella was a practitioner of Ficinian magic and, like Bruno, was committed to a magical reform of Christianity. For him, Christ was simply a magus (albeit a very great one); and Campanella led a revolt in Calabria in 1599 that led to his imprisonment—he spent twenty-seven years of his life behind bars—and torture. In his book, *City of the Sun*, written in prison circa 1602, he envisioned a utopian community governed by the laws of natural magic. Although condemned, as of 1603, to perpetual imprisonment as a heretic, Campanella was in Rome in 1628, practicing Ficinian magic, constructing a sealed room and employing talismans for Pope Urban VIII (!), to protect him from his enemies (this was the same pope who would condemn Galileo only five years later). Campanella's magical practice was apparently of both the ascent and descent variety, and in one of his books he wrote that there was a divine magic that had been used by Moses and the saints, and that it enabled one to reach the higher regions, to move out beyond the limits of the known world and out to Infinity. Campanella talked of divine inspiration and angelic visions, and said that God had allowed him to witness miracles, angels, and demons.[28]

Like Bruno, Campanella saw heliocentricity as a return to ancient truth, and he wrote about this in letters to Galileo. Yet there is a shift here, a shift toward the concerns of materiality and physicality that are the hallmarks of modern science and technology, and it is this that marks Campanella as a watershed figure. Roughly speaking, the goal of watershed figures was to create a heaven on earth, i.e., to use magic for natural ends. In that proto-scientific sense, they were already slipping toward modernity. D. P. Walker notes that Campanella's sealed room, constructed for the pope, was a kind of miniature heaven; yet it also had the characteristics of a working scientific model, analogous to, let us say, a wind tunnel that might be used by a modern aerodynamics laboratory to figure out the mechanics of plane flight. Campanella's operations were not, like Ficino's, simply psychological techniques centered on the imagination, but actual attempts to operate on the physical world through a symbolic or sympathetic medium. It is also the case that much of Campanella's magic was directed to what I have referred to as the fifth body, i.e., the spiritual-political level. His magic was public, says Walker, directed toward practical ends of vast scope. Campanella wrote that "magic is the flower of all the sciences,"[29] but it is likely that he meant the reverse: coming from a magical base, Campanella's goal was perhaps more scientific than it was occult. The purpose of ascent, for Campanella, was to learn what was possible, and then to make it happen materially on this earth. Here again, we can see the "midwife" role of the magical tradition clearly at work.

Girolamo Cardano, or Jerome Cardan (1501–76), a crucial figure in the history of mathematics—he could well be called the founder of probability theory—and a leading physician and astrologer of the sixteenth century, similarly reveals this complex watershed configuration. He too found himself accused of heresy and imprisoned by the Inquisition in 1570, though the next year saw Cardano obtaining a lifetime annuity from the pope. His understanding of nature included a strong belief in an ascent/descent structure, a chain of order that emanated from the One and returned to it. His mathematics, which was very sophisticated, was also a kind of theosophy. Thus Proposition 232 of his *Liber de Proportionibus* (Book of Proportions, 1570; the fifth volume of his mathematical corpus) deals with the kinematics of rotating objects (e.g., a circle) and is supported by theosophical arguments, until it becomes a kind of mathematical ecstasy. The soul, he wrote, "having recognized God and the heavens, descends and creates new order. There is such great bliss in that other world that we cannot compare it with ours. . . . " In a similar fashion, Cardano's *De Subtilitate* (On Subtleness, 1550–51), which was frequently reprinted during the sixteenth and seventeenth centuries, describes the ascension of the mind toward God, to be carried out in nine steps, "to reach the state whereby we may become a torch of God. This," he continued, "Christ taught the eleven disciples and few other men." Cardano advocated fasting and prayer to obtain the "divine fire," and—shades of the *pardes* legend (see Chapter 5)—cautioned against the danger of insanity. The passage is vivid, and his biographer, Markus Fierz, says that it "attests to Cardano's religious experience." The numerology of Ramon Lull, a thirteenth-century Catalan mystic and philosopher, is discussed in the context of certain magical spells, out of which Cardano formulated a major proposition of probability theory.[30]

This wavering between the actual experience of soul travel and "ascent through mathematics," if so it can be called, is truly the crux of the Koestlerian watershed in the transition from magic to science. After Bruno, really, the "divine fire" was extinguished; all that was left of ascent were the formulas, the mathematical ascent of a mechanical ladder—Newton's universal gravitation, for example, or Mersenne's mathematical harmony (see below). But it is fascinating to watch the "wavering" in Cardano, because it reminds us of what we lost in the transition to a mechanico-mathematical substitute for actual mystical ascent. Thus Fierz writes that for Cardano, the art of divination was based on a universe that was unified and alive, and that it "open[ed] the path to God and [made] possible the ascension of the soul. In the pursuit of this goal divination by dreams [was] particularly useful."[31]

Dream interpretation, in fact, was as much a part of Cardano's life as mathematics. He published a book on the subject, recommending that his reader keep a dream journal, and noting that union with God sometimes occurred in dreams. Cardano put dreams in the category of "afflatus," divine influence or ecstatic experience, and said in *De Subtilitate* that the tone and content of the book came to him in a dream.[32]

A full discussion of the nature of "afflatus," and its role in his life, was given by Cardano in his autobiography, *De Vita Propria Liber*, written the year before he died. He described visions he had had as a young boy, and the major dreams he had had at crucial points in his life. He also discussed his own paranormal powers (as we might call them) such as prescient dreams, ESP, and intuitive flashes of direct knowledge. Already, in *De Rerum Varietate*, Cardano had related that he was able to go into trance at will and to see his future in dreams.[33] But Cardano understood that the times were changing, and that the direct experience of such things was becoming a rarity by the late sixteenth century. He may have even understood that posterity would remember him more for his mathematics than for his visionary experience, just as it is Kepler's laws that count for us today, rather than his reconstruction of the "music of the spheres." Kepler himself felt differently about it, and so did Cardano. "One thing alone is sufficient for me," wrote the latter; "to understand and grasp the meaning of all of these wonders would be more precious to me than the everlasting dominion of all the universe; and this I swear by all that is holy."[34]

The final stage in this process was the substitution of mechanico-mathematical ascent for spiritual ascent. In the work of the Cambridge Platonists Ralph Cudworth and Henry More, the cabalistic ladder of emanations—what Cudworth called "plastic natures"—is still present, but as an abstraction, not as a form of magic. Thus in his *True Intellectual System of the Universe* (1678), Cudworth has many passages describing the nature of the soul and how it ascends to heaven; and Gershom Scholem notes that Cudworth's (and More's) cabalistic ideas were derivative of those of a Dutch theosophist by the name of Franciscus Mercurius van Helmont.[35] More argued that gravity could not be explained on strictly mechanical terms, and said that there must be a "spirit of nature" holding the universe together, a "universal soul of the world"; and this (some have claimed) was to have a strong influence on Isaac Newton.[36] Cudworth also held that the existence of plastic natures meant that the world was alive, not just one big clock.[37] Basically, their work was an attempt to combine Neoplatonism and the mechanical philosophy; and despite his similarity to Descartes, it is noteworthy that Cudworth said of the Cartesians that they have "an undiscerned tang of the mechanically-atheistic humor hanging about them."[38] Yet Cudworth was closer to the new world than he was to the old one in one crucial respect: his religion was already dead, mechanical. Cudworth and More were hardly magical practitioners; reference to "plastic natures" or the *anima mundi* were but mere expressions for them. There was no living occult or gnostic experience in their work, no actual soul travel of any kind. What they had done was replace the ladder to God with the theology of ascent, and from there it was a short step to the mechanism of Descartes.

As noted, the theory of plastic natures may have had an influence on Newton, who certainly moved from a world animated by a universal harmony to one controlled by the principle of universal gravitation. Yet long before Newton this tendency was already in effect, and it can be seen clearly in the work of Galileo and, especially, that of Marin Mersenne, who was responsible—as much as any single individual could be "responsible" for such a development—for the birth of the mechanical philosophy.[39]

To take Galileo (briefly) first, then: ostensibly, it would be difficult to find a scientist or philosopher of the seventeenth century who was more mechanically "pure," with the possible exception of Hobbes or Locke. Galileo, with his law of free-fall, analysis of the pendulum, and parabolic curves of projectile motion, is about as modern as you can get: no Keplerian universal harmony for him! He speaks with the voice of the new breed of Italian engineer, and echoes the approach of an updated Archimedes. Thus, when the historian of science Alexandre Koyré attempted, in what has become a classic work, to argue for a Platonistic influence at work on Galileo, he took great pains to make the following point:

> In the history of philosophy there are several Platos and several Platonisms. There are, in particular, these two different versions: the Platonism, or more accurately the Neoplatonism, of the Florentine Academy, a mixture of mysticism, numerology and magic; and the Platonism of the mathematicians, that of Tartaglia and Galileo, a Platonism which is a commitment to the role of mathematics in science but without all these additional doctrines.[40]

The problem, as the Italian historian Eugenio Garin has pointed out, is whether the two Platonisms can really be kept apart; whether you can have the mathematics "without all these additional doctrines." Thus he quotes the following passage from a letter Galileo wrote to Pietro Dini, dated March 24, 1614, which comes as a bit of a surprise to those of us accustomed to thinking of Galileo as the "father of modern science":

> [I]t seems to me that there is in nature a substance that is utterly spiritual, constant, and fast moving. It is diffused throughout the universe and penetrates into everything without distinction. . . . One can reasonably assess that this spirit is something more than light, for it penetrates into all bodily substances, no

matter how thick they are. . . . Hence we can affirm with great likelihood that this fertile spirit and this light diffused throughout the universe come together, and are united in the solar body because it is situated in the centre of the universe. From there, made even more splendid and vigorous, it diffuses itself again.[41]

Garin argues that Galileo's acceptance of Copernican theory represents his connection with philosophers such as Bruno (something Kepler pointed out as early as 1610), and that he was in fact preoccupied with Platonic issues of a nonmathematical kind, issues that cannot be separated from the main body of his work. This, says Garin,

accounts for the long disquisitions on the soul as the divine seat of light and on the manner in which the solar system is constituted in regard to the concentration and expansion of primeval light. It also accounts for his theory of *spiritus*, the soul of the world, of the nourishment of the sun and of universal life.

"All this," continues Garin,

can be found too often in Galileo's writings to be accidental. It clearly demonstrates how difficult it is to distinguish, as Koyré . . . wanted to do, between mystical and geometrical Platonism. . . . [42]

In this regard, it is interesting to read a recent article in *Scientific American*, claiming that it was the shadow of Bruno that brought Galileo before the Inquisition; and that in the public consciousness, Galileo's work seemed very Brunonian.[43] In the context of the failed Campanella revolt, and a general "Rosicrucian scare" that took place in western Europe in the early seventeenth century, Copernicanism was tainted—so the authors of this article claim—with heretical and revolutionary overtones.[44] To make matters worse, the printer of Galileo's *Dialogue on the Two Great World Systems* (1632), the book that led directly to his trial and condemnation, decorated the title page of this work with a triple-fish or dolphin colophon, a symbol associated with Bruno and Hermeticism. The Church reacted at once; Niccolò Riccardi, the pope's theologian, came to see a disciple of Galileo living in Rome, Filippo Magalotti, to tell him "that great offense had been taken at the emblem which was on the frontispiece. . . . " Magalotti assured him that Galileo had no esoteric purposes, and Riccardi was much relieved.[45]

Of course, Galileo was no Brunonian soul traveler, out to "penetrate the skies" or rise on the wings of occult practice. The Hermetic interpretation of his writings—and it is not clear how accurate the *Scientific American* article is on this point—was certainly a mistake. Yet as Garin points out, there were certainly enough Neoplatonic passages in Galileo's work to give one reason to pause. Garin's own interpretation, and it seems highly plausible, is that these passages do not prove that Galileo was a Ficinian magician, but rather that he spoke the cultural idiom of northern Italy, which had already been soaking in such ideas for more than a century. He was a Brunonian in that he took Copernicus' vision seriously, as a physical reality; but in no sense did he believe that we could know the Infinite (much less travel to it). In fact, in Galileo's hands, Copernicanism was a springboard to a new philosophy, one that integrated mathematics with sense experience and that also eliminated God from the world. Galileo had no spiritual aspirations, and certainly no interest in ascent, except in the sense that we have already mentioned, i.e., a mathematico-mechanical "ascent." For the crucial contribution of Galileo to celestial mechanics was the demonstration that physically, at least, there was no absolute contrast between heaven and earth; that the laws of one were the laws of the other.[46] This was, of course, a break with the Aristotelian notion of the sub- and supralunary regions; but in the context of the history of science, magic, and mysticism, it is clearly part of the general trend of soul travel sinking into obscurity, and the ladder presumed to exist between heaven and earth being scaled by more reliable (or material) means. The two strains of Platonism identified by Koyré, the mathematical and the mystical, only became separated in the late sixteenth and early seventeenth centuries. Galileo was part of the process by which one strain fell away and the other got transmuted into a purely descriptive tool for reinterpreting the physical world. This too was part of the watershed, although Galileo was not consciously out to ascend to God by means of equations. In the long run, though, his work had the same effect.

In the case of Marin Mersenne (1588–1648), we can be a lot more specific about the substitution of mathematical "ascent" for the somatic/spiritual variety, for the attack on magic was his avowed aim. This comes out, in particular, in his work on music, a subject that he wrote about voluminously. Yet in a curious way Mersenne, who has been identified as the pivotal figure in the rise of mechanism and scientific positivism, turns out to be more of a watershed figure with respect to this subject than a postwatershed one. The impact of his life, as far as music goes, was certainly to tear down any remaining vestige of the ascent structure and to pave the way for a purely physical, or acoustical, understanding of music; yet he himself could not avoid wavering on the subject to a very great extent. He was not, as was Kepler, arguing for a harmony of the spheres; but his heart did seem to be going in two directions at once.

Why music, of all things? Mersenne's focus on the question of music may seem peculiar, but it must be said that the relevance of this particular issue to the nature of the Scientific Revolution in general has not received sufficient emphasis. In point of fact, nearly all of the leading figures of the first stage of the Scientific Revolution (say, from 1580 to 1650), including Kepler, Galileo, Stevin, Cardano, Bacon, Descartes, and Gassendi, as well as Mersenne, struggled to come to terms with music and music theory.[47] For music embodies a crucial tension, being an affective experience that is nevertheless amenable to mathematical treatment. It is also, because of its affective power, as well as its power to induce altered states of consciousness, traditionally associated with ascent in particular and magical practice in general. That music could lead to ecstatic experience has been known for millennia, though it was largely forgotten after the seventeenth century.[48] This aspect of music, notes Jacques Attali in his book *Noise*, was one that always escaped channelization or classification. It is, he says, a heretical and subversive strain, the music of Dionysian rites and ecstatic cults, always involving marginal people and somehow always managing to survive.[49] In a more watered-down version of this, music in general has been evaluated in terms of its affective power, i.e., its ability to move the listener emotionally. Thus Kepler wrote that the true test of consonance (harmonic proportion) was the reaction of the soul, viz., joy; and for him, this was tied to a larger astronomical scheme, in which the same consonance could be found in the numerical relationships that he believed subsisted between the planets. This macrocosmic/microcosmic tie was the traditional link between music and ascent, and it is a notion that runs at least from Pythagoras through the Renaissance, typically carrying Neoplatonic and sometimes heretical overtones.[50] This is why music was so important to men such as Ficino and Giorgi during the Renaissance, and to Fludd and Kepler (despite their crucial differences) in the seventeenth century. When Kepler explained consonance by saying that harmony was a divine attribute, an activity of the soul itself, and that this in turn was mirrored in the mathematical and physical relationships between the planets, he was affirming a very ancient tradition.[51] Ascent to the heavens would be impossible, of course, if such an "isomorphism" between the individual soul and the "harmony of the world" could not be shown to exist, and in this sense the preoccupation of seventeenth-century scientists with music was, perhaps even unconsciously, an attempt to figure out whether miracles were still possible. For Mersenne, for example, music reflected a harmony that pervaded the world, and that led ultimately to God, whether by listening to it, playing it, or investigating it scientifically. In a similar way, he held that grace could be understood mathematically; that mathematics forced us to recognize the divine.[52] As Isaac Newton would believe a few decades later, Mersenne was (for a time) certain he was onto a secret that had been known to the ancients. Newton, for example, wrote (in his unpublished papers) that Pythagoras had worked out a set of ratios in vibrating strings that gave the ratios of celestial harmony; that the ancient philosophers called God "Harmony"; and that God activated matter harmonically by having Pan (often identified with Dionysus) play on a pipe, thereby inspiring the world with harmonic ratio.[53] The affective relation to music that we all have is, according to this tradition (which lasted until the seventeenth century), the connection between our interior lives, the soul or third body, and the fifth body, the body of the world. Being moved emotionally by music is effectively the first step toward using music as a springboard to the higher regions, to ecstatic and visionary experience. And all this was guaranteed by the harmonic structure of the universe itself. What happens during the Scientific Revolution, of course, is that music, along with everything else, gets mechanized and quantified, and heavenly ascent through magical practice is replaced by the abstractions of acoustics and analysis. One gives up the trip to heaven and settles for the travelogue.

To turn specifically to Mersenne, then, we should note that he lived precisely at that time when magic was on the wane among the educated classes of western Europe, and that he came to embody that transition, being at once a religious man—a priest, in fact—and a proponent of the mechanical philosophy.[54] If, centuries later, Thomas Henry Huxley was Darwin's "bulldog," it might be said that Mersenne fulfilled a similar function for Descartes. He was an indefatigable campaigner against alchemists such as Robert Fludd, and against any form of animism or Hermeticism. In addition to his numerous works on music, mechanism, philosophy, and religion, and his attacks on magic and the occult, Mersenne became a kind of clearinghouse for scientific thought, maintaining a heavy international correspondence, putting proponents of the new philosophy in touch with each other, publishing translations of Galileo's work, presiding over a weekly scientific meeting, and so on. His *Quaestiones in Genesim* (Questions on Genesis, 1623) inveighed heavily against the Renaissance occult tradition; Francesco Giorgi was particularly singled out for attack. His major work on music, the *Harmonie universelle*, sought to replace numerology with mathematical measurement; to do away with Neoplatonic mathematics altogether. As Frances Yates points out, Mersenne was reacting especially to the rise of Rosicrucianism, which was heir to the Neoplatonic tradition of the Renaissance, and which, for a Catholic such as himself (he was a friar in the Minorite order) constituted, along with Christian cabalism, the worst sort of heresy imaginable. This turn toward mechanism was thus politically motivated, part of a fear of religious and social disorder (inextricably linked, in the seventeenth century). Mersenne thus wrote at one point that there were two great reasons for loving God: He gave us science, and He maintained the social order; and we can well understand that he saw these two "gifts" as very much related. The same thing, in fact, applied to musical harmony. Mechanism did not lead to atheism, as so many thought, said Mersenne; just the reverse was true. As Descartes wrote him on April 15, 1630, "God sets up laws in nature just as a king sets up laws in his kingdom." All of this represented a revolution in *mentalité*. As Frances Yates says, " '[T]he emergence of Mersenne out of a banished Giorgi' is one of those transitions from Renaissance to seventeenth century which are fundamental turning points in the history of thought." She continues:

> By eliminating Giorgi and all that he stood for in Renaissance tradition, Mersenne banished the astral linkings of universal harmony, cutting at the roots the connections of the psyche with the cosmos. This appeased the witch-hunters and made the world safe for Descartes, which was what Mersenne was nervously trying to do.

Mersenne was thus a spiritual turning point in the history of Europe; which is to say, a somatic one. If the man or woman of the seventeenth century was going to do any soul travel, it would be by means of the sober equations of Descartes, Galileo, and, later, Sir Isaac Newton.[55]

And yet . . . it is more complicated than this. As Robert Lenoble reveals (much to his own embarrassment), Mersenne was still caught in the network of Renaissance thought; he still hadn't "managed" to leave the fabulous and the occult entirely behind.[56] We see this in various aspects of his work. The same texts, expecially the earlier ones, can be found discussing methods for extracting square roots and for identifying evil spirits. But even Mersenne's later works contain discussions of applying mathematics to the measurement of Noah's ark, of the king's ability to cure scrofula by touch,[57] and of the Copernican hypothesis as evidence of divine grace. The geometry of the parallelogram, said Mersenne, enables us to understand how angels can simultaneously be on earth and in heaven. But if there is a particular drift to Mersenne's life, it is the tendency to resolve miraculous, occult, and religious issues in mechanico-mathematical terms; and nowhere is this conflict of worldviews more present than in his work on music.

It must be said at the outset that Mersenne never played an instrument or composed a line of music himself. His approach was that of the theoretician, and in this field he made a great "contribution" (depending on your point of view), moving music theory away from the affective and ecstatic and toward the abstract and analytical. In this way, he paved the way for the work of Jean-Philippe Rameau, generally regarded as the founder of tonal harmonic theory.[58] Mersenne's first work on the subject, the *Traité de l'harmonie universelle*, appeared in 1627, and his definitive treatment of it was simply called *Harmonie universelle*, published in 1636–37 and later appearing in Latin editions as well. Lenoble called it "one of the masterpieces of the new mechanistic science." In general, Mersenne is credited with reducing music to acoustics, specifically relating the phenomenon of consonance, or harmonious sound, to the mechanics of vibrating bodies. Mersenne was the first to formulate rules governing vibrating strings based on an analysis of length, diameter, tension, and mass, and the first to discern the nature of partials (harmonics) related to a fundamental note. He did research on echoes and resonance, and on the speed of sound; suggested a streamlining of modal systems; and developed rules for the construction of melodies. Sound, he asserted, was nothing more than the movement of air, and thus amenable to mechanical and mathematical treatment. "Just as Descartes distrusted sensory evidence," writes Warren Allen, "so also Mersenne condemned the sensual aspects of music." His goal was to discredit the occult, especially the cabalistic, tradition, as represented by Fludd and Giorgi, and so tied up with ascent and altered states, which claimed that words and sounds had occult powers and that they could influence the soul. Planetary relationships had nothing to do with music, he argued; "the consideration of the Keplerian figures is nowise necessary for the understanding of music."[59] It is not merely that Mersenne set the stage for Rameau; it is that his whole mathematical/harmonic outlook wound up governing Western music well into the twentieth century and, as Yates says, cutting it off from its age-old psychic roots.

The curious thing about all this is that whereas Mersenne's methods were in a totally different world from that of Fludd's or Giorgi's, his goal was pretty much the same: the ascent to God. And this may account for his rage against them, especially Fludd, for what he rejected (he wasn't a priest for nothing) was the actual *experience* of ascent, the real ecstasy induced by music. This was explosive, heretical, unsafe. The safe path was to create not only a mathematical and acoustical bridge (T.O.) to the heavens, but also such a bridge between Aristotelian theology and a dynamic new science, a new system of coding and control. Nevertheless, Mersenne's commitment to the ancient goal of divination—finding God—gives his work an ambivalent character.

According to Robert Lenoble, Mersenne's interest in music stemmed from his belief that the Greeks had been in possession of a secret, a method of altering the human soul via sound. The universal harmony, he said in the *Traité* of 1627, is a doctrine clearly present in the works of Plato and Pythagoras, and this he associated with therapeutic or healing effects. The Greeks, he claimed, knew how to convert the soul by means of sound, and it was necessary to recover these ancient techniques. The true physician, Mersenne went on, is a musician; he knows the relations between musical harmony and the psychophysiology of the soul.

Comparisons with Fludd (1574–1637) are important because Fludd, a physician himself, believed all of this as well. His picture of the universe was that of three regions, or, musically speaking, "octaves," and he held that ascent to the highest region was best understood in musical terms. This sort of thing, he asserted, was known to the Pythagoreans, but was now lost, and had to be restored. Over diagrams of these regions—the supercelestial, the celestial, and the corporeal—Fludd liked to superimpose diagrams of the "divine monochord," based on a one-stringed instrument known from antiquity, which, he said, symbolized the chain of being, from earth to God (Plate 15). In Neoplatonic and cabalistic fashion, ascent of the soul up this ladder or monochord was the ultimate goal of the human being, according to Fludd. Thus in his dedication (to the reader) of the first volume of his *Utriusque Cosmi, Maioris Scilicet et Minoris, Metaphysica,*

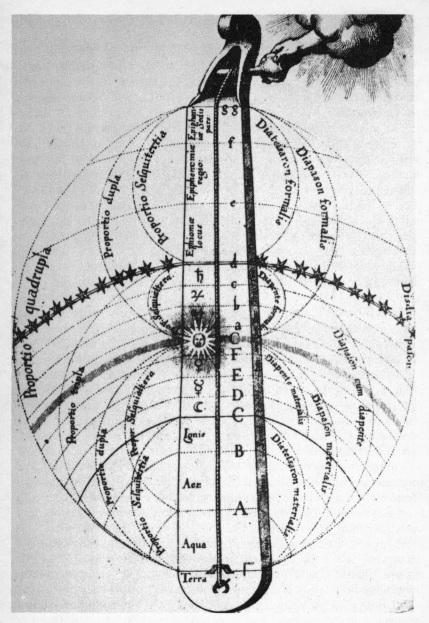

15. Robert Fludd's "divine monochord," symbolizing the ladder of ascent from earth to heaven (1617). From *Robert Fludd* by Joscelyn Godwin, published by Thames and Hudson and Shambhala Publications, Inc., in the U.S.A.

*Physica atque Technica Historia* (An Account, Metaphysical, Physical, and Technical, of Both Worlds, Greater and Lesser) of 1617, Fludd quoted from Ficino's translation of the *Pimander*, from the Hermetic corpus, a passage in which Hermes Trismegistus says that man was given the power to rise to the heavens, and thereby understand all truth, and that when such a man knows himself, he becomes like God. Fludd's diagrams—Yates calls them "ecstatic mystical"—often transpose the three "octaves" into a mathematical scheme, showing how the soul makes the descent and reascent (Plate 16), or map the musical scale and mathematical calculations onto the path of ascent (Plate 17). (These ratios also, according to Fludd, determined the relative distances of the planets and the stars.) Yates is convinced (as was Mersenne) that Fludd was an actual magus, i.e., a full-fledged practitioner of occult techniques, and here again we have the old antagonism between the shaman and the priest. It is interesting that a modern avant-garde composer, Murray Schafer, took the central idea of these diagrams of Fludd, that of "tuning the world," as the title of one of his own books, and states that music is the search for the harmonizing influence of sounds in the world around us. "We must try once again," adds Schafer, "to find the secret of that harmony."[60]

For reasons having nothing to do with new evidence or information, Mersenne underwent a "conversion" to mechanism sometime in the early 1630s, in the same way that English scientists did in the late 1650s and during the early years of the Restoration. And as in this latter case, I believe the reasons can be traced to exaggerated anxiety over political and religious instability.[61] It was in 1630 that Descartes wrote Mersenne about the coincidence of scientific and political law; and in an age of Richelieu, with whom Mersenne was associated, the mechanical philosophy was clearly perceived as an aid to stability. In Mersenne's case, this took the form of persuading himself that the Greeks had lied (!). They had never really succeeded with the soul transformation of which they had boasted, he decided, and thus in short order the Minorite friar underwent a profound conversion, from ancient to modern, but with one curious proviso: retaining the search for the "lost" secret, but in the future. The Greeks, said Mersenne, may have lied about their achievements, but this did not mean that what they claimed was impossible. The answer lay in *future* science; *mechanism would succeed where Greek occultism had failed*. The true role of the musician, he said in *Questions harmoniques* (1634), was to restrain the passions and to encourage piety. Here we have it plainly stated, a classic rerun of an old pattern (from magus to rabbi or priest, in

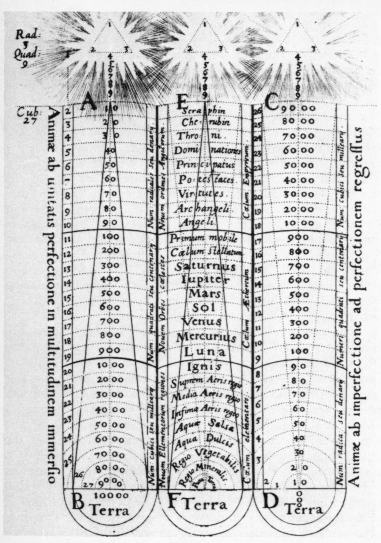

16. Fludd's illustration of the three "octaves," showing the path of descent and reascent of the soul (1619). From *Robert Fludd* by Joscelyn Godwin, published by Thames and Hudson and Shambhala Publications, Inc., in the U.S.A.

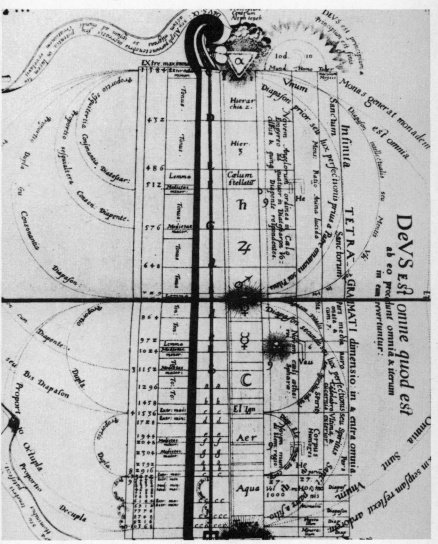

17. Fludd's illustration of a diatonic scale mapped onto the path of ascent to the heavens (1621). From *Robert Fludd* by Joscelyn Godwin, published by Thames and Hudson and Shambhala Publications, Inc., in the U.S.A.

effect): direct ascent, somatic experience, passion, and ecstasy—all of this is pernicious heresy, the sort of thing an "evil magician" like Fludd was up to. Mersenne's attitude shifts: the issue is *harmony*, in the political, musical, and religious worlds, and the keys are mathematics and mechanism. Sound is a matter of air striking the eardrum, he says, and he applauds Hobbes' work as a bold attempt to moralize human beings via science. Ballets should be constructed, said Mersenne in the *Harmonie universelle*, to illustrate the movements of the planets; theology itself can be choreographed. Mersenne claimed that his own rules of composition were so perfect (read: mechanical) that everybody could learn to compose music in less than an hour by means of them.[62] "In Mersenne's hands," writes H. F. Cohen, "a process was completed that had started with father and son Galilei: the musical instrument was turned into a scientific instrument, capable of revealing nature's hidden properties."[63]

The notion of music being tied to political economy is the subject of Jacques Attali's book *Noise*, already referred to, which argues that the music that followed the age of Mersenne, in particular the tonal music of the eighteenth century (Bach, Mozart, etc.), reflected the bourgeoisie's dream of a harmonious world.[64] Attali sees music as anticipatory of new political and economic structures, in any given age; its code predicts the coming ideology and social organization. And the goal of tonal music, he says, is to make people believe in a consensual representation of the world, "to stamp upon the spectators the faith that there is a harmony in order," to "etch in their minds the image of the ultimate social cohesion, achieved through commercial exchange and the process of rational knowledge." The rise of tonality, of mathematical (not just numerical) harmony as the center of musical experience, was in effect a political coup: the bourgeoisie of Europe, he writes, "finessed one of its most ingenious ideological productions: creating an aesthetic and theoretical base for its necessary order, *making people believe by shaping what they hear.*" The two harmonies, he goes on to say, "the divine and the scientific, combine in the image of a universe governed by a law both mathematical and musical." Susan McClary, in her Afterword to Attali's essay, locates this tendency in the early seventeenth century, with the attempt to reduce all music to harmony and all harmony to physics. It was, she says, an attempt to control raw erotic energy by violence, but violence masquerading as order. This is what tonality was about, especially in France. "Exact formulas for the bowing of stringed instruments and for the precise execution of ornaments were codified and enforced. . . . " The sensual, the ecstatic, the somatic, in effect, got co-opted and neutered by the demands of a New Order. Mersenne's goal, says Lenoble, was "the subordination of interior life to the mechanism of nature."[65]

Mersenne did not succeed in attaining his goal; that was left for later generations to accomplish. He himself could not avoid the conclusion that there was no way to reduce the subjective experience of consonance or dissonance—joy or sadness—to acoustics. He was not able to say how the regular striking of the eardrum evoked the experience of beauty, and thus he proposed two separate tables of consonance, a scientific one and an aesthetic one. The emotional or psychic life thus remained inaccessible to the new science, and this was part of the general esoteric/exoteric split that characterized the seventeenth century.

It must be clear by now that what I have called the "Italian" model of heresy was hardly limited to Tuscany or Calabria; it was a phenomenon that occurred in England, France, and Holland as well, in countries that were witnessing the rise of the new capitalist economy and an accompanying drive toward political stability. It was a two-step process that frequently rendered the finest minds of the age completely schizoid, and a process of co-optation that had no specific co-opter, but was rather part of the temper of the times. The "heretical" recovery of ecstatic ascent and magical practice during the Renaissance blew the lid off the dead cover of Church Aristotelianism, and opened up a new role for the human being, that of the operator, or magus. In the early phases, there was much direct experimentation with this "ladder to the stars." This energy enabled a whole "new" worldview to emerge as a possibility, an active and dynamic one. But because of the particular conjunction of all this with major political and economic trends, the liberation embedded in the ecstatic tradition got turned against itself. Ascent was co-opted not by the Church, as in the French model, but by "the age." Ascent got reified; in Galileo's work, as in Newton's, the same laws applied to heaven and earth; this was how the two worlds got sewn together. The theory of universal gravitation was a kind of "lasso," in which a mathematical "rope" was thrown out and the heavens were hauled in. And all of this, finally, was a way of constructing a safe bridge across transitional space. As Donald Winnicott said, the Transitional Object is mapped onto the whole cultural field. The heaven/earth gap, however, is really the nemo, the Self/Other gap, and much of modern science is an attempt to make the (emotional) world forever safe by providing a "reliable"—i.e., nonsomatic—bridge, or ladder of ascent. Historian Frank Manuel captures this very well in his study of Newton when he says that a "chief source of Newton's desire to know was his anxiety before and his fear of the unknown." Newton's goal, says Manuel, was a "structuring of the world in so absolutist a manner that every event, the closest and the most remote, [fit] neatly into an imaginary system. . . ."[66]

The same might be said of Mersenne and Descartes, and for that matter Martin Luther; and the most important characteristic of the Italian model is the acquisition of an insight by playing around (in some form) with the ascent tradition, and then the betraying of that experience by translating the insight obtained into rational or mechanical terms. Descartes' metaphysical commitment to mathematics, his invention of analytic geometry, the formulation of his famous "rules of reasoning"—all this occurred in the months and years following a gnostic illumination that came to him on the night of November 10, 1619. "The experience," writes E. A. Burtt, "can be compared only to the ecstatic illumination of the mystic. . . . " It is also noteworthy that as a young man Descartes had been inspired by the writings of that great Renaissance magician Agrippa von Nettesheim. The following years witnessed Descartes' growing hatred of sensory experience. "I then examined closely what I was," he wrote in 1637, "and saw that I could imagine that I had no body, and that there was no world nor any place that I occupied. . . . " What he took away from his illumination was a commitment to mind, to mathematics, and finally to a mechanical universe. It is also likely that his concept of "intuition"—one of his rules of reasoning—which he defined as a kind of direct and unclouded perception of the truth, and which was then to be followed by "deduction"—was the formal translation of his mystical experience into the world of abstract philosophical analysis.[67]

It is no accident that Descartes is perhaps most famous for his sharp dichotomization of mind and body, seeing them as two separate, mechanically interacting substances (*res cogitans* and *res extensa*). In general, the mind/body split that we live with, and individually suffer from, today is a direct legacy of this two-step process, i.e., using an occult or somatic insight to dislodge an old system, and then reacting with fear to the very tool that made this possible, dropping it like a hot potato, and erecting a new (rigid) system in place of the old one, a system whose very existence depends on the mystical insight now being rejected. The modern period represents, then, a tremendous betrayal and rechanneling of somatic energy, of which witch burnings are only the outward manifestation, the tip of the iceberg. All of us tend to reproduce this history of going from organic experience to abstract system, in our infancy and early childhood. The child's world of fantasy/dream/bodily enjoyment is relentlessly transmuted, by the uptight denizens of modern Newtonian or Cartesian society, into properly controlled behavior. This has had enormous consequences for the nature of Western creativity (see Chapter 10), and it has shaped the modern industrial psyche more than anything else.[68]

The shift from Church Aristotelianism to modern science was not one of a shift from an age of faith to an age of reason, as has so often been said, but from an age of one faith to an age of another faith. The occult and the somatic formed "the crack between worlds." But converted to a system, rendered purely exoteric, magic became modern science, and the magical body became the technical body, captured—neutralized, really—by means of chemical and physical descriptions, and treatment. This story is the real, hidden, and somatic history of the early modern era and ultimately of the whole of what we call "modernity."

The secularized version of ascent, furthermore, is present virtually everywhere we look in modern society. Instead of spiritual ascent and personality transformation, we now use the modern equivalents of the equations and methodology developed by Newton and Galileo to make the ascent to the heavens in a direct, material way: voyages to the moon, space probes to the planets, and so on. Even our architecture reflects this, historically speaking (Plate 18). Prehistory sees ritual dwellings in the form of caves or mounds; early ascent can be seen in the Neolithic stone circles of Europe and later, the pyramids of Egypt and Mesoamerica. A bit later, we have Greek temples and Buddhist stupas, and eventually the clear separation of Above and Below in the domes of the Byzantine period. Romanesque architecture, says the American psychiatrist Charles Johnston in *The Creative Imperative*, gives us "the first gestures toward real ascendant preeminence," made fully manifest in Gothic cathedrals. This later gets secularized, with the structural mass moved further upward still, in the skyscraper, "a perfect monument to the abstract." The goal is still to get to heaven, in other words, but the god is now material and industrial. And finally we have the spaceship, a ritual dwelling, "in which humans not only contemplate the heavens, they inhabit them."[69] Gnostic ascent structure, it would seem, is the template on which the modern Western world, and certainly, modern science, has been built.

Two comments are in order before we turn to our final model of

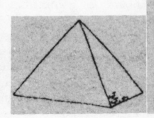

18. The evolution of verticality. Illustration by Anne Gerdes, from Charles M. Johnston, M.D., *The Creative Imperative,* publ. Celestial Arts.

heresy, the case of Nazi Germany. The first is that as in the case of the Greek and French models, we need to be aware of the possibilities of a repeat performance. From the vantage point of our third model, the first two now seem unlikely candidates for heretical experience today, because the ancient and medieval contexts are so different from that of the early modern one. The energy of ecstasy and ascent may be the same, but the world-religion model required a peculiar configuration of imperialism and foreign domination for its success, and the Cathar/romantic love/Inquisition model required a single, powerful religious authority bearing down on the dissenting faction. The Italian model is much closer to us, both in time and texture. Ascent gets co-opted, but not in an overt conspiratorial way. Rather, the somatic energy gets turned loose in an age moving toward new centralized political and economic forms. Its own form gets retained, but its content gets stripped away and replaced. It seems to me that similar diffuse yet convergent tendencies are at work in the Western economies today, as we witness the breakdown of the industrial order and the emergence of a new "information society," with concomitant global alliances along the lines of stable "spheres of influence" that resemble the mentality of Richelieu and the seventeenth-century search for a stable world order. It is the co-optation of the French model, but with a different Establishment and a modern, scientific twist. I shall deal with this at greater length in Chapter 9.

The second point is that we can now recognize that whether we are talking about heresy or orthodoxy, ascent is the name of the game for both. The difference between the two is of course a major one. Heresy says, "You can do it yourself," whereas orthodoxy says, "We'll do it for you" (for a political and economic price). This is no small difference, and it accounts, in part, for the bitter war between heresy and orthodoxy that has characterized so much of Western history, in various forms. One is about direct somatic experience, the other is about fear of the same and about finding substitutes for it. But in one crucial respect, the two camps are identical: reality is regarded as being vertical. The idea, in fact or theory, is that things are not sufficient or satisfactory on earth and that one must somehow go to heaven in order to make them right. If Western religious history is characterized by a somatic/ecstatic breakthrough that then gets recoded as dogma in one form or another, we cannot avoid the conclusion that the code is always a vertical one, always based on ascent. Is this good? Or might a "horizontal" coding make more sense at this point? This is a theme I shall return to in Part III. For now, let me say that there may be more interesting things we can do with our minds than leave our bodies and go to heaven.

The last great heresy in the Christian West was the Fascist experiment of Nazi Germany. It represents the ultimate in vertical structures, with the Führer as a kind of demigod positioned in the celestial realm, at one end, and Jews, Slavs, and other so-called *Untermenschen* literally composted into organic matter at the other. This is not to hold ascent experience per se responsible for this turn of events. As I hope is evident by now, context is much more significant than content in shaping the spiritual/political history of the West. We need, then, to examine the hidden somatic history of the Nazi experience, and see how it interacted with its own particular context to produce such gruesome results.

# 8

# The Twisted Cross

> *Man is becoming God—that is the simple fact.*
> *Man is God in the making. . . . Those who see*
> *in National Socialism nothing more than a*
> *political movement know scarcely anything of*
> *it. It is more even than a religion: it is*
> *the will to create mankind anew.*

> —Adolf Hitler,
> in Hermann Rauschning,
> *Hitler Speaks*

THAT THE REAL STORY OF NAZISM WAS A SOMATIC ONE was recognized by only one writer, the Austrian psychiatrist Wilhelm Reich, in his book *The Mass Psychology of Fascism.* Reich saw the rise of Fascism in Germany as a rechanneled response of repressed sexual energy, and undoubtedly this was a part of the story. Yet it is not the most important part. The actual situation was much larger than this, and a few writers, such as Carl Jung, were much closer to the truth when they argued (as the inner circle of the Nazi Party itself did) that what was going on was an ecstatic phenomenon, the return of repressed pagan (mystical/heretical) tendencies that had been buried by official Christendom for centuries. In what follows, I am going to develop this theme, and argue that the Nazi experiment represented a secular version of the ascent phenomenon that (as we have seen) is central to Western heresy. But the Nazi story is so complex and convoluted that it will not hurt to provide a roadmap of it, and of what I wish to argue, at the outset. Briefly, it goes something like this:

(1) Nazism is actually part of a pattern embedded in the consciousness and religious structure of the West, namely, the ascent phenomenon. Norman Cohn (*The Pursuit of the Millennium*) correctly pegged fascism as part of the Western heretical tradition, but made the mistake of seeing virtually all gnostic heresy as fascistic. Because Cohn had no typology of heresy, he could not perceive differences between movements, only similarities. Hence, in his work, the countercultural tradition gets lumped together into one big (dangerous) category.[1]

(2) A number of historians—George Mosse most notably (*The Crisis of German Ideology*)—have argued that as a doctrine, Nazism represented a sharp break with the mainstream of Western thought, giving particular emphasis to the irrational side of human life. It was, in other words, an ideological rebellion against the dominant (liberal, democratic, rationalist) culture, and the influence of this peculiar brand of racist romanticism can be traced from writers in the late nineteenth century right down to Hitler.[2] While this thesis has much to commend it, it tends to overvalue the importance of intellectuals and ideas for a phenomenon that was violent, pervasive, and grass-roots. Ideas, in and of themselves, are not capable of unleashing energy. To do that, something else must be present.

(3) This missing factor is that of psychological salvation, directly experienced. James Rhodes and Fritz Stern in particular have convincingly argued that Fascism is a gnostic phenomenon, or, at the very least, a redemption psychology.[3] Eric Voegelin analyzed National Socialism as a "political religion" as early as 1938.[4] People became Nazis not because of being persuaded by a certain set of *völkisch* ideas, but because of their immediate existential situation—a situation of cosmic meaninglessness and futility, followed by the emergence of a form of secular, or political, salvation. Like Cohn, however, these writers do tend to lump things together indiscriminately, ignoring many aspects of other millennarian movements that are not analogous to National Socialism.[5] They also analyze the redemption psychology in terms of ideas, even while trying to distance themselves from the type of argument discussed in point (2). In other words, they correctly see Nazism as a form of gnosis, but generally fail to analyze the mode of transmission of the "secret" doctrine.

(4) The attempt to fill this gap, in turn, has been made by a whole host of sensationalist writers arguing for full-blown occultism and occult practice at the heart of the Nazi doctrine and Nazi elite. Ac-

cording to this view, the Nazi elite guard, or SS (*Schutzstaffel*, "Guard Staff"), was a gnostic cult with an elaborate set of magical initiatory practices, and Hitler and other leading Party members were directly involved in occult rites and rituals. Unfortunately, these writers have no evidence to back up this claim. For the most part, their claims are extravagant or completely fraudulent. Nevertheless, Hitler did have a major ascent experience in 1918, in which he was "told" that it was his destiny to save Germany; and a few top-ranking Nazis did flirt with occult ideas and practices.[6]

(5) More to the point, the German historian Klaus Vondung (*Magie und Manipulation*) has recognized that magic *was* a big part of the Nazi agenda, though not in the way this term is usually meant. By means of lighting effects, public rituals, symbolic imagery, and Hitler's own spellbinding oratory, the German public was often thrown into a light (sometimes not-so-light) trance—something quite visible in the films of Leni Riefenstahl, for example (*Triumph of the Will* and others). As the title of Vondung's book suggests, magic and manipulation were crucial to the mass acceptance of the Nazis by the German public, and to the powerful hold of the Party on the public imagination.[7]

(6) Finally, the American historian Robert Pois (*National Socialism and the Religion of Nature*) has been able to demonstrate that there was a split between the beliefs of the inner circle of the Party and what this circle was prepared to leak to the public. Hitler opposed occultism because he felt it could make no headway among the masses, and he understood that the NSDAP (Nazi Party) had to be a mass party in order to succeed. Yet the Nazi elite, Hitler included, did adhere to a mishmash of esoteric ideas related to those Mosse describes (see above, point 2), and to a gnostic/redemption psychology directly opposed to the Catholic Church. But because this would alienate the majority of the German public, it had to go on the back burner until the war was over, after which a more direct assault on Christendom was intended. By way of preparation, however, Nazi "gnosis" was leaked to the public in various ways, as Vondung points out. This also explains the occasional Nazi denunciation, or even persecution, of occult groups, and the fact that the public and private policies of the Third Reich were frequently in conflict.[8]

The main point that emerges here is that we are dealing with the classical Gnostic ascent structure already discussed, but in a modern secular context; and also with the fact that this energy, due to a particular set of political circumstances, got harnessed to a demonic engine of death. Carl Jung, in his famous "Wotan" article of 1936 (see below), and Hermann Rauschning, in his recorded conversations with Hitler, saw that Nazism was a modern form of archaic energy—"the St. Vitus's dance of the twentieth century," as Rauschning put it.[9] Mystical and spiritual longing, felt in the body, is of the same nature here as it was in the other historical situations we have discussed. *The same desire that brought about Jesus Christ brought about Hitler;* let us make no mistake about it. This does not, however, make Christianity equivalent to Fascism; I am talking about the *energy* behind such movements, not the forms that the energy may take. If all the forms were the same, there would be no need to construct a typology. But the same desire for transcendence, and a secularized form of ascent, was fully at work in this drama, and the inner circle of the NSDAP was intuitively aware that this was the key to their appeal. Heinrich Himmler, the head of the SS, sought to model the organization on the Jesuits; and at least in form, the comparison is apt: an elite brotherhood seeking to use a set of symbols to channel somatic energy in a particular direction. The Nazis deliberately cultivated a transpersonal dimension, and this was the source of their popularity. In short, they accurately perceived a fundamental human need; something to which, as Wilhelm Reich noted very early on, competing political parties remained curiously blind.

In what follows I am going to flesh these arguments out in more detail, so that we can again ask the same questions we have asked of our previous models of heresy: is this repeatable in our own time? and, if heretical trends do exist in Western culture today, can we say to what extent they seem to be following the pattern of this model, as opposed to the other ones we have studied? Let us begin here with the history-of-ideas approach (point 2), and see to what extent the explanation I have sketched of the Nazi phenomenon can be regarded as plausible.

It has long been recognized by historians that social and economic conditions, while very important to the rise of Fascism, also fall short as a convincing explanation. Too many other countries have been humiliated in war, or have gone through severe economic inflation and collapse, or have had a vigorous tradition of anti-Semitism, without constructing assembly-line death camps or institutionalizing the gruesome torture and destruction of vast numbers of people classed as "subhuman." Despite the argument of Hannah Arendt on the "banality of evil,"[10] Nazism seems unavoidably demonic in character, a different level of evil from that of mere administrative violence. In terms of its early organizational background, and a certain set of ideas popular in Germany and Austria from the late nineteenth century, the Nazi Party can be seen to be ideologically tied to a particular intellectual trend that is quite obviously anti-Christian in nature.

The political climate that made Adolf Hitler possible antedated the Weimar period by at least thirty years, and had its roots in a conglomeration of ideas and beliefs that in the context of a secular and scientific culture would have to be regarded as a kind of detritus of confused occult and heretical notions.[11] A "steamy subculture of Ariosophy" pervaded Germany and Austria at this time, a "netherworld of fantasy" woven together with a certain set of myths and symbols and adhered to by an odd assortment of sects and cults. It is not merely, as Nicholas Goodrick-Clarke says, that these "abstruse ideas and weird cults anticipated the political doctrines and institutions of the Third Reich," but that this netherworld of fantasy actually managed to get institutionalized; that, as Mosse says, it ultimately came to influence Hitler's thought and to determine the political discussion of an entire nation. The central doctrine was that of "Ariosophy," a term coined by one Jörg Lanz von Liebenfels (1874–1954) to mean occult wisdom concerning Aryans, which was also sometimes referred to as Armanism, Theozoology, or Ario-Christianity. Occultism was crucial to these doctrines, providing a kind of sacred legitimation for political attitudes; and in Germany, from about 1880 on, this was strongly tied to the popularity of Theosophy and the occult writer Madame Helena Petrovna Blavatsky (1831–91), author of works such as *Isis Unveiled* and *The Secret Doctrine*. Blavatsky, who used the swastika in her design for the seal of the Theosophical Society, argued that the earth had witnessed a series of "root races," starting from the most pure (equated with light), which increasingly got enmeshed in matter. The founders of these races, the "Atlanteans," had great psychic powers, she said, but these powers were lost through racial miscegenation. These powers would be restored, she claimed, by the next major race, the Aryans, who would reverse the progressive degradation that had been going on for so long.

All this managed to catch on very quickly. The first German Theosophical Society was established in 1884, and a related journal, *Die Sphinx*, devoted to the scientific study of the paranormal, began publication in 1886 (running to 1895). Between 1892 and 1900, the Theosophist Franz Hartmann edited a journal called *Lotusblüthen* (Lotus Blossoms), which translated Blavatsky's writings and sported the

Theosophical swastika on its cover. Esoteric writings and publications increased sharply from this time on. Paul Zillman's *Metaphysische Rundschau* (Metaphysical Review) began publication in 1896, featuring articles on occult subjects, and Zillman himself founded an occult lodge in 1897 with three levels of initiation. Zillman was an important link between German occultists and the Vienna Ariosophists (discussed below), whose works he published between 1906 and 1908. In general, the first two decades of the twentieth century saw an outpouring in Germany of literature of this kind, and one can rightly characterize the Central Europe of 1880–1914, in particular the Vienna of Hitler's youth, as undergoing something of an occult revival.

Concomitant with the spread of these ideas was the popularity of *völkisch* thought, an aspect of the German romantic tradition that glorified the special qualities of people and place. *Volk* is the German word for people; but as George Mosse notes, it is a mystical term as well, referring to the union of a people with its most inward, creative nature—its unique national character. *Völkisch* writers of the late nineteenth century saw the world as pantheistic, permeated by a life force, and held that the *Volk* was the tangible vessel of that life force. In the works of men such as Paul de Lagarde and Julius Langbehn, a magical ascent/descent structure obtained, in which the life force was pictured as streaming down from the cosmos to the *Volk,* and from it to each individual. The religion of the *Volk* thus linked each person to God.

Ideas such as these easily lent themselves to occultism, and it was in the work of the Austrian writer Guido von List (1848–1919) that occultism and *völkisch* thought were first clearly combined. List claimed to be a practicing magician; in his youth, he was preoccupied with paganism, worship of Wotan (the ancient Teutonic god), and swastika symbolism. He argued that there had once been an ancient Wotan cult that had been the national religion of the Teutons. In historical romances, he popularized ideas of tribal Germanic life, the artificiality of Christianity, and the true religion of pagan sun worship, to which, he said, Germany must return. By the early twentieth century he had created an elaborate cultic mythology, complete with cosmology, esoteric interpretations of folklore, runic and swastika symbolism, and so on. A List society, which included some very distinguished names, was founded in 1908, and it can be said that List's *Weltanschauung* was shared by many Germans and Austrians at the time.

Very possibly, all of this could have remained as innocuous as contemporary Rosicrucian literature. *Völkisch* thought, mysticism, and occultism, in and of themselves, do not lead to National Socialism. Martin

Buber, for example, was a *völkisch* and mystical thinker, but in a Jewish context. But in Germany, for reasons that may partly be social and economic in nature, racism got tied into a whole dualist cosmology, with the Jews being targeted for a special role. For the entire worldview created by List, Lanz, and other Ariosophists was a classic Gnostic/ Manichaean one, according to which there had been an ancient Aryan (Teutonic-Wotanic) race, identified with pure light (blond hair, fair skin, blue eyes), that had lost its psychic/occult powers through mis-cegenation, dragging it down into the dark material world—as Ma-dame Blavatsky had argued; and the agents of this racial pollution were the forces of darkness, the swarthy, greasy, materialistic Jews. As early as 1897 the writer M. F. Sebaldt von Werth began publishing books (illustrated with the swastika) on the sexuality of Aryans, ar-guing for a eugenic program to maintain racial purity. Also influential was the book by Houston Stewart Chamberlain, *Die Grundlagen des XIX Jahrhunderts* (Foundations of the Nineteenth Century), published in 1900, which was destined to become a favorite Nazi text. Cham-berlain argued that race was the key to history; that God was embodied in the Germans, and the devil embodied in the Jews. Germans and Jews, he said—and it would be hard to find a better example of Self/ Other mirroring than this—were the only two pure races on earth, between which only bastard mixtures flourished. Only these two races, the Jews and the Aryans, had retained their purity, and as a result it was these two races that were caught in a titanic struggle to rule the world. Who would be the chosen people was, for Chamberlain, the only historical question left to be decided.

To return to List, it is clear that he was in the mainstream of this sort of thinking, and he was particularly influenced by the writings of Sebaldt von Werth. He propagated the idea of an "Armanist" es-oteric doctrine existing in ancient Germany, whose initiates had total authority over the masses, and whose major concern was racial purity. This Wotanist priesthood, or *Armanenschaft*, he claimed, had stood at the top of society in a neat vertical structure, and movement upward in the hierarchy had depended on gnostic/racial initiation. He argued that the *Armanenschaft* had never really been destroyed, but had sur-vived in secret, waiting for the right moment to come forth (for which, of course, it needed support) and establish pan-Germanic control over Europe. In this vertical, hierarchical state, he said, power would be a function of racial purity. List went on, in 1911, to codify a set of racial and marriage laws that, as Goodrick-Clarke observes, "bear an un-canny resemblance to the Nuremberg racial laws of the 1930s and the

Nazi vision of the future." Much of the Ariosophist vision of a future state controlled by a racially pure elite did, in fact, come to fruition in 1935 with the establishment of the SS.

List apparently had direct experience of ascent. He described a trance in which it was revealed to him that the region of the Danube was the site of ancient Germanic tribes; and in his subsequent researches, List claimed to have traced a network of Wotanist shrines across Austria. In a very real sense, List figured out what heretics had believed for centuries and what is undoubtedly the case: that old Europe was possessed of an archaic, pagan (Great Mother) religion that had occult insight into reality; that folktales and popular customs are the visible debris of this; and that Christianity had wiped much of the old religion out, or driven it underground. To this insight, List added a strong racial component, the idea that the Christian doctrine of love weakened the racial purity of the supposedly original Ario-Germanic race; and also the notion that there was a Germanic priesthood (*Armanenschaft*) that had been persecuted by the Church, which had its members burnt as heretics, but that nevertheless still survived.

All of this found, in the German-speaking countries of the early twentieth century, an enthusiastic bourgeois and aristocratic audience. List's brand of history was something like a rebus, an attempt to uncover a secret Germanic heritage through guilds, heraldry, runes, and other symbols. All of these things, claimed List, were part of an elaborate gnostic cover, coded messages of the magical teaching of a widespread Armanic culture. This culture, he said, could now rise again: a militant, secret force that would restore the Germanic empire. The old world would be restored by reversing the trend of miscegenation and moral decay, and List appealed to a divine dictator who would carry this out. Occultism was important in this effort, for it was (to List) a way of recovering the old culture that Christianity had destroyed. As early as 1891, List predicted that in 1932 a "divine force" would seize the collective unconscious of Germany, transforming a mongrelized, pluralistic society into an aristocratic and monolithic one.

A second key figure in the rise of Ariosophy, already mentioned, was Lanz von Liebenfels, who built on the work of List. Lanz was more directly in the *völkisch* line of thinking than List, and much more blunt in terms of programmatic goals. Plainly put, his theology was a dualist heresy that called for the direct extermination of all racially "inferior" peoples and the restoration of "godlike Aryans" to leadership status. A Cistercian monk (he quit the order in 1899, claiming that it had betrayed its original—by which he meant racist—doctrines), Lanz developed a simplistic Manichaean racist theory that would echo again and again throughout Germany over the next few decades, and which we have already outlined: all evil was dark and animalistic, all good was blond and spiritual. The dark forces worked to promote chaos; the light, to promote order. The original Aryans had copulated with pygmies, resulting in a loss of psychic powers, which could only be restored to the world by the extermination of "inferior races"—etc. This paranoid vision of history, a story of past pollution and future redemption, was popularized by Lanz in books such as *Theozoologie* and in his journal *Ostara,* both of which appeared in 1905. The following year, Lanz purchased a castle in Lower Austria as a headquarters for his activities, and flew the swastika over it; in 1907, he founded the Ordo Novi Templi, or ONT, as a revived version of the medieval Templars, who (he argued) had been a secret Armanist group. The ONT did research into genealogy and esoteric rituals and liturgy, attaining the peak of its activity during 1925–35. *Ostara* itself lasted until 1917, and was revived in the 1920s. The future order depicted in its pages was that of a racist and hierarchical paradise, with Aryans at the top—a vision that persisted in German consciousness and imagination down to the foundation of the Third Reich. *Ostara* was very widely read; as head of the SS, Himmler would later pursue some of the ideas on eugenics that Lanz had outlined in its pages.

How closely Nazi ideology follows the Ariosophical vision of the world is, as we shall see, quite remarkable. Hitler's speeches, his book *Mein Kampf,* Himmler's design for the SS, the writings of Alfred Rosenberg (the Nazi Party ideologist) and of Dietrich Eckart (Hitler's mentor) are so in line with the worldview of List and Lanz that it is easy to conclude that they merely provided a blueprint which Hitler carried out. In the early thirties August Knoll, then a professor at the University of Munich, was ridiculing Hitler's speeches and writings to his students, showing how entire sections had been "borrowed" wholesale from various issues of *Ostara.*

In any event, Aryan occultism grew rapidly in Germany after the First World War.[12] One leading figure was Rudolf John Gorsleben, a man close to Dietrich Eckart and (by 1932) to Julius Streicher, later editor of the infamous newspaper of racial hatred, *Der Stürmer.*[13] Gorsleben's own paper, published in Munich, *Deutsche Freiheit* (German Freedom), propagated the usual mixture of racism and occultism, and his *Hoch-Zeit der Menschheit* (Zenith of Humanity, 1939) described the former glory of an ancient Aryan world. In 1925 Gorsleben founded the Edda Society, an Aryan study group which had many writers and influential people in it, and which declared its commitment to Nazism in 1933. Karl Maria Wiligut, soon to be occult adviser to Himmler and the SS for his supposed clairvoyant knowledge into the German past, was a *völkisch* seer associated with this group. Gorsleben helped found an Ariosophical school in 1931, where courses were given in yoga and breathing exercises.

Actual occult practice, in the form of trance states or (in a few cases) ascent experience, undoubtedly went on in such groups, though its centrality to Nazism is unclear. Thus Friedrich Bernhard Marby founded a school of rune occultism, and devised a system of "rune gymnastics" and mantric recitation; Siegfried Adolf Kummer also founded such a school in 1927, where students practiced magic and meditation. Both men were censured by Wiligut in his capacity as Himmler's magical adviser; but a case can be made for a widespread postwar occult movement that included such disciplines as yoga and dream interpretation. The firm of Johannes Baum published a "New Thought" series during 1920–25, popularizing Eastern religion, breathing exercises, and the like. Herbert Reichstein, another leading occult publisher during this time, was an associate of Lanz. By 1932 he was calling Hitler "an instrument of God." The following year, Reichstein moved to Berlin and began publishing the *Arische Rundschau* (Aryan Review). Ernst Issberner-Haldane, who had an ascent experience in the Andes and then went on to study with a Persian master, opened a racist commune in 1927, which later became an ONT house. Grigorij Bostuničs (later Gregor Schwartz-Bostunitsch) also underwent esoteric instruction—possibly from G. I. Gurdjieff—and returned to Germany to preach about the alleged world Jewish conspiracy and work with Alfred Rosenberg, and later with the SS. Himmler became his patron in the 1930s.

An early link between occult activity and ideology, and the Nazi Party, was a violently anti-Semitic society founded in 1912 called the Germanenorden (Germanic Order), which later added Adolf Hitler to its membership. Its immediate inspiration was Ariosophy; its publications sported a swastika, imposed on a cross. Its lodges spread rapidly throughout Germany, but it did not last much into the First World War. It was, however, revived in Munich ca. 1917 by a man named Rudolf Glauer, a practicing occultist who took the name of Rudolf von Sebottendorff, and who was a staunch admirer of List and Lanz. It was out of the Germanenorden, and its successor organization, the Thule Gesellschaft (Thule Society), a name adopted by the

Germanenorden as a cover (it had gotten into the assassination of public figures), that the Nazi Party arose and from which it took the symbol of the swastika. A Thule-related newspaper, the *Münchener Beobachter* (Munich Observer), later (December 1920) became the official Nazi paper, the *Völkischer Beobachter*, and by 1921 the shares of the corporation were in Hitler's hands.

The *Münchener Beobachter* was crucial in providing its readership with a steady stream of anti-Semitic "documentary evidence" and in acting as a clearinghouse for right-wing events. The issue of May 31, 1919, published the twelve points of Sebottendorff's political program, which contained the essentials of what would become the National Socialist program. (These were elaborated into twenty-five points by Hitler in February of 1920.) The Thule Gesellschaft itself gathered many of the future ideologists of the party, including Alfred Rosenberg and Dietrich Eckart. Eckart founded the journal *Auf gut Deutsch* (In Plain German) in 1918, which attracted leading *völkisch* writers. The same year, the Thule Society organized the Political Workers' Circle under the leadership of the sportswriter Karl Hauer, who introduced his collaborator, a railroad mechanic named Anton Drexler, to the Thule Gesellschaft. In 1919 Drexler and twenty-five railroad workers went on to found the German Workers' Party (DAP), which showed interest in building a mass movement. The DAP often held its meetings in Thule quarters; Hitler was soon recruited as its chairman of propaganda.

That the Nazi Party came out of the Thule Gesellschaft was the claim of Rudolf von Sebottendorff, the guiding force behind this organization. Sebottendorff studied occult and mystical practices in Turkey and Egypt and was also, by his own admission, strongly influenced by the writings of List and Lanz. After being away from Germany from 1919 (he disappeared into Turkey, Mexico, and the United States), he suddenly reappeared in Munich in 1933 with a book entitled *Bevor Hitler kam* (Before Hitler Came), in which he documented the early years of the Nazi Party and claimed that it had emerged out of the Thule Gesellschaft. He identified Hitler as an early associate of the Society, and cited the affiliation of men who were now leading Party members.[14] The book went through a first edition of three thousand copies in 1933, and a second edition (1934) of five thousand copies shortly after, almost all of which (the second edition) were seized by the Gestapo. Sebottendorff mysteriously disappeared after that; his publisher, Hans George Grassinger, who had also published the *Münchener Beobachter*, suspected that the Nazis did away with him. As the historian Karl Bracher suggests, Sebottendorff would have been "an embarrassing witness out of the past."[15]

In an article published in 1963, the American historian Reginald Phelps examined Sebottendorff's claims to the Thule origins of the NSDAP and found that they had some substance.[16] There were, after World War I, a number of parallel racist groups with overlapping memberships, most of which were finally absorbed into the NSDAP. By 1919 there were overlapping memberships among the *Münchener Beobachter*, the Thule Gesellschaft, and the later NSDAP; the paper, that year, moved to the same address as the official Nazi press (Eher-Verlag) and then later to an address that would be a Nazi meeting place. Drexler's DAP often met in Thule quarters, and so on. However, Sebottendorff gave the names of 220 Thule members; fewer than 20 were on the early Nazi lists. Furthermore, the Thule Gesellschaft was effectively dead by 1926, and it was revived only with the Nazi take-over in 1933. Sebottendorff's claim that almost all of Hitler's collaborators were involved with the society is thus unfounded, but it is clear by now that there were many more links than the Nazis wanted to admit. As Phelps notes, the Nazis did not want it known that they had sectarian or occult or elitist origins. Their goal was to build a mass movement, and for that an altogether different strategy was required.

Evidence for Hitler's exposure to occult, *völkisch*, and Ariosophical ideas is largely circumstantial, but it would seem to be fairly persuasive. Eckart was his teacher; Hitler would have consequently read *Auf gut Deutsch* and the writings of men such as Alfred Rosenberg. It is also known that Hitler was a regular guest at the home of Hugo and Elsa Bruckmann in Munich in the 1920s, where the esoteric lecturer Alfred Schuler introduced the ideas of Guido von List. Schuler argued that the "life force" List and others spoke of was in fact the blood, and that it could be revitalized through rituals and spiritual practice. The realization of cosmic forces, said Schuler, could make a person into a magician. Also popular at this time was Ernst Wachler, who promoted the idea of using stage and theater as a setting for spiritual exercises; and as Mosse notes, it is very possible that the early Nazis picked up some of their techniques of mass cult and liturgical frame-work, as later employed at the Nuremberg rallies, from him. These notions—that of the crucial importance of the blood, and the performance of public ritual—proved to be two of the most fundamental ideas of Nazi cosmology and practice.[17]

As for the link between Hitler and Ariosophy, we have already noted August Knoll's claim that Hitler was cribbing his speeches from back issues of *Ostara*.[18] Many historians now accept the argument that the influence was a direct one. The major claim for this was made in *Der Mann, der Hitler die Ideen gab* (The Man Who Gave Hitler His Ideas) by Wilfried Daim, who, along with Knoll, interviewed Lanz in Vienna on May 11, 1951. Lanz claimed that Hitler had visited him at the *Ostara* office in 1909, coming to buy old issues of the journal, and that he (Lanz) had filled in the latter's collection gratis. Josef Greiner, who knew Hitler personally during 1908–14, said that Hitler had a large collection of journal issues in those days and that he debated the ideas presented in them with another boarder in the Vienna hostel in which he was living, a disaffected priest named Grill. Hitler mentions, in *Mein Kampf*, buying "the first antisemitic brochure of my life" during these days, and adds:

> During that time I formed a picture of the world and an ideology which has become the granite foundation of my deeds. I only had to add a little more knowledge to that which I had acquired at that time; I did not have to revise anything.

It is impossible to prove that Hitler met Lanz or even that he ever read *Ostara*; but this may not be necessary. As Daim shows, the congruence between Lanz's ideas and those partially put into practice by Hitler is simply too remarkable for us to conclude that Ariosophy was not a significant part of the latter's "granite foundation." Castration, sterilization, and extermination of "inferior" races are all present in *Ostara*, as are slavery, deportation, and forced labor. Subsidies for "blond marriages" (made available by Hitler in Norway and Holland during the war) are advocated, as well as a ban on interracial ones. Hitler even referred to the Templar Order in a conversation with Hermann Rauschning at one point, saying that in order to arrest racial decay, Germany needed a crusading order, a "brotherhood of Templars round the holy grail of pure blood. . . ."[19] Hitler's personal library contained one of Lanz's books, plus another book given to him by a Party member in 1921, bearing the inscription: "An Adolf Hitler, meinem lieben Armanenbruder" (To Adolf Hitler, my dear Armanen brother).[20] The Manichaean worldview is identical to Lanz's, with history being nothing more than a cosmic combat between "solar" Aryans and "dark" Jews. Blood and race are the keys to this history, and blood and race the keys to its redemption. Also present in the writings of both men is a nightmarish vision, that of the seduction of blond, Nordic girls by dark, repulsive Jews. For both men, this was the ultimate evil, their deepest psychotic fantasy. "In both cases," writes Hitler's biographer Joachim Fest,

> we have the fetid, insipid imagery of the sex-starved daydreamer; and it may well be that the particularly nasty vapors that arise from large tracts of National Socialist ideology derive from the phenomenon of repressed sexuality within the bourgeois world.

The teachings of Lanz and the Thule Gesellschaft, says Fest, dominated Hitler's early years; and while he later freed himself from this sort of thing, it nevertheless remained embedded in his imagination. Fest believes that Daim overestimated Lanz's influence on Hitler, and perhaps this is true; but he notes that in the breeding catalogues kept by the SS, and the practice of exterminating the "unfit," "the weird and murderous notions of Lanz von Liebenfels . . . persisted." As Lanz wrote to one of his ONT brothers in 1932:

> Do you know that Hitler is one of our pupils? You will still live to see that he, and thereby we, also will triumph and kindle a movement that will make the world tremble.[21]

Ariosophy, says Goodrick-Clarke, was probably more a symptom of than an influence on the apocalyptic hysteria existing in Germany and Austria from about 1900 on, but he adds that Nazism was the realization of the fantasies of all of these esoteric groups. Hitler's worldview was profoundly Ariosophical, with race, as we have seen, being the "granite foundation" of his entire cosmology. In a 1931 interview with a Leipzig newspaper editor, Hitler stated that National Socialism was an idea of history "in accordance with the basic principle of the blood." Blood for Hitler (as for earlier occult and mystic writers in Germany and Austria) contained the soul of both the person and the race. In *Mein Kampf*, Hitler talked of Aryans "sojourning in paradise," and falling as a result of pollution. The serpent in this Garden of Eden was the Jew, poisoner of the German blood, and therefore destroyer of the German soul. The "personification of the devil as the symbol of all evil," he wrote, "assumes the living shape of the Jew." All of this was *cosmological* for Hitler, and he said as much on several occasions. The goal of National Socialism, he told Rauschning, was "to create mankind anew," something that could only be realized, he argued, by a return to blood purity.[22]

It is true that Hitler criticized, and finally suppressed, occultists of all sorts, "yet, in his nightly monologues to his assembled guests, [he] revealed his belief in the very ideas that these groups were perpetrating." Rauschning reported that Hitler saw "magic insight" as the goal of human progress and felt that just such insight was the cause of his success. Speculations of the Blavatsky sort, said Rauschning, fascinated him, and he saw his own career "as a confirmation of hidden human power . . . [and] himself as chosen for superhuman tasks. . . ." Ideologically, at least, Hitler was very much a believer in the whole Gnostic notion of ascent, and certainly of dualism and verticality.[23]

Rauschning recorded that Hitler predicted mankind would evolve into two types, a subhuman race and one that would rise above the contemporary human species. He called these the "god-man" and the "mass-animal," and the schema couldn't be more perfectly Manichaean. "What is involved here," wrote Hitler in a memorandum on building up the Party (October 22, 1922),

> is not winning a majority or even so-called political power. What is involved is a life-and-death struggle between two world views that cannot coexist.[24]

"Two worlds face one another," he later said to Rauschning—

> the men of God and the men of Satan! The Jew is the anti-man, the creature of another god. . . . I set the Aryan and the Jew over against each other. . . . The two are as widely separated as man and beast.[25]

"Gods and beasts," he said to Rauschning on another occasion; "that is what our world is made of," a statement which Joachim Fest calls "the most succinct possible summary of the essence of National Socialism."[26] To quote James Webb (*The Occult Establishment*), "Nazi Germany represents the unique spectacle of the partial transformation of the Underground of rejected knowledge into an Establishment."[27]

In terms of overlapping social organizations as well as intellectual or ideological influence, the link between Hitler, the early Nazi Party, and a certain set of occult/Manichaean ideas would seem to be pretty strong. Yet ideas themselves do not create history; and if Ariosophy was passed to the Nazis via various literate and occult groups, it nevertheless remains unexplained how the NSDAP acquired a mass following. Hitler himself rejected these cults and, on occasion, these ideas, precisely because it was clear to him that they were somewhere off on the lunatic fringe, and could not possibly attract solid, middle-class, churchgoing citizens—which is what he very much wished to do. Thus, during the period of the Third Reich, Lanz's ONT was suppressed by the Gestapo and Lanz, apparently, was forbidden to publish. Many occult groups shared this fate. Hitler's interest in "Wotanic nostalgia," if so it may be called, was to take this emotional energy and harness it to a national movement. And this, not ideas per se, is the key: Nazism is an energetic phenomenon, which is to say a somatic one. All of the Ariosophical, *völkisch*, and occult ideas finally did move to center stage in Germany, but only because the energetic configuration of the nation permitted this.

Even on the level of ideas alone, according to J. P. Stern (*Hitler: The Führer and the People*), the appeal of National Socialism is not so surprising. Hitler's views had been the stuff of right-wing extremism in Germany for fifty years prior to 1918, and at least in his nonoccult interests Hitler echoed certain kinds of traditional values.[28] Fritz Stern, like George Mosse, in *The Politics of Cultural Despair* also discusses writers such as Lagarde and Langbehn at length, adding, however, that what these men expressed was not a coherent system, but a leap from despair to utopia, and that this sort of sentiment was present in the German psyche for two generations prior to Hitler as an undercurrent, a subterranean force. As a result, says Stern, we are not really talking about the history of ideas, but of nonpolitical grievances that showed up in politics.[29] All of this had a psychic dimension; it reflected the primary experience of many Germans, and thus an intellectual analysis of these ideas gives us only a fraction of the story. The context, in any event, is clear enough: industrialization hit Germany with a speed not paralleled in other countries, resulting in severe dislocation and alienation and a longing for an earlier, bucolic, and simpler age. In fact, "romantic rebellion" against modernity, against city life, alienation, and bureaucracy, was in full swing by the late nineteenth century. Not that this was necessarily a bad thing: the "romantic rebellion" possessed great insight into the condition of the West, and produced thinkers such as Nietzsche, Ferdinand Tönnies, and Max Weber, all of whom recognized what had happened to the West in the shift from *Gemeinschaft* to *Gesellschaft*. The more specific problem was that this mood inevitably generated a mélange of sects and groups all loosely bound around the notion of a "good," primitive, natural way of life as opposed to a "bad," civilized, artificial one, and this proved to be fertile soil for something as innocuous as the communitarian, back-to-nature Jugendbewegung (Youth Movement) *and* for occult, proto-Fascist organizations such as the Thule Gesellschaft. Concomitant to all this was the fact that it was the Jews, in particular, who rose conspicuously on the modernist, industrial wave, and hence they and the "new Germany" could be seen as being basically un-German, lacking in true *Innerlichkeit* (interiority, inwardness) and pursuing crass material goals instead. The Nazis, says Fritz Stern, had a dynamism and religious tone that spoke to this longing, this *Innerlichkeit*, and that is why (he asserts) pure socioeconomic, psychoanalytic, or intellectual explanations fail. The key to the drama is spiritual/existential. We are dealing with a populace that "craved the certainty of spiritual redemption."[30]

We have met with *Innerlichkeit* before, of course; it is hardly a dirty word. It was a widespread awakening to interiority that, I have argued, underlay the heretical drama of the Albigensian crusades, and it may be central to all gnostic illumination. The difference between the German model and the other three I have discussed, in addition to the racial interpretation of inwardness that was not present in the Greek, French, or Italian cases, and in addition to the very different social and economic context, was that all of this unfolded in a fully secular-scientific world. *Nazism is the ascent phenomenon as a secular religion;* it is, in effect, a secular gnosis. With Hitler, the magic of personality—his voice, says J. P. Stern, was to German audiences "strangely vertiginous"—or personal authenticity, became the touchstone of good politics.[31] In the case of our other three models, we are living in a world in which sacred and secular, religious and political, are all part of the same culture, two sides of the same coin. The Nazi experiment was an attempt to bring these two worlds, split asunder since the Scientific Revolution (the late stage of the Italian model), back together again. It was a demonic attempt to reenchant the world. The language of National Socialism was that of transcendence. Hitler recognized, instinctively, a religious need on the part of the masses and he responded with a gnostic political program, though the gnosis was well disguised.[32] The real story here is one of ecstasy and ascent, salvation and redemption. Let me deal with salvation and redemption first, before we turn to Nazism as an ecstatic ascent phenomenon.

The best case for Nazism being a secular gnosis was made by James Rhodes in his excellent study, *The Hitler Movement*.[33] Nazism, says Rhodes, was an apocalyptic, millennarian, neo-Manichaean heresy, a tendency embedded (he believes) in human nature itself. It was not, as a result, really about ideas in any intellectual sense of the term, because it is not clear to what extent *völkisch* and romantic philosophers really influenced the Germans, and it is also likely that party leaders did not really understand writers like Lagarde and Langbehn and distorted their views, as they surely distorted those of Nietzsche. Rather, on an immediate and existential basis, the Nazis experienced revelations about their historical situation that led them to believe they were caught up in a cosmic drama. In other words, the Brownshirts knew nothing of philosophy or literature. They became millennarians and gnostics on the basis of their own primary experiences, without knowing that any of this had intellectual antecedents. Thus one SS man wrote in a short autobiographical essay: "I was a National Socialist before there was a name for that idea."[34] Nor is it the case, says Rhodes, that all of the Third Reich can be reduced to this, but rather that one type of desire pervaded and integrated all the other factors present.

The phenomenon of "revelation," in the form of ascent or altered state, was apparently present in Nazi Germany to varying degrees. In particular, it happened to Hitler in 1918 as a result of an attack of British mustard gas, and he emerged from it with a "divine" message concerning his historical mission. Rhodes argues that many people experienced some strong or mild form of this, and in that sense, millions of Germans were Hitler in microcosm. Joseph Goebbels, for example, who was Nazi minister of propaganda, records that he underwent a "Damascus"-like conversion to Hitler and his ideas. But if we can put the Nazi elite aside for a moment and deal instead with the rank and file, we do find some variation of "Amazing Grace": I was lost, I got zapped in a moment of illumination, and I saw that I and Germany were saved through National Socialism.

The evidence for this is a set of biographies collected by a Columbia University sociologist, Theodore Abel, who arrived in Germany in June of 1934 and announced, with the encouragement of the Nazi Party, a prize contest to be held under the aegis of Columbia University "for the best personal life history of an adherent of the Hitler movement." Entrants had to have belonged to the party or have sympathized with it prior to January 1, 1933—hence, this would capture "old guard" members, not opportunists who might have joined after the Nazi accession to power. A total of 683 people submitted autobiographies, and these became the basis of a book (it contains actual extracts from about twenty percent of the entries) published in 1938, entitled *Why Hitler Came into Power*. In brief, the documents revealed, in something like sixty percent of the cases, a lost self that was finally saved by stumbling upon National Socialism or hearing a Hitler speech. The voices of these men and women, says Rhodes, are very human. They talk in terms of a dramatic moment, or a moment of illumination, that moved them from aimlessness to self-organization and self-discovery.[35]

This is not *actual* ascent experience. Although trance and occult experiences did float in and around the Nazi Party and Germany for many years, we are for the most part not dealing with the sort of thing described, for example, in the Ascension of Isaiah. National Socialism was, rather, a secular variety of religious apocalyptic. People wound up in a kind of personal/political "heaven" of existential clarity and immense psychic reorganization; they didn't actually "go to heaven." Yet Rhodes does say that mystical visions were present for many of them, in which they "discovered" (a) that their difficulties had been caused by Evil and its agents, to which German society was succumbing; (b) that they had been chosen to defeat these demons, and thereby save Germany and themselves; and (c) that the final battle for total victory or total loss would soon be at hand. As J. P. Stern says, the whole pattern is pseudoreligious, has the quality of an *imitatio Christi*, but the person being imitated is Hitler. The pattern of personal disaster and psychic redemption follows exactly the pattern of Hitler's life as recorded in *Mein Kampf*. The Abel documents, no less than the speeches of Hitler and the biographies of the Nazi elite, reveal the presence of an "ontological hysteria" out of all proportion to the actual danger, and a deliverance from it through a dualist cosmology and an ideology of racial purity. It is almost as though occult practice and ascent experience were not necessary: the Abel writers speak of "the call of the blood," and of "following an inner voice," in much the same way that Hitler told Rauschning of his own "magic insight." None of this was rhetorical; it is clear that these writers "believed that they had experienced personal revelations which guaranteed redemption. . . ." "It is virtually self-evident," says Rhodes, "that the National Socialists were modern, secular gnostics." The presence of a "Jewish enemy" enabled millions of Germans to reconstitute reality, he adds; the eventual extermination of the Jews was an exercise in magic. In other words, they had to find *human* devils because they were living in a secular society; the age of *actual* demons was long over. Yet the structure was still a gnostic one. The murder of the Jews, concludes Rhodes, was a "magical ritual slaughtering."

Seen in these terms, the Nazis' fanatical eagerness to exterminate the Jews even when it was detrimental to the war effort (as was the case by 1944) becomes much more understandable. We are talking about cosmology, eschatology, world-myth, and ultimate salvation. In a cosmic battle between Aryan and Jew, victory could usher in a thousand-year reign, in which the "righteous" would redeem the earth. Eberhard Jäckel, in his book, *Hitler's Weltanschauung*, notes that the extermination of the Jews became the most important aim of the war; and Karl Bracher adds:

> Hitler's fanatical hatred of the Jews . . . cannot be measured by political and pragmatic gauges. The fact that an entire nation followed him and furnished a legion of executioners does demonstrate, however, that we are confronted not merely with the inexplicable dynamics of one man, but with a terrible disease. . . .[36]

Both the Abel documents and published Nazi literature appeal to images of rebirth, eternal life, the creation of a new humanity, and, finally, a rising up toward God. Thus, Goebbels wrote that to become aware of belonging to the *Volk* soul was to become one with the Divinity. Both Goebbels and Hitler, says Rhodes, "viewed heroism as a kind of self-abnegation through which one could merge with the divine. . . ." On the other hand, wrote Hitler in *Mein Kampf*, the "lost purity of blood . . . plunges man into the abyss for all time. . . ." The desire to raise man (i.e., Germans) out of this abyss, and to eventually make him divine, is for Rhodes the single focus that held Nazism together. And it seems obvious that the absorption of the individual German soul into that of the *Volk*, seen as divine, is a modern secular equivalent of the phenomenon of ascent and gnostic illumination.

Of course, most National Socialists did not care about classical Gnostic doctrines or pretend to understand them. The Abel documents show that their concerns were for the most part commonplace, and the electorate that voted for Hitler in 1932 was not in possession of a set of elaborate mythologies, such as Hitler's Manichaean race cosmology. But Hitler was able to present this cosmology in a popular apocalyptic format, such that, for a populace in search of emotional security and Meaning in the world with a capital *M*, it was absorbed at a primitive level. Hitler's 1922 speech, "Die 'Hetzer' der Wahrheit!" (The "Agitators" of Truth!) is a classic example of this, hammering home five basic points that Hitler was to reiterate again and again in the ensuing years. As Rhodes outlines these themes, they look something like this:

| POLITICAL STATEMENT | COSMOLOGICAL TRANSLATION |
|---|---|
| 1. Germany is in danger of imminent collapse and annihilation. | 1. End of Being (ontological destruction) |
| 2. The cause of this is a world Jewish conspiracy. | 2. Demonology (identification of the devil) |
| 3. Resistance is necessary via the *Volk*. | 3. Call for eschatological war |
| 4. Only National Socialism is capable of mounting such a resistance. | 4. Identification of the agents of God |
| 5. This will usher in a new Reich, characterized by both blood improvement and economic improvement. | 5. Salvation, redemption, the new Jerusalem |

In the sense of Robert Masters' theory of the five bodies, Hitler falls into the category of the "great teacher," i.e., he talked to the third body, the unconscious. The real message was somatic, mythological, and the audience knew this intuitively. Christ also talked on this level, as we know; so did many of the Cathar Perfect, and so did Cardano and Pico. The problem remains one of distinguishing between black and white magic. As the Jungian analyst H. G. Baynes put it in 1941 (*Germany Possessed*), the "Wotan-possessed disciples of Hitler are clearly incapable of knowing what is sacred and what is obscene"[37]—something that remains a problem today.

In general, the energetic dimension of the Nazi phenomenon was one that was not lost on Jung and Jungian writers. Jung's own failure to distinguish between black and white magic was responsible for a flirtation with Nazism that is not exactly to his credit. For the most part (not entirely), he got caught up in what J. P. Stern calls the "dynamic fallacy," in which all psychic energy is seen as positive or divine. This fit well with Hitler's view, that authenticity was the supreme value. But Jung had some important things to say about the whole thing. His essential point was that Christianity was alien to German religious thought, and that the true god of the Germans was the Teutonic deity Wotan. Wotan's energy, that of ecstasy and *Ergriffenheit* (possession), was, said Jung, stirring once again, after being dormant for so many years; and this was, for Jung, an archetypal phenomenon:[38]

[W]hat is more than curious [wrote Jung] . . . is that an ancient god of storm and frenzy, the long quiescent Wotan, should awake, like an extinct volcano, to new activity, in a civilized country that had long been supposed to have outgrown the Middle Ages. We have seen him come to life in the German Youth Movement, and right at the beginning the blood of several sheep was shed in honour of his resurrection. . . . The Hitler movement literally brought the whole of Germany to its feet, from five-year-olds to veterans. . . . Wotan the wanderer was on the move.

"I venture the heretical suggestion," Jung continued, "that the un-fathomable depths of Wotan's character explain more of National So-cialism than all three reasonable factors [the economic, the political, and the psychological] put together." "[T]he Germans are in a state of 'fury.' . . ."[39] The impressive thing about the German phenomenon is that one man, who is obviously 'possessed,' has [possessed] a whole nation to such an extent that everything is set in motion and has started rolling on its course [into a dangerous sliding]."[40] Wotan, said Jung,

is a fundamental attribute of the German psyche, an irrational psychic factor which acts on the high pressure of civilization and blows it away. *Despite their crankiness, the Wotan-worshippers seem to have judged things more correctly than the worshippers of rea-son.* . . . A hurricane has broken loose in Germany while we still believe it is fine weather.

"[T]he coincidence of anti-Semitism with the reawakening of Wotan," Jung says at another point in the same essay, "is a psychological subtlety that may perhaps be worth mentioning."[41]

Indeed it is. I find this text overwhelmingly convincing; it speaks to the hidden, somatic sources of Nazism in a way that other expla-nations never could. This is not to say that Fascism and the Holocaust did not have their banal, routine, and bureaucratic aspects, as Hannah Arendt argued; but the amazing thing about the Nazi phenomenon, as Jeffrey Herf has shown (*Reactionary Modernism*), is that the bureau-cratic and the romantic/demonic can actually work together, can ac-tually go hand in hand.[42] Germans were hardly in a state of Wotanic frenzy most of the time; Wotan was rather an undercurrent and an inspiration that the Nazis occasionally tapped, for example, at the Nuremberg party rallies. But one can, as did the Abel writers, emerge from vision or revelation, know what one "has to do," and matter-of-factly set about doing it. The point is that the atmosphere of Germany was pervaded by a lightly altered state. The ascent phenomenon was present to varying degrees on a national scale and, wittingly or not, it constituted a demonic version of a Christian heresy. With National Socialism, wrote H. G. Baynes, "we are living in a world-dream, in which the forces engaged have authentic mythological character."[43]

Nazism was a demonic rerun of an old tape, and the campaign against the Church, well documented by the Canadian historian J. S. Conway, provides ample evidence for this.[44] "The more the absolute authority of the Christian *Weltanschauung* loses its hold," wrote Jung as early as 1918,

> the more audibly can we hear the pacing to and fro of the "blond beasts" in their subterranean dungeon, threatening us with an outburst which is bound to have devastating consequences.

As Baynes put it in 1941, "the present division in Europe has to do with the pagan-Christian conflict within the soul of Christendom." National Socialism, he wrote, is the shadow of Christendom, and it was Hitler's fate to personify it.

How clear all this was in Hitler's mind is quite evident in Rauschning's record of Hitler's private conversations. Hitler was, in fact, almost a classical heretic, who saw Christianity as a civilized veneer that had suppressed a true, pagan Germanic culture. "One is either a Christian or a German," he told Rauschning. "One cannot be both. . . . We want free men, who know and experience that God is within them."[45] It is necessary, as a result, to replace the cross with the swastika.[46] The churches will only be crowded once again, he told Julius Streicher, "when it is *our* religion that is preached there."[47]

> The peasant [said Hitler to Goebbels] will be told what the Church has destroyed for him: the whole of the secret knowledge of nature, of the divine, the shapeless, the daemonic. The peasant shall learn to hate the Church on that basis. Gradually he will be taught by what wiles the soul of the German has been raped. We shall wash off the Christian veneer and bring out a religion peculiar to our race. . . . [I]t is through the peasantry that we shall really be able to destroy Christianity because there is in them a true religion rooted in nature and the blood.

Hitler added, to both Streicher and Goebbels, that there was no rush as far as this agenda was concerned, and indeed, he tried not to move too quickly, so as not to generate Church opposition or alienate the mass of the German people. But he did mount a campaign against the Church, down to the substitution of Nazi rituals for baptism, marriage, the Mass, and so on, and the Church was hardly unaware of this.[48] When pagan celebrations were held in place of Easter in 1937, the Catholic and Evangelical churches wrote Hitler the following month, asking whether "the attempt to de-Christianize the German people is to become the official policy of the Government. . . ."[49] There exists strong evidence, says Robert Pois, "that the eventual goal of National Socialism [was] the extirpation of the entire Judeo-Christian tradition. . . ."[50]

As already noted, Hitler repudiated, on occasion, anti-Christian tendencies within the party, as well as occult ones, and did so in no uncertain terms.[51] It even got to the point that in early June of 1941, Heydrich officially ordered the suppression of all secret societies, and this even included Ariosophical ones. The immediate reason for this was the apparent—and to this day still unexplained—defection to England on May 10, 1941, of Rudolf Hess, whose occult interests, and close relations with astrologers and naturopaths, were widely known. The dragnet sweep of astrologers and other occult practitioners took place on June 9, 1941, and was, in fact, labeled *Aktion Hess:* the Nazis claimed Hess had gone insane, and they scapegoated astrologers as having driven him crazy.[52] But Nazi opposition to sectarian groups had already begun in 1935, if not earlier, so it is clear that Hess' departure was merely an excuse for deeper issues. Specifically, Hitler's goal was to copy the *format* of the Church, the Freemasons, secret societies, and even the Jews (racial purity, tight community, chosen people),[53] but to replace the *content* with his own understanding of the German "magical" heritage. As Conway puts it, the "claim to be the representative of a new paganism was . . . an integral part of all Nazi thinking."[54] And as Hitler often said, there must be no hurry here—the goal was to build a mass following rather than a sectarian one. The masses were not yet ready for the full information about the cosmos, about reality; the party would have to proceed in gradual steps, leaking the information in indirect ways. Addressing the officers' class of 1938, Hitler said that he would here express ideas

which perhaps could be openly stated in later decades or centuries . . . [and] whose official expression in past years and also today still could only do damage to the growing approbation which the movement enjoys among some groups of our people. . . .[55]

It becomes clear, then, that the Nazi elite was very much into a careful orchestration of occult exposure and public "awakening." This is why, very probably, Lanz, Sebottendorff, and Ariosophy were suppressed, for Hitler would hardly wish to point to abstruse mystics or the Thule Gesellschaft as being the sources of his inspiration. This gives much credence to the argument developed by Robert Pois (see note 8) that what was adopted by the Nazi elite was an inner doctrine that retained these obscurantist origins and ideas and a public doctrine that opposed them, with the relationship between the two being stage-managed in ways that were meticulous, the work of a consummate politician. Certainly, the notion of a secret teaching was often repeated, to Rauschning and a few others, such as Otto Wagener, who was told to keep these ideas to himself and "thus become the guardian of the grail, whose innermost truth can be disclosed to only a few." The suppression of (competing) secret societies, which began as early as 1935, thus fits into a coherent pattern and plan.[56]

Hitlerism was, then, an archetypal phenomenon of the gnostic and heretical variety, and the deification of Hitler was a crucial element in the leaking of Fascist "gnosis" to the public at large. It *seemed*, at least on the surface, purely political; and indeed, the cult of personality is hardly limited to fascist regimes. But in the case of Nazism, it went much deeper than this. At the Nazi Party rally in Nuremberg in September of 1937, a huge photo of Hitler was displayed with the inscription beneath it: "In the beginning was the Word. . . ."[57] William Teeling, who visited Germany in the late thirties, was told by the mayor of Hamburg: "We need no priests or parsons. We communicate direct[ly] with God through Adolf Hitler." Dorothy Thompson, writing in the December 1934 issue of *Harper's Magazine* ("Good Bye to Germany"), told the following story:

At Garmisch I met an American from Chicago. He had been at Ober[g]ammergau, at the Passion Play. "These people are all crazy," he said. "This is not a revolution, it's a revival. They think Hitler is God. Believe it or not, a German woman sat next to me at the Passion Play and when they hoisted Jesus on the Cross, she said, 'There he is. That is our Fuehrer, our Hitler.' And when they

paid out the thirty pieces of silver to Judas, she said: 'That is
Roehm, who betrayed the Leader.' "

"There has arisen a new authority as to what Christ and Christianity
really are," said Hans Kerrl, Reichsminister for Church Affairs, on
February 23, 1937; "Adolf Hitler is the real Holy Ghost."

Christ associations were, in fact, everywhere. Walter Langer reports
that an art shop in Berlin had a large portrait of Hitler in its display
window surrounded by paintings of Christ, and the historian Stephen
Roberts tells of seeing, in Munich in the fall of 1936, "coloured pictures
of Hitler in the actual silver garments of the Knight of the Grail. . . ."[58]
The highest circles of the SS were, in the mid-thirties, agreed that
Hitler would take over the role that had historically been that held by
Christ. Indeed, Heydrich said as much to Himmler on one occasion,
and the latter was hardly one to disagree.[59]

It remains for us to examine to what extent Nazism was informed
by actual occult practice, or by the deliberate cultivation of ascent
experience. The argument in favor of this has quite a large, and
sensationalist, literature, its purpose being to show that the Nazis
were inspired and directed by specific occult agencies over the period
1920–45. Not all of this is fanciful. We have already made some reference to these things, and to recapitulate them briefly, we have Guido
von List's trance experience, Goebbel's "Damascus"-like conversion,
Ernst Issberner-Haldane's ascent experience (both psychic and physical) in the Andes, and Hitler's own ascent experience of 1918, in
addition to his strong private interest in occult forces (more on this
below). Lanz and the ONT probably engaged in some esoteric practice;
Rudolf John Gorsleben opened an Ariosophical school in 1931 that
had courses in yoga and breathing exercises, and Friedrich Bernhard
Marby founded a school of rune occultism that included certain esoteric gymnastic exercises and the recitation of mantras. The school of
Siegfried Adolf Kummer (opened in 1927) taught magic and meditation. Grigorij Bostunič had esoteric instruction before working with
Alfred Rosenberg and the SS, and later had Himmler for a patron.
Himmler in particular was very much involved in occult practice (see
below), as was his adviser Karl Maria Wiligut and (to a lesser extent)
Rudolf Hess. Not all of this was deliberate cultivation of the ascent
experience; much of it was designed simply to produce altered states
and paranormal effects, such as ESP. Alfred Schuler, some of whose
lectures Hitler probably attended, said that the life force, which for
him was the blood, could be revitalized through esoteric practices,

and could make the practitioner a magus; but there is no evidence that he (or Hitler) ever performed the rituals involved. Finally, Rudolf von Sebottendorff (as Rudolf Glauer) very probably had esoteric training in Turkey, although there is no evidence that any of this was actually adopted by the Thule Gesellschaft.

The claims made by sensationalist literature for Nazi occult practice, influence by Eastern masters, deliberate engagement in black magical rites, and so on, are quite extensive, and largely without foundation (Himmler remains an important exception).[60] Thus Trevor Ravenscroft (*The Spear of Destiny*) claimed that Hitler took peyote; that under the leadership of Dietrich Eckart the Thule Gesellschaft performed occult rituals on selected victims; and that Eckart opened the centers of Hitler's astral (third) body. No evidence whatsoever is cited for these claims, which are completely outlandish; in fact, at one evening meeting of the Thule Gesellschaft, Sebottendorff performed some "magic pendulum" experiments, and it was later suggested to him that he eschew this sort of thing, as it was a turnoff to the membership.[61] The famous book by Louis Pauwels and Jacques Bergier, *The Morning of the Magicians*, claims that the Nazi leadership was in search of an Eastern occult theocracy, and that the sect chosen to do this was called the Vril Society, which the authors say was an important Nazi organization. Once again, there is no evidence for any of this, and their additional claim, that the Thule Gesellschaft was the secret, guiding agency behind the Third Reich, is also fallacious.[62] The worst example of this sort of thing is undoubtedly René Alleau's book, *Hitler et les sociétés secrètes*, published by a respectable Parisian firm, and from front to back a total lie. The argument of the text is supposedly based on Sebottendorff's work, *Bevor Hitler kam*. Alleau invents a nonexistent subtitle for the book referring to Turkish Freemasonry; claims that the Preface is dated February 3, 1924 (in fact the book was published in 1933 and 1934, and the *Widmung*, or dedication, is dated November 9, 1933); says that Sebottendorff revealed that he was writing the text at the behest of a secret Eastern order, which wished to influence the West; and finally tells his readers that Sebottendorff described a certain type of Islamic yoga based on a set of gestures that generated a series of colors (Alleau reports on these in detail). These exercises were supposedly taught to the SS, says Alleau; and Hitler, who (he claims) studied this practice along with Rudolf Hess when the two men were interned in Landsberg Castle after the failed *putsch* of 1923, later used these gestures in his public speeches to hypnotize his audiences. The problem here (a rather serious one, to say the least) is that none of this appears in *Bevor Hitler kam*. Sebottendorff never described any such exercises in his book, which is simply devoted to arguing that the NSDAP sprang from organizations such as the Thule Gesellschaft. Alleau's entire discussion is a fabrication, presumably based on the assumption that no one would ever read Sebottendorff's book (which is, one must add, not easily obtainable). Thus Dusty Sklar, in *Gods and Beasts*, provides a journalistic account of the usual occult argument, giving no footnotes, and referring her readers to sources that are reliable—e.g., Felix Kersten's *Memoirs* (he was Himmler's personal physician)—as well as to sources such as Alleau, whose claims are uncritically adopted. I take time to explore all of this because I think that an occult case can be made, but not in the way these writers wish to make it. Occult sensibilities and a mild form of ascent experience did pervade the Third Reich, but in no way did they direct day-to-day life. Rauschning was undoubtedly right when he called the regime "magical socialism,"[63] but we need to formulate a historically responsible (that is to say accurate) case here, and lay all the sensationalist claims to rest. In what follows, I am going to attempt a case for the significance of ascent experience, and, more generally, occult practice, for the Third Reich, making clear exactly what is fact and what is speculation.[64]

We can begin with Adolf Hitler himself. The "character of Hitler's compulsive power over men's minds can only be understood in religious terms," writes Joachim Fest;[65] and we have already noted how the Abel documents reveal an odyssey of redemption, an *imitatio Christi*, with Hitler taking the place of Jesus and *Mein Kampf* replacing the Gospels. Hitler's certainty of his role as a spiritual agent, a vessel of a divine power that had chosen him to redeem the German nation, was derived from a war experience in 1918.[66] Hitler himself dated his political calling from this event, and despite his claims for an earlier dating of his anti-Semitism, most historians of the subject agree that his violent feelings toward the Jews date from this time as well. Serving on the front lines in Flanders, Hitler was hit by British mustard gas on October 15 and taken to Pasewalk, a military infirmary north of Berlin, on October 21, from which he was discharged on November 19.

Part of the problem in reconstructing what happened during this period of hospitalization lies in the fact that the hospital records were seized and destroyed by the Gestapo; but there are some indirect testimonials from Hitler himself, as well as from other informants, plus a deposition made in 1943 by Dr. Karl Kronos, a Viennese nerve specialist who had apparently been present at the original medical examination of Hitler, which was conducted by psychiatrist Edmund Forster, then chief of the Berlin University Nerve Clinic.[67] All in all, they add up to the following picture: Hitler lost his sight as a result of the gas attack, which was only slowly restored at Pasewalk, and this was accompanied by depression and mental instability that required Forster's treatment. Forster apparently believed the blindness was hysterical; historian John Toland (*Adolf Hitler*), on the other hand, claims Hitler's initial recovery followed the usual physiological pattern. Nevertheless, says Toland, a second seizure of blindness occurred in November, when Germany was declared a republic, and there was no medical reason for this. This reinforced Forster in his original diagnosis, that Hitler was "a psychopath with hysterical symptoms" (this phrase is from the Kronos report). As Hitler lay in despair on his cot, recovering from Germany's defeat and surrender, he had a "supernatural vision" (this quotation is from the *OSS Hitler Source Book*, cited in note 67). The blindness lifted; in an ecstatic trance, or "inner rapture," Hitler heard voices summoning him to save Germany, to deliver her from defeat.[68]

Ernst Hanfstaengl, who joined Hitler's entourage in 1922, told Franklin Roosevelt twenty years later:

> Hitler made it known early that while in the infirmary of Pasewalk he received a command from another world above to save his unhappy country. This vocation reached Hitler in the form of a supernatural vision.[69]

Ludwell Denny similarly reported (in 1923) that Hitler had been subject to "ecstatic visions";[70] and in remarks which Hitler personally made to Viktor-Adolf von Koerber in 1923, the event is described as "an ecstasy peculiar to the dying seer."[71] "That night in the lonely ward at Pasewalk," writes John Toland, "the most portentious force of the twentieth century was born. Politics came to Hitler, not Hitler to politics."[72]

Hitler emerged from the event as a charismatic with a politico-religious agenda. He changed markedly after this, which is, of course, a common feature of ascent experience. Hitler had not been a talented speaker before the war's end, yet by the spring of 1919 a member of the DAP (German Workers' Party, which Hitler would later join) heard him address a soldiers' council in Munich and noted "his almost occult power of suggestion over the assemblage." [73] Hitler went from someone who was inward and bookish to being a powerful orator. Fritz Wiedemann, his regimental commander, commented on this in 1948, saying that one could tell, in the early twenties, that Hitler had become a different man, and added that his hypnotic gaze was particularly striking. A contemporary account of a meeting with Hitler, says Joachim Fest, had countless parallels: "I looked into his eyes, he looked into mine, and I was left with only one wish—to be at home and alone with the great, overwhelming experience."[74] Hitler's effect was repeatedly described as hypnotic; leading Nazis described their moment of allegiance to Hitler as a kind of religious conversion, and this included Speer, Heydrich, Hess, Hans Frank, Julius Streicher, Göring, Goebbels, Hanfstaengl, Ribbentrop, and many others. In his public addresses in particular, the magic was the message; Speer said that the effect of a Hitler speech went far deeper than the content. The ascent experience got translated into a national, political context, with awesome results. "He felt just what the masses were longing for," said Schwerin von Krosigk, Hitler's minister of finance, "and cast it into incandescent phrases."[75]

It is this public shamanism that qualifies the Nazi experiment as the fourth model of heresy, and this fits in clearly with the ritualistic understanding of magic provided by Klaus Vondung in *Magie und Manipulation* (Magic and Manipulation); I shall say more about it below. It is not that Hitler engaged in deliberate occult practice, but rather that he was possessed, *ergriffen*. At one point Rauschning describes a kind of epileptic seizure Hitler had, rolling on the floor and screaming at something he was apparently seeing in the corner of the room. At other times, Hitler confessed to being carried along by an irresistible force. All of this accords perfectly with what we know of shamanic possession.[76] Rauschning also records a conversation in which a woman in his circle implored him to stay away from black magic, which she saw as leading him on, and Rauschning adds, "we witnessed the development of a man possessed. . . ."[77] True, Hitler was fascinated with occult theories of human force fields that could act interpersonally or bind a community together, or of the existence of an "earth electricity," and teachings about Atlantean civilization, or the so-called "world ice theory" of Hans Hörbiger, were things that totally absorbed him on occasion.[78] But from everything we can gather, Hitler's "occult practice" was limited to occasional involuntary shamanism. He was a trance medium, and his "occult powers" emerged in his public

addresses and his immediate affects on the people around him. The
real occultism, in terms of deliberate practice, that occurred within the
Nazi ranks was that of Heinrich Himmler, which may have had some
impact on the SS.

Himmler's occult interests were notorious.[79] He never actually had
an ascent experience, and the intensity of these interests, as well as
his total identification with Hitler (whom he regarded as a *Gottmensch*),
probably derive from this fact. He regarded himself as a reincarnation
of King Heinrich I (Henry the Fowler, tenth century), and related how
the king's ghost (among others) often appeared to him and gave him
advice. But Himmler's real model was Ignatius Loyola, whose spiritual
exercises and Jesuitical organization he tried to copy for the SS. To
this end, a castle at Wewelsburg, near Paderborn, was taken over in
1934 as a kind of SS monastery and officers' college for ideological
indoctrination, and as a place where the SS elite met regularly to devote
themselves, says Walter Schellenberg, "to a ritual of spiritual exercises
aimed mainly at mental concentration."[80] Schellenberg, who was a
high-ranking member of the SS, recounts the story of General von
Fritsch, army commander-in-chief, who was (according to Schellenberg) unjustly accused of homosexuality and forced to resign. During
this case, writes Schellenberg in his memoirs,

> I witnessed for the first time some of the rather strange practices
> resorted to by Himmler through his inclination toward mysticism.
> He assembled twelve of his most trusted SS leaders in a room
> next to the one in which von Fritsch was being questioned and
> ordered them all to concentrate their minds on exerting a sugges-
> tive influence over the General that would induce him to tell the
> truth. I happened to come into the room by accident, and to see
> these twelve SS leaders sitting in a circle, all sunk in deep and
> silent contemplation, was indeed a remarkable sight.

One wonders whether von Fritsch was aware of what was going on
next door.

The SS practiced an elaborate set of pagan religious ceremonials,
following Himmler's intense interest in Wotan worship, ancient Germanic rituals, and so on. Some of these ceremonials, including the
presentation of the famous SS death's-head ring, were designed by
"Himmler's Rasputin," Karl Maria Wiligut, Himmler's occult adviser
from 1933 to 1939.[81] Mantras were also designed by Wiligut to stimulate
ancestral memory; runes and other occult symbols were employed in

the rituals as well. Otto Rahn (see Chapter 6) was also part of this effort, and worked with Wiligut down to his (Rahn's) death in 1939.[82]

What did all of this amount to? There is no avoiding the possibility that much of this was purely ceremonial. The German historian Heinz Höhne (*The Order of the Death's Head*) says that educational evenings at Wewelsburg were poorly attended, and that the neopagan customs remained primarily a paper exercise. And yet, admits Höhne, Himmler's goal of an elite brotherhood worked. Under his tutelage the SS became a

> bizarre exclusive brotherhood in which the fanaticism of the religious sect, the rites and customs of a feudal age and the romantic cult of Germanism blended oddly with contemporary political and economic management and cold-blooded power politics.[83]

*Something* was working here, and Fest thus argues that the SS liturgy was not just show. Participation in mystic ritual, he claims, held the SS together, bound it into a brotherhood of the elect. "Without a doubt," says Fest,

> the rituals which Himmler staged on the Wevelsburg [*sic*], and at other places dictated by his faith . . . were intended to inspire those states of rapture which are so easily transformed into brutal acts and merciless violence.[84]

It is hard to know what to think here, because if the SS was not actually affected by the demonic—and it was the men of the SS who were the principal murderers of the Jews—it can nevertheless be said that the whole of Germany during these years was pervaded by a kind of demonic atmosphere, part of Hitler's plan to leak the "inner doctrine" slowly to the masses through public spectacle; and the SS was certainly at the center of this effort. The attraction of the SS, says Höhne, was that of

> a secret elite, an all-powerful secret society. To many Germans . . . the words "politics" and "government" meant simply the rule of occult forces, secret circles and *éminences grises*. The SS order was the answer to such daydreams; anyone who joined the SS became overnight one of the lords of the nation, a member of a secret society of selected noblemen, the main prop of the National-Socialist state.[85]

The transcendental impulse is the key here. As James Webb puts it, in the early days the Nazis had the characteristics of an illuminated movement, and when, after 1933, they became the "Establishment," important aspects of the "Underground" became established with them.[86]

The real occult practice of the Third Reich, of which the SS was the key agent, was a mild-to-intense trance or ascent experience, which got diffused through the populace by means of public ritual.[87] This public shamanism, as I have said, constitutes the true occultism of the Third Reich; the magical nature of the Third Reich becomes clear, says Klaus Vondung, if "magic" is understood in anthropological terms. "[E]ven in 'civilized' industrial societies," he writes, "rituals take place that can be analyzed as being magical." Archetypal energy can easily be mobilized by means of stage effects, sounds, colors, symbols, and rhetoric—as Ficino, Pico, and Campanella well knew. Ritual performance is an important element of occult practice, because it affects human physiological responses. Nazi "theater" was not "just theater," in other words. Franz Hermann Woweries' book, *Nationalsozialistische Feier-Stunden* (National Socialist Ceremonials, 1932) provides a list of recommended arrangements for a public celebration that include the use of lights; a stage draped in black; an altar with steps covered with helmets, weapons, and candles; and so on. Visiting Germany from November 1935 to March 1937, Stephen Roberts, who was then a history professor at the University of Sydney, remarked that the Hitlerian style was one soaked in mysticism and Wagnerian ritual. "The mystical trappings of Hitlerism," he reported,

> are always strangely in evidence. . . . [C]onsciously or unconsciously, Hitler uses the very phrases that have been the formulae of occult observations ever since the Middle Ages.

Hitler's speaking abilities, which we have already commented on, were a key factor in all of this. Hitler's effect was repeatedly described as hypnotic, and his oratory evoked a hysterical response. Thomas Aich, in *Massenmensch und Massenwahn* (Mass Man and Mass Madness, 1947) described a mediumistic effect, a mutual frenzy (*Rausch* in German) between Hitler and his audience. Contemporary witnesses commented on the orgiastic atmosphere of these rallies, and described Hitler's subsequent state of exhaustion in sexual terms. "[A]pocalyptic devotion spread like an epidemic," writes J. S. Conway; and if the effect was that of a morphogenetic field, it should be clear by now that its basis was somatic. Albert Speer, describing these events, said that one could almost physically feel the waves that moved through the crowds and feel how this effect bore Hitler along in his speeches from sentence to sentence. "I have been reproached," Hitler once said (as recorded by Rauschning), "for making the masses fanatic and ecstatic. . . . But [he continued] what you tell the people in the mass, in a receptive state of fanatic devotion, will remain like words received under an hypnotic influence, ineradicable, and impervious to every reasonable explanation." All of this followed from the secret, or inner, doctrine of National Socialism: Hitler's "conviction," said Rauschning, "that man exists in some kind of magic association with the universe." To this end, he added, Hitler became "the master-enchanter and the high priest of the religious mysteries of Nazidom."

A good example of this is the annual celebration that was held in Munich every year on November 9, to commemorate the *putsch* of 1923 and honor the blood of the "martyrs." It was, in effect, a passion play. In a ritualistic performance, Hitler walked alone to the sarcophagi of the sixteen "martyrs" of National Socialism, "to linger there," says Klaus Vondung, "in silent remembrance." Following this was a liturgical consecration, a poem by Böhme entitled "Cantata to the Ninth of November," which made reference to Hitler's reemergence from the sarcophagi back into the light. Vondung comments:

> The image given in these lines conjures up association with the shaman, who travels to the realm of the dead and then returns with sacred knowledge, if not also associations with Christ, who entered the realm of the dead, descended into hell, and rose again from the dead.

It was through liturgical and theatrical effects that the deification of Hitler, and the whole Nazi *Weltanschauung*, was imparted to the public in carefully calibrated doses. Hitler's entry at the public rallies, says Langer, "was more befitting a god than a man." Albert Speer, the official National Socialist architect, was responsible for the dramatic lighting effects mounted at the annual Nuremberg rally, and strategically placed 130 searchlights around the field at forty-foot intervals, throwing vertical beams up into the sky to a height of twenty thousand or twenty-five thousand feet. These then merged at the top to create a luminous dome effect, a cathedral of light, or what one witness, the British ambassador Sir Neville Henderson, called "a cathedral of ice" (Plate 19). This pyramid of light hovered over Hitler in the darkness,

19. Albert Speer's lighting effects at the Nazi Party rally at Nuremberg. From Albert Speer, *Inside the Third Reich*.

and was accompanied by colors, flags, and music. A newspaper description of a party rally held in 1937 gives some idea of what was involved here:

As Adolf Hitler enters the Zeppelin stadium, 150 of the Luftwaffe's spotlights, which are distributed about the entire square, light up. From out of the night they cut and then build a baldachin of light which stretches over the entire stadium. For a moment there is dead silence. . . . The wide stadium now acts as a mighty gothic tower of light. From the spotlights there emanates a bluishviolet light. The black blanket of night is suspended between their beams of light. A hundred and forty thousand—there are at least that many gathered here—cannot free themselves from this moment. Is it a dream or is it reality?

The function of the light, says Vondung, which is the dominant theatrical element, is to provide a physical separation between a sphere of light and the surrounding hostile darkness. In this way, the National Socialist doctrine of a Manichaean dualism is "leaked" to the public both physically and symbolically. The "sacred community" is In Here, the hostile environment Out There—a perfect recapturing of the early somatic trauma of Self vs. Other, with swastikas and flags acting as Transitional Objects to provide ontological security. "Flags and light," writes Vondung, "fuse into one magical sphere of influence. . . ."

The same type of thing, on a smaller scale, notes Conway, was practiced in the training camps of the Hitler Youth:

> By means of the pulsating rhythms of the marching columns and the unified singing of Nazi songs endlessly repeated, each boy and girl was initiated into the collective experience which dissolved their individuality and fused them into unity with their comrades . . . and [a] commitment to Adolf Hitler. . . .

These were, as Klaus Vondung says, magical ceremonies unified around the concept of the blood, and they had a powerful somatic component:

> What is essential [he writes] is that in these ceremonies people underwent the psychic and bodily experience that they were in fact all equal, formed one great community, the *Volksgemeinschaft*. . . .

And the Nazis *understood* that these were physical events; they *planned* them as such. "Flags, Sieg Heils, fanfares, marching columns, banners and domes of search lights," writes Joachim Fest—

> the whole arsenal of stimulants, developed with inventive ingenuity, for exciting public ecstasy was ultimately intended to bring about the individual's self-annulment, a permanent state of mindlessness, with the aim of rendering first the party adherents and later a whole nation totally amenable to the leaders' claim to power.

It was not, as I have already indicated, as if all of Germany were at a permanent Hitler rally; daily life was still daily life. But the Nazis were very successful in making a heavy impact on that daily life, by means of a combination of terror (the Gestapo was everywhere) and ecstatic experience. What permeated Germany during these years, says the American historian Rudolph Binion, was "a diffuse sense of empowerment through Hitler," a (generally) mild, but nevertheless frequent, kind of ascent experience. Salvation, redemption, *Deutschland über Alles*. Yet the truth about these magical rallies, as Vondung says, is that they were essentially a form of emotional rape.

And what was the result of all of this ascent experience diffused on a mass scale, and harnessed to a racial-Manichaean ideology and a constant emphasis on blood purity? Heinz Höhne tries to argue the Arendt thesis for the banal and bureaucratic character of the Holocaust, but admits that the Jews were overwhelmed by a "murderous wave of unbridled sadism."[88] "Hour by hour, day by day, week by week," says Höhne, "the SS and their local auxiliaries drove the Jews into the gas chambers, beating, tormenting, insulting and torturing." He records a scene at Auschwitz, described after the war by one of the prisoners there, of a pile of female corpses, many of the women still beautiful, even in death, with breasts cut off and flesh sliced off the thighs with deep incisions. "[W]e were wading in blood way above our ankles," the man reported. There is nothing banal and bureaucratic about this. It takes a certain type of *Rausch*, of frenzy, to make such events happen; and I believe this sort of thing can only emerge from a powerful somatic configuration that is rooted in that profound and painful dichotomy of Self vs. Other, and the drunken, aching longing to heal that split. The Jews were clearly the ultimate Other for Hitler and Germany, the perfect shadow, for they alone had accomplished what Hitler most desperately sought for the Germans, and that was racial, or blood, purity. The logic here was inexorable; there could not be two chosen people, as Hitler once said to Rauschning.[89] If German blood was to be purified once again, then Jewish blood had to run off onto the ground; rivers of it had to flow. All of this was *logical*, it followed "rationally" from Nazi cosmology. Historically speaking, there was nothing aberrant about it, save the total psychosis of this particular form of ascent experience.

With the defeat of Germany, the spell was effectively broken. The SS men in captivity—and of the one million in the SS, perhaps fifty thousand had had a direct hand in the murder of the Jews—were a bit bewildered; not remorseful, of course, but, says Höhne, wondering what the hell had happened. They had become butchers not by force, but in fact with enthusiasm—a word that means, in the original Greek, "full of God." When, in the aftermath of it all, the American psychologist G. M. Gilbert questioned Rudolf Höss, the commandant of Auschwitz, as to whether he thought the Jews had deserved their fate, Höss replied that "there was something unrealistic about such a question, because [we] had been living in an entirely different world." "It never even occurred to us," he told Gilbert.

This analysis is not, it should be understood, an "apology" for Nazism; such a thing quite obviously can never have an apology in any meaningful sense of the term. The argument for *Massenwahn*— mass madness—can obviously be used as an excuse: "The devil made me do it"; and it is out of fear of such a conclusion, I believe, that many historians have shrunk back from talking of National Socialism in terms of magic or enchantment. But *Massenwahn* hardly excuses the Germans from being responsible for the Holocaust, by any means; they *were* responsible, especially if one can say that it is the first responsibility of human beings not to abandon being responsible for any extended period of time. My concern, however, is not the issue of German guilt. Rather, my purpose has been to show that the Nazi experiment falls into the ascent pattern of Western heresy, and is the chief political form that the ascent phenomenon has taken in modern times.

It remains for us to summarize the structural features that are peculiar to this particular form of gnosticism and ascent. In the case of the previous three models, we saw that there was (in each case) a particular configuration of socioeconomic and/or political factors that took the archetypal energy and channeled it in a particular way. The key factors in the Nazi case, beyond those of national humiliation in war and severe economic crisis, were (a) the tying of the ascent structure to a racial cosmology of blood purity; (b) the channeling of the ascent phenomenon into specific political and nationalistic purposes; and (c) the occurrence of this, for the very first time, in a secular and modern context, i.e., a mass technological society. It is these three factors that distinguish the German model from the Greek, French, and Italian ones. In the case of (a), the juxtaposition was that of Aryan blood/light vs. Jewish blood/dark, with miscegenation being the equivalent of an encroachment on transitional space that, like our intermediate species and substances of Chapter 2, evoked existential terror. In the case of (b), politics became not merely a matter of competing social and economic programs, but an arena for religious experience— something totally absent from the West since the Scientific Revolution. And in the case of (c), we have the situation of a nation that, in many ways, never accepted the Enlightenment, never was able to enter fully into the world of Isaac Newton and Thomas Jefferson, and that retained serious unconscious and archetypal longings. This is not necessarily bad; but in an ostensibly secular and scientific context, the eruption of such energy poses an enormous problem, because we moderns have become so spiritually ignorant that we are easily led astray—as the case of Martin Heidegger, and to some extent that of Carl Jung, demonstrate. If you don't have a lot of experience with the sacred, and are always forced to repress it, you are not going to be able to distinguish it easily from the demonic or, as we noted earlier, the obscene, when all of these finally arrive on your doorstep.

Once again, we are faced with the question I have briefly touched on in the case of our other models of heresy: is any of this repeatable? Frankly, I see nothing to prevent the reemergence of some form of race ideology, and certainly nothing to prevent massive economic depression; in fact, I think the latter is likely to occur at some point during the next two decades, probably on a global scale, and when this happens, the search will be on for convenient scapegoats. Furthermore, what J. P. Stern calls the "dynamic fallacy"—the notion that energy, authenticity, and inwardness are enough, and that one does not have to distinguish between types of energy or worry about the context in which it manifests itself—is at present making a very strong comeback in the industrialized nations. Evangelicals, cult followers, guru worshippers, and "channeling groupies" of all sorts in this New Age of ours are only concerned that archetypal energy be present, in politics and everywhere else; they spend very little time worrying about the likelihood that the unleashing of such energy in a mass technological society might easily result in fascism. As H. G. Baynes writes: "a truth that is germane to the problem of individuation may lead to disaster if shouted through loudspeakers to the multitude."[90]

Ultimately, the issue of repeatability hangs on the question of whether the Germans as a people are all that unique. Rauschning certainly thought so:

> Every German [he wrote] has one foot in Atlantis where he can call at least one truly important freehold his own. This German trait . . . this ability to live in two worlds, the imaginary one continually projected onto the real one—all of this applies in a special way to Hitler and his magical socialism. All of these little people who yearn for something and yet find no real fulfillment—nudists, vegetarians, idealists, anti-vaccinationists, atheists, those searching for the meaning of life, reformists—they all want to set up their notions as absolute and make a religion out of their whims. . . . Adhering to a stunted kind of Romanticism, these

little sectarians create a breathless fanaticism from their spite and dogmatism; they promote the collective fanaticism of the Party and keep this fanaticism alive on the mutual confirmation of a dream.[91]

This may, as Rauschning said, be quintessentially German, but it seems to me that ontological insecurity, religious/somatic longing, and—increasingly today—magical thinking and ascent experience are all becoming common characteristics of the Western industrial nations. "National Socialism," writes Robert Pois, "was . . . expressing the wishes of a substantial portion of Western humanity." Or as he says at another point, the "national-socialist Weltanschauung embodied elements that have existed as Western civilization's alter ego for some time."[92]

And the tendencies in this direction are increasing. Born in modern hospitals, lacking the continuum experience that Jean Liedloff speaks of, suffering the confiscation described by Henri Wallon, and yearning for a Transitional Object to "make it all right," modern man and woman are, to my mind, less autonomous and more desperate for salvation than their counterparts were at any other time in history. They are the driest tinder imaginable for fascism, whether they live in Germany, France, Britain, or the United States. "Love," alcohol, television, and drugs tend to be the most popular ways in these and other countries to "solve" the problem of somatic and spiritual hunger, but gurus and cults of all sorts proliferate, and when they do so on a mass scale, they start to resemble Nuremberg rather than Jerusalem, Toulouse, or Florence. The fascism of the Rajneesh cult, to take just one example, is the most recent version of the German model, and its last days found the inner circle poisoning and drugging those who were targeted as dissidents.[93] The whole thing finally collapsed, but what would have happened if its context was not one of basic prosperity and "moderate" bourgeois alienation, but one of worldwide economic depression and inflation, on the scale that hit Germany during the Weimar period? For given the fag-end of capitalism and the inevitable crunch that will hit the industrial nations by the year 2000 or shortly thereafter, we can definitely expect prolonged economic distress at some future point. The worry over economic security is not just worry about money; it is ultimately a *somatic* terror, the ontological anxiety of being wiped out, and in such a context, the Rajneeshee—or any group like them—might have considerably more success. "[J]ust as the individual has neuroses which must not be disturbed," said Hitler to Rauschning, "so the mass has its complexes that must not be awakened. Among them are all reminders of ration cards and inflation."[94] The prevention of this has nothing to do with having a high degree of intellectual ability; the Rajneeshee claimed that ten percent of their ranks held Ph.D.'s (so did many Nazis). What is required is a different kind of intelligence, the ability to be in a position of awareness, or psychic distance, with respect to one's own somatic and energetic longing; the ability to not turn *anything*—computers, ideologies, relationships, spirituality, whatever—into worldviews, but to recognize that they are (like the human ego) just tools, nothing more. It's a tall order, and not an imminent one. For we have lived with vertical ascent structures in the West for at least two millennia, and we are not going to "go horizontal" very easily. But it remains the case that the ultimate redemption of the West is the redemption from the need for redemption itself. This is finally the issue we have to consider.

# PART THREE:
# BREAKING THE MIRROR

---

WHAT AN IMMENSE RIP
IN MY LIFE AND IN ALL THINGS,
IN ORDER TO BE WITH MY ENTIRE SELF,
IN EVERYTHING;
IN ORDER TO NEVER CEASE BEING,
WITH MY ENTIRE SELF, IN EVERYTHING.

—From Juan Ramón Jiménez,
  *Light and Shadows*,
  translated by Dennis Maloney and Clark Zlotchew

I SIT DOWN QUIETLY IN LOTUS POSITION,
MEDITATING, MEDITATING FOR NOTHING.
SUDDENLY, A VOICE COMES TO ME:

"TO STAY YOUNG,
TO SAVE THE WORLD,
BREAK THE MIRROR."

—From Nanao Sakaki,
  "Break the Mirror"

# 9

# The Gesture of Balance

*The neurotic patient does not always*
*want treatment, and when at last his distress*
*drives him to it he does not want it whole-*
*heartedly. This reluctance has been recog-*
*nized in the discussion of resistance and*
*allied phenomena; but the existence of*
*comparable phenomena in societies has not*
*been recognized.*

—W. R. Bion,
   "Intra-Group Tensions in Therapy" (1943)

WE HAVE NOW EXAMINED, in some detail, four basic models of heresy in the West. I have argued that they can best be understood as particular intersections of somatic/spiritual energy and political context. The major question for us now, given our bodily history and the present political or cultural situation, is whether we can expect yet another heretical revival in the near future; and if so, what form it will take, and what response is required of us, somatic or otherwise. It is to this question or these questions that we must now turn.

I hope by now that I have established the fact that Western history is profoundly discontinuous; that it crosses certain watersheds, or undergoes certain system-breaks, such that what is regarded as real or relevant on one side of the "fault line" becomes inconsequential on the other, as a whole new set of realities emerges into view. This is surely the import of much of Michel Foucault's work, and it is certainly implied by Thomas Kuhn's analysis of scientific revolutions—they are really cultural, political, epistemological, socioeconomic revolutions; the whole thing is a package deal. The last major system-break, or paradigm-shift (as Kuhn called it), was the end of the Middle Ages—the collapse of a feudal/Catholic/Aristotelian/animistic world, and the breakthrough to a new world defined by "progress," capital accumulation, mechanistic science, and the denudation of transcendent symbols or archetypes. This is the Italian model, and although Nazism represents the only organized political attempt, in modern times, to reject the Enlightenment and replace it with something else, Fascism was finally only a twenty-year detour, a satanic version of holism that the Allied powers, as the heirs of the Enlightenment, were finally able to defeat. We are, therefore, still living within the world-view of the Italian model, and any system-break that may occur now or in the future must be seen in that context.

I hope I have also established the fact that sectarianism and heterodoxy are among the prime movers of this set of social dynamics, this pattern of rupture and renewal, of crystallization and inevitable dissolution.[1] Moved along by a periodic politicization of the mystical ascent structure, Western culture alternates *entre le cristal et la fumée*, as the French biologist Henri Atlan once put it—between the rigidity of crystal and the evanescence of smoke.[2] Heresy, fueled by vertical, archetypal energy, coalesces within a congealed cultural pattern as an underground force every so often so as to make a new pattern possible. Based as it is on body dynamics, it would seem to be the real source of our innovative capacities. As Shmuel Eisenstadt puts it:

> Out of the combination between the conception of possible alternative ways of salvation, alternative cultural and social orders, and the structuring of the time dimensions, there emerged another element . . . namely that of the utopian vision or visions—the visions of an alternative cultural and social order beyond any given place or time. Such visions contain many of the millen[n]arian and revivalist elements which can be found also in pagan religions, but they go beyond them by combining these elements with a vision stressing the necessity to construct the mundane order according to the precepts of the higher one, with the search for an alternative "better" order beyond any given time and place. . . .[3]

In times of breakdown and incipient discontinuity, vision and transcendence—what amount to the gnosis of ascent—become vehicles for fundamental change. That all of this has been largely ignored by historians is in itself an extremely important indicator of our own culture and its assumptions, though there are indications that things are starting to change. At a recent (1987) meeting of the Organization of American Historians, Robert Abzug, who teaches at the University of Texas, suggested that the emphasis on social or psychological roots of religious experience had led scholars "to ignore what is at religion's heart—the very personal religious experience of the sacred that was so central to historical actors. . . ." We still don't have, he added, a language to undertake such an analysis, "to understand what the sacred meant to people on a personal level."[4] But in fact, many writers— men and women largely outside the "Academy" or considered "quirky" within it, such as Wilhelm Reich or Friedrich Heer—did recognize the significance of "nonordinary reality" for the history of "ordinary reality." "Spirit is the most dangerous thing which exists," wrote Heer in 1953,

> and Nietzsche was right when he considered himself "dynamite." When the old-fashioned guardians of orthodoxy burned a heretic, they knew what they were doing and why. They realized that the spirit is explosive and treated it far more realistically . . . than the pseudo-liberal babblers and advocates of tolerance in the nineteenth century.[5]

Heer understood that Western history is characterized by a periodic political eruption of repressed archetypal energy; he understood that these eruptions produced its discontinuities, and shaped its fundamental contours. Where Heer went "wrong," or at least failed to carry the argument far enough, was in not being able to understand that this energy was somatically based, and this is why he argued (as have others) for an unbroken continuity of the underground tradition. To repeat what I said in Chapter 4, once we realize that the human being has five (or more) bodies, and that these can get activated in such a way as to generate spiritual or psychic energy ("consciousness") that can actually float, can travel in the style of a morphogenetic field, then continuity via the history of ideas becomes unnecessary. This in turn entails the recognition—and this will be part of the "post-Italian" paradigm—that consciousness is a transmittable entity, and that an entire culture can eventually undergo very serious changes as the result of the slow accumulation of enough psychic or somatic changes on an invisible level. Having rightly rejected Hegel's *Zeitgeist* as an unprovable hypothesis, historians were left not being able to explain one of the most common phenomena—and possibly the most crucial one—of Western history, if not all history. Hence the inevitable tendency toward tedium that pervades so much academic history, as I observed in Chapter 3. It is long overdue to put such phenomena back into history, as Professor Abzug says, and on a scientific basis, but not "scientific" in a linear or mechanical sense. Lawrence Durrell writes: "a civilization is simply a great metaphor which describes the aspirations of the individual soul in collective form. . . ."[6] For "soul" I would prefer to substitute "body," but the difference is probably semantic.

That we are living in the midst of a system-break is, as far as I am concerned, too obvious to warrant comment. It has been in progress since the end of the First World War. Its present momentum is inexorable, and it will be with us for much of the next century. We now have a long list of books proclaiming (often in a very naive way) the coming of a "New Age" and a new holistic paradigm; and conversely, numerous economists and ecologists increasingly warn that the "Italian" progress model has no real future, and is bringing us to the abyss faster and faster every day. The most recent report in this genre, for example, the Brundtland Report of 1987 (*Our Common Future*), commissioned by the United Nations World Commission on Environment and Development, links global poverty to the destruction of ecological resiliency and predicts increasingly severe crises that must be arrested if the human race is to survive. In arguing for sustainable development, the report in effect proposes a radical alteration in the way we think and live, and recommends sweeping changes in the institutions of agriculture and industry, business, the military, and government.[7]

There is nothing new in this; it is merely a more strident, and perhaps more detailed and specific, version of what we have been hearing now for nearly thirty years. I would also guess that most people reading this report would suspect that virtually nothing will be done about this situation beyond pious comments in the press and a few useless commissions of inquiry. In fact, if you are reading these words in 1989 or after, the chances are that you will be wondering what the Brundtland Report *was*. There will be no move to arrest the coming system-break because all of the institutions named by the report—industry and agribusiness, for example—are fully committed to the Italian model, and thus hope to solve these problems (if at all) by means of a mind-set that is itself the problem. As a result, the alternatives to this mind-set are emerging from very unconventional quarters, for the most part. In documenting this trend, the Los Angeles journalist Michael Ventura specifically refers to it as a new gnosis, or heresy, which, he says, is "growing in strength and faith, manifesting everywhere, and ready to become the dominant mode of thought as it becomes more unified." At present, he says, the paradigm is totally chaotic, as in the first century A.D.:

> Call it New Age, call it what you will, it combines Eastern thought with relativity physics with cybernetics with Sufic and Franciscan and Zen mysticism with pagan animism with astronomy with biology with Hellenic polytheism with tribal ritual with Jungian and Freudian and Gestalt psychology with ecology with the arts with African aesthetics with Jefferson with Marx with. . . . Well, the point is that one of the historical projects in force now is a planetary movement to form a new faith. . . .[8]

Two things are significant here: unlike many "New Age" polyannas, Ventura is no fool. He understands that, as in the case of the collapse of the Middle Ages, we are not going to get this new paradigm for free, as it were. It will take a century or two to work out, and this "will be a time of upheaval. Wars, famines, depressions, and probably a few atomic bombs, probably dropped by and on Third World countries," are likely to be on the agenda.[9] Secondly, much of what he points to—pagan animism, tribal ritual, and so on—has strong ties to the ascent phenomenon. It is no accident that the same decade that coined the term "paradigm-shift" also discovered LSD and the importance of planetary ecology. All of these are part of a millennarian vision. As in the case of the collapse of the Middle Ages, we have entered a phase of manic-depression so characteristic of the ascent structure. And as Johan Huizinga (*The Waning of the Middle Ages*) reported for that earlier period, depression is everywhere; and just as the black plague, beginning in the fourteenth century, "flushed out" the feudal culture of Europe and decimated it to the point that cultural discontinuity became a lot easier, so are cancer and AIDS creating a similar situation today—the statistics of which are going to be quite unbelievable by the year 2000, certainly by 2010. And elation too is present: the visionary experience provided by drugs and other mystical and occult practices lends itself to renewal once again, to utopian hopes for a new planetary culture. We underestimate how endemic this is in North America and Europe; but in fact, it underlay a good deal of cybernetic and "New Age" thinking. By the mid-seventies, Andrew Greeley was reporting that forty percent of Americans were having mystical or ecstatic experiences (!), and arguing that the psy-chedelic phenomenon of the sixties was a response of American youth to the dominant scientific-technological paradigm, the refusal to con-sider any other forms of knowledge beyond the rational and the tech-nical as valid.[10] That we are caught up in a system-break, and that the ascent phenomenon has been acting as a contributing factor to the shaping of a new post-Italian paradigm, seems clear enough.

Much has been written regarding this new paradigm, although it must be said that in the hands of its leading proponents, writers such as Marilyn Ferguson and Fritjof Capra, its essential definition tends to come off in a vague and rather mushy way. Nevertheless, it draws much of its intellectual inspiration from fields such as modern physics, cybernetics, and brain research, and it argues that a cultural transfor-mation is in the making, one based on a wholly new mode of per-ception. This mode of perception includes the notion that the universe is a "dance" of energy, or a web of relationships (patterned activity); that human beings are participants in nature, not observers of it; and that what I have called the Italian model is breaking down in favor of some new spiritual kind of civilization—a change that these writers view as inevitable and, without qualification, desirable. What lies ahead is unquestionably, in the minds of virtually all New Age proponents, a "good thing," a better life for all.[11]

There are many criticisms that can be made of this vision, in par-ticular its lopsided optimism and its failure to look at the shadow side of the holistic worldview, which to my mind is potentially very dark. As might be expected, writers such as Capra and Ferguson do not lack for critics, and scholars such as Michael Marien and Stephen Jay Gould have done a fairly good job of showing that their arguments lack any real conceptual rigor.[12] My own focus, however, at least at this point, is not on the intellectual flabbiness of the New Age "plat-form," as it were, but—given the centrality of ascent experience that underlies what seems to be a contemporary spiritual awakening—the possible directions in which this latest release of archetypal energy might go. For it was visionary experience and mystical encounter that really gave rise to the "new paradigm" movement in the first place, and this, combined with a lack of any real critical analysis, makes the movement (such as it is) rather problematic. It may indeed be liber-atory, and work, as Ventura hopes it will, in the direction of planetary sustainability. To the extent that this *is* the direction of this latest release of archetypal energy, all well and good. The real naïveté of many New Age thinkers and followers, however, lies in what J. P.

Stern (see Chapter 8) refers to as the "dynamic fallacy"—the idea that all archetypal energy rushes are, *ipso facto,* a good thing. What I have been struggling to provide in this volume is an analysis of the *contexts* of the energetic or somatic phenomenon, for it is context that will determine where the content eventually winds up. And this may not be such an attractive place, as the German model dramatically demonstrates. Hence, our real task here is to try to get a grip on this latest heretical manifestation; to clarify its relationship to our previous four models and ask whether we are simply repeating an old pattern or whether a combination of patterns, or even an entirely new one, is on the agenda for us in the coming century.

None of the four models, it should be said at the outset, can be completely ruled out. Some are less likely to recur than others, but prediction based on the historical record is a very tricky business; a civilization can always wind up in unexpected places. Furthermore, it is possible for any new heretical sect to display more than one tendency. In Chapter 8 I labeled the Rajneeshee fascistic, and I think Frances FitzGerald's reportage on their inner circle speaks for itself;[13] but at least in intent, for what that is worth, the Sannyasin had, as the Moonies or the Scientologists still do, global ambitions—they matter-of-factly declared their intent to become a universal religion, to take over the world. Rajneesh said as much to an ABC-TV reporter in his first public interview (July 1985).[14] As I said earlier, this had no basis in reality; the conditions that produced Christianity were too highly specialized to allow a repeat of such an event, no matter what Rajneesh believed or what any self-styled Christ and his disciples may think. And while the internal dynamics of such groups is often fascistic, it is a different thing when these dynamics come up against the larger political structures in which they have to operate. The Enlightenment is hardly without its virtues, and one of these is a deep distrust of ecstatic experience. If this limits Western scientific culture in ways that finally cripple it spiritually and emotionally, it does serve to protect that culture from the "down side" of the ascent phenomenon. Fascism *could* occur again, especially in the context of massive global chaos and dislocation, but I personally suspect that any overt and centralized ascent tendencies would provoke an armed response. Furthermore, the Holocaust is very recent in Western memory; trials of former Nazis, or those accused of being former Nazis, are still going on, even as I write (Klaus Barbie, John Demjanjuk, et al.). We are simply too wary of the politics of ecstasy for it to gain serious momentum right now.[15] Though models number one and number four *could* be where the New

Age winds up—perhaps even in the name of body consciousness itself—I tend to see them as marginal possibilities. In fact, while we worry about fascism, something else could slip in right under our noses.[16]

If we can recall our French model for a moment, we remember that there were really two phases to it. In the first phase, mostly coinciding with the twelfth century, Catharism spread on the basis of its conscious contact with "God"—its raw, and genuine, somatic energy, which reflected badly on the frozen religiosity of the Church. This is, in many ways, an attractive model, being noncoercive and highly decentralized. It is as though an entire culture, for more than a century, "decided" to give itself over to love; and this shows up clearly both in its poetry and in its sun-drenched, easygoing religious tolerance. The movement possessed no guru figure but rather a host of men and women (the Perfect) who had been touched by the spirit and lived exemplary lives as a result. The destruction of this movement, and of the sheer richness of the southern way of life, was a major loss to the cultural and spiritual history of the West, and the legacy of that catastrophe—that of the Inquisition and the federation of loosely authoritarian nation-states that Europe ultimately became—is an unfortunate one, compared to what could have been.

The second phase of the French model was that of repression combined, as we have seen, with co-optation. With the Cult of the Virgin Mary, the archetypal energy of ascent—which had already been translated into romantic love—got channeled back into the Church of Rome. Crusades aside, the whole thing actually wound up strengthening the powers that be.

Now a repeat of this model in our own time seems, ostensibly, very unlikely. While New Age consciousness, as Ventura points out, is currently chaotic and highly decentralized, ranging as it does from corporate meditation groups to students of tantra or pagan animism, the Church is hardly a significant force on the planet anymore (save in name only), and its ability to co-opt or channel these tendencies seems extremely remote. The only thing is that we may be looking in the wrong place. Today's "Church" is not to be found in Rome but (for example) Brookhaven National Laboratory. Ever since the Italian model, the "Church"—the reigning worldview, in other words—has not been Catholicism, or any other religion, but modern science. The scientific establishment of the twentieth century is the real Church of the West, when you finally get down to it, because it is the ultimate (and official) arbiter of reality. Hence, if we are to look for possibilities

for co-optation, we must think in terms of scientific/industrial/corpo-
rate co-optation. But the meaning of this in our own time is that the
Italian model—the translation of ascent energy into a conceptual, mechanistic, scientific format—is in fact equivalent to the French model,
which is about co-optation by the reigning establishment. The two
coalesce into one here; the somatic energy of holistic thinking becomes
the conceptual structure of cybernetics, or systems theory. This is the
French model in an updated, neo-Italian version. And *that*, not a new
Christianity or fascism, is the real threat facing us today. The New
Age tendencies referred to by Ventura, which seem to be very liberating (and which often are), in many cases prove, on closer examination, to be very much a part of a new "cybernetic holism" and
systems-theory analysis that is arising in our midst.

I do not want, in the concluding sections of this book, to belabor
the negative aspects of the "holistic revolution." They certainly represent a real threat, but I have gone over this territory elsewhere, and
in great detail.[17] My point here is only that we are poised, in the late
twentieth century, on the razor's edge; things could go either way,
and we need to be aware of the general heretical pattern of the Western
ascent structure, that of an explosion of somatic energy followed by
a hardening into fixed forms. Lived experience is not the same thing
as conceptual formulations—dogmas and slogans—of lived experience, and given the Western ascent structure there is an inevitable
pull toward safety, crystallization. What I call "cybernetic holism" is
the tendency of the present Italian model, embodied as it is in the
scientific/corporate establishment, to "buy up" the holistic worldview
and energy, repackage it, and then sell it back to the public in a
"legitimized," "sanitized" form. This then perpetuates the Italian model
under the guise of breaking with it. The world is now no longer seen
as Descartes' clock, but as von Neumann's computer; but it is still, in
the last analysis, a machine. As we shift from an industrial economy
to an "information society," cognition and worldview are getting shaped
along similar lines. Herein lies the co-optation, and it is epitomized
by the position of the artificial intelligence field with respect to things
such as dreams, which one AI representative, Douglas Hofstadter,
refers to as "confused brain patterns." A civilization that starts ignoring its dream life (body number three), that loses sight of oneiric
or somatic information as primary data, is in serious trouble; yet that
is precisely the step that the "new" paradigm is often asking us to
take, in one form or another. In fact, much of the "consciousness
revolution" of the last twenty years has amounted to little more than

a flight from the body. If we have any hope of getting out of this trap, it will be because of clarity rather than charisma; for we are going to have to distinguish between an embodied holism—one that is sensuous and situational—and the cybernetic holism, or abstract "process reality," that is being advanced by many New Age thinkers.

The down side of the latest heretical manifestation is then an updated (neo-Italian) version of the French model, and the social forces working in this direction are very powerful. Formulas are easy, and lived experience frequently painful; catchphrases like "process reality" and "symbolic patterned activity" could become the touchstones of a new authoritarian regime. Systems analysis becomes the reigning ideology, and real body consciousness a taboo subject. Blake remains "quaint," and Reich a "nut case." Universities turn into data banks ("acquisition centers"), knowledge becomes information, and the only thing really new in this New Age is the jargon. It is a depressing scenario, and it could be the order of the day within a mere five decades—or less.

We should be clear as to what this scenario amounts to, should it come to pass. The call for a possible somatic revolution is for real presence, real bodily engagement with the world. The co-optation of archetypal energy for technobureaucratic purposes is a pulling away from somatic life. It is nothing else than the creation of a new Transitional Object, as Ronald Laing has correctly pegged it:

> It was all a machine yesterday. It is something like a hologram today. Who knows what intellectual rattle we shall be shaking tomorrow to calm the dread of the emptiness of our understanding of the explanations of our meaningless correlations?[18]

The "systems view of life" is not life, in other words; it is a way of hiding from the Abyss once again, and from our problems, be they social, sexual, emotional, or environmental. It should come as no surprise that major American corporations are getting more and more interested in the so-called "aquarian conspiracy."[19]

It is not difficult to guess what the victory of the new abstract paradigm might look like. Names of avant-garde holistic scientists and thinkers will replace those of Bacon, Galileo, and Descartes (and Einstein, Dirac, Fermi et al.); a new religion (read: orthodoxy) will be created around the ideas of this new elite; and we shall have a new "intellectual rattle" to play with. We'll shake that rattle for another century or two, and if we are lucky (we may not actually be given another chance), the archetypal energy of the body will break through the bullshit yet one more time. Cybernetic holism will be exposed for what it is—the latest ism for running from reality—and we'll be confronted with the same choice of four heretical models once again; as well as with the option of getting down to the root of the human dilemma once and for all. My own suggestion is that we do this now rather than go round the turnstile one more time, and this would involve a very different scenario than jumping on the New Age bandwagon. This would be a truly liberatory post-Italian-paradigm world, but it requires a refusal of a particular sort, one that will not come easy to any of us, but that contains the real key to freedom. Let me devote the remainder of this chapter to spelling this out.

The linchpin of the Western reality system, as I hope I have been able to demonstrate, is the split between "heaven" and "earth," a split that is nothing more than a projection of the basic fault, and that can only be bridged by an ascent structure, an ecstatic journey capable of traversing transitional space. The religion or philosophy or social system that then gets organized around that vertical journey (or journeyer) then acts as a Transitional Object that holds the culture together for the next few hundred years. Thus far, the West has come up with four variations on this theme; and to my mind, only the Cathar version was genuinely human, though we shall never know how it might have turned out. There is another alternative to recycling the ascent structure one more time, and that is to finally abandon it once and for all. This means, at least initially on the individual level, learning to live with the Abyss; recognizing the gap for what it is. Far more important than finding a new paradigm (T.O.) is coming face to face with the immense yearning that underlies the need for paradigm itself. This means exploring what we fear most, viz., the empty space or silence that exists *between* concepts and paradigms, never *in* them. We are indeed in a system-break, and the temptation to stuff the gap is very strong; but the "road less traveled," which is that of looking at the nature of paradigm itself, is the truly exciting and liberatory path here. There can be no healing of our culture and ourselves without taking this option, and it will not go away, whether we miss it on this "round" or not. Nothing less is at stake than the chance to be finally, fully human, and since that is our destiny, the latest heresy or paradigm-shift is simply not going to cut it.

What does the end of the ascent dynamic really involve? At first glance, it would seem to imply that everything that is meaningful to us would be lost; and indeed, a very good case contrary to what I am advocating can be made. Thus the Jungian analyst H. G. Baynes said that the argument against ascent experience is analogous to the attempt to put out the sun because it gives some people distorted vision. Ecstatic energy, he said, is our "real gold"; we need to learn how to navigate the territory, not to declare that it shouldn't exist.[20]

Certainly, the cognitive insight of ascent experience is earth-shattering; people who have it emerge wondering where they have been all their lives. Purely intellectual or analytical knowing is revealed as being hopelessly incomplete. Life takes on a vivid quality, for one becomes concerned with things that really matter; it is no longer a question of filling up seventy-odd years with "interesting projects" (more often, not so interesting). The event is so numinous, so meaningful, that one's relationship to the world, and to oneself, will never be the same, and thus to talk of abandoning this kind of experience would seem to be, as Baynes said, a great mistake.

The problem is that the very strength of the ascent tradition, viz., the granting of revealed (i.e., certain) knowledge, is also its weakness. The Spanish poet, Antonio Machado, once wrote:

> In my solitude
> I have seen things very clearly
> that were not true.[21]

The "clarity" of archetypal energy is just a bit too wonderful. It is simply too easy to get a "message from God" and be off and running with it. For example, on July 7, 1986, Juan Gonzales, a Cuban refugee who happened to be living in New York and, at the time, riding the Staten Island ferry, killed two people and wounded nine others with a sword in an attack he said was ordered by God. Gonzales said that he was specifically ordered to take control of the ferry in the name of the Father, the Son, and the Holy Ghost.[22] This sort of "amazing grace" gives one moment to pause; and if it occurs as a mass phenomenon, we are in very deep trouble.

A similar type of revelation occurred to Richard Butler, leader, in the United States, of the neo-Nazi Church of Jesus Christ Christian (sic). One evening in 1960 Butler attended a sermon given by the Reverend Wesley Swift and had a born-again experience ("The lights were turned on," he reported). He suddenly "knew" that God had ordered the races to be separate, with (you guessed it) Aryans to reign over all the others.[23]

I know one man who had an ascent experience in a technological context, and now believes that only technology can save us. In California, I met another man who came down off his ecstasy with the belief that he had been contacted by UFOs, and that his job was now to prepare the planet for its salvation via extraterrestrial visitors. My own experience came through a particular type of body meditation; hence, this book. So I am in the position of arguing that the energy of the universe originates in the body, and is generated as a field between bodies, but how can I be sure this is right? It may be much more complicated than this. In certain Oriental traditions, for example, the world is seen as pervaded by a life force—*ch'i, ki, prana*, etc.— and the body is regarded as merely a talented receptacle or "accumulator" for such energy. My approach of the nemo or gap, of Winnicott and Lacan, may be much too narrow, although I admit I have said more than just this. But my point here is that if I decide that ascent experience is the last word, then I can create a religion out of the body and be done with all other alternatives. I may be a lot more harmless than Richard Butler or Juan Gonzales, but—if I am going to base everything on revelation—not a whole lot less rigid. Ascent experience is perhaps not as enlightened as it would at first seem.

This issue is the subject of two very important books on heresy, Umberto Eco's *The Name of the Rose* and Jacob Needleman's *Lost Christianity*. Both authors recognize the "problem" of the Self/Other dynamic, and how it has gotten translated over the centuries into the social arena as the bitter and recurrent struggle of heresy vs. orthodoxy. They suggest that ecstatic dissolution of the Self may not be the best way out of this (binary) game. For Eco, only humor can cut through the blind assurance of revealed experience; it throws us back on ourselves, gives us some psychic distance from the things we are so certain of. (Can you imagine someone like Jerry Falwell poking fun at his own religion? How refreshing—and spiritual—this would be.) I have called this talent "reflexivity," and shall say more about it below (it is not the same thing as cultural relativism);[24] but it is important to note that for Eco this reflexivity, this ability to see ourselves *in* a state of need and commitment, to actually observe it, is the ultimate heresy, much more heretical than any new revelation, any new paradigm. Eco's fictional spokesman, William of Baskerville, tells his assistant, Adso, that the devil is essentially "faith without smile," and adds:

Fear prophets, Adso, and those prepared to die for the truth, for as a rule they make many others die with them. . . . Perhaps the mission of those who love mankind is to make people laugh at the truth . . . because the only truth lies in learning to free ourselves from the insane passion for the truth.[25]

For Jacob Needleman, the real Christianity that got lost and buried somewhere in the first century A.D. was not that of Gnostic ascent, but this same type of reflexive ability—what he calls, following Gurdjieff, "self-remembering."[26] It is, he says, the experience of yourself, *not* the experience of God. Needleman may be correct, historically speaking (I personally tend to doubt it), but he does quote Meister Eckhart in his defense to good effect:

Aware of it or not, people have wanted to have the "great" experiences . . . and this is nothing but self-will. . . . There are thousands who have died and gone to heaven who never gave up their own wills.

"One longs . . . for God, or for Meaning . . .," writes Needleman, "and does not see that the longing itself is the beginning of the answer one is seeking." Ecstasy can bind communities together, he points out, but to what end? We have pursued mystical love, he says, whereas what we need is "ontological love."

This is the crucial point—that true enlightenment is to really know, really feel, your ontological dilemma, your somatic nature. The mystic seeks to go up; the ultimate heresy, to my mind, is to go across, or even down. I recall how, a few years ago, I did a two-week meditation retreat with a former Theravada Buddhist monk, and asked him, in the course of it, where ecstatic experience, or Great Mother consciousness, fit into the whole thing. "Oh," he said with a wave of his hand, "in Buddhism, that is regarded as a very *low* form of consciousness." He went on to say that ascent was regarded in his tradition as *mara*—an obstruction to enlightenment. In the same way, Needleman characterizes ecstasy as a form of bondage. The real goal of a spiritual tradition should not be ascent, but openness, vulnerability, and this does not require great experiences but, on the contrary, very ordinary ones. Charisma is *easy*; presence, self-remembering, is terribly difficult, and where the real work lies. This is the argument that Wally Shawn makes to Andre Gregory in that popular film of a few years ago, *My Dinner with Andre*. Andre goes on about his great rebirth experiences in the forests of Poland; Wally points to the immediacy of cold coffee, which he prepares the night before and then drinks when he gets up in the morning. *Ecstasy lies in details,* in what my friend Jack London calls "the yoga of the household." (When was the last time you observed yourself in the act of dusting the dining room table?) "The highest art," goes an old Tibetan saying, "is the art of living an ordinary life in an extraordinary manner."[27] That this could become the modality of an entire society is an inspiring possibility.

Of course, ascent experience, and what it carries with it, won't go away by fiat, so in this sense Baynes is right—we shall have to learn to navigate the territory. For at least since the binary worldview of Neolithic civilization, we are wired up in a Self/Other dynamic that pulls us toward transcendence, with all its brilliant and destructive possibilities. Yet a much deeper life lies beyond that of the ascent structure, which is finally about salvation, or redemption; for the ultimate heresy is not about redemption but, as I said earlier, about the redemption from redemption itself. It is to be able to live in life as it presents itself, not to search for a world beyond. (Politically, of course, this is very often not possible; but it could be argued that our political forms, and messes, are themselves the results of binary thinking and the ascent mentality.)

The shift away from ascent, and toward bodily presence in the world, implies certain things that go with the territory, as it were. The first of these is an end to the binary contrast mode of consciousness and personality structure. As I have argued, this *seems* inherent, but it is not; it is a Neolithic artifact, a translation of Tame vs. Wild into Self vs. Other and earth vs. heaven. Beneath the dualistic layer of the human psyche is a kaleidoscopic one that I suspect hunter-gatherer cultures possessed, and that is very much about finding ecstasy in details. The American anthropologist, Stanley Diamond, notes that "primitive" life is characterized by direct engagement with nature and bodily functions. The "sense of reality," he writes, "is heightened to the point where it sometimes seems to 'blaze.' "[28] There is no ascent in this "ecstasy"; *all* of life is sacred, not just "heaven." The structure is horizontal rather than vertical, and it has a much greater "feminine" element in it than does our present consciousness. Vertical structures all have a Grail quest behind them; they are all a form of male heroics.[29] So most of our history has been a kind of unnecessary artifact. Self/Other opposition, binary structure, Transitional Objects, what we tend to regard as creativity (see Chapter 10), heresy vs. orthodoxy, ecstatic experience vs. "ordinary" life—all of this may be adventitious, in the last analysis, and certainly not part of "human nature." That meaning for us occurs only by means of conflict, or dialectics, may only reflect a very shallow notion of meaning. This "meaning" is dependent on a mind/body split; without that dichotomous game, most of our history would simply vanish into thin air, since so much of it is about the hero's journey to heal that gap. But journeys are for the most part undertaken out of restlessness; some sort of lack, or need, is typically present. Things are "not right" here, there is something better to be found somewhere else. Vision-quests and ecstatic journeys were perhaps absent from hunter-gatherer societies, or, if present, probably received much less emphasis until the advent of the Neolithic age. Instead, life was its own purpose. Ecstasy is necessary only in a bifurcated world; the hero makes sense only in a religious (binary-mythic) context.

This is why New Age "paradigm-shift" finally won't work; no matter how radically different the content might be (and I am very skeptical on this point anyway), the form is really identical. Paradigm-shift is still part of the salvation mentality, a patriarchal mind-set that tells the hero to persevere, find a new form of consciousness that will give him redemption. The awareness that this whole structure is an illusion is the heresy Needleman and Eco are talking about, the real heresy we need to embrace.

Horizontal consciousness, as well as reflexivity, also implies a society of tools rather than worldviews. The minute anything—science, feminism, Buddhism, holism, whatever—starts to take on the characteristics of a cosmology, it should be discarded. *How* things are held in the mind is infinitely more important than *what* is in the mind, including this statement itself. For there is a big difference between ideas and ideology. An idea is something you have; an ideology, something that has *you*. All of these beliefs, techniques, and ideologies are useful; but they are not "true." What *is* true is our need to stuff the gap, our longing, our drive to create worldviews out of tools so we can be "safe." At least, that is true right now. My guess is that there is a deeper truth, one that could be part of a new culture. This deeper truth is that we really *don't* need to stuff the gap, etc., so that we can be "safe." In this new culture we would observe this need for "safety," but would refuse to give in to it. Safety would come from the body, not from this or that system.

I do not mean to imply by all this that future consciousness would consist in permanent suspended animation, or hanging out in transitional space. Given enough somatic (ontological) security, this might be possible; but a complete *via negativa* is not an answer, and it certainly isn't very complex. The whole notion of "empty space" has its limits, and some form of coding is always necessary for social and psychological life. The argument for the "paradigm of no paradigm" can only be pushed so far; in recent times, Krishnamurti was the great exponent of this, and he became, in fact, the anti-guru guru. In his book *Lying Down*, Marco Vassi pegs the problem of this argument very astutely. It is all, says Vassi, negative intelligence. In denouncing all methods and worldviews, Krishnamurti failed to come up with any positive alternative. Year after year, says Vassi, Krishnamurti would chide his aging fans for having made no breakthrough in terms of their attachments, but he categorically refused to discuss how such a breakthrough might be made. In actual fact, Krishnamurti, as a guru, was the last version of the male heroic structure. As Vassi says, "his mission, ironically, may turn out to have been something like that of a Moses for the horizontal paradigm."[30]

Part of our goal, undoubtedly, is to learn what it means to live without paradigm, but I also sense a much more complex possibility, viz., developing a radical new code that is itself about coding, and is not merely a shift in coding. This is where reflexivity—the awareness of coding as coding, or Gurdjieff's "self-remembering" on a cultural scale—becomes so important. Christianity, Catharism (and romantic love), science, and even cybernetic holism (nature seen as information exchange) are all heuristically valuable, but they are not "true." Only our need for truth is true, and the problem arises when any one of these tools, or codes, is mapped onto our entire ontology. Reflexivity is about the breaking away from this vertical, binary pathology, for it does not (necessarily) say, "Have no codes," but only requires a deliberate awareness of constructing and using a code, and the having of that awareness as part of your code.

Writers such as Gregory Bateson and Henri Atlan are in the vanguard of this, but my favorite remains the late great teller of tales, Jorge Luis Borges. In one short story, "Tlön, Uqbar, Orbis Tertius," he describes a country that chooses a different reality every day (no repeats allowed). One day they are mystics, another, mechanists, another, something else. No one in this country is allowed to publish a book unless they also include in it its counterbook, which is the argument based on opposing premises. Such a life would undoubtedly be a bit too hectic for most of us, but I believe it is a valuable model to contemplate.[31]

Commenting on self-awareness, Lawrence Durrell writes:

Civilizations die in the measure that they become conscious of themselves. They realize, they lose heart, the propulsion of the unconscious motive is no longer there. Desperately they begin to copy themselves in the mirror. It is no use.[32]

"Truth disappears with the telling of it," he adds; "It can only be conveyed, not stated."[33] "Losing heart" is certainly a possibility, but I am not sure it is inevitable, especially if—for the first time in history— we would develop (or grow into) a culture that would accept the fact that the truth can only be conveyed (not stated), and that unconscious process must be allowed to remain unconscious. For reflexivity does not mean making everything conscious; it should include the notion that the code, of which you are aware, is fed by sources that lend themselves only to indirect awareness. This too facilitates the habit of not mistaking tools for worldviews, for one's worldview, in effect, becomes Mystery: there is some sort of larger process operating that we cannot directly apprehend, but that permeates our bodies and moves toward healing. Einstein's question remains the crucial one: "Is the universe friendly?" (What do *you* think?)

This whole subject of coding, and the coding of coding, is addressed from another angle (that of the history of music) by Jacques Attali in his book *Noise*.[34] By "noise" Attali means what I have called silence, i.e., the space between codes. Attali calls for a new form of self-conscious coding which he refers to as "composition," and which could be truly liberatory. Both the history of Western music and that of Western political formations have been characterized by epochs, system-breaks and paradigm-shifts, he says, of new codes violently rupturing and replacing old ones (no surprise there). Attali believes that the next code, "composition," might just be decentralized, independent, and, in effect, radically democratic. Composition, he says,

proposes a radical social model, one in which the body is treated as capable not only of production and consumption, but also of autonomous pleasure. This network differs from all those preceding it. . . .

What may be arising now, he says, is not a new music (read: paradigm), but a new way of *making* music (read: reflexivity). Composition means that

we create our own relation with the world and try to tie other people into the meaning we thus create. . . . Doing solely for the

sake of doing, without trying artificially to recreate the old codes
in order to reinsert communication into them. Inventing new
codes, inventing the message at the same time as the language.
Playing for one's own pleasure, which alone can create the conditions for new communication. A concept such as this seems
natural in the context of music. But it reaches far beyond that; it
relates to the emergence of the free act, self-transcendence, pleasure in being instead of having. . . . [I]t is at the same time the
inevitable result of the pulverization of the networks, without
which it cannot come to pass, and a herald of a new form of
socialization, for which self-management is only a very partial
designation.

Attali's approach is very similar to Vassi's critique of Krishnamurti.
"Announcing the void," he says, ". . . is blasphemy. But blasphemy
is not a plan, any more than noise is a code." Composition is really
about the trust in direct experience, about taking pleasure in the body,
and about creating an exchange between bodies. It "is inscribed not
in a repetitive world, but in the permanent fragility of meaning. . . . It
is also the only utopia that is not a mask for pessimism." Our ultimate
goal, he concludes, is to transform "the world into an art form and
life into a shifting pleasure." This is the ultimate heresy, then, and a
possible outcome of a history of ascent, of system-breaks and paradigm-
shifts that are exciting on one level, tedious on another: life characterized by so much somatic security, so much incarnation, that the
need for "truth" is far less important than the need for love; and
finally, not really in conflict with it. Incarnation means living *in* life,
not transcending it. The last paradigm-shift has to be a shift to a world
in which paradigm-shifts become unnecessary, if not actually banal.

Reflexivity, then, or perhaps what amounts to Jacob Needleman's
notion of "ontological love," opens the door to composition, or what
Dorothy Dinnerstein, in her brilliant essay, *The Mermaid and the Minotaur*, refers to as "enterprise." I think this is similar to what I referred
to, early on, as the "cosmological urge," which should be understood
as not having any edge of desperation attached to it. In terms of how
we have lived on the planet, at least ninety-five percent of our experience has not been about gap-stuffing and the search for Transitional Objects, and this raises the question of what future alternatives
might consist of. The idea here is not to return to some "primitive,"
hunter-gatherer state, but rather to explore the possibilities of a life
grounded in somatic integrity. In his book *Life Against Death*, Norman

Brown raised just this question; but, as Dorothy Dinnerstein notes, Brown fell into the error of regarding all enterprise—the attempt to comprehend the world, or even involve oneself in it—as the attempt of the infant to console itself for the loss of the Primary Unity, or kinesthetic wholeness. All of culture is thus seen as a form of substitute satisfaction.[35] What Dinnerstein argues is that we have to distinguish between enterprise and driven behavior. Enterprise, says Dinnerstein, is actually a healthy thing, a primary satisfaction rather than a secondary one. The problem she says, lies not in enterprise per se but in the situation in which the kinesthetic is renounced to the point that the visual is needed to fulfill compensatory functions. Brown, Róheim, Balint, Merleau-Ponty, Wallon, and Lacan were guilty of what might be called "universalization"—they zeroed in so completely on this one tendency that they mistakenly turned it into the whole of the human condition, and thereby skewed the meaning of human effort.[36] All of these writers, Dinnerstein essentially says, were correct insofar as they recognized that we ruin enterprise by trying to get it to replace a Primary Unity we originally lost, but incorrect insofar as they argued that this is embedded in the structure of the human psyche (or body) itself and that one cannot relate to the world, and to our loss, in a different way. As I shall argue in Chapter 10, there is a way of going about enterprise, particularly as it applies to creativity, in which the activity is *preceded* by wholeness, rather than being a frantic attempt to achieve it. This frantic approach to life, says Dinnerstein, is not inevitable; we really don't have to spend our lives chasing ecstasy in an effort to shut down the nemo. It is in fact possible to embrace enterprise, the cosmological urge, Attali's "composition," and the like in terms of a living out of the ebb and flow of union and separation.[37]

How shall we characterize this? A similar approach to the notion of enterprise is present in certain schools of Buddhism, as I mentioned briefly at the conclusion of Chapter 2. The Pali word *jīvitindriya*, which is sometimes translated as "vitality" or "life principle," is used to stand for the energy that remains in the human being after enlightenment occurs, i.e., after fear, hatred, and delusion are eliminated from the human soul. It is said to arise at the moment of conception and depart at the moment of death. It is a *positive* force, according to the Pali texts.[38] In a similar vein, American Indians often spoke of a "gesture of balance." To clutch at Transitional Objects, regardless of what form they may take, is to lose balance, whereas real liberation is about resiliency, not about "truth". The gesture of balance *should* be a given; my own experience is that unless one works at it, it only emerges at the oddest moments: a joke someone cracks in a railway compartment, at which everyone smiles simultaneously; a simple look of understanding between yourself and a stranger who stops you and asks for the time; the moment you catch yourself, as it were, staring absentmindedly out of the window on a gray Sunday morning, having momentarily forgotten about your coffee and the crossword puzzle you were working on. At such moments, life is neither *this* nor *that*; it just *is*. This is body time, not ego time; the interaction of your Being with reality. What will you remember at the moment of your death? Will it be the moment on the train, or when you interacted with a stranger, or when you looked out of the window on that dull, gray Sunday long ago? What does it mean to be alive right—*now*?

There is only one hope for our situation, and that is that the gesture of balance once again become a way of life; that Self and Other be seen as interrelated aspects of something larger, rather than as opponents. It is a long shot, because this is a still small voice that seems "romantic," or even weak, whereas what is paraded as strength is really a wall of tension, built on a Self/Other opposition. This latter, however, is not a gesture of balance, but rather one of desperation; but it is generally hard to see that. And it is difficult to imagine an entire culture moving in this direction; you can't find the State of Grace anywhere on a map of the known world. But just possibly there is an evolutionary trend here, literally in terms of our own survival, with more and more of us opting for exploration, "enterprise," and some form of reflexivity, rather than for the safety of rote or revealed knowledge and familiar formulas.

A unique opportunity is thus available to us now, perhaps for the first time in our history, and that is to intervene in our own evolution in a creative, and reflexive, way. To come back to John Fowles, he may have put this possibility most clearly when he wrote:

> The nemo is an evolutionary force, as necessary as the ego. The ego is certainty, what I am; the nemo is potentiality, what I am not. But instead of utilizing the nemo as we would utilize any other force, we allow ourselves to be terrified by it, as primitive man was terrified by lightning. We run screaming from this mysterious shape in the middle of our town, even though the real terror is not in itself, but in our terror at it.[39]

The ability to utilize the basic fault creatively is as much an evolutionary option as our history of using it destructively. We are not condemned to the nemo and a whole array of substitute satisfactions. No matter how likely a scenario this is, it is simply not inevitable. It is not so much a matter of mastering the terror Fowles speaks of as being able, for starters, to observe it in a neutral fashion. This one tiny (non)heroic act then opens the door to the world of enterprise, *jīvitindriya*, the going out to the world in a spirit of aliveness and curiosity rather than one of need and desperation. And this act is heroic, not in the ascent or vision-quest sense of the word, but in the sense of something at once necessary and private and extremely difficult, because it requires doing the one thing that we seek to avoid at all costs: we are asked finally to put our entire bodies into a situation; to refuse numbness and protection in favor of risk and immediacy. That is the ultimate meaning of human life on this planet, the hidden history which, down through the ages, the human race has struggled with, and the destiny and choice which now, after all these millennia, stares us uncompromisingly in the face.

# 10

# The Two Faces of Creativity

> [T]he plight of the self of the artist-writer is at
> least in part a historical phenomenon and not an
> essential property of being an artist-writer. . . .
> [T]here may have been other times and other places,
> whether one wishes to call them an age of faith or
> an age of myth, in which men perceived a saving
> relationship to God, the Cosmos, the world, and
> each other. In such times the self did not feel
> displaced, or if it did, it understood its dis-
> placement. The artist-writer did not . . . feel
> the same compulsion to assert his individual genius-
> self as would the artist today. It did not . . .
> occur to the Chartres sculptor to sign his name on
> the toe of an apostle he had finished on the West
> Portal. (Or to the Lascaux Cave painter.)
>
> —Walker Percy,
> Lost in the Cosmos

> An empty stomach is one of the secrets of any creativity.
>
> —Mahatma Gandhi

WHAT, FINALLY, LIES AT THE HEART OF HUMAN IDENTITY? What, finally, *are* the possibilities for the human race, or to narrow it down a bit, for Western culture and civilization? While it may be the case that the story of the West, from the Neolithic revolution to the industrial age, is one of (nonlinear) increasing destructiveness and entropy, it is also the case that this is not the whole story. A quiet moment in an out-of-the-way corner in Paris, and an unknown artist, pen and ink in hand, produces a lovely sketch of trees, buildings, and lampposts in a matter of minutes. We look at the spare lines, the simple beauty of the sketch—it has the "right feel"—and we marvel that this is as much a part of the human repertoire as the willingness to kill condors (or heretics) or to render the planet inert. Are these activities related? Is one "real" and the other, somehow, a "mistake"? Do we really have the option of choosing beauty over madness? What would the act of choosing look like? These are the questions I want to consider in this chapter.

The body, as it turns out, is central to the whole issue, for creativity is a somatic process. The image with which I ended Chapter 2—the child reaching out to the world in a gesture of excited curiosity—shows this. How that expression of curiosity, of creativity, is integrated into the culture at large is the key to understanding the creative "signature" of that culture, and to assessing the possibilities of choosing to love life instead of choosing to fear and hate it. My goal here is to explore Dinnerstein's notion of enterprise, discussed above, in greater detail, and therefore to continue the discussion of what is now possible for us as a culture. So let us start with this infant gesture of curiosity, and see where it takes us.

One of the best treatments of the subject of creativity occurs, curiously enough, in an extraordinarily bad piece of historical writing, a psychobiography of Leonardo da Vinci published by Freud in 1910.[1] As a historical argument, the essay is a complete failure, a mass of unsubstantiated conjecture and speculation. Yet in a few short pages of the text, Freud generates a typology of creativity that strikes me as being immensely suggestive, and it is one that stayed in my mind long after I forgot the discussion of Leonardo per se. Freud's typology is too stark, and it is also incomplete; yet given the available alternatives, it is not a bad place to start. Freud was specifically interested in intellectual activity, and its relationship to sexuality; but I believe that if we are willing to broaden this and talk in terms of sensual experience of the world in general, his anlysis can be extended to all forms of creative work. Let me, therefore, take a bit of poetic license with Freud's exposition, modifying it in certain ways, and see whether it can be helpful to the inquiry at hand.

Freud began his discussion by noting that there is a type of person who pursues creative activity "with the same passionate devotion that another would give to his love. . . ." The crucial event, said Freud, is the fate of what he called the "period of infantile sexual researches," or more generally, the pleasure the child takes in the sensual exploration of its surroundings. This may include curiosity about the birth process, but the larger expression is a tactile-erotic one, and this total lack of inhibition tends to make the parents nervous. Unconsciously, they are stirred to remember when they too were like this, and how this openness toward the world got quashed. Disturbed by this unconscious awareness, they do the same thing to their own children. The impulse then gets thwarted and repressed, and this has three possible outcomes. In the first and overwhelmingly typical case, the child's curiosity gets shut down. The child learns that such openness, such creative expression, is risky business. The result, said Freud, is that creative expression "may be limited for the whole of the subject's lifetime." In the second case, the child's development is sufficiently strong to resist the repression to some degree. This is the classic neurotic artist model. The suppressed sensuality returns from the unconscious "in the form of compulsive brooding, naturally in a distorted and unfree form, but sufficiently powerful to sexualize thinking itself and to colour [creative or artistic] operations with the pleasure and anxiety that belong to sexual processes proper." The brooding never ends; *eros* is transferred to the creative activity and the latter becomes a substitute for it. In the third case, said Freud, "the libido evades the fate of repression by being sublimated from the very beginning." The transition is smooth, the quality of neurosis absent; instinct operates freely in the service of creative activity.

In general, Freud's schema (modified) might look something like the one given on page 322. There is not much to say about Type I creativity (or simply Cr. I), since it is the counterexample, the decision to give up on creativity altogether. The repression is so effective that all creative expression is blocked forever. Most people mask their early defeat with substitute activity, but it shows up somatically when they are caught off guard. Type II, the neurotic model, is—as far as Freud was concerned—typical of most creative work. As we have said, in this case the person fights back, for the spirit was not completely extinguished. But the result of this partial repression is a situation soaking in ambivalent emotions. The creative work has an obsessive quality to it; one is "married" to one's work, as the saying goes. Tension and passion are the characteristic modes of expression here.

Type III is the least familiar case. The repression is very slight, and

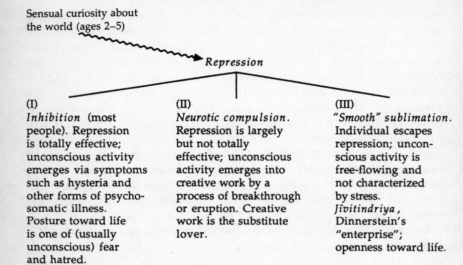

Sensual curiosity about
the world (ages 2–5)

*Repression*

**(I)**
*Inhibition* (most
people). Repression
is totally effective;
unconscious activity
emerges via symptoms
such as hysteria and
other forms of psycho-
somatic illness.
Posture toward life
is one of (usually
unconscious) fear
and hatred.

**(II)**
*Neurotic compulsion.*
Repression is largely
but not totally
effective; unconscious
activity emerges into
creative work by a
process of breakthrough
or eruption. Creative
work is the substitute
lover.

**(III)**
*"Smooth" sublimation.*
Individual escapes
repression; uncon-
scious activity is
free-flowing and
not characterized
by stress.
*Jīvitindriya*,
Dinnerstein's
"enterprise";
openness toward life.

the translation of sensual energy or exploring spirit into creative work
is carried out with a minimum of trauma. Such work has a relaxed,
spontaneous feel to it. In the early pages of the da Vinci biography,
Freud put Leonardo into this category; but by the end of the book,
he was forced to conclude, based on his own evidence, that the Italian
master was a Type II. As a result, Cr. III emerges as an empty category.
It is an intriguing possibility, and Freud's insight here is intuitively
brilliant; but it would seem to be a category without content, hanging
in the middle of nowhere.

One possible candidate for Cr. III might be children's art. I saw such
artwork myself many years ago when I worked in an alternative Montessori nursery for three-year-olds, who had not as yet been hit by
too much repression. As aides or counselors, we were instructed never
to put the children on the spot by asking them what it was they were
painting or constructing, and indeed they exhibited virtually no performance anxiety whatsoever. It was a pleasure to watch their glee as
they immersed themselves in their "work." Looking back, I wouldn't
call it great art, but it certainly was not compulsive or conflict-ridden.
For better or worse, there were no van Goghs in that nursery. The
problem is that if that is all that can be put in this category, then it is
not very interesting. What I wish to argue is that Cr. III constitutes a
mode of expression that includes most medieval art, the art of non-

Western cultures, and the art of traditional societies. It approximates what we call craft, as opposed to art as such. As a result, it throws the creativity of the Western, post-Renaissance world into sharp relief, for it involves a psychodynamic entirely different from that of Cr. II. Modern creativity (Cr. II) should be seen for what it is: a local and in fact fairly recent phenomenon that organizes bodily energy in a particular way. In doing so, it produces a mode of expression that is extremely powerful and focused, but, I shall argue, extremely draining, both for the individual and for the culture at large. And since it *is* recent, and *is* localized, it is possible to claim that the creative process itself has a history, and that much can be revealed about the somatic life of a civilization based on its mode of creative expression. Let us take a look at the pattern of modern creativity in more specific terms.[2]

When I first began thinking about this subject, and specifically about how creativity manifested itself in my own life, there was no avoiding the fact that I fell into the second category. I conformed very well to the popular image of the writer who stayed up all night, fueling himself with coffee and tobacco, pacing the floor in frustration as ideas refused to come, and sitting down and writing things out in a white heat when they finally surfaced. The pattern was clearly addictive/obsessive; neurotic, in short.

Yet as I thought about it more, I began to see that these were the surface manifestations of a deeper drama. The most creative work I had done had resulted from a psychic crisis that ran very deep, and that, once triggered, I was powerless to control. Lacan says that we state our problems on the symbolic level before proceeding to solve them, and this had clearly happened to me. It began with the speculation that if worldviews were artifacts, the magical worldview that antedated modern science must have real validity. The more I began to follow that train of thought, the more archaic consciousness began to take me over. Finally, I was in deep trouble. How does the line from *Faust* go? "Two souls reside within my breast." I was both a modern and an ancient, a scientist and an alchemist, and neither side would release its grip. It was a rocky ride, but I had no choice except to live out those contradictions. Once the traditional/modern gap opened up within my psyche, my fate was sealed: I had to heal that split or die. And this, I believe, is the number-one characteristic of Cr. II: it is a contemporary form of exorcism. (I am not talking here about *productivity*, which has *no* psychic energy behind it, and which merely involves turning out work in a mechanical fashion.) In Cr. II, you are possessed by an internal conflict, and the work is undertaken to resolve it. As far as I can see, the cliché of the suffering artist holds. You create from pain; or as John Fowles puts it in one of his novels, you create from what you lack, not from what you have. It is this that gives modern poetry what Robert Bly has called a "leaping" structure. Chaucer, for example, derived his power from the beautifully crafted language of the narrative. *The Canterbury Tales* are not soaking in unconscious power; they do not "leap," as do, say, many of Bly's own poems.[3]

The second characteristic follows from this: you create yourself out of your work; the work is characterized by "self-expression." In the modern period, art and self-expression (something Chaucer was *not* after) have practically become synonymous. Creative work must bear a personal signature or style, whereas in the Middle Ages it tended to be anonymous. Medieval artists typically did not sign their work. Cennino Cennini's essay of 1400, *Il libro dell' arte*, announced the artist's intention to break with this tradition, and the book is usually regarded as a turning point, marking the end of the craft tradition and the call for modern artistic creativity. Once again, John Fowles is relevant here. "Romantic and post-Romantic art," he writes, "is all pervaded by fear of the nemo; by the flight of the individual from whatever threatens his individuality." "Once artists ran to a centre," he says; "now they fly to the circumference." What we mean today by the word "creative" is simply this: "nemo-killing." Modern creativity is heavily fueled by the desire to prove that one exists.[4]

A third characteristic, which tends to follow from the first two, is that the creative insight is seen to break through, or erupt from, the unconscious. It is this eruption that generates the psychic split that demands to be healed, and that alters the personality structure so that the work of integration becomes self-expression. Traditional creativity would have to be different, since traditional societies tend, in varying degrees, to be swimming in the unconscious already. Hence there is nothing, or at least much less, to erupt.

Fourth, modern creative work has a strong addictive or compulsive component to it; the artist is expected to outdo himself or herself with each succeeding product. ("I work as my father drank," George Bernard Shaw once remarked.)[5] The structure is one of "upping the ante," in other words; work is often "unfinished" because it is done in the pursuit of an inaccessible ideal. It must depart from tradition, must create a new genre, and it gets difficult to keep on doing this. As a result, modern creativity tends to have high psychic costs. A. Alvarez notes in his book *The Savage God* that creativity in the modern period is heavily characterized by suicide, with the most brilliant work being done right before death. In a similar vein, Katinka Matson, in *Short Lives*, gives the reader a series of extremely interesting vignettes that reveal artistic self-destructive tendencies all too clearly. The examples here are literally legion: van Gogh, Modigliani, Dylan Thomas (suicide by alcohol), Janis Joplin and Jimi Hendrix (suicide by drugs), Sylvia Plath, Anne Sexton, and on and on. The work ineluctably moves toward nervous breakdown.[6] It is for this reason, as the American sociologist Elliott Jaques has shown, that so many creative people stop doing what they are doing in their late thirties: they know where it is all leading.[7] This also explains, in part, why the public loses interest in writers such as Norman Mailer. Mailer's first work, *The Naked and the Dead*, remains his best. From the standpoint of modern creativity, the artist is expected to set up and leap over increasingly higher hurdles. This is the structure of an ever-expanding economy; it is not steady-state. Mailer's career was over almost before it began. The modern Western public is trained to expect *novelty* from its creative sector; it quickly loses interest in artists who have nothing "new" to offer.

Finally, modern creativity often involves, as Freud said, the sexualization, or at least eroticization, of the activity. One's work becomes one's lover—one's central, and obsessive, relationship. All the dramas that are typically played out in such a relationship get played out here: the initial romantic rush, the subsequent tapering off, jealousy and possessiveness, and finally disillusion and the search for a new love. There is a heavy overlap of oedipal energy here: male artists are notorious mama's boys, "heroes" winning battles for the mother. And they do this precisely by innovating, by rupturing tradition—i.e., by slaying the father.[8]

We have, in the West, many images that glorify the notion of creativity as being a triumph over adversity. We speak of "the shit that fertilizes roses," or the grain of sand in the oyster that leads to the generation of a pearl. This is the stuff of *Reader's Digest* stories and Ann Landers columns. And these images do capture a truth, though they mask a larger one. The truth they capture is that creative work can and often does emerge out of conflict; the truth they mask is that other psychodynamic patterns of the creative process are possible, and that historically the conflict model may represent an aberration. My goal, however, is not to condemn modern Western creativity as "bad" and to enshrine Eastern or premodern creativity as "good." It is, rather, to argue that there are different somatic processes involved in each case. There is a way, given my own upbringing, that no Indian raga will ever move me as much as Mozart, no Japanese landscape painting resonate for me as deeply as Cézanne's evocative scenes of the Midi. In fact, modern Western art has a brilliance that no medieval icon or Eastern painting can ever approximate, in my view. But my point here is that it takes a particular energy configuration to create such an effect, and if Freud is right about Cr. II, it actually requires early somatic damage that leads to a distrust of the body, and a corresponding shunting of that bodily energy upward, toward the head. The center of gravity is too high, so to speak; there is a way in which the very brilliance of Western creativity depends on its instability, its extremely high level of tension and stress. It is, in essence, an ascent experience, a form of vision-quest coded along the lines of Self/Other opposition. Perhaps, as a result, genius continues (in our culture) to be regarded as being akin to madness, and creative individuals are somehow seen as members of a separate species, inhabiting worlds that most of us will never see or even understand. Art is the activity of a "winner's circle," reserved for a lucky few; and its products, rather than being diffused throughout the culture, are housed in special institutions designed for this purpose. We fail to realize how ahistorical, and ethnocentric, such a view of creativity is.

One exception to this tendency emerges in an important discussion of art—music in particular—in Wilfred Mellers' book, *Caliban Reborn*.[9] Discussing the modern preoccupation with art as self-expression, Mellers writes:

> While this conception of art is our birthright and has gone to make the world we live in, we have to realize that in the context of history the notion is both newfangled and restricted. It is relevant to only about the last five hundred years of Europe's history. . . .

The difference between music as magic (traditional music) and music as expression, he says, is that the former lacks the element of harmonic tension. Such music, he adds, has a strong corporeal component:

> In the music of primitive cultures . . . the rhythm is usually corporeal and the music is never self-expression but rather a communal act of work or play which may have magic[al] as well as social significance.

Mellers goes on to say that "the compositional principles inherent in European music before the Renaissance are not radically distinct from those of Oriental music." In both Gregorian chant and the Indian raga, rhythms such as breath or heartbeat constitute the creative source. The invention of harmony—something that traditional and Oriental cultures were aware of, but that (says Mellers) they never chose to emphasize—ruptured this pattern, i.e. shifted music from a Cr. III structure to one of Cr. II.

Many years ago, living near New York City, I used to play a kind of game, experimenting with the shift between Cr. III and Cr. II energy patterns, without really knowing what I was doing or why. I would go to the Cloisters in upper Manhattan, which is the medieval section of the Metropolitan Museum of Art, and then, having spent several hours there, would go directly downtown to the Museum of Modern Art. I would recommend this experiment to anybody. If you stay tuned to your physical reactions, the effect is quite remarkable. The immersion in a "craft" environment, complete with tapestries, carved wooden doors, stained glass, and illuminated manuscripts creates a very soothing sensation. The body lets go, as it were, and time seems to stand still. The sensation of silence and tranquillity is particularly striking. To follow this up with an immersion in twentieth-century art is to give yourself a real shock. The sensation here is one of excitement and anxiety; the dreamy and magnetic sense of wholeness, or union, is replaced by a chaos and dramatic brilliance that explodes on the canvas, or from the sculptures. As in the case of van Gogh (see below), it is as if the breakdown of the psyche resulted in the breakthrough of art. Two hours in a place such as this leaves one both exhilarated and exhausted. This simple experiment conveys only a fraction (I suspect) of what it means, somatically, to live in one culture as opposed to the other, and how very different the somatic pattern that lies at the root of Cr. II is from that which underlies Cr. III.

Very recently, in December of 1986, I unintentionally repeated this experiment, but in reverse. The Metropolitan Museum had mounted an exhibit of van Gogh's last eighteen months—"Van Gogh at Saint-Rémy and Auvers"—and being in New York at the time, I went to see it. I had originally planned to stay several hours; as it turned out, I was totally exhausted in ninety minutes by the intensity of color and emotion that escalated in van Gogh's paintings in direct proportion to his increasing madness. Whether it was accidental or deliberately planned by the exhibition's organizers, I do not know, but the show exited out onto a very different sort of exhibition, entitled "Individuality and Tradition in Seventeenth-Century Chinese Art." The impact was enormous; I felt a sudden "whoosh" as my entire organism slowed down and my energy returned to ground level. As I sat and looked at the lovely, relaxed prints of mountains and landscapes, a great feeling of peace came over me. I felt a bodily sense of centering, coming home. This was *descent* of the spirit, not ascent; Cr. III is decidedly nonvisionary. I realized that I loved van Gogh, but that I couldn't live with him hanging on my living room walls. The intensity was simply too great; and his creative pattern—which is very typical of Type II creativity—reflected this. In the final seventy days of his life, living under the care of Dr. Gachet at Auvers-sur-Oise, van Gogh turned out no less than forty paintings. By contrast, Kung Hsian, one of the seventeenth-century Chinese painters displayed at the Met, turned out comparatively few; and his comments on this are all of a piece with the Cr. III style. "Little by little is better than more and more," wrote Kung Hsian; "this is the advanced stage of a painter." "When you are afraid of producing too much painting," he wrote, "you will make a good painting." "Being clever is not as good as being dull," he explained. "The uses of cleverness can be grasped at a glance while apparent dullness may embody limitless flavor." These are sentiments that would never occur to van Gogh nor, when you get right down to it, most of us.[10]

My goal here, again, is not to make a judgment, but rather to offer a point of somatic comparison, a cultural juxtaposition. The first four elements I identified as being characteristic of Cr. II—healing a split, self-expression, eruption from the unconscious, and an addictive (escalating) structure—make it clear that modern Western creativity is essentially schismogenic in nature; it has a tendency to move toward climax.[11] Add to this a load of sexual and oedipal or erotic tension, and you have a situation that cannot help but be as brittle as it is brilliant, as neurotic as it is rich. It is thus not that Cr. II is "wrong," but that in the late twentieth century this mode of expression has been pushed to the breaking point and now has no place to go, in an evolutionary sense. As a result, what we are witnessing in a whole variety of fields is not merely the creation of yet another genre, but the transformation of the creative act itself into something else. If creativity has a past, it also has a future, though it is impossible to predict at this stage what it will be. I shall return to this question later on; for now, it might be valuable to try to obtain a deeper understanding of the psychological basis of schismogenic creativity from yet another angle.

The schismogenic nature of Western creativity was first (indirectly) recognized by the Jungian writer Erich Neumann in *The Origins and History of Consciousness*.[12] His essential argument was that the consciousness of the individual passes through the same stages as that of the human race at large, and that mythology is the map of that evolution. (In biological jargon, ontogeny recapitulates phylogeny.) The first myths, said Neumann, are creation myths: the earth is submerged, or nonexistent, and is precipitated out of a watery chaos. This is certainly the drama described, for example, in the opening chapter of Genesis. The second set of myths are hero myths, and these record the process of differentiation. The symbols of the first category are water, or the egg, or the *ourobouros*, reflecting a unitary consciousness or the absence of consciousness: no tension, no opposites, no differentiation. The symbols of the second category are the sun—the entry of light into darkness—and also journeys and conquests. The *Odyssey*, for example, can be read as a psychic journey involving the hero's differentiation from the unconscious and, in general, from the Great Mother. It is the drama of ego vs. unconscious, light vs. dark, male energy vs. female energy, that makes the archetypal journey so fascinating, even to the modern reader. Again and again, Odysseus experiences the enormous pull of that great, unconscious, undifferentiated female power, the desire to melt or merge back into it, to go unconscious, as he once was as a very young infant or a fetus. But what makes him a hero is that he refuses that option. He is not interested in the dark energy of the unconscious, and his "victory" over this is symbolized by the blinding of the Cyclops, whose eye is the "third eye" of intuitive understanding.[13] With the birth of the hero, which is really the birth of the ego,[14] the world becomes ambivalent. It gets split into masculine and feminine, black and white, left and right, God and the devil, ego and unconscious, and this becomes the great drama that all cultures (according to Neumann) have to deal with. In the East, the solution has been characterized as Taoistic, i.e., "both/and"; yin and yang are seen as transformable, interpenetrating, and, as I shall discuss shortly, this has given Eastern creativity a particular style. In the West, most obviously since the Renaissance, the solution has been Manichaean, i.e., "either/or"; the two poles are mortal enemies, locked in combat to the death. And in the West, in particular, this has given rise to a third type of myth that tends to combine the first two: the myth of Set and Osiris, or the twin brothers.

We might diagram the war of the twin brothers as follows:

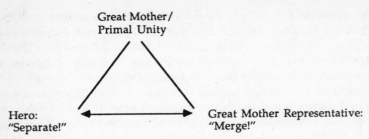

Great Mother/
Primal Unity

Hero:                    Great Mother Representative:
"Separate!"              "Merge!"

This is, of course, a mythological struggle, played out in the Western (Manichaean) psyche. The twin brothers' conflict is intermediate between hero and creation myths. Here a defiant ego has emerged, but it is fearful of complete separation. Set and Osiris, or Cain and Abel, are really two parts of the same person. We hear these conflicting voices particularly at those moments when we are about to give in to an addiction: taking a cigarette, smoking a joint, drinking a martini, eating a slab of cheesecake. The body wants merger; the mind says: resist (or is it the reverse?). This is, in fact, the theme of *Dr. Jekyll and Mr. Hyde*, which is nothing less than a twin brothers' war. Robert Louis Stevenson wrote:

> I thus drew steadily nearer to that truth, by whose partial discovery I have been doomed to such a dreadful shipwreck: that man is not truly one, but truly two. . . . I saw that, of the two natures that contended in the field of my consciousness, even if I could rightly be said to be either, it was only because I was radically both; and from an early date, even before the course of my scientific discoveries had begun to suggest the most naked possibility of such a miracle, I had learned to dwell with pleasure, as a beloved daydream, on the thought of the separation of these elements. If each, I told myself, could be housed in separate identities, life would be relieved of all that was unbearable. . . . It was the curse of mankind that these incongruous faggots were thus bound together—that in the agonised womb of consciousness, these polar twins should be continuously struggling.[15]

What does all this have to do with creativity? The point is that creativity—at least Cr. II—is the *product* of this internal tension. As Neumann put it, "[this] tension is what we call culture." Of course, being a Jungian, Neumann saw this dynamic as universal and archetypal, and perhaps to varying degrees it is. Not all medieval art (or craft) is clearly Cr. III, for example; Gothic architecture reflects an ascent structure very clearly, and it is surely connected to the vision-quest pattern of heresy and religious renewal characteristic of the High Middle Ages. But Neumann did not differentiate between a distinction and an antagonism, and this is no small point. The dynamic of distinction is very probably a part of the cosmological urge (Dinnerstein's enterprise), but different cultures express or deal with it differently, and this may be the crucial issue. Nevertheless, Neumann's formulation of twin brothers arguing over the Abyss is an especially important clue as to what goes on in modern creativity. The "game," so to speak, is to let the whole thing play itself out on the terrain of your psyche, and channel that energy into art, poetry, or whatever. It is this phenomenon that has given Western culture since the time of the Renaissance its distinctive brilliance. But as I have noted, the inherent schismogenic structure means it is pushing up against certain fundamental limits; that in order for his or her work to be increasingly brilliant, the artist has to generate greater and greater twin brothers' splits, or encounters with the Void, from which to recover. Finally, as for Dylan Thomas or Janis Joplin or so many others, the gap becomes too great. The chasm widens beyond their heroic powers, and they cannot manage to get back. Modern creativity is a battlefield of psychic, and often literal, corpses.

A good study of this turbulent or tormented phenomenon in modern art occurs in a work by James Lord called *A Giacometti Portrait*, which is a study of the great sculptor Alberto Giacometti at work. It embodies the first four themes of modern creativity I've noted very clearly. Giacometti is never satisfied with his work; it is never, in his eyes, really finished; he sees his Self totally on the line every time he sits down before an easel or a piece of clay; and so on. Lord writes that he once found Giacometti at a nearby café on a coffee break, with hollow eyes gazing into nowhere, "staring into a void from which no solace could come."[16] Any healing that is engendered tends to be short-lived. As Alvarez notes in *The Savage God*, creative work in the modern period has to be "provisional, dissatisfied, restless." You are constantly challenged to create *yourself*, and this process never ends. The safety valve in Gothic cathedral-building was that ascent structure or not, it was a form of God-expression rather than self-expression. As in the case of romantic love, persons have gotten confused with archetypes. Hence the artist Joan Miró once said of his own creative process:

> I work in a state of passion and compulsion. When I begin a canvas, I obey a physical impulse, a need to act. . . . It's a struggle between me and what I am doing, between me and the canvas, between me and my distress.[17]

The problem with this struggle is that it often ends in death or madness.

It is interesting that this whole structure, which I believe characterizes a number of facets of modern life, including addiction and romantic love as well as creativity, was prefigured in a fragment of Heraclitus, from the sixth century B.C., when ego-consciousness was finally coming into its own on the west coast of Asia Minor. The first part of the fragment reads: "The name of the bow is life." It's a pun, in Greek: *bíos biós*, life is a bow. That is, you can't shoot arrows without the contrary tension of bow and string. But there is more to it than that. The full text of the bow fragment reads: "The name of the bow is life, but its work is death" (i.e., the function of a bow is killing).[18] Western creativity, and especially modern Western creativity, is Manichaean. It is premised on an either/or structure that relentlessly, and schismogenically, moves toward destruction. The creativity of the modern period is not about *jīvitindriya*, or enterprise, not about a free and voluntary going out to life. Cr. II is an acute form of the Grail quest. It has a driven quality to it, and the catastrophic possibilities are endless.

There are numerous examples of Western creativity one can take as illustrations of Type II, and as I indicated earlier, much of this is well documented. The classic example of the tortured genius syndrome, and one that has been worked over in great detail, is that of Vincent van Gogh, whose art was so clearly "a cry of anguish," an attempt to merge with life, a substitute for intimacy. "The more I am spent, ill, a broken pitcher," he wrote, "by so much more am I an artist—a creative artist. . . ."[19] This is one of the paradoxes of modern creativity, viz., that the search for self-expression actually winds up depleting the Self. The artist of the Type II category is like a broken doll, an *imitatio Christi*, exhausting himself (or herself) for the sake of his art, which is "all." In this case, however, he is the agent of his own crucifixion: he makes something greater than himself, seeks the unattainable, and becomes a flawed vessel, ultimately emptied or destroyed. For van Gogh, and many others, acute depression is somehow welcome, a source of creative drama and energy.

A more complex and interesting example of the Cr. II pattern is Wolfgang Amadeus Mozart, about whom so much has been written in recent years. Exactly what happened in Mozart's infancy we shall never know; but there is evidence to suggest the presence of heavy repressed antagonism toward his father Leopold for nearly twenty-five years.[20] Very early on, Leopold Mozart, himself a musician, realized he had a prodigy on his hands, and proceeded to take on the role of impresario, abandoning his own career and dedicating his life to that of his son. He made Wolfgang totally dependent on him, stage-managing virtually every step of Mozart's rise to fame. As a child, Wolfgang was fond of saying, "Next to God comes Papa"; and if antagonism was present, it must have been very deeply buried. Mozart's letters home during this period—about twenty years—were filled with an ostensible love and appreciation of Leopold, and his music during this time was childlike, exuberant, spontaneous. Operas and concerti literally poured from his pen. There is simply no evidence of conflict here, and the style of work reflects this.

All of this gradually began to change in the late 1770s. Wolfgang began to realize that his father had effectively kept him a child all his life, and that Leopold still, after all of his (Wolfgang's) achievements, was disappointed with him. He began to realize also that he feared and resented Leopold, and by 1781 the resulting anger began to surface in some of their correspondence. Yet there was only so much Mozart could say, for Leopold was by now an old man, and Mozart did not want to hurt him. But the conflict that had been so deeply buried finally surfaced, with even more needing to come out; and all of this got channeled into his work. Wolfgang Hildesheimer, one of Mozart's more recent biographers, notes that the four years from 1784 to the end of 1787 were Wolfgang's most prolific and creative ones, and that this was also the period of his greatest experimentation and discovery. Mozart's interest in destroying old genres and creating new ones was at its height during this time. As Hildesheimer writes, "the revolutionary Mozart is the Mozart of his last eight years." Repressed oedipal rebellion surfaced in his two most brilliant operas. In *The Marriage of Figaro* (1786), which was based on a play by Beaumarchais that had long been banned in Vienna, Figaro, the servant of a member of the nobility, Count Almaviva, thwarts the latter in an amorous adventure and emerges the victor. As Hildesheimer tells us, Mozart knew [that] Figaro was no fairy tale. His theme yielded a model for his own behavior; an unconscious drive, probably long latent, came to the surface and tempted him to stop living according to the rules imposed on him from outside. He began "to let himself go."

It was this opera, which so antagonized precisely the class that Leopold had toadied to in order to grease the wheels of his son's career, that marked the beginning of the end of that career: the descent into poverty and, by the end, relative obscurity.

The theme of the upper-class Don Juan character, whose sexual conflicts are so great as to drive him to seduce virtually every woman he meets, and who comes off rather badly for it, was repeated and greatly magnified in Mozart's opera *Don Giovanni*, which appeared the very next year, in 1787, only five months after Leopold's death. It is surely one of the greatest operas of all time; and it is interesting to note that Freud once remarked that it was the only opera that interested him. We need hardly wonder why: one of Mozart's own additions to the libretto was the reappearance of the slain father as an accusing ghost (the statue). Critics said he stole the theme from *Hamlet*, but they hardly had to look that far afield. What we find in Mozart's work, from this point on, with its obvious attack on the aristocracy, its oedipal themes, and its smashing of traditional genres, is the working out of heavy internal conflicts through the creative act itself. Mozart was not necessarily suffering here; indeed, Hildesheimer claims he was getting high off all this conflict. But my point is that the later Mozart was a classic Type II, and that the energy was coming from a place of anger and frustration. This energy—and it had twenty-five years of repression behind it—was clearly phenomenal. Between *Figaro* and *Don Giovanni* (eighteen months), Mozart wrote thirty-five separate works; between *Don Giovanni* and *Così fan tutte* (thirteen months), sixty-three more compositions. These were followed, in 1791, by a mass of chamber music, cantatas, and court dances, plus two more operas, one of which was *The Magic Flute*. And in *The Magic Flute*, the oedipal conflict is revealed as finally resolved: Sarastro, the obvious father figure, is the priest of universal love. As Peter Shaffer has Mozart's arch-rival, Antonio Salieri, say in the play *Amadeus*, when Salieri attends the premiere of the opera and sees the silhouette of Sarastro against the sun: "And in this sun—behold—I saw his *father*! No more an accusing figure but forgiving!—the highest priest of the

Order—his hand extended to the world in love! Wolfgang feared Leopold no longer: a final legend had been made!"[21]

The catharsis was apparently successful. As Hildesheimer notes, the spontaneous, childlike effect of Mozart's earlier years, absent since 1778, reappeared now in the music for the first time in thirteen years; and significantly, *The Magic Flute* would seem to lack the power and brilliance of *Figaro* and *Don Giovanni*. It was, in any event, too late. Believing that someone had poisoned him, Mozart began to write his own requiem, the Requiem Mass, in 1791, which was never completed. He died at age thirty-five, for reasons that remain obscure to this day.[22]

I wish to return, finally, to what I have called traditional creativity, or Cr. III. There are endless examples of this, of course, and I could easily furnish at this point texts of Japanese haiku, photographs of ancient Greek or Egyptian vases, or Hopi or Celtic designs, in addition to the seventeenth-century Chinese landscape painting mentioned earlier. This may, however, not be necessary. By way of illustration I have chosen to reproduce only one particular item here, the famous ink drawing of six persimmons attributed to Mu Ch'i (Plate 20), an artist who lived in Szechwan province (central China) in the late thirteenth and early fourteenth centuries. Here is the commentary of one modern student of Chinese art, Chang Chung-yuan:

This picture of six persimmons is one of the best works ever produced by Chinese artists. Before Mu Ch'i picked up his brush, his mind was in the state of no-thought. Thus, we have in this painting a manifestation of the primary indeterminacy of the uncarved block. What his mind reflected at that moment his brush would put down. First two deep black contours and then to their left two gray contours. To the extreme left and right he placed two plain white contours. The ink wash of the two first contours is pitch dark without any shading at all, and the two contours at the left are all gray with only a light touch. The two outside contours are pure white. The shades of the ink wash from dark to gray and from gray to white correspond to the inner process going on in the painter. When he was still in the depth of the preconscious, the density of his creative night found expression in two dark contours. With the awakening of his consciousness, the inner darkness loses its density and manifests in two gray contours. As he awakens fully, his creative innocence is entirely

20. *Persimmons*, attributed to Mu Ch'i (thirteenth century). From Shin'ichi Hisamatsu, *Zen and the Fine Arts*.

unveiled. So the white contours are its expression. What is expressed in the picture corresponds to what happened in his mind. Through his brush-work, the various states of his mind can be traced from the primary indeterminacy of the uncarved block to transparency.[23]

The first thing that strikes me about this work, and indeed about the whole Cr. III genre, is the absence of what might be called a "Freudian layer." There is seemingly no pent-up sensual or sexual struggle in this material. *Eros* and internal conflict do not play much of a role. What Chang describes is a fairly smooth descent *into* the unconscious, not an eruption from it. Hence it is clear that the dark persimmons would come first, in a state of meditative trance, and the lighter ones after, as the artist comes back to more conscious awareness. The state of "no-mind" familiar to Eastern thought is largely foreign to the modern West (van Gogh was *out* of his mind, not in no-mind). For no-mind is a state of detachment or wholeness, and this indicates that the healing takes *before* the work begins. This material does not reflect the *search* for unity; it is, rather, an artistic expression of psychic unity *previously attained*. To invert John Fowles, you create from what you have, not from what you lack. I think this is implicit in the notion of enterprise.

Also implicit in the notion of enterprise, and in Cr. III, is a lack of any "self-expression." It is not a particular person or healing journey being depicted. If there is a twin brothers' tension here it is fairly muted. The *unity* is what is being expressed, and that is seen as being universal. As already noted, traditional artists, and Western artists prior to the Renaissance, typically did not sign their work. It is all anonymous because it bears the "mark of God," so to speak; a theme pursued by the great French philosopher and mystic, Simone Weil. Weil's ideal of creative work was what she called "decreation"—you "decreate" yourself in order to create the work, as God (she said) diminished Himself in order to create the world. It would be more accurate to say that you don't create the work, but rather that you step out of the way and let it happen. In this way, it is significant that so much Oriental art and poetry is about nature, about the physical world, not about the Self and its dilemmas.[24]

Thirdly, there is no schismogenic or Manichaean structure here. The work is spontaneous and regarded as finished. It is also part of a craft tradition—i.e., the idea is to stay *within* a genre, not to have to constantly invent a new one. And as with craft, all of this is part of daily life; pouring tea, carving wood, cooking persimmons—all activities are considered worthy of craftsmanship. You don't have a special place called a "gallery" to which beauty is assigned for storage and display, nor do you have a special heroic category in society reserved for creative people (the Balinese are an excellent example of a society permeated by art, rather than having art and artists regarded as exceptional). As Ananda Coomaraswamy once put it, "the artist is not a special kind of person; rather, each person is a special kind of artist."[25] And this necessarily means the absence of an addictive or schismogenic structure. This kind of art is continuous with life; it doesn't attempt to "outdo" life by means of psychic acrobatics.

All of this falls into category III, it seems to me, but it is hardly child art. Type III, in fact, can be subdivided into two categories:

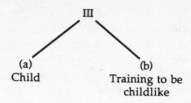

The difference is what the Zen master Shunryu Suzuki labeled as Zen mind vs. beginner's mind. The early Mozart was possessed of beginner's mind. He began composing at age five. When he finally became aware of his conflicts, he switched from III(a) to II. This is not surprising; what else would one expect? It is just that the Eastern pattern, or premodern one, is so different. The goal is not to go unconscious, or to be a three-year-old at a Montessori school, but to pull back enough "yang" energy so that yin and yang can balance out. It is spontaneity of a different sort.

And yet, as I have already suggested (see note 24), the situation may be even more complicated than this. Upon deeper examination, the Cr. II/Cr. III distinction may start to get a bit blurry at the edges. Typologies are useful as "'scaffolding" by which to think, but they often cannot be maintained in real life. It therefore seems to me that Cr. II, as well as Cr. III, can be subdivided into two categories:

**II(a)**—This is what I have described thus far as Cr. II: the healing of the split takes place by the playing out of the struggle in the work itself. The "exorcism" is, in other words, indirect, or unconscious.

**II(b)**—This represents a slight shift away from II(a), in that the exorcism is direct. I.e., one stays fully conscious of the neurotic dramas that have led one to deal with the particular artistic or creative issue at hand, and one goes directly for the liberation from those dramas, through therapy or one's own internal work. In other words, one moves into one's fears. This releases the energy that is tied up in obsessional patterns, which is then available for creative work, and which starts to come out in a more free-flowing way.

The major difference between II(a) and II(b), then, is that II(b) is on the road to Cr. III, so to speak (Cr. III begins when one is finally done with obsessions), whereas II(a) is not. In fact, in II(a), the artist *fears* the loss of obsessions, because he believes that this would mean the end of his career. "Life" and "obsession" are seen as being pretty much identical; the heroic ego whispers in the ear of this person, "Lose me and you'll never create again." And the voice is sincere, because it honestly cannot conceive of a different form of creativity.[26]

The fact that our categories have now developed subcategories, and that these tend to overlap, is possibly an important clue to where our culture is going. Cr. II may be our (i.e., Western) path to Cr. III, at least in its II(b) form; it is not all II(a), not all a dead end, and this suggests that within the evolution of Western creativity itself lies a tendency toward genuine cultural liberation. This is no small point: the way in which our private and cultural neurotic configuration is framed, or dealt with, may actually be the key in the lock. Those who choose to work through their fears and repressions in the service of creative work may (if they do it before they die) break through to a liberating kind of creativity, and in so doing recode the culture along nonschismogenic lines. This is an earthshaking possibility.

If we look around at the artistic and literary scene of the last few decades, especially in the United States, we do find some radical departures from the II(a) model, if only in an attempt to express a unitary type of consciousness. This may be premature; Western culture may have to push through II(b) before it can experiment with III [i.e., III(b)] in a truly unself-conscious way. But the alternative attempts are important nonetheless. Wallace Stevens' work displays obvious "de-creative" tendencies in the field of poetry; Henry Moore's work does the same in the area of sculpture. Postmodern minimalist music is clearly in the Cr. III category. This music, as exemplified by composers such as Philip Glass, Steve Reich, and Terry Riley, has so completely eliminated the tension/resolution structure typical of Western music since the late Middle Ages that the new form has a curious similarity to Gregorian chant. Reich has stated in public interviews that the study of yoga, cabala, African and Balinese music, and classical breathing exercises all had a tremendous impact on his work.[27]

It is not clear what all this means, especially since it can be argued that it represents a retrogression, an attempt to return to an earlier cultural period. For various reasons, I think that unlikely; and we should also keep in mind that a major part of the Renaissance involved a revival of antiquity, or what the English potter Bernard Leach called "revitalization," the going backward in order to go forward. The modern potter, said Leach, takes Sung (twelfth-century Chinese) pottery as a model, not for imitation, as an end in itself, but as a way of revitalizing contemporary techniques.[28] It seems obvious that the limits of Cr. II have been reached, and that beyond the tendencies I have described as Cr. II(b), we are searching around for completely different modes of cultural and creative expression, in the arts as well as the sciences.[29] As in the case of Cr. II(b) this is a hopeful sign; it suggests that there are somatic forces at work in our culture that are antischismogenic, that are working, perhaps unconsciously, to reverse the destructive trajectory of our culture. We are engaged in turning a corner as significant as that which was turned in Western Europe roughly four centuries ago. We can still listen to Gregorian chant, of course, but most of us don't do so very often. In two centuries, Mozart may be in the same category, and the tension/resolution structure of music may be puzzling to our ears. The only suggestion I can make here, in lieu of a crystal ball, is that enterprise in the future may be different from what it was in the past. If we do manage to give up ascent psychology and drivenness, it does not mean that we shall automatically revert to the craft tradition. Something very unexpected may await us on the other side of the watershed. When Attali introduced the concept of "composition," he didn't fill in the blanks.

Beyond the form that creativity will take during the next historical epoch is the question of the human personality structure, and the somatic experience that will underlie it. Who can say what these will be? There seems to be no way to know. But the following lines from Mary Caroline Richards' book, *The Crossing Point*, sound what to me is the most hopeful, and at the same time most realistic, note possible. She writes:

> *Eventually the soul asks to be born again into a world of the*
> *same order as itself—a second coming into innocence, not through*
> *a glass darkly, but face to face, in consciousness. . . .*
> *We pass through cruel ordeals on the way. Estrangement, coldness,*
> *despair. Death.*
> *By going through the experience faithfully, we may come through*
> *on the other side of the crossing point,*
> *and find that our faithfulness has borne a new quality into the world.*[30]

A new quality . . . a new body . . . a new history . . . and a creativity that can be shared by everyone. Let's hope it's still possible.

# EPILOGUE:

## Coming to Our Senses

*Nourishment is to live things that are
unsayable, that cannot be formulated. This
is awareness other than by force of will.
If this is what is in store for us, it will
not be uninteresting. I say this not as a
voyeur but as one whose empathy is to the
cohesion of the voyage. I believe the sign
is displayed in fragments already on the
scene, but the picture has to be put together.
The problem of modern man isn't to escape from
one ideology to another, nor to escape from
one formulation to find another; our problem
is to live in the presence and in the attributes
of reality. Then we will be able to put the
picture together. This picture can only be the
outcome of all the empathy given to many things
observed in common. When many things are
observed in common by the many who constitute a
society, we will have reached a condition worth
celebrating.*

—Frederick Sommer,
*The Poetic Logic of Art and Aesthetics*

WE HAVE INHERITED A CIVILIZATION in which the things that really matter in human life exist at the margin of our culture. What matters?

How birthing takes place matters; how infants are raised matters; having a rich and active dream life matters. Animals matter, and so does ontological security and the magic of personal interaction and healthy and passionate sexual expression. Career and prestige and putting a good face on it and the newest fashion in art or science do not matter. Coming to our senses means sorting this out once and for all. It also means becoming embodied. And the two ultimately amount to the same thing.

Some time ago, a close friend of mine lost his job. Jim was a computer analyst for a large industrial firm. The job was made redundant, and he was laid off. For the first few months, he spent most of his time trying to find another job just like the one he had. I suggested, since money did not seem to be an immediate problem, that he relax about it all. There were so many things he wanted to do; why not enjoy himself, at least for a while? He said he felt he didn't exist without a job; that his job had given him his identity, and that he had to have it back.

But as the months went by, there were no jobs to be had, and Jim was turned down for the few that did come up. Slowly, he began to experiment with therapy, until finally a therapist, a bodyworker, pulled the cork for him, as it were. Jim literally twitched and shook, on and off, for months, as the life energy began to return to a body that had been crushed and repressed since childhood. He was now, in his early thirties, able to face the truth: what really mattered had been so extinguished in his life that he was forced into a total survival mode, which meant creating a career and a persona and a personal snow job that told him that this was what he really wanted out of life. But his body knew better, and ultimately, so did "he." By the end of his year of unemployment, Jim was still unclear as to how he was going to earn a living; but he was clear about one thing: he would never return to the ranks of the walking wounded.

Jim's story is a very common one in our society up to, but not including, the point of getting in touch with the body. Most people do not take this step, and we live in a culture in which it is quite dangerous to do so. The problem is the long run: in the long run, it is much more dangerous *not* to do so. The walking wounded fill our institutions and create our culture. They can be seen in the halls of universities, the offices of government, the corridors of radio and TV studios, on Wall Street, and in Hollywood. They can be seen as well in supermarkets, jails, high schools, factories, and military bases and training camps. We ache to love, but the damage of the basic fault, the loss of kinesthetic awareness, and the relative lack of a happy experience of Otherness, make it very difficult to take chances and very easy to go to sleep in the snow; in effect, to die.

Our hidden history was *always* a somatic one, the "secret life of belly and bone," as Delmore Schwartz put it. Creating a history or a culture we can identify with is no academic exercise; at stake is an entire way of life. Understanding how an entire civilization could banish animals to zoos and Indians to reservations, and plunk five-year-old children down in front of computers is to come to terms with how fucked up we really are, and at least open up the possibility of somatic reconstruction. Coming to a somatic understanding of the historical process, i.e., of our past, could make a rather large difference for what we want to do about our future. We may have to bail out individually, one by one, as Jim did; but enough microconversions of this sort and what could ensue is a whole cultural shift toward health and love and sanity. Whether this can happen fast enough remains an open question.

Somatic understanding also opens up the possibility of somatic grounding, and thus, of the end of the need for some form of ism in our lives to plug the basic fault. When you've lost your body, you need an ism. From there it is a short step to seeing other isms as life-threatening, and to seeing the Other as an enemy. I once asked a friend of mine who had studied the Feldenkrais technique (a major body therapy) for many years what he had gotten out of it. "Hard to say," he replied, "except that after a while I began to notice that it became less and less important for me to win an argument." As I tried to suggest in Chapter 9, this is really the ultimate heresy. Visionary experience is as nothing, compared to this. But it is not an easy point to arrive at, and I know for myself that I'll have to work at it for the rest of my life.

This has been a difficult book for me to write; I struggled a lot with my own body, which I love and hate, as the pages were filling up with ink. And this is fine, but I am left with one lingering doubt that I wish to share with you, the reader, namely that I have perhaps overvalued the body as a vehicle for cultural integrity. For returning to the body, in and of itself, as Paul Ryan once pointed out to me, is a monistic solution—it can only give you monads. This was the great drawback of Wilhelm Reich, and why he tried, at the end of his life, to believe in a universal energy I spoke of earlier, such as *ch'i* or *ki*, by making it scientific (he called it "orgone"). We can recognize the tremendous drawback of the mind/body split, and the severe limits of dualism and a dualistic culture; but body integrity, finally, doesn't necessarily get you into the social or natural environment, and there is no way that these can be ignored. Of course, in the theory of the five bodies, the fifth is that of large-scale influence by means of the spirit, and Gandhi and Hitler are the extreme positive and negative poles of this. But I mean something else; something . . . I don't know, more *scientific*, for lack of a better word. I'm thinking out loud here, and I guess you'll just have to indulge me.

In his remarkable novel, *Jacob Atabet*, Michael Murphy records the following conversation:

> "My body? What do you mean by *my body?*"
> "Just that. The physical body."
> "But where is it?" he asked. "Where does it end or begin? For me it's not that simple. Once you've passed through a cell, once you pass through those ordinary boundaries, it's hard to say where the body leaves off. At the tip of my finger or the edge of a cell? Or somewhere in the DNA? Then the whole world looks like one body. Even the solar system and the galaxy and the view through the *animan siddhi*. All of it still developing, parts dying and being reborn . . . no, I don't know where this body ends."

I am reminded of a remark once made by that great mime, Etienne Decroux, that people should walk down the street as if they belonged to each other. Yet what Murphy is talking about is much larger than this, I think. There is, here, a stretching out to a *Gaia-politik*, the conviction that the flesh of my body is also the flesh of the earth, the flesh of experience. To know your own flesh, to know both the pain and joy it contains, is to come to know something much larger than this. "As our souls, being air, hold us together," wrote Anaximenes in the fifth century B.C., "so breath and air embrace the entire universe." Something obvious keeps eluding our civilization, something that involves a reciprocal relationship between nature and psyche, and that we are going to have to grasp if we are to survive as a species. But it hasn't come together yet, and as a result, to use the traditional labels, it is still unclear whether we are entering a new Dark Age or a new Renaissance.

"In a dark time," wrote Theodore Roethke, "the eye begins to see. . . ." It's a hopeful thought; perhaps, the right note on which to end a book.

# NOTES

**Part I. The Sources of Fragmentation**
CHAPTER 1. THE BASIC FAULT

1. John Fowles, *The Aristos* (rev. ed.; London: Pan Books, 1968), p. 51.
2. Michael Balint, *The Basic Fault* (London: Tavistock, 1968), p. 135.
3. Alice Miller, *Prisoners of Childhood,* trans. Ruth Ward (New York: Basic Books, 1981). This has been reissued in a paperback edition under the original (German) title, *The Drama of the Gifted Child.*
4. Géza Róheim, *The Origin and Function of Culture* (New York: Anchor Books, 1971; orig. publ. 1943). On Balint, see note 2, above. A useful overview of the object-relations school may be found in John D. Sutherland, "The British Object Relations Theorists: Balint, Winnicott, Fairbairn, Guntrip," *Journal of the American Psychoanalytic Association, 28,* 4 (1980), 829–60.
5. Balint, *Basic Fault, passim.* Freud's formulation of this (see Balint, p. 35) is worth quoting here: "All object-discovery is in fact object recovery [Die Objektfindung ist eigentlich eine Wiederfindung]." Some years ago, a friend of mine saw the following graffito on a wall in Strasbourg: "Spectateur! Ce que tu attends, tu l'as déjà perdu! [Passerby! What you are waiting for, you have already lost!]"
6. Erich Neumann, *The Child,* trans. Ralph Manheim (New York: Harper & Row, 1976), pp. 1–25; Kurt Goldstein, "The Smiling of the Infant and the Problem of Understanding the 'Other,' " *The Journal of Psychology, 44* (1957), 175–91; Margaret S. Mahler et al., *The Psychological Birth of the Human Infant: Symbiosis and Individuation* (New York: Basic Books, 1975).
7. Thomas Verny, *The Secret Life of the Unborn Child* (New York: Summit Books, 1981), p. 31; see also p. 33.
8. Charles V. W. Brooks, *Sensory Awareness* (New York: Viking Press, 1974), p. 11.
9. Goldstein, "The Smiling of the Infant," p. 182.
10. Balint, *Basic Fault,* p. 66.
11. On the following see Verny, *Secret Life,* pp. 19–20, 36–37, 64–66, and 75. The most elaborate argument regarding fetal awareness, which sees the womb as basically a kind of trap (especially in the third trimester) and birth as a liberation struggle, is Lloyd deMause's essay "The Fetal Origins of History," *The Journal of Psychohistory, 9,* 1 (Summer 1981), 1–89. I find the argument very weak at points, and heavily tinged with existential bitterness; but it is provocative and does raise the question of a very early imprint of the Self/Other distinction. For useful criticism and commentary, see Thomas Verny

et al., "Symposium: On 'The Fetal Origins of History' by Lloyd deMause," *The Journal of Psychohistory, 10*, 2 (Fall 1982), 213–48.

The existence of intrauterine stress (at least for the late twentieth century) is, however, well established. In addition to Verny, see Arthur Janov, *Imprints* (New York: Coward-McCann, 1983), pp. 25 and 27.

12. Verny, *Secret Life*, p. 98.
13. Frederick Leboyer, *Birth Without Violence* (New York: Alfred A. Knopf, 1975); Michel Odent, *Birth Reborn*, trans. J. Levin and J. Pincus (New York: Pantheon Books, 1984).
14. Janov, *Imprints*, p. 14.
15. Balint, *Basic Fault*, p. 56.
16. Janov, *Imprints*, p. 96.
17. D. W. Winnicott, *Mother and Child* (New York: Basic Books, 1957), and "The Capacity to Be Alone," in *The Maturational Process and the Facilitating Environment* (London: Hogarth Press, 1965), pp. 29–37.
18. Quoted in H. M. Southwood, "The Origin of Self-Awareness and Ego Behaviour," *International Journal of Psycho-Analysis, 54* (1973), 237.
19. Margaret S. Mahler and John B. McDevitt, "Thoughts on the Emergence of the Sense of Self, with Particular Emphasis on the Body Self," *Journal of the American Psychoanalytic Association, 30*, 4 (1982), 837.
20. Joseph D. Lichtenberg, *Psychoanalysis and Infant Research* (Hillsdale, N.J.: The Analytic Press, 1983), p. 159.
21. Seymour Epstein, "The Self-Concept Revisited," *American Psychologist, 28* (May 1983), 405–6.
22. Lichtenberg, *Psychoanalysis and Infant Research*, p. 106.
23. Paul Guillaume, *Imitation in Children*, trans. Elaine P. Halperin (Chicago: University of Chicago Press, 1971; from the 2nd French ed., 1926), p. 150.
24. Charles Darwin, "A Biographical Sketch of an Infant," *Mind, 2* (1877), 285–94; see also Gordon G. Gallup, Jr., "Towards an Operational Definition of Self-Awareness," in R. H. Tuttle (ed.), *Socioecology and Psychology of Primates* (The Hague: Mouton, 1975), pp. 335–36.
25. Guillaume, *Imitation in Children,* pp. 151–53; Maurice Merleau-Ponty, "The Child's Relations with Others," trans. William Cobb, in James M. Edie (ed.), *The Primacy of Perception* (Evanston, Ill.: Northwestern University Press, 1964), pp. 151–53.
26. On Wallon see Merleau-Ponty, "Child's Relations with Others," pp. 113–55, *passim*; Henri Wallon, *Les origines du caractère chez l'enfant* (2nd ed.; Paris: Presses universitaires de France, 1949); H. Wallon, "Comment se développe, chez l'enfant, la notion du corps propre," *Journal de psychologie, 28* (1931), 705–48; H. Wallon, "Importance du mouvement dans le développement psychologique de l'enfant," *Enfance, 9* (March/April 1956), 1–4; and the entire issue of the *International Journal of Mental Health, 1*, 4 (Winter 1972/73), entitled "Henri Wallon: His World, His Work."

It is interesting that most of Wallon's work remains untranslated, and that Wallon, unlike his contemporary Jean Piaget, is virtually unknown. There are reasons for this, ones that reflect Western cultural biases. Piaget was interested in the development of cognitive and intellectual skills, which are so valued in a society organized around achievement and technical mastery. Wallon was interested in ontological development, and he tried to integrate cognitive development with affective development. That Piaget was uninterested in feelings, and became famous, and that Wallon *was* interested, and died in total obscurity, is no accident. See the articles by Gilbert Voyat and Beverly Birns in the Wallon issue of the *International Journal of Mental Health*.

27. Lichtenberg, *Psychoanalysis and Infant Research*, p. ix. The four major studies cited below are as follows: B. Amsterdam, "Mirror Image Reactions Before Age Two," *Developmental Psychobiology*, 5 (1972), 297–305, and also the study with L. M. Greenberg, "Self-conscious Behavior of Infants: A Videotape Study," *Developmental Psychobiology*, 10 (1977), 1–6; A. H. Schulman and C. Kaplowitz, "Mirror Image Response During the First Two Years of Life," *Developmental Psychobiology*, 10 (1977), 133–42; Ann E. Bigelow, "The Correspondence Between Self- and Image Movement as a Cue to Self-Recognition for Young Children," *Journal of Genetic Psychology*, 139 (1981), 11–26 (based on her 1978 Ph.D. dissertation at Simon Fraser University); and Michael Lewis and Jeanne Brooks-Gunn, *Social Cognition and the Acquisition of Self* (New York: Plenum Press, 1979). A useful review of the literature is James R. Anderson, "The Development of Self-Recognition: A Review," *Developmental Psychobiology*, 17 (1984), 35–49.

28. On stages vs. continuous development see Lewis and Brooks-Gunn, *Social Cognition*, pp. 215–19 and 653–70; Anderson, "Development of Self-Recognition," p. 47; B. I. Bertenthal and K. W. Fischer, "Development of Self-Recognition in the Infant," *Developmental Psychology*, 14 (1978), 44–50; and William Damon and David Hart, "The Development of Self-Understanding from Infancy through Adolescence," *Child Development*, 53, 4 (August 1982), 846–48.

29. Daniel N. Stern, "The Early Development of Schemas of Self, Other, and 'Self with Other'," in J. D. Lichtenberg and Samuel Kaplan (eds.), *Reflections on Self Psychology* (Hillsdale, N.J.: The Analytic Press, 1983), p. 56. On the section that follows see this article, pp. 56–57 and 69; Lichtenberg, *Psychoanalysis and Infant Research*, pp. 3–15; T. G. R. Bower, *The Perceptual World of the Child* (Cambridge, Mass.: Harvard University Press, 1977), pp. 19–21 and 28; and Jerome Kagan, "Do Infants Think?," *Scientific American*, 266, 3 (March 1972), 74–82. Stern's most recent work on this subject is *The Interpersonal World of the Infant* (New York: Basic Books, 1985).

30. Stern, "Early Development," pp. 58–70.

31. Gallup, "Towards an Operational Definition," pp. 314ff. and 335.

32. Anderson, "Development of Self-Recognition," p. 36.

33. Is human self-awareness unique? Gordon Gallup at the State University of New York at Albany published a paper in 1977 reviewing all the evidence that suggested that chimpanzees may in fact possess genuine self-consciousness; see Gordon G. Gallup, Jr., et al., "A Mirror for the Mind of Man, or Will the Chimpanzee Create an Identity Crisis for *Homo sapiens*?," *Journal of Human Evolution*, 6 (1977). Adrian Desmond, in *The Ape's Reflection* (London: Blond and Briggs, 1979), argued that self-consciousness exists in varying degrees in different primates, and while human beings are indeed distinctive,

the distinction is less impressive than has generally been believed (see esp. pp. 169–91). To what extent future research will challenge human mental hegemony remains to be seen.

34. There also exist a number of methodological problems with these studies; for example, the question of whether rouge-mark identification really amounts to self-recognition. See remarks on the subject at various points in Gallup, "Towards an Operational Definition," as well as in the articles by Anderson and by Damon and Hart, and the monograph by Lewis and Brooks-Gunn, all cited above.

35. Lewis and Brooks-Gunn, *Social Cognition*, p. 222.

36. From *The Ego and the Id*; quoted in Seymour Fisher and Sidney E. Cleveland, *Body Image and Personality* (2nd ed., rev.; New York: Dover Publications, 1968), p. 42.

37. Herbert Spiegelberg, "On the 'I-Am-Me' Experience in Childhood and Adolescence," *Review of Existential Psychology and Psychiatry*, 4, 1 (1964), 3–21; Don Bannister and Joyce Agnew, "The Child's Construing of Self," in *Nebraska Symposium on Motivation, 1976* (Lincoln: University of Nebraska Press, 1977), pp. 99–125; Lichtenberg, *Psychoanalysis and Infant Research*, pp. 114–16 and 146; and Heinz Lichtenstein, *The Dilemma of Human Identity* (New York: Jason Aronson, 1977), p. 216.

38. Bannister and Agnew, "Child's Construing of Self," p. 116. In *Psychology: The Briefer Course* (1892), the philosopher William James predicted that the "I" would be elusive to empirical research, and that it was better left to philosophy than psychological testing. Of course, James' suggestion was ignored. Reviewing the various tests and studies that have gone on since James' time regarding the subject of self-awareness, Damon and Hart conclude that as James predicted, "I"-awareness slips through the scientific sieve. (Damon and Hart, "Development of Self-Understanding," pp. 843–45.)

39. The dating of eight years of age emerges in two major studies, one by J. Broughton (1978), the other by R. Selman (1980). For details see Damon and Hart, "Development of Self-Understanding," p. 852.

40. Ibid.

41. Kurt Goldstein, "The Smiling of the Infant," pp. 175–91.

42. Merleau-Ponty, "Child's Relations with Others," pp. 120–54. The phrase "lived distance" (quoted on p. 154) is from E. Minkowski.

For a recent set of articles on Merleau-Ponty, including his work on Self/Other relations and an obituary by Jacques Lacan, see *Review of Existential Psychology and Psychiatry*, 18, 1, 2, and 3 (1982–83).

43. That is, the *Christian* West. Heresy is basically foreign to Asian religions. "The idea that one religion is false and another true is essentially Christian, and had not occurred to the Egyptians and Greeks who were living together at Alexandria. Each worshipped his own gods, just as he spoke his own language, but he never thought that the gods of his neighbour had no existence . . ." (E. M. Forster, *Alexandria: A History and a Guide* [New York: Oxford University Press, 1961; orig. publ. 1922], p. 20).

44. Lawrence Durrell, *The Alexandria Quartet* (London: Faber and Faber, 1968), p. 739.

45. Merleau-Ponty, "Child's Relations with Others," p. 119.

46. Paul Schilder, *The Image and Appearance of the Human Body* (New York: International Universities Press, 1950; orig. publ. 1923).

47. Quoted in Norbert Elias, *The History of Manners*, trans. Edmund Jephcott (New York: Pantheon Books, 1978), p. 78.

48. Merleau-Ponty, "Child's Relations with Others," p. 120.

49. For a useful discussion of this point see Andrew M. Greeley, *Ecstasy: A Way of Knowing* (Englewood Cliffs, N.J.: Prentice-Hall, 1974), esp. pp. 56–72.

50. Paul Ryan once pointed out to me that this was why Jimi Hendrix and Janis Joplin destroyed themselves, while John Lennon did not. Lennon brilliantly danced around the basic fault, as is obvious from so many of his lyrics; Hendrix and Joplin fell right into it. This same difference divides philosophers as well as musicians: Sartre and Camus, on the one hand, as opposed to Nietzsche and (to some extent) Kierkegaard, on the other.

51. Merleau-Ponty, "Child's Relations with Others," pp. 136–37.

52. Ibid., pp. 137–38.

53. Pär Lagerkvist, *The Dwarf*, trans. Alexandra Dick (New York: Hill and Wang, 1984; orig. English trans. 1945), pp. 51–52.

54. Paula Elkisch, "The Psychological Significance of the Mirror," *Journal of the American Psychoanalytic Association*, 5 (1957), 238.

55. Merleau-Ponty, "Child's Relations with Others," pp. 132–33.

56. Ibid., pp. 128, 133, and 138.

57. The major text that reviews clinical studies done on body perception, including the use of normal and pathological (alcoholic, schizophrenic, etc.) subjects, and explores how the body image alters under a variety of conditions, is Franklin C. Shontz, *Perceptual and Cognitive Aspects of Body Experience* (New York and London: Academic Press, 1969). Shontz stresses the enormous difficulty of investigating body image by means of measurable clues, as well as the near-impossibility of constructing nonarbitrary definitions of terms such as "body image," "body schema," and "body ego." Circularity, says Shontz, is unavoidable: we need empirical facts to generate a terminology, but the same facts cannot be gathered without a terminology that flows from a philosophical basis. It is also hard to see how the body image *could* be measured, given the fact that it is so polymorphous. Thus it is thought of as both conscious and unconscious, cognitive and affective, as being part of the ego and being something to which the ego reacts, etc. But he adds—and I would have to agree with him—that as a kind of "global concept" that incorporates a whole variety of phenomena, it is usefully integrative; and measurable or not, clearly definable or not, we cannot dispense with it because it is so "pervasively influential," a part of everything we do. That it has hardly been studied is a comment on our methodologies and cultural emphases, not a negation of this very real phenomenon in our lives. (See Shontz, pp. 5, 170–71, and 178.)

On Fisher see below and also note 85.

58. This is discussed in Benjamin Goldberg, *The Mirror and Man* (Charlottesville: University Press of Virginia, 1985), pp. 246–48. For the original research report see A. C. Traub and J. Orbach, "Psychophysical Studies of Body Image,"

*AMA Archives of General Psychiatry, 11* (1964), 53–66; see also *14* (1966), 41–47.

59. Merleau-Ponty, "Child's Relations with Others," p. 129.

60. Ibid.; see also Guillaume, *Imitation in Children*, p. 89.

61. On the following see Jacques Lacan, "The Mirror Stage as Formative of the Function of the I as Revealed in Psychoanalytic Experience," in *Écrits*, trans. Alan Sheridan (New York: W. W. Norton, 1977), pp. 1–7; Arthur Efron, "The Sexual Body: An Interdisciplinary Perspective," *The Journal of Mind and Behavior, 6,* 1–2 (Winter and Spring 1985), 236; and Anthony Wilden, *System and Structure* (2nd ed.; London: Tavistock, 1980), p. 483.

    For a comparison of the approaches of Lacan and Merleau-Ponty, see John O'Neill, "The Specular Body: Merleau-Ponty and Lacan on Infant Self and Other," *Synthese, 66* (1986), 201–18.

62. Michael Eigen, "The Area of Faith in Winnicott, Lacan and Bion," *International Journal of Psycho-Analysis, 62* (1981), 421–22.

    The situation in Eastern cultures would seem to be different, despite the purely ontological nature of the arguments advanced by Lacan and Merleau-Ponty. Merleau-Ponty in fact recognized this; in the original French edition of *The Visible and the Invisible* (p. 274) he wrote: "Le problème moi-autrui, problème occidental" (roughly translated: The problem of Self vs. Other is a Western one). Yi-Fu Tuan argues the same thing in *Segmented Worlds and Self* (Minneapolis: University of Minnesota Press, 1982). In this regard it is instructive to consult the I Ching on the subject of Opposition (Hexagram #38), which turns the discussion into one on the nature of polarity (relatedness).

    I do believe that the Self/Other distinction is an ontological issue, but that it can get dealt with in a whole variety of cultural ways, of which ours is probably the least healthy. Thus, hunter-gatherer societies probably dealt with it "kaleidoscopically" (see Chapter 2); Eastern cultures approach it in a way that we broadly recognize as "Taoistic." The Western style might be called "Manichaean" (see Part II of this volume), which is perhaps the bluntest way of dealing with it. Still, even with its yin/yang structure, Eastern thought does remain dualistic, if not (as in the West) starkly oppositional. To complicate things further, there is, apparently, a Chinese Manichaean tradition as well. See, for example, E. Chavannes and P. Pelliot, "Un traité manichéen retrouvé en Chine," *Journal asiatique* (1911), 499–617 and (1913), 99–199 and 261–394.

    For an interesting comparison of the work of Merleau-Ponty with the thought of the Zen master, Dōgen, see Carl Olson, "The Human Body as a Boundary Symbol: A Comparison of Merleau-Ponty and Dōgen," *Philosophy East and West, 36,* 2 (April 1986), 107–21.

63. For a critique of Merleau-Ponty on this point see Martin C. Dillon, "Merleau-Ponty and the Psychogenesis of the Self," *Journal of Phenomenological Psychology, 9* (Fall 1978), 84–98.

64. Dorothy Dinnerstein, *The Mermaid and the Minotaur* (New York: Harper & Row, 1976).

65. John Bowlby, *Attachment and Loss, Vol. I: Attachment* (Harmondsworth, England: Penguin Books, 1971), p. 436.

66. Efron, "The Sexual Body," pp. 53–54.

67. *The World of the Child* (Toronto: Canadian Broadcasting Corporation, March 1983 "Ideas" Program), transcript p. 21.

68. As an interesting comment on all this, surveys conducted in the U.S. in the 1970s turned up the fact that most people frequented singles bars not in search of sex, but out of the desire to be held. In American culture, however, the request to be held seems weird, so both men and women often find themselves in the curious position of asking for sex, which is "acceptable," in order to achieve a very different objective.

69. As late as 1920, the death rate for infants in the zero-to-one-year-old age group in American foundling institutions, where absolutely no body contact was provided, was nearly one hundred percent. This "disease" was called "marasmus," which literally means "wasting away." See Ashley Montagu, *Touching: The Human Significance of the Skin* (2nd ed.; New York: Harper & Row, 1978), pp. 60, 77–78, and 120–24.

70. Schilder, *Image and Appearance*, pp. 124, 173, 201, 216, and 240.

71. Lecture given at Shaughnessy Hospital, Vancouver, May 30, 1985; see also Odent, *Birth Reborn*.

72. Leboyer, *Birth Without Violence*, p. 62.

73. On the following see Jean Liedloff, *The Continuum Concept* (rev. ed.; Harmondsworth, England: Penguin Books, 1986), pp. 45, 57, 72, 79–80, 114, and 151–52.

74. To belabor the discussion in the text for a moment, an uneasy tension has always existed between object-relations theory and traditional psychoanalysis. As early as 1935, a Scottish physician by the name of Ian Suttie, in *The Origins of Love and Hate* (Harmondsworth, England: Penguin Books, 1963; orig. publ. 1935), argued that the infant had a need for companionship, which was innate and nonsexual in nature. Géza Róheim replied by saying that the relationship to the Other was inevitably libidinal (*Origin and Function of Culture*, pp. 23 and 100). There has been no resolution of the argument; an exhaustive treatment of it may be found in Jay R. Greenberg and Stephen A. Mitchell, *Object Relations in Psychoanalytic Theory* (Cambridge, Mass.: Harvard University Press, 1983). Personally, I don't see any need to adopt an either/or position. In the *Symposium*, Plato put object relations first, but *eros* was a very close second, and in practice they are not easily separable. I think this is the key here: although *eros* and *ontos* (being) are obviously distinguishable, in real life they tend to run together. The matter of physical affect gets mixed into our ontological education from a very early point.

75. The discussion below is based on the following sources: A. Delatte, *La Catoptromancie grecque et ses dérivés* (Paris: Librairie E. Droz, 1932); Elkisch, "Psychological Significance of the Mirror" (see note 54, above); Elias, *History of Manners* (see note 47, above); George T. Emmons, *Slate Mirrors of the Tsimshian*, *Indian Notes and Monographs*, ed. F. W. Hodge (New York: Museum of the American Indian, 1921); Erling Eng, "The Significance of the Mirror and the Self Portrait in Renaissance Developments in Psychology," *Proceedings of the Tenth International Congress of the History of Science* (Ithaca, N.Y., Aug. 26–Sept. 2, 1962), Vol. 2 (1964), pp. 145–47; William F. Fry, Jr., "A Gift of Mirrors: An

Essay in Psychologic Evolution," *The North American Review*, 265 (New Series Vol. 17), 4 (December 1980), 53–58; Goldberg, *The Mirror and Man* (see note 58, above); Frederick Goldin, *The Mirror of Narcissus in the Courtly Love Lyric* (Ithaca, N.Y.: Cornell University Press, 1967); Herbert Grabes, *The Mutable Glass: Mirror-Imagery in Titles and Texts of the Middle Ages and English Renaissance*, trans. Gordon Collier (Cambridge, England: Cambridge University Press, 1982; orig. German ed. 1973); Nancy Thomson de Grummond (ed.), *A Guide to Etruscan Mirrors* (Tallahassee, Fla.: Archaeological News, 1982); Michel Meslin, "Significations rituelles et symboliques du miroir," in *Perennitas: Studi in onore di Angelo Brelich* (Rome: Edizioni dell' Ateneo, 1980), pp. 327–41; and Serge Roche, *Mirrors*, trans. Colin Duckworth (London: Gerald Duckworth, 1957).

76. On the following see D. W. Winnicott, "Transitional Objects and Transitional Phenomena," in *Playing and Reality* (New York: Basic Books, 1971), pp. 1–25.

77. This obsession or anxiety is hardly limited to the individual infant; what such objects can evoke, even in the adult population, is quite instructive. What is one to make of the following news item? In October of 1985, Kevin Bull, age two months, died of bone disease and was buried with a glass case containing his teddy bear placed on top of his grave. Shortly after, the teddy bear was stolen from its case. The child's father, Douglas Bull, asked the police not to intervene, and to simply let the whole thing go. Instead, all of the state troopers at the local barracks went on a search for the missing object, and recovered it two months later. Since the recovery of the object could obviously make no difference for the dead infant, one has to ask why it was important enough for the Connecticut state troopers to go on a dragnet search for a missing teddy bear when they presumably had more urgent tasks confronting them. But laughing at the police here can be too easy. From a psychological point of view, recovering a teddy bear that was keeping a dead infant "company" in his grave can be an urgent matter. (Source: "They Got Back His Teddy," *Vancouver Province*, December 22, 1985.)

78. D. W. Winnicott, *The Maturational Process and the Facilitating Environment* (New York: International Universities Press, 1965), pp. 101 and 188.

79. Efron, "The Sexual Body," p. 52.

80. Wilden, *System and Structure*, p. 23.

81. For a good discussion of this see John Berger, *Ways of Seeing* (New York: Viking Press, 1973).

82. Melanie Klein was the founder of the British object-relations school. For a useful one-volume summary of her work, see Hanna Segal, *Klein* (Glasgow: Fontana, 1979). For an incisive critique of Kleinian psychology see Efron, "The Sexual Body," pp. 43–50. See also Phyllis Grosskurth, *Melanie Klein: Her Work and Her World* (New York: Alfred A. Knopf, 1986).

83. Schilder, *Image and Appearance*, *passim*; Fisher and Cleveland, *Body Image and Personality*, p. 348.

84. Rupert Sheldrake, *A New Science of Life* (Los Angeles: J. P. Tarcher, 1981).

85. See Daniel Goleman, "Body Image," *Times-Colonist* (Victoria, B.C.), April 26, 1985, p. C1 (reprinted from *The New York Times*); Fisher and Cleveland, *Body Image and Personality*; Seymour Fisher, *Body Consciousness* (Englewood Cliffs,

N.J.: Prentice-Hall, 1973); and Fisher's most recent work, summarizing twenty-five years of research on the subject of body perception, *Development and Structure of the Body Image* (2 vols.; Hillsdale, N.J.: Lawrence Erlbaum Associates, 1986).

86. Jean-Louis Barrault, *Reflections on the Theatre*, trans. Barbara Wall (London: Rockliff, 1951), p. 26. It was the French school of mime, which began with the actors Jacques Copeau (1878–1919) and Charles Dullin (1885–1919), that introduced the use of the mask to force the actor or mime to rediscover the expressiveness of the "nonsocial" (esp. nonfacial) parts of the body. Etienne Decroux, also of this school, and a teacher of many great mimes, including Barrault and Marcel Marceau, also adheres to this concept. His students have been required to keep their faces impassive, masklike, so that the rest of the body can come alive. There is an intuitive wisdom in all this; these men understood (understand) that the visual gets in the way of the kinesthetic, and that the process must be reversed. See Annette Lust, "Etienne Decroux and the French School of Mime," *The Quarterly Journal of Speech*, 57, 3 (October 1971), 291–97. I am grateful to Dean Fogal, a Vancouver mime who studied with Decroux, for bringing these references to my attention.

For a full discussion of the French school of mime, see Mira Felnes, *Apostles of Silence* (Cranbury, N.J.: Associated University Presses, 1985).

87. Jean-Claude Dussault, *Le Corps vêtu de mots* (Montreal: Les Quinze, 1980), p. 117.

88. John O'Neill, *Five Bodies* (Ithaca, N.Y.: Cornell University Press, 1985), pp. 22–23.

89. Schilder, *Image and Appearance*, pp. 15–16.

90. Dussault, *Le Corps vêtu de mots*, p. 58.

91. Schilder, *Image and Appearance*, pp. 202–3 and 208–10.

92. Paul Fussell, *Class* (New York: Summit Books, 1983).

93. Schilder, *Image and Appearance*, p. 213. A friend tells me that she is not able to wear red nail polish if she is wearing a red dress; she says it is too much, pushes her right out of her body. In a more extreme way, people who experiment with costumes, such as actors or strippers, can experience a serious type of disembodiment and personality dislocation that can be difficult to shake. It is no accident that most of us are conservative in our dress and that unconventional dress can signal an assault (or attempted assault) on the established order.

94. Schilder, *Image and Appearance*, p. 217.

95. On the following see Fisher, *Body Consciousness*, pp. 23, 25, 40, 63–68, 73, and 78.

96. Apparently, it didn't work; Arbus committed suicide in 1971. Patricia Boswell's biography, *Diane Arbus* (New York: Avon, 1984), makes for very interesting reading if it is approached from a somatic point of view.

97. Paul Shepard, *Nature and Madness* (San Francisco: Sierra Club Books, 1982), p. 165.

98. This information was provided by Brian Sutton-Smith in a talk given at the University of Victoria (British Columbia) on September 28, 1983; see also his *Toys as Culture* (New York: Gardner Press, 1986).

99. "Teddy Bears Play Important Role in Children's Lives," *Montreal Gazette*, August 8, 1980.

CHAPTER 2. THE WILD AND THE TAME: HUMANS AND ANIMALS FROM LASCAUX TO WALT DISNEY

1. Julian Jaynes, *The Origin of Consciousness in the Breakdown of the Bicameral Mind* (Boston: Houghton Mifflin, 1976).
2. Roy Willis, *Man and Beast* (New York: Basic Books, 1974), pp. 7, 9, 31, 66, and 127.
3. Francis Klingender, *Animals in Art and Thought to the End of the Middle Ages*, ed. Evelyn Antal and John Harthan (London: Routledge and Kegan Paul, 1971), p. xxiii.
4. Elizabeth Atwood Lawrence, *Rodeo* (Knoxville: University of Tennessee Press, 1982). The reference here is to the famous essay by Frederick Jackson Turner, "The Significance of the Frontier in American History," read at the American Historical Association meeting in 1893. Turner held that the presence of "raw nature" in each generation, i.e., a receding frontier, determined much that was distinctive in American culture and history. See Ray Allen Billington, *The Genesis of the Frontier Thesis* (San Marino, Calif.: Huntington Library, 1987).
5. Paul Shepard, *Thinking Animals* (New York: Viking Press, 1978); Edmund Leach, "Anthropological Aspects of Language: Animal Categories and Verbal Abuse," in Eric H. Lenneberg (ed.), *New Directions in the Study of Language* (Cambridge, Mass.: MIT Press, 1964), pp. 23–63; Keith Thomas, *Man and the Natural World* (New York: Pantheon Books, 1983).
6. Mary Douglas, *Purity and Danger* (London: Routledge and Kegan Paul, 1966), pp. 165–67.
7. John Berger, "Why Look at Animals?," in *About Looking* (New York: Pantheon Books, 1980), pp. 2–4. On the nature and antiquity of animal sacredness, mythology, and so on see Joseph Campbell, *Historical Atlas of World Mythology*, Vol. 1: *The Way of the Animal Powers* (San Francisco: Harper & Row, 1983).

  In terms of dating, Stanley Diamond provides the following categories: up to 10,000 B.C. is the Paleolithic period, followed by the Paleolithic-Neolithic transition. The second phase, which he calls the "primitive," begins about 9000 B.C. and lasts until the emergence of the archaic civilizations, ca. 5000 B.C. Primitive cultures do not disappear at this time, however, but coexist with the archaic civilizations. The fourth phase, according to Diamond, began in A.D. 1600. See Stanley Diamond, *In Search of the Primitive* (New Brunswick, N.J.: Transaction Books, 1981), pp. 126–29.
8. From "A Doe at Evening," in *The Complete Poems of D. H. Lawrence*, ed. Vivian de Sola Pinto and Warren Roberts (New York: Viking, 1964), Vol. 1, p. 222.
9. Shepard, *Thinking Animals*, pp. 31–32 and 149.
10. From *An Alphabestiary* (Philadelphia: J. B. Lippincott, 1965, 1966).
11. Berger, "Why Look at Animals?," pp. 6–7.
12. Shepard, *Thinking Animals*, p. 32.
13. Ibid., p. 33.
14. Hugh Brody, *Maps and Dreams* (Vancouver: Douglas and McIntyre, 1981), p.

43. Cf. the following passage from José Ortega y Gasset's work, *Meditations on Hunting* (quoted in *The New York Times Book Review* for April 27, 1986):

> It is a "universal" attention, which does not inscribe itself on any point and tries to be on all points. There is a magnificent term for this, one that still conserves all its zest and vivacity and imminence: alertness. The hunter is the alert man. . . . Because of it he lives from within his environment. The farmer attends only to what is good or bad for the growth of his grain or the maturation of his fruit; the rest remains outside his vision and, in consequence, he remains outside the completeness that is the countryside. . . . Only the hunter, imitating the perpetual alertness of the wild animal . . . sees everything. . . .

15. Alan Herscovici, *Second Nature* (Toronto: CBC Enterprises, 1985), p. 66.
16. Ibid., pp. 15 and 60.
17. Paul Shepard, "The Ark of the Mind," *Parabola, 8,* 2 (May 1983), 56; Gerald Carson, *Men, Beasts, and Gods* (New York: Charles Scribner's Sons, 1972), pp. 5–6.
18. Shepard, "Ark of the Mind," p. 55.
19. A theme illustrated very effectively in the 1985 film by John Boorman, *The Emerald Forest*.
20. Joseph Epes Brown, "The Bison and the Mother: Lakota Correspondences," *Parabola, 8,* 2 (May 1983), 7–8 and 11.
21. Shepard, "Ark of the Mind," p. 57.
22. Sonia Cole, "Animals of the New Stone Age," in A. Houghton Brodrick (ed.), *Animals in Archaeology* (London: Barrie and Jenkins, 1972), p. 15.
23. Brodrick, *Animals in Archaeology,* from the Introduction.
24. Carson, *Men, Beasts, and Gods,* p. 10.
25. J. M. Aynard, "Animals in Mesopotamia," in Brodrick, *Animals in Archaeology,* pp. 43 and 66; and Richard Carrington, "Animals in Egypt," pp. 69, 86, and 88 of the same volume.
26. André Leroi-Gourhan, "Animals of the Old Stone Age," in Brodrick, *Animals in Archaeology,* p. 6.
27. Cole, "Animals of the New Stone Age," p. 18.
28. Ibid.; see also Simon J. M. Davis and François R. Valla, "Evidence for Domestication of the Dog 12,000 Years Ago in the Natufian of Israel," *Nature,* 276 (December 7, 1978), 608–10.
29. Strictly speaking, this is not true; or at least, we can make a distinction between aggression (including feuds and skirmishes), which probably does have a Paleolithic history, and war (which involves formation or teamwork, i.e., is organized), which emerged only in the late Paleolithic age or during the transition to Neolithic society. The debate over the innate aggressiveness vs. innate peaceability of Paleolithic humans is an old one, with Raymond Dart, Robert Ardrey, and Konrad Lorenz ranged on one side of the argument and Margaret Mead, Ashley Montagu, and Richard Leakey ranged on the other. Arther Ferrill, in Chapter 1 of *The Origins of War* (London: Thames and Hudson, 1985), says that the evidence is too thin to prove either case.

The evidence regarding warfare per se is much more solid. Ferrill notes that there is no evidence until the final stages of the Paleolithic period that tools or hunting weapons were used by man against man. Cro-Magnon cave paintings (35,000–12,000 B.C.) show virtually no evidence of warfare. But the Mesolithic period, 12,000–8000 B.C., saw a revolution in weapons technology, including the invention of the bow, sling, dagger, and mace. Neolithic cave paintings reveal the use of these against humans, for the first time.

In general, war in the real sense of the term was a Neolithic invention; all the concrete evidence we have for it, whether in art or skeletal remains, is post-Paleolithic in dating. The Neolithic period was in fact ushered in by a burst of warfare, and fortified sites spread out around the eastern Mediterranean from 8000 to 4000 B.C. These fortifications, notes Ferrill (p. 28), may have led to the discovery of agriculture and the domestication of animals. My own guess is that these all arose in an interconnected way, along with a new somatic energy configuration, that of Self vs. Other (of which the fort and the wall are the concrete embodiment).

Self/Other conflict, in any event, can obviously be traced back to Paleolithic times, though I doubt *very* far back. At some point (going backward) it was merely distinction, whereas moving forward in time it turned into organized warfare in the Neolithic period. I suspect also that Paleolithic aggression was a lot more ritualized and contained, and that even if an enemy Other existed at some point, he was still treated with numinous respect, as was done in the case of wild animals. This is a different form of Otherness than the sort that is involved in war, as far as I can see.

30. Shepard, *Thinking Animals*, pp. 148–49 and 154.

31. Aynard, "Animals in Mesopotamia," pp. 43 and 60–61; Cole, "Animals of the New Stone Age," pp. 32 and 38; Ralph B. Little, "Spider Phobias," *The Psychoanalytic Quarterly*, 36, 1 (1967); and Jacques Schnier, "Morphology as a Symbol: The Octopus," *American Imago*, 13 (1956), 3–31. See also James Mellaart, *Çatal Hüyük* (New York: McGraw-Hill, 1967).

32. There is a large literature on the Great Mother, including Erich Neumann's book of the same name and Gertrude Rachel Levy's classic work, *The Gate of Horn* (London: Faber and Faber, 1948). More recent discussions include Marija Gimbutas, *The Goddesses and Gods of Old Europe* (new ed.; London: Thames and Hudson, 1982), and Pamela Berger, *The Goddess Obscured* (Boston: Beacon Press, 1985). Useful discussions bearing on this subject can also be found in Hans Peter Duerr, *Dreamtime*, trans. Felicitas Goodman (Oxford: Basil Blackwell, 1985); A. H. Brodrick, "Animals in the Aegean," in Brodrick, *Animals in Archaeology*, p. 90; Cole, "Animals of the New Stone Age," p. 32; and Max Horkheimer and T. W. Adorno, *Dialectic of Enlightenment*, trans. John Cumming (New York: Herder and Herder, 1972; orig. German ed. 1944), p. 247.

33. Robert Darnton, *The Great Cat Massacre* (New York: Basic Books, 1984), pp. 83, 85, 90, and 92–93.

34. James Fisher, *Zoos of the World* (Garden City, N.Y.: The Natural History Press, 1967), p. 46.

35. Shepard, *Thinking Animals*, p. 109.

36. They are too much to discuss here, but there are two issues I am omitting.

One is the treatment of animals in the Roman Empire; the other is the friendly, rather than fearful, relationship to animals during the Christian Middle Ages. For along with tales of the slaying of dragons and the transformations made possible by witchcraft is the strong use of animals in Christian allegory, or the fairly common practice, at least among the peasantry, of cohabiting with animals, sometimes to absorb their power or particular traits, but also, very likely, because they were so much a part of the natural and social environment. As for Rome, it is generally well known that animals were collected and slaughtered for entertainment in gladiatorial contests. As a culture with a strongly developed ego-consciousness, Rome regarded animals as Others with no significant status or consciousness, and used them in an arbitrary and in fact barbaric way. See Carson, *Men, Beasts, and Gods,* p. 11, and Arnold van Gennep, *The Rites of Passage,* trans. Monika B. Vizedom and Gabrielle L. Cafee (London: Routledge and Kegan Paul, 1960; orig. French ed. 1908), p. 173.

37. Quoted in Kenneth Clark, *Animals and Men* (London: Thames and Hudson, 1977), pp. 154 and 214.

38. Carrington, "Animals in Egypt," p. 73.

39. Sigmund Freud, "The 'Uncanny' " (Das Unheimliche, 1919), in *The Standard Edition of the Complete Psychological Works of Sigmund Freud,* ed. James Strachey (London: Hogarth Press, 1955), Vol. 17, pp. 217–56.

40. I remember reading, some time ago, a very short and quite brilliant story by Junichiro Tanizaki called "Tattoo," in which a young woman, perhaps intending to be a geisha, has a spider tattooed on her back and suddenly seems to take on the qualities of the animal, so that the tattoo artist, who was initially her master, winds up fearing her once the operation is over.

41. Douglas, *Purity and Danger,* pp. 2, 5, 35, 39, 53–56, 115, 121, and 161–63.

42. On the following see Leach, "Anthropological Aspects of Language."

43. I can't recall the particular event, but there was a famous horse race in which a "dead heat" call was decided in favor of one of the two horses because the photo finish revealed a long string of saliva coming out of its mouth and extending over the finish line in advance of the physical boundaries of the other horse. The string of saliva was taken by the judges to be equivalent to the physical boundary of the winning horse.

44. Joseph Needham, "Human Law and the Laws of Nature," in *The Grand Titration* (London: Allen and Unwin, 1969), pp. 329–30. Doris Lessing also discusses the custom of putting nature on trial—including a tree, in France, in 1945—in the opening pages of the 1985 Massey Lectures; see *Prisons We Choose to Live Inside* (Toronto: CBC Enterprises, 1986). For a historical overview of the criminal prosecution of animals, see E. P. Evans, *The Criminal Prosecution and Capital Punishment of Animals* (London: Faber and Faber, 1987; orig. publ. 1906).

45. T. S. Kuhn, *The Structure of Scientific Revolutions* (2nd ed., enl.; Chicago: University of Chicago Press, 1970).

46. The quotation from Mary Douglas is in *Purity and Danger,* p. 102.

A modern equivalent of this combination of fascination with and terror of intermediate species is now surfacing in stories of people who claim to have been abducted by extraterrestrials. It was a bit uncanny for me to discover that some of the major themes of this chapter are present in a very popular book on the subject, the recent best-seller, *Communion*, by Whitley Strieber (New York: Avon, 1988). The author describes these creatures as insectlike, and reports his terror at the prospect of having his body boundaries violated (which he says occurred). He also claims that what these creatures wanted above all else was communion—to look deeply into his soul and know his innermost being. I suspect it is what all of us want, on some level. The psychological resonance here with the search for a nonhuman Other, the longing for communion with a living, nonhuman mirror, strikes me as being a very obvious, and powerful (if unconscious), motivation behind all of this. Strieber himself writes (pp. 238–39): "Maybe the visitor experience [i.e., encounter with extraterrestrials] is what happens when the human mind looks into the mirror . . . and discovers its own reflection is not only real but fearful to see."

47. Leach, "Anthropological Aspects of Language," pp. 40 and 42.

48. Shepard, *Thinking Animals*, p. 100.

49. One investigator, Walter Abell, found that the less any depicted hybrid monster or combination animal form resembled a known species, the greater the anxiety it generated in the observer. See Chapter 10 of his book, *The Collective Dream in Art* (New York: Schocken Books, 1966).

50. James Hillman, "Let the Creatures Be," *Parabola, 8,* 2 (May 1983), 49–53.

51. See note 41, above, for references to the discussion that follows.

52. "Separated" is (according to the Talmud) the second meaning of *kadosh,* which is not that surprising, since the category of holy implies a separation from things that are profane. The word occurs in a number of contexts, including the traditional marriage vows (the bride is to separate herself from others and cleave to the groom), and also in references to holy women, or *kedheshoth,* in ancient Israel. The Jews apparently took over some form of pantheistic sex cult from the Canaanites, and sex rites were performed in the temple to ensure agricultural fertility. Jeremiah, Hosea, and Ezekiel claimed that these women were actually prostitutes, and the *kedheshoth* in fact disappeared from the temple—i.e., were rendered separate from it—sometime after the sixth century B.C. See Johannes Pedersen, *Israel,* trans. Aslaug Møller (Vols. I–II) and Annie I. Fausbøll (Vols. III–IV) (London: Oxford University Press, 1959; orig. Danish ed. 1934), Vol. III, p. 277, and Vol. IV, pp. 469–76.

53. Peter Singer, *Animal Liberation* (New York: Avon, 1977), pp. 207–9.

54. Mary Midgley, *Animals and Why They Matter* (Harmondsworth, England: Penguin Books, 1983), p. 28.

55. Singer, *Animal Liberation,* Chapter 2 and p. 215; see also Richard Ryder, *Victims of Science* (London: Davis-Poynter, 1975).

56. Carson, *Men, Beasts, and Gods,* pp. 77, 79, 82, and 87.

57. Thomas, *Man and the Natural World,* pp. 40 and 95.

58. Clark, *Animals and Men,* pp. 60–61.

59. Berger, "Why Look at Animals?," pp. 9–11; Midgley, *Animals,* p. 12.

60. Singer, *Animal Liberation,* Chapter 3.

61. On the following see David Phillips and Sandra Kaiser, "Animals in Cap-

tivity," *San Francisco Chronicle/Examiner*, "This World" section (January 9, 1986); Solly Zuckerman (ed.), *Great Zoos of the World* (Boulder, Colo.: Westview Press, 1980), pp. 3–10; and Fisher, *Zoos of the World*, pp. 24–52.

62. Phillips and Kaiser, in "Animals in Captivity," note, however, that there was a zoo in the Tower of London in the eighteenth century, admission to which cost threepence.

63. On much of the following see Berger, "Why Look at Animals?," pp. 14–26.

64. Thomas, *Man and the Natural World*, p. 301.

65. Phillips and Kaiser, "Animals in Captivity." The authors report that by 1985, five California condors that had been reared in captivity at the Los Angeles Zoo had become too tame to be released. They had become humanly "imprinted" by the staff—"crippled by a familiarity with humans"—and were thus no longer part of the wilderness community. "Saving" such animals in this way won't work, because it is finally a different animal that gets saved.

   The last wild condor was captured in the United States in April of 1987 and taken to the Los Angeles Zoo to join the twenty-seven other birds still in existence. There is something very sad about this, it seems to me.

66. Quoted in "Other Nations," *Parabola*, 8, 2 (May 1983), 83.

67. Shepard, *Thinking Animals*, p. 240.

68. Midgley, *Animals and Why They Matter*, p. 120.

69. Carson, *Men, Beasts, and Gods*, p. 44; Thomas, *Man and the Natural World*, pp. 108–19; Natalie Angier, "Some Pet Theories About Health," *Eastern Review* (October 1983), 70–74; Lena Williams, "Why America Is Going to the Dogs (and Cats)," *San Francisco Chronicle*, August 19, 1988, p. B4.

70. Karen Miller Allen, *The Human-Animal Bond: An Annotated Bibliography* (Metuchen, N.J.: The Scarecrow Press, 1985), p. ix.

71. Angier, "Some Pet Theories"; Alan Beck and Aaron Katcher, *Between Pets and People* (New York: G. P. Putnam's Sons, 1983); Charles Phineas, "Household Pets and Urban Alienation," *Journal of Social History*, 8 (Spring 1974), 338–43; K. M. Keddie, "Pathological Mourning After the Death of a Domestic Pet," *British Journal of Psychiatry*, 131 (July 1977), 21–25.

72. Paul Cameron et al., *The Pet Threat* (Seattle: The Western Psychological Association, 1977); Paul Cameron and Michael Mattson, "Psychological Correlates of Pet Ownership," *Psychological Reports*, 30 (1972), 286; T. McGinnis, "Why People Own Pets," *Family Health*, 10 (October 1978), 14; Keddie, "Pathological Mourning."

73. Carson, *Men, Beasts, and Gods*, p. 147.

74. Kathleen Szasz, *Petishism: Pets and Their People in the Western World* (New York: Holt, Rinehart and Winston, 1969).

75. Shepard, *Thinking Animals*, pp. 196–204.

76. Berger, "Why Look at Animals?," pp. 12–13.

77. On the following see Lawrence, *Rodeo*, pp. 146, 208–27, and 263–64.

78. Gregory Bateson, *Naven* (2nd ed.; Stanford: Stanford University Press, 1958), and also various essays in *Steps to an Ecology of Mind* (London: Paladin, 1973).

79. On the following see Thomas, *Man and the Natural World*, pp. 38–46, 52, 57, 77, and 134, and W. M. S. Russell and Claire Russell, "The Social Biology of Werewolves," in J. R. Porter and W. M. S. Russell (eds.), *Animals in Folklore*

(Totowa, N.J.: Rowman and Littlefield, 1978), pp. 143–84. Animals as metaphors in Victorian society are discussed by Harriet Ritvo in *The Animal Estate*
(Cambridge, Mass.: Harvard University Press, 1987).

80. From Boyle's *Works* (1772), Vol. 2, p. 182; quoted in Lynn Thorndike, *A History
    of Magic and Experimental Science* (New York: Columbia University Press, 1958),
    Vol. 8, p. 198.
81. This theme is developed very effectively by Paul Shepard in *Nature and Madness*
    (see Chapter 1, note 97).
82. David Foulkes, *Children's Dreams: Longitudinal Studies* (New York: John Wiley
    and Sons, 1982), pp. 48–49, 80, and 115; and E. G. Pitcher and E. Prelinger,
    *Children Tell Stories: An Analysis of Fantasy* (New York: International Univer-
    sities Press, 1963). Humans do appear in Paleolithic art, as it turns out, but
    only as stick figures, and then very few of them. Arther Ferrill notes (*Origins
    of War*, p. 17) that we have several thousand Paleolithic scenes of animals as
    compared to about 130 depictions of human beings, and that these latter are
    very crudely drawn.
83. Midgley, *Animals and Why They Matter*, pp. 118–19.
84. Shepard, *Thinking Animals*, p. 71.

## Part II. Spiritual Politics
### CHAPTER 3. THE BODY OF HISTORY

1. Edmund Leach, "Common Ground," *London Review of Books*, September 19,
   1985, p. 19.
2. Ibid.
3. Cf. David Abram, "The Perceptual Implications of Gaia," *The Ecologist*, 15, 3
   (1985), 96–103. Abram makes a good attempt at describing visceral perceptions
   when he says that if one can get into the space of experiencing one's mind
   as being part of one's body, and can maintain this awareness for some length
   of time, one first begins to experience oneself "as a magic, self-sensing form,"
   and finally "one will begin to experience a corresponding shift in the physical
   environment. Birds, trees, even rivers and stones begin to stand forth as
   living, communicative presences" (p. 100). Martin Buber also discussed this
   phenomenon in the third section of *I and Thou*.
4. Eric Havelock, *Preface to Plato* (Cambridge, Mass.: Harvard University Press,
   1963), pp. 25–27, 45–47, and 150–58.
5. Thomas Goldstein, *Dawn of Modern Science* (Boston: Houghton Mifflin, 1980),
   pp. 156–66.
6. Kurt Goldstein, *Selected Papers/Ausgewählte Schriften*, ed. Aron Gurwitsch et
   al. (The Hague: Martinus Nijhoff, 1971), p. 430.
7. Of course, many historians, such as E. H. Carr (*What is History?* [Harmonds-
   worth, England: Penguin Books, 1964]), claim that objectivity is not strictly
   possible and that the historian's bias inevitably colors the picture; but in the
   end, Carr, like so many others, remains a positivist; he finally does believe
   in a "hard bedrock of reality" that can be contacted via the documents.
8. Lewis Mumford, *The Myth of the Machine* (New York: Harcourt, Brace and
   World, 1966), pp. 3–24; see also pp. 48–71.

9. Charles Darwin, *On the Origin of Species, A Facsimile of the First Edition* (Cambridge, Mass.: Harvard University Press, 1964), p. 288.

10. On the following see R. D. Laing, *The Divided Self* (Harmondsworth, England: Penguin Books, 1965), pp. 25 and 86–87.

11. See Andrei Bely, *Petersburg*, trans. Robert A. Maguire and John E. Malmstad (Bloomington: Indiana University Press, 1978; orig. Russian ed. 1916), pp. 162–68.

   The whole sequence, in fact, is more than just an anxiety reaction, as it involves a classic case of astral projection, and includes strong alchemical overtones, references to Buddhism, and so on. It is almost certain that Bely knew what he was writing about firsthand. He became an active follower of Rudolf Steiner, the German mystic and philosopher, while at work on *Petersburg;* and Steiner's work includes a number of meditations and exercises that enable the practitioner to alter his or her consciousness and experience different realms of reality. Bely had also, apparently, read the occult classic by Annie Besant, *Man and His Bodies* (1896), as well as the Egyptian Book of the Dead, which deals with similar matters. (I discuss the issue of multiple bodies and levels of consciousness in Chapter 4.) This direct experience with mind/body interaction is the key to the hidden history recorded in *Petersburg,* and gives it a dimension that academic studies of the 1905 revolution necessarily miss. See *Petersburg,* pp. 292, 318, 337–40, and 355.

12. Elsa Morante, *History, A Novel,* trans. William Weaver (New York: Vintage Books, 1984), pp. 200–15 and 287–92.

13. There is a good bit of work by, and about, the *Annales* school, whose most famous representative is undoubtedly the late Fernand Braudel. A major study of the school can be found in Traian Stoianovich, *French Historical Method: The* Annales *Paradigm* (Ithaca, N.Y.: Cornell University Press, 1976). In addition, the interested reader might wish to consult the school's journal, *Annales. Economies, Sociétés, Civilisations.*

14. Lucien Febvre, *The Problem of Unbelief in the Sixteenth Century,* trans. Beatrice Gottlieb (Cambridge, Mass.: Harvard University Press, 1983; orig. French ed. 1947); Marc Bloch, *The Royal Touch,* trans. J. E. Anderson (London: Routledge and Kegan Paul, 1973; orig. French ed. 1924).

15. There are a number of discussions of work done in *mentalité* the reader may wish to consult: Stuart Clark, "French Historians and Early Modern Popular Culture," *Past and Present,* 100 (1983), 62–99; Philippe Ariès, "L'histoire des mentalités," in Jacques Le Goff et al. (eds.), *La Nouvelle histoire* (Paris: Retz, 1978), pp. 402–23; André Burguière, "The Fate of the History of Mentalities in the *Annales,*" *Comparative Studies in Society and History,* 24, 3 (1982), 424–37; and other essays by Patrick Hutton, Jacques Le Goff, Alphonse Dupront, Georges Duby, and Robert Mandrou.

16. Foucault's works include *Madness and Civilization, The Birth of the Clinic, Discipline and Punish, The History of Sexuality, The Order of Things,* and *The Archaeology of Knowledge,* and there are numerous studies of his works now available in both French and English. Ariès is the author of *Centuries of Childhood* and *The Hour of Our Death,* among other works; a discussion of his contribution to historiography may be found in André Burguière, "La sin-

gulière histoire de Philippe Ariès," *Le Nouvel observateur*, February 20, 1978, pp. 80–101.

17. Michel Foucault, *The Order of Things* (New York: Vintage Books, 1973), esp. Chapter 2; Patrick H. Hutton, "The History of Mentalities: The New Map of Cultural History," *History and Theory*, 20 (1981), 252.

18. G. Spencer-Brown, *Laws of Form* (New York: E.P. Dutton, 1979), esp. pp. xxix and 105–6.

19. For example, Paola Zambelli, "Uno, due, tre, mille Menocchio?" *Archivio storico italiano*, 137 (1979), 51–90.

20. Carlo Ginzburg, *The Cheese and the Worms*, trans. John and Anne Tedeschi (New York: Penguin Books, 1982), p. 155.

21. Another historian calling for major changes in this direction is Theodore Zeldin. In an article entitled "Personal History and the History of the Emotions" (*Journal of Social History*, 15 [Spring 1982], 339–47), Zeldin asks: "why must historians wear masks when they sit at their typewriters?" and goes on to call for a "humanisation of academia," a "historians' liberation movement," an emphasis on imagination rather than erudition, and "a special variety of history" that encourages the injection of the personal and idiosyncratic into the interpretation of the past. Zeldin himself has written a study of modern France in several volumes (*France, 1848–1945*) that emphasizes things such as ambition, worry, boredom, and pride; and in addition he suggests topics such as love, loneliness, envy, shyness, and smell as reasonable ones for historians to tackle.

This is fine; in fact, coming from someone as eminent as Zeldin, it is nothing less than remarkable. But I don't think it really goes far enough. To begin with, it does not raise the deeper and more embarrassing question of the historian putting his or her own body, personal history, and emotional responses into the picture. Mind/body interaction, body image, the experience of ourselves sensuously and somatically, and knowing our own bodies as part of the process of historical empathy and identification, are all absent from his discussion. My own feeling is that these things should be central. Indeed, I would find a history of the emotions that did not discuss somatic reality, and the historian's own emotions, a bit unreal.

Secondly, Zeldin's "liberation movement" is essentially a call for diversity, for a toleration of freewheeling individuality in topics and approaches. My own concern, like Ginzburg's, is methodological: I seek to forge a new tool of historical investigation, and in that sense I am far less ecumenical than Zeldin is. This may be my problem, of course, rather than Zeldin's, and I would probably agree with his "let's throw open the doors" policy in terms of a transitional period that might serve to free us from traditional methodologies; but I find it personally more exciting to create a new research tool, leading directly to a somatic understanding of the past, than to say "anything goes" and leave it at that. This is *not* to say that such a tool should be turned into a canon or worldview; but that is a different problem altogether.

The closest thing I have found to what I am talking about—and it is not an explicitly somatic approach—is James Rhodes' study of Nazism, *The Hitler Movement* (Stanford: Hoover Institution Press, 1980). Rhodes argues that the real story of the Third Reich requires reading into the hearts and minds of human beings, but that this cannot be done in a rigorous fashion. Rigor, however, may not be the point, according to Rhodes; the procedure he chooses is one of introspection, enabling the investigator to make intelligent guesses. Thus he says that the researcher must permit concepts or symbols to suggest their own experiential meanings, and must move back and forth between situations studied and his or her own reactions to them. "In this procedure," writes Rhodes,

> the investigator infers the motives and experiences of others by examining their situations, behavior, and self-interpretations and by deciding what his own range of possible desires and thoughts would be if his circumstances, actions, and self-explanations were similar. . . . [H]e especially tries to reconstruct their consciousness imaginatively by allowing their words to awaken their wants and perceptions in his own soul. . . .
>
> Although this procedure does not yield the compelling proofs of formal logic or statistics, it does afford a kind of intersubjective transmissibility of its evidence and, in principle, its conclusions are falsifiable; competent readers can evaluate its data and results by repeating its operations.

(See Rhodes, pp. 20 and 207–8, for an extended discussion of this methodology.)

The general issue of empathic understanding, of course, has been raised by a number of historians and philosophers, including Georg Simmel and R. G. Collingwood. For a number of valuable references on the subject, including critiques of the empathic approach, see Thomas A. Kohut, "Psychohistory as History," *American Historical Review, 91*, 2 (April 1986), 347, n. 19.

22. It should be added that the late seventies saw three publications, in French, on the history of fear, by Jean Delumeau, Jacques Le Brun, and Madeleine Läik. Regarding Delumeau's work, *La Peur en Occident, XIVe–XVIIIe siècles* (Paris: Fayard, 1978), Zeldin reports ("Personal History," p. 345): "It is significant that [Delumeau] undertook his study because he wished to understand the terror he felt at the age of ten when a friend suddenly died; a terror so intense that he stayed away from school for three months; the problem of fear has always haunted him; his life has been a search for serenity through acceptance of the inevitable; so this history is very much a reflection on individual experience, giving birth to a massive reflection on the experience of others."

I am not saying that the historian must *necessarily* discuss his or her own life in the course of the historical analysis, but at the very least, the analysis should emerge out of his or her own life experience, or possess strong identification—which is not the same as grinding an ideological axe, a way of being that usually involves *no* personal reflection or soul-searching, and that is all too common among academic "rebels." Rhodes' approach of interior reflection (see note 21, above) can be avoided even in somatic history proper, as a recent book on the history of smell, Alain Corbin's *The Foul and the Fragrant*, trans. Miriam L. Kochan et al. (Cambridge, Mass.: Harvard University Press, 1986), shows. There is nothing whatever of Corbin himself in this book; despite the subject, it remains a "deodorized" kind of history. (Even a few "scratch 'n' sniff" cards supplied with the book might have been a modest step in the right direction.)

23. Zeldin, "Personal History," p. 342.

24. Claude Charron, *Désobéir* (Montreal: VLB Éditeur, 1983), pp. 346–47. Charron's French is a bit idiosyncratic; the last sentence quoted, in particular, is only an approximate translation, but I believe I have captured the sense of the original. ("Elle se tisse discrètement dans les âmes et les coeurs, eux mille fois plus près du vécu quotidien de chacun, de ses succès, de ses échecs, de ses peines et de ses joies.")

25. Although it makes no mention of the body or of experiential identification, a recent article by Peter and Carol Stearns is very useful on the subject of the methodological difficulties involved in generating a history of the emotions. The authors are particularly interested in the evolution of human emotions over time, and see it as something that very much "needs to be woven into the historical fabric." They also suggest that such changes might have an impact on other areas of human behavior, such as politics, which is at least one part of the visible/invisible link I am suggesting in this chapter. The curious thing about the article, however, is its totally antiseptic and scientist tone; there is not a single emotional line in it. And *this* is finally the problem, not merely a lack of analytical studies of the emotions per se.

   See Peter N. Stearns with Carol Z. Stearns, "Emotionology: Clarifying the History of Emotions and Emotional Standards," *American Historical Review*, 90, 4 (October 1985), 813–36, esp. 820 and 829.

26. See Ch. 1, note 98. Sutton-Smith is the author of roughly a dozen books on education, child psychology, games, and play.

27. Quoted in Alice Miller, *For Your Own Good*, trans. Hildegarde and Hunter Hannum (New York: Farrar Straus Giroux, 1983), p. 46.

28. George Mosse discusses the relationship between Fascism and definitions of "respectable" sexual behavior in his recent book, *Nationalism and Sexuality* (New York: Howard Fertig, 1985), which is helpful, although it doesn't deal with the sex-death equation as such.

   There are some suggestions regarding the sex-death equation in L. J. Jordanova's essay, "Natural Facts: a Historical Perspective on Science and Sexuality," in Carol P. MacCormack and Marilyn Strathern (eds.), *Nature, Culture and Gender* (Cambridge, England: Cambridge University Press, 1980), pp. 42–69. In Britain and France in the eighteenth century, boys in their early teens—the majority, presumably, with no sexual experience—were trained to be *accoucheurs* and surgeons, and thus probably had their first view of female genitals in their obstetrical apprenticeship. However, European medical training in general also made use of wax figures of women from the late eighteenth century, and it is also possible that autopsies provided the male medical student with his first view of the female anatomy. Women, apparently, who were trained to be *accoucheurs* and midwives were in their twenties and mostly married, suggesting that at least for those being trained in the healing arts, the sex-death equation (if such existed) applied only to men. It is hard to know what to make of all this, and perhaps it is not too significant, since those studying the healing arts constituted a very small percentage of the population at any given time. How the *majority* of boys and girls learned about sex is still an open question, as far as I know.

I discuss the somatic dimension of the Third Reich in Chapter 8, at length, although my focus is not particularly sexual in nature.

29. Quoted in Elias, *History of Manners* (see Chapter 1, note 47), p. 89.
30. Ibid., p. 256.
31. Wilhelm Reich, *Character Analysis*, trans. Vincent R. Carfagno (3rd ed., enl.; New York: Simon and Schuster, 1972; orig. German ed. 1933), p. xxvi (italicized in the original).

CHAPTER 4. THE GNOSTIC RESPONSE

1. I omit here any discussion of *rational* heresies, such as Socinianism, which denied the Trinity and the efficacy of Church sacraments. Down to the time of the Protestant Reformation and the rise of secular/scientific culture (discussed in Chapter 7), rational heresies played a much less significant role in the history of the Church than did gnostic or mystical ones.
2. There is a story about Al-Hallaj, the twelfth-century Sufi heretic who was about to be put to death by the Islamic orthodoxy, being asked if he wanted to make a final statement. Supposedly, Al-Hallaj turned to his executioner and said: "If what remains concealed from you had remained concealed from me, I wouldn't be here today." Whether apocryphal or not, this story says more about the history of religion—and cognition—than one can possibly imagine.
3. On this and the discussion that follows see Edward Gibbon, *The Decline and Fall of the Roman Empire*, Volume I (Volume 40 of *Great Books of the Western World*, ed. Robert Maynard Hutchins [Chicago: Encyclopaedia Britannica, 1952; orig. publ. 1776]), Chapter 21 and esp. p. 313; and Harold O. J. Brown, *Heresies* (Garden City, N.Y.: Doubleday, 1984), pp. xix, xxiii, 7–8, 105–8, 117–31, 145, and 221 (neither author, however, makes any reference to somatic practice). The doctrine of the Trinity was thus made official in the so-called Nicene Creed, which was reaffirmed at the Council of Chalcedon in 451. After that, the West entered upon centuries of relative doctrinal stability, although the issue continued to emerge. Thus at the Third Council of Toledo in 589, the word *filioque*—"and from the Son"—was added to the Nicene Creed to generate a strict interpretation of consubstantiality. The Creed now read: "and in the Holy Spirit, the Lord and giver of life, who proceeds from the Father *and the Son* [*filioque*], who together with the Father and the Son is worshipped and Glorified." Hence the full identity of the nature of the Father and the Son was emphasized. Controversy in the West over this lasted for two more centuries; the Eastern Church never accepted the doctrine.
4. A beautiful description of this, and its relationship to sexual (tantric) practice, is provided in a remarkable novel of first-century Palestinian politics, *The Illusionist*, by Anita Mason (London: Hamish Hamilton, 1983), pp. 180–82.
5. Robert Masters, "The Way of the Five Bodies," *Dromenon*, 3, 2 (Spring 1981), 16–25. A fuller version of this appears in *The Goddess Sekhmet* (New York: Amity House, 1988).

6. Hans Jonas, *The Gnostic Religion* (2nd ed., rev.; Boston: Beacon Press, 1958), p. 166. For a modern version of the multiple—in this case, seven—body theory, see Rudolf Steiner, *Theosophy* (4th ed.; London: Rudolf Steiner Press, 1973), pp. 17–45, and also *An Outline of Occult Science* (3rd ed.; Spring Valley, N.Y.: Anthroposophic Press, 1972), pp. 21–46. Steiner also entertained a more simplified form of this, that of four bodies (physical, etheric, astral, and egoic) at various points as well. A useful introduction to his work is Colin Wilson, *Rudolf Steiner* (Wellingborough, England: The Aquarian Press, 1985).

7. Christopher Hill, *The World Turned Upside Down* (London: Temple Smith, 1972); see also Lawrence Durrell, *Monsieur* (Harmondsworth, England: Penguin Books, 1984), and Paul Zweig, *The Heresy of Self-Love* (Princeton: Princeton University Press, 1980; orig. publ. 1968), pp. 3–21.

8. The East, just like the West, has not been without distinction between form and essence, and it is doubtful whether Taoism represents any sort of mainstream view. The doctrine most suited to the mandarinate, or bureaucracy of traditional China, was Confucianism, which placed heavy emphasis on concepts of law and justice as making the administration of the state possible.

9. I am omitting, in this exposition, Masters' analysis of the theory in specifically Egyptian terms, and involving the goddess Sekhmet (see above, note 5). According to Michael Crisp, an Egyptologist and expert on the Western magical tradition (personal communication, 1985), Masters has translated terms from the original hieroglyphics incorrectly, and there is no such body mythology connected with Sekhmet. What Masters has done, apparently, is provide a kind of Zoroastrian view of the universe, or a first-to-third century-A.D. view of Egyptian cosmology that most closely resembles the ideas of the Gnostic teacher Basilides. (Cf. the "Paraphrase of Shem," pp. 308–28 of James M. Robinson [ed.], *The Nag Hammadi Library* [San Francisco: Harper & Row, 1978].) In fact, says Crisp, the Egyptians were more Taoistic than Manichaean, contrary to Masters' claims (chaos was part of the order of things, not an enemy); they did not cultivate the later Gnostic idea of the individual merging into a great transpersonal Self; dream and waking states were not sharply distinguished (i.e., they were not early Jungians, as Masters seems to think); and so on. In general, the article is not very reliable as it concerns Egyptian psychic or spiritual life. But Masters is correct in his interpretation of the *ka* (second body) and the spiritual (fifth) body, and he is certainly correct in asserting that some variation of the five-body theory is part of all major spiritual traditions and magical/occult systems.

10. There is a very sensitive discussion of these sorts of exercises as a personal discovery in Joanna Field's book *A Life of One's Own* (Los Angeles: J. P. Tarcher, 1981; orig. publ. 1936), pp. 71 and 73–74:

> Usually this center of awareness seemed to be somewhere in my head. But gradually I found that I could if I chose push it out into different parts of my body or even outside myself altogether. Once on a night journey in a train when I could not sleep for the crowd of day impressions which raced through my head, I happened to "feel myself" down into my heart and immediately my mind was so stilled that in a few moments

I fell into a peaceful sleep. But it surprised me to think that I had lived for twenty-five years without ever discovering that such an internal placing of awareness was possible. . . .

My ordinary way of looking at things seemed to be from my head, as if it were a tower in which I kept myself shut up, only looking out of the windows to watch what was going on. Now I seemed to be discovering that I could if I liked go down inside, go down and make myself part of what was happening, and only so could I experience certain things which could not be seen from the detached height of the tower. . . . [But] I was afraid of it and loath to leave the security of my tower too often.

(Joanna Field is the pseudonym of the British therapist and writer Marion Milner.)

11. On metal bending in particular see J. B. Hasted, *The Metal Benders* (London: Routledge and Kegan Paul, 1981), as well as the very interesting study by H. M. Collins and T. J. Pinch, *Frames of Meaning* (London: Routledge and Kegan Paul, 1982).

12. R. D. Laing, *The Politics of Experience* (New York: Ballantine Books, 1967), p. 190.

13. Sheldrake, *New Science of Life* (see Chapter 1, note 84).

14. See, for example, the *Laws*, sections 942a–d.

15. See Chapter 5, note 16, and also Duerr, *Dreamtime* (see Chapter 2, note 32). On this point it is interesting to note that sexual switching among shamans is well attested to in the anthropological literature.

16. S. N. Eisenstadt, "Heterodoxies and Dynamics of Civilizations," *Proceedings of the American Philosophical Society*, 128, 2 (1984), 104–13.

17. Umberto Eco, *The Name of the Rose*, trans. William Weaver (New York: Harcourt Brace Jovanovich, 1983), p. 248.

18. David E. Aune, "Magic in Early Christianity," in Wolfgang Haase (ed.), *Aufstieg und Niedergang der römischen Welt* (Berlin: Walter de Gruyter, 1980), Vol. 2, 23, 2, pp. 1507–57.

19. "With Qumran," writes Menahem Mansoor, "we are certainly close to Gnosticism, but we have not yet passed the point of transition between pre-*gnosis* and Gnosticism proper." For this article, as well as ones by van Baaren and Hans Jonas, see C. J. Bleeker and Ugo Bianchi (eds.), *Le origini dello gnosticismo: colloquio di Messina 13–18 aprile 1966* (Leiden: Brill, 1967), esp. pp. 90–108, 174–80, and 389–400.

20. A typology of *medieval* heresy was attempted many years ago by Paul Alphandéry in "Remarques sur le type sectaire dans l'hérésiologie médiévale latine," *Transactions of the Third International Congress for the History of Religions* (Oxford, 1908), Vol. 2, pp. 354–57, which has certain things in common with my own four-part typology. Alphandéry's classification is tripartite: world religion, Christian Reformist, and apocalyptic. In the first category he puts the Cathars; in the second, the Waldensians; in the third, the Amalricians, who saw the future as being the inheritance of the chosen few. This may conceivably work for medieval heresy, but it seems to me that it has some serious problems. Catharism *may* have had aspirations of becoming a world

religion, but its defeat at the hands of the orthodoxy doesn't leave much room for speculation on this point. I think it makes more sense to discuss it in terms of outcome rather than intent, and as such, it more clearly falls into the category of defeat/co-optation (discussed at length in Chapter 6). From the point of view of outcome also, Alphandéry's second category need not concern us. "Heresies" of this kind were either neatly channeled away from true heretical directions (the Franciscans are a good example) or easily wiped out (the Waldensians); they never developed enough political power to constitute a "nodal point" in Western history. The apocalyptic-elitist category, as far as I can tell, corresponds to my fourth category, the "German" model. In this case, the human race is politically as well as spiritually divided into the masses, who are "asleep," and a small coterie of the elect who, having attained gnosis, are "awake" and consequently (in this theory) the only people around fit to direct the destinies of the human race.

Still, Alphandéry's emphasis on aspirations is perhaps not so easily dismissed; turning reformers into enemies can become a self-fulfilling prophecy, and this tendency on the part of the Church tends to confirm Michel Foucault's argument that the categorization of Other (usually, a deviant group) as Other is what fuels the oppositional structure of Western culture. Thus historians Jeffrey Burton Russell and Raffaello Morghen have argued that prior to 1140, the Cathars were actually reformers with Puritan interests; it was the Church that made them into heretics (discussed briefly by George H. Shriver in his essay "Images of Catharism and the Historian's Task," in George H. Shriver [ed.], *Contemporary Reflections on the Medieval Christian Tradition* [Durham, N.C.: Duke University Press, 1974], p. 71, and at greater length by Russell in *Dissent and Reform in the Middle Ages* [Berkeley: University of California Press, 1965], pp. 188ff). Carlo Ginzburg develops a similar argument in another context in his book *The Night Battles*, trans. John and Anne Tedeschi (Baltimore: The Johns Hopkins University Press, 1983; orig. Italian ed. 1966); and Russell has a general discussion of the Church turning reformers into heretics, as well as a summary review of some other typologies of heresy, in "Interpretations of the Origins of Medieval Heresy," *Medieval Studies*, 25 (1963), 44–47.

21. To the extent that Protestantism was a front for rationalism, as Keith Thomas and other scholars have argued, the Reformation itself can be subsumed in this category, although the story is obviously much more complex.

22. Stanton Peele, *Love and Addiction* (New York: Signet Books, 1976); Dorothy Tennov, *Love and Limerence* (New York: Stein and Day, 1981).

CHAPTER 5. JEWS AND CHRISTIANS

1. Julian Jaynes, *Origin of Consciousness* (see Ch. 2, note 1), p. 291.

2. E. R. Dodds, *The Greeks and the Irrational* (Berkeley: University of California Press, 1951), pp. 42–43 and 209–11.

3. It is very possible that many of these Greek cults and practices had Egyptian roots. The priestly initiation of ancient Egypt revolved around achieving a deeper embedding of the *ka* into a larger reality, and there are many reports of Greek figures such as Pythagoras (if he indeed existed as an actual person) going to Egypt to acquire esoteric learning and then returning to Greece.

Egypt, however, may not be necessary in terms of historical explanation; Dodds claims that there was a thriving shamanistic tradition in Thrace, and he sees Empedocles (fifth century B.C.) as the last of a long line of Greek shamans. On this, and the diffusion of the idea of the separable Self, see Dodds, *Greeks and the Irrational*, pp. 145ff.

4. Devon H. Wiens, "Mystery Concepts in Primitive Christianity and Its Environment," in Haase, *Aufstieg und Niedergang* (see Ch. 4, note 18), Vol. 2, 23, 2, p. 1249n.

5. Karl Prümm, "Mystery-Religions, Greco-Oriental," in *The New Catholic Encyclopedia* (New York: McGraw-Hill, 1967), Vol. 10, pp. 153–64.

6. Samuel Angus, *The Mystery Religions and Christianity* (New Hyde Park, N.Y.: University Books, 1966; orig. publ. 1925), pp. 45ff.

7. On puritanism and pessimistic gnosticism see Dodds, *Greeks and the Irrational*, pp. 135–78, and Frances Yates, *Giordano Bruno and the Hermetic Tradition* (New York: Vintage Books, 1969), pp. 22 and 128.

8. Plato, *Theaetetus*, section 176b (quotation is from the translation by F. M. Cornford).

9. I recall reading, as a teenager, a book that made an enormous impression on me, namely Milton Steinberg's novel *As a Driven Leaf*. His theme is essentially that everything, even the most rational mathematics, rests on faith, and he reconstructs the Hellenistic-Jewish interaction of antiquity in a very experiential way. Although the Greeks come off as being too rational vis-à-vis the actual historical record, Steinberg's ability to convey the flavor of this syncretistic culture was, as I remember it, quite remarkable; but then, I was "only sixteen."

On the syncretism of this era see Jonas, *Gnostic Religion* (see Chapter 4, note 6).

10. Richard Reitzenstein, *Hellenistic Mystery Religions*, trans. J. E. Steely (Pittsburgh: Pickwick, 1978; from the 3rd German ed. of 1927).

11. Marcel Simon, "The Religionsgeschichtliche Schule, Fifty Years Later," *Religious Studies*, 11 (June 1975); quoted in Wiens, "Mystery Concepts," p. 1253.

12. On this see Alan F. Segal, "Heavenly Ascent in Hellenistic Judaism, Early Christianity, and Their Environment," in Haase, *Aufstieg und Niedergang*, Vol. 2, 23, 2, pp. 1333–94.

13. Ibid., pp. 1334–38. The ascent (*anabasis*, in Greek) is crucial to the hero's journey, but there was also a descent (*katabasis*) that was part of this. The full heroic journey involved a trip to the underworld (e.g., the earth, or Hades) and back.

14. W. Bousset, "Die Himmelsreise der Seele," *Archiv für Religionswissenschaft*, 4 (1901), 136–69.

15. Segal, "Heavenly Ascent," p. 1341. I do not mean to assert here that the ascent tradition is Semitic in origin. As I suggested earlier, the whole multibody structure and accompanying set of esoteric techniques were possibly an Asiatic discovery. Certainly, they antedated Near Eastern practices, and kundalini yoga is undoubtedly the grandfather (or grandmother) of the whole thing. Whether East influenced West, or the discovery was a parallel one, is, however, another matter altogether.

16. Ibid., p. 1370; see also pp. 1342–63 and 1377–78. On Jewish ascent rituals see Naomi Janowitz, "The Language of Ascent: Lévi-Strauss, Silverstein and Maaseh Merkabah," in Robert L. Moore and Frank E. Reynolds (eds.), *Anthropology and the Study of Religion* (Chicago: Center for the Scientific Study of Religion, 1984), pp. 218–20 and 224.

All Western (including Near Eastern) ascent experience has its roots in the pagan and folk practices of Great Mother culture, and this was certainly true for the Jews. It was only later, in the post-Exilic period (the Babylonian exile lasted from 586 to 538 B.C.), that prophecy and ecstatic trance began to fall away, and that Judaism so clearly emerged as a patriarchal religion. What became dominant in Greece—ego-consciousness—was also dominant among the Jews, as both peoples fought to free themselves of the influence of participating consciousness, identified with the feminine. This is what has given the West its strongly masculine bias, and it is why the repressed always tends to return (for men) in feminine form.

The Great Mother roots of Jewish prophecy are discussed by Johannes Pedersen in his classic work, *Israel* (see Chapter 2, note 52). Pedersen points out that one of the later Jewish prophetic books reveals a connection among agriculture, ecstatic prophecy, and a sex cult, and it says that one day the prophets will be ashamed of the visions they have during ecstatic frenzy (Vol. IV, p. 475). He also discusses the numerous Biblical passages that deal with ascent or visionary experience—including Kings, Daniel, Samuel, Jeremiah, and Ezekiel—and notes that Israel's neighbors, especially the Canaanites, Syrians, and Hittites, were very familar with it; it was part of the whole cultural milieu of the Near East (Vol. I, pp. 155–66). Many Jews turned against it in the post-Exilic period, but it never died out completely, continuing on into the second century A.D., perhaps even into the fourth. It was the dynamic tension between legalistic and magical Judaism, in fact, that made the birth of Christianity possible (see below).

17. Scholem is the author of a number of works on Jewish mysticism, including *Major Trends in Jewish Mysticism, The Kabballah and Its Symbolism,* and *Jewish Gnosticism, Merkabah Mysticism and Talmudic Tradition.* In the discussion that follows I am drawing on his article on the cabala (in the entry "Kabbalah") in the *Encyclopaedia Judaica* (Jerusalem: Keter Publishing House, 1971), Vol. 10, cols. 490–654, and in particular cols. 495–503. A useful discussion of Scholem's work can be found in David Biale, *Gershom Scholem: Kabbalah and Counter-History* (2nd ed.; Cambridge, Mass.: Harvard University Press, 1982).

18. E.g., Chapter 1, verse 16: "The appearance of the wheels and their work was like unto the colour of a beryl: and they four had one likeness: and their appearance and their work was as it were a wheel within a wheel." For what it's worth, various UFO cults regard this as evidence that Ezekiel's vision was of a spacecraft. See the *Vancouver Sun*, November 29, 1986, p. B6.

19. Centuries later, Jewish mystics would report their experiences in even greater detail; practices that were, according to Scholem, probably based on this early tradition. See Chapter 6.

20. Segal, "Heavenly Ascent," pp. 1378–83. On Morton Smith see *The Secret Gospel*

(Clearlake, Calif.: The Dawn Horse Press, 1982), and *Jesus the Magician* (San Francisco: Harper & Row, 1978). On the Ascension of Isaiah see Chapter 6.

21. For bibliographical source material the interested reader might begin by consulting the references cited in the articles by David Aune (see Chapter 4, note 18) and William Green (see below, note 30), and in Jack N. Lightstone, *The Commerce of the Sacred* (Chico, Calif.: Scholars Press, 1984), as well as Jonas, *Gnostic Religion*. Works by Cumont, Festugière, Hopfner, and Stucken are classics in this genre.

22. On the following see Martin Hengel, *Judaism and Hellenism*, trans. John Bowden (2 vols.; London: SCM Press, 1974), Vol. 1, pp. 1–4, 56–60, 73–81, 100–108, 113–115, 135, 169–79, and 304–14. I am not, in this discussion, very consistent about transliteration from the Hebrew. Thus "Hasidim" can also be rendered "Chasidim," *halacha* as *halaḥa*, "Chanukah" as "Hanukah" or "Hanukkah," etc.

23. To be precise, the Dead Sea Scrolls are the writings of a sect that was based at Qumran, which most scholars now believe was the Essenes. This has never been proven, but it does seem very likely.

24. Ernest Renan, *Life of Jesus* (New York: Modern Library, 1955; orig. French ed. 1863), pp. 136–38.

25. Charles Guignebert, *The Jewish World in the Time of Jesus*, trans. S. H. Hooke (London: Routledge and Kegan Paul, 1939), pp. 202–5, 222, and 240–60.

26. Quoted in Matthew Black, "The Dead Sea Scrolls and Christian Origins," in Matthew Black (ed.), *The Scrolls and Christianity* (London: S.P.C.K., 1969), p. 98.

27. Ibid., pp. 98–99.

28. E. R. Goodenough, *Jewish Symbols in the Greco-Roman Period* (13 vols.; New York: Pantheon-Bollingen, 1953–68); G. F. Moore, *Judaism in the First Centuries of the Christian Era* (3 vols.; Cambridge, Mass.: Harvard University Press, 1927–30). A useful review of Goodenough vs. Moore is Morton Smith, "Goodenough's *Jewish Symbols* in Retrospect," *Journal of Biblical Literature*, 86 (1967), 53–68.

29. Volume I, Chapter 1 of Goodenough's *Jewish Symbols* contains a helpful summary of his basic thesis. As for his study of Philo, see *By Light, Light! The Mystic Gospel of Hellenistic Judaism* (New Haven: Yale University Press, 1935). One of Goodenough's most formidable opponents was A. D. Nock, who rejected any notion of Jewish mystery religions as being the matrix of Christianity. His strongly critical review of *By Light, Light!* may be found in *Gnomon*, 13 (1937), 156–65 ("The Question of Jewish Mysteries").

    On the Gnostic gospels see Elaine Pagels, *The Gnostic Gospels* (New York: Vintage Books, 1981), and Robinson, *Nag Hammadi Library* (see Chapter 4, note 9).

30. William S. Green, "Palestinian Holy Men: Charismatic Leadership and Rabbinic Tradition," in Haase, *Aufstieg und Niedergang*, Vol. 2, 19, 2, pp. 619–47.

31. See note 17, above.

32. Ben Avuyah is the central figure of Milton Steinberg's novel *As a Driven Leaf*; see above, note 9.

33. Scholem, "Kabbalah," col. 499.
34. Michael E. Stone, "Judaism at the Time of Christ," *Scientific American,* 228, 1 (January 1973), 80.
35. Smith, "Goodenough . . . in Retrospect," p. 65.
36. Biale, *Gershom Scholem,* pp. 71–93.
37. Quoted in Smith, "Goodenough . . . in Retrospect," p. 63.
38. On the following see Hengel, *Judaism and Hellenism,* Vol. 1, pp. 170–254, *passim.* References to five-body theory are, of course, my own.

    The conflict between Goodenough and Moore (or A. D. Nock) is, in fact, a very old one, and the discussion below is only the latest update of this. How much magic, as opposed to how much *halacha,* is to get titrated into "normative" Judaism will probably never get resolved; it may reflect more on the contemporary historian than on ancient Judea. The mystic/rabbinic balance has its own changing historiography and, in addition, that balance may have been very different for Jews in Palestine than for Jews in the Diaspora (Hengel claims not; others, such as Reitzenstein, saw significant differences across the border; see also below, note 41). Scholarly analyses of the influence of Gnosticism on Judaism were pursued in Germany from 1818, and included studies of Philo, Ben Sira, and the Essenes. From 1930, a number of writers, such as Lieberman, Tcherikover, and Bickermann, saw Palestinian Judaism as syncretistic, absorbing Greek ideas. For more on this, see A. D. Momigliano's review of Hengel in the *Journal of Theological Studies,* 21 (1970), 149–53.
39. Cf. Scholem, "Kabbalah," cols. 497–98.
40. Tessa Rajak, in a review of Emil Schürer's work, *The History of the Jewish People in the Age of Jesus Christ,* in the *Times Literary Supplement,* March 13, 1987, p. 278. Schürer, however, was a strong proponent of "normative" Judaism as being *halachic* in nature.
41. Lightstone, *Commerce of the Sacred,* Chapters 2 and 5. In general, Lightstone argues that the situation in Palestine with respect to magical practice was very different from the situation in the Diaspora, because Palestine had a cult based around the Temple and thus had no need of semidivine intermediaries. Hence the shamanistic model was a Diaspora one, he says. Certainly this would help to explain the popularity of Christianity in places like Antioch, as opposed to its unpopularity in Palestine proper. The only trouble is that Lightstone tends to ignore this difference himself, often referring to magical practice in Palestine (as do Hengel and Morton Smith). I suspect it is hard to credit the existence of a really strict dichotomy here.
42. Ibid., Ch. 3.
43. Hengel, *Judaism and Hellenism,* Vol. 1, pp. 309–14.
44. Ibid., pp. 313–14. I have adopted Hengel's model here because to me it offers the most plausible balance of mystic/legalistic Judaism, or of the vertical/horizontal paths, such that Christianity can be seen as being both novel *and* contextual; but the reader should be aware that Hengel is not without his critics. For example, Hengel follows the argument of Bickermann, that it was the Jewish hellenizers who were responsible for the persecution of the Jews under Antiochus IV—they basically wanted a Greek polis and so forced his

hand. But how widespread was this hellenization (Goodenough's problem as well)? For Antiochus IV was met with intense resistance when he attempted to alter *halachic* practice; indeed, Antiochus V abandoned this program completely. Most of Hengel's evidence is literary and philosophical; what we need to know, as Arnaldo Momigliano points out (see above, note 38), is about Jewish institutions, customs, and beliefs. It seems to me that this is an important point, though Hengel does discuss some of these things (including Palestinian graffiti). Thus Fergus Millar argues for the basically un-Greek quality of Palestinian life, and says that although many Jews assented to the paganizing reforms of Antiochus, such changes were not instigated by the Jewish community itself ("The Background to the Maccabean Revolution: Reflections on Martin Hengel's 'Judaism and Hellenism,' " *Journal of Jewish Studies*, 29 [1978], 1–21). All this may be true, but if it is *completely* true, then the emergence of Christ, as well as of other Jewish magicians within Palestine, becomes noncontextual, i.e., miraculous, the more so because the Jewish Great Mother tradition (see above, note 16) had become so significantly weakened in the post-Exilic period. Hengel's claim that by the time of Christ the Torah had rigidified, that it no longer measured up to the visionary message of the prophets, would seem to be a truism. It would then take something like ascent/ecstasy/gnosis to blow the lid off. As Louis Feldman points out, Judaism's quarrel with Paul was that he repealed the law and combined pagan mystery cult ideas with Judaism (notably, the sacrament of the Eucharist). Feldman is very critical of Hengel, but it seems to me that this point is actually evidence for Hengel's thesis: Judaism was frozen and Christianity was made possible by Jews experimenting with ascent practice, which they learned about from their hellenized context. (See Louis H. Feldman, "Hengel's *Judaism and Hellenism* in Retrospect," *Journal of Biblical Literature*, 96 [1977], 371–82.)

45. "Next, It's the World, Bhagwan Says," *Vancouver Sun*, July 18, 1985.

46. For a good discussion of this see Alan Segal's article, "Heavenly Ascent," esp. p. 1337. The relevant works of Lévi-Strauss are *The Raw and the Cooked* and *Structural Anthropology*.

47. One wonders, finally, what to *do* with the anthropology of Claude Lévi-Strauss. As a student of Roman Jakobson, he apparently missed the latter's critique of the Swiss linguist Ferdinand de Saussure, who argued that the most significant aspect of linguistic categories was that they were oppositional. Jakobson argued for a plurality of categories; he studied (for example) the contribution of sound—pure sound—to meaning, a notion that would make no sense in a purely oppositional system. Lévi-Strauss missed all this. For him, as for Saussure, all levels of language were oppositional, and meaning could only emerge in terms of contrast. In this regard, it is interesting that many tribal cultures focus on the importance of sound; it played a major role in hunter-gatherer societies, was part of preoppositional consciousness, and to this day it remains the crucial element in poetry, which should always be real aloud. See Janowitz, "Language of Ascent," pp. 214–15.

48. Robinson, *Nag Hammadi Library*, p. 121; trans. by Thomas O. Lambdin.

49. On the following see Pagels, *Gnostic Gospels*, pp. xv–xvii, xx, and xxxi–xxxii.

50. On this and the following see Frederick Turner, *Beyond Geography* (New York: Viking Press, 1980), pp. 66–68.
51. Pagels, *Gnostic Gospels*, p. 40.
52. Paul Johnson, *A History of Christianity* (New York: Atheneum, 1983), p. 50.
53. Ibid., pp. 53–54 and 87.
54. Ibid., p. 87; Peter Brown, "Society and the Supernatural: A Medieval Change," *Daedalus*, *104*, 2 (Spring 1975), 135, and *The Making of Late Antiquity* (Cambridge, Mass.: Harvard University Press, 1978), pp. 10–12; and Pheme Perkins, *The Gnostic Dialogue* (New York: Paulist Press, 1980), p.6.
55. Perkins, *Gnostic Dialogue*, p. 3: Johnson, *History of Christianity*, pp. 122 and 250.

CHAPTER 6. CATHARS AND TROUBADOURS

1. Julian Jaynes, *Origin of Consciousness* (see Chapter 2, note 1).
2. On the following see Charles M. Radding, "Evolution of Medieval Mentalities: A Cognitive-Structural Approach," *American Historical Review*, *83*, 3 (June 1978), 577–97. The argument has since been expanded into a full-length monograph: *A World Made by Men: Cognition and Society, 400–1200* (Chapel Hill: University of North Carolina Press, 1985). Also relevant is Brown, "Society and the Supernatural" (see Chapter 5, note 54), pp. 133–51.
3. Owen Barfield, *Saving the Appearances* (New York: Harcourt, Brace and World, 1965); Jaynes, *Origin of Consciousness*.
4. The following is discussed in Radding, "Evolution of Medieval Mentalities," pp. 581–85, and in *World Made by Men*, pp. 263–79.
5. A number of scholars have elaborated on some form of nature/nurture interaction as the key to human development, including Paul Shepard *(Nature and Madness)*, Erik Erikson *(Childhood and Society)*, and Daniel Yankelovich and William Barrett *(Ego and Instinct)*.
6. Marie-Dominique Chenu, *Nature, Man, and Society in the Twelfth Century*, trans. Jerome Taylor and Lester K. Little (Chicago: University of Chicago Press, 1968; orig. French ed. 1957), and *L'éveil de la conscience dans la civilisation médiévale* (Montreal: Institut d'études médiévales, 1969); Colin Morris, *The Discovery of the Individual, 1050–1200* (New York: Harper & Row, 1972).
7. On the following see John F. Benton, "Consciousness of Self and Perceptions of Individuality," in Robert L. Benson and Giles Constable (eds.), *Renaissance and Renewal in the Twelfth Century* (Oxford: Clarendon Press, 1982), esp. pp. 263–88. Corroboration of this theme can also be found in the following sources: Pierre Courcelle, *Connais-toi toi-même: De Socrate à saint Bernard* (3 vols.; Paris: Études augustiniennes, 1974–75); George Misch, *A History of Autobiography in Antiquity*, trans. E. W. Dickes and G. Misch (2 vols.; London: Routledge and Kegan Paul, 1950); and Karl Weintraub, *The Value of the Individual* (Chicago: University of Chicago Press, 1978).
8. Benton himself is confused on this point, especially when he criticizes Radding for supposedly underestimating issues of intentionality in early medieval law and penance. Thus on p. 264 he says the new commitment to an inner life in the twelfth century was indeed new, whereas in his comments on Radding (p. 273n), he says this interiority was *not* created anew but simply

reconstructed from the literature of antiquity. I suspect that in this case, as in the case of so many "new" mental developments, the sudden popularity of the literature of antiquity was due to the lived or existential discovery, which was indeed "new."

9. Cf. note 15, below.

10. On this see also Francis B. Sayre, "Mens Rea," *Harvard Law Review*, 45 (1932), 974–1026.

11. Radding, "Evolution of Medieval Mentalities," p. 594. The work of the French historian Etienne Delaruelle (1904–71) is also instructive in this regard. Delaruelle believed that authentic Christian experience in the Middle Ages existed in collective expressions of piety, such as crusades or pilgimages, but that over time medieval religious life moved increasingly toward personal expression, a trend that reached its peak in the thirteenth century. Delaruelle saw this as a political development, i.e., opposition to the Church involved (or took the form of) the emergence of personalities who knew that they possessed a soul, and this knowledge was an important part of their *ressentiment*. He effectively regarded this as part of a dialectic between heresy and orthodoxy, and believed that the religious history of the Middle Ages moved along the line of this tension and resolution. By the fourteenth century, Delaruelle claimed, interiority had effectively been integrated into ("co-opted by" is, I think, more accurate; see below) the structure of the Church.

 See M.-H. Vicaire, "L'apport d'Etienne Delaruelle aux études de spiritualité populaire médiévale," in *La Religion populaire en Languedoc, Cahiers de Fanjeaux*, 11 (1976), 23–36; and Etienne Delaruelle, *La piété populaire au moyen âge* (Turin: Bottega d'Erasmo, 1975), ed. R. Manselli and A. Vauchez, pp. v–xix and 311–12.

12. Benton, "Consciousness of Self," pp. 293–94, and Russell, "Interpretations," (see Chapter 4, note 20), pp. 26–53.

13. Peter Brown argues something similar in "Society and the Supernatural," p. 143. Romantic love and friendship as we experience them today—the existence of an intangible but powerful internal bond between two people—are largely absent from tribal or kinship cultures. Indeed, as Denis de Rougemont has argued (see below), the appearance of romantic love in a culture like traditional China was regarded as a kind of temporary insanity. Things such as this—and I would include humor as well—tend to destabilize the social order because they set up very special bonds between single individuals, an exclusivity of attachment. Camus' famous remark—that if he had to choose between betraying his country and betraying his best friend, he hoped that he would do the decent thing and betray his country—is probably incapable of being translated into the languages of contemporary tribal cultures. This kind of inwardness requires alienation in the first place; it is part of the mental landscape of existential man and woman. In the case of humor, it is interesting that Jorge of Burgos, the defender of the old order in Umberto Eco's novel *The Name of the Rose*, sees it (humor) as dangerous and antisocial. Given the fairly inflexible nature of Western sociopolitical formations he was, it would seem, quite right.

14. Tennov, *Love and Limerence* (see Chapter 4, note 22).

15. Jerzy Kosinski, *Being There* (New York: Bantam Books, 1972). The question of interiority has also been raised in another way by Pheme Perkins (*Gnostic Dialogue;* see Chapter 5, note 54), who, in opposition to Elaine Pagels (*Gnostic Gospels;* see Chapter 5, note 29), has argued that ancient Gnostic experience is not the same as the modern variety, and that it is a mistake to read it as such. The Gnostics, she says, were not primitive Jungian psychologists; for them, the Divine was a concrete, transcendent entity, not a Higher Self or inner god. Modern gnostics, she says, reject the dimension of transcendence present in ancient Gnosticism. In other words, they see salvation in terms of the development of internal integration; they have no interest in the ancient notion of revelation as a divine gift. Figures like Jung have also emphasized the spiritual development of humanity, whereas ancient Gnosticism had a strong element of revolt and alienation (Perkins, pp. 5–6 and 205–16).

   Although Perkins' argument is often confused and contradictory—at one point in her discussion she *defends* Jung and the psychological interpretation, for example—she raises the important point of whether the modern Self can be equated with its ancient variety. The major problem is that gnosticism is an extremely complex phenomenon; it depends on how far you wish to take it, or how much of its doctrine and practice you wish to have. For example, despite his emphasis on internal psychic integration, Jung did, it seems to me, believe in a transcendent divinity, and his work does have much to say about alienation (*Modern Man in Search of a Soul*) and rejection of the modern age—things that saw their concrete expression in the right-wing "revolution" represented by the Nazi experiment (discussed in Chapter 8). Other modern gnostics—many of Jung's followers, for example—would not take the whole thing this far, stress only the "god within," and opt for political quietism. Yet all of this seems to belong to something that can be called gnosticism, which revolves around a common set of attitudes, despite its great syncretistic ability and its diversity of forms. Thus Hans Jonas points out that as early as the third century (this can be found in the Hermetic corpus), techniques are cited to enable the soul to attain the Absolute while still in the body. In this way, transcendence can be turned into immanence, culminating in ecstatic experience (*Gnostic Religion;* see Chapter 4, note 6). But such techniques were available in the area of the Mediterranean basin from at least the second century B.C., as we saw in Chapter 1, and given the nature of human biology, they undoubtedly produced "immanent" effects. Conversely, modern practitioners who have attained ecstatic or visionary experience often tend to find a transcendent source for it, for example, being contacted by the resurrected Christ or by a UFO. It is also the case that the Catharist heresy and the magical activity leading up to the Scientific Revolution (see Chapter 7) had both immanent and transcendent aspects. In general, I don't believe there is any getting away from the fact that constant features of the gnostic worldview, whether ancient or modern, are its emphasis on interiority and its tendency to destabilize formal or institutional structures as a result of this. The real issue we have to struggle with, as I have just been doing, is whether absence of Self is real absence or in fact repression; something that we can never know for sure, but that has significant implications for both the history and the future of Western consciousness.

16. R. I. Moore, "Heresy as Disease," in W. Lourdaux and D. Verhelst (eds.), *The Concept of Heresy in the Middle Ages* (The Hague: Martinus Nijhoff, 1976), pp. 1–11. "Cancer" was also used, not to mean cancer, but as a generic term for skin problems (scores, scabs, etc.), in this case seen as related to the scaly "skin" of the crab.

17. Eco, *Name of the Rose* (see Chapter 4, note 17), pp. 201–3. On the issue of overlap cf. pp. 58–60 or 221–31. The best example of the potential reversal, or mirroring, of the two sides is given in Adso's dream, pp. 426–38.

18. This quote is actually from Russell, "Interpretations," p. 39. I assume the second name cited refers to the Flemish heretic Tanchelm (d. 1115). On Alphandéry see Chapter 4, note 20.

19. On the Marcionites see Steven Runciman, *The Medieval Manichee* (Cambridge, England: Cambridge University Press, 1982; orig. publ. 1947), p. 9.

20. Dualism is a very old religion and certainly antedates Christianity. It can be found in Persia in the sixth century B.C. (Zoroastrianism), as well as in Greek sources: Orphic sects, Empedocles (the war between Love and Strife), Pythagoras, and Plato. The Essenes, referred to in Chapter 5, certainly adhered to a dualist cosmology.

21. With the exception of fish, which the Cathars (and many others in the Middle Ages) did not regard as a flesh food.

22. On Cathar observances see the Inquisition manual by Bernard Gui, trans. in part by Walter L. Wakefield and Austin P. Evans (eds.) in *Heresies of the Higher Middle Ages* (New York: Columbia University Press, 1969), pp. 381–82. Gui was Inquisitor of Toulouse from approximately 1307 to 1324. An extended discussion of Cathar doctrines can also be found in Runciman, *Medieval Manichee*, pp. 147–62. The term *Cathari* was first used by Ekbert (or Eckbert) of Schönau, archbishop of Cologne, 1159–67. The German word for heretic, *Ketzer*, derives from this term.

The Cathars were pessimistic gnostics, and most gnosticism tends to fall into this category. There is, however, an optimistic variety, as represented by Giordano Bruno (see Chapter 7, and also Chapter 5, note 7).

23. Russell, "Interpretations," pp. 44–46 and 51. See also Chapter 4, note 20, and the article cited therein by George Shriver, p. 74.

Peter Waldo, or Valdes, was a wealthy merchant who, like Francis, gave away his property and went about preaching the apostolic ideal. The Waldensians (or Vaudois) originated in Lyons in the late twelfth century. They were formally declared heretics by Pope Lucius III in 1184; burnings of Waldensians began in the early thirteenth century.

24. Wakefield and Evans, *Heresies*, p. 24.

25. Runciman, *Medieval Manichee*, pp. 117–18, and Walter L. Wakefield, *Heresy, Crusade and Inquisition in Southern France 1100–1250* (London: Allen and Unwin, 1974), pp. 20–23 and 31.

26. Friedrich Heer, *The Medieval World*, trans. Janet Sondheimer (New York: New American Library, n.d.; orig. German and English eds., 1961), p. 214.

27. Joseph R. Strayer, *The Albigensian Crusades* (New York: Dial Press, 1971), pp. 3–9. In Provençal one said "oc" for "yes," whereas in the north the word was "oïl" or "oui." Hence, "Languedoc" for the region between Provence and Gascony.

28. Zbigniew Herbert, "Albigensians, Inquisitors and Troubadours," in *Barbarian in the Garden*, trans. Michael March and Jarosław Anders (San Diego: Harcourt Brace Jovanovich, 1985; orig. Polish ed. 1962), p. 106.

29. M. D. Lambert, *Medieval Heresy* (London: Edward Arnold, 1977), p. 111.

30. On the Cathars as healers, see Jean Guiraud, *Histoire de l'Inquisition au moyen-âge* (Paris: Picard, 1935), Vol. 1, pp. 351–53.

31. Strayer, *Albigensian Crusades*, pp. 22–23.

32. Emmanuel LeRoy Ladurie, in *Montaillou*, trans. Barbara Bray (New York: Vintage Books, 1979), pp. 308 and 322, points out that in the region around Montaillou there was a strong identification of Mary with the pagan Earth Goddess, and so ancient fertility cults were incorporated into the Cult of the Virgin. The presence of the Perfect, he claims, opened the way to the emergence of preexisting folklore elements.

33. Wakefield, *Heresy, Crusade and Inquisition*, pp. 77–78.

34. Jonas, *Gnostic Religion*, pp. 21–25 and 42.

35. Heer, *Medieval World*, p. 207.

36. On the following see Fredric L. Cheyette, "Cathars," in Joseph R. Strayer (ed.), *Dictionary of the Middle Ages* (New York: Charles Scribner's Sons, 1982–87), Vol. 3, pp. 181–91; Arno Borst, *Die Katharer* (Stuttgart: Hiersemann, 1953); Jean Duvernoy, *L'Histoire des cathares* (Toulouse: Édouard Privat, 1979); Lambert, *Medieval Heresy*, Chapters 5 and 8; Wakefield, *Heresy, Crusade and Inquisition*; Runciman, *Medieval Manichee*; Strayer, *Albigensian Crusades*; Jonathan Sumption, *The Albigensian Crusade* (London: Faber and Faber, 1978); Walter L. Wakefield, "Inquisition," in Strayer, *Dictionary of the Middle Ages*, Vol. 6, pp. 483–89; Heer, *Medieval World*, pp. 200–20; and the essay by Herbert cited in note 28, above.

37. Wakefield and Evans, *Heresies*, p. 33; Runciman, *Medieval Manichee*, pp. 136–38; and Shriver, "Images of Catharism," p. 72 (see Chapter 4, note 20).

38. Estimate of Napoléon Peyrat, in his *History of the Albigensians*; cited by Herbert, "Albigensians, Inquisitors and Troubadours," p. 115.

39. Eco, *Name of the Rose*, p. 153. Strayer, in *Albigensian Crusades*, p. 62, says that the story is apocryphal, invented by a German monk a few years later; but he adds that it certainly captured the mood of the crusaders. Herbert ("Albigensians, Inquisitors and Troubadours," p. 110) identifies the monk as a fourteenth-century chronicler, Caesarius of Heisterbach. Herbert's figure of the number massacred at Béziers is thirteen thousand. On the political aspect of interiority see above, note 11.

   The same sort of savagery fueled by spiritual bankruptcy was an obvious feature of American involvement in Vietnam in the 1960s. I once saw a Green Beret T-shirt that carried the image of a skull and crossbones, and beneath it the words: "Kill 'em all—let God sort 'em out."

40. Frederick Turner, *Beyond Geography* (New York: Viking Press, 1980), p. 72.

41. Herbert, "Albigensians, Inquisitors and Troubadours," pp. 107 and 112.

42. Turner, *Beyond Geography*, p. 82.

43. Ibid., pp. 72–84; Runciman, *Medieval Manichee*, pp. 143–46.

44. Herbert, "Albigensians, Inquisitors and Troubadours," pp. 101–2.

45. Ibid., pp. 116–21; Sumption, *Albigensian Crusade*, p. 229; and Strayer, *Albigensian Crusades*, pp. 148–49.

46. Wakefield, *Heresy, Crusade and Inquisition*, p. 142; Heer, *Medieval World*, pp. 215–16.

47. Cheyette, "Cathars," pp. 185–86.

48. Lambert, *Medieval Heresy*, pp. 120–21; Strayer, *Albigensian Crusades*, pp. 30–32. See also Ladurie, *Montaillou*, p. 325.

49. Herbert, "Albigensians, Inquisitors and Troubadours," p. 105; Zoë Oldenbourg, *Massacre at Montségur*, trans. Peter Green (New York: Pantheon Books, 1961), p. 33. Sacconi's *Summa on the Cathars and the Poor of Lyons*, written in 1250, can be found in Wakefield and Evans, *Heresies*, pp. 329–46.

50. Shriver, "Images of Catharism," p. 69, and Déodat Roché, *Le Catharisme* (rev. ed.; Narbonne: Cahiers d'études cathares, 1973), Vol. 1, pp. 10 and 97. On Steiner see Chapter 4, note 6.

51. On the following see Runciman, *Medieval Manichee*, pp. v–viii, 5–19, 27–30, and 73–93.

52. On the Bogomils see Milan Loos, *Dualist Heresy in the Middle Ages*, trans. Iris Lewitova (The Hague: Martinus Nijhoff, 1974); Lambert, *Medieval Heresy*, pp. 11–23; and Runciman, *Medieval Manichee*, pp. 73ff.

53. A survey of these debates can be found in Russell, "Interpretations," esp. pp. 35–38.

54. Ibid., p. 38.

55. See Chapter 4, note 2. Ronald Laing writes in the Preface to the 1965 Pelican edition of *The Divided Self* (p. 11): "Among one-dimensional men, it is not surprising that someone with an insistent experience of other dimensions, that he cannot entirely deny or forget, will run the risk either of being destroyed by others, or of betraying what he knows."

56. George Weckman, "Simone Weil: Hinduism and Buddhism," in Thomas A. Idinopulos and Josephine Zadovsky Knopp (eds.), *Mysticism Nihilism Feminism* (Johnson City, Tenn.: Institute of Social Sciences and Arts, 1984), pp. 179–80. See Rudolf Otto, *Mysticism East and West*, trans. Bertha L. Bracey and Richard C. Payne (New York: Macmillan, 1970; orig. English trans. 1932).

57. Oldenbourg, *Massacre at Montségur*, p. 51; Sumption, *Albigensian Crusade*, p. 52. Roché was skeptical of this testimony; see "La Tragédie cathare," *Cahiers d'études cathares*, 11, 8 (1960–61), 34–35.

58. Cheyette, "Cathars," p. 185; Bernard Gui, in Wakefield and Evans, *Heresies*, p. 381; Simone Hannedouche, *Manichéïsme et catharisme* (Arque: Cahiers d'études cathares, 1967), p. 17. The vegetarian diet, however, included fish; see above, note 21.

59. Jean Duvernoy, *Le Catharisme* (Toulouse: Édouard Privat, 1979), Vol. 2, p. 44. The Messalians may have been a variety of Marcionites.

60. Such as standing erect, bending over, joining his hands together, and striking a desk with his hands. See Jean Duvernoy, *Inquisition à Pamiers* (Toulouse: Édouard Privat, 1966), p. 182. Ladurie does not mention this somatic practice

in *Montaillou*. Also, he renders the names differently: Guillaume Bélibaste (junior) and Pierre Maury. (See *Montaillou*, pp. 83 and 364 and *passim*.)

61. Duvernoy, *Le Catharisme*, Vol. 2, p. 186; from Jacques Fournier, *Le Registre d'inquisition de Jacques Fournier, évêque de Pamiers (1318–1325)*, ed. J. Duvernoy (Toulouse: Édouard Privat, 1965), Vol. 3, p. 196. (This is MS. Vat. Lat. 4030, Biblioteca Vaticana.)

62. Duvernoy, *Inquisition à Pamiers*, pp. 193–95, testimony of Pierre Mauri.

63. See Wakefield and Evans, *Heresies*, for the English translation of the text, pp. 447–65 (the ecstatic experience is described on pp. 449–50); also R. H. Charles, *The Ascension of Isaiah* (London: S.P.C.K., 1918).

The Ascension of Isaiah survives as a whole only in an Ethiopian version; otherwise, fragments are available in Greek, Latin, and Slavonic languages. The Latin version was edited by A. Dillman in 1877; there exists a French translation (from the Ethiopian) by E. Tisserant, made in 1909. One version of the text can also be found in René Nelli et al., *Les Cathares* (Paris: Éditions de Delphes, 1965), pp. 91–105.

64. See Gershom Scholem, *Jewish Gnosticism, Merkabah Mysticism and Talmudic Tradition* (New York: Jewish Theological Seminary of America, 1960), Appendix C (transliterated here as *Ma'asseh Merkabah*). The manuscripts used by Scholem date from the fourteenth century, indicating that the tradition was probably kept alive during the Middle Ages. Scholem is able to argue for an earlier date of origin, however, i.e., the early centuries of the Christian era. On much of this see the articles by Segal and Janowitz cited in Chapter 5.

65. Scholem, "Kabbalah" (see Chapter 5, note 17), cols. 518–20, 529–30, and 631.

66. See above, note 22, and also Raoul Manselli, "Églises et théologies cathares," *Cahiers de Fanjeaux, 3: Cathares en Languedoc* (Toulouse: Édouard Privat, 1968), pp. 154 and 157; Marie-Humbert Vicaire, "Les Cathares albigeois vus par les polémistes," pp. 114–15 in the same volume; Hans Söderberg, *La Religion des Cathares* (Uppsala: Almquist & Wiksells, 1949), pp. 7n and 233.

67. Cited in Lambert, *Medieval Heresy*, p. 123.

68. René Nelli, *Le Phénomène cathare* (Toulouse: Édouard Privat, 1964), pp. 104n, 110n, and 112.

69. Söderberg, *La Religion des Cathares*, pp. 229 and 231. Moneta of Cremona, among other contemporaries, reported (*Adversus Catharos et Valdenses*, p. 218) that the "Vision" was in use by the Cathars; see Söderberg, *La Religion*, p. 106, and also J. J. I. von Döllinger, *Beiträge zur Sektengeschichte des Mittelalters* (2 vols.; New York: Burt Franklin, ca. 1960; orig. publ. Munich, 1890), Vol. 2: *Dokumente vornehmlich zur Geschichte der Valdensier und Katherer*, p. 276.

70. Söderberg, *La Religion des Cathares*, pp. 106n and 237–46; von Döllinger, *Beiträge*, Vol. 2, pp. 166f. and 208–10; Roché, *Le Catharisme*, Vol. 1, pp. 37, 52, 58, 121–22, and 193–94; and Wakefield, *Heresy, Crusade and Inquisition*, pp. 36–37.

71. Duvernoy, *Le Catharisme*, Vol. 2, pp. 84n and 86. This document is published in Benjamin E. C. Guérard, *Cartulaire de l'Abbaye de Saint-Père de Chartres* (2

vols; Paris: published by the author, 1840), and is taken from two manuscripts in the Bibliothèque Municipale in Chartres, Numbers 1060 and 1061.

72. Quoted in Heer, *Medieval World*, p. 216.

73. Duvernoy, *Le Catharisme*, Vol. 2, p. 90. The witness who reported this was Adémar de Chabannes; see Jules J. Chavanon (ed.), *Ademarus Cabannensis, 988–1034* (Paris: A. Picard et fils, 1897), p. 185.

74. Duvernoy, *Inquisition à Pamiers*, p. 53, testimony of Béatrice de Planissoles to Jacques Fournier, July 26, 1320. The Cathar who gave her this information was Raimond Roussel.

75. Herbert, "Albigensians, Inquisitors and Troubadours," p. 113.

76. Duvernoy, *Le Catharisme*, Vol. 2, p. 270.

77. Wakefield and Evans, *Heresies*, p. 7; Russell, "Interpretations," pp. 43–46.

78. From Louis Massignon, *Passion de al Hallaj*; quoted in Denis de Rougemont, *Love in the Western World*, trans. Montgomery Belgion (rev. and augmented ed.; Princeton: Princeton University Press, 1983; from the English ed. of 1956), p. 103n.

79. Cheyette, "Cathars," pp. 189–90.

80. Strayer, Preface to *The Albigensian Crusades*.

81. Frederich Heer, *The Intellectual History of Europe*, trans. Jonathan Steinberg (London: Weidenfeld & Nicolson, 1966); from the 1953 Foreword, pp. 1–2.

82. De Rougemont, *Love*, p. 170.

83. On the following see Roger Boase, *The Origin and Meaning of Courtly Love* (Manchester: Manchester University Press, 1977), pp. 21–38.

84. Gabriele P. G. Rossetti, *Sullo spirito antipapale che produsse la riforma . . . Disquisizioni* (1832), was translated into English by C. Ward under the title *Disquisitions on the Antipapal Spirit Which Produced the Reformation* (2 vols.; London: Smith, Elder, 1834), and the theme was further developed in *Il misterio dell' amor platonico del medio evo derivato da' misteri antichi* (5 vols.; London: R. & G. E. Taylor, 1840).

85. *Dante hérétique, revolutionnaire et socialiste* (Paris: Jules Renouard, 1854), and *Les Mystères de la chevalerie et de l'amour platonique au moyen âge* (Paris: Jules Renouard, 1858). Similar ideas were also developed by Anthony Méray and, in 1906, by Joseph Péladan *(Le Secret des troubadours)*. Note also that Eduard Wechssler, in *Das Kulturproblem des Minnesangs* (Halle: Max Niemeyer, 1909), argued that Provençal poetry revealed Neoplatonic influences (on the relevance of Neoplatonism to romantic love see below), and that courtly love was rooted in Christian mysticism. The troubadours, he said, were pursuing an inversion of values, a "courtly asceticism" that ran counter to the worldview of the Church. Love and mysticism, he argued, were united in emotional disposition. See Etienne Gilson, *The Mystical Theology of St. Bernard*, trans. A. H. C. Downes (London: Sheed and Ward, 1949; orig. French ed. 1934), pp. 193 and 195. Gilson, it should be added, was opposed to Wechssler's argument.

86. Rahn's book, *Der Kreuzzug gegen den Graal* (The Crusade Against the Grail), actually elaborated a much larger theme, viz., that Catharism derived from an ancient Teutonic source and was a precursor of Fascism; and more spe-

cifically, that the Grail legend was rooted in Teutonic mythology, of which the Cathars were a link in a historical chain. According to Rahn, the Cathars were in actual possession of the Grail at Montségur and smuggled it out during the final four days of the siege.

Rahn's work became a crucial text for a number of Nazis, who saw themselves as the heirs of a particular occult lineage. Heinrich Himmler, for example, believed that the Catholic Church had become Judaicized over the centuries, and that the Cathars represented the only pure remaining Aryan strain. Rahn himself went off to Montségur in search of the Grail, convinced that the Cathars must have buried it there. He was apparently an early Nazi sympathizer, later (1936) a member of the SS and a guard at Dachau for four months in 1937. For reasons still unclear, Rahn resigned from the SS in February of 1939, and died the following month due to "exposure" he supposedly caught while walking in the mountains. See Nicholas Goodrick-Clarke, *The Occult Roots of Nazism* (Wellingborough, England: The Aquarian Press, 1985), pp. 188–89.

Rahn saw his literary work as purely poetic or mythological in nature. He played with themes, and did not aspire to any real historical accuracy. One writer, Christian Bernadac, claims that Rahn's argument regarding the troubadours was in fact a plagiarization of writings of Déodat Roché, Magre, and Maurice Peyrac; see Christian Bernadac, *Le Mystère de Otto Rahn* (Paris: Éditions France-Empire, 1978). For the Nazi connection, see Duvernoy, *Le Catharisme*, Vol. 2, p. 345, and Paul Ladame's introduction to René Nelli's translation of Rahn's second book, *Luzifers Hofgesinde* (Lucifer's Servants). The study by Jean-Michel Angebert, *Hitler et la tradition cathare* (Paris: Robert Laffont, 1971) (English translation: *The Occult and the Third Reich*), is totally unreliable.

To my knowledge, there is no English translation of *Der Kreuzzug gegen den Graal;* a French translation was undertaken by Robert Pitrou and published under the title *La Croisade contre le graal* (Paris: Librairie Stock, 1934).

87. "Études sur les romans de la Table Ronde. Lancelot du Lac. II. *Le Conte de la Charette*," *Romania*, 12 (1883), 459–534.

88. F. X. Newman (ed.), *The Meaning of Courtly Love* (Albany: State University of New York Press, 1969), p. viii. It is this paradoxical character that many students of the subject seem unable to grasp; hence (in part) their antagonism to de Rougemont. The tendency of the contributors to the Newman volume is to argue that *amour courtois* never really existed, but was merely an invention of literary critics. Thus one writer states that the conception is "inherently absurd"; which may be true from an analytical point of view, but love is not about logic, as de Rougemont well understood. Newman himself is somewhat skeptical of these contributors, noting (p. ix) that they tend to reject the paradoxical tension that Paris argued was the central feature of the whole experience. Similarly, John Heath-Stubbs, in his Foreword to Boase, *Origin and Meaning of Courtly Love*, comments that despite this recent tendency to explain the whole thing away, writers such as de Rougemont and C. S. Lewis (*The Allegory of Love*, 1936) came as a revelation to him, because they were able to grasp the reality of the experience, whether it was

logical or not. This is, I think, a fair comment on most of de Rougemont's critics, though it does not of course prove a necessary relationship between Cathars and troubadours, and it must be stated that no real causal link has ever been substantiated.

For a convincing critique of the Newman volume see Jean Frappier, "Sur un procès fait à l'amour courtois," *Romania, 93* (1972), 145–93.

89. On Tennov see Chapter 4, note 22; for Nygren see *Agape and Eros,* trans. A. G. Hebert and Philip Watson (London: S.P.C.K., 1932–39). It is remarkable how much confusion exists on this point; Erich Fromm's best-seller, *The Art of Loving,* has no real understanding of the distinction at all, and can have only served to confuse people further. For a more sophisticated approach, see the late twelfth- or early thirteenth-century work by Andreas Capellanus, *The Art of Courtly Love,* trans. P. G. Walsh (London: Duckworth, 1982), which asserts that love gets its name *amor* from the word *amus,* hook; hence, to be in love is to be on a hook. (Cited in Susan Griffin, *Made from This Earth* [New York: Harper & Row, 1982], p. 93.) Actually, the Latin word for "hook" is *hamus,* though it is possible that *amus* was a medieval variation of this.

90. Plato, the *Symposium,* sections 189d–193e. For a discussion of the theme of erotic asceticism in the Eastern tradition (specifically, Hindu mythology), see Wendy O'Flaherty, *Asceticism and Eroticism in the Mythology of Śiva* (London: Oxford University Press, 1973).

91. The theory of a direct Neoplatonic influence on the troubadours is generally associated with A. J. Denomy, in studies such as "An Inquiry into the Origins of Courtly Love," *Medieval Studies, 6* (1944), 175–260, and *The Heresy of Courtly Love* (New York: McMullen, 1947). Boase (*Origin and Meaning of Courtly Love,* pp. 81–83) regards this as dubious, in that it is too intellectual. If there was an influence from things such as Sufism or Neoplatonism it was very likely through popular contact rather than abstract doctrine.

The nonsexual nature of romantic attachment in Plato is stressed by Irving Singer in *The Nature of Love,* Vol. I: *Plato to Luther* (2nd ed.; Chicago: University of Chicago Press, 1984), pp. 47–87 and esp. p. 52. Aristophanes' story, he says, is about object relations. The yearning for one's other half occurs *before* Zeus decides to move the sex organs of the bisected "blobs" around to the front, so as to make intercourse possible. As both Plato and the object-relations school argued, there exists a "nonsexual instinct for oneness."

92. René Nelli, *L'Érotique des troubadours* (Toulouse: Édouard Privat, 1963), pp. 228–29, and also his article, "Du Catharisme à l'amour provençal," *Revue de synthèse, 64* (1948), 36 and 38.

93. Duvernoy, *Le Catharisme,* Vol. 2, p. 271. Duvernoy wavers, however, with regard to the de Rougemont thesis; on p. 278 he argues that it was more a case of nostalgia on the part of the southern nobility later on, to look back upon courtly love and its customs and confuse them with those of the condemned religion.

94. Nelli, "Du Catharisme," pp. 36 and 38. There is, it should be noted, a socioeconomic approach to the whole subject of the rise of romantic love that discusses such things as arranged marriages, the shortage of women in the upper strata of society, the prominence of female economic power in the

south, the absence of men due to the Crusades, and the presence of rootless younger sons of the aristocracy without specific goals or financial independence. These factors were certainly present in the south, and such conditions undoubtedly explain why a particular set of ideas would function so well, or get so widely diffused in that particular context. But functional explanations cannot explain motivations of the participants involved; they cannot grasp states of mind (or body) from the inside. For that reason, the discussion below does not deal with the question of socioeconomic context, significant though it may be.

    Nelli and Duvernoy, in particular, have propounded the socioeconomic thesis; see also Herbert Moller, "The Social Causation of the Courtly Love Complex," *Comparative Studies in Society and History*, 1 (1958–59), 137–63; Erich Köhler, "Observations historiques et sociologiques sur la poésie des troubadours," *Cahiers de civilisation médiévale*, 7 (1964), 27–51; and Georges Duby, "Dans la France du Nord-Ouest, au XIIe siècle: les *jeunes* dans la société aristocratique," *Annales. Economies, Sociétés, Civilisations*, 19 (1964), 835–46.

95. Quoted in Keri Hulme, *The Bone People* (London: Pan Books, 1986), p. 65.
96. On the following see de Rougemont, *Love*, pp. 32–38, 41–45, 52, 62–74, 100–101, 153–62, and 238–39.
97. On *chanson de geste* vs. *chanson d'amour* see Heer, *Medieval World*, Ch. 7.
98. Roger Boase reinforces this when he notes that there is no point in saying that the poets of Rome knew about romantic love. Romans, Greeks, and Chinese all knew about it, but in those cultures love was regarded as a sickness as soon as it went beyond sensual pleasure. In this sense, then, the troubadour sentiment *was* a novel one (Boase, *Origin and Meaning of Courtly Love*, p. 1). Also relevant to this discussion is Herman R. Lantz, "Romantic Love in the Pre-Modern Period: A Sociological Commentary," *Journal of Social History*, 15 (Spring 1982), 349–70.
99. Heer, *Medieval World*, p. 170.
100. Ibid., p. 181. This is a very important point, and it receives excellent elaboration in a different context by Caroline Walker Bynum in "Women's Stories, Women's Symbols: A Critique of Victor Turner's Theory of Liminality," pp. 105–25 of Moore and Reynolds, *Anthropology* (see Chapter 5, note 16). So much of the Western psyche is organized around the theme of the "journey," with "liminality" being a threshold phenomenon, a suspension of the journey for a moment of enlightenment, usually experienced and conceptualized as female in nature. But this, as Bynum points out, is only a description of the male psyche. Women are not typically preoccupied with vision-quests and hence the theory of liminality may not really apply to them. Western religious history can be seen as male orthodoxy vs. female heresy (or gnosis), and in some ways this makes sense; but it does suggest that our coding of reality, which is based on the theme of the journey and a vertical ascent structure, is somewhat skewed. See also my discussion of this in Chapter 9.
101. For discussions of overlapping cases see Duvernoy, *Le Catharisme*, Vol. 2, p. 272, and Nelli, *L'Érotique*, pp. 228–29.

102. De Rougemont, *Love*, pp. 102–107; Diane Bornstein, "Courtly Love," in
     Strayer, *Dictionary of the Middle Ages*, Vol. 3, p. 673 (see above, note 36). In
     general, however, I find Bornstein's article unhelpful; it falls into the trap
     of seeing romantic love as a literary device (cf. note 88, above).
        As in the case of the argument for Cathar influence on troubadour poetry,
     *la thèse arabe*, which is the subject of much study, and which was first pro-
     pounded (by Giammaria Barbieri) in the sixteenth century, has not been
     amenable to proof, certainly not of the causal variety. From the end of the
     tenth century there was allegedly no *direct* contact between Provence and
     the Islamic world; troubadours made no references to Arabs (any more than
     they did to Cathars) and did not know Arabic. It has also been argued that
     the concept of *eros* held by these two civilizations was very different (see,
     for example, Nelli, *L'Érotique*, p. 73), although that may not be significant
     from a somatic point of view. Certainly, the "paradoxical asceticism" of
     troubadour lyric, complete with dichotomies of delight and torment, absence
     and presence, everything and nothing, is all present in Arabic mysticism;
     and on the unofficial level, there was a good bit of interaction with Moorish
     musicians and other elements of popular Islamic culture (Boase, *Origin and
     Meaning of Courtly Love*, pp. 64–74). Boase has been able to show how the
     popularity of the Arabic thesis has waxed and waned over the last few
     centuries, being particularly popular, as far as the twentieth century goes,
     during 1912–23 and 1934–48, with de Rougemont being part of this latter
     revival (Boase, pp. 11–21, 29, and 36–37). The case is probably better than
     the one for Cathar influence, though it is in both cases circumstantial; and
     as indicated in the text, acceptance of one hardly precludes acceptance of
     the other.
        For a useful introduction to the Arabic thesis see I.-M. Cluzel, "Quelques
     réflexions à propos des origines de la poésie lyrique des troubadours," *Cahiers
     de civilisation médiévale*, 4 (1961), 179–88. The classic work is A. R. Nykl,
     *Hispano-Arabic Poetry and Its Relations with the Old Provençal Troubadours* (Bal-
     timore: privately printed, 1946). For the contrary viewpoint see Samuel Stern,
     "Literary Connections between the Islamic World and Western Europe in
     the Early Middle Ages: Did They Exist?," pp. 204–30 of his book *Hispano-
     Arabic Strophic Poetry* (Oxford: Clarendon Press, 1974).
103. Nelli, *L'Érotique*, pp. 73 and 222; see also p. 231. On pp. 234–35 Nelli suggests
     that there may have been two separate heresies, one of Catharism and
     another of courtly love, which seems to me to be a dubious argument, and
     a way of simultaneously rejecting and accepting de Rougemont's thesis.
     While the former was (in part) a philosophical system and the latter was
     not, the common bond here, it seems to me, is that of interiority. (See also
     "Les Troubadours et le Catharisme," *Cahiers d'études cathares*, 1 [1949], 22.)
104. Thus far, all note references to de Rougemont have been to the 1983 reprint
     (of the 1956 edition) cited in note 78, above. The first edition of the book,
     *L'amour et l'Occident* (Paris: Plon, 1939; English trans. by M. Belgion 1940,
     published by Harcourt, Brace in the United States and by Faber and Faber
     [as *Passion and Society*] in the United Kingdom), was the narrowest regarding
     the Cathar-troubadour link. As noted below, de Rougemont softened this

in 1956 and again in his Postscript of 1972; but one does have the feeling that this was a concession under duress, forced upon him by his critics, and that he really did hold to a causal (rather than a merely synchronistic) relationship. Certainly, he continued to see Catharism, or some form of Manichaean heresy, as the underlying gnosis of romantic love. This sort of waffling around is not unusual with a thesis of this type, but it does account, at least in part, for the frustration of his critics.

105. Heer, *Medieval World*, pp. 180–81; see above, note 100.
106. This is not to argue, as does Robert Johnson in *We* (San Francisco: Harper & Row, 1983), that since romantic love is a category error, we should avoid it. One might as well tell people not to cry, or dream. There are better solutions to the "problem" of romantic love than denial. Indeed, one of the most telling criticisms of de Rougemont is that he drew the *eros/agape* distinction too starkly. It seems to me that a healthy relationship has significant elements of both, no matter how theoretically incompatible they may be; and at least two mystical writers have discussed the possibility of transcending the distinction by means of a higher unity: Dion Fortune (Violet Firth), in *The Sea Priestess* (New York: Samuel Weiser, 1979; orig. publ. 1938), and Bubba Free John (Franklin Jones), in *Love of the Two-Armed Form* (Middletown, Calif.: The Dawn Horse Press, 1978).

   Irving Singer, in what is otherwise an unconvincing critique of de Rougemont, correctly points out that the major problem with the latter is that he fails to recognize the existence of two major strands in the romantic tradition, one healthy, the other pessimistic. *Eros*, in short, is more than a search for oblivion. See Irving Singer, *The Nature of Love*, Vol. II: *Courtly and Romantic Love* (2nd ed.; Chicago: University of Chicago Press, 1984), p. 298.
107. De Rougemont, *Love* (1983 reprint), p. 331.
108. Alphandéry's contribution on this point is discussed by James Westfall Thompson in "Catharist Social Ideas in Medieval French Romance," *The Romanic Review*, 27, 2 (April–June 1936), 101. The notion of these ideas "penetrating the masses [*la foule*]" may be a condescending one; popular folklore elements may have never *lost* the idea of interiority, for all we know.
109. De Rougemont, *Love* (1983 reprint), p. 111.
110. On this and the following see Marina Warner, *Alone of All Her Sex* (New York: Vintage Books, 1983), pp. 122–33.
111. "Everything happened, therefore, as if in the twelfth century feminine love had already succeeded in softening the masculine instincts, or as if the (male) lovers, around 1150, had learned to enter into sentiments which had been reserved for women up to that time" (Nelli, *L'Érotique*, p. 29).
112. Eleanor McLaughlin, " 'Christ My Mother': Feminine Naming and Metaphor in Medieval Spirituality," *Nashotah Review*, 15, 3 (Fall 1975), 241.
113. Caroline Walker Bynum, *Jesus as Mother* (Berkeley: University of California Press, 1982), pp. 17–18 and 138.

   What are the implications of this for the thesis already advanced, regarding lack of interiority, by Radding, Kohlberg, and Piaget (discussed in the opening pages of this chapter)? It turns out that unintended corroboration of this thesis comes from a rather unexpected source, Carol Gilligan's work *In a Different Voice* (Cambridge, Mass.: Harvard University Press, 1982), esp. pp. 10–32 and 73. Gilligan points out that the six-stage theory of moral development, which evolves from "moral realism" to intentionality/interconnectedness (i.e., understanding the Other) to abstract principles of justice, is a model of *male* development. Women are thus seen to be inferior because they tend not to go beyond stage three; their concern focuses on nonseparateness and relationship, which is the ultimate endpoint (in ecstatic form) of Great Mother consciousness. Thus Gilligan offers a critique of Kohlberg that is quite incisive, and that I think definitely holds up; but it is precisely this critique that confirms the Kohlberg schema as Radding has applied it to medieval culture. This was, after all, a male culture; institutions such as the monastery and the law court had little to offer women, and the *chanson de geste* was a celebration of male military exploits. The early Middle Ages was "stuck," so to speak, in steps one and two, and its subsequent feminization and focus on interiority represents its evolution to stage three. The period 1050–1550 was a very feminine one in the history of the West; what followed was a subsequent "remasculinization" in a new form—the abstract logic of modern science (see Chapter 7).

Was this better? Christopher Hill argued that it was a world turned upside down, and in a different context, Carol Gilligan is saying something similar. Increasing abstraction in the field of human relations is regarded by Kohlberg as progress or "development"; the fact is, from a feminine point of view, someone like Jeremy Bentham would appear to have been a bit of a moron. "Women's moral judgments," writes Gilligan (p. 22), ". . . provide an alternative conception of maturity. . . ." It is this alternative conception, I believe, that attracted a thinker like Jung to the late Middle Ages as something of a high-water mark of cultural development (cf. note 15, above). But the point remains that Western culture, as a male culture, *has* followed the stages Kohlberg lays out, and that the feminine spirituality of the twelfth and thirteenth centuries, as it appeared in the lives of certain female mystics, or in certain aspects of Eucharistic devotion, but especially as it erupted into male consciousness (e.g., Bernard of Clairvaux), can be seen as a kind of developmental stage. If I could venture a guess, it would be that Kohlberg's stages are really tendencies—innate though they may be—and more dependent on culture for their expression than anything else. Historically, the feminization of the High Middle Ages finally got suppressed, co-opted, and reencoded—which is what the French model of heresy is really about—and modern science emerged at the tail end of this process (my Italian model, Chapter 7). Children in modern Western culture thus tend to get "Newtonized," though girls, if Gilligan is right, manage to resist this tendency more successfully than boys do, and Third World peoples (but not their leaders) manage to resist it almost completely. Once dominant, this "Newtonization" process gets increasingly encouraged, until it becomes a sign of "progress" and is then read back into an "innate" program of psychological development. I suspect also that with the current pressure on women to "make it" in male society, the distinction made by Gilligan will start to break down, i.e., women *will* "advance" to stages five and six as part of their development. This is particularly noticeable, ironically enough, in many feminists today who, regardless of the *content* of their arguments, think patriarchally (in form), and have thus, in Kohlberg's sense, "succeeded." The whole thing might be better clarified if energy (or form) were not tied to gender. I.e., it's not a simple question of male vs. female; rather, under certain conditions, women exhibit male energy, and men female energy.

114. Wolfgang Riehle, *The Middle English Mystics*, trans. Bernard Standring (London: Routledge and Kegan Paul, 1981), pp. 107 and 109.

115. I can't remember where I read this. Possibly: J. H. Newman, *Apologia Pro Sua Vita*, ed. David J. DeLaura (New York: W. W. Norton, 1968; orig. publ. 1864). Cf. the following passage from Joanna Field, *A Life of One's Own* (see Chapter 4, note 10), p. 188 (italicized in the original):

> . . . I inherit the earth . . . then I let the sun and sky and waves possess me and emerged feeling they were part of my being . . . "conceived by the Holy Ghost" . . . isn't something born of this? Then, coming home through the vineyards to the village, the air full of the smell of grape pulp, breathing it, tasting it, I remembered the Eucharist. . . . One does want to swallow and be swallowed by one's love.

116. Caroline Walker Bynum, "Fast, Feast, and Flesh: The Religious Significance of Food to Medieval Women," *Representations*, 11 (Summer 1985), 1.

117. Ibid., pp. 15–16; see also *Jesus as Mother, passim*, "Women Mystics and Eucharistic Devotion in the Thirteenth Century," *Women's Studies*, 11 (1984), 179–214, and *Holy Feast and Holy Fast* (Berkeley: University of California Press, 1987), all by Caroline Walker Bynum; Warner, *Alone of All Her Sex*, p. 197; and McLaughlin, " 'Christ My Mother,' " p. 239.

118. Warner, *Alone of All Her Sex*, pp. 115–16, and Hilda Graef, *Mary: A History of Doctrine and Devotion* (2 vols.; London: Sheed and Ward, 1963), Vol. 1, pp. 229–30. *Salve Regina*, composed around A.D. 1100, is indeed remarkable, and the reader might wish to listen to it to capture the flavor of the new interiority. My own copy is a version by Francesco Cavalli (seventeenth century), included on the same tape as Allegri's *Miserere*, by the Westminster Cathedral Choir, Argo recording #KZRDC1013.

119. Warner, *Alone of All Her Sex*, pp. 131, 134, 147, 151–53, 159–60, and 174. René Nelli similarly argues that the Church was able to absorb the heresy of romantic love only after it had half dried it up ("Du Catharisme," p. 38; see also *L'Érotique*, pp. 298–99). Robert Briffault *(Les Troubadours)* claimed that "the Church adopted what she could not suppress" (quoted in Boase, *Origin and Meaning of Courtly Love*, p. 86).

   In addition to Warner on the Cult of the Virgin see Théodore Koehler, "Marie (Saint Vierge)," *Dictionnaire de spiritualité, ascétique et mystique* (Paris: Beauchesne, 1977), Vol. 10, cols. 440–59.

## CHAPTER 7. SCIENCE AND MAGIC

1. This point was first made by Frances Yates in books such as *Giordano Bruno and the Hermetic Tradition* (see Chapter 5, note 7) as well as in numerous articles,

and although a kind of "revisionist attack" has been mounted in recent years on the Yates thesis (see below, note 68), historians of science have been forced to concede that magic is no aberration of Western culture but finally integral to it, and responsible for the rise of modern science in a number of important ways. Despite the editor's introduction, for example, the essays in Brian Vickers (ed.), *Occult and Scientific Mentalities in the Renaissance* (Cambridge, England: Cambridge University Press, 1984), attest to this (see, e.g., p. 165). Even before Yates, Lynn Thorndike had argued the point in his multivolume *A History of Magic and Experimental Science* (see Chapter 2, note 80). My own contribution to the debate can be found in Chapters 3 and 4 of *The Reenchantment of the World* (Ithaca, N.Y.: Cornell University Press, 1981).

2. Paolo Rossi, *Francis Bacon*, trans. Sacha Rabinovitch (London: Routledge and Kegan Paul, 1968).

3. Maurice Aniane, "Notes sur l'alchimie, 'yoga' cosmologique de la chrétienté médiévale," in Jacques Masui (ed.), *Yoga, science de l'homme intégral* (Paris: Cahiers du Sud, 1953), pp. 243–73; D. P. Walker, *Spiritual and Demonic Magic from Ficino to Campanella* (London: University of Notre Dame Press, 1975; orig. publ. 1958), *passim*; Gershom Scholem, "Kabbalah," cols. 490–654 (see Chapter 5, note 17); and David Conway, *Ritual Magic* (New York: E. P. Dutton, 1978).

4. Something pointed out to me by a contemporary magician (or "illusionist," as some would call it), David Abram. This fits in well with my discussion of the esoteric/exoteric split in the shift from magic to science, which can be found in Chapter 3 of *The Reenchantment of the World*. For a summary of the economic background to all this, see Chapter 2 of the same work.

5. Christopher Marlowe, *The Tragedy of Doctor Faustus*, ed. Louis B. Wright and Virginia A. LaMar (New York: Washington Square Press, 1959), p. 3.

6. Yates, *Bruno*, p. 156.

7. Frances Yates, *The Art of Memory* (London: Routledge and Kegan Paul, 1966).

8. On the above, and also in the section below, I am drawing quite liberally from the excellent article by Lawrence S. Lerner and Edward A. Gosselin, "Giordano Bruno," *Scientific American*, *228*, 4 (April 1973), 86–94. See also Yates, *Bruno*, pp. 215 and 236–40. *La Cena de le ceneri* exists in English translation by Stanley L. Jaki (The Hague: Mouton, 1975).

9. It was no contradiction to Bruno that the divine light was an ancient Egyptian one, a Copernican one, and a personal-internal one. Bruno's heresy, which included the notion that God was present within every human being, was in the mainstream of magical beliefs about microcosm and macrocosm, the notion that every human being contains a universe and that the reform of the heavens is the reform of personality as well (cf. Yates, *Bruno*, p. 220). For a critique of the Lerner-Gosselin approach to Bruno as being too Hermetic, see Ernan McMullin, "Bruno and Copernicus," *Isis*, *78*, 291 (March 1987), 55–74 and esp. p. 69.

10. On Bruno's optical "experiments" see Lerner and Gosselin, "Giordano Bruno," p. 89. Copernicus' Hermetic interest is well known, though it is not clear how deep it ran. See, for example, Yates, *Bruno*, p. 154.

11. From the Jaki translation of *La Cena de le ceneri*, p. 61.

12. Yates, *Bruno*, pp. 239–40 and 276–83.

13. Lerner and Gosselin, "Giordano Bruno," pp. 91–92.

14. This is my hypothesis, rather than that of Lerner and Gosselin, though it does (as far as I can see) follow from what they have written.

15. That Western philosophy was searching for a transcendent God, and that Eastern philosophy had no need to search for one because He was immanent, and that this was a principal reason why the West came up with modern science and the East did not, is the theme of a seminal essay by Joseph Needham, "Human Law and the Laws of Nature," in *The Grand Titration*, pp. 299–331 (see Chapter 2, note 44).

16. Lerner and Gosselin, "Giordano Bruno," p. 90. Again, see the reference to Needham in the previous note. If God is conceived of being *in* this world, the major "problem" of Western consciousness—how to reach Him—simply drops away.

17. An English translation of the *Oration* can be found in Ernst Cassirer et al. (eds.), *The Renaissance Philosophy of Man* (Chicago: Phoenix Books, 1956), pp. 223–54. On the section below see Yates, *Bruno*, pp. 84–99, 104, 111, 116, and 145, and also her *Occult Philosophy in the Elizabethan Age* (London: Ark Paperbacks, 1983), pp. 2–3 and 190.

18. See the discussion of Jewish ascent techniques, cabala, and Abraham Abulafia in Chapters 4 and 5.

19. Yates, *Occult Philosophy*, pp. 3 and 20–21, and *Bruno*, p. 145. The trance, according to Pico, can be so intense as to lead to the death of the body—the so-called *mors osculi*, or kiss of death (Yates, *Bruno*, p. 99). Bruno discussed the kiss of death briefly at two points in his *Heroic Furies*, as did Francesco Giorgi (see below) in *De Harmonia Mundi*.

    The doctrine of a ladder of specific steps to God, i.e., the notion of a series of intermediaries, or emanations—*sephiroth*, in the cabala—is discussed by Scholem in the "Kabbalah" article, cols. 563ff. Although ecstatic nuances—i.e., ideas of complete merger into the Godhead—are found in the literature, the doctrine of *devekut*, of a mystical cleaving to God, was one of communion rather than self-annihilation; or in the terminology of de Rougemont (see Chapter 2), one of epithalamian rather than unitive mysticism. See Scholem, "Kabbalah," cols. 613, 624, and 627, and also the discussion of Simone Weil in Chapter 10.

20. Yates, *Bruno*, p. 111.

21. Arthur Koestler, *The Watershed* (Garden City, N.Y.: Anchor Books, 1960). "Watershed" refers to a crossing point, in this case a discontinuous historical shift of the kind represented by the Scientific Revolution.

22. Berman, *Reenchantment of the World*, Chapter 4.

23. Yates, *Bruno*, pp. 62–83; Walker, *Spiritual and Demonic Magic*, Chs. 1 and 2.

24. Walker, *Spiritual and Demonic Magic*, pp. 38–41 and *passim*. See also E. R. Dodds, "The Astral Body in Neoplatonism," in Appendix II of his edition of Proclus, *The Elements of Theology* (2nd ed.; Oxford: Clarendon Press, 1963), pp. 313–21.

25. Yates, *Occult Philosophy*, pp. 29–35.

26. Berman, *Reenchantment of the World*, p. 100; François Secret, *Les Kabbalistes chrétiens de la Renaissance* (Paris: Dunod, 1964), pp. 39–40 and 126–40.

27. On the following see Yates, *Bruno*, pp. 360–83, and Walker, *Spiritual and Demonic Magic*, pp. 205–36. Campanella's discussion of ascent appears in *Del senso delle cose e della magia* (On the meaning of things and of magic), and is quoted in Yates on p. 382.

28. Thorndike, *History of Magic*, Vol. 7, pp. 295 and 297.

29. Quoted in ibid., p. 296.

30. Mario Gliozzi, "Cardano," in C. C. Gillispie (ed.), *Dictionary of Scientific Biography* (New York: Charles Scribner's Sons, 1970–80), Vol. 3, pp. 64–67, and Markus Fierz, *Girolamo Cardano*, trans. Helga Niman (Boston: Birkhäuser, 1983), pp. 59–106.

    Cardano briefly mentioned the experience of witnessing God, but said it was open only to the good and the wise (Fierz, p. 111).

    The proposition referred to, in modern terms, states that the number of possibilities of finding $k$ out of $n$ objects is equal to the binomial coefficient $\binom{n}{k}$, and that the sum of these coefficients is given by

$$\sum_{k=1}^{n} \binom{n}{k} = 2^n - 1.$$

31. Fierz, *Girolamo Cardano*, p. 126.

32. Ibid., pp. 125–26 (the dream book was called *Synesiorum Somniorum Omnis Generis Insomnia Explicantes*), and Ian Maclean, "The Interpretation of Natural Signs: Cardano's *De Subtilitate* versus Scaliger's *Exercitationes*," in Vickers, *Occult and Scientific Mentalities*, pp. 234 and 236.

33. Thorndike, *History of Magic*, Vol. 5, p. 574.

34. Jerome Cardan, *The Book of My Life*, trans. Jean Stoner (New York: E. P. Dutton, 1930), p. 213; see also pp. 147–67.

35. Ralph Cudworth, *The True Intellectual System of the Universe* (3 vols.; London: Thomas Tegg, 1845; orig. publ. 1678); Scholem, "Kabbalah," col. 646. See also Dodds, "Astral Body," p. 321.

36. E. A. Burtt, *The Metaphysical Foundations of Modern Science* (2nd ed.; Garden City, N.Y.: Anchor Books, 1932), p. 140. Both Burtt (pp. 135–48, 150–51, and 163) and Alexandre Koyré (*From the Closed World to the Infinite Universe* [Baltimore: The Johns Hopkins Press, 1957], pp. 109–79 and 190, and esp. pp. 159–60) argued for an influence of the Cambridge Platonists on Newton. See also J. E. McGuire and P. M. Rattansi, "Newton and the 'Pipes of Pan,' " *Notes and Records of the Royal Society of London*, 21 (1966), 129–38.

37. J. A. Passmore, *Ralph Cudworth* (Cambridge, England: Cambridge University Press, 1951), p. 24.

38. Cudworth, *Intellectual System*, Vol. 1, p. 280; quoted in Passmore, *Ralph Cudworth*. See also P. M. Rattansi, "Cudworth," in Gillispie, *Dictionary of Scientific Biography*, Vol. 3, p. 492.

39. Robert Lenoble, *Mersenne ou la naissance du mécanisme* (Paris: J. Vrin, 1943).

40. Alexandre Koyré, *Galileo Studies*, trans. John Mepham (Hassocks, England: The Harvester Press, 1978; orig. French ed. 1939), p. 222. For a critique of Koyré that takes a very different tack from that of Garin (discussed below),

see Ludovico Geymonat, *Galileo Galilei,* trans. Stillman Drake (New York: McGraw-Hill, 1965).

41. Quoted in Eugenio Garin, *Science and Civic Life in the Italian Renaissance,* trans. Peter Munz (Garden City, N.Y.: Anchor Books, 1969), pp. 128–29. On p. 113 Garin notes that another letter to Dini, dated March 26, 1615, is very Ficinian in nature.

42. Ibid., pp. 113 and 130; see also p. 136.

43. Lawrence S. Lerner and Edward A. Gosselin, "Galileo and the Specter of Bruno," *Scientific American,* 255, 5 (November 1986), 126–33.

44. Ibid., p. 131. On the Rosicrucian scare see Berman, *Reenchantment of the World,* pp. 108–9.

45. Lerner and Gosselin, "Galileo," p. 132. It did, however, take Magalotti a bit of time to come up with another book with the same colophon by the same printer, Giovanni Batista Landini, during which time Riccardi's suspicions were revived.

46. Garin, *Science and Civic Life,* pp. 130, 138–39, and 142.

47. H. F. Cohen, *Quantifying Music* (Dordrecht, Holland: D. Reidel Publishing Co., 1984), p. xii. Cohen doesn't mention Cardano, but see Hieronymus Cardanus, *Writings on Music,* trans. and ed. Clement A. Miller (New York: American Institute of Musicology, 1973).

48. Randall McClellan, "Music and Altered States of Consciousness," *Dromenon,* 2, 3–4 (Winter 1979), pp. 3–8.

49. Jacques Attali, *Noise,* trans. Brian Massumi (Minneapolis: University of Minnesota Press, 1985), p. 13.

50. Cohen, *Quantifying Music,* pp. xi and 3; Koestler, *Watershed,* Ch. 9.

51. Cohen, *Quantifying Music,* p. 25; Koestler, *Watershed, passim.*

52. Cohen, *Quantifying Music,* p. 99; Lenoble, *Mersenne,* pp. 237 and 265.

53. McGuire and Rattansi, "Newton," pp. 115–20.

54. On the following see Berman, *Reenchantment of the World,* pp. 109–11, and Yates, *Occult Philosophy,* pp. 172–74. Also useful is William L. Hine, "Marin Mersenne: Renaissance Naturalism and Renaissance Magic," in Vickers, *Occult and Scientific Mentalities,* pp. 165–76.

55. Lenoble, *Mersenne,* pp. 265 and 276; Yates, *Occult Philosophy,* pp. 173–74.

56. On the following see Lenoble, *Mersenne,* pp. 67, 77n, 92, and 236. I put "managed" in quotes to emphasize how loaded our terminology is. A future age might possibly regard Mersenne's lingering occultism as his saving grace.

57. Cf. the discussion of Marc Bloch's treatment of this subject in Chapter 3.

58. Rameau's classic work, the *Traité de l'harmonie,* appeared in 1722. On the discussion below see Lenoble, *Mersenne,* pp. 44, 304–5, 367–71, and 522–31; A. C. Crombie, "Mersenne," in Gillispie, *Dictionary of Scientific Biography,* Vol. 9, pp. 316–22; Albion Gruber, "Mersenne and Evolving Tonal Theory," *Journal of Music Theory,* 14, 1 (1970), 36–67; Cohen, *Quantifying Music,* pp. 100–15 and 158–60; Albert Cohen, "Marin Mersenne," in Stanley Sadie (ed.), *The New Grove Dictionary of Music and Musicians* (New York: Grove's Dictionaries of Music, 1980), Vol. 12, pp. 188–90; Warren D. Allen, *Philosophies of Music History* (New York: Dover Publications, 1962; orig. ed. 1939), pp. 15–18; and Hellmut

Ludwig, *Marin Mersenne und seine Musiklehre* (Halle: Buchhandlung des Wais-
enhaus GmbH, 1935).

59. Marin Mersenne, *Harmonie universelle*, trans. Roger E. Chapman (The Hague:
Martinus Nijhoff, 1957), p. 46. This is a translation of the seven books of
instruments from the full text of the *Harmonie universelle*. Cf. Lenoble, *Mersenne*, p. 369.

60. Allen Debus, "Fludd," in Gillispie, *Dictionary of Scientific Biography*, Vol. 5,
pp. 47–49; Joscelyn Godwin, *Robert Fludd* (London: Thames and Hudson,
1979), pp. 19, 42, 48–50, and 53; Murray Schafer, *The Tuning of the World* (New
York: Alfred A. Knopf, 1977), p. 6; Allen Debus (ed.), *Robert Fludd and His
Philosophicall Key* (New York: Science History Publications, 1979), pp. 6 and
13; Yates, *Bruno*, pp. 404–6 and 425.

61. Berman, *Reenchantment of the World*, Ch. 4.

62. Lenoble, *Mersenne*, p. 522n.

63. Cohen, *Quantifying Music*, p. 102. On the Fludd-Mersenne controversy see
Yates, *Bruno*, pp. 437–39.

64. On this see Attali, *Noise*, pp. 5, 10, 46, and 61, the Afterword by Susan
McClary, and Chapter 10, note 33, below.

65. Lenoble, *Mersenne*, p. 531.

66. Frank E. Manuel, *A Portrait of Isaac Newton* (Cambridge, Mass.: Harvard University Press, 1968), p. 380.

67. See René Descartes, *Discourse on Method*, trans. Laurence J. Lafleur (2nd ed.;
Indianapolis: Bobbs-Merrill, 1956), p. 21; Burtt, *Metaphysical Foundations*, pp.
105–8; Yates, *Bruno*, pp. 452–53; and Garin, *Science and Civic Life*, p. 148.

68. Interestingly enough, this process has gotten played out in the historiography
of the Scientific Revolution itself. Many historians who embraced the Yates
thesis, or the notion of magico-Hermetic influence, in the heyday of the sixties,
subsequently got nervous and, with virtually no new historical evidence,
furiously began backpedaling, as the implications of their work became clear.
I have, as a result, not said very much about the critics of the Yates thesis
because their critiques seem so transparent. Thus C. B. Schmitt writes of a
"Hermetic madness," "an extremism which all but went over the edge,"
though he concedes that the work of Yates, Garin, Walker, and Rossi cannot
easily be dismissed. Robert Westman attacks the Yates thesis by defining it
in terms Frances Yates would not have recognized; J. E. McGuire questions
whether alchemy can be called Hermetic, while admitting that he has not
read B. J. T. Dobbs' definitive study of Newton's alchemy. "What is depressing
about [all this]," writes P. M. Rattansi, "is the anxiety of the authors to return
to a 'respectable' ancestry for some seminal transformations in early-modern
scientific thought." That is, indeed, the point. Undoubtedly, the worst example of this is Brian Vickers, in his introduction to the *Occult and Scientific
Mentalities* volume, in which he establishes two supposedly disparate categories—"scientific" and "occult"—and then puzzles over the "problem" that
men such as Bacon, Kepler, and Mersenne seem to have been in both camps
(!). This "return to such a crude bipolarity," writes Patrick Curry, obliterates
(again without any new evidence whatever) what Yates et al. managed to

establish: that there are no "stable and enduring epistemological entities as . . . 'science' and 'magic,' existing in a universal or transcendental way and amenable to universal definition." Vickers' approach represents the worst sort of Whig history, and the most obvious sort of fear of a living, magical tradition. The approach is totally anachronistic and ahistorical, imposing modern categories on a time period that simply did not make such distinctions. Schmitt similarly, says Curry, has returned to a naive, cheerfully Popperian position, that of seeing science as uniquely progressive (as opposed to the magical tradition, which is supposedly "protective"); and indeed, Schmitt's review of the Westman-McGuire volume reveals a positivistic, Sartonian bias underneath it all. Once again, what we have in all this is "an attempt to protect the purity of *modern* science . . . from the pollution of 'occult' or 'mystical' influence." As it turns out, many of the papers in the Vickers volume— to their credit—contradict the arguments of the editor's own introduction.

See C. B. Schmitt, "Irrational Undercurrents" (review of Vickers, *Occult and Scientific Mentalities*), *Times Literary Supplement*, November 2, 1984, p. 1243; Robert S. Westman and J. E. McGuire, *Hermeticism and the Scientific Revolution* (Los Angeles: The William Andrews Clark Memorial Library, 1977), and the reviews of this volume by P. M. Rattansi in the *Journal of the History of Philosophy*, 19 (1981), 392–96, and P. B. Wood in the *British Journal for the History of Science*, 13 (1980), 70–72; B. J. T. Dobbs, *The Foundations of Newton's Alchemy* (Cambridge, England: Cambridge University Press, 1975); Patrick Curry, "Revisions of Science and Magic," *History of Science*, 23 (1985), 299–325; and C. B. Schmitt, "Reappraisals in Renaissance Science" (review of Westman-McGuire), *History of Science*, 16 (1978), 200–14.

69. Charles M. Johnston, *The Creative Imperative* (Berkeley: Celestial Arts, 1984/ 86), pp. 174–76.

CHAPTER 8. THE TWISTED CROSS

1. Norman Cohn, *The Pursuit of the Millennium* (London: Paladin, 1970; orig. publ. 1957).
2. George L. Mosse, *The Crisis of German Ideology* (New York: Schocken Books, 1981; orig. publ. 1964).
3. Rhodes, *Hitler Movement* (see Chapter 3, note 21); Fritz Stern, *The Politics of Cultural Despair* (Berkeley: University of California Press, 1961).
4. Erich Voegelin, *Political Religions* (Lewiston, N.Y.: E. Mellen, 1986; orig. German ed. 1938). See also Eric Voegelin, *The New Science of Politics* (Chicago: University of Chicago Press, 1952) and *Science, Politics and Gnosticism* (Washington: Regnery Books, 1968).
5. See the review of Rhodes by T. L. Brink in the *American Historical Review*, 87, 2 (April 1982), 483–84.
6. For references to the sensationalist literature on Nazi occultism see below, notes 60 and 64.
7. Klaus Vondung, *Magie und Manipulation* (Göttingen: Vandenhoeck & Ruprecht, 1971); see also his article, "Spiritual Revolution and Magic: Speculation and Political Action in National Socialism," *Modern Age*, 23, 4 (Fall 1979), 394–402.

8. Robert A. Pois, *National Socialism and the Religion of Nature* (London: Croom Helm, 1986); see also his article, "Man in the Natural World: Some Implications of the National-Socialist Religion," in Seymour Drescher et al. (eds.), *Political Symbolism in Modern Europe* (New Brunswick, N.J.: Transaction Books, 1982), pp. 256–72.

9. Hermann Rauschning, *Hitler Speaks* (London: Thornton Butterworth Ltd., 1939), p. 249; publ. in the United States as *The Voice of Destruction* (New York: G. P. Putnam's Sons, 1940). This book is a (not completely exact) translation of *Gespräche mit Hitler* (Zurich: Europa Verlag, 1940). Rauschning was, in the 1930s, a Nazi *Gauleiter* (district leader) and Hitler confidant who subsequently defected to the Allies. Historians generally regard him as an authentic source. See J. S. Conway, "Hermann Rauschning as Historian and Opponent of Nazism," *Canadian Journal of History, 8* (1973), 67–78.

10. Hannah Arendt, *Eichmann in Jerusalem* (New York: Viking Press, 1963).

11. The following discussion is taken from Mosse, *Crisis of German Ideology*, pp. vi, viii, 4, 14–17, 34, 41, 63, 72–73, and 93–96, and Goodrick-Clarke, *The Occult Roots of Nazism* (see Chapter 6, note 86), pp. x, 1–5, 18–57, 60–100, 109, and 194. On Lanz von Liebenfels see also Karl D. Bracher, *The German Dictatorship*, trans. Jean Steinberg (New York: Praeger, 1970), p. 62, and note 18, below.

12. On the following see Mosse, *Crisis of German Ideology*, pp. 228–33, 296, and 306; Goodrick-Clarke, *Occult Roots of Nazism*, pp., 60–62, 109–10, 122–23, 127–29, 133, 138–49, and 155–75; and Bracher, *German Dictatorship*, pp. 80–83.

13. Difficult to translate. Literally, "The Stormer"; but in German, the word has associations with *Sturm und Drang*, struggle, and effort. It implies enthusiasm, dedication to a cause.

14. Rudolf von Sebottendorff, *Bevor Hitler kam* (Munich: Deukula-Verlag Grassinger, 1933; 2nd ed. 1934).

15. Bracher, *German Dictatorship*, p. 80. Grassinger made his suggestion in a letter to Reginald Phelps (see below).

16. Reginald H. Phelps, " 'Before Hitler Came': Thule Society and the Germanen Orden," *Journal of Modern History, 35* (1963), 245–61.

17. Mosse, *Crisis of German Ideology*, pp. 75–80.

18. On the following see Bracher, *German Dictatorship*, p. 62; Goodrick-Clarke, *Occult Roots of Nazism*, pp. 194–203; Joachim C. Fest, *Hitler*, trans. Richard and Clara Winston (New York: Vintage Books, 1975), pp. 37, 40, 226, and 770; Wilfried Daim, *Der Mann, der Hitler die Ideen gab* (Munich: Isar Verlag, 1958), pp. 12–41 and 198–209; and Josef Greiner, *Das Ende der Hitler-Mythos* (Zurich: Amalthea-Verlag, 1947). According to James Webb, however (see note 27, below), this last text is not regarded as being all that reliable by historians of the Nazi period.

19. Rauschning, *Hitler Speaks*, p. 227.

20. Jackson Spielvogel and David Redles, "Hitler's Racial Ideology: Content and Occult Sources," *Simon Wiesenthal Center Annual, 3* (1986), 246. This is a very useful article, and I am grateful to Michael Kater of York University for bringing it to my attention.

21. Daim, *Der Mann*, p. 12; translated in Spielvogel and Redles, "Hitler's Racial Ideology," p. 229. On the discussion below see this article, pp. 227–46.

22. Rauschning, *Hitler Speaks*, p. 242.
23. Spielvogel and Redles, "Hitler's Racial Ideology," p. 233; and Rauschning, *Hitler Speaks*, p. 240.
24. Quoted in Rudolph Binion, *Hitler Among the Germans* (New York: Elsevier, 1976), p. 59.
25. Rauschning, *Hitler Speaks*, p. 238.
26. Ibid., p. 242; Joachim C. Fest, *The Face of the Third Reich*, trans. Michael Bullock (London: Weidenfeld & Nicolson, 1970), pp. 291–92.
27. James Webb, *The Occult Establishment* (La Salle, Ill.: Open Court Publishing Company, 1976), p. 275. Webb reviews the story of List, Eckart, Lanz, and the Thule Gesellschaft on pp. 275–344.
28. J. P. Stern, *Hitler: The Führer and the People* (London: Flamingo, 1984; orig. publ. 1975), p. 17.
29. On this and the following see Fritz Stern, *Politics of Cultural Despair*, pp. xiv, xxv–xxviii, and 292–94.
30. Ibid., p. 295. Cf. p. 293: "The various attempts to understand the triumph of national socialism have consistently underestimated the deeply rooted spiritual longing, which inspired so many of Hitler's followers. . . ." Fritz Stern does, however, go on to say that Nazism was derived from the ideas of men such as Lagarde and Langbehn, so he doesn't completely escape what James Rhodes, whose analysis is based on primary experience of the rank and file (see below), calls the "miseducation thesis." Fritz Stern also makes the same mistake made by J. P. Stern, saying that it all ended in nihilism, whereas Rhodes argues quite convincingly that the Nazi worldview was consistent right down to the end. Extermination of the Jews was the *logical* outcome of the Ariosophical race ideology.
31. J. P. Stern, *Hitler*, pp. 10 and 24.
32. Ibid., pp. 93 and 97. See also the writings of Eric Voegelin cited in note 4, above.
33. The following discussion is taken from Rhodes, *Hitler Movement*, Preface and pp. 6, 14–21, 26–30, 37–41, 50, 56–60, 64–71, 76–78, 110–15, 130–34, 174–75, 193–94, and 209.
34. This is from the Abel documents (see below); quoted in Rhodes, *Hitler Movement*, p. 100.
35. On this, in addition to Rhodes, *Hitler Movement*, see J. P. Stern, *Hitler*, pp. 185–94. Abel's book (originally published by Prentice-Hall) was reprinted as *The Nazi Movement: Why Hitler Came to Power* (New York: Atherton, Atheling Books, 1966), and a second time as well, as *Why Hitler Came to Power* (Cambridge, Mass.: Harvard University Press, 1986). Abel donated the original essays to the Hoover Institution at Stanford University after the the war; in 1951, the FBI seized about one hundred of these, never returned them, and later claimed they were lost. On the reliability of the essays for historical testimony see J. P. Stern, *Hitler*, pp. 186–88.
36. Eberhard Jäckel, *Hitler's Weltanschauung*, trans. Herbert Arnold (Middletown, Conn.: Wesleyan University Press, 1972), p. 64; Bracher, *German Dictatorship*, p. 63.

37. H. G. Baynes, *Germany Possessed* (London: Jonathan Cape, 1941; New York: AMS Press, 1972), p. 88.
38. See J. P. Stern, *Hitler*, pp. 108–10. The original article by Jung may be found in the *Neue Schweizer Rundschau* (Zurich), Neue Folge III, Heft 11 (March 1936), pp. 657–69, and reprinted in Jung's *Aufsätze zur Zeitgeschichte* (Zurich: Rascher Verlag, 1946), pp. 3–23. The English version, which is somewhat misleading at one or two points (see below, note 40), is included in Jung's *Collected Works*, Vol. 10: *Civilization in Transition*, trans. R. F. C. Hull (2nd ed.; Princeton: Princeton University Press, 1970), pp. 179–93. Quotations that follow are from the Hull translation, pp. 180–81 and 184–86.
39. *Wütens*, in the original German version, which I presume is derived from Wotan. The word has the sense of rabidity, of foaming at the mouth.
40. I have retranslated Jung's original German here because Hull rendered it stronger and more negative than it actually is. Hence Hull uses the word "infected" for *ergriffen*, which really means "possessed"; and the sentence in the original German ends with the words *"in gefährliches Rutschen"* ("into a dangerous sliding"), which Hull rendered as "towards perdition."
41. Statements like these make one realize that Jung's attitude toward National Socialism was a complicated one. The "Wotan" essay was used at the Göring Institute (established in Berlin in 1933 for the practice of psychotherapy) by one therapist, Lucy Heyer-Grote, on patients who were opposed to the Nazi regime. She reported that it had a comforting effect on them. By September of 1939 Jung was writing: "Hitler is reaching his climax and with him the German psychosis." See Geoffrey Cocks, *Psychotherapy in the Third Reich* (New York: Oxford University Press, 1985), p. 133.
42. Jeffrey Herf, *Reactionary Modernism* (Cambridge, England: Cambridge University Press, 1984).
43. Baynes, *Germany Possessed*, p. 15. Quotes from Baynes below, including the one from Jung, are taken from pp. 62, 75, and 294.
44. J. S. Conway, *The Nazi Persecution of the Churches* (Toronto: Ryerson Press, 1968).
45. Rauschning, *Gespräche*, p. 50. Hitler used the word *spüren* here, which I have translated as "experience," but it could also be rendered as "perceive" or "sense."
46. Ibid., p. 51.
47. On this and the following quote see Rauschning, *Hitler Speaks*, pp. 58 and 63.
48. J. P. Stern, *Hitler*, p. 107; Conway, *Nazi Persecution*, pp. 153–55; and Vondung, *Magie und Manipulation*, pp. 97, 118, and 154–55.
49. Quoted in Stephen H. Roberts, *The House That Hitler Built* (6th ed.; London: Methuen, 1938), p. 277. According to Conway, the churches were heavily persecuted by the Nazi regime, but they also capitulated to National Socialism and betrayed Christian ideals. Both the churches and the Nazis, says Conway, shared anti-Semitic and antidemocratic ideologies. "As for the Jews," remarked Hitler, "I can just carry on with the same policy which the Catholic Church has adopted for fifteen hundred years, when it has regarded the Jews as dangerous and pushed them into ghettos . . ." (quoted in Conway, p. 26)—clearly, something to think about.

50. Pois, *National Socialism*, p. 28.

51. For example: "It seems to me that nothing would be more foolish than to reestablish the worship of Wotan. Our old mythology had ceased to be viable when Christianity implanted itself. Nothing dies unless it is moribund. . . ." (From Adolf Hitler, *Hitler's Secret Conversations 1941–44* [first published as *Hitler's Table Talk*] [New York: Octagon Books, 1972], p. 51. See also pp. 33, 49, 51, and 417.) Regarding Himmler's mythologizing tendencies (see below), Hitler's architect, Albert Speer, recorded Hitler as saying: "What nonsense! Here we have at last reached an age that has left all mysticism behind it, and now he wants to start that all over again. We might just as well have stayed with the church. At least it had tradition. To think that I may some day be turned into an SS saint! Can you imagine it? I would turn over in my grave. . . ." (From Albert Speer, *Inside the Third Reich*, trans. Richard and Clara Winston [New York: Macmillan, 1970], p. 112.) In point of fact Hitler *was* transformed into an SS saint, with his full encouragement and participation. Cf. Vondung, *Magie und Manipulation*, pp. 43–44.

52. Hess, who died on August 17, 1987 (at age ninety-three), apparently by his own hand, in Spandau Prison, after having spent nearly forty-one years there, was certainly not insane, as the Nazis tried to make out, but was clearly what we might call "flaky." His occultism, which included astrology, dowsing, homeopathy, Anthroposophy, yoga, herbology, and the like, was more a form of hypochondria than anything else. It certainly had no ascent experience attached to it. See Wulf Schwarzwäller, *Rudolf Hess* (Vienna: Verlag Fritz Molden, 1974), p. 159; James Leasor, *Rudolf Hess* (London: George Allen and Unwin, 1962), pp. 37 and 137; J. Bernard Hutton, *Hess* (London: David Bruce and Watson, 1970), p. 112; Roger Manvill and Heinrich Fraenkel, *Hess* (London: MacGibbon and Kee, 1971), pp. 49, 64–66, 104, 128, and 131–2; and Walter Schellenberg, *The Labyrinth*, trans. Louis Hagen (New York: Harper and Row, 1956), p. 185.

53. On Hitler's actual admiration of the Jews see Henry Ashby Turner, Jr. (ed.), *Hitler—Memoirs of a Confidant*, trans. Ruth Hein (New Haven: Yale University Press, 1985), pp. 206–7. The confidant was Otto Wagener (1888–1971), who was close to Hitler from 1929 to 1933, and the memoirs (written in a POW camp in Wales in 1946) are preserved in Munich's Institut für Zeitgeschichte.

54. Conway, *Nazi Persecution*, p. 140.

55. Quoted in Fest, *Face of the Third Reich*, p. 384, n. 25.

56. Rauschning, *Gespräche*, p. 5; and Turner, *Hitler*, pp. 324–25. For more on the subject of the suppression of secret societies see Conway, *Nazi Persecution*, pp. 372 and 378–82.

　　The thesis of an inner doctrine that could be "leaked" to the public only in small doses first appeared in Rauschning's records of conversations with Hitler, and the evidence provided there seems to support it very well. More analytical presentations of the argument can be found in Aryeh Unger, *The Totalitarian Party* (London: Cambridge University Press, 1974) and, as noted, the work of Robert Pois.

57. This and the following quotations are taken from Walter C. Langer, *The Mind of Adolf Hitler* (New York: New American Library, 1972), pp. 64–65. This was

a wartime report commissioned by the OSS in 1944. The rally of 1937 was reported by William Teeling in his 1939 book, *Know Thy Enemy!*; Ernst Röhm was head of the SA and a close friend of Hitler, until he and a number of other men in the SA were murdered in the famous Röhm *putsch* of 1934.

58. Langer, *Mind of Adolf Hitler*, p. 64; Roberts, *House That Hitler Built*, p. 10n.
59. Joseph Ackermann, *Heinrich Himmler als Ideologe* (Göttingen: Musterschmidt, 1970), p. 78 and note 229: "Passen Sie auf" [said Heydrich] ". . . in zehn Jahren wird Adolf Hitler in Deutschland genau die Stellung einnehmen, die heute noch Jesus Christus bekleidet" ("You wait and see . . . in ten years Adolf Hitler will take over in Germany the same position that Jesus Christ occupies today").
60. On the following see Trevor Ravenscroft, *The Spear of Destiny* (New York: G. P. Putnam's Sons, 1973); Louis Pauwels and Jacques Bergier, *The Morning of the Magicians*, trans. Rollo Myers (London: Granada Publishing, 1971; orig. French ed. 1960; alternative title, *The Dawn of Magic*), pp. 127–210; René Alleau, *Hitler et les sociétés secrètes* (Paris: Éditions Bernard Grasset, 1969), pp. 156–85; Dusty Sklar, *Gods and Beasts* (New York: Thomas Y. Crowell, 1979); and Goodrick-Clarke, *Occult Roots of Nazism*, 217–25.
61. Phelps, " 'Before Hitler Came,' " p. 251.
62. As already noted, the Thule Gesellschaft had disbanded by 1926. The bit about the Vril Society is based on an exaggeration of a memory of Willy Ley, a German engineer who emigrated to the United States in 1935, referring to a sect in Berlin engaged in a type of meditation designed to learn about a life-force energy it called "vril." See Willy Ley, "Pseudoscience in Naziland," *Astounding Science Fiction* (New York), 39 (1947), 90–98.
63. Rauschning, *Gespräche*, p. 208.
64. Other examples of sensationalist or undocumented literature along these lines are as follows: Dietrich Bronder, *Bevor Hitler kam* (1964); Werner Gerson, *Le Nazisme, société secrète* (1969); Elisabeth Antebi, *Ave Lucifer* (1970); Jean-Claude Frère, *Nazism et sociétés secrètes* (1974); J. H. Brennan, *Occult Reich* (1974); Jean-Michel Angebert, *Les Mystiques du soleil* (1971); and Nigel Pennick, *Hitler's Secret Sciences* (1981).

In *Das Ende der Hitler-Mythos*, Josef Greiner, who knew Hitler personally, claimed that Hitler was interested in Eastern teachings, attended lectures on occultism while in Vienna, studied dowsing, hypnosis, numerology, astrology, and so on (see esp. pp. 86–96). This was supposedly eyewitness testimony, but was probably a fabrication (see above, note 18).
65. Fest, *Face of the Third Reich*, p. 298.
66. The following account is taken from John Toland, *Adolf Hitler* (Garden City, N.Y.: Doubleday, 1976), pp. xviii–xx, 71, and 925; and Binion, *Hitler Among the Germans*, pp. 3–6 and 120–26. This latter work is regarded by many historians as unreliable, being for the most part an exercise in speculative Freudian psychohistory, and arguing that Hitler's alleged mother fixation, especially after her death following treatment for breast cancer in 1907, determined his entire life and interlocked with a national neurosis. This trauma, says Binion, was repressed, and only got released after Hitler's gas poisoning in 1918. I tend to be skeptical of this type of history, but there is really no need to get

into the debate. For our own purposes, Binion's discussion of the concrete events of Pasewalk poses no problem; it is amply documented and seems reliable enough.

67. Binion (*Hitler Among the Germans*) reproduces some of these testimonials on pp. 136–38. The Kronos report, with information on Forster, comes from a restricted United States Navy intelligence report, #31963, declassified in 1972, from the OSS files of the National Archives in Washington, D.C. It is entitled "A Psychiatric Study of Hitler." See also the *OSS Hitler Source Book*, esp. p. 901, also in the National Archives; the *Frankfurter Zeitung* of January 27, 1923, p. 1; and Adolf-Viktor von Koerber, *Adolf Hitler* (Munich: E. Boepple, 1923), pp. 6–7.

68. There is a possibility, though it cannot be substantiated, that this vision was induced by Forster himself. For what it is worth, a friend and colleague of Forster, Ernst Weiss, subsequently published a novel, *The Eyewitness*, in which a soldier, "A.H.," arrives at Pasewalk military hospital in 1918, having been gassed, and in whom a psychiatrist induces a hallucination by means of hypnosis.

69. Quoted in Binion, *Hitler Among the Germans*, p. 137.

70. Ibid.; see also Ludwell Denny, "France and the German Counterrevolution," *The Nation*, 116 (1923), 295–97.

71. Quoted in Binion, *Hitler Among the Germans*, p. 138. On Koerber see note 67, above.

72. Toland, *Adolf Hitler*, p. xx.

73. Binion, *Hitler Among the Germans*, p. 1. Binion notes however (p. 148 n. 4) that the recollection may have been spurious, but there are certainly many others like it.

74. Fest, *Face of the Third Reich*, p. 4.

75. Binion, *Hitler Among the Germans*, pp. 124–26; cf. Speer, *Inside the Third Reich*, p. 18.

76. Baynes, *Germany Possessed*, p. 37.

77. Rauschning, *Hitler Speaks*, p. 213.

78. Ibid., p. 240, and Turner, *Hitler*, pp. 35–38 and 313–19. On Hörbiger and the Nazi interest in his *Welteislehre* see Webb, *Occult Establishment*, pp. 326–33.

79. On the following see Mosse, *Crisis of German Ideology*, p. 306; Ackermann, *Heinrich Himmler*, p. 34 n. 85 and p. 78; Goodrick-Clarke, *Occult Roots of Nazism*, pp. 177–88; Webb, *Occult Establishment*, pp. 318–27; and Schellenberg, *The Labyrinth*, pp. 14–15.

80. Similar testimony was provided by a man named Rupprecht, the castle warden. See Heinz Höhne, *The Order of the Death's Head*, trans. Richard Baug (London: Secker and Warburg, 1969), p. 152.

The anthropologist Agehananda Bharati, who grew up in Germany during this era, informs me that a major center for this sort of activity was Bad Tölz, in Bavaria, where the Nazis practiced yoga and breathing techniques. Bharati says that knowledge of this activity was fairly widespread by 1943 (private communication, September 1988).

81. Wiligut had been institutionalized for insanity during 1924–27. He joined Himmler's entourage as Karl Maria Weisthor in 1933. There is a full-scale

biography of him by Rudolf J. Mund, *Der Rasputin Himmlers* (Vienna: Volk-stum-Verlag, 1982), which tends to exaggerate his influence on Himmler and the SS (or so it seems to me) and which is, despite its insight into Himmler's occultism, a questionable source, because the material for it is based on personal conversations and correspondence between Mund and people who knew Wiligut. No footnotes are provided, and none of this material is on file in a library or state archive.

82. Much of this, however, was uninspired and even pedantic; for example, the *Ahnenerbe*, or Ancestral Bureau, which Himmler set up in 1935 to investigate and publish on the subject of Germanic researches. See Michael H. Kater, *Das "Ahnenerbe" der SS 1935–1945* (Stuttgart: Deutsche Verlags-Anstalt, 1974). Webb (*Occult Establishment*, pp. 323–24) says that the Ahnenerbe did keep occult records, but that they have vanished, and were probably destroyed.

83. Höhne, *Order of the Death's Head*, pp. 148–49 and 154–57.

84. Fest, *Face of the Third Reich*, p. 113.

85. Höhne, *Order of the Death's Head*, p. 582.

86. Webb, *Occult Establishment*, p. 309.

87. On the following see Fest, *Face of the Third Reich*, p. 83; Binion, *Hitler Among the Germans*, pp. 118–22; Roberts, *House That Hitler Built*, p. 10; J. P. Stern, *Hitler*, p. 36; Conway, *Nazi Persecution*, pp. 143–45 and 149–52; Rauschning, *Hitler Speaks*, pp. 209–10, 219, and 248; Vondung, *Magie und Manipulation*, pp. 7, 37–38, 156, 171–75, and 190–94, and also his article, "Spiritual Revolution and Magic," p. 400; and Speer, *Inside the Third Reich*, pp. 19 and 69.

88. On this and the following see Höhne, *Order of the Death's Head*, pp. 380, 389, and 581.

89. Rauschning, *Hitler Speaks*, p. 238.

90. Baynes, *Germany Possessed*, p. 96.

91. Rauschning, *Gespräche*, pp. 208–9. This section was not translated in the English version of the text (see *Hitler Speaks*, pp. 219–20).

92. Robert Pois, *National Socialism*, p. 29, and "Man in the Natural World," pp. 263 and 265.

93. Frances FitzGerald, "A Reporter at Large (Rajneeshpuram)," *The New Yorker*, September 22 and 29, 1986, reprinted in *Cities on a Hill: A Journey Through Contemporary American Cultures* (New York: Touchstone, 1987); Hugh Milne, *Bhagwan: The God That Failed* (London: Methuen, 1986); and James S. Gordon, *The Gold Guru* (Harmondsworth, England: Penguin Books, 1987). Interestingly enough, in the last few months of the commune's existence, it became obsessed by pollution, by a preoccupation with what happened to its bodily fluids and wastes, and by a fanatical desire to ensure purity. This fits in well with Fascist obsessions discussed in this chapter, and also with the discussion of pollution in Chapter 2.

94. Rauschning, *Hitler Speaks*, p. 210.

## Part III. Breaking the Mirror
### CHAPTER 9. THE GESTURE OF BALANCE

1. Cf. Eisenstadt, "Heterodoxies and Dynamics of Civilizations" (see Chapter 4, note 16).

2. Henri Atlan, *Entre le cristal et la fumée* (Paris: Éditions du Seuil, 1979).

3. Eisenstadt, "Heterodoxies and Dynamics of Civilizations," p. 108.

4. Quoted in *The Chronicle of Higher Education*, April 15, 1987, pp. 7–8.

5. From the 1953 Foreword to Heer's *Intellectual History of Europe* (see Chapter 6, note 81), p. 3.

6. Durrell, *Alexandria Quartet* (see Chapter 1, note 44), p. 764 (from the novel *Clea*).

7. *Our Common Future* (Oxford: Oxford University Press, 1987). The report was discussed in many major newspapers; see, e.g., the coverage in *The Globe and Mail* (Toronto), April 27, 1987, pp. A1–2, and A10–11.

8. Michael Ventura, *Shadow Dancing in the U.S.A.* (Los Angeles: J. P. Tarcher, 1985), p. 224.

9. Ibid., p. 230.

10. I don't have the exact citation, but Greeley's article first appeared ca. 1975 in the Sunday *New York Times Magazine*. See also his book *Ecstasy: A Way of Knowing* (see Chapter 1, note 49).

11. Marilyn Ferguson, *The Aquarian Conspiracy* (Los Angeles: J. P. Tarcher, 1980); Fritjof Capra, *The Turning Point* (New York: Simon and Schuster, 1982).

12. Michael Marien, "The Transformation as a Sandbox Syndrome," *Journal of Humanistic Psychology*, 23, 1 (Winter 1983), 7–15; Stephen Jay Gould, "Utopia (Limited)," *The New York Review of Books*, March 3, 1983, 23–25. See also M. Berman, "The Cybernetic Dream of the 21st Century," *Journal of Humanistic Psychology*, 26, 2 (Spring 1986), 24–51, and "Nature Is Not a Paradigm," *Whole Earth Review*, No. 55 (Summer 1987), 29–33.

13. See Chapter 8, note 93.

14. "Next, It's the World, Bhagwan Says" (see Chapter 5, note 45).

15. One guru I know of, a major figure in the human potential movement, led a workshop in Germany in the early 1980s with five hundred people, and had them goose-stepping, in trance, in short order. She turned to a friend of mine, a German, who was watching this display, and said enthusiastically, "I'd like to do this with twenty thousand people." He looked at her with amazed horror and replied, "Not in *this* country you don't!" I doubt it would be a good idea in *any* country.

16. On fascistic tendencies in the New Age, in addition to the items already cited in Chapter 8, note 93, the reader might wish to look at Richard Behar, "The Prophet and Profits of Scientology," *Forbes, 138,* 9 (October 27, 1986), on the cult started by L. Ron Hubbard. In addition, Swami Muktananda's brand of fascism, which included the accumulation of firearms and the use of goon squads, was exposed by Matthew Rodarmor in *Co-Evolution Quarterly*, No. 40 (Winter 1983), 104–11. Cultic abuses of the spirit are, of course, legion, yet we watch millions being drawn into these groups time and again. Dennis Stillings discusses the sham aspects of "channeling" in his very perceptive article, "Strip-Mining the Psyche," *Artifex* (Minneapolis), 5, 5 (October 1986), 1–5; Arthur Deikman and John Welwood make an attempt at establishing criteria for evaluating spiritual groups in the *Journal of Humanistic Psychology*, 23, 3 (Summer 1983), 8–18, and 42–60. There are also a number of books now

that reveal the United States government's interest in the occult for military purposes, e.g., *Psychic Warfare*, by Martin Ebon (New York: St. Martin's Press, 1984). The amenability of mysticism to totalitarian manipulation was also commented upon by Max Horkheimer in his essay on Aldous Huxley, "Means and Ends," in *Eclipse of Reason* (New York: Seabury Press, 1974; orig. publ. 1947), pp. 3–57 (see esp. p. 57).

17. See items cited in note 12, above.

18. R. D. Laing, *The Voice of Experience* (New York: Pantheon Books, 1982), p. 66.

19. By Marilyn Ferguson's own admission in her reply to Michael Marien in the *Journal of Humanistic Psychology*, 23, 1 (Winter 1983), 16–17.

20. Baynes, *Germany Possessed* (see Chapter 8, note 37), pp. 83 and 96.

21. Antonio Machado, *Times Alone*, ed. and trans. by Robert Bly (Middletown, Conn.: Wesleyan University Press, 1983), p. 147.

22. Reported in the *Vancouver Province*, July 8, 1986, p. 9.

23. Reported in the *Seattle Post-Intelligencer*, January 6, 1985, p. F4. Part of the problem with the ascent tradition, as Agehananda Bharati points out in *The Light at the Center* (Santa Barbara, Calif.: Ross-Erikson, 1976) (see also my discussion, below), is that despite any religious experience a person may have, it proves nothing about the ontological status of the framework in which that experience occurred. The ascent experience is not tied to any specific worldview, ism, or ideology, and is, in this sense, amoral, despite its enormous transformative power. Hence J. P. Stern's telling phrase, "dynamic fallacy."

24. M. Berman, "Updating the Three R's: Toward a Post-Modern Epistemology," *IS Journal* (Los Angeles), 2, 1 (June 1987), 2–12.

25. Eco, *The Name of the Rose* (see Chapter 4, note 17), pp. 477 and 491.

26. On the following see Jacob Needleman, *Lost Christianity* (New York: Bantam Books, 1982), pp. 23, 35, 140, 171, 180, 193, and 213–16.

27. Quoted in Marco Vassi, *Lying Down* (Santa Barbara: Capra Press, 1984), p. 61. The topic of what really constitutes a miracle was also the theme of a more low-key and amusing film, *Heavenly Pursuits* (1987), starring Tom Conti as a Glasgow schoolteacher who makes remarkable strides with his supposedly backward class while the school board is busy pursuing stigmata, visions, and miraculous cures.

28. Diamond, *In Search of the Primitive* (see Chapter 2, note 7), p. 170.

29. See Vassi, *Lying Down*, and also Chapter 6, note 100.

30. Ibid., pp. 82–83.

31. Jorge Luis Borges, "Tlön, Uqbar, Orbis Tertius," in *Ficciones* (New York: Grove Press, 1962; orig. Spanish ed. 1941), pp. 17–35.

32. Durrell, *Alexandria Quartet*, p. 764.

33. Ibid.

34. Attali, *Noise* (see Chapter 7, note 49). Much of Attali's argument is based on the work of Henri Atlan, cited in note 2, above. I should say that there are a number of problems with Attali's thesis; one of the most serious of these is tying "composition" to a philosophy of pure hedonism, or egotism, which I see as a serious mistake. Nevertheless, he has hit on something important

here, similar to Dorothy Dinnerstein's concept of "enterprise" (discussed below), that is very valuable. On the discussion in the text see pp. 10, 19, 32, 134, 137, 142–43, and 147.

35. Discussed in Dinnerstein, *Mermaid and the Minotaur* (see Chapter 1, note 64), pp. 121–22, 129–30, and 135; see also Norman O. Brown, *Life Against Death* (Middletown, Conn.: Wesleyan University Press, 1959), esp. pp. 87–109.

36. Dinnerstein, *Mermaid and the Minotaur*, pp. 139–41. An interesting discussion of "enterprise," or what he calls "epistemic curiosity," may be found in D. E. Berlyne, "Curiosity and Exploration," *Science, 153*, 3731 (July 1, 1966), 25–33.

The term "universalization"—turning a partial explanation into a total one—was coined by Kurt Goldstein; see his *Selected Papers/Ausgewählte Schriften*, p. 414 (see Chapter 3, note 6).

37. Dinnerstein, *Mermaid and the Minotaur*, p. 144.

38. Narada Thera, *A Manual of Abhidhama* (2 vols.; Rangoon: Buddha Sāsana Council, 1970), Vol. 1, pp. 86–87, and Vol. 2, pp. 7 and 24. See also Nyanatiloka, *Buddhist Dictionary* (Colombo: Frewin and Co., 1950), p. 63. I am grateful to Alan Clements, an American Buddhist teacher, for first mentioning the concept of *jīvitindriya* to me, and for referring me to these texts.

I do want to add, however, that there are souls and there are souls; Eastern and Western traditions do not coincide here, which could obviously make a difference for how the soul is experienced in different cultures. In particular, the Christian concept of the soul as a "thing," a fixed entity or immortal essence, is foreign to, say, Indian thought. For a useful discussion of this issue, see Karel Werner, "Indian Concepts of Human Personality in Relation to the Doctrine of the Soul," *Journal of the Royal Asiatic Society*, No. 1 (1988), 72–97.

39. Fowles, *Aristos* (see Chapter 1, note 1), pp. 59–60.

CHAPTER 10. THE TWO FACES OF CREATIVITY

1. Sigmund Freud, *Leonardo da Vinci and a Memory of His Childhood*, trans. Alan Tyson (New York: W. W. Norton, 1964). See esp. pp. 27–30 for the discussion that follows.

2. Still and all, Freud must be credited, at so early a date, with seeing that an alternative to Cr. II was at least conceivable. Most Western writers on the subject cannot escape their own cultural categories. Otto Rank, for example, who had much to say on the subject of creativity, essentially saw it as the triumph of the artist's will over obstacles that confronted him; see Esther Menaker, "The Concept of Will in the Thinking of Otto Rank and Its Consequences for Clinical Practice," *The Psychoanalytic Review*, 72 (1985), 254–64. In a similar fashion, Rollo May, in *The Courage to Create* (New York: W. W. Norton, 1975), sees the creative act as the overcoming of anxiety, and regards meditation as something that attenuates the creative impulse. (See also his recent book, *My Quest for Beauty* [Dallas: Saybrook Publishing Company, 1985], esp. pp. 141–42.) In general, the conflict model (Type II) seems to dominate the field, regardless of how much these studies differ in other ways. See, for example, Arthur Koestler's classic work, *The Act of Creation* (London:

Hutchinson, 1964), or the more recent study by Albert Rothenberg, *The Emerging Goddess* (Chicago: University of Chicago Press, 1979).

An interesting approach to the problem of creativity is provided by the American psychiatrist Gilbert Rose in his book *The Power of Form* (New York: International Universities Press, 1980). At first, I thought it would be a very useful source for my own study, since it is essentially a somatic analysis of creativity based on concepts such as the Transitional Object, labile body image and body boundary, and the dialectic between symbiosis and individuation. Yet Rose, like others, discusses only Cr. II without realizing his cultural limitations: art for him is primarily self-expression, the working out of the Self/Other (for him, in fact, Self/Mother) dividing line, and not much else. A similar analysis is carried out by Arnold Modell in his article, "Transitional Object and the Creative Act," *The Psychoanalytic Quarterly*, 39 (1970), 240–50, with the important exception that Modell does distinguish between two styles of creativity.

Finally, the same problem of an exclusively Western focus appears in one of the richest books ever written on the subject of creativity, *The Meaning of the Creative Act*, trans. Donald A. Lowrie (London: Gollancz, 1955; orig. Russian ed. 1914), by the Russian philosopher Nicolas Berdyaev. All of Indian culture, for example, is lumped under the heading of yoga, which is then summarily dismissed: "In all its forms," writes Berdyaev, "this mysticism denies man, his 'I' and his creativeness" (p. 302). Somehow, the view of the West (or rather, *from* the West) always comes back to the assertion that creativity is a manifestation of the "I," and that the absence of this is equivalent to noncreativity.

3. On "leaping" see, for example, Bly's essay, "Spanish Leaping," in his journal *The Seventies*, No. 1 (Spring 1972), 16–21.

4. Fowles, *Aristos* (see Chapter 1, note 1), pp. 52–53.

5. Quoted in Erik H. Erikson, *Young Man Luther* (New York: W. W. Norton, 1962), p. 45.

6. A. Alvarez, *The Savage God* (New York: Bantam Books, 1973), esp. pp. 227–52; Katinka Matson, *Short Lives: Portraits in Creativity and Self-Destruction* (New York: William Morrow, 1980).

7. Elliott Jaques, *Work, Creativity and Social Justice* (London: Heinemann, 1970), Chapter 3 ("Death and the Mid-Life Crisis").

8. On overmothering as an important factor in the genesis of creativity see Matthew Besdine, "The Jocasta Complex, Mothering and Genius," *The Psychoanalytic Review*, 55 (1968), 259–77 and 574–600. Besdine identifies a whole number of individuals who seem to display this syndrome, including Michelangelo, Poe, Dylan Thomas, Proust, van Gogh, Goethe, Einstein, Shakespeare, Freud, Balzac, and Sartre. My own guess is that for the modern period, i.e., that of Cr. II, this list could be extended almost indefinitely. Robert Bly has argued most cogently that the modern period in the West is conspicuously devoid of any male initiation rites, the result of which is that men typically feel excluded from their fathers' world. A boy who is not initiated into his father's world is forced to become a hero in his mother's, and this lends modern creativity a sharp neurotic edge. (See the interview with Bly in *New*

*Age Journal,* May 1982.) I am not convinced that this is limited to males alone; it seems to me that there is a female equivalent of the Jocasta complex, of which someone like Sylvia Plath is the obvious, and probably extreme, case. (See the memoir of Plath by Alvarez in the opening pages of *The Savage God.*)

9. On the following see Wilfred Mellers, *Caliban Reborn: Renewal in Twentieth Century Music* (New York: Harper & Row, 1967), Chapter 1.

10. Quotations from Kung Hsian are taken from translations of texts that were displayed as part of the exhibition at the Metropolitan Museum of Art during 1986–87.

11. On schismogenesis see Chapter 2, note 78.

12. On the following see Erich Neumann, *The Origins and History of Consciousness,* trans. R. F. C. Hull (Princeton: Princeton University Press, 1970; orig. German ed. 1949), Introduction and pp. 5–41 and 88–127.

13. I am grateful to Michael Crisp for this very imaginative, and I think accurate, interpretation.

14. Or perhaps, of a certain type of ego. There may be such a thing as a nonheroic ego, as I tried to suggest at the conclusion of Chapter 9.

15. Robert Louis Stevenson, *Dr. Jekyll and Mr. Hyde* (New York: Bantam Books, 1981; orig. publ. 1886), pp. 79–80. The splitting of the Great Mother was discussed by Neumann in *Origins and History,* pp. 96–97. The terminology "Great Mother Representative" is my own; Neumann's own phrase, which strikes me as being a loaded one, is "destructive male consort."

16. James Lord, *A Giacometti Portrait* (New York: Museum of Modern Art, 1965), p. 38. See also Lord's recent study, *Giacometti, A Biography* (New York: Farrar Straus Giroux, 1985).

17. Miró died in 1984; this quotation (from 1959) appeared in several obituaries that ran in a number of North American newspapers.

18. Philip Wheelwright (ed.), *The Presocratics* (New York: The Odyssey Press, 1966), p. 78 (Fragment 115; Hermann Diels' Fragment 48).

19. Quoted in Albert J. Lubin, *Stranger on the Earth* (New York: Holt, Rinehart and Winston, 1972), pp. 3 and 16.

20. The following discussion is based on Charlotte Haldane, *Mozart* (New York: Oxford University Press, 1960), and Wolfgang Hildesheimer, *Mozart,* trans. Marion Faber (London: Dent, 1983), esp. pp. 131, 138, 175, 178, 180–85, 235, 351, and 357.

21. Peter Shaffer, *Amadeus* (New York: Harper & Row, 1980), p. 83.

22. Was Mozart in fact poisoned? He himself, says Hildesheimer (p. 357), believed that someone had given him aqua tofana, a slow-working arsenic poison common enough in the eighteenth century. Shaffer's play is built around the possibility that Salieri was the villain, and it is certainly curious that Salieri *denied* poisoning Mozart on his (Salieri's) deathbed (Haldane, *Mozart,* p. 129). An inquest on Mozart's death held in London in May of 1983 concluded that he could have been poisoned, not by Salieri, but by a married woman with whom he was having an affair. (This was reported on the BBC.) Dr. Peter J. Davies argued against the possibility of poisoning in a two-part article published in the British journal *Musical Times* in 1984; see also Donald Henahan,

"Rest in Peace, Salieri, No One Killed Mozart," *The New York Times*, November 11, 1984, Section H. The issue will probably never be resolved.

23. Chang Chung-yuan, *Creativity and Taoism* (New York: Harper & Row, 1970), page facing Plate 4.

24. Weil wrote: "We participate in the creation of the world by decreating ourselves." Unfortunately, Weil gave no exact definition of "decreation" (a word apparently coined by Charles Péguy); and insofar as the present study is concerned, this raises certain problems. Thus Weil distinguished decreation—making something created pass into the realm of the uncreated—from destruction—making something created pass from nothingness, what she called a "blameworthy substitute for decreation." Yet her paradigm case was that of Christ, whose heroism (in the pejorative sense) seems evident (on this see Joseph L. Henderson, *Thresholds of Initiation* [Middletown, Conn.: Wesleyan University Press, 1967], pp. 71 and 180 and *passim*), and whose path led to crucifixion. Weil wrote: "It is necessary to uproot oneself. To cut down the tree and make of it a cross, and then to carry it every day." It thus seems that decreation, which is *ideally* (I believe) an important element of Cr. III, could easily slip into Cr. II, especially if the creative act is seen as an *imitatio Christi*, the broken vessel van Gogh speaks of.

To make this a bit clearer: I believe that this confusion, or ambiguity, arises from the heroic dynamic of Western culture itself. Christ is the model hero, which status he achieved by means of anti-heroics. The Eastern notion of getting the Self out of the way so that creativity can proceed has little to do (at least theoretically; practice may be a different matter) with the erasure of the Self. Instead, the idea is to remain aware of the "I" even while putting it aside. The psychology is very different from that of Western mysticism. Eastern art actually strengthens the Self by means of putting it on the back burner, so to speak. Cr. II sacrifices the Self completely, wipes it out for "art." Cr. III is a lot gentler; as there is no need for heroics, there exists no corresponding need for ego-destruction.

I suspect that Weil's theory has more in common with Cr. II than Cr. III, because its sources are apparently those of *Western* mysticism, specifically the Jewish "underground" magical tradition, the cabala. In the cabalistic doctrine of ẓimẓum (contraction), God is seen as creating the world out of self-diminution. That is, the Infinite, or *Ein-Soph*, undertakes an act of limitation, so that something finite can take its place, thus leaving room for the creative process. Weil believed that our duty to God was to reverse the process, i.e., allow Him to reenter the world by decreating our Selves; and to that end, she died of anorexia in 1943. However, this was probably a misinterpretation of the cabala, as well as of the Eastern concept of the Void, or the "No-Self," in that the annihilation of personality or ego does not mean the literal destruction of the physical body, but rather the holding of the ego in a different relationship from that in which it is usually held. Much Christian mysticism, in fact, may be based on a misinterpretation of Eastern thought. Yet it may also be the case that an East-West overlap exists, and if so, it may imply a confusion or blurring of Cr. II and Cr. III. Denis de Rougemont, in fact, claimed that even within the Western gnostic traditions, you could always find a position more "Eastern" than the one that you were examining at the moment. Weil's neo-Cathar tendencies might also be relevant to all this (see Chapter 6).

The same ambiguity surfaces in a famous 1917 essay by T. S. Eliot, "Tradition and the Individual Talent," in which he states at one point that the "progress of an artist is a continual self-sacrifice, a continual extinction of personality"—which I would take to be a form of Cr. II. Then later on he writes: "Poetry . . . is not the expression of personality, but an escape from personality." As already noted, Cr. III does not involve extinction, but setting aside. If one escapes personality, one still has it—can use it as a tool, for example—but is no longer attached to it. It is only (heroic) attachment that dialectically brings on the desire for extinction. Etc.

For a fuller discussion of these issues see the following: John Hellman, *Simone Weil* (Waterloo, Ontario: Wilfred Laurier University Press, 1982), esp. pp. 93–94 and 101; W. Rabi, "La conception weilienne de la création: Rencontre avec la Kabbale juive," in Gilbert Kahn (ed.), *Simone Weil: philosophe, historienne et mystique* (Paris: Aubier Montaigne, 1978), pp. 141–54; Simone Weil, *Gravity and Grace*, trans. Emma Craufurd (London: Routledge and Kegan Paul, 1952; orig. French ed. 1947), pp. 28–34; Miklos Vetö, *La Métaphysique religieuse de Simone Weil* (Paris: J. Vrin, 1971), pp. 19–43 (see p. 20n for a reference to the parallel between Weil's ideas and Jewish mysticism); T. S. Eliot, "Tradition and the Individual Talent," in *Points of View* (London: Faber and Faber, 1941), pp. 23–34; Scholem, "Kabbalah," cols. 588–89 (see Chapter 5, note 17); and Judith van Herik, "Looking, Eating and Waiting in Simone Weil," in Idinopulos and Knopp (eds.), *Mysticism Nihilism Feminism*, pp. 56–89, as well as some of the other essays in this text (see Chapter 6, note 56).

25. I have substituted the word "person" for "man," which appears in the original. See Ananda Coomaraswamy, "Meister Eckhart's View of Art," in *The Transformation of Nature in Art* (2nd ed.; New York: Dover Publications, 1956; orig. publ. 1934), p. 64.

26. In general, the typology being employed here is probably not actually fulfilled in practice, even in this form, which is subtler than the one in which we originally had it. For example, someone engaged in II(b) could occasionally slide back into unawareness [II(a)], or could be engaged in III(b) from time to time. This latter situation would be a mixture of Eastern and Western approaches, of meditative practice and traditional psychoanalytic work, and this is probably not all that uncommon in the art world.

The whole issue of overlap vs. distinctness of Types II and III strikes me as being a fascinating one, and it may be rooted in the issue of Eastern vs. Western varieties of mysticism (see note 24) or in the complicated relationship between traditional psychoanalysis and object-relations theory noted in Chapter 1. It could also be attributable to both. But it is revealing to see how artists themselves occasionally struggle with this. In an interview held in 1985, Federico Fellini stated that "the cinema, like all other manifestations of creativity, ought to be a state of combustion, a metabolism of the unconscious, a journey toward the center of ourselves and the world." The scrambling of categories is evident here: "combustion" sounds like Cr. II, "metabolism" like Cr. III. Similarly, to go toward the center of ourselves to the exclusion of the world is narcissistic. Yet metabolism is a (very slow) form of combustion, and Self and World (like the Transitional Object) are part of the same reality. Hence the same man who made $8\frac{1}{2}$, a film that explodes with unconscious power ("combustion") and self-expression, also made *Amarcord*, which is gentle ("metabolic") and oriented to the external world. *La Strada* seems to be somewhere in between, and remains, at least for me, Fellini's most profound and moving film.

See "Fellini: 'Per il primo amore sono svenuto,' " *Corriere della Sera* (Milan), October 20, 1985.

27. On minimal art, see Gregory Battcock (ed.), *Minimal Art: A Critical Anthology* (New York: E. P. Dutton, 1968). Philip Glass is perhaps best known for his opera *Einstein on the Beach* and for composing the sound track of Godfrey Reggio's film, *Koyaanisqatsi* (1983). Terry Riley's most famous work (Steve Reich worked on it as well) is probably *In C;* for an interesting interview with Riley see Jon Pareles, "Terry Riley's Music Moves to Improvisation," *The New York Times*, September 24, 1982. Reich discussed his sources and his own musical development in an interview/performance at the Exploratorium, San Francisco, December 15, 1982; see also the excellent article by Ingram Marshall in *Stagebill* (San Francisco), 2, 4 (December 1982), and the interview with Reich in *Parabola*, 5, 2 (May 1980), 60–72. Reich has stated that he is interested in music that evokes a physiological response; that if music doesn't give you goose bumps, it isn't working. It is also noteworthy that Reich spent a good bit of time studying the work of Ludwig Wittgenstein, which probably enabled him to focus his attention on the phenomenon of silence, and to step outside the Western historical mainstream in his creative work. In that regard the following passage, from the Foreword (1930) to Wittgenstein's *Philosophical Remarks*, ed. Rush Rhees and trans. Raymond Hargreaves and Roger White (Chicago: University of Chicago Press, 1975), is very striking inasmuch as it contains the germ of the Cr. II vs. Cr. III notion elaborated in this chapter:

> This book is written for such men as are in sympathy with its spirit. This spirit is different from the one which informs the vast stream of European and American civilization in which all of us stand. *That* spirit expresses itself in an onwards movement, in building ever larger and more complicated structures; the other in striving after clarity and perspicuity in no matter what structure. The first tries to grasp the world by way of its periphery—in its variety; the second at its centre—in its essence. And so the first adds one construction to another, moving on and up, as it were, from one stage to the next; while the other remains where it is and what it tries to grasp is always the same.

28. Bernard Leach, *A Potter's Book* (2nd ed.; London: Faber and Faber, 1945), p. 42.

29. It would require a very long discussion at this point, but it seems to me that in terms of the cultural evolution of Western creativity, we are not really witnessing a return to earlier forms as much as a kind of "bifurcation effect,"

of which this return is only one part. Minimal music, as I have said, has a trancelike quality reminiscent of Gregorian chant; the movement is toward wholeness, unity. (In his early days, Steve Reich used to say that he wasn't very interested in Western music composed after A.D. 1200.) The other aspect of the bifurcation process is (in the case of music) the work of composers such as John Cage, which incorporates heavy elements of chance and improvisation—a trend that began in the 1950s and that is known as Indeterminacy. One very astute student of music history, Romulus Franceschini, describes the background to this movement as follows (personal communication, October 1982):

> The notion that the musical score represents a "complete" realization of a composer's ideas is a relatively recent one. It is found only in European cultural ideology, its canonization exactly synchronous with the establishment of the bourgeoisie as ruling class. It began, roughly, in the Renaissance (Palestrina, Monteverdi, etc.), developed in the 17th, 18th, and 19th centuries (Italian opera, the rise of secular and instrumental music, Bach, Handel, Haydn, Mozart, Beethoven, etc.), and reached its apex in the post-Wagnerian world (Richard Strauss, Mahler, etc.) and the establishment of the symphonic tradition as the dominant one in Europe.

At the heart of Cage's efforts is a revolt against the "tyranny" of the score and the composition process itself. The minimalist movement (Reich, Glass, etc.) was in turn a revolt against this; for it represents a rejection of intellectualism in music, really beginning with Arnold Schönberg (one of Cage's teachers) and Anton von Webern. In some ways, however, the Cage school is the intellectual version of the minimalist trend, it seems to me. Morton Feldman, for example, was both a pioneer of Indeterminacy and a "spiritual father" of minimalism, according to Franceschini. It is also the case that in atonal music, there is no home key, but rather the controlled juxtaposition of equally valued tones, and there is also an attempt to deal with silence in a formal kind of way (see Cage's collection of essays, *Silence* [Middletown, Conn.: Wesleyan University Press, 1961]). This is what I mean by a "bifurcation effect"—the same process going on at two levels, one experiential (it is very easy to "get into" minimal music), the other intellectual, and largely geared to a professional audience interested in the solution of technical problems within the discipline. The same split can be seen in the sciences: you have a magical revival and a holistic/cybernetic paradigm, which are isomorphic to each other (possess the same formal properties), erupting in the culture almost simultaneously. All of this is evidence that Western creativity itself has arrived at a crossroads; the two sides of the bifurcation, in art, music, and science as well as literature, are the manifestations of this.

For a more detailed discussion of recent trends in the history of music see Leonard B. Meyer, *Music, The Arts, and Ideas* (Chicago: University of Chicago Press, 1967); Michael Nyman, *Experimental Music: Cage and Beyond* (London: Studio Vista, 1974); and the interviews with John Cage in Daniel Charles, *For the Birds*, trans. Richard Gardner (Salem, N.H.: M. Boyers, 1981).

Despite the attempted erudition of this footnote, I don't know very much about the history of recent music, and I want to express my gratitude to John Clauser and Romulus Franceschini for their help in guiding me through this difficult territory.

30. M. C. Richards, *The Crossing Point* (Middletown, Conn.: Wesleyan University Press, 1973), pp. 63–64.

# INDEX

Abel, Theodore, 270–271, 272; *Why Hitler Came into Power*, 270–271
Abzug, Robert, 299–300
Adams, Henry, *Mont-Saint-Michel and Chartres*, 221
Agrippa von Nettesheim, 248
Aich, Thomas, *Massenmensch und Massenwahn*, 285–286
Aimeric de Belenoi, 178
Albigensians, 154, 189, 202, 203, 206, 269; *see also* Catharism; Crusades; and Troubadours
Alchemy, 112–113, 148, 150, 188, 223; *see also* Fludd, Robert
Alexander of Neckam, *De Naturis Rerum*, 47
Alleau, René, *Hitler et les sociétés secrètes*, 279–280
Allen, Warren, 240
Alphandéry, Paul, 187, 215, 367–368
Alvarez, A., *The Savage God*, 324–325, 331
Anaximenes, 344
Andersen, Hans Christian, "The Emperor's New Clothes," 36–37
Animals, 70, 81–92, 97–98, 100–102, 356–357; and antivivisectionism, 83; bullfights, 92; children, 100–102; destruction of, 85; in dreams, 100; and Industrial Revolution, 83–84; as pets, 90–92; in rodeos, 92–95; and scientific research, 83–86; werewolves, 96; zoos, 87–90, 97–98
Annales School, 120–121, 361
Anti-Semitism, 262–263, 265–267, 271–274, 280–281, 289; *see also* Nazism
Antiochus IV, 162
Apocalyptic tradition, 167, 170
Apuleius, *The Golden Ass*, 73
Aquinas, Thomas, 233; *see also* Scholasticism

Arbus, Diane, 60, 353
Architecture, gothic, 331; modern, 249
Arendt, Hannah, 256–257, 274
Arian heresy, 138–139
Ariès, Philippe, 122, 361
Ariosophy, 257–261, 262–278; and Germanenorden, 262; and Hitler, 264–265; and Vienna Ariosophists, 258
Armanist doctrine, 259–261
Aroux, Eugène, 206, 209
Aryan occultism 261–263; *see also* Nazism
Ascent, 169, 222, 226–230, 232, 247, 369–370, 403; Cathars, 202–203; ecstatic, 247–248; Hitler, 267, 278, 281; mechanico–mathematical, 233, 236–237; music, 237; Nazism, 253–254, 260, 269–271, 275, 278–293; New Age paradigm, 302, 307–313; secular, 249
Atlan, Henri, 298, 313
Attali, Jacques, 237, 246, 314–315, 316, 340; and composition, 314, 340; *Noise*, 237, 314–315
Aune, David, 150
Aura, 143–144; *see also* Ka
A-Voidance, 20–22

Bacon, Francis, 222, 237; *Novum Organum*, 222
Balint, Michael, 23–24, 26–27, 42, 316, 345; *The Basic Fault*, 23
Barbarossa, Emperor Frederick, 191
Baren, Th.P. van, 152
Barfield, Owen, 179
Barrault, Jean-Louis, 56
Bateson, Gregory, 94, 313
Bauer, Walter, *Orthodoxy and Heresy in Earliest Christianity*, 176
Baum, Johannes, 262

Baynes, H.G., 273, 275, 291, 308; *Germany Possessed*, 273
Bélibaste, Pierre, 198
Bely, Andrei, *Petersburg*, 119
Benton, John, 182–183, 374–375
Berger, John, 65–66, 85, 89; on pets, 91; "Why Look at Animals?" 65
Bergier, Jacques, *The Morning of the Magicians*, 279
Bernard of Clairvaux, 189, 191, 215, 217, 218
Bernard, Claude, 83
Biale, David, *Gershom Scholem: Kabbalah and Counter-History*, 105
Binion, Rudolph, 288–289, 400
Bion, W.R., "Intra-Group Tensions in Therapy," 297
Blake, William, 71, 77, 140, 156; "The Everlasting Gospel," 156
Blau, L., *Das altjüdische Zauberwesen*, 163
Blavatsky, Helena Petrovna, 257–258, 259, 267; *Isis Unveiled*, 257; *The Secret Doctrine*, 257
Bloch, Marc, 121
Bly, Robert, 118, 324
Boehme, Jacob, 140
Bogomils, 196; and Cathars, 196
Borges, Jorge Luis, 313
Bosch, Hieronymus, 73, 75, 76; *The Temptation of St. Anthony*, 75
Bostunič, Grigorij (Gregor Schwartz–Bostunitsch), 262, 278
Bordelon, Abbé, 96; *Monsieur Oufle*, 96
Bousset, Wilhelm, 160
Boyle, Robert, 97
Bracher, Karl, 264, 272
Brody, Hugh, 68–69
Brooks, Charles, 25
Brooks-Gunn, Jeanne, 33
*The Brothers Karamazov* (Dostoevsky), 147
Brown, Norman, *Life Against Death*, 315–316
Brown, Peter, 177
*The Brundtland Report of 1987*, 300
Bruno, Giordano, 154, 225–229, 231, 232, 235; *La Cena de le ceneri*, 225
Buber, Martin, 258–259

Buddhism, 101, 149, 150, 192–193, 316–318; and enterprise, 316–318
Burtt, E.A., 248
Bynum, Caroline Walker, 217–218

Cabala, 151–152, 160, 199–200, 228–230, 233, 390; Catharism, 199–200; and Cudworth, Ralph, 233; natural magic, 228–230
Campanella, Tommaso, 154, 225, 229, 230–231; and magic, 230–231; *City of the Sun*, 230
Campbell, Joseph, 211
Capra, Fritjof, 302
Cardano, Girolamo, 154, 225, 229, 231–233, 237, 273; *Liber de Proportionibus*, 231–232; *De Rerum Varietate*, 233; *De Subtilitate*, 232; *De Vita Propria Liber*, 232
Cartesians, 233; *see also* Descartes, René; Mechanism
Castelnau, Peter (Pierre) de, 191
Catharism, 150, 152–154, 172, 173, 178–220, 222, 225, 251, 304, 377, 381–382, 385–386; body practice, 198; Bogomils, 196; Cathar church, 189 (*see also* French model); somatic history, 195–197; iconography, 201–202 (*see also* Inquisition); and modern science, 225; the Perfect, 188, 191–192, 194–195, 200–201; and romantic love, 207–209, 212–213; and troubadours, 206, 209
Cathars. *See* Catharism
Cennino Cennini, *Il libro dell' arte*, 324
Chadwick, Edwin, 84
Chamberlain, Houston Stewart, *Die Grundlagen des XIX Jahrhunderts*, 259
Chang Chung-yuan, 335–337
Chansons d'amour, 210
Chansons de geste, 209–210
Charron, Claude, 127–128
Chaucer, *The Canterbury Tales*, 324
Cheyette, Fredric, 204
Chivalry. *See* Romantic love
Chrétien de Troyes, 210
Christianity, 153–154, 156–180, 182–205, 210–220, 228–230, 255–257, 275–278, 313; and Cathar heresy,

188–205; and the cult of the Virgin Mary, 154, 156–180, 214–220; and French model, 186–187, 205; heresy in, 123–124, 138–140, 150–153, 162–177, 182–205; and magic, 151, 228–230; and Nazism, 225–256; New Age paradigm, 313; and romantic love, 210–220

Church Aristotelianism, 222–223, 226, 247, 249

Cohen, H.F., 246

Cohn, Norman, *The Pursuit of the Millennium*, 254

Composition, 314, 340, 404–405

Comtean Positivism, 113

Confiscation, 36, 44, 49–50, 52, 98, 148, 185, 291; *see also* Wallon, Henri

Consolamentum, 194–195, 198–200; *see also* Catharism

Conway, J.S., 285, 288

Cooley, C.H., *Human Nature and the Social Order*, 29

Coomaraswamy, Ananda, 338

Copernican theory; and Bruno, Giordano, 225–226; and Galileo, 235–236, 240

Copernicus, Nicolas, 226

*Corporéalité*, 134–135; *see also* Somatic history

Cosmic anonymity, 25–26, 32; *see also* Infant-world unity; Neumann, Erich

Cosmological urge, 42, 100, 315–316

Courtly love. *See* Romantic love

Craft, 323, 327, 330–331

Creativity, 316, 320–340, 404–405; Freud on, 320–322; modern, 323–331; and music, 326–327; Type I, 321–322; Type II, 321–324, 326–328, 330, 332–334, 404–405, 408–409; Type III, 322–323, 327–328, 331, 335–339, 408–409

Crime of conscience (thought crime), 186, 204–205, 215, 216; *see also* Inquisition

Crusades, 191, 193–194, 202–203, 205, 218; Albigensian, 202, 218

Cudworth, John, 229, 233; *True Intellectual System of the Universe*, 233

Cult of the Virgin Mary, 154, 205, 214–220, 304; romantic love, 216; *see also* Christianity

Cybernetic holism, 305–307, 313

Cybernetics, 301–302, 305

Daim, Wilfried, *Der Mann, der Hitler die Ideen gab*, 265–266

DAP. *See* German Workers' Party

Darwin, Charles, 29–30, 45, 115–116

Decroux, Etienne, 344

Dee, John, 229

della Porta, Giambattista, 225, 229

Descartes, René, 82, 233, 237, 238, 240, 243, 248; *see also* Mechanical philosophy

Diamond, Stanley, 311, 354

Diaspora, 161–162, 168

*Die Sphinx*, 257

Dinnerstein, Dorothy, 42, 100, 315, 322; *The Mermaid and the Minotaur*, 42, 315

Disney, Walt, 63, 66, 68, 100

Dodds, Eric, 157

Douglas, Mary, 65, 79, 81, 82; *Purity and Danger*, 81

Dreams, animals in, 100; interpretation of, Cardano, 232–233; interpretation and Nazism, 262

Drexler, Anton, 263–264

Durrell, Lawrence, 37, 300, 313–314

Dussault, Jean-Claude, 56

Dynamic fallacy, 291, 302–303; *see also* Stern, J.P.

Eckart, Dietrich, 261, 263, 279; *Auf gut Deutsch*, 263

Eco, Umberto, 150, 185–186, 309–310, 312; *The Name of the Rose*, 185, 309

Eco-radicals, 55

Ecstatic experience, 38, 310, 329; *see also* Ascent

Edda Society, 262

Efron, Arthur, 51

Eigen, Michael, 41

Einstein, Albert, 41, 314

Eisenstadt, S.N., 149–150, 298

Ekbert of Schönau, 200

Elias, Norbert, 48–49, 111, 131, 134; *The History of Manners*, 48

Enterprise, 315–318; see also Dinner-
stein, Dorothy
Erasmus, 37, 131; De Civilitate Morum
Puerilium, 131
Essenes, 150, 153, 160–164, 166–168,
196; see also Greek model

Fascism, 150, 153, 172, 233–234, 298,
303; and gnosticism, 234; see also
Nazism
Febvre, Lucien, 121
Ferenczi, Sándor, 21, 27
Ferguson, Marilyn, 312
Fest, Joachim, 266, 280, 282, 288
Ficino, Marsilio, 154, 224, 225, 229–
231, 237; Hermetica, 224
Fiedler, Leslie, Freaks: Myths and Im-
ages of the Secret Self, 60
Field, Joanna, A Life of One's Own,
366–367
Fierz, Markus, 232
Fisher, Seymour, 40, 56, 59–60; Body
Consciousness, 59
FitzGerald, Frances, 303
Five body theory. See Theory of five
bodies; and Masters, Robert
Fludd, Robert, 229, 237, 238–239, 240,
241–243; Ultriusque Cosmi, Maioris
Scilicet et Minoris; Metaphysica, Phys-
ica atque Technica Historia, 241–243
Fodor, Nándor, The Search for the Be-
loved: A Clinical Investigation of the
Trauma of Birth and Prenatal Condi-
tioning, 26
Foucault, Michel, 61, 122, 137, 297,
361; Les Mots et les choses, 122
Fowles, John, 20, 24, 317–318, 324,
337; see also Nemo
Frank, Hans, 282
French model (heresy), 154, 186–187,
205–207, 214–215, 219–220, 223, 247,
251, 269, 303–306; see also Chapter 6
French School, 29, 30–31, 36, 49; see
also Mirroring; Lacan, J.; Wallon,
H.; Merleau-Ponty, M.
Freud, Sigmund, 26, 34, 37, 60, 61,
78, 123, 143, 147, 320–322, 326, 345;
Civilization and Its Discontents, 37; on
Leonardo da Vinci, 320–321; and
Oedipus complex, 61
Fussell, Paul, Class, 57

Gaia-politik, 344, 360
Galileo Galilei, 221–222, 229, 230,
234–236, 237, 239, 247; Dialogue on
the Two Great World Systems, 235–
236; Letters on Sunspots, 221
Gallup, Gordon, 347–348
Gandhi, Mahatma, 144–145, 319
Garin, Eugenio, 234–236
Geopolitics, 57
Germanenorden, 262–263
German model (heresy), 154, 290–293,
303–304
German Workers' Party, 263, 281
Gibbon, Edward, The Decline and Fall
of the Roman Empire, 139
Gilligan, Carol, In a Different Voice,
387–388
Ginzburg, Carlo, 111, 121, 123–125,
134; The Cheese and the Worms, 123–
125
Giorgi, Francesco, 225, 229–230, 237,
240, 241; De Harmonia Mundi, 230
Glass, Philip, 339
Gogh, Vincent van, 51, 327–328, 332–
333, 337
Gnosis, 139, 152; see also Gnosticism
Gnosis of ascent, 298–299
Gnostic Gospels, 175–176, 371
Gnosticism, 138–140, 143–148, 151–
155, 157–177, 229, 298–299; and
modern science, 229; pessimistic,
158; see also Heresy
Goebbels, Joseph, 270, 272, 276, 278,
282
Goldsmith, Oliver, An History of the
Earth and Animated Nature, 97
Goldstein, Kurt, 25, 26, 35; infant-
world unity, 25, 26
Goldstein, Thomas, 112
Goodenough, Erwin, 164–167, 169–
170; Jewish Symbols in the Greco-
Roman Period, 164
Goodrick-Clarke, Nicholas, 257, 259–
260, 266
Göring, H., 282
Gorsleben, Rudolf John, 261–262, 278;
and Ariosophy, 278; and Edda Soci-
ety, 262; Deutsche Freiheit, 261; Hoch-
Zeit der Menschheit, 261
Gosselin, Edward, 226–227
Gould, Stephen Jay, 302

Grassinger, Hans George, 263
Great Mother societies, 64, 69, 71–73, 76, 148, 211–212, 310, 329, 356; and Christianity, 211–212; and ecstatic experience, 310, 329; and magic, 156–157
Greek model (heresy), 154, 173–174, 186–187, 214, 219–220, 223, 251, 269, 303–304; and ascent, 174; *see also* Chapter 5
Greeley, Andrew, 301–302
Green, William, 165
Greenacre, Phyllis, *Trauma, Growth and Personality*, 26
Greiner, Josef, 265, 399
Grolnick, Simon, 61
Guigenbert, Charles, 163
Guillaume, Paul, 29, 30–31, 40, 45
Gurdjieff, G.I., 262, 313

Haida cosmology, 110
*Halacha*, 162–166, 170
Hanna, Thomas, 15, 58; *Bodies in Revolt*, 15
Harding, D.E., *The Hierarchy of Heaven and Earth*, 19
Hartmann, Franz, 257
Hasidism, 161–162
Hasmoneans, 162, 167
Hauer, Karl, 263
Havelock, Eric, *Preface to Plato*, 112
Heer, Friedrich, 189, 190, 211–212, 213–214, 299
Hegel, G.W.F., 144–146, 299
Heidbreder, Robert, *Don't Eat Spiders*, 101
Heidegger, Martin, 155, 291
Heliocentricity, 225–228, 231
Hengel, Martin, 167–172; *Judaism and Hellenism*, 167
Heraclitus, 332
Heresy, 79–82, 137–179, 184–206, 207, 219–220, 221–252, 290–293, 315 (*see also* Catharism; French model; German model; Greek model; Italian model); and modern science, 221–252; and Nazism, 290–292; and New Age paradigm, 315; and romantic love, 207
Heretical movements. *See* Heresy

Herf, Jeffrey, *Reactionary Modernism*, 274
Hermetic soul travel, 228–229
Hermetical tradition, 172, 226–229, 235–236; and Galileo, 236
Hess, Rudolf, 278–282, 398
Heydrich, Reinhard, 276, 278, 282
Hidden history. *See* Somatic history
Hildesheimer, Wolfgang, 333–335
Hill, Christopher, 141
Hillman, James, 81
Himmler, Heinrich, 256, 262, 278, 280, 283–284; and the occult, 283–284
Historical fiction, 118–120
Historiography, 107–111, 117–125, 363, 364, 393, 394; Annales School, 120–121; contemporary, 108–112; experiential identification, 125–126; *mentalité*, 121–123; and nemo, 23; and objectivity, 116–117; professionalization of , 113–114; *see also* Somatic history
History of Religions school, 159
Hitler, Adolf, 144, 145, 155, 216, 253, 255, 257, 261, 262–293; and Ariosophy, 264–265; and ascent, 278, 281; and Germanenorden, 262; and heresy, 282; *Mein Kampf*, 261, 265, 266, 271, 272; and the occult, 264–266, 282–286; and the Theory of five bodies, 273, 275–279
Hobsbawm, Eric, 119
Hofstadter, Douglas, 305
Hogarth, William, *The First Stage of Cruelty*, 74
Höhne, Heinz, 284, 289; *The Order of the Death's Head*, 284
Holt, John, 42
Homer, 73, 76; *The Odyssey*, 73, 329
*Homoousios*, 138–139, 177
Hopkins, Gerard Manley, 211
Horizontal path, 164–166, 168, 251, 311–312
Höss, Rudolf, 289–290
Hsian, Kung, 328
Huizinga, Johan, *The Waning of the Middle Ages*, 301
Hunter-gatherer societies, 65, 66–72, 149–150; *see also* Paleolithic society
Hutton, Patrick, 122
Huxley, Thomas Henry, 238

Illich, Ivan, 45
Infant-world unity, 25–26; *see also* Cosmic anonymity; Goldstein, Kurt
Information society, 251, 305–306
Inquisition, 154, 186, 191, 192–195, 200–202, 204, 225, 251
Isadore, Bishop of Seville, 47
Issberner-Haldane, Ernst, 262, 278
Italian model (heresy), 154, 222–224, 247–248, 251, 269, 298, 302–305; and ascent, 251; *see also* Inquisition

Jäckel, Eberhard, *Hitler's Weltanschauung*, 272
Jaques, Elliott, 325
Jalal, ed-Din Rumi, 209
James, William, 348
Janov, Arthur, 27
Jaynes, Julian, 63–64, 156–157, 179
Jiménez, Juan Ramón, *Light and Shadows*, 17, 295
Johnson, Paul, 177
Johnson, Samuel, 53
Johnston, Charles, *The Creative Imperative*, 248, 250
Jonas, Hans, 190, 193; *The Gnostic Religion*, 190
Judaism, 81, 153–154, 156–177, 221, 372–373; *see also* Anti-Semitism; Hasidism
Jugendbewegung, 268
Julian of Norwich, 217
Jung, Carl, 60, 71, 143, 155, 216, 253, 256, 273–274, 291, 397; and anti-Semitism, 274; and Nazism, 273–274, 291

Ka, 47, 143–145
Kabbalah. *See* Cabala
Kafka, Franz, *Metamorphosis*, 73
Kaiser, Sandra, 90
Kepler, Johannes, 229, 233, 237–238
Kerrl, Hans, 278
Kersten, Felix, *Memoirs*, 280
Kinsey, Alfred, 117
Klein, Melanie, 54, 61
Klingender, Francis, *Animals in Art and Thought to the End of the Middle Ages*, 64–65
Knoll, August, 264–265

Koestler, Arthur, 229
Kohlberg, Lawrence, 181, 183
Kosinski, Jerzy, *Being There*, 184
Koyré, Alexandre, 234–236
Krishnamurti, 313, 315
Kuhn, Thomas, 79, 297–298
Kummer, Siegfried Adolf, 262, 278
Kundera, Milan, *The Incredible Lightness of Being*, 116
Kurosawa, Akira, *The Seven Samurai*, 58

Lacan, Jacques, 23, 29, 36, 40–41, 42, 49, 51, 54, 143, 146, 186, 309, 316, 323; Self/Other split, 41; *sevrage*, 42; *stade du miroir*, 41, 186
Ladurie, Emmanuel LeRoy, 121
Lagarde, Paul de, 258, 268, 270
Lagerkvist, Pär, *The Dwarf*, 39
Laing, R.D., 23, 29, 37, 61, 116–117, 145, 306; *The Divided Self*, 116–117
Lamashtu, 72
Lambert, M.D., 190
Langer, Walter, *The Mind of Adolf Hitler*, 277, 398–399
Langbehn, Julius, 258, 268, 270
Lanz von Liebenfels, Jorg, 257, 259, 260–263, 265, 266, 268, 277–278
Lao-tzu, *Tao Te Ching*, 141
Lawrence, D.H., 65–66
Lawrence, Elizabeth, 65, 92–94; *Rodeo*, 92–94
Leach, Bernard, 339–340
Leach, Edmund, 65, 78–80, 94
Leboyer, Frederick, 27, 43–44; and soft birthing techniques, 27
Lennon, John, 19, 24
Lenoble, Robert, 239–240
Lerner, Lawrence, 226–227
Lévi-Strauss, Claude, 60, 159, 173–174, 373; *The Raw and the Cooked*, 60
Lewis, Michael, 33
Liedloff, Jean, 44, 62, 292; *The Continuum Concept*, 44; and Yequana Indians, 44
Lightstone, Jack, 168
Limerence, 207–208, 210, 211; *see also* Romantic love
List, Guido von, 258–260, 263, 264–265, 278

Looking-glass self, 29; see also Cooley, C.H.

Lord, James, A Giacometti Portrait, 331

Lotusblüthen, 257

Lull, Ramon, 232

Luther, Martin, 248

Maaseh Merkabah, 199; see also Scholem, Gershom

Machado, Antonio, 308

Magical socialism, 280; see also Rauschning

Magical tradition, 73, 144, 151–154, 156, 163, 168, 222–224, 228–231, 247–249, 323; Ficinian, 230–231, 389; and Great Mother society, 156; Jewish, 163, 168; and medieval Europe, 73; modern science, 154

Mailer, Norman, The Naked and the Dead, 325

Manichaeanism, 148, 152, 154, 187, 193, 196, 200, 203, 205, 211, 265; and Lanz, 265; Saint Augustine, 177

Manifest destiny, 56–57

Manuel, Frank, 248

Marby, Friedrich Bernhard, 262, 278; and rune occultism, 262

Marcel, Gabriel, Metaphysical Journal, 15

Marien, Michael, 302

Marryat, The Phantom Ship, 96

Marx, Karl, 53, 60, 71, 146; The Communist Manifesto, 60; Das Kapital, 53

Massignon, Louis, 203

Masters, Robert, 140–146, 273; "The Way of the Five Bodies," 140–146; see also Theory of five bodies

Matson, Katinka, Short Lives, 325

McClary, Susan, 246–247

Mead, George, Mind, Self and Society, 29

Mechanical philosophy, 82–83, 113, 233–234, 236–240, 243, 248 (see also Descartes, René; Mersenne, Marin); and Neoplatonism, 233–234

Medici, Catherine de, 49

Medieval mysticism, 203

Mellers, Wilfred, Caliban Reborn, 326–327

Mentalité, 109, 121–123, 131–134, 179, 361

Mercurius van Helmont, Franciscus, 233

Merkabah, 160, 169

Merkabah mysticism, 199–200

Merleau-Ponty, Maurice, 23, 36, 37, 38–39, 41, 143, 316

Mersenne, Marin, 229, 234, 236–237, 238–241, 243–248; Harmonie universelle, 240; Questions harmoniques, 243; Quaestiones in Genesim, 239; Traité de l'harmonie universelle, 240

Metempsychosis, 157–158

Midgley, Mary, 90, 101–102

Miller, Alice, 22, 61, 129–130; For Your Own Good, 129–130; Prisoners of Childhood, 22

Mimesis, 112

Miró, Joan, 331–332

The Mirour of Good Manners, 48

Mirror, and ankh, 47; and etiquette, 48; history of, 45–49, 82; as metaphor for the soul, 46; and Narcissus myth, 46; in Renaissance, 48; and Scientific Revolution, 48

Mirror foiling, 48

A Mirror for Magistrates, 48

Mirroring, 28–36, 38–41, 43, 45, 51, 54, 64–66

Modern science, New Age paradigm and, 304–305

Monasticism, 181–182, 186

Moneta of Cremona, Adversus Catharos et Valdenses, 200

Montfort, Simon de, 191

Moore, G.F., 164, 170

Moore, Henry, 339

Morante, Elsa, La Storia, 120

More, Henry, 97, 229, 233; and gravity, 233

Morphogenetic fields, 146; see also Sheldrake, Rupert

Morris, Colin, 181, 215

Mosse, George, 254, 255, 258, 264, 268; The Crisis of German Ideology, 254

Mozart, Leopold, 333–335

Mozart, Wolfgang Amadeus, 333–335, 338, 406–407; Così fan tutte, 334; Don Giovanni, 334; The Magic Flute, 334; The Marriage of Figaro, 333

Mu Ch'i, Plate 20, 336
Mumford, Lewis, 115
*Münchener Beobachter*, 262, 263
Murphy, Michael, *Jacob Atabet*, 344
Music, 233, 237–238, 239–247, 326–
   327, 333–338, 339, 410–411; and as-
   cent, 237; Fludd on, 243; and Mer-
   senne, 243–247; mathematical
   harmony, 243, 246; modern creativ-
   ity, 326–327, 333–334; Mozart, 333–
   338; postmodern minimalist, 339
Mussolini, Benito, 58–59
*My Dinner with Andre*, 310–311
Mystery cults, 156–161
Mysticism, 131, 170; Jewish, 170

National Socialism. *See* Nazism
Nazi cosmology, 60
Nazism, 154–155, 251, 252, 253–293;
   ascent, 253, 289–293; Christianity,
   275–278; Eastern religion, 262;
   gnosticism, 260, 269–273, 290–293;
   *Innerlichkeit*, 269; the occult, 254–
   255, 261–267, 269, 276–280, 283–289
Needham, Joseph, 79
Needleman, Jacob, 309, 310, 312, 315;
   *Lost Christianity*, 309
Nelli, René, 201, 209, 213
Nemo, 20–21, 23, 24, 36, 42, 48, 54,
   143, 247–248, 309, 317–318; *see also*
   Fowles, John
Neolithic society, 70–71, 76–77
Neo-Nazi Church of Jesus Christ
   Christian, 308–309
Neoplatonism, 233–236, 239, 242
Neumann, Erich, 25–26, 148, 208, 329,
   330–331; and cosmic anonymity,
   25–26, 208; *The Origins and History
   of Consciousness*, 329
Neusner, Jacob, 167
*The New Left Review*, 53
New Age cults, 172–173, 303
New Age paradigm, 300–302, 304–
   318; and ascent experience, 302;
   and fascism, 402–403
Newman, F.X., 206–207
Newman, John Henry Cardinal, 217–
   218
Newton, Sir Isaac, 113, 155, 229, 232–
   234, 238, 247–248
Newtonian Puritanism, 227

Nietzsche, F., 268, 270
Nock, A.D., 150–151
Nuclear holocaust, 98–100
Nuremburg rally, Plate 19, 286–287
Nygren, Anders, *Agape and Eros*, 207

Object-relations school, 23, 61; *see also*
   Self/Other relationship
Occult, 153, 154, 197, 200, 223, 230,
   255, 260–262; *see also* Catharism;
   Nazism
Odent, Michael, 27, 43; and soft birth-
   ing techniques, 27
Oest, J., *For Your Own Good*, 129–130;
   *see also* Miller, Alice
O'Neill, John, 56
Otto, Rudolf, *Mysticism East and West*,
   197

Paleolithic society, 66–70, 71, 81, 115,
   149, 156; and art, 67
*Palingenesia*, 140, 157–158
Pauwels, Louis, *The Morning of the
   Magicians*, 279
Percy, Walker, *Lost in the Cosmos*, 319
Perfect, the, 188–192, 194–195, 197–
   199, 200–202, 206, 273; *see also* Ca-
   tharism
Perkins, Pheme, *The Gnostic Dialogue*,
   376
Perls, Fritz, 147
Pets, 90–92, 97–98
Pharisees, 162–164, 168, 176
Phelps, Reginald, 264
Phillips, David, 90
Philo Judaeus, 164–165
Piaget, Jean, 42, 180–181, 202; *The
   Moral Judgment of the Child*, 180
Plastic natures, theory of, 233–234
Plato, 147, 157–158, 164, 207–208, 241;
   *The Symposium*, 207, 217
Pois, Robert, 255, 276, 277, 292; *Na-
   tional Socialism and the Religion of Na-
   ture*, 255
Political Workers' Circle, 263
Preyer, William, 30, 33, 45
Pythagoras, 238, 241

Quantum mechanics, 124–125
Qumran sect, 160–162, 367, 371; *see
   also* Essenes

Radding, Charles, 179–183, 185, 190, 375
Rahn, Otto, 206, 209, 213, 284
Rajneesh, Bhagwan, 172–173, 292–293, 303, 410
Rameau, Jean-Philippe, 240, 241
Rank, Otto, 24, 26; *The Trauma of Birth*, 26
Ranke, Leopold von, 113, 119
Rauschning, Hermann, 256, 265–267, 271, 275, 277, 280, 282, 286, 291–293, 395
Ravenscroft, Trevor, *The Spear of Destiny*, 279
Ray, John, 97
Rebirthing, 25, 140
Reich, Steve, 339
Reich, Wilhelm, 23, 25, 57, 61, 134, 185, 253, 256, 299, 343; *The Mass Psychology of Fascism*, 253; modal personality, 57; Reichian bodywork, 25
Reichstein, Herbert, *Arische Rundschau*, 262
Reitzenstein, Richard, 159; *see also* History of Religions school
Renan, Ernest, 163
Reynold, George, *Wagner the Wehrwolf*, 97
Rhodes, James, 254, 269–273; *The Hitler Movement*, 269
Richards, Mary Caroline, *The Crossing Point*, 340
Riefenstahl, Leni, 145, 255; *The Triumph of the Will*, 255
Riley, Terry, 339
Roberts, Stephen H., *The House That Hitler Built*, 397
Roché, Déodat, 195–196, 200
Rodeos, 65, 92–95
Roethke, Theodore, 344
Róheim, Géza, 23, 51, 316; *The Origin and Function of Culture*, 23
Romantic love, 186–187, 205–220, 251, 304, 313, 375, 382–384; and Cathars, 208, 212–213
Rosenberg, Alfred, 262–263, 264, 278
Rosicrucianism, 235, 239, 258
Rossetti, Gabriele, 206, 209
Rougemont, Denis de, 186, 205–216, 226; *Love in the Western World*, 186, 205; *see also* French model
Rousseau, Jean-Jacques, 61
Runciman, Steven, 190, 193, 196
Russell, Jeffrey Burton, 188–189, 196

Sacconi, Rainer, 195, 200
Saint Augustine, 46, 177, 179, 182; *Confessions*, 46, 179
Saint Benedict, 182–183
Saint Francis, 21, 183
Sakaki, Nanao, "Break the Mirror," 295
Sartre, Jean-Paul, 37
Schafer, Murray, 243
Schellenberg, Walter, 283
Schilder, Paul, 37, 43, 55–56, 58; *The Image and the Appearance of the Human Body*, 37
Schismogenesis, 94, 328–329, 337
Scholasticism, 222–224; *see also* Aquinas, Thomas
Scholem, Gershom, 160, 165–167, 170, 199, 233; *Jewish Gnosticism, Merkabah Mysticism and Talmudic Tradition*, 199
Schuler, Alfred, 264, 278
Schwartz, Delmore, 107, 343; "The Heavy Bear Who Goes With Me," 107
Scientific naturalism, 97
Scientific positivism, 236–237; *see also* Mersenne, Marin
Scientific Revolution, 73, 76, 83, 112–114, 131–132, 229–237, 237–252; and ascent, 229–237
Sebaldt von Werth, M.F., 259
Sebottendorff, Rudolf von (Rudof Glauer), 262–264, 277, 279–280; *Bevor Hitler kam*, 279–280; and Germanenorden, 263
Segal, Alan, 160, 174
Self/Other relationship, 38–66, 69–70, 71–91, 175–177, 185–186, 309–311, 350, 351; childhood, 28–37 (*see also* Confiscation); fetal, 26–27; Neolithic revolution, 76–77; Scientific Revolution and, 82–84, 90–94; sexuality and, 42–43
Set and Osiris, 329–330
Sheldrake, Rupert, 56, 146
Shepard, Paul, 65, 66, 68–70, 72, 78, 80, 91, 102; "The Pet as Minimal Animal," 91; on totemic cultures, 66

Shontz, Franklin, 40; *Perceptive and Cognitive Aspects of Body Experience*, 349

Shriver, George, 195

Simon, Marcel, 159; *see also* History of Religions school

Singer, Peter, 83, 86

Sklar, Dusty, *Gods and Beasts*, 280

Smith, K.F., 96

Smith, Morton, 161, 166

Soft birthing techniques, 27, 43–44; *see also* Leboyer, F.; Odent, M.

Somatic history, 55–65, 72, 100–102, 107–125, 152, 195–197, 202, 342–345, 363–364; *see also* Historiography phy

Sommer, Frederick, *The Poetic Logic of Art and Aesthetics*, 341

*Song of Songs*, 215, 217

Speer, Albert, 282, 286–287

Spencer-Brown, G., *Laws of Form*, 122

*Stade du miroir*, 41, 146, 186; *see also* Lacan, Jacques

Steiner, Rudolf, 195

Stern, Daniel, 32–33

Stern, Fritz, 254, 269

Stern, J.P., 268–269, 271, 291, 302–303; and dynamic fallacy, 291, 302–303; *Hitler: The Führer and the People*, 268–269, 271

Stevens, Wallace, 339

Stevenson, Robert Louis, *Dr. Jekyll and Mr. Hyde*, 96, 330

Storytelling. *See* Historical fiction

Strayer, Joseph, 204

Streicher, Julius, 261, 275, 282; *Der Stürmer*, 261

Sutton-Smith, Brian, "The Role of Toys in the Modern World," 128–129

Suzuki, Shunryu, 338

Symbiosis, 25–26; *see also* Cosmic anonymity; Infant-world unity

Syncretic sociability, 36, 38

Szasz, Kathleen, *Petishism*, 91


Telesio, Bernardino, 225

Templar Order, Hitler and, 265

Tennov, Dorothy, 207–208, 210; *Love and Limerence*, 207; *see also* Limerence

Teresa of Avila, 140, 203, 212

Tertullian, 176–177, 180; *De Anima*, 176

Theory of five bodies, 140–146, 152, 166, 168–173, 203, 273, 299–300, 344

Theosophy, 257

Third Reich, *see* Nazism; and the occult, 279–280, 285

Thomas Keith, 65, 84, 89–90, 95, 97; *Man and the Natural World*, 65

Thompson, Dorothy, 277–278

Thompson, Lewis, *The Deepest Ground*, 90

Thought crime. *See* Crime of conscience

Thule Gesellschaft, 262–264, 265, 269, 277, 279, 280

Toland, John, *Adolf Hitler*, 281, 399–400

Tönnies, Ferdinand, 268

Torah ontology, 167, 170–171

Toynbee, Arnold, 192–193

Transformation, principle of, 102

Transitional Object, 50–53, 61, 62, 64, 68, 76–77, 80, 90, 100, 149, 174, 208, 241, 247, 306–307, 311, 315–316; and Nazism, 292–293

Transitional space, 81, 149

*Tristan and Iseult*, 209–210

Troubadours, 186–187, 206, 208–213; and Cathars, 212–213

Turner, Frederick, 176, 178, 191–192; *Beyond Geography*, 178

Type I creativity, 321–322

Type II creativity, 321–324, 326–328, 330–334, 338–340, 404–405, 408–409

Type III creativity, 322–323, 327–328, 331, 335–339, 408–409


Universal gravitation, theory of, 247


Varela, Francisco, 116

Vassi, Marco, 313, 315; *Lying Down*, 313

Ventura, Michael, 301, 302, 304, 305

Verny, Thomas, 26–27, 345; *The Secret Life of the Unborn Child*, 26–27

Vertical path, 164, 166–168, 176, 293, 311
Vinci, Leonardo da, 39, 320–321
Visceral history. *See* Somatic history
Voegelin, Eric, 138, 254
*Volk*, 258–259, 268, 272
*Völkischer Beobachter*, 262; *see also Münchener Beobachter*
Vondung, Klaus, 255, 282, 285, 286–289; *Magie und Manipulation*, 255, 289
Vril Society, 279

Wachler, Ernst, 264
Wagener, Otto, 277
Wakefield, Walter, 190
Walker, D.P., 229, 231
Wallon, Henri, 23, 30–32, 36, 37, 40–41, 44–45, 49, 143, 292, 316, 346–347; and confiscation, 36; and syncretic sociability, 36
Warner, Marina, 218–219
Webb, James, 267, 276, 285; *The Occult Establishment*, 267
Weber, Max, 150, 268
Weil, Simone, 337, 407–408
Whitehead, Alfred North, 157
Wiedemann, Fritz, 282

Wiligut, Karl Maria, 262, 278, 283–284, 400–401
Willis, Roy, 64
Winnicott, Donald, 23, 28–29, 37, 42, 49–53, 61, 247, 309; and self vs. mother, 42; and transitional objects, 50–53, 61; *see also* Transitional Object
Wiseman, Frederick, 85–86; *Meat*, 85; *Primate*, 85
Witchcraft, 73–74, 79, 96, 112, 148, 151, 152; *see also* Occult; Magical tradition
Wotan, 258–260, 268, 273–274, 397, 398; and the SS, 283–284
Woweries, Franz Hermann, *Nationalsozialistische Feier-Stunden*, 285

Yates, Francis, 158, 224–225, 226, 228–229, 239, 243
Yequana Indians, 44, 61
Yevtushenko, Yevgeny, 80

Zbigniew, Herbert, 193, 195
Zeldin, Theodore, 126, 362–363
Zillman, Paul, *Metaphysische Rundschau*, 258
Zoos, 87; history of, 87–90, 97–98

# ABOUT THE AUTHOR

MORRIS BERMAN received his B.A. in mathematics from Cornell University and his Ph.D. in the history of science from Johns Hopkins. He has taught at several universities in the United States and Canada and has lectured widely in Europe and North America on the themes of personal and cultural change. He is the author of *Social Change and Scientific Organization* (1978) and *The Reenchantment of the World* (1981), which has been translated into German, Dutch, Spanish, and Japanese. Dr. Berman resigned from university teaching in 1988 to devote himself to research and writing on a full-time basis.